AMERICAN LITERATURE

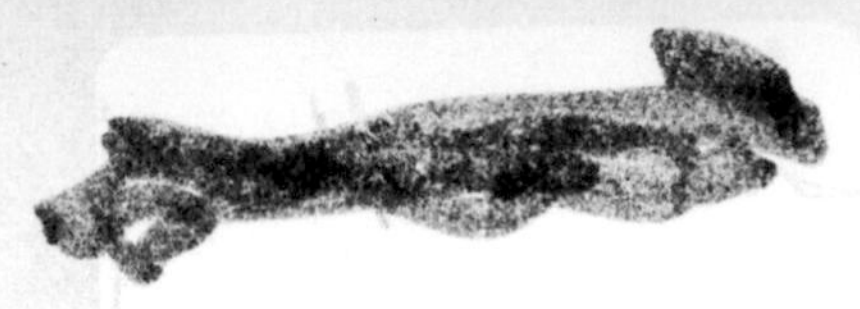

About the Authors

Bartholow V. Crawford received his B.A. degree from Cornell College, Iowa and his M.A. and Ph.D. degrees from Harvard University. He has taught at the University of Minnesota and at Rice Institute. In 1921 he joined the faculty of the University of Iowa, where he is now Professor of English. He is the author of *Henry David Thoreau: Representative Selections.*

Alexander C. Kern received his B.A. degree from Yale University and his M.A. and Ph.D degrees from the University of Wisconsin. He has taught at the University of Wisconsin, Allegheny College, the University of Maryland, and the University of Iowa, where he is now Associate Professor of English.

Morriss H. Needleman has many years of teaching experience and has received his B.A. degree and M.S. degree in Education. He is the co-author of another Outline in the College Outline Series: *An Outline-History of English Literature.*

COLLEGE OUTLINE SERIES

AMERICAN LITERATURE

BARTHOLOW V. CRAWFORD

ALEXANDER C. KERN

MORRISS H. NEEDLEMAN

BARNES & NOBLE, Inc. NEW YORK

Publishers • Booksellers • Since 1873

Reprinted, 1964

L. C. Catalogue Card Number: 53-1513

This book is an original work (Number 49) in the original College Outline Series. It was written by distinguished educators, carefully edited, and produced in the United States of America in accordance with the highest standards of publishing.

PUBLISHER'S FOREWORD

The outline-history of *American Literature* covers the field, we believe, with an eclectic adequacy not attempted by any other manual. All three authors read in manuscript the work of each of their colleagues, weighed the criticisms made, and finally rewrote any part or parts that needed freshness of point of view, better balance, and richer interpretation.

As the result of several such years of intensive collaboration, the authors have achieved their common purpose of helping the student appreciate better the ideas and the ideals of American literature.

In the opinion of the editor, Bartholow V. Crawford, Alexander C. Kern, and Morriss H. Needleman have succeeded in:

1. Placing emphasis upon those authors most frequently anthologized, because it will be those about whom the student will seek specific aid. In addition, a large body of significant minor authors who too frequently have been neglected is also treated, on the belief that a knowledge of less well-known writings may be necessary to bring into focus the whole complex literary picture.

2. Devising a book that lends itself to immediate use for further study. Such editorial aids as cross-references and footnotes have been utilized at strategic points so as to reduce to a minimum the necessity of directing students to other books. It is not difficult, when advisable, to disregard the footnotes; yet the footnotes themselves, while stimulating the student's interest in specific literary problems, are a concise, up-to-date bibliography ready to serve as a point of departure for supplementary readings and explorations.

3. Presenting material that in each case grows out of both the nature of the subject and the needs of the student. To avoid narrowness of subject matter, the authors present a large body of desirable omnibus material.

4. Bringing the treatment of the subject abreast of modern research and criticism. This has involved considerable effort and expense, since additions have had to be made several times while the work was in page proof. But both the editor and the authors

have felt that every effort must be made to issue a work distinguished by significant immediacy, quick serviceability, and sound scholarship.

5. Designing an outline-history of *American Literature* in a fashion permitting adjustment to the needs of *all* students, both those who purpose to go no further than the first course and those who plan to go beyond. Those who wish some minimal signposts may give heed to the works marked by an obelisk (†); those who wish to enrich the mininal requirements may make the reference notes the basis of additional work; and, finally, those who plan to do graduate work may follow up for themselves the various problems raised throughout the outline.

6. Relating the literature to life, vitalizing ideas and ideals, and integrating broad intellectual and philosophical connections. The textbook itself should avoid undue stress on material apparently intended to yield entertainment suitable for adolescents rather than to provoke thinking on an adult level. Indiscriminate mastery of the material in the outline-history, *American Literature,* is not the desideratum. The student is not to work for the memorization of biographical facts, dates of literary works, or even critical judgments, except in a naturally subordinate degree. If a choice is offered, the student, as did the three authors, should favor intellectually stimulating ideas rather than factual matter barren of ideas. Not only is literature related to life: literature is life itself.

Moreover, while designed primarily for the college undergraduate and the majoring or even the graduate student, it is felt that the outline-history of *American Literature* is useful as well for all who do not have access to adequately equipped libraries or who may find it convenient to have in succinct form a representative discussion of American literature.

The publisher will be glad to receive the reader's criticisms and suggestions for revisions to be incorporated in future editions of the text.

THE EDITOR

PREFACE

Objectives sought by the authors of the outline-history of *American Literature* have been several. They have endeavored to provide for the undergraduate a compact and clearly outlined manual which will put at his disposal accurate information with which he may fill out lecture notes and prepare for tests. For the more advanced student they have tried to make clear through chronological arrangement and outline treatment the trend and sweep of development, and juxtaposition of authors and works in a variety of literary fields and against a background of historical events. Through critical judgments, time-tested rather than personal, they have suggested the estimate of less familiar works, while, at the same time, where considered judgment is at variance, summarizing critical judgments pro and con. To the teacher and the professional scholar they have made available extensive current bibliographies.

In the preparation of the outline-history of *American Literature* there has, of course, been free consultation among the authors. Responsibility for Chapters I-IV (except for the article on Herman Melville, which was contributed by M. H. Needleman), has, however, fallen to Alexander C. Kern; for Chapters V-VIII, to Bartholow V. Crawford; and for Chapters IX-XIV (except for the article on Henry James, which was contributed by B. V. Crawford), to Morriss H. Needleman, who has also undertaken extensive editorial tasks.

B. V. C.
A. C. K.
M. H. N.

TABLE OF CONTENTS

Page

Editor's Foreword v

Preface vii

Key to Symbols and Abbreviations xiii

THE COLONIAL PERIOD (1607-1763)

Chapter

I **Renaissance and Puritan Influences** 1
Historical Background 1
General View of the Literature 1
Southern Writers: Captain John Smith; John and Ann Cotton 2
The Puritans 2
Description, Annals, and History of New England: William Bradford; Thomas Morton; John Winthrop; Mary Rowlandson 4
Seventeenth Century Theologians: Thomas Shepard; Roger Williams; John Davenport 5
The Mather Dynasty: Richard Mather; Increase Mather; Cotton Mather 7
Miscellaneous Prose: Thomas Brattle; Robert Calef; Nathaniel Ward; Samuel Sewall 9
Puritan Poetry: Ann Bradstreet; Michael Wigglesworth; Edward Taylor 10
Supplementary List of Authors 12

II **The Rise of Rationalism and Democracy** 14
Historical Background 14
General View of the Literature 14
Religious Writing in New England: John Wise; Jonathan Edwards; Charles Chauncey 14
History and Annals in New England: Sarah Kemble Knight 17
The Southern Colonies: Alexander Spotswood; William Byrd of Westover 18
The Middle Colonies: Thomas Godfrey 18
Journalism in the Colonies 19
Supplementary List of Authors 19

THE REVOLUTIONARY PERIOD (1763-1810)

III **The Struggle for Independence: Deism, National Issues, and the Beginnings of Belles Lettres** 22
Historical Background 22
General View of the Literature 23

Chapter Page

Prose of the Enlightenment: John Woolman; William Bartram; Alexander Wilson; Meriwether Lewis; Hector St. John de Crèvecoeur; Benjamin Franklin; James Otis; Patrick Henry; John Dickinson; Samuel Adams; Francis Hopkinson; Thomas Paine; William Smith; Thomas Jefferson; Alexander Hamilton; James Madison; George Washington; John Adams; John Marshall . . . 24

Poetry: Nathaniel Evans; Philip Freneau; John Trumbull; Timothy Dwight; Joel Barlow 37

Drama: Royall Tyler 41

The Novel: William Hill Brown; Charles Brockden Brown; Hugh Henry Brackenridge 41

Miscellaneous Prose: Noah Webster; Joseph Dennie . . 44

Supplementary List of Authors 45

THE ROMANTIC PERIOD (1810-1865)

IV **Early Sentiment and Romance** 48

Historical Background 48

General View of the Literature 49

The Knickerbocker School: Washington Irving; Nathaniel Parker Willis; Fitz-Greene Halleck; Joseph Rodman Drake; George Pope Morris; James Kirke Paulding 49

Poetry: William Cullen Bryant; John Pierpont; James Gates Percival; Richard Henry Dana, Sr.; John Gardiner Calkins Brainard; Thomas Buchanan Read; Richard Henry Stoddard; Thomas William Parsons; Edgar Allan Poe; Stephen Collins Foster; Henry Timrod; Paul Hamilton Hayne 54

Novelists: James Fenimore Cooper; Herman Melville; Richard Henry Dana, Jr.; John Pendleton Kennedy; William Gilmore Simms 65

Dramatists: George Henry Boker 74

The West 75

American Humor: Josh Billings; Artemus Ward . . . 76

Historians: William Hickling Prescott; John Lothrop Motley; Francis Parkman 77

Other Writing: Dorothea Dix; Elihu Burritt; John Neal; Charles Fenno Hoffman; John Godfrey Saxe; Henry Charles Carey; William Wirt; James Kent; Washington Allston 79

Supplementary List of Authors 80

V **Transcendentalism: Its Major and Minor Figures** . . 85

Origin of Concept 85

Group Activities 86

Major Figures: William Ellery Channing (1780-1842); Ralph Waldo Emerson; Henry David Thoreau; Bronson Alcott; Margaret Fuller 87

Minor Figures: Theodore Parker; Henry Hedge; Jones Very; Christopher Pearse Cranch; William Ellery Channing (1818-1901); Orestes Augustus Brownson; James Freeman Clarke 104

Chapter Page

VI **The Genteel Tradition of New England: Its Major Figures** 107

Henry Wadsworth Longfellow; John Greenleaf Whittier; Nathaniel Hawthorne; Oliver Wendell Holmes; James Russell Lowell 107

VII **Walt Whitman: Prophet of Democracy** 134

VIII **Mid-Century Minor Figures: Romancers, Essayists, Poets** 143

Harriet Beecher Stowe; James T. Fields; George William Curtis; Bayard Taylor; Louisa May Alcott; Thomas Bailey Aldrich; Elizabeth Stuart Phelps . . . 143

THE TRIUMPH OF REALISM: 1865-1914

IX **The Local-Colorists** 152

Historical Background 152

General View of the Literature 157

The West: Bret Harte; Edward Eggleston; John Hay; Joaquin Miller; Other Local-Colorists 161

The South: Joel Chandler Harris; Lafcadio Hearn; George W. Cable; James Lane Allen; Other Local-Colorists 172

New England: Sarah Orne Jewett; Mary E. Wilkins Freeman; Other Local-Colorists 182

X **The Gilded Age: Conservatism and Iconoclasm** . . . 187

Mark Twain; William Dean Howells; Henry James; Hamlin Garland; Stephen Crane 187

Reformers, Historians, and Philosophers 209

XI **Democracy and the Common Man: Novelists and Short-Story Writers** 214

Ambrose Bierce; Edward Bellamy; Francis Marion Crawford; H. C. Bunner 214

Other Novelists and Short-Story Writers 224

XII **Convention and Revolt in Poetry** 231

Emily Dickinson; Sidney Lanier; Edward Rowland Sill; John B. Tabb; Bliss Carman; Richard Hovey; William Vaughn Moody 231

Other Lyrists 249

XIII **Nationalism and Cosmopolitanism: Essayists, Critics, and Playwrights** 254

John Burroughs; Henry Adams; Gamaliel Bradford . . 254

Other Essayists and Critics 261

Playwrights 264

YESTERDAY AND TODAY

XIV **Representative Authors** 268

Historical Background 268

General View of the Literature 268

Short-Story Writers and Novelists 269

Poets 279

Important Playwrights 285

Chapter Page
Essayists, Critics, Educators, and Philosophers 288
APPENDIX: SUPPLEMENTARY BIBLIOGRAPHIES 296
INDEX 311

KEY TO SYMBOLS AND ABBREVIATIONS USED IN THIS HANDBOOK

NOTE: The dagger-mark or obelisk denotes an author's more important works.

AB. .... American Bookman
ABC. .... American Book Collector
AC. .... Americana Collector
ACQ. .... American Catholic Quarterly
AGR. .... American Germanic Review
AHR. .... American Historical Review
AIM. .... Annals of Internal Medicine
AJ. .... Appleton's Journal
AL. .... American Literature
AM. .... American Mercury
Americana .... Americana
AMH. .... Annals of Medical History
AN. .... Alienist and Neurologist
An.R. .... Antioch Review
AP. .... American Parade
A.Pr. .... American Prefaces
APSR. .... American Political Science Review
AR. .... American Review
Arena .... Arena
AS. .... American Speech
A.Schol. .... American Scholar
ASR. .... American-Scandinavian Review
Atl. .... Atlantic Monthly
AUP. .... Annales de l'Universite de Paris

BBDI. .... Bulletin of Bibliography and Dramatic Index
BFHA. .... Bulletin of Friends' Historical Association
Blackwood's .... Blackwood's
BLM. .... Book League Monthly
BMJ. .... British Medical Journal
BMSJ. .... British Medical and Surgical Journal
BNM. .... Book News Monthly
Bookman .... Bookman
Britannica .... Britannica; in Verbindung mit dem Seminar für englische Sprache und Kultur an der Hamburgischen Universität. (*Also:* Britannica; Herausgegeben vom Seminar für englische Sprache und Kultur an der Hansischen Universität)
BRLC. .... Bibliothèque de la Revue de Littérature Comparée
BS. .... Bibliotheca Sacra
BSP. .... Boston Society Publications

Cath.HR. .... Catholic Historical Review
CCP. .... Colorado College Publications

CE. .... College English
Century .... Century
CH. .... Church History
CHAL. .... Cambridge History of American Literature
Chaut. .... Chautauquan
CHR. .... Canadian Historical Review
CHSP. .... Cambridge Historical Society Publications
CHSR. .... Clarendon Historical Society Reprints
CJ. .... Classical Journal
CL. .... Canada Lancet
CLR. .... Columbia Law Review
CMHS. .... Collections of the Massachusetts Historical Society
Colophon .... Colophon
Critic .... Critic
CSM. .... Christian Science Monitor
Cu.H. .... Current History
CUQ. .... Columbia University Quarterly
CW. .... Catholic World
C.Weekly .... Classical Weekly

DAB. .... Dictionary of American Biography
Dial .... Dial
DR. .... Dalhousie Review

EA. .... Etudes Anglaises
Eco.R. .... Economic Review
EIHC. .... Essex Institute Historical Collections
EJCE. .... English Journal (College Edition)
EL. .... English Leaflet
Eng.R. .... English Review
ER. .... Edinburgh Review
ES. .... English Studies (Amsterdam)
Ethics .... Ethics

FM. .... Frontier and Midland
FR. .... Fortnightly Review
Freeman .... Freeman
Frontier .... Frontier
FT. .... Frontier Times

GBDP. .... Giessener Beiträge zur deutschen Philologie
GH. .... Good Housekeeping
GHQ. .... Georgia Historical Quarterly
GMHC. .... General Magazine and Historical Chronicle
GR. .... Germanic Review
Graham's .... Graham's

Harper's .... Harper's
HGM. .... Harvard Graduates' Magazine
HH. .... Hound & Horn
HJ. .... Hibbert Journal
HLB. .... Huntington Library Bulletin
HLQ. .... Huntington Library Quarterly
HM. .... Harvard Monthly
HMNQ. .... Historical Magazine, and Notes and Queries
HMS. .... Harvard Medical School
HR. .... Homiletic Review
HSNPL. .... Harvard Studies and Notes in Philology and Literature
HTR. .... Harvard Theological Review

IHS. .... Iowa Humanistic Studies
IJHP. .... Iowa Journal of History and Politics

IMH. .... Indiana Magazine of History
IMJ. .... Indiana Medical Journal
Ind. .... Independent
IR. .... International Review

JAF. .... Journal of American Folklore
JAH. .... Journal of American History
JEGP. .... Journal of English and Germanic Philology
JHAM. .... Johns Hopkins Alumni Magazine
JHHB. .... Johns Hopkins Hospital Bulletin
JHSHPS. .... Johns Hopkins Studies in History and Political Science
JISHS. .... Journal of the Illinois State Historical Society
JMH. .... Journal of Modern History
JMMS. .... Journal of the Michigan Medical Society
JSH. .... Journal of Southern History

KR. .... Kenyon Review

Landmark .... Landmark
LHJ. .... Ladies' Home Journal
LHQ. .... Louisiana Historical Quarterly
LLT. .... Life and Letters To-Day
LM. .... London Mercury
LMM. .... Lippincott's Monthly Magazine
LW. .... Literary World (Boston)

Macmillan's .... Macmillan's
MAH. .... Magazine of American History
MB. .... More Books (Boston Public Library Bulletin)
Med.R. .... Medical Record
MH. .... Mental Hygiene
M.Hist. .... Minnesota History
MHM. .... Maryland Historical Magazine
MHR. .... Missouri Historical Review
MHS. .... Massachusetts Historical Society
Mi.HM. .... Michigan History Magazine
MLN. .... Modern Language Notes
MLQ. .... Modern Language Quarterly
MLR. .... Modern Language Review
MM. .... Massachusetts Magazine
Mod.HM. .... Modern History Magazine
Mod.M. .... Modern Monthly
Month .... Month
MP. .... Modern Philology
MQ. .... Musical Quarterly
MR. .... Methodist Review
MRR. .... Medical Review of Reviews
MVHR. .... Mississippi Valley Historical Review

NAR. .... North American Review
Nation .... Nation
Nationalist .... Nationalist
NCR. .... New-Church Review
NEM. .... New England Magazine
NEQ. .... New England Quarterly
NQ. .... Notes and Queries
NR. .... New Republic
NSN. .... New Statesman and Nation
NYT. .... New York Times
NYTBR. .... New York Times Book Review
NYTM. .... New York Times Magazine

OHSQ. .... Oregon Historical Society Quarterly
OM. .... Overland Monthly
OSAHQ. .... Ohio State Archaeological and Historical Quarterly
Outlook .... Outlook

PAAS. .... Proceedings of the American Antiquarian Society
PBSA. .... Papers of the Bibliographical Society of America
PCSM .... Publications of the Colonial Society of Massachusetts
Personalist .... Personalist
PH. .... Pennsylvania History
PHR. .... Pacific Historical Review
PHSA. .... Proceedings of the Huguenot Society of America
PHSD. .... Papers of the Historical Society of Delaware
PIHS. .... Publications of the Ipswich Historical Society
PL. .... Poet-Lore
PMASAL. .... Papers of the Michigan Academy of Science, Arts and Letters
PMHB. .... Pennsylvania Magazine of History and Biography
PMHS. .... Proceedings of the Massachusetts Historical Society
PMLA. .... Publications of the Modern Language Association of America
PNJHS. .... Proceedings of the New Jersey Historical Society
Poetry .... Poetry
PQ. .... Philological Quarterly
PR. .... Partisan Review
PS. .... Physician and Surgeon
PSQ. .... Political Science Quarterly
PUB. .... Pacific University Bulletin
PVHS. .... Proceedings of the Vermont Historical Society
PW. .... Publishers' Weekly
Putnam's .... Putnam's

QQ. .... Queen's Quarterly
QR. .... Quarterly Review
QRB. .... Quarterly Review of Biology

RAA. .... Revue Anglo-Américaine
RCR. .... Reformed Church Review
RH. .... Revue Hispanique
RIHSC. .... Rhode Island Historical Society Collections
RIP. .... Rice Institute Pamphlet
RL. .... Religion in Life
RP. .... Review of Politics
RR. .... Review of Reviews
R.Rev. .... Romanic Review
RUL. .... Rutgers University Library

SAQ. .... South Atlantic Quarterly
SB. .... Southern Bivouac
Scribner's .... Scribner's
SF. .... Social Forces
SHJ. .... Southern History Journal
So.R. .... Southern Review
SP. .... Studies in Philology
SR. .... Sewanee Review
SRL. .... Saturday Review of Literature
SS. .... Science & Society
SSN. .... Scandinavian Studies and Notes
SSR. .... Sociology and Social Research
St.BHJ. .... St. Bartholomew's Hospital Journal
SUAN. .... Syracuse University Alumni News

Sunset .... Sunset
Sw.R. .... Southwest Review

TA. .... Theatre Arts
Thought .... Thought
TLS. .... Times Literary Supplement (London)
TR. .... Texas Review
TRSL. .... Transactions of the Royal Society of Literature
TWASAL. .... Transactions of the Wisconsin Academy of Sciences, Arts, and Letters

UBS. .... University of Buffalo Studies
UCC. .... University of California Chronicle
UCFP. .... Union College Faculty Papers
UIS. .... University of Iowa Studies
UISLL. .... University of Illinois Studies in Language and Literature
UKHSB. .... University of Kansas Humanistic Studies Bulletin
UKSE. .... University of Kansas Studies in English
U.Ma.S. .... University of Maine Studies
U.Mi.S. .... University of Missouri Studies
UNDQJ. .... University of North Dakota Quarterly Journal
UNGB. .... University of Nebraska Graduate Bulletin
Uni.R. .... Unitarian Review
UNSLLC. .... University of Nebraska Studies in Language, Literature and Criticism
UPB. .... University of Pittsburgh Bulletin
UR. .... University Record
USCHRS. .... U.S. Catholic Historical Records and Studies
UTB. .... University of Texas Bulletin
UTQ. .... University of Toronto Quarterly
UTSE. .... University of Texas Studies in English
U.Wa.PLL. .... University of Washington Publications in Language and Literature
U.Wi.SLL. .... University of Wisconsin Studies in Language and Literature

VJUS. .... Vassar Journal of Undergraduate Studies
VMHB. .... Virginia Magazine of History and Biography

WMH. .... Wisconsin Magazine of History
WR. .... Westminster Review
WUV. .... Washington University Studies

YR. .... Yale Review
YULG. .... Yale University Library Gazette

THE COLONIAL PERIOD

(1607-1763)

Chapter I

RENAISSANCE AND PURITAN INFLUENCES

HISTORICAL BACKGROUND

1603: Accession of James I. *1607:* Settlement of Virginia. *1609:* Separatists go to Holland. *1620:* Settlement of Plymouth by Separatist Pilgrims. *1630:* Settlement of Massachusetts Bay. *1632:* Maryland chartered. *1633:* Laud in power over all England. *1635:* Connecticut founded. *1636:* Providence settled. *1649—1660:* Commonwealth in England: Puritans in power. *1660:* The Restoration. *1663:* Carolina chartered. *1664:* New Jersey and New York established. *1675—1676:* King Philip's War and Bacon's Rebellion. *1681:* Pennsylvania chartered. *1684:* Massachusetts charter revoked. *1689:* Revolt against Andros. *1689—1697:* King William's War against the French.[1]

GENERAL VIEW OF THE LITERATURE

The earliest colonial literature was written by Englishmen who wrote in English literary forms. Their writing was not good, partly because it was imitative and partly because it was a side line. The literature was utilitarian. In style it followed English models, but there was a cultural lag and progress was slower. At the end of the seventeenth century, the American writer was closer to the Elizabethans than to Dryden.[2]

Literature in the South. Since exploration was a phase of the Renaissance, the first Southern authors were Elizabethan in energy, curiosity, and versatility. They were adventurers writing excitedly of disasters, new scenery, and Indians. Their prose, describing adventures or history, was vigorous, elaborate, and racy; their poetry was doggerel or full of conceits — and their models for both were the fanciful styles of *Euphues* and the metaphysical

1 For historical background see: C. M. Andrews, *The Colonial Period of American History* (four volumes, 1934-1938); C. P. Nettels, *The Roots of American Civilization* (1938), the best one-volume colonial history, with extensive bibliographies.

2 Most useful of the works on colonial literature are the following: M. C. Tyler, *A History of American Literature during the Colonial Time* (rev. ed., two volumes, 1897); M. C. Tyler, *The Literary History of the American Revolution, 1763-1783* (two volumes, 1897), still the best study of its time; V. L. Parrington, *Main Currents in American Thought*, I (1927). *The Cambridge History of American Literature*, I (1917), has excellent essays by authorities. Perry Miller and T. H. Johnson (editors), *The Puritans* (1938) supersedes earlier works.

poets.[3] Lack of printing and wide separation of settlers kept down both culture and writing.

SOUTHERN WRITERS

CAPTAIN JOHN SMITH, 1579/80—1631, annalist, romancer. Accompanied the first expedition to Jamestown (1607); a narrator of force. *A True Relation of Such Occurences and Accidents of Note as Have Happened in Virginia . . .* (1608). Graphic style. The first book in American literature. *A Map of Virginia* (1612). *A Description of New England* (1616), a glowing account. *The General History of Virginia, the Summer Isles, and New England*† (1623), has the complete story of Smith's rescue by Pocahontas.[4] *The True Travels* (1629).[5] *Advertisements for the Unexperienced Planters of New-England, or Anywhere* (1631), good advice, crisply written. Excellent description. Smith commended by such persons as Donne and Wither. He is Elizabethan in energy, versatility, and style — a lesser Ralegh.[6]

JOHN and ANN COTTON, authors and colonists, reacted to Bacon's Rebellion. Their long lost accounts found in the *Burwell Papers* contain the elegy "Bacon's Epitaph, Made by his Man,"† and "Upon the Death of G. B. [General Bacon]." The prose and perhaps the poems may be ascribed to John Cotton of "Queen's Creek."[7] Prose style is good, though pedantic. The poem, worthy of Marvell, is metaphysical in the style of Donne, Jonson, Cowley, and Henry King, and remarkably smooth and masterly.

THE PURITANS

Colonization was the last phase of the Reformation as well as of the Renaissance. The Pilgrims and Puritans hoped to set up in America a commonwealth, ideal according to their essentially Calvinistic theology.[8] The chief points of Puritan theology are:

---

3 For discussion of Southern writers see: W. M. Baskervill, *Southern Writers: Biographical and Critical* (1897-1903); *A Library of Southern Literature*, edited by E. A. Alderman and others (seventeen volumes, 1908-1923); M. J. Moses, *The Literature of the South* (1910). For historical background see: P. A. Bruce, *Economic History of Virginia in the Seventeenth Century* (two volumes, 1896); T. J. Wertenbaker, *Virginia under the Stuarts* (1914), and *The First Americans* (1929).

4 Fuller's *Worthies of England* points out that Smith is the sole authority for his fabulous adventures. As for the complimentary verses published with the *General History*, R. B. Botting does not believe them to be by John Donne: see *TLS.*, March 14, 1936, p. 224, col. 3.

5 See *Travels and Works of Captain John Smith*, edited by A. C. Bradley (1910); E. K. Chatterton, *Captain John Smith* (1927); S. E. Morison, *Builders of the Bay Colony* (1930), Chapter I.

6 For material on all American writers see the new and excellent *Dictionary of American Biography* (twenty volumes, 1928-1936).

7 J. B. Hubbell, "John and Ann Cotton, of 'Queen's Creek,' Virginia," *AL.*, X (1938-1939), pp. 179-201, gives all that is known of these writers.

8 The New Englanders studied Calvinism through the treatises of William Perkins, John Preston, and William Ames, men who modified the original doctrines of John Calvin's *Institutes of the Christian Religion*. See Perry Miller, *The New England Mind: The Seventeenth Century* (1939), Appendix B, and *passim*.

1. Absolute sovereignty of God.

2. Predestination: An omniscient Deity knows from the beginning who will be saved.

3. Providence: God directly intervenes in the world. Example: God responsible when mice ate Anglican prayer book but not the New Testament.

4. Natural depravity: Since Adam's fall all men are born in sin and deserve damnation.

5. Election: Through God's mercy a few are saved, but by grace alone, not by their own efforts.

6. Evil is inner: Man needs reform of himself, rather than of institutions.

7. God is revealed in the Bible.[9]

These tenets had certain practical effects. The Puritans sought to establish a Godly commonwealth developed in the Federal School of political theory: (1) Because man was naturally bad, God established government by a covenant, for His own glory. (2) Rulers as well as subjects had to obey the covenant. (3) Government included all spheres: church-going, amusements, dress, business practices, and prices. No religious freedom was permitted. (4) Church government in America was based upon the congregational system taken over from the Pilgrims. This ultimately led toward democracy in church and state, though the aims of the Puritans were far from democratic.

Despite theological agreement, the Puritans and Pilgrims showed differences: (1) The Puritans sought to reform the Anglican Church from within. The Pilgrims were Separatists who withdrew from the corrupt state church. (2) The Puritans were prosperous, with a university man for each thirty families. The Pilgrims were poor and in general less educated.

To insure the success of the Godly state, a highly educated clergy was developed. Result, Harvard College founded in 1636, and New England began to foster a culture of its own. In the arts, content took precedence over form. While music[10] and poetry were not frowned upon, the main emphasis was on utility, which dictated the literary types. History, defense, and promotion of the colony were common, and much of the religious writing — sermons, poems, diaries, biographies — was utilitarian in purpose. Adoption of the logic and rhetoric of Ramus encouraged a "plain style"[11] in Puritan

9 For the religious background see Perry Miller and T. H. Johnson (editors), *The Puritans* (1938), with bibliographies.

10 J. H. Kouwenhoven, "Singing in New England," *NEQ., VI* (1933), pp. 567-588.

11 S. E. Morison, *Harvard College in the Seventeenth Century* (two parts, 1936), Part I, pp. 169-193; Perry Miller and T. H. Johnson (editors), *The Puritans* (1938), Introduction, pp. 1-79.

prose, as opposed to the fanciful style of *Euphues* or the elaborate Anglican prose of Taylor, Donne, or Andrewes. Puritan poetry imitated the metaphysical conceits of English religious poets like Quarles and Herbert. Anagrams, puns, and tortured figures were common. The most popular poems were written in sing-song, jolting meter which was easy to memorize, if not appropriate to the subject matter; moral aims completely subdued form.

DESCRIPTION, ANNALS, AND HISTORY OF NEW ENGLAND

WILLIAM BRADFORD, *c.* 1588—1657, Pilgrim, statesman, annalist. Became a Separatist, and migrated to Leyden in 1609. Was a weaver; read theology. Migrated to New England (1620) and was governor, except for five years, from 1621 until his death. Had shrewd discretion and great generosity. Acquainted with French, Dutch, Latin, and Greek; studied Hebrew in old age. Possessed a silver beer bowl, red waistcoat, and violet cloak—items which do not fit modern misconceptions of Puritans.

Bradford, devout, conscious of providence, and nobly simple of character, was the greatest of early historians. His style, studiously clear, is based on the Geneva Bible (not the King James), and is enlivened by humor, irony, and alliteration.[12] But its quality is dependent primarily upon his greatness of character.

History of the Plymouth Plantation† (*c.* 1630—1651; first completely published in 1856).[13] Bradford's masterpiece. Kindliness and piety, care in sketching background, make his description of the sentiments of the disembarking settlers a high mark in eloquence.

THOMAS MORTON, *fl.* 1622—1647, adventurer, set up a colony at Wollaston or Merry Mount. His May-pole dances, debauchery, and sale of fire arms to Indians caused trouble. Was arrested several times and sent to England.[14] Died in Maine. *New English Canaan* (1637; edited by C. F. Adams, 1883) is, in part, a vigorous statement of Morton's side of the quarrel. Hawthorne used this career in "The Maypole of Merry-Mount," and Howard Hanson has written an opera on the same subject with a libretto by Richard L. Stokes.

JOHN WINTHROP, 1588—1649, statesman, diarist. Born in Suffolk of prosperous ancestry. At Cambridge two years, was justice of the peace, and attorney and squire. Discouraged by loss of attorneyship and the plight of the Puritans, he led movement

12 E. F. Bradford, "Conscious Art in Bradford's *History of Plymouth Plantation,*" *NEQ.*, I (1928), pp. 133-158.

13 Best editions are by W. T. Davis, *Original Narratives of Early American History* (1908), and W. C. Ford (two volumes, 1912). For biography see P. H. Plumb, *William Bradford of Plymouth* (1920).

14 Henry Adams, *Three Episodes in Massachusetts History*, I (1892).

to emigrate, was elected governor in 1629, and re-elected almost constantly. Censured for leniency in 1636, he afterwards acted more rigorously.

Letters.[15] Written to wife. The correspondence shows great depth of emotion combined with charm and religious sentiment.

Journal.†[16] Kept intermittently from 1630 to death. A great work embodying history, theology, political theory, economics,[17] providences, and daily life. The primary source for the early years of Massachusetts Bay. Covers ideals, controversies, hardships. The classic statement of Puritan political theory appears in 1645. Winthrop, no believer in democracy, which as John Cotton said was not supported by the Bible, distinguished between natural and civil liberty. Natural liberty, possessed by the unregenerate, is liberty to do evil as well as good; it resists authority and degrades man. Civil liberty, based on God's covenent with man, is liberty for good. In it obedience to authority exists and has meaning. In the subjection to civil liberty man is made free, and the magistrate who does less than his best to maintain his responsibility, should be censured.

MARY ROWLANDSON, *c.* 1635—1678, wife of the minister at Lancaster, captured by Indians in 1676 and ransomed after eleven weeks. *The Sovereignty & Goodness of God Together . . . ; Being a Narrative of the Captivity and Restoration of Mrs. Mary Rowlandson* (1682) went through more than thirty editions. Her idiomatic and sinewy English conveys a good picture of Indian life, the pathos of her situation, and the contemptuous attitude of the colonists toward the "noble savage."

SEVENTEENTH CENTURY THEOLOGIANS[18]

THOMAS SHEPARD, 1605—1649. Son of a grocer. B.A., Cambridge (Emmanuel College) in 1624; M.A. in 1627. Came to America in 1635 and was a leader against the Antinomians. Interested in education. His style is clear, strong, and good. *The Sincere Convert* (1641) ran through twenty editions.[19]

ROGER WILLIAMS, *c.* 1604—1683, minister, son of a tailor. Patronized by Sir Edward Coke. Went to Charterhouse;

15 J. H. Twichell, *Some Old Puritan Love-Letters* (1893); A. M. Earle, *Margaret Winthrop* (1895); *Winthrop Papers* (*MHS.*, two volumes, 1929-1931), I.

16 *The History of New England from 1630 to 1649*, edited by James Savage (two volumes, 1825-1826; revised, 1853); *Winthrop's Journal, "History of New England," from 1630 to 1649*, edited by J. K. Hosmer (two volumes, 1908).

17 E. A. J. Johnson, "Economic Ideas of John Winthrop," *NEQ.*, III (1930), pp. 235-250; Stanley Gray, "The Political Thought of John Winthrop," *NEQ.*, III (1930), pp. 681-705.

18 See C. K. Shipton, "The New England Clergy of the 'Glacial Age,'" *PCSM.*, XXXII (1937), pp. 24-54.

19 *The Autobiography of Thomas Shepard*, edited by Nehemiah Adams (1832); cf. S. E. Morison, *Builders of the Bay Colony* (1930), pp. 105-134.

B.A., Cambridge (1627). Went to Plymouth. Became pastor at Salem in 1633, where he got into trouble insisting: (1) that the New England churches separate, (2) that land be bought from the Indians to validate the charter, (3) that a magistrate refuse to receive an oath from an unregenerate man (this would have wrecked the judicial system of the colony), (4) that the civil government was without authority to punish persons for religious reasons. Such views would abolish the theocratic pretensions of the state. Ordered banished in 1635, on Winthrop's advice he fled to Rhode Island in the winter of 1636 and established a colony. Was a Baptist for a time; became and remained a seeker for truth. In 1643 he went to England, was befriended by Milton, obtained a charter, and advocated religious freedom. Was friendly with the Indians. Later he engaged in a controversy with the Quakers.

Williams was noble and magnanimous, had great personal charm, but was emotional and uncompromising. His views on religious liberty are well ahead of his time; so in his own day his influence was small.[20] His literary style is uneven, often verbose, elaborate, and tiring, but at its best richly eloquent.

Works include: *A Key into the Language of America* (1643); *The Bloody Tenent of Persecution for Cause of Conscience* (1644); *The Bloody Tenent Yet More Bloody: by Mr. Cotton's Endeavor to Wash It White in the Blood of the Lamb* (1652).[21] The last two books defend freedom of conscience in a powerful, if diffuse, style; the first is a dialogue between Truth and Peace. The second takes up the nature of persecution, the limits of civil power, and the rights already granted by parliament, with the conclusion that persecution for cause of conscience is unchristian. *Queries of Highest Consideration* (1644), advocates separation of church and state. *George Fox Digg'd out of His Burrows* (1676), written in language often violent, is addressed to the Quakers.[22] *The Writings of Roger Williams* (six volumes, 1866—1874) also contain many revealing letters.

JOHN DAVENPORT, 1597—1670, preacher, B.D., Oxford (1625), first minister in ultra-Puritan New Haven. Opposed Half-Way Covenant. Advent to Boston in 1668 split the First Church. See *A Sermon Preach'd at the Election . . . 1669* (1670).

---

20 J. E. Ernst, "The Political Thought of Roger Williams," *UWPLL.*, VI (1929), pp. 1-229; and *Roger Williams* (1932); F. B. Wiener, "Roger Williams' Contribution to Modern Thought," *RIHSC.*, XXVIII (1935), pp. 1-20; S. H. Brockunier, *The Irrepressible Democrat* (1940).

21 H. B. Parks, "John Cotton and Roger Williams Debate Toleration," *NEQ.*, IV (1931), pp. 735-756; Michael Freund, "Roger Williams, Apostle of Complete Religious Liberty," *RIHSC.*, XXVI (1933), pp. 101-133; E. F. Hirsch, "John Cotton and Roger Williams: Their Controversy concerning Religious Liberty," *CH.*, X (1941), pp. 38-51.

22 J. M. Ives, "Roger Williams, Apostle of Religious Bigotry," *Thought*, VI (1931), pp. 478-492.

THE MATHER DYNASTY

The decline of the Puritan "theocracy" is spanned by the Mather Dynasty. Lack of persecution, growth of prosperity, and decline in spirituality made for changes in New England. *The Half-Way Covenant* (*c.* 1662), drafted by Richard Mather, a clear concession to toleration, permitted children of non-regenerate, though baptized, parents to be baptized.[23] The loss of the Massachusetts Bay charter eliminated religious qualifications for voting. The Mathers attempted unsuccessfully to stem the trend.

RICHARD MATHER, 1596—1669. Pastor at Dorchester. Able, ambitious. Drew up the Cambridge Platform (1646) and backed the Half-Way Covenant.[24] *Church-Government and Church-Covenant Discussed* (1643). *A Platform of Church Discipline*† (1649). Helped edit *The Whole Book of Psalms* [*The Bay Psalm Book*] (1640).

INCREASE MATHER, 1639—1723, son of Richard.[25] B.A., Harvard (1656); M.A., Trinity College, Dublin (1658). Preached in England until 1661, then at Second [North] Church in Boston. As agent for the colony he obtained a new charter, but his popularity declined. Was President of Harvard (1685—1701), then forced out of office. Had prodigious learning and industry. One hundred fifty publications[26] couched in a lucid, forceful, and direct style. An able writer and administrator.

Writings include: *An Essay for the Recording of Illustrious Providences* (1684). On a suggestion from England he collected examples of providences which he classified scientifically. Generally known as "Remarkable Providences." *Cases of Conscience concerning Evil Spirits* (1693) claims that two witnesses (not possessed) are necessary to establish guilt of witch. *Several Reasons Proving that Inoculating or Transplanting the Small Pox Is a Lawful Practice* (1721); *Diary* (pub. 1900).

COTTON MATHER, 1663—1728, son of Increase.[27] M.A., Harvard (1681). From 1685 on associated with his father's church. An indefatigable worker; produced five hundred books and pamphlets. Was an active philanthropist, a clerical politician, and a promoter of science. Played some part in the Salem witchcraft trials, was opposed to the admission of spectral evidence, but made

---

23 Perry Miller, "The Half-Way Covenant," *NEQ.*, VI (1933), pp. 676-715.

24 Williston Walker, *Ten New England Leaders* (1901).

25 For biographical material see: Cotton Mather, *Parentator* (1724); K. B. Murdock, *Increase Mather, the Foremost American Puritan* (1925).

26 T. J. Holmes, *Increase Mather, a Bibliography of his Works* (two volumes, 1931).

27 Samuel Mather, *The Life of . . . Cotton Mather* (1729); Barrett Wendell, *Cotton Mather, the Puritan Priest* (1891, 1926); Ralph and Leslie Boas, *Cotton Mather* (1928); K. B. Murdock, "Cotton Mather, Parson, Scholar, Man of Letters," in A. B. Hart (editor), *Commonwealth History of Massachusetts* (1927-1930), II, pp. 323-354.

no open protest.[28] Public revulsion of feeling against the execution of twenty witches and two dogs helped break the power of the clergy. Conscious of this fact, Mather wrote the *Magnalia* to call the people back to the great days of New England.

His character is difficult to evaluate, for he possessed the usual Puritan virtues in exaggerated form. Had industry and ambition, but his vanity was inordinate. Was a mystic and a man of excellent ability.

His style, quaint and fantastic, tending toward Elizabethan elaboration, heavily decorated with quotations and allusions, did not conform to the "simple style" of the ordinary Puritan divines.[29] He emphasized providences; nevertheless, he was interested in science, accepted Copernican cosmography, advocated inoculation despite personal danger, and was elected to the Royal Society.[30] His openness to scientific advance tended to modernize his theology.

***Magnalia Christi Americana; or The Ecclesiastical History of New-England*†** (1702).[31] Greatest work. Has books on: the settlement of New England, lives of governors and magistrates, lives of sixty famous divines, history of Harvard College and its famous graduates, faith and polity of the churches, providences, conflicts with religious opponents, and the Indians. Though credulous, it is a deep mine of information, the most famous and most remarkable book of the time. Monumental in scholarship.

Bonifacius (1710). Reached many editions as *Essays to Do Good*. A treatise on organized philanthropy; influenced Franklin. Shows humanitarian impulse.

The Christian Philosopher; a Collection of the Best Discoveries in Nature with Religious Improvements (1721).[32] Attempts to reconcile science and religion. Outlines recent developments. Maintains that God's benevolence is manifest in nature and apparent to man through reason. God can interfere with man's affairs. Cf. *Sentiments on Small Pox Inoculation* (1721), favoring the innovation.

Manuductio ad Ministerium (1726). Handbook for preachers. The chapter on "Poetry and Style" is the best literary criticism of

---

28 C. W. Upham, "Salem Witchcraft and Cotton Mather," *HMNQ.*, Second Series, VI (1869), pp. 129-219; J. P. Quincy, "Cotton Mather and the Supernormal in New England History," *PMHS.*, Second Series, XX (1907), pp. 439-453; G. L. Burr (editor), *Narratives of the Witchcraft Cases* (1914), contains many documents. G. L. Kittredge, *Witchcraft in Old and New England* (1929), gives the general setting and examples. Cf. S. E. Morison, *The Puritan Pronaos* (1936), pp. 248-257.

29 Perry Miller, *The New England Mind: The Seventeenth Century*, pp. 331-362.

30 G. L. Kittredge, "Cotton Mather's Election into the Royal Society," *PCSM.*, XIV (1913), pp. 81-114.

31 Texts: *Magnalia* (two volumes, 1853-1855); *Selections from Cotton Mather*, edited by K. B. Murdock (1926). For Coleridge's use of the *Magnalia*, see David Davies, "Coleridge's Marginalia in Mather's *Magnalia*," *HLQ.*, II (1939), pp. 233-240.

32 For text, see *Selections from Cotton Mather*, edited by K. B. Murdock (1926). Cf. Theodore Hornberger, "The Date, the Source, and the Significance of Cotton Mather's Interest in Science," *AL.*, VI (1934-1935), pp. 413-420.

the colonial period. Praises Richard Blackmore's style; defends his own as containing substance, not only in thought, but in the profitable references.

Diary of Cotton Mather.†[33] A chronicle of his spiritual state rather than of external events.

MISCELLANEOUS PROSE

THOMAS BRATTLE, 1658—1713, merchant, son of the wealthiest man in New England. An able liberal. Helped the Brattle Street Church, opposed the witch trials, and wrote *A Full and Candid Account of the Delusion Called Witchcraft* (published 1798).

ROBERT CALEF, 1648—1719, merchant, author of *More Wonders of the Invisible World* (1700). Claimed that Cotton Mather had purposely fomented the witchcraft trials to regain spiritual control, a charge which is now, on the whole, dispelled.

NATHANIEL WARD, 1578—1652, minister's son.[34] B.A., Emmanuel College, Cambridge (1600); M.A. (1603). Studied and practiced law. Became a minister in 1618. Came to America (1634). Preached (1634—1636) at Ipswich (Indian name, Aggawam). Wrote *The Body of Liberties* (1641), the first law code of Massachusetts. Returned to England (1646), and became a minister again.

The Simple Cobbler of Aggawam in America. Willing to Help 'Mend His Native Country, Lamentably Tattered, Both in the Upper-Leather and Sole, with All the Honest Stitches He Can Take† (begun in 1645; 1647), by "Theodore de la Guard." Reached four editions in the first year.[35] Professed to be reflections of a self-exiled cobbler on religious dissensions. Is really a protest against toleration, women's fashions, and long hair on men. Looks forward to Presbyterian uniformity in England. The style is sincere, droll, pungent, vigorous, crotchety; Elizabethan in its puns, word coinage, learning, racy homeliness, and metaphors. Not typically Puritan. The most amusing work of the seventeenth century.

SAMUEL SEWALL, 1652—1730, jurist, merchant, diarist.[36] Like the Mathers he covers the transition. Born in England. B.A., Harvard (1671). Trained for but did not enter the ministry.

---

33 Published in *PMHS.*, Seventh Series, VII (1911), VIII (1912).

34 J. W. Dean, *Nathaniel Ward* (1868); S. E. Morison, *Builders of the Bay Colony* (1930), pp. 217-243.

35 *The Simple Cobbler of Aggawam in America*, edited by L. C. Wroth (1937).

36 N. H. Chamberlain, *Samuel Sewall and the World He Lived In* (1877); J. L. Sibley, *Biographical Sketches*, II (1881), pp. 345-364; H. C. Lodge, *Studies in History* (1884); H. W. Lawrence, "Samuel Sewall, Revealer of Puritan New England," *SAQ.*, XXXIII (1934), pp. 20-37.

Married daughter of the wealthy John Hull. Was a judge at the witchcraft trials, later publicly recanted his error. Member of the colonial council (1691—1725). Chief justice of the colony (1718—1728).

***Diary of Samuel Sewall, 1674—1729*†** (First published, 1878—1882). The American Pepys, but not his equal, Sewall is mercantile, conventional, religious, fond of dwelling on death, introspective, but affectionate and charming. Records daily events, summarizes sermons, attacks the wearing of wigs, and gives details of his courtship of Madam Winthrop and others. His interest in the comforts of life, in a less zealous religion, in humanitarianism, shows the emergence of eighteenth century secularism from the Reformation.

PURITAN POETRY

General View. Puritan poets were brought up on Horace and Virgil, read Sidney, Spenser, Quarles, Herbert, Sylvester's translation of Du Bartas, but were not interested in the fleshly poets. There was no lack of Puritan poetry, but there was a lack of genuine inspiration. Their conception of the poet's office emphasized content, not form; edification, not beauty. They were mainly metaphysical poets. When the use of conceits went out of fashion, their reputation suffered.[37]

The Whole Book of Psalms Faithfully Translated into English Metre (1640), better known as the ***Bay Psalm Book,*** by Thomas Weld, John Eliot, and Richard Mather. Ran to seventy editions; revised 1651, 1752. The object was, while adhering closely to the Hebrew, to put the Psalms into rhyme and meter so that they could be sung to set tunes. Result is comparable to similar attempts of Donne and Milton. Often considered a good example of bad poetry. The first *book* published in the colonies.

ANN BRADSTREET, *c.* 1612—1672, daughter of Thomas Dudley, later governor of Massachusetts. Married Simon Bradstreet. Emigrated to America (1630), lived near Andover (1644—1672). A sensitive woman transplanted to a wilderness and the mother of eight children, she nevertheless found time to write poetry,[38] often metaphysical and based upon a knowledge of Spenser, Sidney, Herbert, Quarles, and Sylvester's translation of Du

---

37 For a discussion of Puritan poetry see: M. C. Tyler, *History of American Literature* (rev. ed., two volumes, 1897), I, pp. 264-292; II, pp. 5-63; K. B. Murdock, *Handkerchiefs from Paul* (1927); Perry Miller and T. H. Johnson (editors), *The Puritans* (1938), pp. 545-552.

38 H. S. Campbell, *Anne Bradstreet and Her Time* (1891); L. Caldwell, *An Account of Anne Bradstreet* (1898); S. E. Morison, *Builders of the Bay Colony* (1930), pp. 320-336, are good biographies.

Bartas. Often bookish, but at her best when recording her own feelings and observations.[39]

The Tenth Muse Lately Sprung Up in America (1650). A later edition, *Several Poems . . . By a Gentlewoman in New-England* (1678), adds "Contemplations," "The Flesh and the Spirit," and verses on her family.[40] "The Four Elements," "The Four Constitutions," "The Four Seasons," and "The Four Monarchies" are written in tedious, cramped heroic couplets. They are full of erudition, which for a woman then was amazing. "The Four Monarchies" is based upon the Bible, Plutarch, Usher, and Ralegh's *History of the World.* "Contemplations" is her best poem, written in a seven line stanza with an Alexandrine, showing the influence of Sidney and Spenser. The descriptions of nature are charming and are employed, not only for moralization, but for their own sake, though the introduction of "philomel" shows her close adherence to poetic tradition. Good command of metrics. "To My Dear and Loving Husband" and some other poems show a tenderness and depth of feeling not commonly expressed in the colonial period. "Upon the Burning of Our House" is a deeply felt expression of loss, ending with the consolation that her treasures are in heaven. "Longing for Heaven" has pathos, simplicity, and grace. "In Honor of . . . Queen Elizabeth" shows resentment at the imputation that women are not capable, as does the "Prologue" to *The Tenth Muse.*

MICHAEL WIGGLESWORTH, 1631—1705, minister, doctor, poet.[41] Born in England. B.A., Harvard (1651); went to Malden (1654). A kindly and cheerful man, who studied medicine to care for his flock. This gentle parson wrote the most terrifying poem of the colonial period — and by far the most popular.

***The Day of Doom*†** (1662; best edition by K. B. Murdock, 1929). Written in galloping fourteeners with internal rhyme, a measure suited to popular appeal and easy memorization, but not to the subject. Describes Christ's descent upon an unsuspecting world, the terror of the sinners, the resurrection of the dead, and Christ's judgment. The children who die without committing sins are also judged, but are allowed by the kind-hearted author (who here breaks with rigid Calvinism) the easiest room in hell. The damned are rushed off to torment, and the blessed spend eternity in bliss. Despite its crude form, this poem has flashes of vitality and imagination.

---

39 Marcia Wheelock, "Mistress Anne Bradstreet," *VJUS.*, V (1931), pp. 26-29.

40 *The Works of Anne Bradstreet,* edited by J. H. Ellis (1867, 1932), is definitive. See also *The Poems of Anne Bradstreet,* Introduction by C. E. Norton (1897).

41 J. W. Dean, *Sketch of the Life of Rev. Michael Wigglesworth, A.M.* (1863); J. L. Sibley, *Biographical Sketches,* I (1873), pp. 259-286; F. O. Matthiessen, "Michael Wigglesworth, a Puritan Artist," *NEQ.,* I (1928) pp. 491-504.

God's Controversy with New-England.[42] Pictures the founding of a New England Canaan through prosperity, decline, threat of punishment, and the actual chastisement. Deplores the spiritual decline. Iambic pentameter used.

Meat out of the Eater (1670). In couplets of fourteeners, takes Christian comfort in sorrow.

EDWARD TAYLOR, *c.* 1645—1729, minister, poet. Born in England. B.A., Harvard (1671). Pastor and physician at Westfield. Most gifted of the Puritan poets. Work was unpublished at his own request. Four hundred pages of manuscript poetry found in Yale library (1937).[43] Writing belatedly in the school of Herbert, Crashaw, and Quarles, Taylor left poems of remarkable intensity, striking and often sustained imagery, and a certain American homeliness.

"Huswifery." Smoothest poem, built upon the sustained image of the stages in manufacturing a robe of glory. Based on fact that weaving was done in the home. Has deep emotion.

"The Ebb and Flow." God is flint and steel, author the tinder catching the sparks, which seem to die, but are fanned by God's spirit. Intense, with figure well maintained; one of the best.

"The Glory of, and the Grace in the Church Set Out." Flowers grow in the garden of the church, and are improved by the minister's art, but Christ makes them thrive. Verse compact almost to crabbedness.

"Meditation Eight" (1684). Tries to discern in astronomy a link between heaven and man, but truth and sustenance are in Christ, the bread of life. First stanza echoes the *"flamantia moenia mundi"* of Lucretius; last three extend the extravagant image of Christ made into bread. Perhaps best of all.

"Meditation Three" (Second Series, 1693). Begins beautifully, then becomes involved. Emphasizes humility.

SUPPLEMENTARY LIST OF AUTHORS

SOUTHERN WRITERS

GEORGE SANDYS, 1578—1644, traveler, poet. *Ovid's Metamorphosis Englished by G. S.* (1626).

FATHER ANDREW WHITE, 1579—1656, Catholic cleric, chronicler. *A Declaration of the Lord Baltemore's Plantation in Mary-land* (1633).

42 In *PMHS.*, XII (1871-1873), pp. 83-93.

43 For selections see: T. H. Johnson, "Edward Taylor: a Puritan 'Sacred Poet,'" *NEQ.*, X (1937), pp. 290-322; Perry Miller and T. H. Johnson (editors), *The Puritans* (1938), pp. 650-657; *The Poetical Works of Edward Taylor*, edited by T. H. Johnson (1939). See also Austin Warren, "Edward Taylor's Poetry: Colonial Baroque," *KR.*, III (1941), pp. 355-371.

WILLIAM STRACHEY, *fl.*1606—1618, annalist. *Wracke and Redemption of Sir Thomas Gates* (1625).

GEORGE PERCY, 1580—*c.*1632, chronicler. *Discourse of the Plantations of the Southern Colony of Virginia* (1607, 1619).

RICHARD RICH, *fl.*1609—1610, balladist. *Newes from Virginia* (1610).

ALEXANDER WHITAKER, 1585—1616/17, rector. *Good News from Virginia* (1613).

JOHN HAMMOND, *fl.*1635—1656, pamphleteer. *Leah and Rachel* (1656).

COLONEL HENRY NORWOOD, *fl.*1649, chronicler. *A Voyage to Virginia* (*c.*1649).

GEORGE ALSOP, *fl.*1658—1666, poet, adventurer. *A Character of the Province of Mary-Land* (1666).

JOHN GRAVES, Quaker poet. *A Song of Sion* (1662).

EBENEZER COOK [or Cooke], *fl.*1708—1730, poet. *The Sot-Weed Factor* (1708), and perhaps *Sot-Weed Redivivus* (1730).

NEW ENGLAND WRITERS

WILLIAM MORRELL, *fl.*1623—1625, poet. *New-England* (usually cited as *Nova Anglia;* 1625).

JOHN JOSSELYN, *fl.*1638—1675, chronicler. *New England's Rarities Discovered* (1672).

THOMAS LETCHFORD, annalist. *Plain Dealing* (1642).

JOHN COTTON, 1584—1652, theologian. *The Bloody Tenent Washed* (1647).

THOMAS HOOKER, *c.*1586—1647, theologian. *A Survey of the Sum of Church Discipline* (1648).

JOHN WILSON, *c.*1590—1667, clergyman, poet. *A Song of Deliverance* (1680).

CHARLES CHAUNCEY, 1592—1672, clergyman. *God's Mercy* (1655).

EDWARD WINSLOW, 1595—1655, annalist. *Mourt's Relation* (1622).

CAPTAIN JOHN UNDERHILL, *c.*1597—1672, soldier, annalist. *News from America* (1638).

EDWARD JOHNSON, 1598—1672, chronicler. *The Wonder-Working Providence of Sions Saviour in New England* (1653).

CAPTAIN JOHN MASON, *c.*1600—1672, soldier. *Brief History of the Pequot War* (1677, 1736).

JOHN NORTON, 1606—1663, clergyman. *The Heart of N-England Rent* (1659).

DANIEL GOOKIN, *c.*1612—1687, historian. *Historical Account of the Doings and Sufferings of the Christian Indians in New England, 1675-77* (1836).

PETER FOLGER, 1617—1690, non-Puritan poet. *A Looking-Glass for the Times* (1676).

THOMAS WHEELER, *c.*1620—1686, annalist. *Narrative* (published, 1827).

WILLIAM HUBBARD, *c.*1621—1704, historian. *Narrative of Troubles with the Indians* (1677).

JONATHAN MITCHELL, *c.*1624—1668, clergyman. *A Discourse* (1677).

SAMUEL LEE, 1625—1691, clergyman. *The Joy of Faith* (1687).

SAMUEL DANFORTH, 1626—1674, almanac poet.

URIAN OAKES, *c.*1631—1681, cleric, poet. *Elegie* (1677).

JOHN ROGERS, 1631—1684, poet. *Upon Mrs. Anne Bradstreet* (1678).

COLONEL BENJAMIN CHURCH, 1639—1718, chronicler. *King Philip's War* (1716).

JASPER DANCKAERTS, 1639—*c.*1703, traveler. *Journal* (in collaboration; published 1867, 1913).

BENJAMIN TOMPSON, 1642—1714, poet. *New England's Crisis* (1676).

JOHN NORTON, 1651—1716, poet. *A Funeral Elegy* (1678).

Chapter II

THE RISE OF RATIONALISM AND DEMOCRACY

HISTORICAL BACKGROUND

Migration of Germans and Scots into the Middle and Southern Colonies. *1702—1713:* Queen Anne's War. *1732:* Georgia chartered. *1734:* Beginning of the Great Awakening. *1740:* Massachusetts land bank established. *1744—1748:* King George's War. *1755:* Deportation of Acadians. *1756—1763:* French and Indian War. *1760:* Accession of George III. *1763—1765:* Pontiac's conspiracy.[1]

GENERAL VIEW OF THE LITERATURE

Early eighteenth century American literature shows few significant changes from that of the seventeenth. In New England, especially, the prose style grew simpler,[2] while Pope and the neoclassicists influenced the poetry. Newtonianism and deism affected upper-class thought. In the South, a cultivated class was arising (William and Mary College established, 1693); the wealthiest planters educated their sons in England. The Middle Colonies also became prominent culturally (King's College, now Columbia, was established, 1754; the Philadelphia Academy was founded in 1749; and the Presbyterians began the College of New Jersey, now Princeton, in 1746).

RELIGIOUS WRITING IN NEW ENGLAND

JOHN WISE, 1652—1725, clergyman, son of an indentured servant.[3] B.A., Harvard (1673). Minister in Ipswich from 1682. Led protest against taxes laid by Andros, was arrested. Attacked plan for rigid church government; favored use of paper money, and inoculation. Style is clear, logical, interesting.

---

1 For historical background see again p. 1, footnote 1. Also Francis Parkman, *The Conspiracy of Pontiac* (1851), *Montcalm and Wolfe* (1884); J. T. Adams, *Provincial Society* (1928); Charles and Mary Beard, *The Rise of American Civilization* (rev. ed., 1933); H. L. Osgood, *The American Colonies in the Eighteenth Century* (four volumes, 1934).

2 See H. M. Jones, "American Prose Style: 1700-1770," *HLB.*, No. 6 (1934), pp. 115-151.

3 See: H. M. Dexter, *The Congregationalism of the Last Three Hundred Years, as Seen in Its Literature* (1880), pp. 494-507; J. M. Mackaye, "The Founder of American Democracy," *NEM.*, N. S. XXIX (1903), pp. 73-83; T. F. Waters, "John Wise of Chebacco," *PIHS.*, No. 26 (1927), pp. 1-23.

The Churches Quarrel Espoused (1710). Attacks the Mathers' plan for clerical control of churches. Overwhelming in vigor and semi-Miltonic eloquence.

A Vindication of the Government of New-England Churches† (1717). A closely reasoned exposition of the Congregational system of democratic church government. Showed a new trend by separating theology and rational argument. Established the law of nature on reason equally with revelation. Civil governments are set up by men, for the good of men, not for the glory of God. Men follow natural laws discernible through reason. In a state of nature, men are free and equal; in joining a society they give up some natural rights for the general good. Of three types of society — democracy, aristocracy, and monarchy — democracy is first and best. Wise carried this argument from civil to church government, used Pufendorf's *De Jure Naturae et Gentium* (translated, 1703) as source. Wise was republished in 1722 to aid the Revolutionary cause.

JONATHAN EDWARDS, 1703—1758, clergyman, theologian, mystic.[4] The greatest American mind of the colonial period. Son of a preacher at East Windsor, Connecticut. Precocious, educated at home. Was graduated from Yale (1720). Studied theology until 1722. Presbyterian minister in New York City (1722—1723). Tutor at Yale (1724—1726). Became colleague of his grandfather, Solomon Stoddard, in Northampton (1726). Married Sarah Pierrepont (1727). Conducted religious revivals at Northampton (1734 *ff.*). Felt that sudden conversion, frowned upon by the Puritans, was a sign of election. In difficulties with his parish partly because he insisted only the regenerate be given communion. Resigned parish (1750). Missionary at Stockbridge (1751—1757). Family poor; sold lace, painted fans, and embroidery. Appointed president of College of New Jersey. Died as result of smallpox inoculation.

Edwards was deeply mystical and at the same time a great logician. Was adept in science,[5] psychology, and philosophy. This complexity makes him difficult to treat. He was not a typical Calvinist. He was an idealist in philosophy, and used a logical system not typical of the Puritans. Read Locke at Yale, and was greatly

4 S. E. Dwight, *The Life of President Edwards* (Volume I of the *Works*, edited by Dwight, 1829); "Jonathan Edwards' Last Will and the Inventory of His Estate," *BS.*, XXXIII (1876), pp. 438-447; A. V. G. Allen, *Jonathan Edwards* (1889) is excellent; H. N. Gardiner (editor), *Jonathan Edwards: A Retrospect* (1901); A. P. Stokes, *Memorials of Eminent Yale Men*, I (1914), pp. 19-29; S. T. Williams (editor), "Six Letters of Jonathan Edwards to Joseph Bellamy," *NEQ.*, I (1928), pp. 226-243; H. B. Parks, *Jonathan Edwards, the Fiery Puritan* (1930); A. C. McGiffert, *Jonathan Edwards* (1932); T. H. Johnson, "Jonathan Edwards and the 'Young Folks' Bible," *NEQ.*, V (1932), pp. 37-54; O. A. Winslow, *Jonathan Edwards, 1703-1758; a Biography* (1940) is best for the facts of his life.

5 C. H. Faust, "Jonathan Edwards as a Scientist," *AL.*, I (1929-1930), pp. 393-404; Theodore Hornberger, "The Effect of the New Science upon the Thought of Jonathan Edwards," *AL.*, IX (1937-1938), pp. 196-207.

influenced by him. By using part, and attacking part of Locke's ideas, Edwards became leading defender of Puritanism against Arminian and deistic attacks. Mystical experiences confirmed his belief in the absolute sovereignty of God; he spent much of his life glorifying God and debasing man. His renown as a hell-fire preacher represents this aspect of his work. He initiated the Great Awakening,[6] entertained Whitefield, and defending his own course against Charles Chauncey, he favored good works, not writhings, as proof of conversion. His importance lies in two divergent directions: He reinforced Calvinistic theology and philosophy, exerting a wide influence in Scotland and Holland as well as America.[7] Also, by promoting the Great Awakening, he exerted a liberalizing political effect, since the uneducated were more likely to have emotional experiences than the rich. The Great Awakening was important for fastening a rigorous morality, often called Puritan but really evangelical, upon the American people.[8] He was also an early American idealist.

Edwards' style is lucid and compact, patterned on the Tillotson school, and especially on the Bible. Never ornate, it has few figures, and no straining for effect. His early work is often emotional and eloquent, but his later controversial writing is bare logic. Late in life he read *Sir Charles Grandison,* and expressed regret at having paid too little attention to style.

Writings[9] include: *Of Insects* (1751), brilliant observations on flying spiders by a boy of eleven. *Of Being* and *Notes on the Mind,* both college essays; latter shows philosophical idealism, the source of which has been mooted but is probably not Berkeley but Edwards' own mind working on Locke;[10] contends that reality is in the mind of God and is communicated to man by His will. *Resolutions* (1722—1723) lays out a rigorous spiritual regimen. *Narrative of Surprising Conversions* (1735; rev. 1736), originally a letter to Charles Chauncey describing the Northampton revival. Later version included account of the spiritual wrestlings of Phoebe Bartlett, a child of four. *A Treatise concerning Religious Affections* (sermons of 1742—1743; 1746). His thesis: men are

---

6 E. H. Byington, "Jonathan Edwards and the Great Awakening," *BS.*, LV (1898), pp. 114-127.

7 Leslie Stephen, *Hours in a Library,* Second Series (1876), pp. 44-106; G. P. Fisher, *Discussions in History and Theology* (1880), pp. 227-252; F. H. Foster, *A Genetic History of the New England Theology* (1907), pp. 47-103; I. W. Riley, *American Philosophy: The Early Schools* (1907); H. W. Schneider, *The Puritan Mind* (1930), pp. 102-155; H. G. Townsend, *Philosophical Ideas in the United States* (1934), pp. 35-62.

8 H. M. Jones, "The European Background," in *The Reinterpretation of American Literature,* edited by Norman Foerster (1929).

9 *The Works of President Edwards,* edited by S. E. Dwight (ten volumes, 1829-1830); *Benjamin Franklin and Jonathan Edwards: Selections from Their Writings,* edited by Carl Van Doren (1920); *Jonathan Edwards: Representative Selections,* edited by C. H. Faust and T. H. Johnson (1935), has an excellent critical analysis of Edwards' thought, pp. xi-cxv (pp. xi-cxlii).

10 For bibliography on the sources of Edwards' ideas see C. H. Faust and T. H. Johnson, *op. cit.*

governed by passions (an un-Puritan doctrine derived from Shaftesbury and Hutcheson), so the best affections should be instilled in them by conversion which bestows a new spiritual sense. This concept probably an answer to Locke's sensationalism. *Sinners in the Hands of an Angry God* (1741), celebrated picture of man suspended over hell. *Farewell Sermon* (1750), eloquent. *The Great Christian Doctrine of Original Sin Defended* (1758) contends men act out of self-love and are therefore bad. *The Nature of True Virtue* (1765), claims that virtue is disinterested benevolence; man, being motivated by self-love, is incapable of altruism. Influenced by Hutcheson, Shaftesbury, Cudworth.

***Personal Narrative*†** (1739). Describes Edwards' conversion about twenty years before. Radiates serenity and sweetness of his state after conversion. A most attractive work.

***A Careful and Strict Enquiry into the Modern Prevailing Notions of that Freedom of Will Which Is Supposed to Be Essential to Moral Agency, Virtue and Vice, Reward and Punishment, Praise and Blame*†** (1754). One of the greatest philosophical works written in America. Attacked the Arminian believers in freedom of the will, like Clarke, Taylor, and Chubb. Edwards' analysis is based on Hobbes, Collins, and Locke, though he may have known the first two only through their attackers. He contends, with Locke, that will is subject to the strongest motive. A man can do what he wills, but he cannot will what he wills. Since a man does an act willingly, he is responsible to God for it. (Hobbes made those two points.) Completely tears down the Arminian argument. Note Dr. Johnson's comment on Boswell's statement that Edwards puzzled him: "All theory is against the freedom of the will, all experience for it."

CHARLES CHAUNCEY, 1705—1787, Boston minister, a leading antagonist of Edwards in controversy over the Great Awakening.[11] Chauncey was urbane, cultivated, socially conservative; in religion he pointed towards Unitarianism. Wrote: *Enthusiasm Described and Caution'd Against* (1742), "A Letter from a Gentleman in Boston, to Mr. George Wishart" (1742),[12] and *Seasonable Thoughts on . . . Religion in New-England* (1743).

HISTORY AND ANNALS IN NEW ENGLAND

SARAH KEMBLE KNIGHT, 1666—1727, schoolmistress of Benjamin Franklin.[13] Took a round trip from Boston to New

11 See C. H. Maxson, *The Great Awakening in the Middle Colonies* (1920); W. M. Gewehr, *The Great Awakening in Virginia* (1930); J. C. Miller, "Religion, Finance, and Democracy in Massachusetts," *NEQ.*, VI (1933), pp. 29-58; M. H. Mitchell, *The Great Awakening* (1934).

12 In *CHSR.*, First Series, No. 7 (1883).

13 A. Titus, "Madam Sarah Knight, Her Diary and Her Times," *BSP.*, IX (1912), pp. 99-126.

York alone in 1704—1705. Her *Journal,* which went through four editions, gives a sharp, racy account of the people away from civilization, their manners, speech, and habits. An early example of American humor.

THE SOUTHERN COLONIES

ALEXANDER SPOTSWOOD, 1676—1740, governor of Virginia, did exploring in the Shenandoah valley and made treaties with the Indians.[14]

WILLIAM BYRD OF WESTOVER, 1674—1744, planter, author, official.[15] Educated in England by his wealthy family. Aristocratic, cultivated book collector and amateur scientist. *History of the Dividing Line Run in the Year 1728* describes the survey of boundary between Virginia and North Carolina. Contains satirical sketches of the indolent frontiersmen of Carolina,[16] and excellent description of nature. Written in urbane, cultivated eighteenth century style. *A Journey to the Land of Eden in the Year 1733* (1841) describes trip to his holdings in Carolina, ironically called Eden. Contains more clever attacks on Lubberland. *A Progress to the Mines, in the Year 1732* (1841),[17] another account of a trip written with his usual wit. New writings have recently been discovered.[18]

THE MIDDLE COLONIES

The Friends, founded by George Fox, and steadily persecuted for their religious beliefs, had obtained a haven in Pennsylvania.[19] The principles of Quakerism were: (1) A loving God. (2) The inner light; *i.e.,* God revealed himself to individuals directly, not only through the Bible, churches, and nature. (3) Equality before

---

14 See *The Official Letters of Alexander Spotswood,* edited by R. A. Brook (two volumes, 1882-1885); Leonidas Dodson, *Alexander Spotswood, Governor of Colonial Virginia, 1710-1722* (1932).

15 R. C. Beatty, *William Byrd of Westover* (1932); M. H. Woodfin, "William Byrd and the Royal Society," *VMHB.,* XL (1932), pp. 23-34, 111-123; G. R. Lyle, "William Byrd, Book Collector," *ABC.,* V (1934), pp. 163-165, 208-209; J. R. Masterson, "William Byrd in Lubberland," *AL.,* IX (1937-1938), pp. 153-170; L. B. Wright ,"The 'Gentleman's Library' in Early Virginia: The Literary Interests of the First Carters," *HLQ.,* I (1937), pp. 3-61, furnishes background; C. L. Cannon, "William Byrd II of Westover," *Colophon,* N. S., III (1938), pp. 291-302; L. B. Wright, "A Shorthand Diary of William Byrd of Westover," *HLQ.,* II (1939), pp. 489-496; L. B. Wright and Marion Tinling, "William Byrd of Westover: An American Pepys," *SAQ.,* XXXIX (1940), pp. 259-274.

16 Carl Holliday, *The Wit and Humor of Colonial Days* (1912), pp. 145-152.

17 All three were published in *Westover Manuscripts* (1841). Cf. *The Writings of "Colonel William Byrd of Westover in Virginia, Esq.,"* edited by J. S. Bassett (1901), which includes excellent biographical sketch; *A Journey to the Land of Eden and Other Papers,* edited by Mark Van Doren (1928); *Byrd's History of the Dividing Line betwixt Virginia and North Carolina,* edited by W. K. Boyd (1929), which contains for the first time the "Secret History of the Line."

18 *The Secret Diary of William Byrd,* edited by L. B. Wright and Marion Tinling (1941); *Another Secret Diary of William Byrd,* edited by M. H. Woodfin (1942).

19 See M. K. Jackson, *Outlines of the Literary History of Colonial Pennsylvania* (1906); R. M. Jones, *The Quakers in the American Colonies* (1911); Luella Wright, *The Literary Life of the Early Friends* (1932).

God. Made Quakers democratic. (4) Salvation open to all who seek it; opposed to predestination. (5) Freedom of the will. (6) Objection to war, violence, and persecution. (7) Charity and humanitarianism.

THOMAS GODFREY, 1736—1763, watchmaker, poet, dramatist. Son of a philosophical glazier. Became soldier, later factor in North Carolina, where he died. *Juvenile Poems . . . with The Prince of Parthia, a Tragedy* (1765) was edited by Nathaniel Evans, another poet in William Smith's coterie.[20] Smith wrote an introduction to the play. Godfrey's poems are conventional, imitating Pope and his school. *The Prince of Parthia* (*c.*1759; 1765) is in blank verse modeled on Shakespeare, Beaumont and Fletcher, and Rowe.[21] The plot moves rapidly, and the characterization is not bad. Verse uneven but often good. Staged in 1767, the first American tragedy performed in the colonies.

JOURNALISM IN THE COLONIES[22]

The first American newspaper, *Publick Occurrences* (Boston, 1690), was suppressed after only one issue. The *Boston News-Letter* (1704—1776) was the first successful paper. The *Boston Gazette* (1719—1741) and James Franklin's liberal *New England Courant* (1721—1726) were early papers, and others were established in Philadelphia (1719) and New York (1725). Thirty-seven papers were published in the colonies by 1775.

Magazines were slower in starting.[23] Andrew Bradford's *American Magazine,* which lasted three issues, appeared at Philadelphia in 1741. Benjamin Franklin's *General Magazine and Historical Chronicle* was first published in the same year and lasted for six issues. Perhaps the most important from a literary point of view was the *American Magazine* (Philadelphia, 1757—1758), edited by William Smith, who used it to encourage the work of a group of young writers. Contributions to these early periodicals are more significant for social history than for literary merit.

SUPPLEMENTARY LIST OF AUTHORS

NORTHERN COLONIES

RICHARD STEERE, poet. *The Daniel Catcher* (1713).

SAMUEL PENHALLOW, historian. *History of the Wars . . . with the Eastern Indians* (1726).

20 A. F. Gegenheimer, "Thomas Godfrey: Protégé of William Smith," *PH.*, IX (1942-1943), pp. 233-251; X (1943-1944), pp. 26-43.

21 T. C. Pollock, "Rowe's *Tamerlane* and *The Prince of Parthia*," *AL.* VI (1934-1935), pp. 158-162.

22 C. A. Duniway, *The Development of Freedom of the Press in Massachusetts* (1906); E. C. Cook, *Literary Influences in Colonial Newspapers, 1704-1750* (1912) is excellent; W. G. Bleyer, *Main Currents in the History of American Journalism* (1927); W. S. Hoole, *A Check-List and Finding-List of Charleston Periodicals, 1732-1864* (1936); F. L. Mott, *American Journalism* (1941).

23 See F. L. Mott, *A History of American Magazines, 1741-1850* (1930); L. N. Richardson, *A History of Early American Magazines, 1741-1789* (1931).

SAMUEL WILLARD, 1640—1707, theologian. *A Compleat Body of Divinity* (1726).
SOLOMON STODDARD, 1643—1729, minister, theologian. *An Answer to Some Cases of Conscience* (1722).
JOHN DUNTON, 1659—1733. *Letters from New England* (1867).
JOHN WILLIAMS, 1664—1729, minister. *The Redeemed Captive* (1707).
ZABDIEL BOYLESTON, 1669—1766, physician. *Some Account of Inoculation* (1721).
BENJAMIN COLMAN, 1673—1747, clergyman. *The Government and Improvement of Mirth* (1707).
PAUL DUDLEY, 1675—1751, scientist.
JOHN BULKLEY, 1679—1731. *The Necessity of Religion in Societies* (1713).
ROGER WOLCOTT, 1679—1767, poet. *Poetical Meditations* (1725).
JOHN BARNARD, 1681—1770, clergyman. *The Throne Established by Righteousness* (1734).
THOMAS PRINCE, 1687—1758, historian. *Chronological History of New England* (1736—1755).
WILLIAM DOUGLASS, *c.*1691—1752, historian. *Summary* (1748—1753).
EBENEZER TURELL, 1702—1778, biographer.
JOHN ADAMS, *c.*1705—1740, poet. *Poems on Several Occasions* (1745).
JOSEPH GREEN, 1706—1780, poet. *The Loss of His Cat* (1733).
MATHER BYLES, 1707—1788, Tory poet, preacher. *Poems on Several Occasions* (1744); *The Conflagration* (1755).
NATHANIEL AMES, 1708—1764. *Astronomical Diary and Almanac* (1725—1764).
JOHN SECCOMB, 1708—1792, poet. "Father Abbey's Will" (1731).
JANE TURELL, 1708—1735, poet. *Reliquiae Turellae et Lachrymae Paternae* (1735; reprinted as *Memoirs of the Life . . . of Jane Turell,* 1741).
JOHN WINTHROP, 1714—1779, scientist.
JONATHAN MAYHEW, 1720—1766, liberal clergyman. *The Snare Broken* (1766).
JOHN MAYLEM, *b.*1739, poet. *Gallic Perfidy* (1758); *Conquest of Louisberg* (1758).

SOUTHERN COLONIES

JOHN LAWSON, *d.*1711, historian. *A New Voyage to Carolina* (1709).
JAMES BLAIR, 1655—1743, educator, historian. *The Present State of Virginia* (1727).
HUGH JONES, *c.*1670—1760, teacher. *The Present State of Virginia* (1724).
ROBERT BEVERLEY, *c.*1673—1722, historian. *History and the Present State of Virginia* (1705, 1722).
ALEXANDER GARDEN, 1685—1756, Charleston minister. *Six Letters* (1740); *The Doctrine of Justification* (1742).
JAMES E. OGLETHORPE, 1696—1785, colonizer, annalist. *A New and Accurate Account of . . . South Carolina and Georgia* (1733).
WILLIAM DAWSON, 1704—1752, poet. *Poems on Several Occasions* (1736).
PATRICK TAILFER, *fl. c.*1740, historian of Georgia. *A True and Historical Narrative . . . of Georgia* (1740).
WILLIAM STITH, 1707—1755, historian. *History of the First Discovery and Settlement of Virginia* (1747).

MIDDLE COLONIES

DANIEL DENTON, *d. c.*1696. *A Brief Description of New York* (1670).
DANIEL LEEDS, 1652—1720. Almanacs.
DANIEL COXE, 1673—1739, traveler. *A Description of . . . Carolana* (1722).
CADWALLADER COLDEN, 1688—1776. *History of the Five Indian Nations* (1727).
JONATHAN DICKINSON, 1688—*c.*1747. *Familiar Letters* (1745).
WILLIAM LIVINGSTON, 1723—1790, lawyer, poet. *Philosophic Solitude* (1747).
SAMUEL DAVIES, 1723—1761. *Sermons* (three volumes, fifth edition, 1792).
WILLIAM SMITH, 1728—1793, historian. *History of . . . New York* (1757).

THE REVOLUTIONARY PERIOD
(1763-1810)

Chapter III

THE STRUGGLE FOR INDEPENDENCE: DEISM, NATIONAL ISSUES, AND THE BEGINNINGS OF *BELLES LETTRES*

HISTORICAL BACKGROUND

General View. (1) Increasing tension with England. (2) The Revolutionary War. (3) Establishment of federal government and the Constitution. (4) Rise of political parties. (5) The beginnings of American nationalism. (6) Expansion into the Ohio valley.

The Revolution (1763—1783). *1761:* James Otis attacks writs of assistance. *1763:* Proclamation of 1763 forbids settlement in the West. *1764:* The Sugar Act and the Currency Act. *1765:* Quartering Act. Stamp Act. Non-importation agreements. *1766:* Repeal of Stamp Act. *1767:* Townshend Act. *1770:* Repeal of Townshend Act except its tea duties. Boston Massacre. *1773:* East India Act and Boston Tea Party. *1774:* Coercive Acts. Quebec Act. First Continental Congress adopts Declaration of Rights; Continental Association. *1775:* Battles of Lexington and Concord (April). Battle of Bunker Hill (June). *1776: Declaration of Independence* (July 4). Battle of Trenton. *1777:* Burgoyne's surrender at Saratoga. *1777—1778:* Valley Forge hardships. *1778:* Alliance with France. *1781:* Articles of Confederation ratified. Surrender of Cornwallis at Yorktown. *1783:* Peace of Paris recognizes independence.

The New Nation (1783—1810). *1786:* Annapolis Convention. *1787:* Constitutional Convention works out a new frame of government. The Ordinance of 1787. Struggle for ratification of the Federal Constitution. *1787—1788: The Federalist* papers. *1787—1797:* Washington in office. *1792:* Hamilton's scheme of government in operation. *1793:* Jefferson resigns from cabinet. *1797:* John Adams inaugurated as president. *1798:* Alien and Sedition Acts. *1801:* Jefferson becomes president. *1803:* Louisiana Purchase. *1807:* Embargo on shipping. *1809:* Repeal of Embargo Act. Madison becomes president.

Political and Social Conditions. The Enlightenment marks the transition from colonial status to independence and successful federation. The colonies, squeezed by the mercantile system, took steps toward resistance. While independence was being won with foreign aid, an internal revolution against the aristocracy was going on. This conflict halted when the Constitution again put the conservatives in the saddle. Two major political parties emerged: the Federalists, conservative, pro-English, representing commercial and financial interests; the Republicans, liberal, pro-French, representing the agrarian interests. Jefferson led the latter into office, but did not permanently destroy Hamilton's eonomic and financial system. Threats of war with England darkened early nineteenth century optimism.[1]

GENERAL VIEW OF THE LITERATURE

The eighteenth century marked the break in thought between medieval survivals and modern trends. Newtonian science strengthened deism and gave birth to the idea of progress. Natural rights and democracy went hand in hand. Aesthetic primitivism adopted the idea of the noble savage. Classicism and neoclassicism gave way before the impact of science and sentimentalism. America was also influenced by the frontier, Quakerism, political conflicts, and a growing nationalism. This period was marked by the decline of Puritan influence, the rise of Philadelphia, Hartford, and finally New York as literary capitals, and by the appearance of the novel and drama.

Prose. The writing was still predominantly utilitarian, and often heavy in style. Works resulting from the rationalism of the age were dominant. Travel literature and scientific works found a large sale, but most prose was political, turning on issues of the Revolutionary war and the adoption of the Constitution. The journalistic essays have not, in general, survived.

Poetry. Through much of this period the previous standards were in force; Butler, Dryden, Pope, Pomfret, and Churchill were models of satire; and Goldsmith, Akenside, Young, and Macpherson influenced other writers. Satire was popular. Freneau, the best poet of the period, showed a romantic concreteness of imagery in his best poems, but the Hartford wits used older models for their political verse and deadly epics.

Drama. Religious opposition to drama was so stubborn in America that plays were not legally presented in Philadelphia until

---

1 For historical, political, and social background see p. 1, footnote 1. Also S. G. Fisher, *The True History of the Revolution* (1902); C. E. Merriam, *A History of American Political Theories* (1903); G. O. Trevelyan, *The American Revolution* (four volumes, 1899-1907); Carl Becker, *The History of Political Parties in the Province of New York* (1909) and *The Eve of the Revolution* (1918); A. M. Schlesinger, *The Colonial Merchants and the American Revolution* (1918); R. G. Adams, *The Political Ideas of the American Revolution* (1922); C. H. McIlwain, *The American Revolution* (1923); S. E. Morison, *Sources . . . Illustrating the American Revolution* (1923); Allan Nevins, *The American States during and after the Revolution* (1924); J. F. Jameson, *The American Revolution Considered as a Social Movement* (1926); R. G. Gettell, *History of American Political Thought* (1928).

1787, and in Boston until 1791. The Revolution produced a number of plays on war subjects, but it was not until Tyler's *Contrast* (1787) that comedy of manners appeared. From that time there was a steady production of plays, though their literary quality was not great.

The Novel. Objections to frivolous or immoral fiction colored the earliest novels, which were heavily didactic. Many were influenced by Richardson's sentimental code and seduction plots. Brockden Brown imitated the Gothic romances and Godwin, while Brackenridge modeled his work on Cervantes and Swift. Despite the American scenes, the early novels were derivative in technique.

PROSE OF THE ENLIGHTENMENT

The development of rationalism had a great effect upon religious and political thought in America. Newtonian rationalism[2] embodied the following points: (1) A universe operating by unchanging laws. (2) A harmonious system. (3) A benevolent deity. (4) Man seeking inner harmony corresponding with the cosmos. (5) Probable immortality. This scheme was at first used by Cotton Mather and others to re-enforce Biblical revelation.

It was an easy step to deism, which accepted Newtonian assumptions but gave them a different application: (1) A transcendant God operating by natural law rather than by providential intervention. (2) A benevolent God. (3) God revealed in nature, not in the Bible. (4) Freedom of the will. (5) Man naturally altruistic. (6) Men are equal. (7) Evil is result of corrupt institutions, not of man's natural depravity. (8) Man is perfected by education. (9) Humanitarian aid to man is the best service of God. (10) Distrust of existing religious systems.

Deism[3] was an aristocratic movement until the Revolution, but it then made serious inroads upon religion from 1791 to 1810. Primitivism, the idea that man in the state of nature is superior to man in civilization, was common. Popularized by Rousseau and the Abbé Raynal, the view was conditioned in America by contact with the Indians.[4] The idea of progress[5] was also prevalent in

2 See: C. S. Duncan, *The New Science and English Literature in the Classical Period* (1913); E. A. Burtt, *The Metaphysical Foundations of Modern Physical Science* (1925); H. M. Jones, *America and French Culture* (1927); Elie Halévy, *The Growth of Philosophic Radicalism*, translated by Mary Morris (1928); Carl Becker, *The Heavenly City of the Eighteenth-Century Philosophers* (1932); Joseph Haroutunian, *Piety versus Moralism; The Passing of the New England Theology* (1932); H. H. Clark, "An Historical Interpretation of Thomas Paine's Religion," *UCC.*, XXXV (1933), pp. 56-87.

3 G. A. Koch, *Republican Religion* (1932); A. O. Lovejoy, "The Parallel of Deism and Classicism," *MP.*, XXIX (1932), pp. 281-299; H. M. Morais, *Deism in Eighteenth Century America* (1934).

4 Albert Keiser, *The Indian in American Literature* (1933).

5 J. B. Bury, *The Idea of Progress* (1932); Lois Whitney, *Primitivism and the Idea of Progress in English Popular Literature of the Eighteenth Century* (1934).

American thought, and Locke's doctrine of natural rights was of primary importance in political development.[6]

Non-Political Prose

JOHN WOOLMAN, 1720—1772, Quaker diarist.[7] Born and raised on a farm in New Jersey; became a tailor in order to earn a modest living. Feeling the call, he traveled through the South, where he became a sincere opponent of slavery. Later went to England, where he died of smallpox. He deplored the techniques used to obtain luxuries, and his humanitarianism put him well ahead of his time. A simple, noble soul expressed itself in a pure and limpid style and in heart-felt action. His wide fame is reflected in Charles Lamb's statement, "Get the writings of John Woolman by heart." *Some Considerations on the Keeping of Negroes* (1754; 1762). *Journal* (1774)[8] has richly deserved its thirty-four republications. *A Word of Remembrance and Caution to the Rich*† (1793), republished by the Fabians in 1897, is today the most impressive of his essays.

WILLIAM BARTRAM, 1739—1823, naturalist, writer, informally educated.[9] *Travels through North and South Carolina, Georgia, East and West Florida* (1791), a delightful book, written in a lush and concretely vivid style, almost makes a religion of nature; was read by Chateaubriand, and furnished imagery for Coleridge's "Kubla Khan" and Wordsworth's "Ruth."[10]

ALEXANDER WILSON, 1766—1813, ornithologist, poet.[11] Came from Scotland (1794). Influenced by William Bartram. "The Foresters" (1805), a pretentious, protracted poem on a trip to Niagara Falls. *American Ornithology* (nine volumes, 1808—1814), clear, accurate, charming, fine plates. *Poems; Chiefly in the Scottish Dialect* (1816) is distinguished only by fidelity to nature.

---

6 B. F. Wright, *American Interpretations of Natural Law: A Study in the History of Political Thought* (1931); R. S. Crane, "Anglican Apologetics and the Idea of Progress," *MP.*, XXXI (1934), pp. 273-306, 349-382; Merle Curti, "The Great Mr. Locke: America's Philosopher, 1783-1861," *HLB.*, No. 11 (1937), pp. 107-151.

7 E. C. Wilson, "John Woolman: A Social Reformer of the Eighteenth Century," *Eco.R.*, XI (1901), pp. 170-189; Ann Sharpless, *John Woolman, a Pioneer in Labor Reform* (1920); E. E. Taylor, *John Woolman, Craftsman Prophet* (1920); F. V. Morley, *The Tailor of Mount Holly: John Woolman* (1926); Muriel Kent, "John Woolman, Mystic and Reformer," *HJ.*, XXVI (1928), pp. 302-313; Janet Whitney, *John Woolman, American Quaker* (1942).

8 *The Journal of John Woolman*, with an Introduction by J. G. Whittier (1871); *The Journal and Essays of John Woolman*, edited by A. M. Gummere (1922).

9 N. B. Fagin, *William Bartram: Interpreter of the American Landscape* (1933); Ernest Earnest, *John and William Bartram, Botanists and Explorers* (1940).

10 Joseph Bédier, *Études Critiques* (1903), pp. 196-294; E. H. Coleridge, "Coleridge, Wordsworth and the American Botanist William Bartram," *TRSL.*, Second Series, XXVII (1906), pp. 62-92; Lane Cooper, *Methods and Aims in the Study of Literature* (1915), pp. 100-125; Gilbert Chinard, *L'Exotisme Américain dans l'Oeuvre de Chateaubriand* (1918); *The Travels of William Bartram*, edited by Mark Van Doren, with an Introduction by J. L. Lowes (1940).

11 J. S. Wilson, *Alexander Wilson: Poet-Naturalist* (1906).

MERIWETHER LEWIS, 1774—1809, explorer. A Virginian who became Jefferson's secretary and leader of the expedition to the West. *History of the Expedition under the Command of Captains Lewis and Clark* (1814).[12]

MICHEL-GUILLAUME JEAN DE CRÈVECOEUR, known as, **HECTOR ST. JOHN DE CRÈVECOEUR,** 1735—1813, author, farmer.[13] Born near Caen of good family; was well educated. Came to America (1754); settled in Orange County, New York, with an American wife (1769). A Loyalist, he went to England (1780), returned (1783 or 1784), found his home burned, his wife dead, and his children gone. Returned to France (1790).

Crèvecoeur's writing[14] is that of a philosophical and cultivated man, a primitivist, Rousseauist, and physiocrat. His delightful style and delicate nature description add to the charm of his view that the settler can get close to primitive nature. *Letters from an American Farmer*† (1782) contains twelve letters, partly idyllic descriptions of various colonies, of farm life, and of animals. He recognized the force of the frontier in shaping man, and talked of the forthcoming composite American nationality. The preliminaries of the Revolution shattered his dream. A dedication to the Abbé Raynal betrayed the author's predeliction to primitivism. He was also physiocratic, believing that the soil is the source of wealth and virtue, and he was sensitive to abuses of the slaves and the Indians. *Sketches of Eighteenth Century America*[15] contains unpublished material emphasizing his disillusionment when the Revolution showed that men close to nature were still susceptible to corruption.

BENJAMIN FRANKLIN, 1706—1790, printer, scientist, author, editor, organizer, diplomat, statesman.[16] Born in Puritan Boston, the son of a chandler, he was apprenticed to his brother James as a printer (1718). Reworking Addison developed his style; imitating Socrates improved his argument; reading Shaftes-

---

12 Best edition is *Original Journals of the Lewis and Clark Expedition, 1804-1806,* edited by R. G. Thwaites (eight volumes, 1904-1905).

13 J. P. Mitchell, *St. Jean de Crèvecoeur* (1916); H. C. Rice, "Le Cultivateur Américain," *Bibliothèque de la Revue de Littérature Comparée,* LXXXVII (1933); F. B. Sanborn, "Hector St. John, an Old Evasive Planter," *MM.,* IX (1916), pp. 163-183.

14 See: P. H. Boynton, "A Colonial Farmer's Letters," *NR.,* III (1915), pp. 168-170; J. B. Moore, "Crèvecoeur and Thoreau," *PMASAL.* (1926), pp. 309-333; and "The Rehabilitation of Crèvecoeur," *SR.,* XXXV (1927), pp. 216-230; H. C. Rice, "Some Notes on the American Farmer's Letters," *Colophon,* Part XVIII, No. 3 (1934); P. A. Shelley, "Crèvecoeur's Contribution to Herder's 'Neger-Idyllen,'" *JEGP.,* XXXVII (1938), pp. 48-69; J. R. Masterson, "The Tale of the Living Fang," *AL.,* XI (1939-1940), pp. 67-73.

15 *Sketches of Eighteenth Century America,* edited by H. L. Bourdin, R. H. Gabriel, and S. T. Williams (1925); H. L. Bourdin and S. T. Williams, "The American Farmer Returns," *NAR.,* CCXXII (1925), pp. 135-140; "Crèvecoeur, the Loyalist," *Nation,* CXXVI (1925), pp. 328-330; "Crèvecoeur on the Susquehanna, 1774-1776," *YR.,* XIV (1925), pp. 552-584.

16 Biographies: James Parton, *Life and Times of Benjamin Franklin* (two volumes, 1864); P. L. Ford, *The Many Sided Franklin* (1899); W. C. Bruce, *Benjamin Franklin Self-Revealed* (two volumes, 1917); Bernard Faÿ, *Benjamin Franklin* (1929); Carl Van Doren, *Benjamin Franklin* (1938).

bury and Collins made him a doubter; Mather's *Essays to Do Good* helped him organize philanthropic institutions. He anonymously contributed the *Dogood* papers to the *New England Courant.* Fled to Philadelphia (1723) to escape his brother's harshness. Worked in London (1724—1726), where he wrote *A Dissertation on Liberty and Necessity, Pleasure and Pain* (1725). On his return to Philadelphia, he set up his own press, and, because of his thrift and industry, he succeeded. In 1727 he formed the Junto club for the improvement of the members and their community. With Breintnall, he wrote the *Busy-Body* papers for Bradford's *American Weekly Mercury.* In 1729 he purchased the *Pennsylvania Gazette.* He founded the Philadelphia Library Company, the first subscription library in America (1731); began publishing *Poor Richard's Almanac* (1732); established the Union Fire Company (1736); issued the *General Magazine and Historical Chronicle,* the second magazine in the colonies (1741); invented the Franklin stove (1742); established the American Philosophical Society (1744); and retired from business (1748).

From this time he was active in public life. In 1749 he founded the Philadelphia Academy. He proved the identity of lightning and electricity by means of his famed kite experiment, and invented the lightning rod (1752); became deputy-postmaster general of the colonies (1753); proposed the Albany plan of union (1754); aided Braddock in obtaining supplies (1755); and was colonial agent for Pennsylvania from 1757. In that year appeared *The Way to Wealth,* a compilation of prudent principles from the annual *Almanacs.* In England (1757—1763 and 1764—1775) as agent for the colonies, he associated with intellectuals. He mildly opposed the Stamp Act, supported paper money, and began the *Autobiography.* His *Rules by Which a Great Empire May be Reduced to a Small One,* a brilliant, humorous, Swiftian attack on colonial policy, appeared in 1773. He helped frame the *Declaration of Independence,* and went to France as a commissioner (1776). At the French court his scientific reputation and rustic simplicity made him a favorite. Such charming sketches as *The Ephemera, The Whistle, Morals of Chess, Dialogue between Franklin and the Gout* appeared (1778—1780). He helped negotiate the treaty of peace with England (1783), wrote *On the Causes and Cure of Smoky Chimneys,* returned to America, and became president of Pennsylvania (1785). In 1787 he was president of an antislavery society, and before his death he also wrote observations on education. Even such an incomplete list of Franklin's activities indicates not only his energy and versatility but also the direction of his interests.

In all respects Franklin was the embodiment of the Enlightenment and of the Age of Reason. His practical bent was not only American, but also a phase of eighteenth century humanitarianism. Although his energy and organization, his tabulation of characteristics for self-improvement show the influence of Puritanism,

Franklin was neither introspective nor mystical. His religion followed the pattern of scientific deism with emphasis on a benevolent creator manifest in nature, and best served by doing good to fellow men. Of the immortality of the soul, he was fairly certain. Franklin was tolerant of organized sects because of the good they did. At times he doubted freedom of the will, and at others he emphasized self-control, but in general he thought that men could be improved by improvement of their surroundings.

Franklin represented, in his early life, a form of economic individualism which emphasized thrift, industry, system, sobriety, and the appearance of diligence as *The Way to Wealth*.[17] The *Autobiography,* which runs only to 1759, also tends to confirm this picture, but it does not tell the whole story. Franklin was an economic individualist, liberal for his day. He was opposed to the mercantile system, since he was a colonial; he thought slavery was unsound;[18] he backed the labor theory of value, which he derived from Sir William Petty; and he advocated the use of paper money. He was also interested in the physiocrats, believing that agriculture was the only real source of wealth, but he was at the same time interested in colonial manufacturing. He believed in free trade and *laissez-faire,* individualistic doctrines growing out of reactions to mercantilism. These ideas he shared with Adam Smith.[19]

In politics, Franklin was liberal, but not radical. He did not subscribe to the theory of natural goodness, and had a certain distrust of the mob. Yet he opposed the proprietors of Pennsylvania, objected to many of the acts of the British Government,[20] and advocated a unicameral legislature. He based his arguments upon English law rather than upon natural rights.[21]

As a writer[22] Franklin represented the ideals of the time. His reading included Defoe, Bunyan, Swift, Addison, Locke, Collins, Shaftesbury, Thomson, Cowper, Cotton Mather, Goldsmith, Waller, Milton, Watts, Plutarch, the classics, and the Bible. His style

17 These individualistic virtues are the essence of capitalism and Puritanism. Max Weber, *The Protestant Ethic and the Spirit of Capitalism*, translated by Talcott Parsons (1930), uses Franklin as a major example.

18 V. W. Crane, "Benjamin Franklin on Slavery and American Liberties," *PMHB.*, LXII (1938), pp. 1-11.

19 W. A. Wetzel, "Benjamin Franklin as an Economist," *JHSHPS.*, 13th Series, IX (1895), pp. 425-476; F. W. Garrison, "Franklin and the Physiocrats," *Freeman*, VIII (1923), pp. 154-156; L. J. Carey, *Franklin's Economic Views* (1928); W. R. Riddell, "Benjamin Franklin and Colonial Money," *PMHB.*, LIV (1930), pp. 52-64.

20 V. W. Crane, "Benjamin Franklin and the Stamp Act," *PCSM.*, *XXXII* (1936), pp. 56-77.

21 S. R. Eiselen, *Franklin's Political Theories* (1928); cf. V. W. Crane, *Benjamin Franklin, Englishman and American* (1936); F. L. Mott and C. E. Jorgenson, *Benjamin Franklin. Representative Selections* (1936), pp. lxxxii-cx.

22 J. B. McMaster, *Benjamin Franklin as a Man of Letters* (1887); William MacDonald, "The Fame of Franklin," *Atl.*, XCVI (1905), pp. 450-462; C. A. Sainte-Beuve, *Portraits of the Eighteenth Century*, translated by K. P. Wormeley (two volumes, 1905), I, pp. 311-375; P. E. More, *Shelburne Essays*, Fourth Series (1907), pp. 129-155; Frederic Harrison, *Memories and Thoughts* (1906), pp. 119-123; S. P. Sherman, *Americans* (1922), pp. 28-62; L. M. MacLaurin, *Franklin's Vocabulary* (1928); H. S. Canby, *Classic Americans* (1931), pp. 34-45, has Quaker bias.

was simple, concise, clear, direct, and graceful. Grammatically he was a purist, using few Americanisms. He often employed a Swiftian device of straightforward irony, as in *An Edict of the King of Prussia* (1773), in which Prussia claimed England by right of settlement. All that cool logic, common sense, grace, and wit could do was done by Franklin, but he showed no lofty flights of imagination. Though he was a scientist as renowned as Einstein is today, a statesman, diplomat, and humanitarian, and incidentally a writer, he would live for his writings alone.

The Autobiography of Benjamin Franklin† (written 1771, 1784, 1788—1789). A permanent classic, including his utilitarian moral philosophy, instructions on how to succeed, religious views, literary experiences, and adventures. The style is easy and flowing, and its literary quality and breadth of view lift it from the class of success stories. The text had a chequered career from 1789, when a portion was published, to 1868, when a good complete English text finally appeared. His other more strictly literary productions include: the *Dogood* series, which show a heavier wit than his later works; the *Busy-Body* series; and the delicate and playful essays put out at Passy.

SUGGESTED MERITS

1. Clarity, ease, and force of style.
2. Charming fancy, as in the Passy papers.
3. Sense of humor.
4. Gift for sententious, didactic aphorism.
5. Sound common sense.
6. Attractive didacticism.

SUGGESTED DEFECTS

1. Lack of imaginative richness of expression.
2. Lack of Addisonian elegance.
3. Excessive materialism with lack of emphasis on higher values.

Political Prose[23]

The colonies attempted to obtain changes in laws regulating the colonial system and sought justification of their claims in (1) the

23 See p. 23, footnote 1, for bibliography. Also: Henry Adams, *A History of the United States . . .* (1885-1891)—see p. 257, footnote 13; C. A. Beard, *Economic Interpretation of the Constitution* (1913) and *Economic Origins of Jeffersonian Democracy* (1915); W. A. Dunning, *A History of Political Theories*, III (1920); Claude Bowers, *Jefferson and Hamilton* (1925), pro-Jeffersonian in bias; J. T. Adams, *New England in the Republic* (1926); Bernard Faÿ, *The Revolutionary Spirit in France and America* (1927); J. B. McMaster, *A History of the People of the United States* (nine volumes, 1883-1927); R. B. Morris, "Legalism versus Revolutionary Doctrine in New England," *NEQ.*, IV (1931), pp. 195-215; B. F. Wright, *American Interpretations of Natural Law* (1931); J. M. Jacobson, *The Development of American Political Thought* (1932); C. F. Mullett, *Fundamental Law and the American Revolution, 1760-1776* (1933); Claude Bowers, *Jefferson in Power* (1936).

English Constitution, and (2) the doctrine of natural rights.[24] Each English move was countered by the Americans, but consistent argument was not encouraged by the technique of answering specific measures. The Loyalists, upper-class Americans whose interests were English, presented a strong logical case for their side, but appeal by the patriots to mobs resulted in violence to Loyalists who were forced to flee, abandoning their property. Sentiment for freedom did not arise until late in the controversy.

The war gained independence, but it did not solve political problems since England's strong government induced the colonists to set up a weak system under the Articles of Confederation. Conservatives and practical men drafted the Constitution, and wrote brilliant defenses to secure its adoption. Tension again developed, as major political parties emerged and carried on a heated controversy throughout the period.

JAMES OTIS, 1725—1783, political writer, leader.[25] His *Speech against Writs of Assistance* (1761) began the opposition to England. *Rights of the British Colonists Asserted and Proved* (1764)[26] claims that rulers must regard their subjects and that the colonists, having the rights of Englishmen, cannot be taxed without consent. This was the basis of early arguments against England.

PATRICK HENRY, 1736—1799, orator, patriot. Born on Virginia frontier. A great spontaneous orator, like Otis. His speeches have not been preserved verbatim, but have been reconstructed by William Wirt.[27]

JOHN DICKINSON, 1732—1808, pamphleteer, statesman.[28] Born in Maryland, studied law at the Middle Temple (1753—1757). Refused to sign the *Declaration of Independence,* but fought in the Revolution. Governor of Pennsylvania (1782—1785). Member of the Constitutional Convention; presented a conservative plan. Aided in getting ratification of the Constitution in Pennsylvania and Maryland. Later governor of Maryland. Though he advocated conciliation, he is known as "The Penman of the Revolution." *Late Regulations respecting the British Colonies . . .*

---

24 The natural rights arguments derived mainly from Locke, though the old Federal school of Puritan theology, which emphasized a compact theory, made it easier for the clergy to take over the newer ideas. See: C. H. Van Tyne, "The Influence of the New England Clergy, and of Religious and Sectarian Forces on the American Revolution," *AHR.*, XIX (1913), pp. 44-64; E. F. Humphrey, *Nationalism and Religion in America, 1774-1789* (1924); Alice Baldwin, *The New England Clergy and the American Revolution* (1928).

25 William Tudor, *The Life of James Otis* (1823); E. E. Brennan, "James Otis: Recreant and Patriot," *NEQ.*, XII (1939), pp. 691-725.

26 C. F. Mullett, "Some Political Writings of James Otis," *U.Mi.S.*, IV, Nos. 3 and 4 (1929).

27 William Wirt, *Sketches of the Life and Character of Patrick Henry* (three volumes, 1817).

28 See Wharton Dickinson, "John Dickinson, LL.D.: The Great Colonial Essayist." *MAH.*, X (1883), pp. 223-234; C. J. Stillé, *The Life and Times of John Dickinson* (1891); R. H. Richards, "The Life and Character of John Dickinson," *PHSD.*, III, No. 30 (1901); C. F. Himes, *The True John Dickinson* (1912); J. H. Powell, "John Dickinson and the Constitution," *PMHB.*, LX (1936), pp. 1-14.

Considered (1765) attacks the Stamp Act as inexpedient for England. *Letters from a Farmer in Pennsylvania* (1767—1768), published in twelve numbers. Cautious, cultivated, conciliatory. Contended that although regulation of trade was legal, revenue acts were not, and the Townshend Acts were revenue acts. Dickinson hoped to obtain modifications of policy to preserve the empire. "A Song for American Freedom" (1768), known as the "Liberty Song," was popular just before the Revolution. *Letters of Fabius* (two series, 1788, 1797).[29]

SAMUEL ADAMS, 1722—1803, agitator, pamphleteer.[30] Harvard, B.A. (1740); M.A. (1743). A failure in business. Industrious, resourceful, friendly, a brilliant politician. Drafted resolutions and instructions. Wrote incessantly under many pseudonyms. His work kept colonial resistance alive (1771—1773), until his organization of the Boston Tea Party. *The Writings of Samuel Adams*[31] contain his well-written, topical pamphlets.

FRANCIS HOPKINSON, 1737—1791, essayist, poet, musician, painter, scholar, jurist, gentleman.[32] A Philadelphian, first graduate of the College of Philadelphia. Signed the *Declaration of Independence*. Designed the U. S. flag.[33] An urbane writer, often imitative of Addison, but also interested in mathematics and science. *A Pretty Story* (1774),[34] a clever satire on British conduct; told as the account of the owner of an Old Farm who gave the worthless New Farm to one of his sons; the son developed it laboriously, only to have the father make demands at the instance of his wife. Perhaps modeled on Arbuthnot's *History of John Bull*. *Letter . . . on the Character of the English Nation* (1777), another satire. "The Battle of the Kegs" (1778) was a famed poem of no great merit. A supporter of the Constitution in later years, he wrote *The New Roof* to satirize attacks on that document. Was a composer; wrote *Seven Songs* (1788). A cultivated man, not a dilettante, friend of Franklin[35] and Jefferson, Hopkinson was of the finest type of the period.

---

29 Texts: *The Political Writings of John Dickinson* (1801, 1914); *The Writings of John Dickenson, 1764-1774,* edited by P. L. Ford (*c.*1894).

30 W. V. Wells, *The Life and Public Services of Samuel Adams* (three volumes, 1865); R. V. Harlow, *Samuel Adams* (1923); J. C. Miller, *Sam Adams, Pioneer in Propaganda* (1936).

31 Edited by H. A. Cushing (four volumes, 1904-1908).

32 O. G. T. Sonneck, *Francis Hopkinson, the First American Poet-Composer, and James Lyon, Patriot, Preacher, Psalmodist* (1905); A. R. Marble, *Heralds of American Literature* (1907), pp. 19-58; G. E. Hastings, *The Life and Works of Francis Hopkinson* (1926) and "Francis Hopkinson and the Anti-Federalists," *AL.*, I (1929-1930), pp. 405-418.

33 G. E. Hastings, "Francis Hopkinson and the American Flag," *GMHC.*, XLII (1939); pp. 46-63.

34 In *The Miscellaneous Essays and Occasional Writings of Francis Hopkinson* (three volumes, 1792). Cf. G. E. Hastings, "Two Uncollected Essays by Francis Hopkinson," *GMHC.*, XLI (1939), pp. 416-422.

35 See Dixon Wecter, "Francis Hopkinson and Benjamin Franklin," *AL.*, XII (1940-1941), pp. 200-217.

THOMAS PAINE, 1737—1809, radical thinker and writer.[36] Son of a Quaker staymaker; entered the same trade. Became an exciseman. Came to America with a letter from Franklin. Helped edit the *Pennsylvania Magazine; or, American Monthly Museum.* Was not at first in favor of independence, but changed his mind and published *Common Sense*, the title supplied by Rush, in January, 1776. This pamphlet had tremendous effect in swinging the public to the thought of independence. Paine joined the army, where he encountered plenty of discouragement. To strengthen the morale of the soldiers, he wrote his stirring series, *The Crisis* (1775—1783). The first of sixteen numbers began with the challenge, "These are the times that try men's souls." He advocated nationalization of the Western lands, attacked paper money, and supported the plan to strengthen the powers of the Continental Congress.[37] In England, Paine met Burke, Fox, Horne Tooke. Replied to Burke's *Reflections on the French Revolution* in *The Rights of Man* (1791—1792). He was forced to flee to France where he had been elected a deputy, but as a moderate he fell into disfavor, and in prison wrote *The Age of Reason* (1794—1796), attacking Christianity. Paine returned to America at Jefferson's invitation; was ostracized because of his supposed atheism and his attack on Washington. He died in poverty.

Primarily a journalist, and one of the greatest, Paine had the virtues and defects of his craft. He was direct, simple, clear, candid, bold, witty, appealing to emotion and understanding, fitting language to thought, and preserving order.[38] His defects lay in excessive brashness, lack of restraint in language, and in frequent superficiality. His writing was by no means so crude as has been contended. His turbulent career was produced, not by native destructiveness, but by the scientifically deistic view that man should return to a primitive state of harmony with natural law, by eliminating corrupt governments.[39] Not interested in history, Paine ruthlessly attacked existing governments on the *a priori* rationalistic belief that men are good and institutions are bad. He is important in both political and intellectual history.

Writings include: *The Case of the Officers of Excise* (1772); *Epistle to the People Called Quakers* (1776); *Public Good* (1780), on public lands; *Dissertations on Government, the Affairs of the Bank, and Paper Money* (1786); *Decline and Fall of the English*

36 M. D. Conway, *The Life of Thomas Paine* (two volumes, 1892); Hasketh Pearson, *Tom Paine: Friend of Mankind* (1937); H. H. Clark, *Thomas Paine: Representative Selections* (1945); W. E. Woodward, *Tom Paine: America's Godfather* (1945).

37 See especially, *Six New Letters of Thomas Paine* (1939), edited by H. H. Clark, with an excellent introduction.

38 H. H. Clark, "Thomas Paine's Theories of Rhetoric," *TWASAL.*, XXVIII (1933), pp. 307-339.

39 H. H. Clark, "An Historical Interpretation of Thomas Paine's Religion," *UCC.*, XXXV (1933), pp. 56-87, and "Toward a Reinterpretation of Thomas Paine," *AL.*, V (1933-1934), pp. 133-145; V. E. Gibbens, "Tom Paine and the Idea of Progress," *PMHB.*, LXVI (1942), pp. 191-204.

System of Finance (1796); *Letter to George Washington* (1796); *Agrarian Justice* (1797); *Answer to the Bishop of Llandaff* (1810); *Miscellaneous Poems* (1819).

Common Sense (1776). Cut through legal arguments and explained the necessity of independence and its utility on economic grounds. *Plain Truth* (1776), an anonymous Tory pamphlet, was a feeble reply to *Common Sense.*

The Rights of Man† (1791—1792). Clever combination of propaganda and political theory, attacking royalty and arguing democracy from the state of nature and the Bible. Denied that England had a constitution. Suggested abolition of property, universal education, old-age pensions. Paine's theory, perhaps derived from Lord Kames, that only social rights are surrendered to the government shows him a capable thinker.[40]

The Age of Reason (1794—1796).[41] An attack on Christianity and a defense of deism written perhaps to wean France from atheism, or to undermine the buttress of privilege in the established church. Much execrated, but still influential among small-town free-thinkers.

WILLIAM SMITH, 1727—1803, Provost of the College of Philadelphia, center of a literary circle, the author of *The Letters of Cato* (1776), a hostile discussion of Paine's work.

THOMAS JEFFERSON, 1743—1826, statesman, architect, educator.[42] Born on Virginia frontier. Graduated from William and Mary College (1762). He read widely[43] in the classics, English law, Harrington, Milton, Hobbes, Locke, Voltaire, Helvetius, and Montesquieu, but not in Rousseau. In 1775 he went to the Continental Congress and in 1776 drafted the *Declaration of Independence.* In the Virginia Legislature, he led successful attacks on entail, primogeniture, and the established church, and an unsuccessful attack on slavery. Minister to France (1784—1789). Secretary of State under Washington (1789—1793). President of the United States (1801—1809). He carried on an extensive corre-

---

40 C. E. Merriam, "Thomas Paine's Political Theories," *PSQ.*, XIV (1899), pp. 389-403; C. E. Persinger, "The Political Philosophy of Thomas Paine," *UNGB.*, Sixth Series, No. 3 (1901), pp. 54-74; Norman Sykes, "Thomas Paine," in *The Social & Political Ideas of Some Representative Thinkers of the Revolutionary Era*, edited by F. J. C. Hearnshaw (1931), pp. 100-140; Joseph Dorfman, "The Economic Philosophy of Thomas Paine," *PSQ.*, LIII (1938), pp. 372-386.

41 *The Writings of Thomas Paine*, edited by M. D. Conway (four volumes, 1894-1896); *Selections from the Writings of Thomas Paine*, edited by Carl Van Doren (1922); *Selections from the Works of Thomas Paine*, edited with Introduction by A. W. Peach (1928); *Thomas Paine: Representative Selections*, edited by H. H. Clark (1944), with an excellent introduction.

42 Biographies: H. S. Randall, *The Life of Thomas Jefferson* (three volumes, 1858); A. J. Nock, *Jefferson* (1926); Gilbert Chinard, *Thomas Jefferson* (1929); J. T. Adams, *The Living Jefferson* (1936).

43 Gilbert Chinard (editor), *The Commonplace Book of Thomas Jefferson* (1926) and *The Literary Bible of Thomas Jefferson* (1928).

spondence, and established the University of Virginia, even drawing the architectural plans.

More than any American except Franklin, Jefferson embodied the ideals of his day. He accepted the main tenets of deism: belief in natural rights, political equality, natural altruism. He was deeply interested in science, experimental agriculture,[44] architecture,[45] scholarship, and education.[46] Politically he was the father of the democratic spirit of this country. He believed that an educated electorate would choose officials from among the most capable men. He thought that the best government was that which governed least, without aiding any particular class, and he was the advocate of states rights and *laissez-faire*. His agrarianism was sociological. He thought that cities produced depressed groups which easily could become mobs. The physiocrats seem only to have re-enforced ideas he had gained previously.[47] His correspondence was of tremendous influence and is still of vital interest. In literature he liked the classics.[48] He gave up an early interest in poetry and novels, but wrote an article on prosody. Anglo-Saxon and the philology of Indian languages interested him. Authors whom he liked included Shakespeare, Milton, Swift, Sterne, Macpherson, Akenside, Blair, besides the political philosophers. As a writer he showed dignity, flexibility, clarity, lyrical appreciation of nature, and command of generalization, but was occasionally prolix. On the whole he followed his theory of putting force before pedantic correctness.

A Summary View of the Rights of British America (1774). Argues from the British Constitution and also from natural rights.

***The Declaration of Independence*†** (1776).[49] A loftily eloquent expression of the American viewpoint. Argues from both natural right and English law. Jefferson's change of the Whiggish "Life, liberty, and property" to "Life, liberty, and the pursuit of happiness" shows his idealism.

Notes on . . . Virginia (1781—1782; 1784).[50] Written in reply

---

44 See Paul Wilstach, *Jefferson and Monticello* (1925).

45 S. F. Kimball, *Thomas Jefferson, Architect* (1916), discusses this phase of his activity.

46 On education, see: C. F. Arrowood, *Thomas Jefferson and Education in a Republic* (1930); R. J. Honeywell, *The Educational Work of Thomas Jefferson* (1931); O. W. Long, *Thomas Jefferson and George Ticknor* (1933). Consult also Adrienne Kock, *The Philosophy of Thomas Jefferson* (1943).

47 Cf. *The Correspondence of Jefferson and Du Pont de Nemours*, edited by Gilbert Chinard (1931).

48 See especially Gilbert Chinard (editor), *The Literary Bible of Thomas Jefferson* (1928), Introduction; and C. A. Smith, *Southern Literary Studies* (*c.*1933).

49 Carl Becker, *The Declaration of Independence* (1922); J. P. Boyd, *The Declaration of Independence* (1945).

50 Three standard editions of *The Writings of Thomas Jefferson* are edited by: H. A. Washington (nine volumes, 1853-1854), still useful; P. L. Ford (ten volumes, 1892-1894), the best text; A. L. Bergh (twenty volumes, 1903), the most inclusive. Cf. *Alexander Hamilton and Thomas Jefferson: Representative Selections*, edited by F. C. Prescott (1934); Bernard Mayo, *Jefferson Himself* (1942); a complete, fifty-volume edition of Jefferson's writing is projected by Princeton University.

to a series of questions by the Marquis de Barbé-Marbois. Contains excellent expressions of Jefferson's principal theories.

ALEXANDER HAMILTON, 1757—1804, statesman.[51] Born in the West Indies. Arrived in New York (1772); entered King's (Columbia) College (1773). *A Full Vindication* (1774) and *A Farmer Refuted* (1775) were replies to Samuel Seabury. Joined army in 1775 and became a member of Washington's staff. Married Elizabeth Schuyler (1780). Gave up Lockean for Hobbesian principles. A conservative, if not a monarchist, he supported the Constitution in *The Federalist* papers. As secretary of the treasury, he made his great reports: *Report on Public Credit* (1790); *Report on a National Bank* (1790); *Report on Manufactures* (1791). These laid out the basis of the Federalist system and the economic future of the country. He resigned his office in 1795, opposed John Adams, and was killed in a duel with Aaron Burr (1804).

Naturally aristocratic, Hamilton built his scheme of government on Hobbes's belief that people are motivated by self-interest. No adherent to *a priori* principles, he was an historical relativist. The rich, he felt, must be persuaded to help the new state by receiving a financial stake in it. Checks and balances were desirable in protecting this minority. Hamilton's economic vision in foreseeing and providing for the industrial development of the country surpassed Jefferson's.

Hamilton's literary ideals as exemplified in his writings include: calm appeal to reason, dignified language, clarity and brevity, appeal to emotions (especially in his youth), appeal to experience, coherent orderliness in organization, appeal to the interests of men. The reading which produced these theories included Hume, Hobbes, Cudworth, Rousseau, Grotius, Vattel, Pufendorf, Montesquieu, Junius, Adam Smith, and the classics, especially Aristotle's *Politics* and Plutarch. Hamilton is vital to an understanding of America.

The Federalist (1787—1788). Written by Hamilton, Madison, and Jay to support the ratification of the Constitution by New York State, is the greatest American work on political theory. Minimizing natural rights arguments, the authors show how the Constitution sets up a republican rather than a democratic government, one which through checks and balances will prevent factions from oppressing minorities. Appealing to reason, vigorously written, this document retains its interest and importance.

---

51 Biographies: J. C. Hamilton, *The Life of Alexander Hamilton* (two volumes, 1834-1840) and *History of the Republic* (six volumes, 1857-1860); H. C. Lodge, *Alexander Hamilton* (1883); W. G. Sumner, *Alexander Hamilton* (1890); Gertrude Atherton, *The Conquerer* (1902), fiction but useful; F. S. Oliver, *Alexander Hamilton* (1906); H. J. Ford, *Alexander Hamilton* (1931). Also useful are: R. I. Warshow, *Alexander Hamilton* (1931); J. J. Smertenko, *Alexander Hamilton* (1932); R. E. Bailey, *An American Colossus* (1933); R. G. Tugwell and Joseph Dorfman, "Alexander Hamilton: Nation-Maker," *CUQ.*, XXIX (1937), pp. 209-226; XXX (1938), pp. 59-72; D. G. Loth, *Alexander Hamilton* (1939); Bower Aly, *The Rhetoric of Alexander Hamilton* (1941).

JAMES MADISON, 1751—1836, statesman.[52] Educated at Princeton. Important member of the Constitutional Convention, where he took notes on the debates. A co-author of *The Federalist,*† he wrote "No. X," a classical analysis of interest groups in society.[53]

GEORGE WASHINGTON, 1732—1799, general, statesman.[54] Primarily a man of action. His voluminous writings improved steadily in style, though always formal and rather heavy. The *Farewell Address,*[55] written in consultation with Hamilton, has become a classic statement of American foreign policy, and a warning against the danger of factional conflict.

JOHN ADAMS, 1735—1826, statesman.[56] Harvard, A.B. (1755). In 1811 he renewed his friendship with Jefferson through a notable exchange of letters.[57] *A Defence of the Constitutions . . . of the United States of America* (1787—1788) and *Discourses on Davila* (1790—1791) set forth his aristocratic view of government. He felt that the rich, the well-born, and the able should rule, and expressed as great a fear of mobs as of kings. He was charged with monarchism. He favored the elaborate checks and balances which were employed in the Constitution.[58] In thought he resembled Harrington and Hobbes; his writing was solid, logical, well designed in architecture, but frequently too detailed and turgid.[59]

JOHN MARSHALL, 1755—1835, jurist.[60] A Virginia Fed-

---

52 W. C. Rives, *History of the Life and Times of James Madison* (three volumes, 1859-1868); Gaillard Hunt, *The Life of James Madison* (1902); A. E. Smith, *James Madison: Builder* (1937); J. J. Spengler, "The Political Economy of Jefferson, Madison, and Adams," in *American Studies in Honor of William Kenneth Boyd* (1940); Irving Brant, *James Madison: The Virginian Revolutionist* (1941); A. T. Prescott, *Drafting the Federal Constitution* (1941).

53 *The Writings of James Madison*, edited by Gaillard Hunt (nine volumes, 1900-1910).

54 Biographies include: John Marshall, *The Life of George Washington* (five volumes, 1804-1807); Washington Irving, *Life of George Washington* (five volumes, 1855-1859); G. W. P. Custis, *Recollections and Private Memoirs of Washington* (1860); P. L. Ford, *The True George Washington* (1896); Rupert Hughes, *George Washington* (three volumes, 1926-1930); Bernard Faÿ, *George Washington* (1931). Cf. A. B. Hart, "A Study of Washington Biography," *PW.*, CXIX (1931), pp. 820-822; John Hay, Jr., "George Washington, Literary Man," *PW.*, CXXI (1932), pp. 943-944; G. K. Chesterton, "George Washington," *FR.*, CXXXVII; N.S. CXXXI (1932), pp. 303-310; M. J. Moses, "His Excellency, George Washington," *TAM.*, XVI (1932), pp. 137-146.

55 *The Writings of George Washington*, edited by P. L. Ford (fourteen volumes, 1889-1893); also *The Diaries of George Washington* (four volumes, 1925), edited by J. C. Fitzpatrick, who is preparing the definitive collection of writings.

56 Biographies: J. T. Morse, *John Adams* (1885); J. Q. and C. F. Adams, *The Life of John Adams* (two volumes, 1871); Gilbert Chinard, *Honest John Adams* (1933). Cf. J. T. Adams, *The Adams Family* (1930).

57 See *Correspondence of John Adams and Thomas Jefferson (1812-1826)*, edited by Paul Wilstach (1925).

58 C. M. Walsh, *Political Science of John Adams* (1915): F. N. Thorpe, "The Political Ideas of John Adams," *PMHB.*, XLIV (1920), pp. 1-46.

59 *The Works of John Adams*, edited by C. F. Adams (ten volumes, 1850-1856), the first volume of which also contains a biography. *Familiar Letters of John Adams and His Wife Abigail Adams, during the Revolution* (1876).

60 A. J. Beveridge, *The Life of John Marshall* (four volumes, 1916-1919) is a monumental history of this period, Federalist in bias. See also: B. W. Palmer, *Marshall and Taney: Statesmen of the Law* (1939), pp. 43-141, 256-275; Max Lerner, "John Marshall and the Campaign of History," *CLR.*, XXXIX (1939), pp. 396-431; B. M. Ziegler, *The International Law of John Marshall* (1939); B. H. Levy, *Our Constitution: Tool or Testament?* (1941), pp. 3-58.

eralist. Chief Justice (1801—1835), Marshall greatly extended the powers of the national government and in particular of the Supreme Court by his decisions,[61] written in clear, vigorous style, and permanently influenced American historical development. Also wrote *The Life of George Washington* (five volumes, 1804—1807).

POETRY[62]

NATHANIEL EVANS, 1742—1767, poet, cleric, friend of Godfrey.[63] His *Poems on Several Occasions* (1772) were imitative of Milton, Cowley, Prior, Gray, Collins. The best were called forth by the French and Indian War. He showed promise, but died young.

PHILIP FRENEAU, 1752—1832, poet, editor, seaman.[64] Of a Huguenot family. Graduated from the College of New Jersey in 1771, with Madison and Brackenridge. With the latter he wrote a prose romance, *Father Bombo's Pilgrimage,* and a commencement poem, "The Rising Glory of America." He was the most "hellishly keen" satirist of the British during the War. Voyage to the West Indies resulted in his fine poems, "The Beauties of Santa Cruz" (1776; 1786), "The Jamaica Funeral" (1776; 1786), and "The House of Night" (1779). Was captured and incarcerated by the English in a hulk which he excoriated in "The British Prison Ship" (1781). His satire continued to appear in the *Freeman's Journal* until 1784, when he returned to the sea.[65] He edited the *Daily Advertiser* (1789—1791), and was aided by Jefferson in setting up the militantly anti-Federalist paper the *National Gazette* (1791—1793).[66] He later contributed to the *Jersey Chronicle* and

---

61 *John Marshall, Complete Constitutional Decisions,* edited by J. F. Dillon (1903); cf. E. S. Corwin, *John Marshall and the Constitution* (1921).

62 For collections of verse of this period see: Frank Moore, *Songs and Ballads of the American Revolution* (1856) and *Illustrated Ballad History of the American Revolution* (1876); W. B. Otis, *American Verse, 1625-1807* (1909); M. A. DeW. Howe, *Yankee Ballads* (1930); O. E. Winslow, *American Broadside Verse from Imprints of the 17th and 18th Centuries* (1930); Louise Pound, *American Ballads and Songs* (1932); L. M. Miner, *Our Rude Forefathers: American Political Verse (1783-1788)* (1937).

63 E. L. Pennington, *Nathaniel Evans: A Poet of Colonial America* (1935).

64 Studies include: E. F. De Lancey, "Philip Freneau, the Huguenot Patriot Poet of the Revolution and His Poetry," *PHSA.,* II (1891), pp. 66-84; M. S. Austin, *Philip Freneau, the Poet of the Revolution* (1901); S. E. Forman, "The Political Activities of Philip Freneau," *JHSHPS.,* Series XX, No. 9-10 (1902); P. E. More, *Shelburne Essays,* Fifth Series (1908), pp. 86-105; F. L. Pattee, *Sidelights on American Literature* (1922), pp. 250-292; S. B. Hustvedt, "Philippic Freneau," *AS.,* IV (1928), pp. 1-18; F. L. Pattee, "Philip Freneau as Postal Clerk," *AL.,* IV (1932-1933), pp. 61-62; J. M. Beatty, "Churchill and Freneau," *AL.,* IV (1932-1933), pp. 270-287; Frank Smith, "Philip Freneau and *The Time-Piece and Literary Companion,*" *AL.,* IV (1932-1933), pp. 270-287; Rica Brenner, *Twelve American Poets* (1933), pp. 3-22; V. F. Calverton, "Philip Freneau, Apostle of Freedom," *Mod.M.,* VII (1933), pp. 533-546; G. W. Allen, *American Prosody* (1935), pp. 1-26; H. H. Clark, *Major American Poets* (1936), pp. 781-787; P. M. Marsh, "Was Freneau a Fighter?" *PNJHS.,* LVI (1938), pp. 211-218, and "Philip Freneau and His Circle," *PMHB.,* LXIII (1939), pp. 37-59. The best biography is L. G. Leary, *That Rascal Freneau* (1941).

65 P. M. Marsh, "Philip Freneau's Personal File of *The Freeman's Journal,*" *PNJHS.,* LVII (1939), pp. 163-170.

66 P. M. Marsh, "Freneau and Jefferson: *The Poet-Editor Speaks for Himself about the* National Gazette *Episode,*" *AL.,* VIII (1936-1937), pp. 180 189.

the *Time-Piece* (1797—1799). In this period before 1800 he was a supporter of the French Revolution. As he grew older, Freneau took to drinking, lost much of his wealth, and finally died of exposure in a snowstorm.

Freneau was much more than a Revolutionary satirist. His genuine and original lyrical gift made him the father of American poetry, and he has also been called the father of American prose.[67] His political satire and his poems of "romantic fancy" stem from the same source — eighteenth century scientific deism. Freneau believed in a benevolent creator, the natural goodness and equality of man, the noble savage, the evil of institutions, the idea of progress through harmony with God's laws, and in the capricious genius of great men. Widely read in classical and neoclassical literature, Freneau is a transitional figure in the approach to Romanticism, both in diction and in his treatment of the sea, the noble savage, and nature.[68]

He believed that the removal of tyrannical governments would permit a natural harmony; he used violent language to further this utopian end. Among his best revolutionary satires were "American Liberty," "A Political Litany," "A Midnight Consultation," "America Independent," "George the Third's Soliloquy," and "The British Prison Ship,"[69] The same spirit made Freneau a sympathizer with the French Revolution, a defender of Genêt after Jefferson had given him up, and the author of "On the Anniversary of the Storming of the Bastile" (1793), "The Republican Genius of Europe" (1795), and "God Save the Rights of Man" (1795). His fierce editorial attacks on the Federalists sprang from sincere conviction.[70]

Freneau's lyric poetry, though minor, is often haunting in beauty. Using the contemporary themes of nature, evanescence, interest in both humanity and solitude, primitivism and the supernatural, he achieved a real charm, which is at odds with the harsh satire for which he was best known in his own day. Both types are marred by a restless, perhaps romantic, lack of discipline and control of his medium.

Freneau's non-political prose is smooth and pleasant. "The Philosopher of the Forest" series depicts a man living close to nature, avoiding the evils of pride which are the cause of wars. The eloquent description shows a knowledge of seventeenth century as well as Addisonian rhythms. "The Essays of Robert Slender" are

67 H. H. Clark, "What Made Freneau the Father of American Prose?" *TWASAL.*, XXV (1930), pp. 39-50.

68 See H. H. Clark's interpretations: *Poems of Freneau* (1929), Introduction; "The Literary Influences on Philip Freneau," *SP.*, XXII (1925), pp. 1-33; "What Made Freneau the Father of American Poetry?" *SP.*, XXVI (1929), pp. 1-22.

69 Dorothy Dondore, "Freneau's *The British Prison Ship* and Historical Accuracy," *EJ.*, XXVIII (1939), pp. 228-230; P. M. Marsh and Milton Ellis, "A Broadside of Freneau's 'The British Prison Ship,'" *AL.*, X (1938-1939), pp. 476-480.

70 Cf. *Letters on Various Subjects*, edited by H. H. Clark (1934), for some of Freneau's more temperate political writings.

really sketches. "Tomo Cheeki, the Creek Indian in Philadelphia" uses the Goldsmith device of having a stranger describe ridiculous customs.

"The Power of Fancy."[71] Is in the good eighteenth century tradition of versified poetic theory, imitating Joseph Warton, and showing Freneau's knowledge of Milton. His individualistic and nationalistic poetic theory also found expression in "To Sylvius," "To an Author," and the essay "Advice to Authors."

"The Beauties of Santa Cruz." Excellent lyric. Its concrete nature imagery shows him the precursor of a new poetic style.[72]

"The House of Night." Related to Blair and the graveyard school, and modelled on Sackville's *Induction,* it is a powerful macabre poem.

"To the Memory of the Brave Americans," or **"Eutaw Springs"** (1781). Solemn and enduring elegy to the Revolutionary heroes.

"To a Wild Honeysuckle" (1786). Perhaps his finest lyric, is a lament for the mutability of nature, conveying the emotion of transience delicately and with restraint. The diction as well as the mood, pensive and poignant, is akin to seventeenth century poets like Marvell.

"The Indian Burying Ground" (1788). Captures his feeling for the noble savage, which he obtained partly from Addison and partly from observation. Both Scott and Thomas Campbell borrowed a line from this poem.

Freneau's sea poems, which emphasize the dangers as much as the mystery of the deep, include "Hatteras," "The Hurricane," and the stirring naval poems, "The Memorable Victory of Paul Jones," "Captain Barney's Victory," and "The Battle of Lake Erie."

The Connecticut Wits[73]

JOHN TRUMBULL, 1750—1831, poet, jurist.[74] M.A., Yale (1770); remained as tutor and sought introduction of English literature in curriculum. *The Progress of Dulness* (1772—1773),

71 The best editions are: *The Poems of Philip Freneau,* edited by F. L. Pattee (three volumes, 1902-1907); *Unpublished Freneauana,* edited by C. F. Hartman (1918); *Poems of Freneau,* edited by H. H. Clark (1929).

72 See C. A. Moore, "The Return to Nature in English Poetry of the Eighteenth Century," *SP.,* XIV (1917), pp. 243-291. For another precursor to Romanticism, see Leon Howard, "Thomas Odione: An American predecessor of Wordsworth," *AL.,* X (1938-1939), pp. 417-436.

73 See: A. M. Marble, *Heralds of American Literature* (1907); H. A. Beers, *The Connecticut Wits and Other Essays* (1920); *The Connecticut Wits,* edited by V. L. Parrington (1926), with a hostile introduction; Leon Howard, *The Connecticut Wits* (1943).

74 J. H. Trumbull, *The Origin of M'Fingal* (1868); Alexander Cowie, *John Trumbull, Connecticut Wit* (1936) and "John Trumbull as a Critic of Poetry," *NEQ.,* XI (1938), pp. 773-793; K. A. Conley, "A Letter of John Trumbull," *NEQ.,* XI (1938), pp. 372-374; Leon Howard, *The Connecticut Wits* (1943), pp. 37-78.

a Hudibrastic satire on education. *An Elegy on the Times* (1774) attacked British economic policies. *M'Fingal* (two cantos, 1775; complete, 1782) was a satire on the Tories in the Revolution. Based on *Hudibras* and Churchill's *The Ghost,* from which he unwisely borrowed a Scotch instead of a native protagonist; it lacked the bite if not the wit of its prototypes. Trumbull was too genial to be an influential satirist, but his poem is still highly entertaining.

TIMOTHY DWIGHT, 1752—1817, author, educator, cleric, patriot, Calvinist, Federalist.[75] Educated at Yale. Chaplain in the Revolution. Wrote song, "Columbia" (1784; 1793). *The Conquest of Canaan* (1785) is a dull epic on the wars of Joshua. *Greenfield Hill* (1794) is modelled on Denham's *Cooper's Hill.* The first book is like Thomson, the second like Goldsmith, but instead of bewailing the deserted village, Dwight praised the changes in America, the general prosperity, and the leaders of the people. The poem has some pleasant description.

From 1795 he was president of Yale; revived Calvinism, yet he was a humanitarian, fostered missions, and set up charitable institutions. His *Theology Explained and Defended* (five volumes, 1818—1819) was important. His best work was *Travels in New-England and New-York* (four volumes, 1821—1822), a clear-sighted and unfavorable picture of provincial and frontier conditions. Dwight was an ardent nationalist seeking to set up an *American* literature.

JOEL BARLOW, 1754—1812, poet, statesman.[76] Graduated from Yale (1778) with Noah Webster. Chaplain in Revolution; a Hartford lawyer. Became a Rousseauistic democrat. Sent to France as land agent (1788). Met Paine in England.[77] Was United States consul to Algiers (1795—1805). Died as minister to France. *The Vision of Columbus* (1787) was an ambitious patriotic poem in nine books, subsequently enlarged into *The Columbiad* (1807), a long, dull effort to glorify democracy and peace, as well as the young nation. Written in heroic couplets. *The Hasty Pudding* (1793; 1796), an amusing mock-heroic piece

---

75 See: M. C. Tyler, *Three Men of Letters* (1895), pp. 69-127; D. D. Addison, *The Clergy in American Life and Letters* (1900), pp. 157-190; M. A. DeW. Howe, *Classic Shades* (1928), pp. 3-40; A. W. Griswold, "Three Puritans on Prosperity," *NEQ.*, VII (1934), pp. 475-493; C. E. Cuningham, *Timothy Dwight, 1752-1817* (1942); Leon Howard, *The Connecticut Wits* (1943), pp. 79-111, 342-401.

76 Studies include: C. B. Todd, *Life and Letters of Joel Barlow* (1886); M. C. Tyler, *Three Men of Letters* (1895), pp. 129-188; T. A. Zunder, "Six Letters of Joel Barlow to Oliver Wolcott, *NEQ.*, II (1929), pp. 475-489; V. C. Miller, "Joel Barlow: Revolutionist, London, 1791-92," *Britannica,* VI (1932); T. A. Zunder, *The Early Days of Joel Barlow . . . 1745-1787* (1934); M. R. Adams, "Joel Barlow, Political Romanticist," *AL.*, IX (1937-1938), pp. 113-152; Leon Howard, *The Vision of Joel Barlow* (1937) and "Joel Barlow and Napoleon," *HLQ.*, II (1938), pp. 37-51; M. E. Kempton, "The Tom Barlow Manuscript of the Columbiad," *NEQ.*, XI (1938), pp. 834-842; T. A. Zunder, "A New Barlow Poem," *AL.*, XI (1939-1940), pp. 206-209; John Dos Passos, *The Ground We Stand On* (1941), pp. 256-380; Leon Howard, *The Connecticut Wits* (1943), pp. 133-165, 271-341.

77 See T. A. Zunder, "Notes on the Friendship of Joel Barlow and Tom Paine," *ABC.*, VI (1935), pp. 96-99.

celebrating the American dish, cornmeal mush. *Advice to the Privileged Orders* (1792—1793)[78] was a brilliant analysis of political evils, written by an ardent democrat who thought the French Revolution would cause a general improvement of governments.

DRAMA[79]

ROYALL TYLER, 1757—1826, dramatist, novelist, jurist.[80] Few of his plays have survived. Best known for *The Contrast* (acted 1787; published 1790), the first performed American comedy. It contrasted an American officer, Colonel Manly, with Dimple, who affects English fashions. Has Jonathan, the prototype for the stage Yankee. Examples of his closet-type religious drama are: *The Origin of the Feast of Purim, Joseph and His Brethren,* and *The Judgement of Solomon.* Also wrote *The Algerine Captive* (1797), a picaresque novel satirizing education, medical quacks, slavery, and the treatment of prisoners in Algeria. Wrote poetry as "Colon" of "Colon and Spondee," his literary partnership with Joseph Dennie. Attacked Della Cruscans. Long poem, *The Chestnut Tree* (1824; 1931) gave a good picture of village life and a prophecy of the results of the machine age.

THE NOVEL[81]

WILLIAM HILL BROWN, 1765—1793, wrote *The Power of Sympathy* (1789, 1937), which has been designated as the first American novel.[82]

---

78 P. H. Boynton, "Joel Barlow Advises the Privileged Orders," *NEQ.*, XII (1939), pp. 477-499.

79 William Dunlap, *History of the American Theatre* (1832); G. O. Seilhamer, *A History of the American Theatre, 1749-1797* (three volumes, 1888-1891); T. A. Brown, *History of the New York Stage, from 1732 to 1901* (three volumes, 1903); Arthur Hornblow, *A History of the Theatre in America* (two volumes, 1919); A. H. Quinn, *A History of American Drama from the Beginning to the Civil War* (1923); M. J. Moses, *The American Dramatist* (1925); G. C. D. Odell, *Annals of the New York Stage* (1927-); Oral Coad and Edwin Mims, *The American Stage* (1929); R. D. James, *Old Drury in Philadelphia: A History of the Philadelphia Stage, 1800-1835* (1932); T. C. Pollock, *A History of the American Theatre in the Eighteenth Century* (1933); F. P. Hill, *American Plays Printed 1714-1830: A Bibliographical Record* (1934); M. J. Moses and J. M. Brown (editors), *The American Theatre as Seen by Its Critics, 1752-1934* (1934); C. G. Hartman, *The Development of American Social Comedy from 1787 to 1936* (1939).

Anthologies have been edited by: M. J. Moses, *Representative Plays by American Dramatists* (three volumes, 1918-1921) and *Representative American Dramas* (revised by J. W. Krutch, 1941); A. G. Halline, *American Plays* (1935); A. H. Quinn, *Representative American Plays* (revised, 1938).

80 See Frederick Tupper, "Royall Tyler, Man of Law and Man of Letters," *PVHS.*, I (1928), pp. 63-101; A. H. Nethercot, "The Dramatic Background of Royall Tyler's *The Contrast*," *AL.*, XII (1940-1941), pp. 435-446.

81 L. D. Loshe, *The Early American Novel* (1907, 1930); Oscar Wegelin, *Early American Fiction, 1774-1830* (1929); Pelham Edgar, *The Art of the Novel from 1700 to the Present Time* (1933); G. F. Singer, *The Epistolary Novel* (1933); A. H. Quinn, *American Fiction* (1936); Carl Van Doren, *The American Novel* (1939); L. H. Wright, "A Statistical Survey of American Fiction, 1774-1850," *HLQ.*, II (1939), pp. 309-318.

82 Milton Ellis, "The Author of the First American Novel: William Hill Brown," *AL.*, IV (1932-1933), pp. 359-368.

CHARLES BROCKDEN BROWN, 1771—1810, novelist, editor, first professional man of letters in the United States.[83] Of wealthy Quaker family. Read omnivorously as a boy. Planned epics on Columbus, Pizarro, and Cortez. Was impressed by English liberals like Mary Wollstonecraft and William Godwin, and by Condorcet, Raynal, Helvetius. Wrote novels feverishly from 1798—1801. Edited magazines both before and after.

Brown sought to write truly American novels, but he failed in technique and treatment, though not in setting. From Godwin he took a plot idea of having an innocent person hounded by a wealthy man. He was influenced by the Gothic romance to use horror and the pre-Byronic hero. Richardsonian influence is seen in seductions, introspection, and sensibility. His style was unhappily heavy, Latinate, stilted. But he did have power, even if the characters were too often undifferentiated and the circumstances too improbable.

Showed a notable interest in scientific and pseudo-scientific topics like sleep-walking, ventriloquism, and spontaneous combustion.

Alcuin (1798). First feminist work in America. Argued for mutuality and against indissoluble marriages. Influenced by Mary Wollstonecraft.

Wieland† (1798).[84] Attack on superstition is the theme of this exciting romance. Theodore thinks God has commanded him to kill his family, but the voice is that of Carwin, a ventriloquist. The rational characters have the least trouble, and Wieland comes to grief more because of fanaticism than the ventriloquist's deceptions, which serve chiefly to maintain interest despite the many halts while Clara, the narrator, analyzes her feelings. Has power.

Ormond (1799).[85] Plot resembles that of Godwin's *Caleb Williams*. Constantia Dudley, the poor heroine, is pursued by Ormond, who is rich but loses his benevolence. She finally kills him when he assaults her.[86]

Arthur Mervyn (1799—1800). Has an inextricably complicated plot with murder, seduction, a chase of the young country lad, and

---

83 For studies see: William Dunlap, *The Life of Charles Brockden Brown* (two volumes, 1815), unsympathetic; H. T. Tuckerman, *Mental Portraits* (1853), pp. 271-286; W. H. Prescott, *Biographical and Critical Miscellanies* (1903), pp. 1-52; M. S. Vilas, *Charles Brockden Brown: A Study of Early American Fiction* (1904); John Erskine, *Leading American Novelists* (1910), pp. 3-49; Carl Van Doren, "Minor Tales of Brockden Brown," *Nation*, C (Jan. 14, 1915), pp. 46-47; D. L. Clark, *Charles Brockden Brown* (1923) and "Brockden Brown's First Attempt at Journalism," *UTSE.*, VII (1927), pp. 155-174; Tremaine McDowell, "Scott on Cooper and Brockden Brown," *MLN.*, XLV (1930), pp. 18-20; *The Rhapsodist*, edited by H. R. Warfel (1943). Cf. H. R. Warfel's forthcoming biography of Brown (*c.*1946).

84 Edited by F. L. Pattee (1926), with Introduction. Cf. J. C. Hendrickson, "A Note on *Wieland*," *AL.*, VIII (1936-1937), pp. 305-306.

85 Edited by Ernest Marchand (1937).

86 Shelley was influenced by Brown in *The Revolt of Islam* and in his prose romances. See M. T. Solve, "Shelley and the Novels of Brown," *The Fred Newton Scott Anniversary Papers* (1929), pp. 141-156; Eleanor Sickels, "Shelley and Charles Brockden Brown," *PMLA.*, XLV (1930), pp. 1116-1128.

a terrible, realistic picture of the yellow fever epidemic in Philadelphia. Its effect is strong but chaotic. Again the theme is the problem of natural innocence beset by villainy.

Edgar Huntly; or Memoirs of a Sleep-Walker (1799).[87] Contains dangers in the forest, Indian depredations, and crimes committed in a state of somnambulism. Believing that native material should be used, Brown introduced the Indian, treating him not as the noble savage, but as a ruthless fighter when disturbed. As befits romance, his Indians are bad, but easily killed.

Clara Howard (1801) and ***Jane Talbot*** (1801). Both in letter form, they mark recession from Brown's previous sensationalism. They probe character well, but are less interesting. Mildly feministic, but less so than *Alcuin*.[88]

Despite Brown's philosophical radicalism, he was no literary rebel.[89] He edited and wrote most of the *Monthly Magazine and American Review* (1799—1800); *American Review and Literary Journal* (1800—1803); *Literary Magazine and American Register* (1803—1807); and the *American Register, or General Repository* (1807—1810). His criticism was fairly conventional, and he found it expedient to avoid controversial matters in politics.

HUGH HENRY BRACKENRIDGE, 1748—1816, author, jurist.[90] Came from Scotland (1753); graduated from Princeton (1772). A chaplain in the army, taught school, edited the *United States Magazine* (1779), wrote blank verse dramas: *The Battle of Bunkers Hill* (1776) and *The Death of General Montgomery* (1777). Went to Pittsburgh as a lawyer (1786). Misfortunes in politics caused him to begin *Modern Chivalry* (1792—1815), written in installments to satirize political and social conditions on the frontier. He tried to please both sides during the Whiskey Rebellion, and wrote a justification of his conduct. He collected a volume of fugitive writings before his death.

Brackenridge was a classicist, a believer in balance. He opposed both democratic excesses and aristocratic pretensions. He read widely in the classics and in English literature.

Modern Chivalry (1792—1815). Based on Don Quixote, contains the adventures of Captain Farrago and his ignorant servant Teague O'Regan. Teague runs for Congress, is elected to the American Philosophical Society, is tarred and feathered as an exciseman, sets up a newspaper, etc. With humor that is still appealing, Brackenridge satirizes all the excesses of his day — attacks

---

87 Edited by D. L. Clark (1928).

88 D. L. Clark, "Brockden Brown and the Rights of Women," *UTB.*, No. 2212 (1922).

89 Ernest Marchand, "The Literary Opinions of Charles Brockden Brown," *SP.*, XXXI (1934), pp. 541-566.

90 C. M. Newlin, *The Life and Writings of Hugh Henry Brackenridge* (1932) is definitive.

on judges, on property qualifications for voting, on pride in ignorance. A believer in Jeffersonian democracy and education, he represents a happy balance between aristocracy and mobocracy.

MISCELLANEOUS PROSE

NOAH WEBSTER, 1758—1843, journalist, educator, lexicographer.[91] Graduated from Yale (1778). An ardent nationalist,[92] his first spelling book, *A Grammatical Institute of the English Language* (1783), contains in an introduction his declaration of literary independence. *Sketches of American Policy* (1785—1786) strongly argued for potent central government. In his lectures (1785—1786) he argued in the interests of American language and educational system and attracted the attention of Franklin. Founded the *American Magazine* (1787—1788) and became a critic. *An Examination into the Leading Principles of the Federal Constitution* (1787) was another argument for a strong and stable government. *Dissertations on the English Language* (1789) advocated American language and institutions to implement the new government. *A Collection of Essays and Fugitiv Writings* (1790) and *The Prompter* (1791) inculcated Federalistic and nationalistic ideals. Founded and edited the *American Minerva* (1793—1803). In 1802 he began to work for an American copyright. Worked on *An American Dictionary of the English Language* from 1800—1828, meanwhile issuing a *Compendious Dictionary* (1806), and helping to found Amherst College. His *Spelling Book* sold one hundred million copies.

JOSEPH DENNIE, 1768—1812, essayist, editor.[93] Born in Boston, father a merchant. Graduated from Harvard (1790), but disliked it. Admitted to the bar in New Hampshire. Wrote "Colon and Spondee" papers with Royall Tyler; "Farrago" essays (1792), combining Goldsmith's vivacity and Addison's sweetness;[94] "The Eagle" (1793—1794) partly reprinted in *The Tablet* (1795); "Lay Preacher," a pro-Federalist series for the *New Hampshire Journal: or the Farmer's Weekly Museum.* He edited this journal (1795—1799), and later the *Port Folio* (1801—1812), as "Oliver Oldschool, Esq." This was the chief American literary magazine till 1815. Printed ms. poems of Campbell, Moore, Hunt, "Monk"

91 E. E. F. Ford, *Notes on the Life of Noah Webster* (1912); H. R. Warfel, *Noah Webster, Schoolmaster to America* (1936) is excellent; E. C. Shoemaker, *Noah Webster, Pioneer of Learning* (1936).

92 On Webster's nationalism, see H. H. Clark, "Nationalism in American Literature," *UTQ.*, II (1933), pp. 492-519; also R. W. Bolwell, "Concerning the Study of Nationalism in American Literature," *AL.*, X (1938-1939), pp. 405-416.

93 See W. W. Clapp, *Joseph Dennie* (1880); H. M. Ellis, "Joseph Dennie and His Circle," *TUSE.* No. 3 (1915), pp. i-vii, 9-285; L. G. Pedder (editor), "The Letters of Joseph Dennie, 1768-1812," *U.Ma.S.*, XXXVIII, Second Series, No. 36 (1936); Bernard Smith, *Forces in American Criticism* (1939), pp. 19-21.

94 Cf. E. C. Coleman, *The Influence of the Addisonian Essay in America before 1810* (1936).

Lewis, and selections of Wordsworth and Coleridge, showing Dennie's interest in romanticism. Though he published approval of Tom Moore and the romantic poets, he loved the classics, and was a political conservative.

SUPPLEMENTARY LIST OF AUTHORS

PROSE WRITERS

SAMUEL JOHNSON, 1696—1772, philosopher. *Elementa Philosophica* (1752).

JOHN BARTRAM, 1699—1777, naturalist. *Observations in His Travels* (1751); *Description of East Florida* (1769).

STEPHEN HOPKINS, 1707—1785, governor, patriot. *Rights of Colonies Examined* (1765).

RICHARD BLAND, 1710—1776, patriot. *An Enquiry into the Rights of the British Colonies* (1766).

JONATHAN CARVER, 1710—1780. *Travels* (1778).

ANTHONY BENEZET, 1713—1748, humanitarian. *A Historical Account of Guinea* (1771).

DANIEL DULANY, 1722—1797, lawyer. *Considerations on the Propriety of Imposing Taxes* (1765).

JOHN WITHERSPOON, 1723—1794, scholar. *The Works of John Witherspoon* (nine volumes, 1804—1805).

SAMUEL SEABURY, 1729—1796, loyalist. *The Westchester Farmer* (1774—1775).

JOSEPH GALLOWAY, 1731—1803, loyalist. *A Candid Examination* (1775).

ANN HULTON, loyalist. *Letters of a Loyalist Lady* (1927).

ETHAN ALLEN, 1738—1789, soldier, deist. *Reason the Only Oracle of Man* (1784).

JONATHAN BOUCHER, *c.*1738—1804, loyalist. *Reminiscences of an American Loyalist* (1925).

DANIEL LEONARD, 1740—1829, loyalist. *Massachusettensis Letters* (1774—1775).

JAMES WILSON, 1742—1798, jurist. *Selected Political Essays of James Wilson* (1930).

BENJAMIN RUSH, 1745—1813, physician. *Essays* (1798).

FISHER AMES, 1758—1808, politician. *Works* (1809; enlarged, 1854).

POETS

GEORGE COCKINGS, *fl.*1758—1802, poet. *War* (1758); *The Conquest of Canada* (1766).

JONATHAN ODELL, 1737—1818, loyalist. *The Old Year and the New* (1779).

NATHAN MILES, 1741—1828, poet. *The American Hero* (1775).

THOMAS COOMBE, 1747—1822, loyalist. *The Peasant of Auburn; or, The Emigrant* (1783).

LEMUEL HOPKINS, 1750—1801, poet. *The Guillotina* (1796).

JOSEPH STANSBURY, *fl.*1776—1780, loyalist. *Lords of the Main* (1780).

DAVID HUMPHREYS, 1752—1818, poet. *On the Happiness of America* (1780).

ANN ELIZA BLEEKER, 1752—1783. *The Posthumous Works* (1793).

PHILLIS WHEATLEY, *c.*1753—1784, Negro poet. *Poems* (1773).

SARAH WENTWORTH MORTON, 1759—1846. *Ouâbi* (1790).

RICHARD ALSOP, 1761—1815, poet. *The Charms of Fancy* (1788); *The Echo* (with Theodore Dwight, 1807).

JOHN WILLIAMS, 1761—1818, satirist. *Hamiltoniad* (1804).

JOSEPH BROWN LADD, 1764—1786. *Poems of Arouet* (1786).

Samuel Low, *b.*1765, poet, dramatist. *Poems* (1800); *The Politician Outwitted* (1789).

Thomas Green Fessenden, 1771—1837, poet. *Democracy Unveiled* (1805).

William Clifton, 1772—1799. *The Group* (1796); *Poems* (1800).

Robert Treat Paine, 1773—1811, poet. *Works* (1812).

Paul Allen, 1775—1826, poet. *Original Poems* (1801); *Noah* (1821).

John Shaw, 1778—1809, poet. *Poems* (1810).

DRAMATISTS

Mercy Otis Warren, 1728—1814, dramatist. *The Adulateur* (1773); *The Group* (1775).

John Leacock, dramatist. *The Fall of British Tyranny* (1776).

Major Robert Rogers, 1731—1795, dramatist, Indian fighter. *Ponteach* (1766).

Colonel Thomas Forrest, *d.*1828, dramatist. *The Disappointment* (1767, 1796).

William Dunlap, 1766—1839, dramatist, biographer, painter. *Ribbemont* (acted, 1796); *André* (1798).

Peter Markoe, *c.*1752—1792, dramatist, poet. *The Reconciliation* (1790).

John D. Burk, 1775—1808, dramatist. *Bunker Hill* (1797); *Bethlem Gabor* (1807).

James Nelson Barker, 1784—1858, dramatist. *Superstition* (1824).

Joseph Hutton, 1787—1828, dramatist. *The Orphan of Prague* (1808).

NOVELISTS

Enos Hitchcock, 1745—1803. *Memoirs of the Bloomsgrove Family* (1790).

Ebenezer Bradford, 1746—1801. *The Art of Courting* (1795).

James Butler, *c.*1755—1842. *Fortune's Football* (1797—1798).

Hannah W. Foster, 1759—1840. *The Coquette* (1797).

Sarah Sayward Barrell Keating Wood, 1759—1855. *Julia and the Illuminated Baron* (1800).

Isaac Mitchell, 1759—1812. *The Asylum; or, Alonzo and Melissa* (serial, 1804; two volumes, 1811).

Susanna Haswell Rowson, 1762—1824. *Charlotte, a Tale of Truth* (1791).

Tabitha Tenney, 1762—1837. *Female Quixotism* (two volumes, 1801).

Caroline Matilda Warren, *c.*1787—1844. *The Gamesters* (1805).

MISCELLANEOUS PROSE

Lindley Murray, 1745—1826, educator. *English Grammar* (1795).

Judith Sargent Murray, 1751—1820, essayist, dramatist. *The Gleaner* (three volumes, 1798), poems and essays; *The Medium* (1795), drama.

Anne McVickar Grant, 1755—1838, author. *Memoirs of an American Lady* (1808).

THE ROMANTIC PERIOD

(1810-1865)

CHAPTER IV

EARLY SENTIMENT AND ROMANCE

HISTORICAL BACKGROUND

General View. (1) The War of 1812 freed the United States from danger of foreign domination, and attention was turned to internal expansion. The West was settled rapidly, internal improvements were demanded, and "manifest destiny" became obvious to the people. (2) The common man came into his own under Jackson. (3) The industrial revolution transformed the Northeast and combined with a reform epoch to set the North and South against each other on the issue of slavery. (4) The Civil War settled the question of secession and started the country on a new path.

The Romantic Period (1810—1865). *1812—1815:* The War of 1812. *1817—1825:* Monroe's era of good feeling. *1820:* The Missouri Compromise. *1823:* The Monroe Doctrine. *1825:* Erie Canal completed. *1827:* First railroad completed, Quincy, Massachusetts. *1829—1837:* Jacksonian democracy. *1832:* South Carolina Nullification Ordinance. *1834:* McCormick invents reaper. *1837—1841:* Van Buren administration. *1837:* Financial panic. *1841—1845:* Tyler administration. *1844:* Telegraph line. *1845:* Annexation of Texas. *1845—1849:* Polk administration. *1845—1847:* Irish immigration. *1846—1848:* Mexican War. *1848:* German immigration. *1849—1853:* Taylor and Fillmore in office. *1849:* Gold rush to California. *1850:* Compromise of 1850. Enforcement of Fugitive Slave law enrages the North. *1853:* Railroad complete from New York to Chicago. *1853—1857:* Pierce's administration. *1854:* Kansas-Nebraska bill results in another contest over slavery. *1857—1861:* Buchanan in office. *1857:* Dred Scott decision. Panic and depression in North. *1858:* First successful marine cable to Europe. *1859:* John Brown's raid. *1860:* Election of Lincoln. Secession begins. *1863:* Emancipation Proclamation. Battle of Gettysburg. *1865:* Lee's surrender. Assassination of Lincoln.[1]

---

1 For historical background see: J. F. Rhodes, *A History of the United States, 1850-1877* (eight volumes, 1899-1919); J. R. Commons *et al., History of Labor in the United States* (two volumes, 1918); W. E. Dodd, *The Cotton Kingdom* (1919), a very good little book; Claude Bowers, *The Party Battles of the Jackson Period* (1922); Merle Curti, *The American Peace Crusade, 1815-1860* (1929); C. R. Fish, *The Rise of the Common Man, 1830-1850* (1929); U. B. Phillips, *Life and Labor in the Old South* (1929); E. D. Branch, *The Sentimental Years, 1836-1860* (1934); A. C. Cole, *The Irrepressible Conflict* (1934); *Sources of Culture in the Middle West*, edited by D. R. Fox (1934).

GENERAL VIEW OF THE LITERATURE

Literature finally emerged. Whereas seventeenth century writing had been primarily religious and eighteenth century writing primarily political, nineteenth century writing was belletristic, centered in art. Romanticism was the dominant strain, with emphasis on individualism, emotionalism, use of the past in historical novels and extravagant romances, and new emphasis on nature. But American conditions were such that the form of the movement was disguised. The fact that the United States had already achieved a democracy, and that the presence of the frontier kept working conditions good, prevented the political radicalism of the European romantics. American natural beauty was celebrated when interest in nature arose, and the American past, as well as foreign settings, was used in romance. A set of national ideals was developed by men like Emerson and Whitman. American society was agrarian, which produced both idyllic pictures of rural life and humorous treatments of rusticity. But as a young country, the United States had a sense of inferiority, a "colonial complex" which led to literary nationalism and an emphasis on refinement and decorum.[2] Sectional differences remained or developed as a result of the large size of the country. Then, too, the absence of international copyright and the presence of many periodicals, annuals, and gift books affected writing, the former by putting English authors into competition with American, the latter by chaining the writers to the sentimental tastes of the middle classes. Finally evangelical religion in its deprecation of carnal sins, kept moral conduct within strict bounds, and in its distrust of frivolous writing imposed an aggressive didacticism upon literature to demonstrate its utility.[3]

THE KNICKERBOCKER SCHOOL

WASHINGTON IRVING, 1783—1859, author, essayist, story writer, historian, biographer.[4] Born of prosperous merchant

---

2 See V. F. Calverton, *The Liberation of American Literature* (1932).

3 See Paul Kaufman in *The Reinterpretation of American Literature*, edited by N. F. Foerster (1928), pp. 114-138, for a good chapter on Romanticism. Merle Curti, *The Growth of American Thought* (1943) is excellent on intellectual trends.

4 Biographies: P. M. Irving, *Life and Letters of Washington Irving* (four volumes, 1862-1864; three volumes, 1869); C. D. Warner, *Washington Irving* (1881); R. H. Stoddard, *Life of Washington Irving* (1883); G. S. Hellman, *Washington Irving, Esquire* (1925); S. T. Williams, *Washington Irving* (two volumes, 1935), the best critical biography.

Letters and Journals include: *Letters of Henry Brevoort to Irving* and *Letters from Irving to Henry Brevoort*, edited by G. S. Hellman (1918); *Journals of Washington Irving*, edited by W. P. Trent and G. S. Hellman (three volumes, 1919); for other items, edited by S. T. Williams, see his *Washington Irving*. Of especial interest is *The Journal of Emily Foster*, edited by S. T. Williams and L. B. Beach (1938), finally proving that Irving did propose to her and was rejected.

Writings: The standard edition is *The Works of Washington Irving* (twenty-one volumes, 1860-1861). The best volume of selections is *Washington Irving*, edited with bibliographies and a critical introduction by H. A. Pochmann (1934).

Bibliographies: W. R. Langfeld and P. C. Blackburn, *Washington Irving: A Bibliography* (1933). Cf. W. R. Langfeld (editor), *The Poems of Washington Irving* (1931), reprinted from *Bulletin of New York Public Library*, XXXIV (1930), pp. 763-779.

stock. Was frail in health. Read for law instead of attending college. On first trip to Europe (1804), went frequently to the theatre. Began desultory law practice on his return, though he soon devoted more time to literature than to law. Was popular in society both here and abroad (his tour in 1821 was the beginning of his social triumph in England). Traveled often on Continent, especially in Germany and Spain. Remained a bachelor, and was indolent by his own admission. He lived a leisurely life as a recognized man of letters. Appointed attaché to American legation at Madrid (1826). Became Secretary of the Legation to the Court of St. James (1829). Minister to Spain (1842—1845).

Irving, a far cry from the ethical ideal of the Puritans, was a man of sentiment, pleased by the amenities of upper-class life, which made him a cultural Federalist and inclined him toward antiquarian research. Beginning as a neoclassicist, he became a romantic as a result of contact with German Gothicism[5] and Scott. He lives today because of his blend of sensibility and humor, and because of his charming and carefully wrought style. He was a slow worker, for he lacked a creative imagination, and in addition he was a perfectionist. His outlook was genial (he did not share the Federalists' distrust of human nature), and by virtue of his charm, he had tremendous influence as the literary ambassador of America to Europe. The characteristics he contributed to the form of the short story include: (1) definiteness of locality, (2) absence of didacticism, (3) unity of atmosphere and time, (4) humor, (5) vivid characterization, and (6) finished style.[6] Such qualities as these keep him alive despite his lack of deep insight into human nature, lofty ideas, or moral earnestness.[7]

Letters of Jonathan Oldstyle (1802—1803; 1824). Juvenilia.

Salmagundi; or, The Whim-Whams and Opinions of Launcelot Langstaff, & Others (1807—1808). By Washington and William Irving and James Kirke Paulding, a serial miscellany of essays and poems comprising Addisonian memoirs of the Cockloft family, and satirical letters from a Turkish exile in New York, after the model of Goldsmith and Montesquieu.[8]

---

5 See H. A. Pochmann, "Irving's German Sources in *The Sketch Book*," *SP.*, XXVII (1930), pp. 477-507, and "Irving's German Tour and Its Influence on his Tales," *PMLA.*, XLV (1930), pp. 1150-1187.

6 F. L. Pattee, *The Development of the American Short Story* (1933), pp. 1-26.

7 J. G. Lockhart, "On the Writings of Charles Brockden Brown and Washington Irving," *Blackwood's*, VI (1820), pp. 554-561; C. D. Warner, W. C. Bryant, and G. P. Putnam, *Studies of Irving* (1880); E. W. Bowen, "Washington Irving's Place in American Literature," *SR.*, XIV (1906), pp. 171-183; W. M. Payne, *Leading American Essayists* (1910), pp. 40-143; H. W. Boynton, "Irving," in *American Writers on American Literature*, edited by John Macy (1931), pp. 58-71; H. S. Canby, *Classic Americans* (1931), pp. 67-96; I. T. Richards, "John Neal's Gleanings in Irvingiana," *AL.*, VIII (1935-1936), pp. 170-179; "A Master of the Obsolete: Washington Irving in the Shadows," *TLS.*, No. 1781 (1936), p. 229.

8 H. W. Mabie, *The Writers of Knickerbocker New York* (1912); Stockton Axson, "Washington Irving and the Knickerbocker Group," *RIP.*, XX (1933), pp. 178-195.

A History of New York . . . by Diedrich Knickerbocker † (1809).[9] Begun as a parody, continues as a burlesque,[10] with fact and fiction mingled in an "American manner." His kindly satire of the Dutch offended their descendants. Diedrich was of this line, an eccentric bachelor with diverting idiosyncrasies. Book IV satirized Thomas Jefferson as Governor Kieft. The style is classic eighteenth century English with echoes of everything imaginable.[11]

The Sketch Book of Geoffrey Crayon, Gent. † (1819—1820). An immediately popular collection of sketches, short stories, and essays, containing the immortal "Rip Van Winkle," "The Legend of Sleepy Hollow," "The Spectre Bridegroom," "Stratford on Avon," and "Westminster Abbey."

Bracebridge Hall (1822). Charming, but more dated than *The Sketch Book*. "The Stout Gentleman" is one of its best tales.

Tales of a Traveller (1824). Contains a number of Gothic stories of which "Adventure of the German Student" and "The Devil and Tom Walker" are the most effective. Criticized as inferior to its predecessors.

A History of the Life and Voyages of Christopher Columbus (1828). Though now superseded, reveals Irving's diligence. Based chiefly on the work of Navarrete.

A Chronicle of the Conquest of Granada (1829). A semi-fictionized history.

The Alhambra † (1832). Contains delightful sketches and stories founded on Irving's experiences in the old palace and on oral tradition. Many of the romantic tales are based on legends of buried Moorish treasure, and emphasize the cupidity of churchmen. Irving discovered a romantic past with castles and a departed glory which America lacked. Notable are "The Rose of the Alhambra,"† "Legend of the Arabian Astrologer,"† and "Legend of Two Discrete Statues."†

The Crayon Miscellany (1835). Series of three volumes. Introduces the new element of the American West in *A Tour on the Prairies,*† based on Irving's own experiences.

Astoria (1836). The first biography of an American business magnate (J. J. Astor), written at a time when interest in the West was increasing.

---

9 The first edition was reprinted with a critical introduction by S. T. Williams and Tremaine McDowell (1927).

10 C. G. Laird, "Tragedy and Irony in Knickerbocker's History," *AL.*, XII (1940-1941), pp. 158-172, shows that the work becomes more serious as it progresses.

11 See Edwin Greenlaw, "Washington Irving's Comedy of Politics," *TR.*, I (1916), pp. 291-306; Tremaine McDowell, "General James Wilkinson in the *Knickerbocker History of New York*," *MLN.*, XLI (1926), pp. 353-359; Clarence Webster, "Irving's Expurgations of the 1809 History of New York," *AL.*, III (1931-1932), pp. 293-295.

Adventures of Captain Bonneville (1837).[12] No longer looked to as a source for Indian customs. Irving's Western books were less popular than his previous sketches.

The Life of Oliver Goldsmith (1840; revised, 1846). Perhaps because of Irving's sympathies with the inconsistencies of his subject, this is the most successful of his biographies. ***Mahomet and His Successors*** (1850). ***Wolfert's Roost*** (1855) contains assorted sketches written long before. ***Life of Washington*** (five volumes, 1855—1859). A labor of love, which Irving found difficulty in completing. It was based on careful research, though facilitated by the publication of *The Writings of Washington,* edited by Jared Sparks.

SUGGESTED MERITS	SUGGESTED DEFECTS
1. Irving himself thought that his style was his most important characteristic. It is smooth, euphonious, lucid, and, while carefully wrought, it is easy, natural, and charming.	1. Diction tends to be a mosaic of old expressions and thus to lack originality.
2. Humor of several sorts: Satire in *Salmagundi* and *Knickerbocker* is usually kindly, at times sharp. Geniality is more characteristic, as in *Rip Van Winkle.* Even his Gothic horror stories end with a comic turn.	2. Lacks emotional depth or intensity; of course he did not try to achieve either.
3. Sentiment often blended with humor. Frequently expressed as nostalgia for a romantic past, as in England and Spain. Explains his early idealization of Indians.	3. Sentimentality occasionally excessive. See "The Pride of the Village." At home in the past, not in the reality of the present. Books on the West are clear, for example, but lack charm of earlier work.
4. Skill in short story and sketch based on careful handling of details which round out the slender plot.	4. Inventive power slight. His plots are usually borrowed.
5. Conscientious as a historian and biographer, though most at home in freer forms.	5. Needed basis of a previous work as structural frame for his history and biography.
6. Literary ambassador to Europe. Irving's geniality, tolerance, humor, liking for tradition, and elegance of style made him popular with literary leaders and the reading public of Europe, thus aiding the acceptance of later American authors.	6. Sought perhaps too much to please. His work shows changing taste of time, but carefully avoids controversial issues.

12 Title of the first edition is: *The Rocky Mountains: or, Scenes, Incidents, and Adventures . . . of Captain B. L. E. Bonneville.* See J. A. Russell, "Irving: Recorder of Indian Life," *JAH.,* XXV (1931), pp. 185-195.

NATHANIEL PARKER WILLIS, 1806—1867, poet, dramatist, New York editor.[13] Maine born, educated at Andover and Yale; became known as beau and writer of Scriptural poetry. As editor (1829—1831) of the *American Monthly Magazine* and its successor the *New-York Mirror* he acquired prominence. *Pencillings by the Way* (1835), *Loiterings of Travel* (1839), *Letters from Under a Bridge* (1840) had a popularity today difficult of explanation. So too his poetry: *Melanie and Other Poems* (1835), *The Lady Jane and Other Poems* (1844), *The Poems, Sacred, Passionate, and Humorous* (third edition, 1844), and his novel *Paul Fane* (1857). Most likely to endure are his plays *Bianca Visconti* (played, 1837) and *Tortesa the Usurer* (1839). Both plays show: 1. free treatment of history; 2. diffuse and badly articulated plot; 3. wordy and high-flown style. Association with G. P. Morris on the *New Mirror* (1843—1844), *New-York Mirror* (1844—1845), and with the *Home Journal* (1846—1867) is important in journalism. His contemporary popularity shows the false standards of his day.

FITZ-GREENE HALLECK, 1790—1867.[14] Born at Guilford, Connecticut. Son of a Tory. Went to New York at the age of twenty-one. Worked in banks, but educated himself and wrote as a side line. Had a charming personality and wit. Campbell his ideal, but influenced also by Scott and Byron. Wrote the "Croaker Papers" with J. R. Drake for the *Evening Post* and *National Advertiser* (1819); he called these satirical poems "harmless pleasantries luckily suited to the hour of their appearance." *Alnwick Castle, with Other Poems* (1827) tries to unite Byron's satiric realism with Scott's romance. *The Poetical Works of Fitz-Greene Halleck* (1847). "Fanny" (1819) is a clumsy imitation of "Beppo." "Marco Bozzaris" is somewhat better. Excellent is the elegy, "On the Death of Joseph Rodman Drake."

JOSEPH RODMAN DRAKE, 1795—1820, poet.[15] Father died and rest of family went to New Orleans. He remained in New York state and studied medicine. Died of tuberculosis. Friend of Halleck with whom he wrote "Croaker Papers" (1819). *The Culprit Fay, and Other Poems*† (1835). Title poem was written in three days; is charming but imperfect. Drake was a spontaneous poet interested in using the American scene. He showed promise.

GEORGE POPE MORRIS, 1802—1864, poet, journalist. Co-founded *New-York Mirror* (1823), important as vehicle for

13 [G. Paston], "Willis's Writings," *NAR.*, XLIII (1836), pp. 384-412; H. A. Beers, *Nathaniel Parker Willis* (1885); J. G. Wilson, *Bryant and His Friends* (1886); Granville Hicks, "A Literary Swell," *AM.*, XVI (1929), pp. 361-369.

14 See N. F. Adkins, *Fitz-Greene Halleck: An Early Knickerbocker Wit and Poet* (1930), for a general discussion of the Knickerbocker school; cf. H. W. Mabie, *The Writers of Knickerbocker New York* (1912).

15 See F. L. Pleadwell, *The Life and Works of Joseph Rodman Drake* (1935).

the Knickerbocker school. Author of "Woodman, Spare that Tree" and "Near the Lake." Also wrote *Briar Cliff* (1826), a drama of the Revolution, and a volume of humorous prose.

JAMES KIRKE PAULDING, 1778—1860, poet, novelist, friend of Irving with whom he wrote *Salmagundi* series.[16] Important in politics and literature (1807—1850). Chief Dutch interpreter of New York Dutch. *The Diverting History of John Bull and Brother Jonathan* (1812), allegorical anti-English satire in the wave of nationalism.[17] *The Lay of the Scottish Fiddle* (1813), a poetic parody of Scott. *The Backwoodsman* (1818), a poem. *Westward Ho!* (1832), a tale.[18] *The Old Continental* (1846), often considered better than *The Spy*. *The Bucktails* (1847), satirical play.

POETRY

Northern Poets

WILLIAM CULLEN BRYANT, 1794—1878, poet, editor.[19] Born at Cummington, Massachusetts; grew up on a farm as a Federalist, a Calvinist, and a classicist; he gradually changed his beliefs until he ended as a Democrat, a Unitarian, and a romanticist.[20] His satire, *The Embargo; or, Sketches of the Times,* was published in Boston (1808). Studied for college (1809—1810), partly with Rev. Moses Hallock. Entered Williams College as a sophomore (1810), and spent one year there. "Thanatopsis" written (1811). Wrote Byronic poetry, studied law, and was a practicing attorney in Plainfield (1815—1816), and in Great Barrington (1816—1825). Left for New York City where he helped edit the *New York Review* and the *United States Review.* Later he obtained a position on the New York *Evening Post* of which he was an editor (1829—1878). The rest of his life was as steady as Poe's was unstable. He wrote countless reviews, did editorial work on the

---

16 W. I. Paulding, *Literary Life of James Kirke Paulding* (1867); A. L. Herold, *James Kirke Paulding, Versatile American* (1926); N. F. Adkins, "James Kirke Paulding's *Lion of the West*," *AL.*, III (1931-1932), pp. 249-258.

17 See E. K. Brown, "The National Idea in American Criticism," *DR.*, XIV (1934), pp. 133-147; also, J. C. McClosky, "The Campaign of Periodicals after the War of 1812 for National American Literature," *PMLA.*, L (1935), pp. 262-273.

18 N. F. Adkins, "A Study of James K. Paulding's *Westward Ho*," *AC.*, III (1927), pp. 221-229.

19 Julia Hatfield, *The Bryant Homestead Book* (1870), gossipy and not reliable; G. W. Curtis, *The Life, Character, and Writings of William Cullen Bryant* (1879); Parke Godwin, *A Biography of William Cullen Bryant* (two volumes, 1883), the standard biography; J. G. Wilson, *Bryant and His Friends* (1886), pp. 11-127 and *passim;* John Bigelow, *William Cullen Bryant* (1890); W. A. Bradley, *William Cullen Bryant* (1905), better on poetry than on the life; Tremaine McDowell, "The Ancestry of William Cullen Bryant," *Americana*, XXII (1928), pp. 408-420; also "Cullen Bryant at Williams College," *NEQ.*, I (1928), pp. 443-466, "The Juvenile Verse of William Cullen Bryant," *SP.*, XXVI (1929), pp. 96-116, "William Cullen Bryant and Yale," *NEQ.*, III (1930), pp. 706-716; "Cullen Bryant Prepares for College," *SAQ.*, XXX (1931), pp. 125-133.

20 See Tremaine McDowell, *William Cullen Bryant: Representative Selections* (1935), p. xv *f.*

paper, issued poems, took six trips to Europe, and died wealthy. His chief volumes of verse were: *The Fountain and Other Poems* (1842); *The White-Footed Deer and Other Poems* (1844); *Thirty Poems* (1864); *Hymns* (1864); *The Iliad of Homer* (1870); *The Odyssey of Homer* (1871—1872).

In politics, Bryant discarded his early conservatism which had induced him to support the New England threat of secession in 1812. Reading Ricardo, Smith, and Say led him to a belief in free trade. On the *Post* he was a steady liberal, advocating penal reforms, freedom of speech, the rights of labor, currency and banking reforms, and the abolition of slavery. He became a Free-Soiler and a "black Republican"; during the War he felt that Lincoln moved too slowly, though he came to appreciate him.

In religion, Bryant abandoned Calvinism for deism and Unitarianism, but retained a slight tinge of Puritanism all his life. Volney was still popular at Williams when Bryant was there,[21] and he became something of a deist and stoic as "Thanatopsis" attests. Later he embraced Unitarianism. He was not entirely clear in his thoughts on nature. He occasionally saw it as an emanation of God ("A Forest Hymn"), but he was not a pantheist. Nature was at times evil, as in storms, and he felt it only as a secondary manifestation of God. In general his relation to nature was joyous, even when it reminded him of the transcience of life, for he appreciated a certain amount of flux, and thought that creation was ever renewed in the cycle of change which gave things an impersonal immortality.

His romanticism, which is demonstrated in his attitude toward nature, developed early.[22] He was influenced by the transitional English figures — Blair, White, Cowper, Thomson, and Alison;[23]

---

21 Tremaine McDowell, "Cullen Bryant at Williams College," *NEQ.*, I (1928), pp. 443-466.

22 Materials for criticism include: John Wilson, *Essays Critical and Imaginative* (1856), II, pp. 191-223, sane Scottish view; J. V. Cheyney, *That Dome in Air* (1895), pp. 127-143; Harriett Monroe, "Aere Perennius," *Poetry*, VI (1915), pp. 197-200, and "Bryant and the New Poetry," *Dial*, LIX (Oct. 14, 1915), p. 314 *f.*, strongly opposed; J. L. Hervey, "Bryant and 'The New Poetry,'" *Dial*, LIX (Aug. 15, 1915), pp. 92-93, favorable; A. H. Strong, *American Poets and Their Theology* (1916), pp. 3-48; E. J. Bailey, *Religious Thought in the Greater American Poets* (1922), pp. 10-32; Allan Nevins, *The Evening Post* (1922), shows Bryant's political liberalism; Norman Foerster, *Nature in American Literature* (1923), pp. 7-19; Rémy de Gourmont, *Deux Poètes de la Nature: Bryant et Emerson* (1925), pp. 25-50, approves Bryant's interest in death; Rica Brenner, *Twelve Poets* (1933), pp. 23-47; C. I. Glicksberg, "William Cullen Bryant, a Reinterpretation," *RAA.*, XI (1934), pp. 495-503; "William Cullen Bryant and Communism," *Mod.M.*, VIII (1934), pp. 353-359; "Bryant and the *United States Review*," *NEQ.*, VII (1934), pp. 687-701; "William Cullen Bryant and Fanny Wright," *AL.*, VI (1934-1935), pp. 427-432; "Bryant the Poet of Humor," *Americana*, XXIX (1935), pp. 364-374; G. W. Allen, *American Prosody* (1935), pp. 27-55; C. I. Glicksberg, "New Contributions in Prose by William Cullen Bryant," *Americana*, XXX (1936), pp. 573-592, also "Bryant and Whittier," *EIHC.*, LXXII (1936), pp. 111-116, and "Bryant and the Sedgwick Family," *Americana*, XXXI (1937), pp. 626-638; H. L. Drew, "Unpublished Letters of William Cullen Bryant," *NEQ.*, X (1937), pp. 346-355; Tremaine McDowell, *William Cullen Bryant* (1935), gives in its critical introduction, pp. xiii-lxviii, the best materials so far for a critical estimate, also "Bryant's Practice in Composition and Revision," *PMLA.*, LII (1937), pp. 474-502; C. I. Glicksberg, "Bryant on Emerson the Lecturer," *NEQ.*, XII (1939), pp. 530-534.

23 W. P. Hudson, "Archibald Alison and William Cullen Bryant," *AL.*, XII (1940-1941), pp. 59-68.

he imitated Byron for a time; and by 1812 he was a permanent admirer of Wordsworth, from whom he derived more in technique than in thought. He is remembered as the celebrator of the wilder aspects of nature — the storms and rugged hills, as well as the flowers and birds.

Bryant was skillful in the use of verse forms; in his own day he was considered an innovator. He wrote stately and sonorous blank verse, adopted the Spenserian stanza, showed great mastery of the octosyllabic couplet, and worked out a number of other stanza forms. The influence of Wordsworth on his diction is obvious. Aside from the use of a variety of forms, his work did not show progress. He wrote as well at the end of his life as ever, but without entirely fulfilling his early promise, and he could never sustain a long poem. Since the American climate was not congenial to the professional poet, Bryant turned to journalism to make a living, though it could be wished that he had been as willing to starve for his art as Poe. If not one of the great, he was at least the first American to attain an international reputation as a poet.

For years Bryant was an important critic, delivering lectures on poetry and writing reviews, many of them only recently identified.[24] His literary theories can be outlined as follows: (1) Appeal to feeling, imagination, and understanding. (2) Opposition to neoclassical, second-hand, bookish imitation. (3) Use of imaginative synthesis. (4) Attack on metaphysical subtleties. (5) Need for selection to attain elevation and suggestiveness. (6) Use of nature as a means of bodying forth ideas. (7) Flexibility and freedom in metrics. (8) Concern with timeless elements. (9) Emphasis on ethical beauty.[25]

"Thanatopsis"† (1817 version enlarged in 1821). The main body was written in 1811, but the beginning which makes nature the speaker, and the conclusion were added in 1821. A sonorous, deistic, stoical meditation on death.[26]

"The Yellow Violet" (1814). Uses American not English nature. Though not orthodox, Bryant is accused of over-moralizing. If so, he was in the Burns and Wordsworth tradition.

"Inscription for the Entrance to a Wood" (1815). Blank verse, sensuous description of nature, claiming that the forest is consolation for those who find men evil.

"I Cannot Forget with What Fervid Devotion." A lament on the fact that urban life shatters the dream engendered by walks in the woods.

---

24 Tremaine McDowell, *William Cullen Bryant* (1935), pp. 359-362, lists over fifty.

25 See *The Prose Writings of William Cullen Bryant*, edited by Parke Godwin (two volumes, 1884); and Tremaine McDowell, *William Cullen Bryant* (1935).

26 See Carl Van Doren, "The Growth of 'Thanatopsis,'" *Nation*, CI (Oct. 7, 1915), pp. 432-433.

"To a Waterfowl"† (1815; 1818). Often considered Bryant's masterpiece. Has sure command of metrics. The flight of the bird gives the poet an idea of a protecting power.

"Green River" (1820). In four foot couplets. Theme: the healing powers of nature.

"Oh Fairest of the Rural Maids." Written to Frances Fairchild, later Bryant's wife.

"A Winter Piece." A cheerful description of a snow-covered New England landscape.

"Monument Mountain." Retells an Indian legend of a girl who, because of an unhappy love, cast herself off a cliff.

"A Forest Hymn"† (1825). A stately and dignified celebration of nature's sanative effect on man. God is the creator, but there are also some pantheistic hints here. Poe praised its rhythmical beauty.

"To the Fringed Gentian" (1829; 1832). A charming lyric with a moral turn. Gives evidence of Bryant's close association with nature, the result of botanizing expeditions begun in his youth.

"Song of Marion's Men," "The Battle-Field," "Our Country's Call," and **"Death of Lincoln."** Reveal his patriotism.

"The Fountain" (1839). Works out the theme of permanence in flux. The fountain continues to flow even though the surroundings change.

"A Lifetime" and **"The Flood of Years"** (1876). Written in a retrospective mood. The latter is a contemplation of the past which overwhelmed countless people, and of the future in which they will be made happy once more.

SUGGESTED MERITS

1. Lofty nobility and eloquence of style.

2. Technical mastery of many verse forms.

3. Dignified treatment of expansive subjects such as the beauties of nature and the fate of man.

4. A classical emphasis upon exactness and correctness of form which produced, in spite of his general romanticism, a uniform excellence.[28]

5. A courageous stoicism as expressed in "Thanatopsis," changing to the long-range optimism of "The Flood of Years."

SUGGESTED DEFECTS

1. Lack of that concentration which marks the greatest poets.

2. Narrow range of subject matter.

3. Dullness. Many readers find Bryant lacking in emotional and intellectual fire.[27]

4. Excessive moralizing, as at the end of "To a Waterfowl" and "To a Fringed Gentian."

---

27 E. C. Stedman, *Poets of America* (1885), pp. 62-94.

28 H. H. Clark, *Major American Poets* (1936), pp. 788-797.

JOHN PIERPONT, 1785—1866, poet, Unitarian clergyman, reformer.[29] An accomplished prosodist and humorist; had a vigorous mind. *The Portrait* (1812) and *Airs of Palestine* (1816) established him as a poet. *Anti-Slavery Poems* (1843). Famous: "Warren's Address to the American Soldiers."

JAMES GATES PERCIVAL, 1785—1856, poet, geologist of Connecticut.[30] B.A., Yale (1815). *Poems* (1821) contained the Spenserian "Prometheus." *Clio I and II* (1822), not good lyrics. *Prometheus Part II with Other Poems* (1822), *Clio III* (1827), *The Dream of a Day, and Other Poems* (1843). Was the ranking poet until Bryant's *Poems* (1832). Turned to geology in later life.

RICHARD HENRY DANA, Sr., 1787—1879, poet, essayist. Born in Cambridge of distinguished ancestry. Harvard (1804—1807). *The Buccaneer and Other Poems* (1827), its title-poem praised by *Blackwood's* as powerful and original. Influenced by Crabbe, Wordsworth, Coleridge. Wrote in simple, direct style, not fashionably florid. Edited *North American Review.*

JOHN GARDINER CALKINS BRAINARD, 1796—1828, poet. Edited *Connecticut Mirror* in Hartford (1822). *Poems* (1825) and *Literary Remains* (1832)[31] contain popular pieces like "On the Connecticut River," "The Black Fox of Salmon River," and "The Sea Bird's Song." Used ballad form; possessed delicacy and humor.

THOMAS BUCHANAN READ, 1822—1872, painter, poet.[32] Wrote "Sheridan's Ride" (1865), one poem likely to escape oblivion. "Drifting," "The Attack," "The Maid Who Binds Her Warrior's Sash" are other poems not without merit. Read's only venture in prose was *Paul Redding: A Tale of the Brandywine* (1845). *The Female Poets of America* (1849) is an anthology with brief introductory notices. His complete poetical works were published in 1883.

RICHARD HENRY STODDARD, 1825—1903, poet, critic, editor.[33] Self-educated, worked in factories, was an iron-moulder. Received customs house position (1853) through Hawthorne.

---

29 See sketch in S. A. Eliot, *Heralds of a Liberal Faith* (1910), II; J. T. Winterich, "Savonarola of Hollis Street," *Colophon,* Part Twenty, No. 4 (1935).

30 W. H. Pearson, "James Gates Percival," *WMH.,* VIII (1925), pp. 131-145; A. B. Benson, "James Gates Percival, Student of German Culture," *NEQ.,* II (1929), pp. 603-624.

31 Edited by J. G. Whittier, with Introduction (1832).

32 See H. C. Townsend *et al., A Memoir of T. Buchanan Read* (1889); R. H. Stoddard, *Recollections Personal and Literary* (1903); C. L. Moore, "A Neglected American Poet," *Dial,* LVI (1914), pp. 7-9; A. E. Smith, "Letters of Thomas Buchanan Read," *OSAHQ.,* XLVI (1937), pp. 68-80.

33 See J. B. Gilder in *Authors at Home,* edited by J. L. and J. B. Gilder (1889), pp. 293-312; H. C. Vedder, *American Writers of Today* (1894), pp. 275-287; E. C. Stedman, *Genius and Other Essays* (1911), pp. 141-153, 166-173; W. P. Fenn, "Richard Henry Stoddard's Chinese Poems," *AL.,* XI (1939-1940), pp. 417-438.

Reviewer for New York *World* (1860—1870). Literary editor of *Mail and Express* (1880—1903). Poetry not great. Ear bad, imagination limited and imitative. "The Dead Master" addressed to Bryant and "Abraham Lincoln: An Horatian Ode" have real power. Used Oriental themes. Bridged the generations of Bryant and Taylor. Criticism good considering its journalistic nature. *Poems* (1852); *Songs of Summer* (1857); *The Book of the East and Other Poems* (1871); *The Poems of Richard Henry Stoddard* (1880); *The Lion's Cub: With Other Verse* (1890); *Under the Evening Lamp* (1892); *Recollections Personal and Literary* (1903).

THOMAS WILLIAM PARSONS, 1819—1892.[34] A Boston dentist whose real interest lay in scholarship and religion. Translated Dante's *Inferno,*† ten cantos of which appeared in 1843, to be followed by the remaining seventeen in 1865, almost simultaneously with Longfellow's translation of the *Divine Comedy.* In 1893, his *Inferno* and *Purgatorio*† were published together, while his original poems appeared in a separate volume. Enshrined as "The Poet" in Longfellow's *Tales of a Wayside Inn,* Parsons himself wrote *The Old House at Sudbury* (1870). A collection of his letters has recently been published.[35]

Southern Poets

EDGAR ALLAN POE, 1809—1849, poet, short-story writer, critic.[36] Born in Boston; parents were actors. In 1811 he was taken into the home of John Allan of Richmond, but not legally adopted; thus his future was insecure. Educated in England (1815—1820). Attended University of Virginia (1826), but soon left after a quarrel with Allan over gambling debts. He left foster home (1827), published *Tamerlane and Other Poems* in Boston, and joined the army. After Mrs. Allan's death (1829) he resigned and obtained an appointment to West Point in 1830. Fearing that he would lose right to property if Allan remarried and hoping to prevent the step, Poe refused to obey orders and was expelled from

34 T. B. Aldrich, "A Portrait of Thomas William Parsons," *Century,* XLVIII; N.S., XXVI (1894), p. 323 *f.*; M. S. Porter, "Thomas William Parsons, with Unpublished Poems by Dr. Parsons, and Letters by Dr. Holmes," *Century,* LXII; N.S., XL (1901), pp. 934-938; Austin Warren, "T. W. Parsons, Poet and Translator of Dante," *MB.,* XIII (1938), pp. 287-303.

35 *Letters by T. W. Parsons,* edited by Zoltán Haraszti (1940).

36 Biographies include: J. H. Ingram, *Edgar Allan Poe* (two volumes, 1880); J. A. Harrison, *Life and Letters of Edgar Allan Poe* (two volumes, 1903), one of the best; G. E. Woodberry, *The Life of Edgar Allan Poe* (two volumes, 1909), best literary life; J. W. Robertson, *Edgar Allan Poe; a Psychopathic Study* (1921); *Edgar Allan Poe Letters till Now Unpublished, in the Valentine Museum,* edited by M. N. Stanard (1925); J. W. Krutch, *Edgar Allan Poe* (1926), Freudian; M. E. Phillips, *Edgar Allan Poe* (two volumes, 1926), original material, poorly arranged; Hervey Allen, *Israfel* (two volumes, 1926), vivid, perhaps too romantic; Una Pope-Hennessy, *Edgar Allan Poe* (1934), sensible; J. H. Birss, "Poe in Fordham: A Reminiscence," *NQ.,* CLXXIII (1937), p. 440; H. E. Spivey, "Poe and Lewis Gaylord Clark," *PMLA.,* LIV (1939), pp. 1124-1132; A. H. Quinn, *Edgar Allan Poe* (two volumes, 1942), contains new material and is temperate in tone.

West Point. Thereafter he was permanently estranged from his foster father. From 1831 to 1833 he probably lived with his aunt, Maria Clemm, in Baltimore. "MS. Found in a Bottle" won the Baltimore *Saturday Visitor's* one hundred dollar prize (1833). Through John Pendleton Kennedy, he obtained a position on the *Southern Literary Messenger* (1835), and began his editorial career. He married Virginia Clemm, his thirteen-year-old cousin, in 1836, and lost his position (1837), possibly because of alcoholism. After a financially barren year in New York, he went to Philadelphia where he helped edit *Burton's Gentleman's Magazine* (1839—1840) and *Graham's Magazine* (1841—1842). *Tales of the Grotesque and Arabesque* appeared (1840). In 1844 he moved to New York to work on the *Evening Mirror*. *The Raven and Other Poems* and *Tales* appeared (1845). *Godey's Lady's Book* published his series on "The Literati" of New York (1846). The next year his wife died after a long illness in extreme poverty. He sought refuge in other women, especially Mrs. Whitman and Mrs. Shelton. Some of his best poems and some of his most successful lectures are the product of his last year before he died in Baltimore, perhaps intoxicated or perhaps drugged and robbed.

Despite such unhappy circumstances, Poe distinguished himself in three fields — criticism, short story, and poetry. It is difficult to estimate Poe's works because they are hard to separate from the man, who is not any too well known. Unfortunately, Poe left his papers to Griswold, who disliked him and defamed him thoroughly. Thus the truth about Poe is still not easy to get at,[37] especially since most of the search has been for abnormalities. It is, after all, his work that counts, and more light can still be thrown upon his

---

37 The nature of Poe criticism is significant. Beginning with Rufus Griswold, the first defaming biographer and critic, too much attention has been given to attack and defense, to debunking and equally dangerous romanticizing. At the other pole are the hundreds of short articles dealing with sources for particular poems. These may be found listed in the bibliographies appearing in each issue of *AL.* Among the significant estimates and worth-while discoveries are: Charles Baudelaire, "Edgar Poe, Sa Vie et Ses Oeuvres," in *Histoires Extraordinaires par Edgar Poe* (1856; translated by H. C. Curwin, 1872); L. E. Gates, *Studies and Appreciations* (1900), pp. 110-128; Gustav Gruener, "Notes on the Influence of E. T. A. Hoffmann upon Edgar Allan Poe," *PMLA.*, XIX (1904), pp. 1-25; W. C. Brownell, *American Prose Masters* (1909), pp. 207-267, very unfavorable; C. A. Smith, *Edgar Allan Poe, How to Know Him* (1921); F. L. Pattee, *Sidelights on American Literature* (1922), pp. 327-342; Margaret Alterton, *Origins of Poe's Critical Theory* (1925), the basis for an intellectual defense of Poe; Killis Campbell, "Poe's Reading," *UTSE.*, V (1925), pp. 166-196; Floyd Stovall, "The Women of Poe's Poems and Tales," *UTSE.*, V (1925), pp. 197-209; Napier Wilt, "Poe's Attitude toward His Tales, a New Document," *MP.*, XXV (1927), pp. 101-105, shows Poe's tales based on study of current magazines; Norman Foerster, *American Criticism* (1928), pp. 1-51, important; S. F. Damon, *Thomas Holley Chivers, Friend of Poe* (1930); W. L. Werner, "Poe's Theories and Practice in Poetic Technique," *AL.*, II (1930-1931), pp. 157-165; L. C. Bell, *Poe and Chivers* (1931), reply to Damon; H. S. Canby, *Classic Americans* (1931), pp. 263-307; Killis Campbell, *The Mind of Poe and Other Studies* (1933), sane and sound, the best single book for Poe criticism; W. F. Taylor, "Israfel in Motley: A Study of Poe's Humor," *SR.*, XLII (1934), pp. 330-340; Ernest Marchand, "Poe as Social Critic," *AL.*, VI (1934-1935), pp. 28-43; D. K. Jackson, *Poe and the Southern Literary Messenger* (1934); G. W. Allen, *American Prosody* (1935), pp. 56-90; *Edgar Allan Poe: Representative Selections*, edited by Margaret Alterton and Hardin Craig (1935), with critical introduction, bibliography, and notes, is important; R. L. Hudson, "Poe and Disraeli," *AL.*, VIII (1936-1937), pp. 402-416; M. G. Evans, *Music and Edgar Allan Poe* (1939); W. K. Wimsatt, Jr., "Poe and the Chess Automaton," *AL.*, XI (1939-1940), pp. 138-151, and "What Poe Knew about Cryptography," *PMLA.*, LVIII (1943), pp. 754-779.

writing. The nature of Poe's genius further complicates the problem, for he worked brilliantly in a narrow field. Those who seek Shakespeare's breadth or even Hawthorne's depth of ethical probing will find Poe wanting. But he will be remembered as a skillful poet, as the most important critic of his generation, and as the father of the American short story and detective story.

CRITICISM

In his lifetime Poe was most renowned as a critic,[38] for he was a vigorous reviewer who spared no names. His criticism is still important because he made use of principles in judging a work. He developed a Newtonian conception of the oneness of the universe (see *Eureka*), and he may have tried to make art fit into this scheme.[39] Beauty, not truth, he claimed, was the end of art; his poetic principle was aspiration for supernal beauty. A poem: (1) should not be didactic, (2) should be short, (3) should be a rhythmical creation of beauty, (4) should make the ideal beautiful, and elevate the soul, (5) should be melancholic in its beauty, and (6) should have a beautiful woman as its best subject. His equally clear precepts governing the short story (see *Hawthorne and the Story-Teller's Art*) are that it should: (1) have totality of effect, (2) begin with the first sentence, (3) aim at truth, (4) be short, (5) have no loose ends. All these principles were exemplified in his own work,[40] perhaps too well, since the theory fits Poe and very few others. It hardly deals with ethics.

POETRY[41]

Poe was a skillful metrist, and a careful reviser who achieved the effects he aimed at. His subjects show a similarity, and at times he is too much interested in sound alone. He has had special influence on Baudelaire.

"Al Aaraaf" (1829). A difficult poem emphasizing as a desirable objective the elevation of the soul through contemplation of the beautiful. Has a melody characteristic of his subsequent work; defective structure, obscuring style.

"To Helen"† (1831). Expresses his grief at the death of Mrs. Jane Stanard. It is one of his finest poems, showing unusual restraint and compression.[41a]

---

38 See J. B. Moore, *Selections from Poe's Literary Criticism* (1926); also A. I. Cooke, "The Popular Conception of Edgar Allan Poe from 1850 to 1890," *UTSE.*, No. 4226 (1942), pp. 145-170.

39 See Margaret Alterton, *Origins of Poe's Critical Theory* (1925).

40 This theory was influenced by Newtonianism, Coleridge, Shelley, and Byron. See Floyd Stovall, "An Interpretation of Poe's 'Al Aaraaf,'" *UTSE.*, IX (1929), pp. 106-133, his "Poe's Debt to Coleridge," *UTSE.*, X (1930), pp. 70-127, and his "Poe as Poet of Ideas," *UTSE.*, XI (1931), pp. 56-62.

41 Killis Campbell, *The Poems of Edgar Allan Poe* (1917), is the best edition.

41a W. C. Brown, "The English Professor's Dilemma," *CE.*, V (1944), pp. 379-385.

"Israfel"† (1831). On the ideal poet. One of the best examples of his liquid diction and rhythmical perfection.

"The City in the Sea" (1831).[42] Perhaps a city of sin or a city of the dead. Is a marvel of tone. Has some echoes of Shelley.

"The Haunted Palace"† (1839). Was used in *The Fall of the House of Usher* and was intended to symbolize a disordered mind. It has been often praised.

"The Raven"† (1845). Most famous of Poe's poems. Chivers claimed that Poe plagiarized it. The raven probably came from Dickens' *Barnaby Rudge* and some effects from Mrs. Browning's "Lady Geraldine's Courtship." Poe wrote an essay, "The Philosophy of Composition,"† purporting to describe his technique in writing this poem. The familiar theme of mourning for the death of a beautiful lover is skillfully applied.

"Ulalume"† (1847). Written on the death of his wife, but generalized into indefiniteness by the dialogue of his soul, in which he tries to console himself, but meets only the finality of the tomb.

"The Bells" (1849). A neat exercise in onomatopoeia, whose first version was only eighteen lines long.

"Eldorado" (1849). Expresses the never-ending quest for happiness, or, as some would have it, an unattainable ideal.

"Annabel Lee"† (1849). On the favorite theme of death, with the feeling so well generalized that it is unimportant whether his own wife or another was meant.

SHORT STORIES

Poe's tales have no less vogue than his poetry. This is deserved because of his unexampled skill in narration. He conceived the short story like the poem as a unit, every portion of it contributing to the final effect. Naturally he improved technically as he wrote more. He always lavished care on his work even when it did not thereby become more saleable. The stories may be divided into: (1) tales of terror, (2) tales of beauty in color and rhythm, (3) tales of ratiocination.

The tale of terror, a hangover from Gothicism,[43] was adopted by Poe partly because it would sell, but doubtless also because it fitted his temperament. "The Descent into the Maelstrom" describes the adventures of a fisherman who escapes the whirlpool. "Ligeia"[43a] is again on his favorite theme, the death of a beautiful

42 Louise Pound, "On Poe's 'The City in the Sea,'" *AL.*, VI (1934-1935), pp. 22-27.

43 See Oral Coad, "The Gothic Element in American Literature before 1835," *JEGP.*, XXIV (1925), pp. 72-93.

43a R. P. Basler, "The Interpretation of 'Ligeia,'" *CE.*, V (1944), pp. 363-372.

woman, who this time triumphs over the grave and returns. For continuous building of atmosphere this tale is not surpassed. "MS. Found in a Bottle," which won him a prize, had power but not the fine form of his later tales. "The Cask of Amontillado" neatly describes a gruesome revenge. "Berenice," "The Fall of the House of Usher," "The Tell-Tale Heart," and "The Black Cat" all belong in this category, but all of them also deal with diseased minds. This use of psychological abnormality to heighten the effect of terror is one of Poe's favorite devices.

His tales of beauty or prose-poems include: "Shadow," "Eleanora," "The Domain of Arnheim," and even "The Masque of the Red Death," which is grotesque and terrible but depends for its effect upon the writing.

The tales of ratiocination show Poe exercising his sharp, logical mind. No great cryptographer,[44] he was nevertheless able to work out fine stories like "The Gold Bug,"† one of the least terrifying and most popular, a tale of buried treasure. Even more lastingly important, for better or worse, were such detective stories as "The Murders in the Rue Morgue," "The Mystery of Marie Roget," and "The Purloined Letter." These established the technique of the modern detective tale.

SUGGESTED MERITS	SUGGESTED DEFECTS
1. In *poetry* Poe is a master creator of moods through skillful use of internal and external rhyme, regular rhythm, carefully chosen sound, onomatopoeia, and suggestively vague description. His influence through the French symbolists is still felt on American poetry.[45]	1. To many, Poe's metrical effects seem crude, his vocabulary meagre and repetitious, his rhymes obvious. (Emerson called Poe the "jingle man.") These critics feel he subordinated sense to sound, and that his intentional vagueness is often less successful than sharp, clear imagery.[46]
2. Poe's *short stories* are praised for their concision, unity of effect, and tension. They generally evoke gripping excitement through brilliantly imagined events and carefully wrought style.	2. Detractors point out Poe's forte is not humane but abnormal psychology, that he does not understand normal people, that his range is consequently narrow, and that his style is labored and artificial.[47]
3. Poe's *criticism* has been highly regarded because he judged by a coherent set of aesthetic and technical standards. He was not limited by American nationalism to patriotic praise of American authors.	3. Poe's criticism was often unduly censorious, nor was his taste unerring.

44 W. F. Friedman, "Edgar Allan Poe, Cryptographer," *AL.*, VIII (1936-1937), pp. 266-280; C. S. Brigham, "Edgar Allan Poe's Contributions to Alexander's Weekly Messenger," *PAAS.*, LII (1942), pp. 45-125; W. K. Wimsatt, Jr., "What Poe Knew about Cryptography," *PMLA.*, LVIII (1943), pp. 754-779.

45 Oscar Cargill, *Intellectual America* (1940), pp. 176-180, and *passim.*

46 See Yvor Winters, *Maule's Curse* (1938), pp. 93-122; Cleanth Brooks and R. P. Warren, *Understanding Poetry* (1938), p. 358 *ff.*

47 See W. C. Brownell, *American Prose Masters* (1909), pp. 207-267.

STEPHEN COLLINS FOSTER, 1826—1864, composer.[48] Songs include: "Susanna" (*c.* 1848); "Old Uncle Ned" (*c.* 1848), also "Uncle Ned" (*c.* 1848); "Away Down South," (*c.* 1848); "Nellie Was a Lady" (*c.* 1849); "Nellie Bly" (*c.* 1849); "Gwine to Run All Night; or, De Camptown Races" (*c.* 1850); "Old Folks at Home" (*c.* 1851); "My Old Kentucky Home, Good Night" (*c.* 1853); "Jeanie with the Light Brown Hair" (*c.* 1854); "Come Where My Love Lies Dreaming" (*c.* 1855); "Old Black Joe" (*c.* 1860); "Beautiful Dreamer" (*c.* 1864).

HENRY TIMROD, 1828—1867, poet of South Carolina.[49] Was a tutor on plantations and a member of Simms's coterie during vacations. Became the laureate of the Confederacy. His writing improved when he had something to say. "A Cry to Arms" (1862) and "Carolina" (1862) are representative of stronger note. The War ruined him financially, but did not make him morbid. Magnolia Cemetery "Ode" dates from this period, one of his best poems. To be noted are "Ethnogenesis" (1861) and "The Cotton Boll" (1861), two odes. *Poems of Henry Timrod* (memorial edition, 1899) shows him to be one of the best Southern poets. Good lyricist. Poetry carefully polished, clear, quotable, but lacking in profundity. His critical theory was that the source of poetry could not be reduced to beauty alone. Power and truth were also important. His faults are too strong a didactic vein, too much sweetness, and a slavish imitation of English romantic poets.

PAUL HAMILTON HAYNE, 1830—1886, poet of prominent Charleston family.[50] Read for law. After the War he lived in a shack and wrote for a living. *Poems* (1855). *Sonnets and Other Poems* (1857). *Avolio, a Legend of the Island of Cos* (1860). *Legends and Lyrics*† (1872). *Poems of Paul Hamilton*

---

48 R. P. Nevin, "Stephen C. Foster and Negro Minstrelsy," *Atl.*, XX (1867), pp. 608-616; W. W. Whittlesey and O. G. Sonneck, *Catalogue of First Editions of Stephen Collins Foster* (1915); H. V. Milligan, *Stephen Collins Foster* (1920); J. T. Howard, *Stephen Foster, America's Troubador* (1934); J. G. Bowman, "A Singer to Pioneers," *Atl.*, CLVI (1935), pp. 83-88; R. W. Walters, *Stephen Foster* (1936); E. N. C. Barnes, *Near Immortals* (1940), pp. 3-14; Alexander Woollcott, *Long, Long Ago* (1943), pp. 183-185.

49 *The Poems of Henry Timrod*, edited by P. H. Hayne (1873), with good biography; *Poems of Henry Timrod* (1899); Henry Timrod, "The Character and Scope of the Sonnet," *Outlook*, LXXVII (1904), pp. 706-709, also "A Theory of Poetry," *Atl.*, XCVI (1905), pp. 313-326; G. A. Wauchope, *Henry Timrod, Man and Poet* (1915); H. T. Thompson, *Henry Timrod* (1928), G. P. Voigt, "Timrod's Essays in Literary Criticism," *AL.*, VI (1934-1935), pp. 163-167; E. W. Parks, "Timrod's College Days," *AL.*, VIII (1936-1937), pp. 294-296; Lewis Patton, "An Unpublished Poem by Henry Timrod," *AL.*, X (1938-1939), p. 222 *f.*; G. P. Voigt, "Timrod in the Light of Newly Revealed Letters," *SAQ.*, XXXVII (1938), pp. 263-269; *The Uncollected Poems of Henry Timrod*, edited by G. A. Cardwell, Jr. (1942); *The Essays of Henry Timrod*, edited by E. W. Parks (1942).

50 M. J. Preston, "Paul Hamilton Hayne," *SB.*, II (1886), pp. 222-229; T. W. Higginson, "Paul Hamilton Hayne," *Chaut.*, VII (1887), pp. 228-232; W. H. Hayne, "Paul H. Hayne's Methods of Composition," *LMM.*, L (1892), pp. 793-796; Maurice Thompson, "The Last Literary Cavalier," *Critic*, XXXVIII (1901), pp. 352-354; C. R. Anderson, "Charles Gayarre and Paul Hayne: The Last Literary Cavaliers," *American Studies in Honor of William Kenneth Boyd* (1940), pp. 221-281; D. M. McKeithan, "A Correspondence Journal of Paul Hamilton Hayne," *GHQ.*, XXVI (1942), pp. 249-272.

Hayne (1882), completed edition. *The Broken Battalions* (1885), a Confederate memorial. Was good at the sonnet, but on the whole uneven, without talent of the higher order. A friend of Whittier.

Men Noted for Single Poems

FRANCIS SCOTT KEY, 1779—1843, "The Star-Spangled Banner"† (1814).[51] **SAMUEL FRANCIS SMITH**, 1808—1895, "America"† (1832).

NOVELISTS

The novel grew luxuriantly in the middle period. After Cooper had shown the way, themes from American history and tales of the Indians were commonly used. Meanwhile the didactic novel continued in popularity and the sentimental story, most frequently written by women, produced a wave of tears which reached its crest in the fifties.[51a] The South began to use its past culture and history in romance.[52] Hawthorne showed what could be done in probing the souls of his characters in novels, the more remarkable in the light of what had preceded them in American fiction, and Melville went his curious and unappreciated way.

Major Novelists

JAMES FENIMORE COOPER, 1789—1851, novelist, social critic.[53] Born in Burlington, New Jersey, of prosperous parents. Moved to Cooperstown (1790). Studied with an anti-Puritan, Tory tutor (1790). At Yale (1803—1806); dismissed for perpetrating idle pranks. A sailor and naval officer (1806—1811). Married Susan DeLancey, of Loyalist family (1811); and she kept him off the sea. Moved to Cooperstown (1814) as squire.

---

51 Victor Weybright, *Spangled Banner: The Story of Francis Scott Key* (1935); E. S. Delaplaine, *Francis Scott Key: Life and Times* (1937).

51a See H. R. Brown, *The Sentimental Novel in America, 1789-1860* (1940). Sentimental women novelists include Lydia Maria Child, Susan Bogert Warner, Emma Southworth, Maria Susanna Cummins.

52 See J. G. Johnson, *Southern Fiction prior to 1860: An Attempt at a First-Hand Bibliography* (1909); W. S. Jenkins, *Pro-Slavery Thought in the Old South* (1935).

53 Biographies: T. R. Lounsbury, *James Fenimore Cooper* (1882); R. E. Spiller, *Fenimore Cooper, Critic of His Times* (1931), emphasizes social thought; H. W. Boynton, *James Fenimore Cooper* (1931). Cf. *Correspondence of James Fenimore Cooper*, edited by J. F. Cooper (two volumes, 1922).

For a biography, criticism, and bibliography, see Warren S. Walker, *James Fenimore Cooper: An Introduction and Interpretation* (Barnes & Noble, 1962).

Criticism includes: W. G. Simms, *Views and Reviews* (1845), pp. 210-238; J. E. Cooke, "Cooper's Indians," *AJ.*, XII (1874), pp. 264-267; D. L. Maulsby, "Fenimore Cooper and Mark Twain," *Dial*, XXII (1897), pp. 107-109; W. C. Brownell, *American Prose Masters* (1909), pp. 3-60; John Erskine, *Leading American Novelists* (1910), pp. 51-129; E. E. Hale, "American Scenery in Cooper's Novels," *SR.*, XVIII (1910), pp. 317-332; J. DeL. Ferguson, *American Literature in Spain* (1916), pp. 32-54; Joseph Conrad, *Notes on Life and Letters* (1921), pp. 53-57; E. E. Leisy, *The American Historical Novel (on American Themes) before 1860: The Early Novels of James Fenimore Cooper* (1923); *A History of Cooperstown*, edited by S. M. Shaw and W. R. Littell (1929); R. E. Spiller, "Cooper's Defense of Slave-Owning America," *AHR.*, XXXV (1930), pp. 575-582; Gregory Paine, "Cooper and *The North American Review*," *SP.*, XXVIII (1931), pp. 267-277.

In 1817 the family estate was divided, and Cooper returned to Westchester county. Invested in a whaling venture (1819). Disgusted by a novel he was reading aloud (apparently he had covered Jane Austen and Mrs. Opie),[54] he said he could do better himself, whereupon he accepted his wife's challenge and wrote *Precaution* (1820), a poor but not unsuccessful novel of English manners. The next year he published *The Spy,* which established his reputation. Moved to New York and became the center of the Bread and Cheese Club.[55] House at Cooperstown burned (1823). Took his family to Europe (1826) for their education; met Scott and Lafayette (1826—1827); visited in France, Switzerland, Italy, Germany, England until 1833, attempting meanwhile to explain Americans to Europe. Somewhat disillusioned on his return, he proceeded to justify his views to Americans. Purchased Otsego Hall at Cooperstown (1834). In 1837 a controversy developed with the people of Cooperstown over the use of Three Mile Point, which he owned; the quarrel was continued by the New York City Whig papers (1838).[56] His *History of the Navy* (1839) caused criticism of his interpretation of the Battle of Lake Erie; Cooper sued his attackers for libel and won most of the cases. He became for a time engrossed in social criticism, and wrote less successfully. Near the end of his career he wrote *Satanstoe,*† one of his best novels. *Upside Down, or Philosophy in Petticoats,* his only attempt at drama, was played in New York (1850). A few months before his death, he joined the Episcopal church (1851).

Cooper's reputation has risen of late, (1) because a study of his social criticism shows his penetrating mind,[57] (2) because of his epic treatment of the frontier in the Leather-Stocking Tales, and (3) because he began the realistic sea story. As the son of a judge, Cooper was a patrician from birth. He believed that all classes should be regulated, and that the aristocracy had duties as well as privileges. He was a member of the Democratic party, despite his Federalist and Quaker background.[58] He believed in class distinctions, in squirearchy, in the soil; he hated the middle class which was gaining power on Wall Street, squatters, and New Englanders. He was no rationalist in religion, advocated humility and tolerance, but was impatient with Puritan extremism. In art, Cooper, like Wordsworth, preferred plain and simple diction, though he failed to put his theory into practice. This may partly explain his popularity in translation.

---

54 G. E. Hastings, "How Cooper Became a Novelist," *AL.*, XII (1940-1941), pp. 20-51.

55 See: N. F. Adkins, "James Fenimore Cooper and the Bread and Cheese Club," *MLN.*, XLVII (1932), pp. 71-79; A. H. Marckwardt, "The Chronology and Personnel of the Bread and Cheese Club," *AL.*, VI (1934-1935), pp. 389-399.

56 See: E. R. Outland, "The 'Effingham' Libels on Cooper," *U.Wi.SLL.*, No. 28 (1929); Dorothy Waples, *The Whig Myth of James Fenimore Cooper* (1938).

57 *James Fenimore Cooper: Representative Selections*, edited by R. E. Spiller (1936), contains his chief social views and has an excellent introduction and bibliography.

58 H. S. Canby, *Classic Americans* (1931), pp. 97-142.

SOCIAL CRITICISM

When Cooper arrived in Europe, he found prevalent misconceptions of the America he loved. These he began to correct in *Notions of the Americans* (1828) in semi-novel epistolary form. He thought the United States was like his aristocratic ideal, and offended both English and Americans by his work. *The Bravo* (1831), *The Heidenmauer* (1832), and *The Headsman* (1833) followed to show the defects of feudal society and dependence on hereditary aristocracy. *A Letter to His Countrymen* (1834) outlined his belief in the Constitution, in checks and balances, in popular freedom, and in recognition of the worth of leaders. Tone was hot-headed. Five volumes of travel: *Sketches of Switzerland* (two parts, 1836), *Gleanings in Europe: France* (1837), *Gleanings in Europe: England* (1837), and *Gleanings in Europe: Italy* (1838) all make the same point: that America should not imitate European customs. *The American Democrat*† (1838) was a complete statement of his social ideal of equality of rights, not of condition; and while not "a complete repudiation of democracy," as H. L. Mencken points out, "it went into the defects and dangers of democracy with acrid realism."[59] A landed class is thus compatible with democracy. His novel *The Monikins* (1835) attacks Europe for corruptions, and America for vulgarity and materialism. *Homeward Bound* (1838) and its sequel *Home as Found* (1838) contrast American reality with American ideals, the latter taking up the development of Cooperstown. *Afloat and Ashore* (1844) and *Miles Wallingford* (1844), good novels, deal with impressment of seamen and also take up questions of social classes. The "Littlepage Manuscripts" social trilogy works out Cooper's theory of the protection of property over three generations. *Satanstoe* (1845),[60] the best of the three tales, treats colonial New York brilliantly. *The Chainbearer* (1845) is less good, and *The Redskins* (1845—1846), attacking the anti-rent party's protest against the patroon system, is dull.[61] *The Crater* (1847), a failure, shows Cooper's turn toward religion, as do *The Oak Openings* (1848), an underrated novel of bee-hunters in the Old Northwest, and *The Sea Lions* (1849).

THE LEATHER-STOCKING TALES

Cooper's fame as a novelist will rest on the five works of the Leather-Stocking series, not written in the order of the story, which give a broad and noble picture of the woodsman and the Indian. Here there is a feeling for nature which Balzac commended, a sweep of narrative, and a development of character which give Cooper rank as a novelist. Formative factors for the character of Natty were: (1) Youthful memory of a real character. (2) The

59 *The American Democrat,* with an Introduction by H. L. Mencken (1931), pp. xi-xx.
60 Edited with critical introduction by R. E. Spiller and J. D. Coppock (1937).
61 See also *The Lake Gun,* edited by R. E. Spiller (1932), pp. 7-23.

Daniel Boone legend. (3) The idea of the natural man (Rousseauistic primitivism). (4) An idealistic conception of American manhood. Taken in narrative order:

***The Deerslayer*†** (1841). One of the best. Written last, it shows conscious art in rounding out the character of Natty Bumppo, who acquires the name Deerslayer, is made ill when he shoots his first man, refuses the advances of Judith Hutter, because of his self-respect. Hetty Hutter, a subnormal girl, is also well done.

***The Last of the Mohicans*†** (1826). Has the best executed plot of the series. Has noble Indians in Uncas and Chingachgook,[62] a fine chase story, good minor characters in Cora, Adam, Heyward. The feeling for nature and the excitement of the action are remarkable, but less so than the nostalgia of the Indians who have to leave their home.

***The Pathfinder*†** (1840). Partly a water story. Natty, in love with Mabel Dunham, wisely gives her up for his real love, the forest. Cooper anticipated Howells in breaking the romantic cliché.

***The Pioneers*†** (1823). First written of the series, created the novel of the frontier. Though Leather-Stocking and Chingachgook do not have the breadth they later attain, and though there is too much conversation, there is good technique, and one of Cooper's better heroines. Old Leather-Stocking, arrested for shooting out of season, saves people from a panther and a forest fire.

***The Prairie*†** (1827). Ennobles the aged Hawkeye who has gone to the upper Missouri to flee civilization. Has force like Hardy's Egdon Heath. Hawkeye rescues a bride from some kidnapping squatters. His death as he stands up facing the setting sun and calling "Here!" was imitated by Thackeray in *The Newcomes*.

SEA STORIES

The Pilot*†** (1823). As a seaman Cooper was dissatisfied with Scott's *The Pirate* and decided to do better. Wrote *The Pilot* and other romances, not emphasizing the mystery of the sea so much as the details of seamanship. The love stories are weak, but the humor is good, the unnamed hero (John Paul Jones) is well done, and Long Tom Coffin is an excellent character. Cooper's mastery of sailing technique gives veracity and atmosphere, even when the reader does not understand the technical terminology. ***Red Rover (1827) is a tale of adventure with the gentlemanly Captain Heidegger giving up piracy to aid the Americans.[63] ***The Water Witch*** (1830) has privateering, propaganda for American ships, and satire on the commercial classes in Alderman Breverout. ***The Two Admirals*** (1842) is one of his greatest sea stories, depicting whole fleets in action. ***Wing-and-Wing*** (1842), a favorite of Cooper, is

62 See Gregory Paine, "The Indians of the Leather-Stocking Tales," *SP.*, XXIII (1926), pp. 16-39.

63 See Thomas Philbrick, *James Fenimore Cooper and the Development of American Sea Fiction* (1961).

a Mediterranean story with an excellent character, Bolt, the impressed seaman from New Hampshire.

HISTORICAL NOVELS

***The Spy*†** (1821). Cooper's first success, it started a whole succession of novels on the Revolution, none of them matching the original. Cooper's wife came of a Loyalist family which enabled him to show impartiality. Harvey Birch, the self-sacrificing patriot, is one of his best characters.[64] Betty Flanagan is a well-drawn comic, and the picture of society is good. Fearing the work would fail, Cooper wrote and paged the last chapter; then led up to it from the middle.

Lionel Lincoln (1825). Despite good descriptions of Lexington and Bunker Hill, was a failure. Meant as the first of a series of thirteen, with one hero for each colony, it was also the last.

The Wept of Wish-ton-Wish (1829). Partly historical on Goffe and King Philip's War, partly on the Indian.

Wyandotté (1843). Describing an Indian attack on the Wyoming Valley, is as moderately successful as *The Wept of Wish-ton-Wish*. *Wyandotté* shows both the virtues and vices of the Indian affected by whites.

SUGGESTED MERITS	SUGGESTED DEFECTS
1. Cooper achieved success in maintaining suspense through use of the chase type of plot. He is, at his best, a master of rapid action. Really originated the sea story with use of technical mastery of sailing terms, at which he has hardly been surpassed.	1. Kept re-using same[65] devices to the point of monotony. Action often improbable. Wrote too rapidly to be critical.
2. Description often gives feeling of the majestic expanse of the wilderness.	2. Description often excessively lengthy and dull.
3. Large variety of vigorous characters from all races and classes. Good at comic and low types. Heroines courageous and active. One great epic character in Natty.	3. Characters external. Heroines clinging and fainting. Comic creations boring.
4. Rapid narrative style which improved with writing experience.[66]	4. Dialogue atrociously stilted. Style crude, with eighteenth century formality.
5. Vigorous and unified social criticism of both Europe and American democracy.	5. Social views unpopular because aristocratic.

64 See Tremaine McDowell, "The Identity of Harvey Birch," *AL.*, II (1930-1931), pp. 111-120.

65 See Mark Twain, "Fenimore Cooper's Literary Offenses," in *How to Tell a Story* (1897), pp. 78-96.

66 Yvor Winters, *Maule's Curse* (1938), pp. 25-50.

HERMAN MELVILLE, 1819—1891, poet, novelist; "the literary discoverer of the South Seas."[67] Born at No. 6 Pearl Street, New York City. Moved to Albany (1830), where he attended Albany Academy (1830—1834). Father died (1832), leaving the family almost destitute. Clerk (1834—1836). Shipped as a cabin boy on a merchantman bound for Liverpool (1837), a voyage described in *Redburn.* Taught at Greenbush, New York, and Pittsfield, Massachusetts (1837—1841). After nineteen months on the whaler *Acushnet,* which he had boarded at New Bedford bound for the South Seas (1841), he jumped ship at Nukuhiva, the Marquesas Islands (1842), described in *Typee* and *Mardi.* Escaped a month later from the friendly cannibals in the Taipi valley. Seaman on the man-of-war *United States* at Honolulu (1843),[68] mirrored in *White-Jacket.* Discharged (1844). Married Elizabeth Shaw, daughter of Chief Justice Lemuel Shaw of Boston (1847). Settled in New York City. Occasional reviewer for the *Literary World* (1847—1850). On trip to England (1849), he visited several places including Paris and Coblentz. Moved to "Arrowhead," a farm near Pittsfield, Massachusetts (1850—1863), where he became a friend of Hawthorne. Plates of his books destroyed in the Harper fire (1853); not reprinted, his books were gradually forgotten by public. To the Holy Land via Constantinople and Liverpool (1856).[69] Returned to America (1857). Sailed to San Francisco on the clippership *Meteor,* whose captain was his brother (1860). Failed to obtain an appointment in the United States Consular Service (1861). Moved to New York City (1863). Customs Inspector (1866—1885). Died at 104 East 26th Street, New York City (1891).[70]

PROSE

Typee: A Peep at Polynesian Life (1846). Realistic-romantic

---

67 The first Melville biography is the rare account written in 1891 by J. E. A. Smith for the *Evening Journal,* Pittsfield, Massachusetts.
Consult R. M. Weaver, *Herman Melville, Mariner and Mystic* (1921); Meade Minningerode, *Some Personal Letters of Herman Melville and a Bibliography* (1922); John Freeman, *Herman Melville* (1926): thereby becoming the first American to be included in the English Men of Letters Series: "I," says John Freeman, "hope America will pardon the inclusion of an American writer among English men of letters"; Lewis Mumford, *Herman Melville* (1929); Willard Thorp, *Herman Melville* (1938); C. R. Anderson, *Melville in the South Seas* (1939); Jay Leyda, *The Melville Log* (two volumes, 1951); Lawrance Thompson, *Melville's Quarrel with God* (1952). *Letters,* ed. Davis Gilman (1960).

68 R. S. Forsythe, "Herman Melville in Honolulu," *NEQ.,* VIII (1935), pp. 99-105.

69 See his *Journal up the Straits* (from October 11, 1856 — May 5, 1857), edited by Raymond Weaver (1935). Because written in a poor handwriting that defied deciphering, it was excluded from the Constable (definitive) edition of Melville's works.

70 His financial circumstances have been exaggerated in different directions: see William Charvat, "Melville's Income," *AL.,* XV (1943-1944), pp. 251-261.

yarn based on experiences when he deserted the *Acushnet* is also of value for its description of a primitive culture.[71]

Omoo: A Narrative of Adventures in the South Seas (1847). With *Typee,* forms a continuous fictional account of Melville's derring-do in the Society Islands (1842). Good dialogue, sharp ear for dialect, skilful character drawing.

Mardi: And A Voyage Thither (1849). Satirical, chaotic allegory[72] interspersed with amorphic lyrics and rhapsodic passages: while it lacks the humanizing qualities of *Moby-Dick,* it fits among his better intellectual achievements. Several sources.

Redburn: His First Voyage (1849). A rambling novel based on experiences during his 1837 voyage.

White-Jacket; or, The World in a Man-of-War**†** (1850). Loosely-knit novel compounded of autobiography and fiction, energized by powerful situations and astringent character-portrayals, and weighted down by propaganda: *e.g.,* the *Neversink* is the frigate *United States;*[73] Jack Chase is the actual name of the captain of the man-of-war on which Melville served; the purpose is to reform naval abuses.[74]

Moby-Dick; or, The Whale**†** (1851). Realistic narrative of whaling is swept along by powerful currents of commonplace details and melodramatic events, familiar style and heightened overtones, sprawling patches and epic rhythms, hundreds of digressions and prose apostrophes and sustained metaphors, documented cetology and transcendental subtleties: currents propelled by Ahab's overwhelming monomania: the will of man pitted against infinite

---

71 It is true that Barrett Wendell stated: "Herman Melville, with his books about the South Seas, which Robert Louis Stevenson is said to have declared the best ever written, and with his novels of maritime adventure, began a career of literary promise, which never came to fruition." But it is not true that from the beginning both American and English critics were predominantly hostile to Melville. Barrett Wendell, *A Literary History of America* (1900), p. 229; J. J. Firebaugh, "Humorist as Rebel: The Melville of Typee," *Nineteenth Century Fiction,* IX (1954), pp. 108-120.

72 See M. R. Davis, "The Flower Symbolism in Mardi," *MLQ.,* II (1941), pp. 625-638; David Jaffé, "Some Sources of Melville's *Mardi,*" *AL.,* IX (1937-1938), pp. 56-69.

73 *Journal of a Cruise to the Pacific Ocean, 1842-1844, in the Frigate "United States,"* edited by C. R. Anderson (1937).

74 According to Admiral Samuel R. Franklin, U.S.N., the book had more influence in abolishing flogging in the Navy than anything else. Consult Livingston Hunt, "Herman Melville as a Naval Historian," *HGM.,* XXXIX (1930-1931), pp. 22-30.

Fundamentally a sociologist, Melville often presented an inspiring vision of democracy: H. W. Wells, "An Unobtrusive Democrat: Herman Melville," *SAQ.,* XLIII (1944), pp. 46-51.

evil in the universe (the whale).[75] Directly influenced by the final tragic voyage of the *Essex*.[76]

Pierre; or, The Ambiguities† (1852). Self-revealing, clinical, somber, symbolic tragedy,[77] more carefully plotted than written. Latter part is less artificial than earlier, and revelatory of human insight. Some critics consider it an excellent book; others dispute the statement.

Israel Potter: His Fifty Years of Exile (1855). Historical romance livened by some adventures has its source in the *Life and Remarkable Adventures of Israel R. Potter* (1824).[78]

The Piazza Tales (1856). Collection of short stories and sketches, some of which demonstrate the essence of Melville's loneliness and superb technical achievement: *teste,* "Benito Cereno,"† based in part on the *Journal of Amasa Delano* (1816),[79] has a well-poised and well-sustained plot, without Melville's lavish allusions and ornate metaphors; "Bartleby the Scrivener," an allegorical tale of a Wall Street clerk who creates emotional tension with his "I would prefer not to"; "The Encantadas, or Enchanted Isles,"† composed of ten sketches[80] of the Galapagos Islands in the Pacific and of three people who temporarily inhabit them: excellent descriptive power and mythopoetic creativeness. "The Lightning-Rod Man" has been interpreted as being an attack upon organized religion, "a declaration of independence of the orthodox creeds."[81]

---

75 As Willard Thorpe and C. R. Anderson have individually stated, practically every reader indulges in a personal interpretation of the theme or symbolical meaning of *Moby-Dick,* which is more of an epic than a novel. Various critics emphasize that *Moby-Dick* (1) is a "definite account of the short-lived whaling industry," (2) represents man's eternal struggle against nature, (3) epitomizes the romantic generation's "pursuit of death," (4) is a parable on the mystery of evil and the accidental malice of the universe, (5) represents through every one of its characters such abstractions as Fate and Revenge, (6) presents the heroic struggle between man and moral evil, (7) reveals the spiritual disillusionment of its author, (8) exposes the universal struggle of man's dual ego. Present opinion is weighted in the direction of Clifton Fadiman's appraisal in *Moby-Dick; or, The Whale* (1943), p. ix (pp. v-ix): "It has towering faults of taste, it is often wilful and obscure, but it will remain, I think, America's unarguable contribution to world-literature, so many-levelled is it, so wide-ranging in that nether world which is the tortured, defiant, but secretly terror-stricken soul of man, alone and appalled by his alone-ness."

For an explanation that seeks the essential greatness of *Moby-Dick* in terms of Ahab's monomania and its apparent defect rather than in hazy symbols and under-the-surface analogies, see H. A. Myers, "Captain Ahab's Discovery: The Tragic Meaning of *Moby-Dick,*" *NEQ.*, XV (1942), pp. 15-34. Consult, too: Lincoln Colcord, "Notes on Moby Dick," *Freeman*, V (1922), p. 584 *f.* (pp. 559-562, 585-587); D. H. Lawrence, *Studies in American Classic Literature* (1923), pp. 214-240; W. S. Glein, *The Meaning of Moby-Dick* (1938), pp. 24-37, 183-190; René Galland, "Herman Melville et 'Moby Dick,'" *RAA.*, V (1927-1928), pp. 1-9. See also page 70, footnote 67.

76 *Narratives of the Wreck of the Whale-Ship Essex* (Golden Cockerel Press, London, 1935).

77 E. L. G. Watson, "Melville's *Pierre,*" *NEQ.*, III (1930), pp. 195-234; *Pierre; or The Ambiguities,* edited by Robert Forsythe (1930), pp. ix-xi, xix-xxxviii.

78 R. P. McCutcheon, "The Technique of Melville's *Israel Potter,*" *SAQ.*, XXVII (1928), p. 162 (pp. 161-174).

79 H. H. Scudder, "Melville's *Benito Cereno* and Captain Delano's Voyages," *PMLA.*, XLIII (1928), pp. 502-532.

80 Russell Thomas, "Melville's Use of Some Sources in *The Encantadas,*" *AL.*, III (1931-1932), pp. 432-456. The first to recognize the supreme artistry of "Benito Cereno" and "The Encantadas" was Michael Sadleir in 1922, and since then most critics, including Raymond Weaver, have voiced the same opinion.

81 B. D. Kimpel, "Two Notes on Herman Melville," *AL.*, XVI (1944-1945), pp. 29-32.

The Confidence-Man: His Masquerade (1857). Unfinished, inept, satirical treatise, tedious as narrative and abortive as philosophy. As in the case of *Pierre,* there are two camps of opinion as respects its worth.

Billy Budd (written *c.* 1889; published 1924). Symbolic novelette of a handsome sailor whose hanging passes into legendry, grew out of his experiences in 1843—1844 and his reading in 1888.[82]

POETRY[83]

(1) *Battle-Pieces and Aspects of the War* (1866), ineffectual if direct poems about the Civil War, supplemented by a prose plea for a decent attitude toward Southern Reconstruction. (2) *Clarel* (1876),[84] an excellent religious narrative poem in two volumes inspired by his "Pilgrimage in the Holy Land." (3) *John Marr and Other Sailors* (1888), sea poems better than his previous attempts. (4) *Timoleon, etc.* (1891), about twoscore poems inspired by his travels in Greece and Italy (1856).

INDIVIDUAL POEMS

"Sheridan at Cedar Creek," "Shiloh," "Art," "Chattanooga," "On the Slain at Chickamauga," "The 'Temeraire,' " "The Enviable Isles," "Immolated," "Monody," "Formerly a Slave," "To Ned," "Epilogue to *Clarel.*"

Minor Novelists

RICHARD HENRY DANA, Jr., 1815—1882, author, lawyer.[85] A trip as a sailor (1834—1836) resulted in *Two Years Before the Mast*† (1840), a classic, since a sensitive man was describing his adventures in an exciting fashion. Has directness, romantic charm, humanitarian aim of stopping the practice of flogging.

JOHN PENDLETON KENNEDY, 1795—1870, author, statesman.[86] *Swallow Barn*† (1832)[87] gives idyllic but accurate picture of plantation life in Virginia. *Horse-Shoe Robinson*

---

82 E. L. G. Watson, "Melville's Testament of Acceptance," *NEQ.*, VI (1933), pp. 319-327; C. R. Anderson, "The Genesis of Billy Budd," *AL.*, XII (1940-1941), pp. 328-346.

83 John Freeman, *Herman Melville* (1926), pp. 155-169; Willard Thorp, *Herman Melville* (1938), pp. lxxxiv-xcvi (pp. xi-cxxix); *Selected Poems of Herman Melville,* edited by William Plomer (1943), pp. 6-8.

84 H. W. Wells, "Herman Melville's *Clarel,*" *CE.*, IV (1942-1943), pp. 478-483.

85 C. F. Adams, *Richard Henry Dana* (two volumes, 1890-1891); J. D. Hart, "The Other Writings of Richard Henry Dana, Jr.," *Colophon,* Part 19, No. 6 (1934), and "The Education of Richard Henry Dana, Jr.," *NEQ.*, IX (1936), pp. 3-25; J. S. Johnson, *On Richard Henry Dana and Two Years Before the Mast* (1936); G. W. Smalley, *Anglo-American Memories* (1911), pp. 36-44.

86 H. T. Tuckerman, *The Life of John Pendleton Kennedy* (1871); E. M. Gwathmey, *John Pendleton Kennedy* (1931).

87 Edited by J. B. Hubbell (1929), with introduction.

(1835),[88] on battle of King's Mountain, vividly written. Also wrote *Quodlibet* . . . (1840), a Whig satire on politics.

WILLIAM GILMORE SIMMS, 1806—1870, South Carolina poet, critic, editor, and novelist.[89] Spent youth in poverty. Became drug clerk. Admitted to the bar (1827). Published verse in 1825 and 1827. Became journalist in 1828. Married into planter class, but was not accepted by the best people. Home burned during Civil War, so he had to write for a living, and composed too rapidly to maintain his standards. This was also true of Cooper, whose work Simms's resembles. Edited *Southern Quarterly Review* and *Russel's Magazine.* Wrote criticism, *Views and Reviews* (1845). Wrote novels of the Revolutionary War in South Carolina. *The Yemassee*† (1835),[90] perhaps his best novel with a fine picture of the Indians when debauched by the white man. Simms's Indians are less idealized than Cooper's. *The Partisan* (1835), first of a series on the Revolution including *Mellichampe* (1836); *The Scout* (1841; reissued 1854); *Woodcraft* (1854); *The Forayers* (1855); *Eutaw* (1856). The plots in these novels are similar: a partisan and a loyalist are in love with the same woman. Simms is good at describing warfare and nature. The aristocratic characters are unreal, while rowdies like Porgy are more convincing. Wrote other novels about the Southern border, in Alabama, *Richard Hurdis* (1838); Mississippi, *Border Beagles* (1840); and Kentucky, *Beauchampe* (1842). *Charlemont* (1856) is probably his most sensational tale.

DRAMATISTS

American drama was still characterized by quantity rather than quality. Most plays were written for entertainment and had few literary pretensions. The serious plays were set in the romantic past, while comedies of manners concentrated on the stage Yankee. American history, the Indian, and Italy were popular subjects. Boker was the only dramatist of consequence.

GEORGE HENRY BOKER, 1823—1890, dramatist, sonnet-sequence writer.[91] Graduated from Princeton, 1842. *Calaynos* (1848), a blank verse tragedy laid in medieval Spain. Based on fear of Moorish taint. *The Betrothal* (1850), a charming comedy. *Leonor de Guzman* (1853) has good characterization in the contrast between Leonor, the mistress, and Queen Maria after the King's death. *The Widow's Marriage* (1852; 1856), an unpro-

---

88 Edited by E. E. Leisy (1937), with critical introduction.

89 W. P. Trent, *William Gilmore Simms* (1892) is the standard biography. See also J. W. Higham, "The Changing Loyalties of William Gilmore Simms," *JSH.*, IX (1943), pp. 210-223.

90 See *The Yemassee,* edited by Alexander Cowie (1937), with critical introduction.

91 See J. W. Krutch, "George Henry Boker," *SR.*, XXV (1917), pp. 457-468; E. S. Bradley, *George Henry Boker, Poet and Patriot* (1927); J. B. Hubbell, "George Henry Boker, Paul Hamilton Hayne, and Charles Warren Stoddard: Some Unpublished Letters," *AL.*, V (1933-1934), pp. 146-165, and "Five Letters from George Henry Boker to William Gilmore Simms," *PMHB.*, LXIII (1939), pp. 66-71.

duced comedy. *Francesca da Rimini*† (written 1853; played 1855; published 1856)[92] used the situation outlined by Dante but switched the emphasis to Paolo's deformed brother, Lanciotto. Has been called the best verse drama in English produced in the nineteenth century. The characters are alive, especially the malevolent jester Pepe, whose relation to his master is excellently portrayed. *Plays and Poems* (two volumes, 1856). *Nydia: A Tragic Play*[93] and *Glaucus* are based on the destruction of Pompeii. Two other plays[94] are *The Bankrupt* (1940) and *The World a Mask* (1940). *Poems of the War* (1864). *Sonnets: A Sequence on Profane Love,* edited by E. S. Bradley (1929)[95] help explain why Boker achieved greater intensity in *Francesca da Rimini* than in his other plays. Sonnets include: "My heart is sad today; I know not why"; "O weary watches of the dismal night!" "'O for my sake do you with fortune chide' "; "Love sat at ease upon Time's bony knee." An excellent dramatist, Boker is also one of our best sonneteers.

THE WEST[96]

The seaboard states had the new West introduced to them by a series of descriptions and tales. TIMOTHY FLINT's *Recollections of the Last Ten Years* (1826)[97] opened up the Mississippi valley. He wrote many novels. *Francis Berrian, or the Mexican Patriot* (1826) is typical of the romantic pattern, showing early illusions changing to disillusionment, with consolation in nature. ALEXANDER ROSS (1783—1856) is the sole first-hand authority for early Oregon history in *Fur Hunters of the Far West* (two volumes, 1855) and other books. PETER CARTWRIGHT's unvarnished *Autobiography* (1857) gives another picture of early settlers. He was a Methodist preacher not afraid to beat up the rowdies who disturbed his meetings, and his account is boastful but vigorous.[98]

92 C. J. Metcalf, "An Old Romantic Triangle, Francesca da Rimini in Three Dramas," *SR.*, XXIX (1921), pp. 45-58. Cf. A. H. Quinn, *A History of the American Drama from the Beginning to the Civil War* (1923), pp. 337-364.

93 Edited by E. S. Bradley (1929).

94 Included in *Glaucus and Other Plays,* edited by [E.] Sculley Bradley (1940).

95 E. S. Bradley, "A Newly Discovered American Sonnet Sequence," *PMLA.*, XL (1925), pp. 910-920.

96 R. L. Rusk, *The Literature of the Early Middle Western Frontier* (two volumes, 1925); D. A. Dondore, *The Prairie and the Making of Middle America* (1926); C. B. Spotts, "The Development of Fiction on the Missouri Frontier (1830-1860)," *MHR.*, XXVIII (1933-1934), pp. 195-205, 275-286; XXIX (1934-1935), pp. 17-26, 100-108, 186-194, 279-294; D. R. Fox, *Sources of Culture in the Middle West* (1934); R. C. Buley, "Glimpses of Pioneer Mid-West Social and Cultural History," *MVHR.*, XXIII (1937), pp. 481-510.

97 Edited by C. H. Grattan (1932).

98 H. H. Grant, *Peter Cartwright: Pioneer* (1931).

AMERICAN HUMOR[99]

The native brand of humor, depending partly on exaggeration and violent contrast, developed slowly, and the comic types emerged only gradually. The stage Yankee appeared by 1787; foppish English characters were satirized after the War of 1812. But not until SEBA SMITH's *Life and Writings of Major Jack Downing* (1833) did the Down East Yankee really take form, with the knowing rustic laughing at city sophistication. "Downing" set the type of cracker-barrel philosopher employed by Lowell and many others.

The Southwestern school of frontier humor emphasized the wildly, if imaginatively, exaggerated yarn.[100] Western humorists furnish marvellous material for social history, since their elaborated stories grow out of typical frontier backgrounds which are invariably included in the stories. They are direct ancestors of Mark Twain.

The Civil War brought politics back into humor on both sides of the border. DAVID ROSS LOCKE, 1833—1888, as editor of the Toledo *Blade,* invented Petroleum V. Nasby, a copperhead preacher, ignorant, corrupt, a bad speller, who always ruined the proslavery case. The writing, which Lincoln enjoyed, was malicious in its humor. *The Nasby Papers* (1864); *Divers Opinions of Yours Trooly, Petroleum V. Nasby* (1865; 7th edition by 1866).

HENRY WHEELER SHAW, 1818—1885, humorist known as **JOSH BILLINGS.**[101] Born in Massachusetts. Wrote at Poughkeepsie, N. Y. Successful when he adopted bad spelling. Poor at characterization and narrative; excellent at homely aphorism. *Josh Billings, His Sayings* (1865) and *Josh Billings, Farmers Allminax* (annual, 1870—1880) include his best work.

CHARLES FARRAR BROWNE, 1834—1867, **"ARTEMUS WARD,"** humorist.[102] Maine born, a compositor and printer. Gained recognition while employed on the Cleveland *Plain Dealer* as a writer of humorous sketches. From this he proceeded, as did Clemens after him, to win fame as a humorous lecturer; popular, first in America, and finally in England, where he died. In print a humorous impression of illiteracy and provincial-

---

99 For material on American humor see: J. R. Tandy, *Crackerbox Philosophers in American Humor and Satire* (1925); Constance Rourke, *American Humor* (1931); Walter Blair and F. J. Meine, *Mike Fink, King of Mississippi Keelboatmen* (1933); Walter Blair, *Native American Humor* (1937), with excellent bibliography; E. S. Bradley, "Our Native Humor," *NAR.*, CCXLII (1937), pp. 351-362; P. D. Jordan, "Humor of the Backwoods, 1820-1840," *MVHR.*, XXV (1938), pp. 25-28; T. D. Clark, *The Rampaging Frontier* (1939); Walter Blair, *Horse Sense in American Humor* (1942).

100 *Ring-Tailed Roarers,* edited by V. L. O. Chittick (1941). David Crockett, *A Narrative of the Life of David Crockett* (1834), and Augustus B. Longstreet, *Georgia Scenes* (1835, 1840) are representative of Southern frontier humor.

101 Cyril Clemens, *Josh Billings, Yankee Humorist* (1932).

102 E. P. Hingston, *The Genial Showman* (1870); D. C. Seitz, *Artemus Ward: A Biography and Bibliography* (1919).

ism was achieved through the device of dialectical misspelling. *Artemus Ward, His Works Complete* (1875); *Complete Works* (1890).

HISTORIANS

WILLIAM HICKLING PRESCOTT, 1796—1859, historian.[103] Of good family. Schooled at Harvard. Suffered an accidental loss of one eye and serious injury to the other. Nevertheless, he deliberately entered upon a career as a historian, grounding himself in English literature and general backgrounds. Choice of Spain came about partly through the influence of Ticknor. *History of the Reign of Ferdinand and Isabella, the Catholic*† (three volumes; published 1837 but dated 1838), enthusiastically received and widely translated. *A History of the Conquest of Mexico*† (three volumes, 1843); *History of the Conquest of Peru*† (two volumes, 1847); *History of the Reign of Philip the Second, King of Spain* (three volumes, 1855—1859); *History of the Reign of Charles V* (1857).[104] *Biographical and Critical Miscellanies* (1845), reviews and historical articles, includes a brief "Life of Charles Brockden Brown" (1834).[105]

Prescott is still fairly well regarded by professional students. Fresh material has qualified acceptance of conclusions in the *Mexico;* the *Peru* has been less affected. But he is weak on social and economic phases which he tried to cover.

JOHN LOTHROP MOTLEY, 1814—1877, historian, diplomat, novelist.[106] Of cultured family. A.B., Harvard (1831). Studied in Germany. Stimulated by Prescott's work; turned to writing history. Minister to Austria (1861—1867). Minister to England (1869—1870). Wrote two novels: *Morton's Hope* (two volumes, 1839); *Merry-Mount* (two volumes, 1849). His histories, which were widely popular, include: *The Rise of the Dutch Republic* (three volumes, 1856); *History of the United Netherlands* (1860—1867); *The Life and Death of John of Barneveld* (two volumes, 1875). His work exemplified his theories:[107] that history revolved around great men, that it should be well written, and that

---

103 Thomas Powell, *Living Authors of America* (1850), pp. 169-188; George Ticknor, *Life of William Hickling Prescott* (1864); Rollo Ogden, *William Hickling Prescott* (1904); H. T. Peck, *William Hickling Prescott* (1905); J. S. Bassett, *The Middle Group of American Historians* (1917), pp. 211-223; William Charvat and Michael Kraus, *William Hickling Prescott: Representative Selections* (1943), pp. xi-cxlii; B. D. Wolfe, "Prescott's Pageant of Aztec and Conquistador," *NYTBR.*, October 17, 1943, pp. 9, 32.

104 *William Hickling Prescott: Representative Selections,* edited by Michael Kraus and William Charvat (1943), gives an excellent introduction and convenient excerpts.

105 Cf. H. H. Clark, "Literary Criticism in the *North American Review,* 1815-1835," *TWASAL.*, XXX (1940), pp. 299-350.

106 O. W. Holmes, *John Lothrop Motley, a Memoir* (1879); E. P. Whipple, *Recollections of Eminent Men* (1887), pp. 155-203; G. W. Curtis, *Correspondence of John Lothrop Motley* (two volumes, 1889); J. S. Bassett, *The Middle Group of American Historians* (1917); O. W. Long, *Literary Pioneers* (1935), pp. 199-224.

107 *John Lothrop Motley: Representative Selections,* edited by C. P. Higby and B. T. Schantz (1939), has excellent analysis.

it should embody the idea of the growth of mental freedom. He was anti-Spanish and anti-Catholic. He wrote in the tradition of great literary historians, with careful accuracy, and fluently elaborate style.

FRANCIS PARKMAN, 1823—1893, historian.[108] Boston born; educated at Harvard (A.B. 1844; LL.B. 1846), and by travel. *The Oregon Trail*† (1849). *The Conspiracy of Pontiac*† (1851). With *Pioneers of France in the New World* (1865) Parkman undertook his great series of historical works. Other volumes are *The Jesuits in North America in the Seventeenth Century* (1867); *The Discovery of the Great West* (first published 1869; revised 1879 as *La Salle and the Discovery of the Great West,* following publication of important documents hitherto unavailable); *The Old Régime in Canada* (1874); *Count Frontenac and New France under Louis XIV* (1877); *Montcalm and Wolfe* (1884); *A Half-Century of Conflict* (1892).

Along with unusual powers as a historian Parkman disclosed significant limitations. He was conservative. With Holmes, he preferred a settled society dominated by those of inherited means, culture, and intelligence. He feared extension of the suffrage, was lukewarm to anti-slavery agitation, vigorously opposed woman's suffrage. Yet he stood strongly against anything approaching political, intellectual, and spiritual despotism. Consequently, his sympathies were with the English rather than the French. His agnostic tendency also lessened his sympathy for the Catholic Church. Parkman's attitude toward the Indian was realistic, not sentimental. To him the Indian was no "noble savage," as Rousseauism had conceived him, but merely savage. In his field of American history Parkman remains supreme. His first-hand acquaintance with the life of the Indians added vividness to passages based on carefully gained documentary material, which he used with exemplary accuracy. Subsequent investigation has resulted in no serious correction of his writings. His emphasis was not economic or sociological.[109] His tone is at once romantic and scientific, and notably vivid.[110] His fascinating series is often called the best piece of history ever written in America.

---

108 Biography and criticism: G. W. Cooke, "Francis Parkman," *NEM.*, N.S., I (1889), pp. 248-262; O. B. Frothingham, "Memoir of Francis Parkman," *PMHS.*, Second Series, VIII (1894), pp. 520-562; John Fiske, *A Century of Science and Other Essays* (1899), pp. 194-264; C. H. Farnham, *A Life of Francis Parkman* (1900); G. M. Gould, *Biographic Clinics* (1904), II, pp. 131-202; E. G. Bourne, *Essays in Historical Criticism* (1913), pp. 277-287; Bliss Perry, "Some Personal Qualities of Parkman," *YR.*, XIII (1924), pp. 443-448; Joseph Schafer, "Francis Parkman, 1823-1923," *MVHR.*, X (1924), pp. 351-364; Albert Keiser, *The Indian in American Literature* (1933), pp. 126, 142-143, 294-295, 299; W. L. Schramm, *Francis Parkman: Representative Selections* (1938), pp. xiii-cxliv; Mason Wade, *Francis Parkman* (1942).

109 Cf. his only novel, *Vassell Morton* (1856), as noted in W. L. Schramm, *Francis Parkman: Representative Selections* (1938), p. xcii.

110 Allan Nevins, "Prescott, Motley, Parkman," in *American Writers on American Literature,* edited by John Macy (1931), p. 239.

OTHER WRITING

Statesmen of Literary Note

In the golden age of public speaking DANIEL WEBSTER, 1782—1852, was famous as an orator of rhetorical excellence, though his fame has subsequently declined; HENRY CLAY, 1777—1852, as a debator; JOHN C. CALHOUN, 1782—1850, as a brilliant logician; ABRAHAM LINCOLN,[111] 1809—1865, as the simple and profound exponent of great truths. Lincoln's speech on departing from Springfield, the *Gettysburg Address,* and the *Second Inaugural Address* are immortal for their combination of human understanding, deep insight, fundamental sincerity, elemental soundness, abiding faith, and boundless compassion.

Miscellaneous Writing

DOROTHEA [LYNDE] DIX, 1802—1887, reformer, author of moral tales and gift books like *The Pearl* (1829).[112] *Memorial to the Legislature of Massachusetts* (1843) is a plain account of her discoveries in prisons and institutions. It produced immediate reforms.

ELIHU BURRITT, 1810—1879, blacksmith, editor, ran the *Christian Citizen* (1844—1851), a peace newspaper, and *Olive Leaves* (1850), a pro-working-class paper. Active in any international peace movement.[113]

Journalists, Editors, Publishers

JOHN NEAL, 1793—1876, editor, critic, novelist, poet. "Battle of Niagara" (1818), poem. *Otho* (1819), verse tragedy. *Logan* (1822), Indian novel. *Seventy Six*† (1823), historical romance. Wrote on "American Writers" for *Blackwood's* (1824—1825);[114] gave ten pages to Irving; eight to himself; four to Brockden Brown; and one-half page to Cooper. *The Down-Easters* (1833), later novel. Important as a critic and editor.

---

111 Useful works on Lincoln include: William Herndon and J. W. Weik, *Herndon's Lincoln* (two volumes, 1896); J. G. Nicolay and John Hay, *Abraham Lincoln* (ten volumes, 1890); Lord Charnwood, *Abraham Lincoln* (1916); N. W. Stephenson, *Lincoln* (1922), the best one-volume life; A. J. Beveridge, *Abraham Lincoln, 1809-1858* (two volumes, 1928), sound; R. P. Basler, "Abraham Lincoln — Artist," *NAR.*, CCXLV (1938), pp. 144-153, and "Abraham Lincoln's Rhetoric," *AL.*, XI (1939-1940), pp. 167-182; Carl Sandburg, *Lincoln* (four volumes, 1940); *The Life and Writings of Abraham Lincoln,* edited by P. Van D. Stern, with an Introduction by Allan Nevins (1940).

112 Francis Tiffany, *Life of Dorothea Lynde Dix* (1890); H. E. Marshall, *Dorothea Dix, Forgotten Samaritan* (1937).

113 M. E. Curti, *The American Peace Crusade: 1815-1860* (1929); and *The Learned Blacksmith: The Letters and Journals of Elihu Burritt* (1937).

114 See *American Writers,* edited by F. L. Pattee (1937). Cf. William Charvat, *The Origins of American Critical Thought, 1810-1835* (1936), for a discussion of early critical work.

CHARLES FENNO HOFFMAN, 1806—1884, editor, poet, novelist.[115] *Greyslaer: A Romance of the Mohawk* (1839), based on the Beauchamp murder, had four editions in one year. *The Vigil of Faith and Other Poems* (1842) went through four editions in three years. *The Echo* (1844), *Love's Calendar, Lays of the Hudson, and Other Poems* (1847) were light, delicate, musical, lilting.

JOHN GODFREY SAXE, 1816—1887, contributed to Journals. *Progress: A Satirical Poem* (1846) is typical of his poetry. He was a better humorist than versifier. See: *The Fly-ing Dutchman* (1862), *Clever Stories of Many Nations* (1865).

HENRY CHARLES CAREY, 1793—1879, publisher, economist. Paid Carlyle and Scott for American issues of their work. He became *laissez-faire* in sympathy, but in 1844 returned to protection without adopting the pessimism of the classical economists. *The Harmony of Interests, Agricultural, Manufacturing, and Commercial* (1851). Best economic thought of his day.

WILLIAM WIRT, 1772—1834, wrote essays, *The Letters of a British Spy,* (1803); *The Rainbow* (1804); *The Old Bachelor* (1812). The *Letters* went through twelve editions. *Sketches of the Life and Character of Patrick Henry* (1817) was laudatory and ornate.

JAMES KENT, 1763—1847, Chancellor of New York State.[116] His *Commentaries on American Law* (four volumes, 1826—1830) was a great guide to the law of equity, and had fourteen editions.

WASHINGTON ALLSTON, 1779—1843, painter, poet, critic. *Lectures on Art, and Poems* (1850). *The Sylphs of the Seasons, with Other Poems* (1813). *Monaldi* (1841) is a short novel patterned after Mrs. Radcliffe. His verse was praised by Coleridge.

SUPPLEMENTARY LIST OF AUTHORS

POETRY

Northern Poets

JAMES MCHENRY, 1785—1845, poet, novelist. *Waltham* (1823), poems; *O'Halloran* (1824), novel.

EMMA HART WILLARD, 1787—1870, educator, poet. "Rocked in the Cradle of the Deep."

LYDIA HUNTLEY SIGOURNEY, 1791—1865, poet, journalist. *Poems Religious and Elegiac* (1841).

MARIA GOWEN BROOKS, *c.*1794—1845. *Judith, Esther, and Other Poems* (1820).

CARLOS WILCOX, 1794—1827. *Remains* (1828).

GEORGE HILL, 1796—1871. *Ruins of Athens* (1831).

---

115 H. F. Barnes, *Charles Fenno Hoffman* (1930).

116 J. T. Horton, *James Kent: A Study in Conservatism, 1763-1847* (1939).

GRENVILLE MELLEN, 1799—1841. *The Martyr's Triumph* (1833).

WILLIAM WILSON, 1801—1860. *Poems* (1869).

ALBERT GORTON GREENE, 1802—1868. *The Militia Muster.*

RUFUS DAWES, 1803—1859. *Geraldine* (1839).

EMMA CATHERINE MANLEY EMBURY, 1806—1863. *Guido* (1828); *Poems* (1869).

WILLIS GAYLORD CLARK, 1808—1841. *Literary Remains* (1844).

LEWIS GAYLORD CLARK, 1808—1873, editor, poet. *Knick-Knacks from an Editor's Table* (1852).

CHARLES TIMOTHY BROOKS, 1813—1883, poet, translator. *William Tell* (1837).

THOMAS DUNN ENGLISH, 1819—1902, poet, dramatist. "Ben Bolt" (1843); *The Mormons* (1858), drama.

JULIA WARD HOWE, 1819—1910. "The Battle Hymn of the Republic" (1862).

WILLIAM WETMORE STORY, 1819—1895, poet, sculptor. *Graffiti d'Italia* (1868).

ALICE CARY, 1820—1871, and PHOEBE CARY, 1824—1871. *The Poems of Alice and Phoebe Cary* (1849).

GEORGE FREDERICK ROOT, 1820—1895, composer, poet. "Tramp, Tramp, Tramp, the Boys Are Marching."

HENRY HOWARD BROWNELL, 1820—1872. *Lines of Battle* (1912).

MARIA WHITE LOWELL, 1821—1853. *Poems* (1855).

WILLIAM ALLEN BUTLER, 1825—1902. *Nothing to Wear* (1857).

FRANCIS MILES FINCH, 1827—1907. "The Blue and the Gray" (1867).

CHARLES GRAHAM HALPINE, 1829—1868. "Sambo's Right to Be Kilt."

HENRY CLAY WORK, 1832—1884. "Marching through Georgia" (1865).

WALTER KITTREDGE, 1834—1905. "Tenting on the Old Camp Ground" (1864).

Southern Poets

CLEMENT CLARKE MOORE, 1779—1863. " 'Twas the Night before Christmas" (1823).

WILLIAM JOHN GRAYSON, 1788—1863. *The Hireling and the Slave* (1854).

RICHARD HENRY WILDE, 1789—1847. "My Life Is Like the Summer Rose."

MIRABEAU BUONAPARTE LAMAR, 1798—1859. "The Daughter of Mendoza."

GEORGE DENNISON PRENTICE, 1802—1870. *The Poems of George D. Prentice* (1876, 1883).

EDWARD COOTE PINCKNEY, 1802—1828. "A Health."

THOMAS HOLLEY CHIVERS, 1809—1858, physician, poet. *Eonchs of Ruby* (1851).

ALEXANDER BEAUFORT MEEK, 1814—1865. "Red Eagle"; "Balaklava."

PHILIP PENDLETON COOKE, 1816—1850. *Froissart Ballads and Other Poems* (1847).

WILLIAM WILBERFORCE LORD, 1819—1907. *Christ in Hades* (1851).

AMELIA BALL COPPUCK WELBY, 1819—1852. *Poems* (1845).

MARGARET J. PRESTON, 1820—1897. *Beechenbrook* (1865); *Old Song and New* (1870).

THEODORE O'HARA, 1820—1867. "The Bivouac of the Dead."

FRANCIS ORRAY TICKNOR, 1822—1874. "Little Giffen" (1867).

JAMES MATTHEWS LEGARÉ, 1823—1859. *Orta-Undis and Other Poems* (1848).

ETHEL LYNN BEERS, 1827—1879. "The Picket-Guard" (1861).

JAMES BARRON HOPE, 1829—1887. *A Wreath of Virginia Bay Leaves* (1895).

ABRAM JOSEPH RYAN, 1838—1886. "The Conquered Banner" (1865).

JAMES RYDER RANDALL, 1839—1908. "Maryland, My Maryland" (1861).

NOVELISTS

Northern Novelists

REBECCA RUSH, *fl.*1812. *Kelroy, a Novel* (1812).

WILLIAM AUSTIN, 1778—1841. "Peter Rugg, the Missing Man" (1824).

SUSAN RIDLEY SEDGWICK, 1789—1867. *The Young Emigrants* (1830).

CATHARINE MARIA SEDGWICK, 1789—1867. *The Linwoods* (1835).

DANIEL PIERCE THOMPSON, 1795—1868. *The Green Mountain Boys* (1839).

NICHOLAS MARCELLUS HENTZ, 1797—1856. *Tadeuskund, the Last King of the Lenape* (1825).

WILLIAM WARE, 1797—1852. *Zenobia* (1837); *Aurelian* (1838); *Julian* (1841).

JOSEPH C. HART, 1798—1855. *Miriam Coffin; or, The Whale-Fisherman* (1834).

RALPH INGERSOLL LOCKWOOD, 1798—1858. *The Insurgents* (two volumes, 1835).

LYDIA MARIA CHILD, 1802—1880. *Hobomok* (1824).

JACOB ABBOTT, 1803—1879. The *Rollo* series. *Rollo Learning to Read* (1835).

CHARLES F. BRIGGS, 1804—1877. *Adventures of Harry Franco* (1839).

FREDERICK WILLIAM THOMAS, 1806—1866. *Clinton Bradshaw* (1835).

THEODORE SEDGWICK FAY, 1807—1898. *Hoboken, a Romance* (1843).

WILLIAM STARBUCK MAYO, 1811—1895. *Kaloolah* (1849); *The Berber* (1850).

PETER HAMILTON MYERS, 1812—1878. *The First of the Knickerbockers* (1848).

SYLVESTER JUDD, 1813—1853. *Margaret* (1845); *Richard Edney* (1850).

ROBERT TRAILL SPENCE LOWELL, 1816—1891. *The New Priest in Conception Bay* (1858).

CHARLES WILKINS WEBBER, 1819—1856. *Old Hicks, the Guide* (1848).

HENRY AUGUSTUS WISE, 1819—1869. *Los Gringos* (1849).

SUSAN BOGERT WARNER, 1819—1885. *The Wide, Wide World* (1850).

EMMA D. E. N. SOUTHWORTH, 1819—1899. *The Hidden Hand* (1859).

CAROLINE CHESEBROUGH, 1825—1873. *The Foe in the Household* (1871).

MARIA S. CUMMINS, 1827—1866. *The Lamplighter* (1854).

THEODORE WINTHROP, 1828—1861. *Cecil Dreeme* (1861); *John Brent* (1862).

Southern Novelists

GEORGE TUCKER, 1775—1861. *A Voyage to the Moon* (1827).

NATHANIEL BEVERLEY TUCKER, 1784—1851. *The Partisan Leader* (1836).

HENRY JUNIUS NOTT, 1797—1837. *Novellettes of a Traveller* (two volumes, 1834).

WILLIAM ALEXANDER CARRUTHERS, *c.*1800—*c.*1846. *The Cavaliers of Virginia* (1834—1835).

JOHN ESTEN COOKE, 1830—1886. *The Virginia Comedians* (1854); *Henry St. John, Gentleman* (1859); *Surry of Eagle's Nest* (1866).

DRAMATISTS

GEORGE WASHINGTON PARKE CUSTIS, 1781—1857. *Pocahontas; or, The Settlers of Virginia* (1830).

SAMUEL WOODWORTH, 1784—1842. *The Forest Rose* (1825); *The Widow's Son* (1825).

MORDECAI MANUEL NOAH, 1785—1851. *Marion; or, The Hero of Lake George* (1821); *The Grecian Captive* (1822).

DAVID PAUL BROWN, 1795—1872. *Sertorius; or, The Roman Patriot* (1830).

JAMES LAWSON, 1799—1880. *Giordano* (1832).

CAROLINE LEE WHITING HENTZ, 1800-1856. *De Lara, or the Moorish Bride* (1831).

ROBERT MONTGOMERY BIRD, 1806—1854. *The Gladiator* (1831); *The Broker of Bogota* (1834): *Nick of the Woods* (novel, 1837).

JOSEPH STEVENS JONES, 1809—1877. *The Carpenter of Rouen* (1840); *Moll Pitcher* (1855).

ROBERT TAYLOR CONRAD, 1810—1858. *Jack Cade* (1835, 1841).

ANNA CORA MOWATT [RITCHIE], 1819—1870. *Fashion; or, Life in New York* (1845; 1850).

MRS. SIDNEY FRANCES BATEMAN, 1823—1881. *Self* (1856); *Geraldine; or, Love's Victory* (1859).

CLIFTON W. TAYLEURE. *Horseshoe Robinson* (1856), based on J. P. Kennedy's novel.

MINOR WESTERN WRITERS

JAMES HALL, 1793—1868. *Legends of the West* (1832).

HENRY R. SCHOOLCRAFT, 1793—1864. *Indian Tribes of the United States* (six volumes, 1851—1857).

CAROLINE MATILDA STANSBURY KIRKLAND, 1801—1864. *A New Home—Who'll Follow?* (1839, 1874).

WILLIAM JOSEPH SNELLING, 1804—1848. *Tales of the Northwest* (1830, 1936).

HUMORISTS

DAVY (DAVID) CROCKETT, 1786—1836. *A Narrative of the Life of David Crockett* (1834).

ASA GREENE, 1789—*c.*1837. *The Life and Adventures of Dr. Dodimus Duckworth* (1833).

AUGUSTUS B. LONGSTREET, 1790—1870. *Georgia Scenes* (1835, 1840).

THOMAS CHANDLER HALIBURTON, 1796—1865. *Sam Slick* (1837, 1838, 1840).

WILLIAM TAPPAN THOMPSON, 1812—1882. *Major Jones's Courtship* (1843).

BENJAMIN P. SHILLABER, 1814—1890. *Life and Sayings of Mrs. Partington* (1854).

THOMAS BANGS THORPE, 1815—1878. "The Big Bear of Arkansas" (1841).

JOHNSON JONES HOOPER, 1815—1862. *Some Adventures of Captain Simon Suggs* (1845).

JOSEPH GLOVER BALDWIN, 1815—1864. *Flush Times of Alabama and Mississippi* (1853).

MRS. FRANCES WHICHER. *Widow Bedott Papers* (1856).

FREDERICK S. COZZENS, 1818—1869. *The Sparrowgrass Papers* (1856).

GEORGE HORATIO DERBY, 1823—1861. *Phoenixiana* (1855); *The Squibob Papers* (1865).

CHARLES GODFREY LELAND, 1824—1903. *Hans Breitmann's Ballads* (collected 1914).

CHARLES HENRY SMITH, 1826—1903. *Bill Arp, So Called, a Side Show of the Southern Side of the War* (1866).

MORTIMER NEAL THOMSON, 1831—1875. *Doesticks: What He Says* (1855).

ROBERT HENRY NEWELL, 1836—1901. *The Orpheus C. Kerr Papers* (three volumes, 1862—1865).

JOURNALISTS

MASON LOCKE WEEMS, 1759—1825, biographer. *Life . . . of George Washington* (*c.*1800).

MATHEW CAREY, 1760—1839, editor, economist. *The Porcupiniad* (1799).

SARAH JOSEPHA B. HALE, 1788—1879. Edited *Godey's Lady's Book* (1837—1877).

SAMUEL GRISWOLD GOODRICH, 1793—1860. Edited *The Token* (1827—1842).

HUGH S. LEGARÉ, 1797—1843. Established *Southern Review* (1828).

ROBERT CHARLES SANDS, 1799—1843, journalist, author. *Tales of Glauber-Spa* (1832).

William Cox, *d.*1851. *Crayon Sketches* (collected, 1833).

William Leggett, 1801—1839. *Leisure Hours at Sea* (1825).

Epes Sargent, 1813—1880, journalist, author. *Fleetwood* (1845).

Rufus Wilmot Griswold, 1815—1857. *The Poets and Poetry of America* (1842).

Cornelius Mathews, 1817—1889. Co-founder of *Arcturus* (1840).

Edward Z. C. Judson, 1823—1886, "Ned Buntline." Began the dime novel.

Oliver Bell Bunce, 1828—1890. *A Bachelor's Story* (1859).

MISCELLANEOUS AUTHORS

John James Audubon, 1785—1851, naturalist. *The Birds of America* (four volumes, 1827—1838).

Eliza Leslie, 1787—1858. *Pencil Sketches* (three series, 1833, 1835, 1837).

George Ticknor, 1791—1871, scholar. *History of Spanish Literature* (1849).

Charles Robert Leslie, 1794—1859. *A Handbook for Young Painters* (1855).

Horace Mann, 1796—1859, educator. *Lectures on Education* (1845).

William Lloyd Garrison, 1805—1879, reformer. Edited *The Liberator* (1831—1865).

Horace Greeley, 1811—1872, journalist, reformer. Edited the New York *Tribune* (1841—1872).

Delia S. Bacon, 1811—1859. *Philosophy of the Plays of Shakespeare Unfolded* (1857).

Henry Theodore Tuckerman, 1813—1871, critic. *Thoughts on the Poets* (1846).

Emily C. Judson, 1791—1871, "Fanny Forester," journalist. *Trippings in Author-land* (1846).

Chapter V

TRANSCENDENTALISM: ITS MAJOR AND MINOR FIGURES

ORIGIN OF CONCEPT

The German Influence Direct. The movement known as Transcendentalism, though deriving from Germany and England, with an infusion of Oriental philosophy, and, at certain points, of French Fourierism, found its most significant development in America. This took place during the decade beginning with the publication of Emerson's *Nature* (1836). Confined largely to New England, and more narrowly to the vicinity of Boston and Concord, it involved a body of individuals, few in number, but, for so small a group, of exceptional intellectuality and prominence.

The name *Transcendental* marks the indebtedness of the movement as respects stimulus and central thought to the German philosopher, Immanuel Kant, whose *Critique of Pure Reason* (1781) made use of the word.

Direct acquaintance with Kant's work involved either, as in the case of Hedge, personal contact with German philosophy through foreign travel, or, as with Margaret Fuller, Theodore Parker, and a few others, ability to read the language with freedom.[1]

The German Influence Indirect. For Emerson, Thoreau, and the majority, however, the teachings of Kant arrived in the writings of Coleridge (chiefly *The Friend*) and the German essays of Carlyle, while its general approach found illustration in certain poems of Wordsworth such as "Tintern Abbey" and the "Ode on Intimations of Immortality."

Proceeding from the basis of the limitation of the powers of pure reason to phenomena alone, Kant found the demand of human nature for great guiding principles such as God, Freedom, and Immortality, the need of a *transcendental* knowledge to be supplied

1 Acquaintance with the German language, all authorities are agreed, was not by any means common, and the movement to remedy this deficiency of very recent date. The New England intellectuals "discovered" German literature, much as had Scott, William Taylor (the translator of Bürger's "Lenore"), Carlyle, Coleridge, Crabb Robinson, M. G. Lewis, and other Englishmen during the last decades of the eighteenth century. Margaret Fuller, encouraged by Hedge to continue her studies, translated, according to R. C. Burton (*Margaret Fuller's Criticism: Theory and Practice*, Ph.D., Iowa, 1941), "the *Conversations with Eckermann*, Bettina von Arnim's *Günderode*, and hundreds of pages of Uhland, Novalis, and Körner, with poems of her own as commentaries." Also familiar with German were Ripley, Francis, and Bartol. See René Wellek, *Immanuel Kant in England, 1793-1838* (1931); "Emerson and German Philosophy," *NEQ.*, XVI (1943), pp. 41-62.

through communion with the encompassing Universe (what Emerson memorably termed the "Over-Soul"). This communion was to be achieved, partly through contact with Nature, the garment of God, partly through attending to the dictates of instinct and the "Inner Light."

The Oriental Contribution. Contemporaneous with the interest in Kantian philosophy and its English derivatives was the interest of leading Transcendentalists in the Oriental Scriptures, evidenced in the pre-*Dial* reading of Emerson and Thoreau, and in the translations contributed to the pages of the *Dial*.[2]

Foundation in the Spirit of the Times. Historically, Transcendentalism, which included in its inner circle several of the Unitarian clergy, was an outgrowth and an extension of the reaction against Puritanism initiated by Unitarianism. Whereas Unitarianism, rejecting the authority of the clergy, had asserted the right of the individual to think and believe what he pleased, and had adopted a definitely sceptical position as respects the miracles and the authority of Scripture not far removed from that of the English deists, Transcendentalism, by its emphasis on the instinctive and mystical, had supplied something previously wanting in the cold intellectualism out of which it had grown.[3] It added, too, an element of confidence in the benevolent attitude of the Creator toward his world, the wonders and complexity of which the Transcendentalist appreciated without the disillusioning concept of "Nature red in tooth and claw" which was to follow the discoveries of Darwin and his associates. The belief in the divinity of the individual soul, arising from its capacity for communicating directly with stores of universal Truth, led naturally to a disregard for the accumulated wisdom of the past, and a heretical attitude in politics as well as theology.[4] Because Transcendentalism was profoundly idealistic, and because it sought to achieve an ideal level of living, it occurred naturally to the Transcendentalists to enter the reform movements then so numerous. Hence their presence in the abolitionist ranks, as well as in such co-operative enterprises as Brook Farm.

GROUP ACTIVITIES

Transcendental Club. The nickname applied by outsiders to an informal discussion group more often called by its members

---

2 F. I. Carpenter, *Emerson and Asia* (1930); Arthur Christy, *The Orient in American Transcendentalism* (1932).

3 Van Wyck Brooks, *The Flowering of New England 1815-1865* (1936), p. 191 *f.*, makes clear the relationship of the philosophers Fichte, Schleiermacher, and Herder to the Transcendental point of view. As regards Schelling and Hegel, neither accepts the Kantian distinction between *transcendent* and *transcendental.*

4 Tersely, then, Transcendentalism stemmed from the romantic movement; it set itself up against Lockean empiricism, orthodox New England Calvinism, deism, and Trinitarianism, and against materialism, rationalism, and bourgeois commercialism. Idealistic and intuitive is its doctrine of knowledge; unitarian is its theology.

"The Symposium" or "Hedge's Club" after Henry Hedge, who with Dr. Channing and George Ripley used his influence to bring about its establishment. Maintained for several years, it nevertheless had neither officers nor regular time nor place of meeting. Its membership was elastic, including with varying regularity: Emerson, Thoreau, Alcott, Theodore Parker, Margaret Fuller, W. H. Channing, Ripley, Hedge, Brownson, Clarke, Convers Francis, J. S. Dwight, C. A. Bartol, Elizabeth and Sophia Peabody, Hawthorne, Charles T. Follen.

The Dial.[4a] Quarterly periodical, issued sixteen times between 1840 and 1844. Organ of the Transcendental movement. Edited for the first two years by Margaret Fuller, thereafter by Emerson with the assistance of Thoreau. Small at the start, the subscription list, which constituted the entire support of the periodical, steadily dwindled. Though the chief contributors were the three editors, others were Alcott, Theodore Parker, Ripley, C. P. Cranch, Charles Lane, Jones Very, and C. A. Dana.

Brook Farm. Famous Transcendental co-operative experiment, launched (1841) under leadership of George Ripley who, in addition to practical experience as a farmer, had devoted himself to the study of co-operatives. It was finally (1847) liquidated as a result of economic difficulties and after changes aligning it more definitely with Fourieristic theory had alienated many of those originally sympathetic. Among the participants were: C. A. Dana (later of the *Sun*), J. S. Dwight, Isaac T. Hecker (later founder of the Paulist Fathers), and, for a time, Hawthorne. Emerson, Margaret Fuller, Alcott, and Brownson visited but did not join. Thoreau held aloof. G. W. Curtis was a pupil in the excellent school. Included also were "several Harvard students, an English baronet's son, a Spaniard, two Filipinos, the son of a Louisiana planter." [5]

TRANSCENDENTALISM: MAJOR FIGURES

WILLIAM ELLERY CHANNING, 1780—1842, clergyman, philosopher.[6] Born in Newport, Rhode Island, graduate of Harvard, for a time resident in Virginia, became at twenty-three minister of the Federal Street Society, Boston. This post he retained till death. His bent toward reform, and profound belief in the virtues of unrestricted discussion he owed to a youthful acquaintance with the perfectionist philosophy of Godwin and Mary Wollstonecraft. Far more than a Unitarian concerned narrowly

---

4a C. L. F. Gohdes, *The Periodicals of American Transcendentalism* (1931), pp. 17-37.

5 Lindsay Swift, *Brook Farm* (1906); Lewis Mumford, *The Story of Utopias* (1922); Van Wyck Brooks, *The Flowering of New England 1815-1865* (1936); Katherine Burton, *Paradise Planters: The Story of Brook Farm* (1939); V. F. Calverton, *Where Angels Dared to Tread* (1940); J. B. Wilson, "The Antecedents of Brook Farm," *NEQ.*, XV (1942), pp. 320-331.

6 For bibliography, see page 296.

with the nature of the Godhead, he marks a definite development toward Transcendentalism in his justification of a belief in God by what Man finds in his own soul. A kindly God plus a Rousseauistically noble concept of Man made up his formula for life. Reluctant to seem a schismatic, he was slow in declaring himself, the memorable statement at the ordination of Jared Sparks (1819) being deferred until his fortieth year. This position he expanded in a sermon, "Unitarian Christianity Most Favorable to Piety" (1826). Always a courageous and original thinker, Channing expressed in *Remarks on American Literature* (1830) a demand for independence of European domination considerably preceding that voiced by Emerson in *The American Scholar* (see p. 91). Though out of sympathy with such practical reformers as Garrison, and an early opponent of war, Channing made three important contributions to the antislavery cause between 1835 and 1837, a period when the agitation was still far from its height. These were: *Slavery* (1835) aimed at the theoretical defenses of the institution, many of them Southern; *The Abolitionist* (1836), expressing sympathy with one James Birney, printer victim of an Ohio mob; a letter addressed to Henry Clay, and opposing Texas annexation.[7] Like Emerson, he found allegiance to a government intolerable when it outraged the consciences of its people. At the famous Faneuil Hall meeting held in protest over the Lovejoy murder, Channing and Wendell Phillips spoke from the same platform.

Channing was no visionary, but was ahead of his time in his concern over prison discipline, pauperism, child labor, and working conditions generally. Acquainted through foreign travel with life in England, France, and Italy, he was also widely known abroad; and was personally acquainted with Wordsworth and Coleridge, whose works had played a large part in his own intellectual development, and with Richter, Schiller, and Goethe.

RALPH WALDO EMERSON, 1803—1882, poet, essayist, philosopher.[8] Born in Boston into a family of position if not of wealth, Emerson had behind him the prestige of a line of preacher ancestors. The premature death of his father, the Reverend William Emerson (1811), enforced strictest economy; yet Waldo, like his three brothers,[9] went through the Boston Latin School and proceeded (1817) to Harvard. Less promising than either Charles or Edward, he made good use of his time, read heavily in Plato and Plotinus, in Shakespeare,[10] in the Metaphysical Poets,[11] in Mon-

7 Cf. Granville Hicks, "Dr. Channing and the Creole Case," *AHR.*, XXXVII (1931-1932), pp. 516-525; Fulmer Mood and Granville Hicks, "Letters to Dr. Channing on Slavery and the Annexation of Texas, 1837," *NEQ.*, V (1932), pp. 587-601.

8 For full bibliography, see pages 296-297.

9 The Emersons were not of a sturdy stock. Three children died in infancy. Bulkeley remained of undeveloped mentality. Edward died in 1834, Charles in 1836.

10 R. P. Falk, "Emerson and Shakespeare," *PMLA.*, LVI (1941), pp. 532-543.

11 Cf. N. A. Brittin, "Emerson and the Metaphysical Poets," *AL.*, VIII (1936-1937), pp. 1-21.

taigne (his lifelong favorite),[12] and, initially, in the Oriental Scriptures.[13] Following graduation (1821) he taught for a short time in a girls' school conducted by his brother William, studied theology, married (1829), became (1829) pastor of the Second Church of Boston. Unable to convince himself of the divine institution of the sacrament of the Lord's Supper,[14] he resigned (1832) and, still grieving over the complete breakdown (1828) of his brilliant brother Edward — to die in 1834 — and the pathetic death of his lovely young wife, Ellen Louisa Tucker (February, 1831),[15] set out (December, 1832) for Europe. He was disappointed in his encounters with Landor, Coleridge, Wordsworth; profoundly stirred by his visit to Carlyle.[16] The years immediately following his return, his marriage to Lydia Jackson (1835), and his settling at Concord were the most fruitful in his career. In 1836 he saw through the press, with an introduction of his own writing, the first edition of Carlyle's *Sartor Resartus.* In the same year he wrote *Nature,* little read, but compact and fundamental statement of his whole Transcendental position. Also in 1836 he helped found the so-called Transcendental Club from which sprang (1840) the *Dial,* to which he contributed importantly and which he edited during its last two years. In 1837 he delivered his Harvard Phi Beta Kappa address, *The American Scholar;* in 1838 his less familiar but perhaps more important *Divinity School Address.* The two series of *Essays,* 1841 and 1843, come closest to encompassing the Emerson of any but the most thorough readers.

During 1847—1848 he lectured in England, and renewed his contacts with Carlyle on a more equal if perhaps on a less cordial and completely sympathetic basis.[17] Perhaps as a result he pub-

12 W. L. Ustick, "Emerson's Debt to Montaigne," *WUS.*, IX, Fourth Series (1922), pp. 245-262; C. L. Young, *Emerson's Montaigne* (1941).

13 J. S. Harrison, *The Teachers of Emerson* (1910); F. T. Thompson, "Emerson's Indebtedness to Coleridge," *SP., XXIII* (1926), pp. 55-76. F. T. Thompson shows that the more careful reading followed college days. J. B. Moore, "Emerson on Wordsworth," *PMLA.*, XLI, N.S. XXXIV (1926), pp. 179-192; Arthur Christy, *The Orient in American Transcendentalism* (1932), pp. 61-183.

14 Cf. "Letter to the Second Church and Society" (1832); A. C. McGiffert, Jr., *Young Emerson Speaks* (1938). "This is the end of my opposition that I am not interested in it. I am content that it stand to the end of the world if it please men and please Heaven and I shall rejoice in all the good it does."

15 "Shall I ever again be able to connect the face of outward nature, the mists of morn, the star of eve, the flowers, and all poetry, with the heart and life of an enchanting friend? No. There is one birth, and one baptism, and one first love, and the affections cannot keep their youth any more than men." *Journal,* February, 1832.

16 Townsend Scudder, *The Lonely Wayfaring Man* (1936).

17 On the general question of the relationship of Emerson and Carlyle see: C. E. Norton (editor), *The Correspondence of Thomas Carlyle and Ralph Waldo Emerson, 1834-1872* (revised edition, 1888); H. F. Lowry and R. L. Rusk (editors), *Emerson-Clough Letters* (1934); Townsend Scudder, III, "Emerson in Dundee," *A.Schol.*, IV (1935), pp. 331-334; Townsend Scudder, III, "Emerson's British Lecture Tour, 1847-1848," *AL.*, VII (1935-1936), pp. 15-36; W. S. Vance, "Carlyle in America before *Sartor Resartus,*" *AL.*, VII (1935-1936), pp. 363-375; Townsend Scudder, III, "Emerson in London and the London Lectures," *AL.*, VIII (1936-1937), pp. 22-36; Townsend Scudder, III, "A Chronological List of Emerson's Lectures on His British Lecture Tour of 1847-1848," *PMLA.*, LI (1936), pp. 243-248; George Kummer, "Anonymity and Carlyle's Early Reputation in America," *AL.*, VIII (1936-1937), pp. 297-299; P. W. Brown, *Middlesex Monographs* (1941) pp. 3-23. Carlyle's inducing Clough to return to England after he had followed Emerson to America as a disciple occasioned

lished in 1850 *Representative Men,* in plan reminiscent of that used by Carlyle in the series of lectures *On Heroes, Hero-Worship, and The Heroic in History* (1841). The lecture platform from which the *Essays* were derived, and for which these Addresses were designed, was a field steadily cultivated by Emerson over three decades, which did much to extend his fame through the Middle West, as well as in nearer regions.[18]

English Traits (1856), more informal than the most of Emerson, is full of amused and keen comments on the mother country.[19] *The Conduct of Life* (1860) and *Society and Solitude* (1870) and additional volumes of essays were overshadowed by their more memorable predecessors. Three volumes of poems appeared: *Poems* (1847), *May-Day and Other Pieces* (1867), and *Selected Poems* (1876). Additional poems are included in the collected editions of 1883 and 1904.

During the decade preceding the Civil War, Emerson's opposition to slavery, once lukewarm, passed from dislike into hatred. Like his friends, Alcott, Thoreau, Parker, and Sanborn, he knew and supported John Brown, encouraged violation of the Fugitive Slave Law, helped slaves to freedom.[20] None, or little, of this, however, finds its way into his remembered prose or verse.

Following the war he resumed his lectures, but about 1872 there began an unmistakable breakup of his faculties and eventually his memory quite failed him.

ESSAYS AND ADDRESSES

Nature† (anonymously, 1836). Long unread except by the discriminating few, it is, like Carlyle's *Sartor Resartus,* the essence of its author. Style lyric and impassioned, essentially that of a prose poem; but, because of compression and abstract reasoning,

---

bad feeling between the old friends. See F. T. Thompson, "Emerson and Carlyle," *SP.*, XXIV (1927), pp. 438-453; Townsend Scudder, III, *The Lonely Wayfaring Man* (1936).

18 See J. R. Lowell, "Emerson the Lecturer," in *My Study Windows* (1871), pp. 375-384; H. H. Hoeltje, "Ralph Waldo Emerson in Iowa," *IJHP.*, XXV (1927), pp. 236-276; H. H. Hoeltje, "Emerson's Venture in Western Land," *AL.*, II (1930-1931), pp. 438-440; H. H. Hoeltje, "Ralph Waldo Emerson in Minnesota," *M.Hist.*, XI (1930), pp. 145-159. Clarence Gohdes (editor), *Uncollected Lectures by Ralph Waldo Emerson: Reports of Lectures on American Life and Natural Religion.* Reprinted from *The Commonwealth* (1932); H. H. Hoeltje, "Emerson in Virginia," *NEQ.*, V (1932), pp. 753-768, dealing with the University of Virginia address in 1875; L. H. Meeks, "The Lyceum in the Early West," *IMH.*, XXIX (1933), pp. 87-95; R. G. Silver, "Emerson as Abolitionist," *NEQ.*, VI (1933), pp. 154-158; By The Editor [R. T. Flewelling], "Emerson and the Middle Border," *Personalist* XVI (1935), pp. 295-309; Louise Hastings, "Emerson in Cincinnati," *NEQ.*, XI (1938), pp. 443-469; C. I. Glicksberg, "Bryant on Emerson the Lecturer," *NEQ.*, XII (1939), pp. 530-534; L. M. Wright, "Culture through Lectures," *IJHP.*, XXXVIII (1940), pp. 115-162; E. E. Sandeen, *Emerson as an American* (Ph.D., Iowa, 1940).

19 "With the exception of 'English Traits,' nearly everything that Emerson wrote was an embroidering of a few very simple ideas. . . . God as moral law; the world as an emanation from God; man as having divinity within himself; 'self-reliance'; and a religion not of authority but of the spirit." H. B. Parkes, *The Pragmatic Test* (1941), p. 48 *f.*, (pp. 39-62).

20 Raymer McQuiston, "The Relation of Ralph Waldo Emerson to Public Affairs," *UKHSB.*, III, No. 1 (1923); R. G. Silver, "Emerson as Abolitionist," *NEQ.*, VI (1933), pp. 154-158, recounting the hostile reception of an abolitionist address by Emerson; W. A. Huggard, "Emerson and the Problem of War and Peace," *UIS.*, V, No. 5 (1938).

often difficult to read. Most tangible are the sections on Commodity — the "advantages which our senses owe to Nature" — and Language. Section on Discipline presents a distinction in its use of the terms, Reason and Understanding, derived from Coleridge's *The Friend;*[21] sections on Idealism and Spirit are too abstract to be easily grasped. Dated by its kindly view of Nature.[22] Twenty-five years later the influence of Darwin's *Origin of Species* (1859) would doubtless have made itself felt.

***The American Scholar*†** (1837). Not the first,[23] but the most memorable[24] and influential[25] demand for American independence of European domination in thought and creative art. Emerson was already a well-known speaker and the occasion a great one. So far as the title is concerned, *Scholar* should not be mistaken for *student* or for the *researcher* of present-day lingo. It is rather, in Emerson's phrase, "Man Thinking"; and that is its central theme.[26] Nor should it be assumed that the address is devoted specifically to the need of severing the leading strings of Europe. Actually this aspect of the address ("We have listened too long to the courtly muses of Europe") occupies only a small concluding portion. As "Man Thinking" the Scholar is shown to be subjected to three major influences: Nature; The Past (*i.e.,* Books) which may make the Scholar a bookworm, but which, correctly used, serve as an inspiration ("Books are for the Scholar's idle time"); Action (*i.e.,* Life). The age calls to the Scholar for active participation and leadership; it emphasizes as never before the importance of the individual. "Like Locke, Paine, and Jefferson, he [Emerson] felt that each generation should legislate for itself, and should not be ruled from the grave."

***Divinity School Address*†** (1838). Delivered at the request of the handful of graduates of the Harvard Divinity School, this address resulted in what Emerson himself called a "storm in our

---

21 F. T. Thompson, "Emerson's Indebtedness to Coleridge," *SP.*, XXXIII (1923), pp. 55-76.

22 Norman Foerster, *Nature in American Literature* (1923), pp. 27-68.

23 The same position had already been taken by William Ellery Channing in *Remarks on American Literature* (1830). G. H. Orians, in *A Short History of American Literature* (1940), pp. 121-123, cites Longfellow's article, "Defense of Poesy" in the *North American Review* (1832), Cooper's *Letter to his Countrymen* (1834), and Verplanck's *The American Scholar* (1836) as evidence that the subject was in the air. B. T. Spencer, "A National Literature, 1837-1855," *AL.*, VIII (1936-1937), pp. 125-159, shows the topic not new, and Emerson more moderate than some. Cf. also H. N. Smith, "Emerson's Problem of Vocation: A Note on 'The American Scholar,'" *NEQ.*, XII (1939), pp. 52-67.

24 Lowell called it an "event without any former parallel in our literary annals, a scene to be always treasured in the memory for its picturesqueness and its inspiration. What crowded and breathless aisles, what windows clustering with eager heads, what enthusiasm of approval, what grim silence of foregone dissent!"

25 On the occasion of the approximate centennial of its delivery (1936), addresses were delivered by President W. A. Neilson (Smith) and by Dean (later President) G. S. Ford (Minnesota), both entitled "The American Scholar Today." Cf. also C. F. Thwing, "The American Scholar: Emerson's Phi Beta Kappa Address (1837)," *HJ.*, XXXVI (1937-1938), pp. 119-131.

26 Jerome Nathanson, *Forerunners of Freedom* (1941), pp. 11-40.

washbowl" and in what H. S. Commager has termed[27] a "Tempest in a Boston Tea Cup." Most obvious point of attack was the fact that by asserting the divinity and inspiration of all men it relegated Christ to a definitely human position.[28] This feeling found fresh support in the fact that he neither quoted nor discussed the Scriptures, that he denied the truth of miracles as taught by the church, and used no prayer. As a result he antagonized important elements within the Unitarian Church itself. Andrews Norton, father of Charles Eliot Norton, responded first in the Boston *Daily Advertiser,* and a year from the date of Emerson's address in a deliberately planned reply from the same platform, "The Latest Form of Infidelity." Emerson's utterances were, however, as has recently been pointed out,[29] "mere notes in a general discord." Like *The American Scholar* and "Self-Reliance" it emphasizes the majesty and divinity of the individual soul. ("If a man is at heart just, then in so far is he God; . . . "). Here appears one of the important expressions regarding the purely negative character of evil.[30] If evil is merely the absence of good, it "flees before virtue as darkness does before light." Other passages definitely look forward to "The Over-Soul."[31] The address is also important in its Transcendental insistence on the importance of Intuition. This meant, of necessity, denial to any church of authority to assert or communicate truth. The conclusion constitutes a surprisingly practical discussion of the profession of preaching.

Essays† (First Series, 1841). Best-known titles form a group treating major Emersonian ideas. Taken together they constitute a fairly complete statement of the Transcendental position. Stylistically, they illustrate the Emersonian manner in its most characteristic aspect: its tendency to reiteration with plentiful, varied illustration rather than logical argument; its employment of sparkling paradox, half statement, and half overstatement; its fragmentary, gem-like sentences, both memorable and quotable. When the ordinary man refers to Emerson, he is referring to this volume.

---

27 In *NEQ.*, VI (1933), pp. 651-675. See, also, D. E. Trueblood, "The Influence of Emerson's Divinity School Address," *HTR.*, XXXII (1939), pp. 41-56.

28 Cf. C. W. Cannon, *The Influences determining Emerson's Conception of Jesus* (Ph.D., Iowa, 1936-1937). Consult, too, C. H. Foster, "Emerson as American Scripture," *NEQ.*, XVI (1943), pp. 91-105.

29 Clarence Gohdes, "Some Remarks on Emerson's *Divinity School Address,*" *AL.*, I (1929-1930), pp. 27-31. He emphasizes Emerson's indebtedness to an article by the Reverend S. D. Robbins, "Thoughts on Unity, Progress, and Government," which appeared three months before in the *Boston Quarterly Review.* On the general relationship of Emerson to New England religious thinking, see Perry Miller, *The New England Mind* (1939), p. 278 *f.*; L. H. Downs, *Emerson and Dr. Channing* (Ph.D., Iowa, 1940). In certain of its more general aspects see G. H. Hartwig, "Emerson on Historical Christianity," *HJ.*, XXXVII (1938-1939), pp. 405-412; C. C. Charvat, *Emerson and Catholicism* (Ph.D, Iowa, 1940).

30 "Good is positive. Evil is merely privative, not absolute: it is like cold, which is the privation of heat." See, however, the important article of C. E. Jorgenson, "Emerson's Paradise under the Shadow of Swords," *PQ.*, XI (1932), pp. 274-292.

31 "When he says, 'I ought'; when love warms him; when he chooses, warned from on high, the good and great deed; then deep melodies wander through his soul from Supreme Wisdom."

Of special significance are the following: "Love," "Friendship," "Prudence," "Heroism," "Circles," "Intellect," "Art,"[32] and those discussed immediately below.

"History." Interprets the term broadly, much as do some modern social historians, including therein virtually everything that, viewed in the large, constitutes human progress, which, in its evolution, parallels the evolution of the individual, and, partly on this account, is to be measured in terms of what it means to him. Parallelism between portions of this essay and *The American Scholar* is striking.

"Self-Reliance."† Epitome of Emerson's practical philosophy, most popular, most quoted. Emphasizing note of severe individualism, of nonconformity ("Trust thyself") basic in Emerson's Puritan inheritance and character. In keeping, on the one hand, with his toleration of the economic *laissez-faire,* and tacit acceptance of wealth as an indication of merit; on the other, with his demands for opportunity for all, his growing suspicion of the industrial civilization of his day, his Jeffersonian dislike of strong centralized government, his suspicion of political parties as such.[33] Now and then he tends to deflate social and reform movements.[34] In later life Emerson was himself conscious of the opposition between this

32 Of the remaining essays in the First Series, "Prudence" and "Heroism" may well be considered together, for Emerson interprets his term broadly, including under Prudence a balanced grouping of most of the virtues, and a sensible acceptance of the Universe and its ways with Man. "Friendship" and "Love," too, should be read together, and balanced by the exquisite poems, "To Ellen at the South," "Thine Eyes Still Shined," from the days of his first courtship and marriage. These show what is often not realized, that in his verse Emerson's native reticence vanished. There is, however, a balancing note, disclosed from time to time in the *Journals* and expressed in "Give All to Love." "Circles" is made up of a whimsically miscellaneous collection of illustrations. "Intellect" and "Art" are the lesser essays of the volume.

33 Emerson's attitudes, expressed and implied, on these various matters have occasioned confusion and some controversy. Though his "Essay on Politics" forms a compressed statement, other observations, at least superficially hard to reconcile, will be found scattered through his works. Clearly he had little faith in mere political machinery as security for the liberties of the individual, and still less trust in the will of the majority. He rebelled personally against the Fugitive Slave Law, yet later, during the Civil War, he at least tacitly conceded the function of the state in acting for the individual in times of national emergency. Similar inconsistencies appear in his attitude toward wealth and poverty, commerce, industrial progress. Cf. A. C. Kern, "Emerson and Economics," *NEQ.*, XIII (1940), pp. 678-696. Cf., also E. W. Emerson, *Emerson in Concord* (1889); G. E. Woodberry, *Ralph Waldo Emerson* (1907), p. 144; O. W. Firkins, *Ralph Waldo Emerson* (1915), p. 22; Raymer McQuiston, "The Relation of Ralph Waldo Emerson to Public Affairs," *UKHS.*, III, No. 1 (1923); Lucy Hazard, *The Frontier in American Literature* (1927), p. 150 *ff.*, V. L. Parrington, *Main Currents in American Thought,* II (1927), p. 392; J. T. Adams, "Emerson Re-Read," *Atl.*, CXLVI (1930), p. 492 (pp. 484-492); H. H. Clark, "Emerson and Science," *PQ.*, X (1931), p. 247 (pp. 225-260); Ernest Marchand, "Emerson and the Frontier," *AL.*, III (1931-1932), pp. 149-174; V. F. Calverton, *The Liberation of American Literature* (1932), p. 248; Clarence Gohdes, *Uncollected Letters of Ralph Waldo Emerson* (1932); F. I. Carpenter, *Emerson* (1934), p. xlvi; J. T. Flanagan, *Emerson and the State* (Ph.D., Minnesota, 1934); Townsend Scudder, *The Lonely Wayfaring Man* (1936), p. 148; J. T. Flanagan, "Emerson and Communism," *NEQ.*, X (1937), pp. 243-261; William Charvat, "American Romanticism and the Depression of 1837," *SS.*, II (1937-1938), p. 80 (pp. 67-82); Mildred Silver, "Emerson and the Idea of Progress," *AL.*, XII (1940-1941), p. 7 (pp. 1-19); A. I. Ladu, "Emerson: Whig or Democrat," *NEQ.*, XIII (1940), pp. 434-437 (pp. 419-441); E. E. Sandeen, "Emerson's Americanism," printed 1940 in *Critical Studies in Arnold, Emerson, and Newman,* U.I.S. Hum., Ser. V.

34 Cf. passage beginning, "Society is a wave. . . ."; cf. also "In like manner the reformers summon conventions and vote and resolve in multitude. Not so O friends! will the God deign to enter and inhabit you, . . ."; cf. also Bliss Perry, *Emerson Today* (1931), pp. 108-109.

view, at points not unlike that of Thoreau,[35] and the acknowledged necessities of democratic social organization.[36] As Emerson's encouraging message to youth, this has been subjected to specific attack as bad advice and a plain disregard of facts,[37] and has been defended vigorously.[38] Attention has been called to the clear indebtedness of two adjoining paragraphs to Wordsworth's "Ode on Intimations of Immortality" and to "The Everlasting No" chapter in Carlyle's *Sartor Resartus*.[39]

"Compensation."† Facing the problem of the existence of a moral order in the Universe, Emerson undertakes, through the citation of a multitude of instances, to demonstrate that "the dice of God are always loaded." Names an astonishingly varied collection of parallels, illustrating balance or polarity, but quite without moral significance. Concludes that no crime goes cosmically unpunished; that success in this world may not be ultimate success; that what is to the individual immediate grief or disillusionment or tragedy may operate to the maturing or solidifying of character.

"Spiritual Laws." In certain respects the bridge between the extremes represented by the glorified individualism of "Self-Reliance" and the cosmic, enveloping "Over-Soul." Contains amusingly sharp and contemporary criticism of the busy activities of men — even of himself and his Concord neighbors[40] — when measured by the majestic standards of Nature.[41] By putting oneself in alignment with the Universe, by developing the talent which is Nature's indication of a call to a vocation, by being one's own self (Carlyle's "sincerity" and "unconsciousness"), by being independent and fearless, Man can attain to his highest possibilities. Stress upon passivity and calm is Oriental. First series of *Essays* appeared during publication of the *Dial*, which is full of material from the Oriental Scriptures.

"The Over-Soul."† Standing at the opposite extreme from "Self-Reliance," presents another and more mystical[42] side of Transcendentalism. The title is Emerson's phrase for the deeps of encompassing spiritual nature, the Over-Soul, to which the soul

---

35 Cf. passage near end of Chapter One, *Walden* (*Works*, II, p. 86).

36 See "Society and Solitude," concluding paragraph. *Works*, VII, p. 15 *f.*; also, Phillips Russell, *Emerson: The Wisest American* (1929), p. 250.

37 J. T. Adams, "Emerson Re-Read," *Atl.*, CXLVI (1930), pp. 484-492.

38 Newton Dillaway, *Prophet of America: Emerson and the Problems of Today* (1936). Cf. also By The Editor [R. T. Flewelling], "Emerson and Adolescent America," *Personalist*, XX (1939), pp. 343-352.

39 Cf. also G. R. Elliott, "On Emerson's 'Grace' and 'Self-Reliance,'" *NEQ.*, II (1929), pp. 93-104.

40 "Nature does not like our benevolence, or our learning, much better than she likes our frauds and wars. When we come out of the caucus, or the bank, or the Abolition Convention, or the Temperance Meeting, or the Transcendental Club, into the fields and woods, she says to us, 'So hot? my little sir.'"

41 By this term Emerson means, as in *Nature* (1836) and elsewhere, something distinctly beyond mountains and valleys, trees and flowers and grass.

42 E. A. Warren, Jr., "The Teachings of Emerson: A Critique from the Standpoints of Christianity and Humanism," *NCR.*, XXIX (1922), pp. 275-293.

lies open. Suggestive of the "trailing clouds of glory" of Wordsworth's "Ode on Intimations of Immortality" is the sentence, "Man is a stream whose source is hidden." So, too, the half-conscious state of awareness so eloquently described in "Tintern Abbey"[43] suggests that glorification of the ecstatic moment — Alcott was actually subject to trances — and by implication, of instinct as a source of truth which fits in so well with the doctrine of "Self-Reliance."

Essays (Second Series, 1844). Less widely read than the First Series, the Second contains several distinguished essays.

"The Poet." View of poetry is Transcendental; notable for emphasis which, in common with Carlyle, he lays on insight and wisdom and the poet's message; notable, too, for disregard of technical considerations.[44] "For it is not metres but a metre-making argument that makes a poem, ..." To Emerson, Poe was "the Jingle Man." Note, however, Emerson's praise of the Poet as the language-maker. Ends on a national note, stresses our "incomparable materials" for poetry, materials such as were later utilized, in all their variety, by Whitman.

"Experience." Long, brilliant, and varied essay, marked by a practicality and concreteness suggestive of Thoreau,[45] and an eloquence of direct address reminiscent of Carlyle.[46] Notable also for its frank allusion to the death of his son two years before as having left the father essentially untouched.[47]

"Nature." Prose poem containing passages of exceptional loveliness, and suggestive in many ways of the *Nature* of 1836. Nevertheless, acknowledgment of the ruthlessness of Nature, of her laws which she will never contravene, of her wastefulness of the individual seed to achieve perpetuity of the species, of the sex urge as Nature's device for continuing life.

"New England Reformers." Historical in approach; showing a certain coolness and detachment in dealing with the reforming

43 ". . . that serene and blessed mood,
In which the affections gently lead us on, —
Until, the breath of this corporeal frame
And even the motion of our human blood
Almost suspended, we are laid asleep
In body, and become a living soul:
While with an eye made quiet by the power
Of harmony, and the deep power of joy,
We see into the life of things."

44 Cf. Charles Cestre, "Emerson Poete," *EA.*, IV (1942), pp. 1-14.

45 "In the morning I awake and find the old world, wife, babes, and mother, Concord and Boston, the dear old spiritual world, and even the dear old devil not far off." "A collector recently bought at public auction, in London, for one hundred and fifty-seven guineas, an autograph of Shakespeare: but for nothing a school boy can read Hamlet, and can detect secrets of highest concernment yet unpublished therein."

46 "Thy sickness, they say, and thy puny habit, require that thou do this or avoid that, but know that thy life is a flitting state, a tent for a night, and do thou, sick or well, finish that stint."

47 The effect of the death of little Waldo appears from trustworthy testimony to have been quite otherwise. Forty years later, the last words on the lips of the dying Emerson are said to have been, "O! that beautiful boy!"

movements which had flowered so luxuriantly in New England and involved acquaintances and neighbors. Emerson's aversion to parties, projects, and movements is here easily discernible. His profound conviction that it is less important that some evil be attacked than that the individual shall be right in his own mind, leads to a curious digression — an attack on classical training in colleges, as pointless, because useless.

Of the remaining essays, "Character" and "Nominalist and Realist" are sound but undistinguished; "Politics" is important as a part of the confused and confusing picture of Emerson's attitude toward the State;[48] "Manners" and "Gifts" are closer to the level and tone of the familiar essay.

Representative Men (1850). Though compressed in preparation for the press, the oral quality of the original lectures is still to be detected. A close comparison with Carlyle's *On Heroes, Hero-Worship, and The Heroic in History* discloses similarity of plan. "On the Uses of Great Men," for instance, corresponds to the first paragraphs of Carlyle's "Hero as Divinity." Of Emerson's six Representative Men (Plato, Swedenborg, Montaigne, Shakespeare, Napoleon, and Goethe), two — Shakespeare and Napoleon — had already been discussed by Carlyle. Carlyle's reasons for failing to include Goethe have been termed by his editor unsatisfactory,[49] but it is to be remembered that he had already translated the *Wilhelm Meister*. The two differ significantly in their attitude toward the Great Man, who, according to Carlyle, would have forced his way to the top anywhere, any time; but is, with Emerson, the product of the mass. In this the characteristic differences in the attitudes of the two toward Democracy are thrown into relief. That heroes are men of insight and self-reliance and sincerity, they are agreed.[50]

The Conduct of Life (1860). Given first at Pittsburgh (1851), these lectures were later delivered in Boston.[51] I — "Fate." Brilliant example of Emerson's appropriation of the discoveries of Science, specifically Evolution, which figures here as a kind of environing Necessity.[52] II — "Power." Reiterates doctrine of Compensation, of Over-Soul, in a statement that power comes from alignment of the individual with the Universe. To this is added an acknowledgment, suggestive of the later Carlyle of "Cromwell" and "Frederick," that Power may be pardoned for the neglect of

48 Cf. A. C. Kern, "Emerson and Economics," *NEQ.*, XIII (1940), pp. 678-696; also page 93, footnote 33.

49 Archibald MacMechan (editor), *Carlyle on Heroes and Hero-Worship, and the Heroic in History* (1901), p. 344. Cf. also F. W. Wahr, *Emerson and Goethe* (Ph.D., Michigan, 1915).

50 For discussion of individual portraits see Régis Michaud, *Emerson: The Enraptured Yankee* (1930), p. 341; Clarence Hotson, "The Christian Critics and Mr. Emerson," *NEQ.*, XI (1938), pp. 29-47 (dealing especially with Swedenborgianism).

51 J. P. Abbott, *Emerson and the Conduct of Life* (Ph.D., Iowa, 1939).

52 H. H. Clark, "Emerson and Science," *PQ.*, X (1931), pp. 225-260; J. W. Beach, "Emerson and Evolution," *UTQ.*, III (1934), pp. 474-497.

details. III — "Wealth." Practical Yankee side of Emerson is revealed in an understanding of the necessities of Commerce. IV — "Culture." Shown as correcting the theory of success. Develops ideas from *The American Scholar*. V — "Behavior." Approaching the tone of the familiar essay, and drawing upon experiences of the manners of the South and West. VI — "Worship." The naturalness of Faith presented in passages of extraordinary vividness and eloquence. Then a discussion of the transitional state in which the faiths of men now are. The solution is faith in the universal scheme of things, and the worthiness of every individual. VII — "Considerations by the Way." Of minor significance. VIII — "Beauty." Concerned with some of the principles of Art. IX — "Illusions." The Transcendental view of Life as a phantasmagoria to which the observer contributes the most important part.

Society and Solitude† (1870). Based on lectures previously given. Contents: "Society and Solitude," "Civilization," "Art," "Eloquence," "Domestic Life," "Farming," "Works and Days," "Books," "Courage," "Success," "Old Age."

POETRY

His poetry divides itself into several fairly well defined groups:

NATURE POEMS. These bulk large both in number and in length. Such are "Woodnotes I" (1840), "Woodnotes II" (1841), "To the Humble-Bee"† (1839), "The Snow-Storm" (1841), "The Titmouse" (1862), the more extended "May-Day" (1867), "Musketaquid" (1847), and "Sea-Shore" (1864). "The Rhodora"† (1839) and "Forerunners" (1846) have about them a Transcendental flavor. "Fable" (1846) is an exquisite bit, almost unique in adult American poetry.

TRANSCENDENTAL. Often cryptic; often with an Oriental source or flavor, these include: "The Sphinx"† (1841), "Uriel" (1847) — interpreted by some scholars as a parable of the excitement occasioned by delivery of the Divinity School Address, "Hamatreya" (1847),[53] "Brahma"† (1857), "Days"† (1857), "Experience" (1867).

PERSONAL. Includes his love poems, "To Ellen at the South" (1843), "Thine Eyes Still Shined" (1847); his comments upon love, "Each and All"† (1839), and "Give All to Love" (1847); his poem of lament over his son, five-year-old Waldo, "Threnody"† (1847); his acquiescence in old age, "Terminus" (1867); his statement regarding religious toleration, "The Problem" (1840).

PUBLIC AND PATRIOTIC. Such are the immortal "Hymn"†

53 George Williamson, "Emerson the Oriental," *UCC.*, XXX (1928), pp. 271-288; F. I. Carpenter, "Immortality from India," *AL.*, I (1929-1930), pp. 233-242; Arthur Christy, *The Orient in American Transcendentalism* (1932), pp. 61-185.

(1837) at Concord Bridge, "Ode Inscribed to W. H. Channing" (1847), "Boston Hymn" (1863), and "Voluntaries" (1863). "Bacchus" (1847) deserves special mention as a superb drinking song, something in the manner of the "Ode to a Nightingale." In the field of epigrams and quatrains Emerson has shown a talent unmatched in America and strikingly reminiscent of his master, Landor.

Emerson had an authentic poetic gift,[54] not greatly appreciated in his lifetime. This resulted from (1) his fame as prose writer, (2) technical irregularities, and (3) deficiency of emotional concreteness. In college he was devoted to Shakespeare and the Metaphysical poets, came quickly to know and admire Wordsworth[55] and Coleridge as the greatest poets and thinkers of the age. Wordsworth's "Ode on Intimations of Immortality" and "Tintern Abbey" had special appeal to Transcendental readers, and were popular throughout the Concord circle. Coleridge furnished Emerson food for thought with *The Friend* and the *Biographia Literaria.* From him he learned the distinction between Reason and the Understanding, Talent and Genius, Fancy and the Imagination.[56] It is probable that the reading of Wordsworth stimulated Emerson to the writing of nature verse. Certainly the influence of Walter Savage Landor (see the essay on that poet) is felt in his quatrains and epigrams. Emerson himself exercised a great and significant influence upon Whitman, both in early recognition and encouragement and in a disregard for technical metrical restrictions.

HENRY DAVID THOREAU, 1817—1862, poet, essayist, naturalist.[57] Born in Concord, Massachusetts, which became from 1823 on the family home. Of all the famous residents of the village, he alone was native born.[58] There Thoreau grew up, worked in his father's pencil factory, attended Concord Academy, learned surveying, and in 1837, following graduation from Harvard, took his brief fling at school teaching. Association with Emerson (Thoreau was seventeen when Emerson moved to Concord) led to membership in the Transcendental Club, contribution to the *Dial,* residence for at least two extended periods in Emerson's household,[59] and intimate lifelong friendship, cooling only in the last

54 Joel Benton, *Emerson as a Poet* (1883); F. T. Thompson, "Emerson's Theory and Practice of Poetry," *PMLA.*, XLIII (1928), pp. 1170-1184; Alfred Kreymborg, *Our Singing Strength* (1929), pp. 67-83; G. W. Allen, *American Prosody* (1935), pp. 91-126; C. H. Foster, *Emerson's Theory of Poetry* (1939).

55 J. B. Moore, "Emerson on Wordsworth," *PMLA.*, XLI, N.S. XXXIV (1926), pp. 179-192.

56 F. T. Thompson, "Emerson's Indebtedness to Coleridge," *SP.*, XXIII (1926), pp. 55-76.

57 For full bibliography, see pages 297-299.

58 H. H. Hoeltje, "Thoreau in Concord Church and Town Records," *NEQ.*, XII (1939), pp. 349-359.

59 H. S. Canby, "Two Women," *NAR.*, CCXLVIII (1939-1940), pp. 18-32, offers evidence indicating on Thoreau's part a more than "brotherly" affection for Mrs. Lydia Emerson and her sister. This theory has not, however, gone unchallenged. See review by Raymond Adams of Canby's *Thoreau* (1939), *AL.*, XII (1940-1941), p. 113 *f.* (pp. 112-115).

years. Close friendship continued to his death with Alcott, Louisa Alcott, Ellery Channing, Hawthorne, and Sanborn. High points in the externally unexciting narrative of his life were: the death (1842) of his beloved brother John; his trip (1843) to Staten Island, where he tutored the children of William Emerson for a time; his overpublicized residence at Walden Pond (July, 1845 — September, 1847); his trip to New York (November, 1856), when he saw Whitman, Greeley, and Beecher; and his longest trip, that to Minnesota (1861),[60] barely completed before his death. His vacation expeditions were, however, often turned to literary account. *A Week on the Concord and Merrimack Rivers*† (1849) records an actual journey taken with his brother John (1839). His trips to Maine (1846; 1853, 1857) resulted in "Ktaadn and the Maine Woods" (*Union Magazine,* 1848), "Chesuncook" (*Atlantic Monthly,* 1858) and "The Allegash and East Branch," published with the others as *The Maine Woods*† (1864). His trip to Canada (1850) with Ellery Channing is recorded in part as "Excursion to Canada" (*Putnam's Magazine,* 1853); entire in *A Yankee in Canada, with Anti-Slavery and Reform Papers*† (1866). His trips to Cape Cod (1849, 1850, 1855, 1857) inspired the papers published in *Putnam's Monthly Magazine* as "Cape Cod"† (1855), and in the *Atlantic Monthly* (1864) as "The Wellfleet Oysterman" and "The Highland Light."

PROSE

His three discussions of the slavery issue: "Civil Disobedience"† (1849), "Slavery in Massachusetts" (1854), and "A Plea for Captain John Brown" (1859) are courageous and even violent — evidence that he could be roused to action. In general, however, his attitude toward government, as toward all co-operative enterprises, was one of nonparticipation. Thoreau's social criticism aims its barbs specifically at preoccupation with nonessentials and too great absorption of time and energy in industrial development and the accumulation of wealth. Thoreau had a Yankee love of inventiveness and thrift, a respect for the mastering of difficulties; but he insists that the price paid for wealth and material progress is too high. For the complexities of modern civilization his remedy is simplification, a more leisurely existence, with time in it for communion with Nature, and development of the individual to his highest possibilities.

Walden; or, Life in the Woods† (1854). May be read simply as a narrative — with regrettable digressions — of two years spent close to Nature, and of the efforts required to provide the minimum essentials of food and shelter. As such, it appeals to something elemental and primitive in the reader. May be read as the record

60 J. T. Flanagan, "Thoreau in Minnesota," *M.Hist.*, XVI (1935), pp. 35-46.

of an experimental demonstration of a theory — that life can be lived fruitfully on a far less complex, crowded, and expensive level than the conventional. As such, its conclusiveness may be questioned. Thoreau's experiment was carried on in close proximity to the village whither he went frequently, and with some assistance from friends and family. Actually, this purpose was quite secondary, the primary objective being quiet, and favorable surroundings for meditation and literary composition. In that sense, the philosophical observations scattered through *Walden,* though often drawn from the Journals of preceding years, may properly be regarded as the chief fruit of the experiment, and, in the aggregate, his message to his age. Chiefly, these observations are individual rather than doctrines of Transcendental philosophy. Thoreau was called a Transcendentalist and used the word freely. His love of solitude, of contemplation, and of communion with Nature is Oriental and Transcendental though he more than others put them into practice.[61] The rhapsodic passages, less common here than in *A Week,* are often of exquisite beauty. He was, however, basically, a believer in Free Will and individual responsibility rather than Oriental passivity, and he combined with a strain of the mystic a high degree of physical competence as farmer, surveyor, and general handy man, together with an insatiable scientific curiosity. None of his works, though highly valued by experienced readers of Thoreau, approaches in importance or popularity *Walden,* named by H. S. Canby[62] along with *Moby-Dick,* Emerson's *Essays,* Poe's *Poems, Leaves of Grass,* and *The Scarlet Letter* "one of the six most remarkable books of our single century of national existence."

PROSE STYLE. The style of Thoreau is grounded in the classics and the best of English literature, not entirely uninfluenced by that of Emerson, but essentially original. It is crisp, vigorous, allusive, colorful in diction, full of subtle harmony. At its best it is unsurpassed in American literature.

POETRY

Though he expressed himself freely on the nature of poetry,[63] Thoreau wrote comparatively little verse deserving to be ranked above the mediocre. Nature pictures contributed to the *Dial* include "Within the circuit of this plodding life" (1842), "The river

61 Thoreau's interest in Oriental literature, initiated by passages in Chalmers' *English Poets* read before entering Harvard, stimulated by Emerson in 1838, reaching its peak in 1841 (cf. R. W. Adams, "Thoreau's Literary Apprenticeship," *SP.*, XXIX [1932], pp. 617-629) persisted through life. The Oriental Scriptures he read in French translations; his other sources of information were English. First published works showing such influence appear in 1843 in the *Dial.* What he knew of German Transcendentalism he got through Coleridge and Carlyle, whom he first read in college; Thoreau was not, like Theodore Parker and Margaret Fuller, at home in German.

62 *Classic Americans* (1931), p. 216.

63 F. W. Lorch, "Thoreau and the Organic Principle in Poetry," *PMLA.*, LIII (1938), pp. 286-302.

swelleth more and more" (1842), "The sluggish smoke curls up from some deep dell" (1843), and the unusually rhythmical "When Winter fringes every bough" (1843). Most effective personal expressions in the *Dial* are "Great God, I ask thee for no meaner pelf" (1842), "Light-winged Smoke, Icarian bird" (1843), and "Woof of the sun, ethereal gauze" (1843). The two last named are there printed under the heading, "Orphics." "Conscience is instinct bred in the house" (1849, *A Week*) in language approximating prose expresses characteristic revolt against super-sensitive goodness. "The Atlantides" (1849, *A Week*) asserts in eloquent classic imagery the solitary dignity of the soul. Poems of a highly personal nature, perhaps addressed to Ellen Sewell, include "Low in the eastern sky" (1842, *The Dial*), "The Breeze's Invitation" (1839; printed 1905), "I'm guided in the darkest night" (1840; printed 1939). The well known poem, "Sympathy" (1840, *The Dial*), long thought directed to Ellen Sewell, has been assigned[64] on adequate grounds to her brother, Edmund. Poignant expression of grief for his brother John appears in "Brother where dost thou dwell" (1843; printed 1895). "Inspiration" ("Whate'er we leave to God, God does"; printed 1863) expresses Transcendental theory of original composition, negatived in practice.

[AMOS] BRONSON ALCOTT, 1799—1888, lecturer, educator, philosopher.[65] Of rural Connecticut origin, and with education rudimentary as respects formal schooling, Alcott learned much of life from youthful peddling expeditions into various Southern states. Having experienced the inadequacy of existing educational methods, he set out to improve teaching, first in his native state (1823—1827), then in Boston (1828—1830), in Germantown, Pennsylvania (1831—1833), and again in Boston (1833—1839). Notable among these schools was the Temple School, conducted (1834—1838) in the Masonic Temple, Boston. Assisted by the intelligent and devoted Elizabeth Peabody,[66] he here introduced such novelties as organized play and gymnastics, physiology, libraries, and the honor system. His methods, characterized by an unconventional emphasis upon the "unfoldment" theories of Pestalozzi, and involving a combination of physical, artistic, ethical, and intellectual instruction through "Conversations," she described in 1835 as *The Record of a School.* To this he added (1836—1837) his own *Conversations on the Gospels Held in Mr. Alcott's School, Unfolding the Doctrine and Discipline of Human Culture.* So

---

64 H. S. Canby, *Thoreau* (1939), p. 110 *f.*; Carl Bode, *Collected Poems of Henry Thoreau* (1943), p. 347. For a more general discussion, see H. W. Wells, "An Evaluation of Thoreau's Poetry," *AL.*, XVI (1944-1945), pp. 99-109.

Cf. also Raymond Adams, review of Bode's 1943 volume, *NEQ.*, XVII (1944), p. 116 (pp. 115-117).

65 For bibliography, see page 299.

66 J. E. Roberts, "Elizabeth Peabody and the Temple School," *NEQ.*, XV (1942), pp. 497-508.

violent was the public reaction to this work, and to the unconventional trend of his teaching, that in 1838 he closed the school. From his "Conversations" with children came as a parallel development the idea of "Conversations" with adults. At first the occasion of considerable merriment, these took him in later years out of New England into many Middle Western communities where his handsome presence and sonorous voice brought him a welcome even among those who could not understand what he said. Of the New England Transcendentalists Alcott was one of the most prominent and active. He was one of the half-dozen who organized (September, 1836) the Transcendental Club and the first regular meeting was held at his house. The name of the periodical, the *Dial,* founded (1840) by the group, was his suggestion; fifty of his "Orphic Sayings" were in the first number (July, 1840). In 1842 Alcott visited England at the invitation of certain admirers who had named Alcott House in his honor. Returning home with two English friends, Lane and Wright, he established with them the next year the ill-fated project in farming and "consociate family life" known as "Fruitlands" at Harvard, Massachusetts. Late in 1844 the family moved to Concord to remain three and one-half years, a long stay for this roving family. During the following seven years they resided in six different places. Eventually, late in 1857, just before the death of his daughter Elizabeth ("Beth"), they returned to Concord to occupy Orchard House, preserved today by admirers of his more famous daughter, Louisa. Thanks to the increasing returns from her books, he enjoyed here and at the Thoreau house on Main Street, to which they moved in 1877, an increasing measure of security and comfort. Here, too, in the Concord School of Philosophy (1879—1888) he found an outlet for his peculiar talents, and achieved a measure of recognition.

[SARAH] MARGARET FULLER (Marchioness Ossoli), 1810—1850, translator, critic, editor, feminist;[67] most important American woman of letters before 1850; born at Cambridgeport, Massachusetts. Her lawyer father, a Congressman (four terms), but intellectually and politically independent, gave her, even from childhood, a severe masculine education with little or no relaxation. The result was intellectual development probably without an equal in any American woman of her day, attained, however, at the sacrifice of physique and social charm.[68] Familiar from her teens with Jefferson, Rousseau, Wollstonecraft, and the other revolutionary thinkers, she grew to womanhood, well acquainted with the German authors Novalis, Richter, Goethe (whom she profoundly admired) and, to a less degree, with Kant and Fichte.

---

67 For bibliography, see page 299.

68 Thomas Carlyle: "Yesternight there came a bevy of Americans from Emerson, one Margaret Fuller, the chief figure of them, a strange, lilting lean old maid, not nearly such a bore as I expected." Susan Coolidge (editor), "A Gallery of Contemporary Portraits," *LW.*, XVI (1885), p. 186 *f.* (pp. 185-187).

An early feminist, she took over (1839—1844) the "Conversations" initiated by Elizabeth Peabody in the latter's bookshop. Out of them grew her book, *Woman in the Nineteenth Century*† (1844), comparable in purpose and significance to Wollstonecraft's *Vindication of the Rights of Women,* and bringing its author notoriety, if not fame. A member of the so-called Transcendental Club, she became (July, 1840) editor of the *Dial,* to be succeeded by Emerson (April, 1842) when need of more lucrative employment forced her to resign. As editor she was indefatigable and herself a liberal contributor. A trip to Illinois and Wisconsin (1843), at the invitation of the J. F. Clarkes, bore fruit in *Summer on the Lakes* (1844).[69] From 1844 to 1846 she was the literary critic of the New York *Tribune* under Horace Greeley, occupying the space formerly utilized by Albert Brisbane in expounding Fourierism.[70] Her criticism was courageous and high principled, if not well written. The attacks upon the youthful Lowell and the popular idol, Longfellow, reluctantly delivered, won the praise of Poe, but brought also the storm of reproof she had anticipated. A long-deferred trip abroad (1846) took her to England, where she studied social conditions and visited the Carlyles, to Paris, and to Italy. There she became embroiled in the Italian revolution; took charge of a hospital; met, fell in love with, and married Giovanni Angelo, Marquis Ossoli, by whom she had a child. On a return journey to America (1850) all were drowned in a shipwreck within sight of her native land.

The career of Margaret Fuller and her personal contacts are more important than her works. Little that she has written will live. Her familiarity with languages, in particular with German, made her a valuable member of the Transcendental circle.[71] With Emerson she was long intimate, and, while she sought his friendship from selfish motives, the seer was frank to acknowledge the benefit he derived, and his admiration for her character.[72] Her contacts with Hawthorne, almost certainly occasioning the portraiture of Zenobia in *The Blithedale Romance,* have been the subject of some speculation.[73] Whatever the explanation, it would appear that she possessed characteristics which irritated Hawthorne, though other elements may well have entered into his feeling. Miss Fuller was unattractive physically, and mentally arrogant. She was, however, intellectually honest, and profoundly interested in the affairs of the mind and of the spirit.

---

69 R. V. Carpenter, "Margaret Fuller in Northern Illinois," *JISHS.*, II (1910), pp. 7-22.

70 H. N. McMaster, *Margaret Fuller as a Literary Critic, UBS.*, VII, No. 1 (1928); Margaret Wallace, "Margaret Fuller: Critic," *Bookman,* LXIX (1929), pp. 60-67; Roland Burton, *Margaret Fuller as a Literary Critic* (unpublished Ph.D., Iowa, 1941).

71 F. A. Braun, *Margaret Fuller and Goethe* (1910); Harry Slochower, "Margaret Fuller and Goethe," *GR.*, VII (1932), pp. 130-144.

72 H. R. Warfel, "Margaret Fuller and Ralph Waldo Emerson," *PMLA.*, L (1935), pp. 576-594.

73 Cf. page 121, footnote 62.

TRANSCENDENTALISM: MINOR FIGURES

THEODORE PARKER, 1810—1860, liberal clergyman, Abolitionist, fearless popular orator.[74] Descendent of Captain Parker, commander of colonial forces in the Lexington skirmish. Scholar and linguist, acquainted with German philosophy in the original, possessed of a huge private library, largely in other languages. Nevertheless, a practical reformer, ready to attack any evil whether slavery, war, drunkenness, poverty, severe penal codes, injustice to women.[75] Hated because of free use of personalities in pulpit, and active assistance to escaping slaves. Friend of Lincoln, who used a sentence of Parker's, with slight emendation, as the immortal conclusion of the *Gettysburg Address.*

[FREDERIC] HENRY HEDGE, 1805—1890, clergyman, scholar.[76] Born in Cambridge, Massachusetts. Precocious, he learned of the philosophy of Fichte, Schleiermacher, and Schelling by a visit to Germany (1818) with young Bancroft. Following his A.B. (Harvard, 1825), he became a clergyman, returning (1857) as professor in the Divinity School. Having encouraged Margaret Fuller, Ripley, and Clarke to study German philosophy in the original, he founded the Transcendental Club, at first nicknamed Hedge's Club. Aside from religious works (cf. *Ways of the Spirit and Other Essays,* 1877) he published *Prose Writers of Germany* (1848) made up of translations with critical introductions, and an edition of Goethe's *Faust* (1882).

JONES VERY, 1813—1880, poet.[77] Born and reared in Salem, Massachusetts, and as a lad sailed with his father on voyages to New Orleans and to Russia. Though known to few of his classmates at Harvard, he was a prize man and was invited to remain as a tutor in Greek. Unquestionably eccentric, he insisted that his Sonnets were "communicated" by the Holy Ghost, and for a time (1838) was voluntarily confined to an asylum. He was, however, to Emerson, who edited his works, "profoundly sane." W. C. Bryant pronounced his Sonnets "among the finest in the language." Though criticism has not supported this judgment, there are signs of a revival of interest in his verse and personality.

CHRISTOPHER PEARSE CRANCH, 1813—1892, minister, painter, critic, poet.[78] A graduate in theology from Harvard, he preached in the Eastern states and in St. Louis, Cincinnati, and Louisville, where he succeeded James Freeman Clarke in his pulpit

---

74 For bibliography, see page 300.

75 Cf. Russell Blankenship, *American Literature* (1931), pp. 317, 318 (315-319), who characterizes Parker as "an agrarian democrat" and places him halfway "between the two American democrats whom he most resembled, Jefferson and Lincoln."

76 O. W. Long, *Frederic Henry Hedge: A Cosmopolitan Scholar* (1940).

77 For bibliography, see page 300.

78 Cf. Leonore C. Scott, *The Life and Letters of Christopher Pearse Cranch* (1917).

and as editor of the *Western Messenger.* Contributor to the *Dial,* and associated with Brook Farm, though not an active participant. As an artist travelled abroad until 1873, when he retired to Cambridge, Massachusetts. Known chiefly for his *Poems* (1844) and his translation of Virgil's *Aeneid* (1872), he was also the author and illustrator of two amusing juveniles: *The Last of the Huggermuggers* (1856) and *Kobboltozo* (1857).

WILLIAM ELLERY CHANNING, 1818—1901, essayist, poet.[79] Born in Boston, the son of a prominent doctor, and nephew to the more famous William Ellery Channing (1780—1842) after whom he was named, Ellery Channing (as he was commonly called) distinguished himself from boyhood by his general irresponsibility in all matters of a practical character. Leaving his Harvard course incomplete, he went to live for a time in the country, then wandered to far-off Cincinnati. Returning to Concord in 1842 he became an intimate of Emerson and Thoreau, who loved him, and a trial to his wife, Ellen Fuller, to his sister-in-law, Margaret Fuller, and to Nathaniel Hawthorne, who criticized him sharply. Aside from his biography, *Thoreau: The Poet-Naturalist* (1873), his only claim to attention consists in his verse. Though irregular and faulty beyond all excuse, it possesses freshness and unconventionality which have pleased some readers. Volumes include *Poems* (1844); *Poems: Second Series* (1847); *The Woodman and Other Poems* (1849); *Near Home* (1858); *The Wanderer* (1871); *Eliot* (1885); *John Brown and the Heroes of Harper's Ferry* (1886).

ORESTES AUGUSTUS BROWNSON, 1803—1876, journalist, clergyman.[80] Vermont born. Reared a Presbyterian, he was ordained (1826) a Universalist clergyman, but, after filling several pulpits in New England and New York, drifted into Unitarianism. For a time sympathetic with the Owenites and then with plans for organizing a Workingmen's Party, he established (1836) in Boston the Society for Christian Union and Progress, a church for workers. His *New Views of Christianity, Society, and The Church* (1836) was matched in radical tone by his magazine, the *Boston Quarterly Review,* which began appearing in January, 1838. From 1842 to 1844 merged into the *United States Democratic Review* of New York, it was re-established in Boston as *Brownson's Quarterly Review,* and, despite loss of popularity resulting from his conversion (1844) to Catholicism, continued until January, 1865, and resumed in October, 1872. Though a spirited controversialist whose shifts of belief alarmed his friends, Brownson was highly regarded as a man of originality, sincerity, and social conscience.

---

79 For bibliography, see page 300.

80 For bibliography, see page 300.

Six others of his books are *Charles Elwood: or, The Infidel Converted* (1840); *The Mediatorial Life of Jesus* (1842); *The Spirit-Rapper: An Autobiography*† (romance, 1854); *The Convert: or, Leaves from My Experience*† (1857); *The American Republic: Its Constitution, Tendencies, and Destiny* (1865); *Conversation on Liberalism and the Church* (1870).

JAMES FREEMAN CLARKE, 1810—1888, Unitarian pastor, writer on religious subjects.[81] Born in Hanover, New Hampshire. Educated at the Boston Latin School and at Harvard, where he was a classmate of O. W. Holmes in the class of 1829. Graduation from the Divinity School (1833) was followed by removal to Louisville, Kentucky, where he remained until 1840, serving also (1836—1839) as editor of the *Western Messenger,* to which Channing and Emerson contributed. From 1840 on a clergyman in Boston, prominent in Transcendental circles. Among his publications are *The Christian Doctrine of Forgiveness of Sin* (1852); *The Christian Doctrine of Prayer* (1854); *Ten Great Religions*† (1871—1883); *Common Sense in Religion* (1874); *Essentials and Non-Essentials in Religion* (1878); *Self-Culture* (1882); *The Problem of the Fourth Gospel* (1886).

81 Cf. E. E. Hale, *James Freeman Clarke* (1891).

Chapter VI

THE GENTEEL TRADITION OF NEW ENGLAND: ITS MAJOR FIGURES

HENRY WADSWORTH LONGFELLOW, 1807—1882, poet.[1] Born in Portland, Maine, into a well-to-do, prominent, and cultivated family of Puritan antecedents. Prepared mostly at private schools, he attended Bowdoin College (1821—1825), where he had as classmates Hawthorne and Franklin Pierce, made a good record, read spottily in English poetry — there is no indication in his letters that he knew the leading Romantic poets — and showed an early fondness for Indian lore. Elected to the chair of Modern Languages at Bowdoin, he spent three years (1826—1829) in France, Spain,[2] Italy,[3] and Germany. Until his appointment (1834) to the chair of Modern Languages at Harvard, he was busy with teaching, translating, preparation of texts for classes, publishing only some essays and the Irvingesque *Outre-Mer* (1833—1834). On his second European trip (1835—1836), his wife, Mary Storer Potter, a Portland girl whom he had known from childhood and married in 1831, died at Rotterdam. Fame came in 1839 when he followed the mediocre prose romance, *Hyperion,* with his first collection of verse, *Voices of the Night.* His third foreign visit (1842) preceded his marriage (1843) to the lovely and well-connected Frances Elizabeth Appleton of Boston. Until his resignation of his professorship (1854) the chief events were the successive appearance of uniformly successful volumes of poems: *Ballads and Other Poems* (1841); *The Spanish Student* (1843); *Poems* (1845); *The Belfry of Bruges and Other Poems* (published December, 1845; dated 1846). *Evangeline* (1847); *The Seaside and the Fireside* (1850). In 1855 he published *The Song of Hiawatha;* in 1858 *The Courtship of Miles Standish and Other Poems.* Despite the tragic death (1861) of Mrs. Longfellow, he did not cease writing.[4]

---

1 For detailed bibliography, see pages 300-301.

2 I. L. Whitman, *Longfellow and Spain* (1927).

3 Emilio Goggio, "Italian Influences on Longfellow's Works," *R.Rev.*, XVI (1925), pp.208-222.

4 *Tales of a Wayside Inn* (1863, 1872, and in *Aftermath,* 1873); *Household Poems* (1865); *Flower-de-Luce* (1866; dated 1867), *Christus* (1872); *Three Books of Song* (1872); *The Hanging of the Crane* (1874); *The Masque of Pandora, and Other Poems* (1875); *Kéramos and Other Poems* (1878); *The White Czar and Other Poems* (1878); *From My Arm-Chair* (1879); *Bayard Taylor* (1879); *Ultima Thule* (1880); *In the Harbor* (*Ultima Thule,* Part II, 1882), the year of his death; and *Michael Angelo* (1883). His great translation of Dante's *Divina Commedia,* the work of years, appeared 1865-1867.

Longfellow's prose is consistently undistinguished. *Hyperion* (1839), aside from thinly veiled allusions to his own romantic situation,[5] is stilted sentimentalism of the German school, then widely copied. His essays contributed to the *North American Review* (1837—1838), too, are forgotten.

The popularity of Longfellow the poet was, however, enormous. By 1857 the aggregate sales of these too-frequent volumes of verse were more than 300,000 copies;[6] and in London 10,000 copies of *The Courtship of Miles Standish* were sold the first day.[7] When, in 1868, accompanied by six of his immediate family, he went abroad, his experiences resembled those of a triumphal tour. In England, following great honors on the Continent, he met every prominent literary and public man, received honorary degrees at Oxford and Cambridge, and had an audience with the Queen. Such popularity, to no small degree arising from his charming personality, could not be expected to last. But of more importance than declining sales since his death is the change in critical attitude. While Longfellow was alive, the criticisms of Poe, Simms, and Margaret Fuller, concentrating on his imitativeness (which Poe magnified into plagiarism), found little support among competent critics.[8] Today criticism is predominately unfavorable.[9] The very qualities which made him popular are today the basis of attack.

(1) Longfellow's themes were unquestionably familiar and close to people's hearts; today they are termed trite. (2) His ideas are never surprising, difficult to grasp, or daring; as such they are pronounced superficial and commonplace. (3) His treatment of love between the sexes is marked by (a) the presentation of sincere, enduring love, as in *Evangeline, Hiawatha, Miles Standish, The Hanging of the Crane;* (b) the avoidance of any acknowledgment of the facts of bodily charm or physical passion; (c) the lack of any strongly lyrical impulse, as shown in love poems directed to individuals and the like. These characteristics were to a large degree those of his age and as such made him acceptable in every family circle. It need not be pointed out that today they are out of line with trends in poetry as well as prose. (4) His didactic, moralistic observations, welcome to his generation, constituting him "a good influence," help to explain his tremendous vogue in the schools. Here, as a conspicuous instance of a tendency, Longfellow suffers the modern condemnation visited on an entire age. (5) His clearness, simplicity, tunefulness, and regularity of style, metrical

5 Lawrence Thompson, *Young Longfellow* (1938).

6 H. S. Gorman, *A Victorian American: Henry Wadsworth Longfellow* (1926), p. 279.

7 W. C. B[ronson], "Longfellow, Henry Wadsworth," *DAB.*, XI (1933), pp. 382-387. By 1900 thirty-three different translations had been made into German, including eight of *Evangeline*, and five of *Hiawatha*. Clarence Gohdes, "Longfellow and His Authorized British Publishers," *PMLA.*, LXV (1940), pp. 1165-1179.

8 Some correspondence of Lowell indicates that his private estimate may not have been one of unqualified admiration.

9 Consult, for example, Alfred Kreymborg, *Our Singing Strength* (1927), pp. 97-115.

and stanzaic form, made him quotable and easily memorized.[10] During the vogue of free verse, now subsiding, he suffered for his regularity and conventionality. (6) His preoccupation with European legendary and folk material and with the work of well-known writers needed no defense in a day when America had less culture than today and knew all too little of any other. This led, however, to much translation and downright imitation charged up today as lack of proper originality and national spirit. (7) Longfellow's employment of Nature in his verse is pleasant, but incidental and superficial; agreeable to the taste of his age without being significant of any consciously held opinion. Like Keats, he finds pleasure in Nature, but his reaction is not similarly ecstatic, nor marked by like sensuous richness. There is nothing to suggest a consciousness of Nature as a beneficent presence bringing subtle influence to bear through ecstatic moments such as Wordsworth mentions in "Tintern Abbey." Nor is there conspicuous technical facility in the use of botanical and other physical detail, as with Bryant or Tennyson. Though charming scenes and descriptive phrases of accuracy and beauty can easily be assembled from his works, Longfellow is only casually and incidentally a nature poet. (8) Burdened with his share of poignant personal losses, Longfellow nevertheless lived a sheltered life. Public issues seldom attracted his attention. Aside from a small group of antislavery poems (*Poems on Slavery,* 1842) written at the insistence of his abolitionist friend, Sumner, he took no part in the movement. Not completely uninterested as was his archcritic Poe, [11] he did not voice the convictions he confided to his Journals. For this he has been criticized, perhaps with justice. Taken in the aggregate, these qualities, good and bad, characterize the age almost as much as the man.

Beyond this, however, it has been maintained[12] that Longfellow possessed neither great intellectual power nor great creative originality. He made no profound observations upon life, wrote nothing calculated to task the comprehension of any reasonably mature mind, and tended unquestionably to lean on the work of others.[13] Another critic[14] has spoken of Longfellow's shallowness of poetic feeling. Interpreted as absence of a consuming urge toward expression, this complaint finds support in the fact that for a decade following his first European tour, in what should have been his most productive years, he wrote almost nothing but prose. He was, to be sure, busy teaching, translating, establishing himself at Bow-

10 When he was a royal guest in 1868, Queen Victoria discovered to her surprise that many of the palace servants knew his poems by heart.

11 Cf. Paul Kaufman in Norman Foerster, *The Reinterpretation of American Literature* (1928), p. 127 (pp. 114-138).

12 V. L. Parrington, *Main Currents in American Thought,* II (1927), pp. 439-441.

13 L. R. Thompson, "Longfellow's Original Sin of Imitation," *Colophon,* N.S. I (1935), pp. 97-106.

14 Van Wyck Brooks, *The Flowering of New England 1815-1865* (1936), p. 508 *ff.*

doin. Yet, at the age for love poetry, no lyrics are addressed to the childhood sweetheart he married. His interest in Indians, exhibited in college, later to flower in *Hiawatha,* lies quite in abeyance. The poetic urge was not strong.

To Longfellow's credit it may be maintained: (1) that he treated a few native themes effectively and memorably. *Evangeline, Hiawatha,* and *The Courtship of Miles Standish* are three of the four best-known long poems (*Snow-Bound* the other) in American literature, all dealing, as it happens, with solidly American themes; (2) that Longfellow did invaluable service to the culture of his native land through his foreign borrowings, even though often from second-rate authors;[15] (3) that he bids fair to retain his leadership as a popular American poet for years to come, whatever the coolness of the critics; (4) that in two fields disregarded by the public — his great Dante translation and his sonnets, including the Petrarchan sequence of six in the "Divina Commedia" — he has done first-rate work, as good as has yet been done in America.

Coplas de Manrique (1833). First published work. Is a careful translation from the Spanish of Don Jorge Manrique of what the poet terms "the most beautiful moral poem of that language," and Percy H. Boynton (*Literature and American Life,* p. 545) "a transparently veiled Spanish homily on the vanity of human wishes."

"A Psalm of Life"† (anonymously in *Knickerbocker Magazine,* 1838). Designed as self-encouragement in a period of gloom following the death of his first wife.[16] Didactic.

"The Wreck of the Hesperus"† (1840). Composed December 30, 1839, and published a few days later in the *New World,* it was based on an actual disaster on the reef of Norman's Woe near Gloucester but a few days before. Definitely an imitation of authentic popular ballads such as "Sir Patrick Spens" (see lines 13-20), the style is less literary than that of "The Skeleton in Armor" (1841).[17]

---

15 O. W. Long, *Early American Explorers of European Culture* (1935) treats George Ticknor, Edward Everett, J. G. Cogswell, George Bancroft, Longfellow, J. L. Motley; "their intellectual experiences in Germany, and — their part in the advancement of American culture in later life." Moreover, Longfellow's catholic sympathies are evident from his many poems on Oriental themes: Arthur Christy in his "Introduction" to *The Leap of Roushan Beg* (1931).

16 C. L. Johnson, "Three Notes on Longfellow," *HSNPL.*, XIV (1932), pp. 249-271; F. L. Pattee, *The First Century of American Literature, 1770-1870* (1935), p. 524 *f.*, says: ". . . had first been made public in a lecture to his Harvard class on Goethe — doubtless to illustrate the spirit of *Wilhelm Meister*. . . . Life is no longer a dream (as in the *Sorrows of Werther*) but a place for work"; William Charvat, "Let us then be up and doing," *English Journal*, XXVIII (1939), pp. 374-383.

17 In its dialogue not unlike Goethe's "Erlkönig," set to music by Schubert. Cf. Henry Beston, "The Real Wreck of the Hesperus," *Bookman*, LXI (1925), pp. 304-306 [Anonymous], "Longfellow's 'Wreck of the Hesperus': 'The Reef of Norman's Woe,'" *NQ.*, CLXVII (1934), p. 59; L. R. Thompson, *Young Longfellow* (1938), p. 309 G. L. White, Jr., "Longfellow's Interest in Scandinavia during the Years 1835-1847," *SSN.*, XVII (1942), p. 74 ff. (pp. 70-82).

The Spanish Student (1840—1842; published 1842 in *Graham's Magazine*).[18] Longfellow's first venture in drama, it afforded no encouragement to the author to continue in the field. In 1844 Poe charged that it contained passages plagiarized from "The Raven."

Evangeline† (1845—1847; 1847). Based on a story told to Longfellow by a Boston clergyman who had it from a parishioner. Hawthorne, who brought the visitor to Longfellow, had been asked to write the story but had declined. Whittier abandoned a like project.[19] Unacquainted by contact with any of the regions described,[20] Longfellow read T. C. Haliburton's *An Historical and Statistical Account of Nova Scotia* (1829), books on the Mississippi and the great plains, visited a "diorama" of the Mississippi region currently on exhibition in Boston, and, reportedly, interviewed a Harvard student from Louisiana. Resemblances in treatment between *Evangeline* and Goethe's *Hermann und Dorothea* have aroused comment, including the hexameter verse in which Longfellow's success was so outstanding. Events recorded, less brutal and more defensible than indicated, occupied years 1763—1855, involved 6,000 persons. Was originally to have been named "Gabrielle." [21]

The Building of the Ship† (1850). Outstanding (1) as one of Longfellow's few vigorous poems devoted to national issues; (2) because of the timeliness of its admonitions in a year when the Fugitive Slave Bill was being signed, the Free Soil Party being formed, and Webster's Seventh of March speech delivered; (3) because of Longfellow's familiarity as a Maine man with the process of ship-building, including technical terminology; (4) because of the superb peroration.[22] In structure, resemblance has been noted to Schiller's *Song of the Bell.*[23]

The Song of Hiawatha† (1855).[24] Reflects a lifelong interest in

---

18 L. R. Thompson, "Longfellow Sells *The Spanish Student*," *AL.*, VI (1934-1935), pp. 141-150.

19 J. W. Bowker, Jr., and J. A. Russell, "The Background of Longfellow's Evangeline," *QQ.*, XXXIX (1932), pp. 489-494.

20 Other than the Philadelphia setting of the final scene which he had visited immediately before sailing on his first trip to Europe.

21 For additional information see Archibald MacMechan, "Evangeline and the Real Acadians," *Atl.*, XCIX (1907), pp. 202-213; M. G. Hill, "Some of Longfellow's Sources for the Second Part of Evangeline," *PMLA.*, XXXI (1916), pp. 161-180; Clifford Millard, "The Acadians in Virginia," *VMHB.*, XL (1932), pp. 241-258; J. B. Brebner, "The Brown Mss. and Longfellow," *CHR.*, XVII (1936), pp. 172-178.

22 O. S. Coad ("The Bride of the Sea," *AL.*, IX [1937-1938], pp. 71-73) points out striking resemblance of the stanzas describing the launching to a Whittier poem, "The Ship-Builders" (*United States Magazine, and Democratic Review*, April, 1846).

23 "Ein Längeres Gedicht *The Building of the Ship*, steht in seinem Aufbau Schillers *Glocke* nahe. . . ." J. T. Hatfield, *Four Lectures* (1936), p. 51 (pp. 43-55).

24 Stith Thompson, "The Indian Legend of Hiawatha," *PMLA.*, XXXVII (1922), pp. 128-140; H. S. Gorman, *A Victorian American: Henry Wadsworth Longfellow* (1926), p. 275; J. A. Russell, "Longfellow: Interpreter of the Historical and the Romantic Indian," *JAH.*, XXII (1928), pp. 327-347; W. L. Schramm, "Hiawatha and Its Predecessors," *PQ.*, XI (1932), pp. 321-343; Dorothy Werner, *The Idea of Union in American Verse* (1932), p. 49; P. H. Boynton, *Literature and American Life* (1936), p. 548; F. L. Pattee, *The Feminine Fifties* (1940), p. 167 *ff.*
Parodies of Hiawatha include W. N. Lettsom, *The Song of Floggawaya* (1856),

Indians. In college Longfellow read Heckewelder's *Account of the History, Manners, and Customs of the Indian Nations of Pennsylvania and the Neighboring States* and absorbed the kindly Moravian's romantic attitude. At eighteen he wrote "The Burial of the Minnisink" (1825). Had often encountered Indians as a boy, had seen Black Hawk in Boston in 1837, and conversed with an Ojibway chief in 1849. But chief dependence was on H. R. Schoolcraft's *History of the Indian Tribes of the United States.* Like Schoolcraft, Longfellow confuses the Iroquois Hiawatha with the less admirable Ojibway Manabozho. He also introduces incongruous sentimentalism in the love story and employs names from far separated tribes. Setting of the poem is on the south shore of Lake Superior. The meter, unrhymed trochaic tetrameter, was frankly borrowed from the *Kalevala,* a Finnish epic. Two sections have been used by the Negro composer Samuel Coleridge-Taylor for tuneful choral compositions, "Hiawatha's Wedding Feast" and "The Death of Minnehaha."

The Courtship of Miles Standish† (1858). Based on careful reading of Bradford's *History of Plymouth Plantation* and several other authoritative works, it deals with ancestral figures; hence, perhaps, its kindly treatment of a Pilgrim romance. Less sentimental than *Evangeline.*

"My Lost Youth"† (1855; 1858). Exquisite tribute to his romance-tinged youth of ships and sturdy seafaring folk. The famous refrain is a precise translation of Herder (*Stimmen der Völker in Liedern*), who got it from Johannes Scheffer of Upsala's *Lapponia* (1673, Latin), who had translated it from a Lapp original.[25]

Tales of a Wayside Inn† (Part I, 1863; Second Day, 1872; Third Part, in *Aftermath,* 1873). Series of narrative poems written in the pattern of the *Decameron,* was to have been called "Sudbury Tales" after the Howe Tavern at Sudbury, Massachusetts, its setting. It included the previously written "Paul Revere's Ride,"† "The Legend of Rabbi Ben Levi," and "The Saga of King Olaf." Also included are "King Robert of Sicily" and "The Birds of Killingworth."

The Divine Comedy (1867). Produced with the assistance of C. E. Norton, J. R. Lowell, and W. D. Howells, who passed upon the translation line by line. The device was perhaps suggested, says Van Wyck Brooks (*The Flowering of New England,* p. 331), by the gathering in Dresden at which Ticknor heard Tieck read aloud his translation of Dante into German.

[Anonymous], *Kwai! Ong-We-Ong-We! Oushat. Halloo! An Indian! Winter!* (1856), Lewis Carroll, "Hiawatha's Photographing" (1857), J. W. Ward, *The Song of Higher Water* (1868), C. B. M. Heywood, "Hiawatha at Cambridge," *LM.*, XXVII (1932-1933), pp. 6-30, and Owen Rutter, *Tradatha* (revised, 1935).

25 J. T. Hatfield, "Longfellow's 'Lapland Song,'" *PMLA.*, XLV (1930), pp. 1188-1192.

***Christus: A Mystery*†** (1872). One of Longfellow's most ambitious projects, but one of his most labored and unsuccessful. Three parts: I — "The Divine Tragedy," the Gospel story, published separately the year previous; and introducing a miracle play, "The Nativity"; II — "The Golden Legend"† (1851) made up of nine episodes like a miracle cycle, and telling "a typical mediaeval tale of a sick Prince, aided by Lucifer, and then saved by a pure maiden"; III — "The New England Tragedies" (1868) treating colonial episodes in dramatic form and made up of the five-act plays, "John Endicott" and "Giles Corey of the Salem Farms." Apparently influenced by *Der Arme Heinrich.*[26]

The Hanging of the Crane (published 1874, but, according to T. B. Aldrich whose new home suggested the idea, conceived early in 1867). Tenderness of such passages as that numbered III parallels the poet's sonnet "Nature." An interesting musical parallel may be noted in John Alden Carpenter's orchestral sketch, "Adventures in a Perambulator."

"Morituri Salutamus"† (1875). Read by the poet at the fiftieth anniversary exercises of his college class, that summer at Brunswick, Maine. The comparison with Tennyson's "Ulysses" (1842) and Browning's "Rabbi Ben Ezra" (1864) is obvious. Note the quality of versified oratory, conspicuous in the close-knit progressive thought. Rhymed pentameter.

"Three Friends of Mine" (1875). Touchingly records the loss of C. C. Felton, one of Longfellow's oldest Cambridge friends; Louis Agassiz, a member of the Saturday Club and also celebrated in Lowell's "Agassiz"; and Charles Sumner, Longfellow's closest friend. Allusions to the meanderings of the Charles River, and to Mount Auburn Cemetery give the poem a local flavor.

Sonnets. Longfellow's success with the sonnet form is outstanding.[27] "Mezzo Cammin" (1842; 1886) is autobiographical, written at the age of 35; The six *Divine Comedy* sonnets† (1864—1867; 1867) were used, the first two to preface the "Inferno," the next two the "Purgatorio," and the final two the "Paradiso." The sonnets translated from Michael Angelo were originally designed to be included in *Michael Angelo: A Fragment,* left incomplete at the poet's death.

JOHN GREENLEAF WHITTIER, 1807—1892, poet.[28] Born near Amesbury, Massachusetts, of a family settled in America in 1638; Quaker for some generations. His permanent handi-

---

26 J. T. Krumpelman, "Longfellow's 'Golden Legend' and the 'Arme Heinrich' Theme in Modern German Literature," *JEGP.*, XXV (1926), pp. 137-192.

27 P. E. More, *Shelburne Essays,* Fifth Series (1908), pp. 132-157.

28 For a biography, criticism, and bibliography see John B. Pickard, *John Greenleaf Whittier* (Barnes & Noble, 1961); see also bibliography on pp. 301-2 of this work.

caps were several: ill health resulting from exposure and over-exertion; partial deafness; color blindness;[29] a meagre education; and, from various factors including poverty and family responsibilities, a resulting narrow and provincial experience. Early contact with W. L. Garrison developed a native dislike of slavery into aggressive opposition;[30] diverted him at least partially from the field of practical politics in which he had ambition and natural skill. Too fluent a pen, and too ready a medium in the various papers he edited;[31] produced quantities of forgotten verse and prose, much of it only recently collected. The prolific, varied, and ill-controlled nature of his creative impulse may be suggested by the fact that the list of individual volumes published during his lifetime numbers no fewer than forty.[32] Of his best verse[33] little is controversial, much religious, rural, and regional. Despite his earnestness, Whittier's personal kindliness kept him free of wartime hates. His old age was sunny and marked by nation-wide tributes.

IMPORTANT PROSE PIECE

Leaves from Margaret Smith's Journal† (1848). Semi-fictional romance is an admirable picture of colonial times, perhaps Whittier's best piece of creative prose.[34]

IMPORTANT POEM

Snow-Bound† (1865; 1866). Occupies a unique place in American poetry as an accurate but charming regional and period picture, counterpart of Burns's "Cotter's Saturday Night." The house mentioned, Whittier's birthplace, still stands, but the barn described is not that first erected on the site. The uncle referred to died from a blow by a tree he was felling. The aunt, who had lost her betrothed years before, had seen a ghostly visitor the night of his

---

29 Desmond Powell, "Whittier," *AL.*, IX (1937-1938), pp. 335-342.

30 Cf. "To William Lloyd Garrison" (1831) in which he acknowledges his debt.

31 Bertha-Monica Stearns, "John Greenleaf Whittier, Editor," *NEQ.*, XIII (1940), pp. 280-304.

32 *Legends of New-England* (1831); *Moll Pitcher* (1832); *Justice and Expediency* (1833); *The Song of the Vermonters* (1833); *Mogg Megone* (1836); *Poems Written during the Progress of the Abolition Question in the United States, between the Years 1830 and 1838* (1837); *Narrative of James Williams* (1838); *Poems* (1838); *Lays of My Home* (1843); *Ballads and Other Poems* (1844); *The Stranger in Lowell* (1845); *Voices of Freedom* (1846); *The Supernaturalism of New England* (1847); *Poems* (1849); *Leaves from Margaret Smith's Journal* (1849); *Old Portraits and Modern Sketches* (1850); *Songs of Labor and Other Poems* (1850); *The Chapel of the Hermits* (1853); *Literary Recreations and Miscellanies* (1854); *The Panorama* (1856); *Poetical Works* (1857); *The Sycamores* (1857); *Home Ballads* (1860); *In War Time and Other Poems* (1864); *National Lyrics* (1865); *Snow-Bound* (1866); *The Tent on the Beach* (1867); *Among the Hills* (1869); *Miriam and Other Poems* (1871); *The Pennsylvania Pilgrim* (1872); *Hazel-Blossoms* (1875); *Mabel Martin* (1876); *Centennial Hymn* (1876); *The Vision of Echard* (1878); *The King's Missive* (1881); *The Bay of Seven Islands* (1883); *Saint Gregory's Guest* (1886); *At Sundown* (1890); *The Demon Lady* (1894).

33 W. T. Scott, "Poetry in America: A New Consideration of Whittier's Verse," *NEQ.*, VII (1934), pp. 258-275.

34 C. B. Williams, *Margaret Smith's Journal* (Ph.D., Chicago, 1933); also, G. R. Carpenter, *John Greenleaf Whittier* (1903), p. 245; V. L. Parrington, *Main Currents in American Thought*, II (1927), p. 363 *f.*

death much as did the maiden in Bürger's "Lenore." The sister whose death is mentioned with such tenderness had died the year preceding the writing of the poem.[35] Its persisting popularity has resulted in part from the halo of memory which the author has thrown over scenes familiar to hosts of New Englanders scattered over America; but also from its touching genuineness and the exquisite beauty of the conclusion.[36]

SHORTER POEMS

SLAVERY. "Massachusetts to Virginia"† (1843), occasioned by the arrest in Massachusetts of George Latimer, alleged fugitive slave, is a powerful poem (notably ll. 69-84) illustrating the influence of an intrinsically unimportant incident in crystallizing wavering public opinion. Cf. also "A Sabbath Scene" (1850). "Randolph of Roanoke" (1847)[37] pays tribute to a proud Virginian who, dying, freed his slaves rather than risk their passing into unkind hands. "Ichabod"† (1850), occasioned by Webster's Seventh of March speech, "in support of the 'Compromise' and the Fugitive Slave Law" (Whittier), should be balanced by the later and kindlier poem, "The Lost Occasion" (1880). "Brown of Ossawatomie" (1859) and "Barbara Frietchie"† (1863)[38] are ballads with a dubious factual basis. "Laus Deo!"† (1865) celebrated that year's ratification of the Constitutional amendment abolishing slavery. Another excellent antislavery poem is "The Farewell of a Virginia Slave Mother" (1838).

COLONIAL. "Cassandra Southwick" (1843) recounts persecution (1658) of a rebel against the established church. "The Garrison of Cape Ann" (1857) retells an incident from Cotton Mather's *Magnalia* designed to illustrate the triumph of godliness over the supernatural forces of darkness. "The Wreck of Rivermouth" (1864) narrates a disaster at sea predicted by a witch; the "Father Bachiler" of the poem may be a reminiscence of a Stephen Bachiler in Whittier's own ancestry. Whittier's interest in colonial themes and times turns often in the direction of witchcraft.[39] Among such poems are "The Weird Gathering" (1831), "Moll Pitcher"† (1832), "Mabel Martin" (1857), "The Prophecy of Samuel Sewall" (1859), "The Witch of Wenham" (1877), and "Calef in Boston" (1849). "The Palatine" (1867) recounts the reappearance

35 N. L. Sayles, "A Note on Whittier's *Snow-Bound*," *AL.*, VI (1934-1935), p. 336 *f.*; H. L. Drew, "The Schoolmaster in *Snow-Bound*," *AL.*, IX (1937-1938), p. 243 *f.*

36 "The portraits given are drawn with affectionate care against a background of consummate fidelity. Here is the simple, vivid rendering of a Flemish canvas. Here is simplicity and elemental poetry." G. S. Bryan, "Foreword," p. 5 (pp. 3-5), in *Snow-Bound* (1930).

37 M. H. Coleman, "Whittier on John Randolph of Roanoke," *NEQ.*, VIII (1935), pp. 551-555.

38 D. M. Quynn and W. R. Quynn, *Barbara Frietschie* (1942).

39 G. H. Orians, "New England Witchcraft in Fiction," *AL.*, II (1930-1931), p. 54 *ff.* (pp. 54-71).

of a blazing ship, lured to disaster a century before by false lights placed by "wreckers." Cf. Clemence Dane's play, *Granite* (1926), and Daphne du Maurier's *Jamaica Inn* (1937), dealing with those of Cornwall. "The Sisters" (1858) is a stirring ballad of two sisters loving the same man, betrothed to one, but so much better loved by the other that she knows by telepathy the moment of his death at sea. "Abraham Davenport" (1866) repeats a colonial incident. Quieter pictures are "The Shoemakers" (1845) and "The Huskers" (1847). "Skipper Ireson's Ride"† (1828, 1857; 1857),[40] one of the poet's best ballads, with a rich dialect, deals with a Marblehead occurrence of almost his own day. "Amy Wentworth" (1862), commending a marriage of wealth with poverty, perhaps expresses a personal attitude.

PERSONAL. Treasured pictures of boyhood years appear in "In School-Days" (1870) and "The Barefoot Boy"† (1855).[41] "My Playmate" (1860) alludes to a distant relative, Mary Emerson Smith, married in 1832, with whom he was once passionately in love, even to willingness to marry her "out of meeting." "Memories" (1832, 1841; 1843) either refers to Mary or recalls his close friendship with Lucy Hooper, who died in 1841.[42] "Telling the Bees"† (1858), one of his loveliest poems, preserves an old-country folk custom transplanted to rural New England. Presenting a mature view, more poised and philosophical, are "Benedicite" (1851), "Among the Hills" (1868), and "The Waiting" (1862). "Proem"† (1847; 1849) and "Response" (1878), the latter read at a dinner given for him on his seventieth birthday, are excellent self-criticism and deserve close study. Marked, too, with a strongly personal flavor are the poems in which he acknowledges his essentially provincial devotion to the immediate region of his birth. Such a poem is "The Last Walk in Autumn" (1857). "Our River" (1861) and the rather Byronic "The Merrimack" (1841) deal with the same stream. "Hampton Beach" (1843) and "Sunset on the Bearcamp" (1876) are Wordsworthian in their love of nature. "Summer by the Lakeside" (1853) introduces a note of religious faith.

RELIGIOUS. Whittier's interest in Oriental literature has recently been emphasized.[43] Outstanding is the definitely Transcendental "The Over-Heart" (1859), close in thought to Emerson's "The Over-Soul." "Miriam" (1871) has a background of comparative religions, with some paraphrased Oriental philosophy at the end. Similar is the material included in "Oriental Maxims" (1881).

40 E. E. Ericson, "'John Hort' and 'Skipper Ireson,'" *NEQ.*, X (1937), p. 531 *f.*

41 N. F. Adkins, "Whittier's 'The Barefoot Boy,'" *NQ.*, CLXV (1933), p. 78 *f.*

42 Albert Mordell, "Whittier and Lucy Hooper," *NEQ.*, VII (1934), pp. 316-325.

43 Arthur Christy, "Orientalism in New England: Whittier," *AL.*, I (1929-1930), pp. 372-392; "The Orientalism of Whittier," *AL.*, V (1933-1934), pp. 247-257.

Others in the group are "The Two Rabbi[n]s" (1868), "Rabbi Ishmael" (1881), "The Khan's Devil" (1879), and "Requital" (1885). Definitely Quaker are "The Meeting" (1868) and "First-Day Thoughts" (1853). "My Psalm" (1859) shows mature adjustment to things as they are. "The Preacher" (1859) is a fair and understanding character sketch of George Whitefield, the great English evangelist of the mid-eighteenth century, buried in the Federal Street Church, Newburyport, close to Whittier's birthplace. Whitefield accomplished great good but gave tacit approval to the slave trade by soliciting its profits for the support of his own work. "The Eternal Goodness" (1865) and "Our Master" (1866) are hymns now often heard in the services of other sects.

MISCELLANEOUS. Included among the poems must be the popular but hastily written "Maud Muller"† (1854); the narratives, "The Pipes at Lucknow" (1858) and "The Angels of Buena Vista" (1847); and his tributes to personalities, notably "Kossuth" (1851), "Burns" (1854), and "Our Autocrat" (1879).

NATHANIEL HAWTHORNE, 1804—1864, short-story writer, novelist.[44] Born in Salem, Massachusetts, Hawthorne inherited from seafaring ancestors, then named Hathorne, a familiarity with nautical affairs and a capacity for business. The first is sparingly revealed in the opening of *The House of the Seven Gables;* the second helped him through his official duties at Boston, Salem, and Liverpool; inspired the opening chapter of *The Scarlet Letter;* and occasioned the volume *Our Old Home.* Two years of boyhood inactivity resulting from an injury, and long visits over several years to the Maine Woods, doubtless strengthened, even before college days, an ingrained fondness for solitude. At Bowdoin, where he had as friends Longfellow, Franklin Pierce, and Horatio Bridge, he won, it is true, a certain reputation for conviviality as well as literary talent; but when, following graduation (1825), he returned to Salem, it was to a retirement unbroken, except for the anonymous appearance of *Fanshawe* (1828), until the publication of *Twice-Told Tales* in 1837.

Products of college days and those immediately following are *Seven Tales of My Native Land* (1825, unpublished) and *Fanshawe* (1828), which he called in and destroyed.[45] Other stories, including "The Gray Champion," appeared in *The Token,* the *Salem Gazette,* and the *New England Magazine.* The second series of *Twice-Told Tales* (1842) was followed in 1846 by *Mosses from an Old Manse,* a collection different only as respects the greater length and imaginative range of the stories included. Hawthorne had in the meantime (1839—1840) occupied the position of measurer in the Boston Custom House; published (1841) *Grandfather's*

44 For analysis of Hawthorne's mind and work, see Arlin Turner, *Nathaniel Hawthorne* (Barnes & Noble, 1961). Full bibliography is on pp. 302-3 of this work.

45 G. H. Orians, "Scott and Hawthorne's *Fanshawe,*" *NEQ.,* XI (1938), pp. 388-394.

Chair, first of several successful volumes of stories for children; resided (1841) for a few months at Brook Farm; married Sophia Peabody (1842) and moved to the "Old Manse," Concord. In 1846 he returned to Salem as governor of the port. The change was important, not only because it was here that he completed *The Scarlet Letter* (1850), but because it contributed descriptive detail to *The House of the Seven Gables* (1851). Deprived of his post (1849), he resided for a time at Lenox in western Massachusetts, at West Newton, and at "Wayside," Concord, which he purchased as a home. As a reward for writing a campaign life of his classmate Franklin Pierce, then candidate for president, he was appointed U.S. consul (1853—1856) in Liverpool, England. Residence in Rome (1858—1859) provided inspiration and setting for *The Marble Faun* (1860). Following return (1860) to Wayside, Hawthorne struggled against declining health, publishing recollections of his English experiences in *Our Old Home* (1863), and attempting other projects which he left uncompleted when he died (1864) while driving through New Hampshire with Pierce.

Hawthorne was thirty-three when his first important work, the first (1837) edition of *Twice-Told Tales,* was published; forty-six when fame found him with the printing of *The Scarlet Letter.* By that date Poe was dead and Cooper about to die; and there was no fictional artist in America to dispute his sway. Nor did any rival appear subsequently, though absence from the country, declining creative powers, and the public preoccupation with great national issues lessened his popularity.

With respect to his technical attainments, critics are in substantial agreement. More than with most, his style was a natural gift, recognized even in college. It was, however, perfected by years of conscious effort before any of his finished work became widely known. His vocabulary is superbly adequate without the offensive repetition of pet words encountered in Poe. The contribution of verbal art to the mass effect of his outstanding scenes is not to be denied. Less can be said for his achievement in other directions. Though the creator of a few memorable characters, Hawthorne cannot be called a master of characterization. Pearl, a shadowy copy of his own daughter Una, convinces many critics that Hawthorne could not draw children. Still less was he a plot maker. *The Scarlet Letter,* an expanded short story, is a series of tableau-like scenes. *The Blithedale Romance* is marred by mechanical manipulation of characters of an obvious sort. *The House of the Seven Gables* shows bad distribution of space. His superlative, and indeed his unique, achievement lies in the dignity of his themes, in the creation of effects, in the perfect adaptation of every detail to the production of a single impression.

SHORT STORIES

Among his best tales are "The Great Stone Face" (1851), "Wakefield" (1835), "The Gray Champion"† (1837), "Dr. Heidegger's Experiment"† (1837), "Drowne's Wooden Image" (1846), "The Birthmark"† (1846), "Rappaccini's Daughter"† (1846), "The Celestial Railroad"† (1846), and "The Ambitious Guest"† (1842). Speaking generally, the themes of his stories fall into the following classifications: (1) incapacity to mingle with men; (2) hidden sin; (3) the scientific impulse run riot;[46] (4) pure fantasy; (5) episodes from colonial history. This variety of themes and materials results[47] from fairly extensive vacation trips to the Berkshires, White Mountains, Connecticut, Niagara Falls, on which he had a much better time than has been assumed on the basis of the emasculated journals published by his wife.[48] Hawthorne was not blind to a pretty face nor unresponsive to a salty masculine joke.

On the other hand it would be foolish to deny the preponderant element of history and tradition. Not only has investigation shown that he was a voluminous, though casual, reader of colonial literature,[49] but that upon occasion he leaned heavily upon particular sources. G. Harrison Orians[50] and Miss F. N. Cherry[51] have traced "Young Goodman Brown"† (1846) to a Cervantes story, "El Coloquio de los Perros." Arlin Turner[52] traces it to Cotton Mather's *Wonders of the Invisible World*. "The Gray Champion," which had its basis in a historic Indian attack just 100 years before the beginning of the American Revolution, retells an incident which G. H. Orians says[53] had appeared in a series of historical works beginning with Governor Thomas Hutchinson's *History of Massachusetts* (1765). Randall Stewart shows[54] that "The Birthmark" (1846) drew heavily upon a passage in Combe's *Physiology* cited in the notebooks. Similar investigations have been directed at "Lady Eleanore's Mantle"† (1837),[55] "Dr. Heidegger's Experiment" (1837),[56] "The Maypole of Merry-Mount"† (1837),[57]

---

46 Hawthorne's best tales, says F. L. Pattee (in *The Development of the American Short Story* [1923], pp. 91-115), are "sermons, each with a test to which its author rigidly adheres. . . ."

47 Carl Van Doren, *The American Novel* (1940), p. 61.

48 Randall Stewart, *The American Notebooks of Nathaniel Hawthorne* (1932).

49 [Anonymous], "Books Read by Nathaniel Hawthorne, 1828-1859," *EIHC.*, LXVIII (1932), pp. 65-87; also, G. P. Lathrop, *A Study of Hawthorne* (1876).

50 "New England Witchcraft in Fiction," *AL.*, II (1930-1931), pp. 54-71.

51 "The Sources of Hawthorne's 'Young Goodman Brown,'" *AL.*, V (1933-1934), pp. 342-348.

52 "Hawthorne's Literary Borrowings," *PMLA.*, LI (1936), pp. 543-562.

53 "The Angel of Hadley in Fiction," *AL.*, IV (1932-1933), pp. 257-269.

54 *The American Notebooks of Nathaniel Hawthorne* (1932), XXV.

55 F. N. Cherry, "A Note on the Source of Hawthorne's 'Lady Eleanore's Mantle,'" *AL.*, VI (1934-1935), pp. 437-439.

56 Louise Hastings, "An Origin for 'Dr. Heidegger's Experiment,'" *AL.*, IX (1937-1938), pp. 403-410; A. L. Cooke, "Some Evidences of Hawthorne's Indebtedness to Swift," *UTSE.*, (1938), p. 143 *ff.* (pp. 140-162).

57 G. H. Orians, "Hawthorne and 'The Maypole of Merry-Mount,'" *MLN.*, LIII (1938), pp. 159-167; D. F. Connors, "Thomas Morton of Merry Mount: His First Arrival in New England," *AL.*, XI (1939-1940), pp. 160-166.

"Roger Malvin's Burial"† (1846),[58] "Fancy's Show Box" (1837),[59] "Howe's Masquerade"† (1837).[60] Proper names throughout his stories and novels have been traced by Arlin Turner to Mather and Sewall, including Goodman Brown, Dr. Dolliver, Judge Pyncheon, Matthew Maule, and Ethan Brand.

ROMANTIC NOVELS

The Scarlet Letter† (1850). Doubtless inspired by the narrative in John Winthrop's journal of the punishment of one Mary Latham, it was the outgrowth of an earlier short story, "Endicott and the Red Cross" (1837), in which an embroidered *A* is mentioned. *The Scarlet Letter* illustrates the precise nature of Hawthorne's interest in the past. Instead of the continuous narrative of the historian, it consists of a series of vivid scenes from which the antiquarian data he could so easily have supplied have been rigorously excluded. Emphatically not a love story, it is concerned with conscience and the effects of concealed sin rather than with sin itself. Interrelations of the characters are secondary to the struggle of each character with his own conscience. Hawthorne does not pronounce judgment, yet none escapes punishment of one kind or another. Considering the date of writing and the rigid morality of the author, the treatment of sex sin, and in particular of an erring woman, is remarkably sympathetic and charitable; indeed, Chillingworth the husband, who commits no offense against public morals, is punished for violating a principle sacred to Hawthorne in tyrannizing over another personality. Sin is thus broadly interpreted; but in the conception of the inevitability of punishment the book is essentially Puritan.

The House of the Seven Gables† (1851). With a Salem setting, makes use of family history in the form of a curse traditionally hurled at the author's witch-hanging great-grandfather, stresses descriptive elements, introduces in Judge Pyncheon a character avowedly modeled upon the Reverend Charles W. Upham, a politician whom Hawthorne thought responsible for his removal from his post at the Salem Custom House. Evils of heredity and inbreeding are stressed in the Judge, Hepzibah, and Clifford, who are contrasted with the normal, if not highly developed, natures of Phoebe and Holgrave. Gothic touch appears in the description of the portrait seeming about to leave its frame, and concealing a secret compartment.

The Blithedale Romance† (1852). Hawthorne made use of Brook Farm as a setting "merely to establish a theatre, a little re-

---

58 G. H. Orians, "The Source of Hawthorne's 'Roger Malvin's Burial,'" *AL.*, X (1938-1939), pp. 313-318.

59 N. F. Doubleday, "The Theme of Hawthorne's 'Fancy's Show Box,'" *AL.*, X (1938-1939), pp. 341-343.

60 H. E. Thorner, "Hawthorne, Poe, and a Literary Ghost," *NEQ.*, VII (1934), pp. 146-154.

moved from the highway of ordinary travel, where the creatures of his brain may play their phantasmagorical antics without exposing them to too clear a comparison with the actual events of real lives."[61] Though not consciously misleading, this seems to most scholars an understatement. Hollingsworth may be Theodore Parker; more plausibly, Coverdale may be the author. Aside from her beauty, which scarcely fits, Zenobia has striking points of resemblance to Margaret Fuller; the unfavorable portrait seemingly resulted from a dislike of long standing. Some attempt has also been made to identify the original as Fanny Kemble, the actress, whom Hawthorne knew at Lenox, Massachusetts, in 1851.[62]

Termed by Henry James "the lightest, the brightest, the liveliest" of Hawthorne's books, *The Blithedale Romance* suffers from lack of any absorbing theme, and from a badly articulated plot. Coverdale, the narrator, a prejudiced participant in the action, cannot reveal what goes on in the minds of others. In some novels unimportant, this technique is here a serious obstacle. The satire upon Hollingsworth exhibits a disbelief in philanthropists, paralleling that expressed by Thoreau near the end of the first chapter of *Walden.*

***The Marble Faun*†** (1860). Last and longest novel, published in England as *Transformation,* is really misnamed, since a faunlike human being, not the marble faun of Praxiteles, is its central character. The ravages of guilt in his nature — in Miriam, who permitted the crime to be committed; and in Hilda, who had knowledge of what was done — constitute the real theme. Symbolism like that of the *Scarlet Letter* reappears in the adroit hinting at animallike ears on the head of Donatello. Partly because of the writer's inexperience, partly because such material had then reader interest, extensive — indeed disproportionate — use is made of the artistic background. Conspicuous is his Protestant bias against religious paintings and the Catholic Church, his provincial prejudice against the nudity of classical sculpture.

OLIVER WENDELL HOLMES, 1809—1894, essayist, poet,[63] novelist. Of fine English and Dutch colonial ancestry, closely connected with half a dozen of the best Boston families, the son of a prominent and scholarly Cambridge clergyman, and bearing the name of his maternal grandfather, the Hon. Oliver Wendell, Holmes had justifiable bases for his pride in family. From Phillips

---

61 Quoted in Carl Van Doren, *The American Novel* (1940), p. 75.

62 Cf. Van Wyck Brooks, *The Flowering of New England 1815-1865* (1936), pp. 382-383, 431; Oscar Cargill, "Nemesis and Nathaniel Hawthorne," *PMLA.*, LII (1937), p. 849 (pp. 848-861); W. P. Randel, "Hawthorne, Channing, and Margaret Fuller," *AL.*, X (1938-1939), pp. 472-476; Austin Warren, "Hawthorne, Margaret Fuller, and 'Nemesis,'" *PMLA.*, LIV (1939), p. 615 (pp. 615-618).

63 For full bibliography, see pages 303-304.

Andover he went to Harvard (1825); graduating (1829) in a class for which he wrote close to forty reunion poems. After a trial year in the Harvard Law School he studied medicine, first in Boston, then (1833—1835) in Paris, taking his M.D. (1836) at Harvard. In 1837 and 1838 he won Boylston prizes for three medical essays. From 1838—1840 he was Professor of Anatomy at Dartmouth. In 1847, following private practice and teaching, he became Professor of Anatomy and Physiology at Harvard, dropping the latter branch in 1871, and retiring, emeritus, in 1882. The essay "The Contagiousness of Puerperal Fever," read before the Boston Society for Medical Improvement and published (1843) in the *New England Quarterly Journal of Medicine and Surgery,* aroused controversy, but caused important reforms in hospital procedure.[64] Holmes had an important part in founding (1857) the *Atlantic Monthly,* contributing to its first number an instalment of the *Autocrat*. The Lowell Institute Lectures on *The English Poets of the Nineteenth Century* were delivered in 1853. Holmes visited Europe in 1886, receiving honorary degrees from both English universities. He died in 1894. Dates of his chief works are as follows: *Old Ironsides* (1830); *Poems* (1836); *Boylston Prize Dissertations* (1838); *Homeopathy and Its Kindred Delusions* (1842); *The Contagiousness of Puerperal Fever*† (1843); *Poems* (1846); *Urania: A Rhymed Lesson* (1846); *Poems* (1849); *The Autocrat of the Breakfast Table* (1858); *The Professor at the Breakfast Table* (1860); *Elsie Venner* (1861); *Songs in Many Keys* (1862); *Soundings from the Atlantic* (1864); *Humorous Poems* (1865); *The Guardian Angel* (1867); *The Poet at the Breakfast-Table* (1872); *Songs of Many Seasons* (1875); *John Lothrop Motley: A Memoir* (1879); *The Iron Gate, and Other Poems* (1880); *Medical Essays 1842—1882* (1883); *Pages from an Old Volume of Life* (1883); *A Mortal Antipathy* (1885); *Ralph Waldo Emerson,* American Men of Letters (1885); *Our Hundred Days in Europe* (1887); *Before the Curfew and Other Poems* (1887); *Over the Teacups* (1891).

---

64 The career of Holmes as a medical man, too often neglected, is of importance (1) because it was his major interest — to which literature was secondary; (2) because it brought professional fame, unrealized in literary circles. His Boylston prize essays (1836, 1837) were entitled: "Facts and Traditions respecting the Existence of Indigenous Intermittent Fever in New England," "The Nature and Treatment of Neuralgia," and "The Utility and Importance of Direct Exploration in Medical Practice." For relation of his essay on Puerperal Fever to the subsequent work of Semmelweis, see S. I. Hayakawa and H. M. Jones: *Oliver Wendell Holmes: Representative Selections* (1939), p. xxxii. For further discussion, see W. S. Walsh, *Literary Life* (1882), II, pp. 135-149; J. G. Whitter, *The Writings of John Greenleaf Whittier* (seven volumes, 1888), VII, pp. 374-382; also, *The Prose Works of John Greenleaf Whittier* (three volumes, 1892), III, pp. 374-382; D. W. Cheever, "Oliver Wendell Holmes, the Anatomist," *HGM.*, II (1894-1895), pp. 154-159; J. H. M. Knox, Jr., "The Medical Life of Oliver Wendell Holmes," *JHHB.*, XVIII (1907), pp. 45-51; W. B. Jennings, "Oliver Wendell Holmes," *MRR.*, XV (1909), pp. 107-114; Stewart Lewis, "A True Story of Oliver Wendell Holmes," *IND.*, LXVII (1909), p. 1313; H. R. Viets, "Oliver Wendell Holmes, Physician," *A.Schol.*, III (1934), pp. 5-11.

ESSAYS AND NOVELS

The Autocrat of the Breakfast-Table † (1831—1832; 1858).[65] Formally launched in the first number of the *Atlantic* (1857), had its actual beginning in two papers published in the *New England Magazine* (November, 1831; February, 1832). Lacking the charm of the later continuation, these first papers still had the characteristic mixture of prose and verse. For the general pattern Holmes may have found a suggestion in the Sir Roger de Coverley papers of Addison. The device of a conversational framework was peculiarly adapted to the needs of one of the most brilliant conversationalists of the age. It provided a natural atmosphere and made easy the shift from one topic to another. The incidental interest which developed in the table itself was fed by an increasing emphasis on the story element as the *Professor*,[66] the *Poet*, and *Over the Teacups* followed the *Autocrat*. The grouping of diverse personalities — always some rough blurter of startling truths, always a sweet feminine figure, etc. — kept alive the elements of surprise and variety. Revealed against this background is the fascinating mind of the Autocrat, quick to surround any idea or thing with suggestions of the greatest variety and interest supplied out of his wide reading and practical experience. These suggestions, too, have often the element of contrast, so common but unrealized a factor in life.

Elsie Venner † (1861),[67] ***The Guardian Angel*** † (1867), ***A Mortal Antipathy*** (1885). Holmes's "medicated" novels are alike in faults of construction, in the use of inconsistently happy endings, in the weighting of the narrative in order to show that what men do is often determined for them by outside causes or forces. This, Holmes's comment on the orthodox theology of his day, he states even more vigorously in his essay (1870), "Mechanism in Thought and Morals" (1883). However, despite their faults, his novels have interest, and are among the first in American literature to utilize a scientific approach.[68]

POETRY

PUBLIC AFFAIRS. When scarcely out of college, Holmes attained fame with his ringing poem "Old Ironsides"† (1830), which pre-

---

65 J. T. Winterich, "Romantic Stories of Books: *The Autocrat of the Breakfast-Table*," *PW.*, CXIX (1931), pp. 317-321; Robert Withington, "A Note on the *Autocrat*, III and IV," *MLN.*, XLVI (1931), p. 293. "A whole submerged continent of contemporary life and thought is revealed by the reefs and islets of allusion in *The Autocrat*. . . . That Holmes' book remains lively and entertaining reading . . . is evidence that he was much more than the *flâneur* which some modern critics hold him to be": DeLancey Ferguson, "The Unfamiliar Autocrat," *Colophon*, N.S. I, No. 3 (1936), p. 396 (pp. 388-396).

66 C. K. Shorter, Introduction to *The Professor at the Breakfast Table* (1928).

67 [Anonymous], a review of "Elsie Venner," *Atl.*, VII (1861), pp. 509-511; J. M. Ludlow, " 'Elsie Venner' and 'Silas Marner,' " *Macmillan's*, IV (1861), pp. 305-309.

68 C. P. Oberndorf, *The Psychiatric Novels of Oliver Wendell Holmes* (1943).

served this historic frigate *Constitution* down to our own day.[69] This interest in public affairs continued through mature years but never reached enthusiasm. His themes were at times merely reminiscent, as in "Lexington" (1849) and "A Ballad of the Boston Tea-Party" (1873), and in the delightful "Grandmother's Story of Bunker-Hill Battle" (1875). "The Statesman's Secret" (*c.* 1850; 1862) parallels Whittier's "Ichabod" in criticism of Webster, laying the emphasis on his ambition; but his "Birthday of Daniel Webster" (1855—1856; 1862) shows a disposition to forget at death all that was unworthy. As the Civil conflict neared we find the emphasis laid on the idea of Union imperilled.[70] The titles, "Brother Jonathan's Lament for Sister Caroline"† (1861), "Voyage of the Good Ship Union" (1862), "Union and Liberty" (1861), indicate this. Loftier in tone is the "Prologue to 'Songs in Many Keys'" (1862). It may be remarked here that, perhaps because he felt the medium ill adapted to such discussion, political questions were resolutely excluded from the familiar essays.

MEDICAL. Holmes's life work as a physician suffered at the beginning from report that he had written a volume of verse. In "The Stethoscope Song" (1849) he had even turned his humor upon a young physician. Recollections of student days in Paris are touched with pathos in "La Grisette" (1863), but in general his profession and his poetry are kept well separated.

HUMOROUS. The comic approach has given us much of Holmes's most treasured verse. Early in point of time are "The Ballad of the Oysterman"† (1830), a satire on the romantic ballads of the day, and the rather self-conscious "Height of the Ridiculous" (1830). "To an Insect" (1831) should be compared with Freneau's "To a Caty-Did" which it curiously resembles. "Latter-Day Warnings" (1857)[71] and "Contentment"† (1858) are alike in the device of crowding details of varied and contrasting character into humorous juxtaposition. "The Deacon's Masterpiece"† (1858) deals delightfully with the poet's own grandfather, David Holmes, captain in the French and Indian War, and surgeon in the Revolution, who built the "One-Hoss Shay." The shay constitutes for Holmes a symbol of the dry, logical perfection of Calvinism.[72] "How the Old Horse Won the Bet" (1876) reminds us of Holmes's lifelong enthusiasm for fast horses. Two of Holmes's family reminiscences, "My Aunt"† (1831) and "Dorothy Q."† (1871), illustrate a blending of kindly humor with pathos which seems characteristic. Such

---

69 Holmes regarded the writing of poetry as an occupation in which very ordinary people could attain reasonable success; this idea may have arisen from his own early and spectacular achievement and his continued composition of verse in advanced old age.

70 Robert Withington, "The Patriotism of the Autocrat," *HGM.*, XXXVI (1927-1928), pp. 523-532; D. L. Werner, *The Idea of Union in American Verse 1776-1876* (1932).

71 Forrest Wilson, *Crusader in Crinoline* (1941), p. 215 *f.*; I. V. Brown, "The Millerites and the Boston Press," *NEQ.*, XVI (1943), pp. 592-614.

72 But see J. T. Morse's answer to W. S. Merrill's query: "Centenary of the Autocrat," *CW.*, CXXXIV (1931-1932), p. 586 (pp. 581-586).

are the elements, in perfect balance, in "The Last Leaf"† (1831). Not less touching than his later poems, "The Voiceless" (1858) and "Under the Violets" (1859), it treats its central figure, Major Thomas Melville, of Boston Tea Party fame, with a whimsicality which lightens without disspelling the charming note of regret.

OCCASIONAL. Of *vers de société*[73] Holmes wrote a great deal. Much of it was drawn forth by special occasions. Such were the reunions of his college class.[74] Of the close to twoscore poems the best are: "The Boys"† (1859), "All Here" (1867), "Bill and Joe"† (1868), and the last, "After the Curfew" (1889; 1890). Similar in purpose, though with some added dignity, is his richly descriptive "At the Saturday Club" (1884). Of verse called forth by more miscellaneous and more public occasions examples are: "Poetry: A Metrical Essay" (1836), "Bryant's Seventieth Birthday" (1864), "For the Burns Centennial Celebration" (1862), "For Whittier's Seventieth Birthday" (1877; 1880), "The Iron Gate" (1879; 1880 — for his own Seventieth Birthday Breakfast, given by the *Atlantic* in 1879 — and pieces concluding his Lowell Institute lectures: "After a Lecture on Wordsworth" (1862) and "After a Lecture on Shelley" (1862).

RELIGIOUS. While Holmes vigorously rebelled against the orthodox Calvinistic faith of his father, and attacks it in both his essays and his novels,[75] he makes much less use in his verse of strictly religious or broadly philosophical ideas than do Emerson, Whittier, or even Longfellow. Like Whittier, however, in their simple faith are his occasional hymns: "A Hymn of Trust" (1859), "A Sun-Day Hymn"† (1859), and "Parting Hymn" (1861). "The Living Temple"† (1858), too, is illustrative of his devout attitude as a practicing scientist. "The Chambered Nautilus"† (1858) stands in a unique position among Holmes's poems. Written in a moment of creative enthusiasm, rare with Holmes, it nevertheless deserves close study because of its compact but beautiful statement of what has recently been termed a humanistic point of view.[76]

---

73 "Light verse is to poetry what the familiar essay is to prose": W. F. Taylor, *A History of American Letters* (1936), p. 208.

74 Samuel May, "Dr. Holmes with His Classmates," *HGM.*, III (1894), pp. 159-162.

75 Actually, his social, political, and literary views were conservative; his religious and philosophical views, radical: H. H. Clark, "Dr. Holmes: A Re-Interpretation," *NEQ.*, XII (1939), pp. 19-34.

76 ". . . Like all humanism, self-dependent and individualistic, the soul trusts to its own powers." S. I. Hayakawa and H. M. Jones, *Oliver Wendell Holmes: Representative Selections* (1939), p. lv. For further discussion see N. F. Adkins, " 'The Chambered Nautilus': Its Scientific and Poetic Backgrounds," *AL.*, IX (1937-1938), pp. 458-465. On his place as a religious poet see M. J. Savage, "The Religion of Holmes's Poems," *Arena*, XI (1894), pp. 41-54; F. S. Townsend, "The Religion of Oliver Wendell Holmes," *MR.*, XCI (1909), pp. 605-611; E. S. Turner, "The Autocrat's Theology: Unpublished Letters of Holmes," *Putnam's*, VI (1909), pp. 662-667; A. H. Strong, *American Poets and Their Theology* (1916), pp. 321-367; E. J. Bailey, *Religious Thought in the Greater American Poets* (1922), pp. 137-157; W. V. Gavigan, "The Doctor Looks at Religion: Dr. Holmes and the Church," *CW.*, CXXXVII (1933), pp. 53-59; Van Wyck Brooks, "Dr. Holmes: Forerunner of the Moderns," *SRL.*, XIV (June 27, 1936), pp. 3-4, 13-15 (an expansion of which appears in his *The Flowering of New England 1815-1865* [1936]).

MISCELLANEOUS. "At Dartmouth" (1839; 1940) has autobiographical interest and anticipates the *Autocrat*.[77] "To My Readers" (1862) is of importance because of its frank discussion of the difficulties and even the defeats accompanying creative composition. "Nearing the Snow-Line" (1870) is a notable success among Holmes's infrequent experiments with the sonnet. "The Girdle of Friendship" (1884) employs a conceit with conscious art. "Too Young for Love" (1890) and "La Maison d'Or" (1890) have a Landor-like compression and finish.

GENERAL ESTIMATE AS A POET

MERITS: (1) Technical mastery within self-imposed limits; metrical correctness; accuracy and grace of diction. (2) Balance of the serious and the comic, and perfection of tone in occasional verse. (3) Broadly humorous treatment of a variety of themes; revealing shrewd knowledge of human foibles, and enriched by skillful use of contemporary allusions and plays on words.

DEFECTS: (1) Metrical traditionalism and monotonous regularity. (2) Refusal to attempt any project of size; poetry definitely a side line. (3) Absence of deep thought, religious or philosophical, of "high seriousness," of "criticism of life." (4) Neoclassic tendency to expend effort on trivial subjects. (Cf. sonorous lines near end of "To an Insect.") (5) Substitution of rhetoric for poetry, especially in poems dealing with public affairs. (Cf. "The Statesman's Secret.")

JAMES RUSSELL LOWELL, 1819—1891, poet, essayist, diplomat.[78] Eminent Cambridge family. Prepared at the Cambridge Latin School, he graduated at Harvard in 1838. There he had edited *Harvardiana,* and had read Carlyle, the Romantic poets, and the first beginnings of Victorian poetry, but did not at once discover his special fitness for an academic career. Two years of study gave him (1840) a Harvard law degree, and he attempted practice but without satisfaction. Following publication (1841) of his first volume of verse, *A Year's Life,* he (with Robert Carter) launched (1843) the *Pioneer,* which survived through January, February, and March only. In 1844 he married Maria White, whose strongly abolitionist[79] and Transcendental influence is traceable in Lowell from their first acquaintance in 1840. That year he published *Poems* (1844), and the year following his *Conversations on Some of the Old Poets* (1845), a considerable part of which had already been printed in Nathan Hale's *Boston Miscellany.*

---

77 *At Dartmouth,* with an Introduction by E. M. Tilton (1940).

78 For full bibliography, see page 304.

79 Lowell's own grandfather, John Lowell, was responsible for introducing into the Massachusetts Bill of Rights a sentence taken from that of Virginia, "All men are created free and equal," thus setting free every slave in Massachusetts.

Shortly after his marriage Lowell was for a time in Philadelphia, where he wrote editorials for the *Pennsylvania Freeman,* of which Whittier had for a time been editor.[80] Published *Poems, Second Series* (1847; dated 1848). The year 1848 was notable also for appearance of *The Vision of Sir Launfal, A Fable for Critics,* and *The Biglow Papers* (First Series). For fifteen months beginning in 1851 he was with his invalid wife in Europe, but the hopes for her recovery failed with her death in 1853. In 1855, the year of the Lowell Institute lectures on the English Poets (published 1897), Lowell became Smith Professor of Modern Languages at Harvard, a post held until 1886. From June, 1855, to August, 1856, he studied in Germany and Italy, taking up his duties in 1857,[81] the year of his marriage to Frances Dunlap. Simultaneously he assumed editorship of the newly founded *Atlantic Monthly* (1857—1861). Retiring, he entered (1862) into a similar but less onerous relationship with the *North American Review,* of which he was joint editor (1864—1872). From 1877 until transferred to London (1880—1885)[82] he was minister to Spain. In both posts his urbanity, his eloquence, and his political astuteness made him conspicuously successful.[83] Following his wife's death in 1885 he returned to America. Literary and public duties, notably the address on the 250th anniversary of the founding of Harvard University (November, 1886) and the Lowell Institute lectures on the Old English Dramatists (1887; 1892) occupied his flagging powers. Death came in 1891. Chief works not already noted: *Fireside Travels* (1864); *Ode Recited at the Commemoration of the Living and Dead Soldiers of Harvard University* (1865); *Under the Willows and Other Poems* (1869); *The Cathedral* (1870); *Among My Books* (1870; Second Series, 1876); *My Study Windows* (1871); *Three Memorial Poems* (1877); *Democracy and Other Addresses* (1887); *Political Essays* (1888); *Heartsease and Rue* (1888); *Latest Literary Essays and Addresses* (1891); *Last Poems* (1895); *Early Prose Writings* (1902); *Four Poems* (1906); *The Round Table* (1913); *The Function of the Poet and Other Essays* (1920).

---

80 These, along with editorials printed in the *National Anti-Slavery Standard,* were printed as *The Anti-Slavery Papers of James Russell Lowell* (two volumes, 1902). For comment on Lowell's radical prose, see V. L. Parrington, *Main Currents in American Thought,* II (1927), p. 464 *f.*

81 Barrett Wendell, *Stelligeri and Other Essays concerning America* (1893), pp. 205-217; C. W. Eliot, "James Russell Lowell as a Professor," *HGM.,* XXVII (1919), pp. 492-497; W. R. Thayer, "James Russell Lowell as a Teacher," *Scribner's,* LXVIII (1920), pp. 473-480.

82 Beckles Willson, *American Ambassadors to England (1785-1928)* [1928], pp. 374-388 (pp. 374-397).

83 G. W. Smalley, "Mr. Lowell in England," *Harper's,* XCII (1895-1896), pp. 788-801; F. S. A. Lowndes, "The Literary Associations of the American Embassy," *FR.,* LXXXIII; N.S. LXXIII (1905), pp. 1031-1043.

MAJOR WORKS

Biglow Papers, First Series*†** (1848). Nine numbers published separately, beginning June 17, 1846, in the Boston *Courier;* last four in *National Anti-Slavery Standard.* Purpose: opposition to the war with Mexico and the annexation of Texas.[84] Despite ulterior purpose, character interest attached to Ezekiel and Hosea Biglow, father and son, and the Reverend Homer Wilbur — this last a private joke of Lowell's on his father's family pride. Hosea humorously exposes editorial and political pretense. The Yankee dialect excited controversy.[85] ***Second Series (1867). Consists of "The Courtin'," an amusing narrative in dialect verse, and eleven satirical numbers. More serious in tone; attacks slavery; urges strengthening of Union. First number written in poignant grief over death of three dear nephews; second number, thinly disguised attack on English attitude by author. Following papers expose contemporary politics, voice need for a great leader, praise Emancipation Proclamation.[86] Though he wearied of the misspellings and of the serial appearance, Lowell maintained his effectiveness.[87]

Of historic importance as an outstanding instance of poetic, regional, comic satire,[88] the *Papers* are generally regarded as Lowell's most original, perhaps most enduring, work.

***A Fable for Critics*†** (1848). Published anonymously, but at once generally credited to Lowell. Metrical resemblances in measure and comic rhyme to Pope's *Dunciad,* to Leigh Hunt's *The Feast of the Poets;* to Byron's *English Bards and Scotch Reviewers* and, near the beginning, *The Vision of Judgment.* In turn influenced Amy Lowell's *A Critical Fable* (1922). Same device of comic rhyme employed (1857) in his own "The Origin of Didactic

---

84 For author's statement see letter to Thomas Hughes in H. E. Scudder, *Complete Poetical Works,* Cambridge Edition, p. 166. For discussion of Lowell's primacy in the employment of poetic satire and the effectiveness of the *Papers,* see Ferris Greenslet, *James Russell Lowell* (1905), p. 85; E. M. Chapman, "The Biglow Papers Fifty Years After," *YR.,* VI (1916), pp. 120-134; J. T. Winterich, "Romantic Stories of Books: *The Biglow Papers,*" *PW.,* CXIX (1931), pp. 1605-1610.

85 Lowell avowed his own exactness. C. H. Grandgent, eminent linguist, "From Franklin to Lowell; A Century of New England Pronunciation," *PMLA.,* XIV, N.S. VII (1899), pp. 207-239, in general supports the genuineness of the dialect. So also Henry James, *Essays in London and Elsewhere* (1893). Cf., however, J. H. Gilmore, "The Biglow Papers," *Chaut.,* XXIII, N.S. XIV (1896), pp. 19-23; G. R. Carpenter, *John Greenleaf Whittier* (1903), p. 227. More recently, see L. H. Chrisman, "Permanent Values in *The Biglow Papers,*" in *John Ruskin, Preacher, and Other Essays* (1921), pp. 163-176; J. A. Heil, "Die Volkssprache im Nordosten der Vereinigten Staaten von Amerika dargestellt auf Grund der Biglow Papers von James Russell Lowell," *Giessener Beiträge zur Erforschung der Sprache und Kultur Englands und Nordamerikas,* III, No. 2 (1927), pp. 205-311; A. G. K[ennedy], (a review of J. A. Heil's work on Lowell's *Biglow Papers*), *AS.,* III (1927-1928), p. 462 *f.*; Marie Killheffer, "A Comparison of the Dialect of 'The Biglow Papers' with the Dialect of Four Yankee Plays," *AS.,* III (1927-1928), pp. 222-236; R. B. Nye, "Lowell and American Speech," *PQ.,* XVIII (1939), pp. 249-256; Harold Blodgett, "Robert Traill Spence Lowell," *NEQ.,* XVI (1943), p. 585 (pp. 578-591).

86 For an analysis of the eighth number (Second Series), see F. D. Smith, "Mr. Wilbur's Posthumous Macaronics," *UNDQJ.,* X (1920), pp. 436-443.

87 P. H. Boynton, *Literature and American Life* (1936), p. 555.

88 J. F. Jameson, "Lowell and Public Affairs," *RR.,* IV (1891), pp. 287-291; Jeanette Tandy, "The Biglow Papers," in *Crackerbox Philosophers in American Humor and Satire* (1925), pp. 43-64.

Poetry." Criticisms reckoned today opinionated but shrewd and vigorous; keen in distinguishing first-rate from second-rate ability. Comment on Bryant regretted by Lowell as unduly severe; Margaret Fuller roughly handled, perhaps because of sharp criticisms of his verse contained in her *Papers on Literature and Art,* Part II (1846), p. 132; criticisms of Cooper and Poe, severe but just. The charge of imitativeness brought against unnamed disciples of Emerson is generally thought to refer to Thoreau and Ellery Channing.[89]

The Vision of Sir Launfal † (1848). Plot of verse parable based on Malory. Chiefly notable as an illustration of the duality of Lowell's nature: (1) mystical;[90] (2) didactic; with its emphasis on sympathy and brotherly love. Prized also for its passages of nature description and its rare emphasis on narrative.[91] Chief meter is iambic tetrameter; varied cadences and subtle effects achieved by shifting meters.

Letters. Among the best in our literature. Spontaneous, natural, spirited.

OTHER PROSE

POLITICAL. Numerous youthful contributions to the *Courier,* the *Pennsylvania Freeman,* and the *National Anti-Slavery Standard* are marked by earnestness, vigor, opposition to slavery, but primary concern for the preservation of the Union; regarded by extreme abolitionists as too moderate. Attitude maintained in Civil War essays in *Atlantic Monthly* and *North American Review;* early appreciation of the greatness of Lincoln; less readiness to concede sincerity of Johnson.[92]

Democracy (1886). Address delivered in October, 1884, at Birmingham, England. Belongs to a difficult time for him and for America. It may be regarded as a defense of Democracy as a form of government, with special reference to the American experiment.

CRITICAL. "Cambridge Thirty Years Ago" (1853) and "A Moosehead Journal" (1853), both of pleasantly narrative quality, were contributed to *Putnam's Monthly,* launched (1853) by G. W. Curtis and Parke Godwin. "Keats" appeared in 1854. Otherwise. almost all the best essays were written following 1865 and collected

89 For discussion of veiled allusion to Thoreau, and comments occasioned, see B. V. Crawford, *Henry David Thoreau: Representative Selections* (1934), p. xi *f.* See also E. J. Nichols, "Identification of Characters in Lowell's 'A Fable for Critics,'" *AL.*, IV (1932-1933), pp. 191-194.

90 Cf. Lowell's own admission, "one half of me clear mystic," Ferris Greenslet, *James Russell Lowell* (1905), p. 82.

91 Cf. L. A. Sloan, *Lowell's "The Vision of Sir Launfal," a Study and Interpretation* (1913).

92 J. F. Jameson, "Lowell and Public Affairs," *RR.*, IV (1891), pp. 287-291; Edward Grubb, "The Socialism of James Russell Lowell," *NEM.*, N.S. VI (1892), pp. 676-678; W. G. Jenkins, "Lowell's Criteria of Political Values," *NEQ.*, VII (1934), pp. 115-141.

in the volumes, *Among My Books* (1870, 1876)[93] and *My Study Windows* (1871). "Gray" has the late date of 1886. Of the better known essays two are devoted to famous New England associates — the valuable and richly reminiscent "Emerson the Lecturer" (1868), and the sparkling but dangerously prejudiced "Thoreau" (1865).[94] "Carlyle" (1866), one of Lowell's most brilliantly written essays, is devoted to a man for whom he exhibits a sympathy much cooled from the enthusiasm of youth. Telling phrases are still quoted, and the essay reads well even today. "Wordsworth" (1854) has many of the same virtues of style. Emphasis is laid on the shocking inequality of Wordsworth and on his colossal egotism. Pointed out is something now generally realized, the small benefit derived by Wordsworth from his 1798 trip to Germany. Two essays, "On a Certain Condescension in Foreigners" (1869) and "A Good Word for Winter" (1869), are among the best familiar essays written in America, marked in both instances by the apparent aimlessness, the informality, and the allusiveness expected in the form. "Witchcraft" (1868) in its treatment of a New England theme is filled with a wealth of illustrative material suggestive of a modern scientific worker.[95] "Rousseau and the Sentimentalists" (1867), one of Lowell's most admired critical essays, suggests by the second half of the title its chief object, Lowell finding in sentimentalism an unmistakable strain of exhibitionism. "Shakespeare Once More" (1868) says much that is now familiar, but that was far less so when written. The attitude toward the First Folio is in keeping with modern scholarship. The treatment of *Hamlet* shows rare understanding. Two assertions of dubious soundness are: (1) that the style of no modern author reminds one of him (Lowell must have forgotten *The Cenci* and *Virginius*), and (2) that the style of Shakespeare "never curdles into mannerism." "Chaucer" (1870), "Dryden" (1868), "Pope" (1871), "Milton" (1876)[96] are extensive, scholarly, historically sound, genuinely appreciative essays of the sort which has given most satisfaction to critical readers.

OTHER VERSE

YOUTHFUL. Representative of the two strongest influences on his youthful writing are (1) his early sonnets, "My Love, I have no fear that thou shouldst die" (1841; 1844), "Our love is not a fading earthly flower" (1842; 1844), "Beloved, in the noisy city here" (1842; 1844), full of Shakespearean echoes in conceit and

93 Ray Palmer, "James Russell Lowell and Modern Literary Criticism," *IR.*, IV (1877), pp. 264-281.

94 For comment see Austin Warren, "Lowell on Thoreau," *SP.*, XXVII (1930), pp. 442-461; B. V. Crawford, *Henry David Thoreau: Representative Selections* (1934), pp. xi-xiv, liv-lvi.

95 Cf. G. L. Kittredge, *Witchcraft in Old and New England* (1929).

96 R. C. Pettigrew, "Lowell's Criticism of Milton," *AL.*, III (1931-1932), pp. 457-464.

phrase; "The Shepherd of King Admetus" (1842), "A Legend of Brittany" (1843; 1844), "Rhoecus" (1844), "To the Dandelion" (1854) — Keatsian in theme and treatment.[97] Examples of his love of Nature are: "An Indian-Summer Reverie" (1846; 1847), which presents a detailed, localized picture of his Cambridge environment, and "The First Snow-Fall" (1849), which adds a poignant personal note.[98] "An Incident in a Railroad Car" (1842), while expressing that admiration for Burns which Lowell shared with Whittier (cf. "At the Burns Centennial," 1859), stresses also, more generally, a growing realization of the powers of verse and its capacity for service.

ABOLITIONIST. Lowell's enthusiasm for Abolitionism, intensified by association with Maria White, bears fruit in "Prometheus" (1843; termed "radical" by Lowell himself), "A Glance behind the Curtain" (1843), "Stanzas on Freedom" (1843; 1844), "Wendell Phillips" (1843; 1844), "Great truths are portions of the soul of man" (1841; 1842). In 1845 appeared "The Present Crisis" (wr. 1844), one of Lowell's most quoted and rhetorically effective poems. "On the Capture of Certain Fugitive Slaves near Washington" (1845) also approximates versified oratory more nearly than pure poetry. "To W. L. Garrison" (1849) expresses a qualified admiration for its subject. "The Washers of the Shroud" (1861)[99] strikes a tone of tolerance and gentleness.[100] "Masaccio" (1855) draws a lesson from a French chapel. Much of his most powerful comment was, of course, reserved for the *Biglow Papers* and for the Odes.

RELIGIOUS. Little of Lowell's verse deserves a specifically religious classification. "Bibliolatres" (1849) presents a broad conception, free from Bible worship or credal narrowness. References in poems of personal grief such as "On the Death of a Friend's Child" (1844) and others of a more intimate character have nothing unconventional or noticeably ardent. His mystical strain shows in "The Vision of Sir Launfal" (1848) mingled with that love of the mediaeval exemplified even much later in "The Cathedral"† (1869; 1870).[101]

---

97 For indication of critical reception of 1844 volume, see Zoltán Haraszti, "Letters by T. W. Parsons," *MB.*, XIII (1938), p. 348 *f.* (pp. 343-367). Lowell is accused by a writer in the Boston *Transcript* of dangerously radical tendencies, of "'great faults in nearly everything,'" of a style burdened with "'obsolete, quaint, odd, fantastic words, and of words coined for the occasion'"; while Parsons himself found in Lowell "'a too ready faculty of imitation.'"

98 Most representative of later nature poems are: "Pictures from Appledore" (1851, 1855; 1868), "Under the Willows" (1868), and portions of "The Cathedral" (1870), the last two both showing Wordsworthian influence. Cf. Norman Foerster, *Nature in American Literature* (1923), pp. 143-175.

99 Source of the title and initial idea is indicated by Louise Pound, "Lowell's 'Breton Legend,'" *AL.*, XII (1940-1941), pp. 348-350.

100 W. G. Jenkins, "Lowell's Criteria of Political Values," *NEQ.*, VII (1934), pp. 115-141.

101 M. J. Savage, "The Religion of Lowell's Poems," *Arena*, IX (1893-1894), pp. 705-722; H. E. Scudder, *James Russell Lowell*, II (1901), p. 311; A. H. Strong, *American Poets and Their Theology* (1916), pp. 267-317; L. M. Shea, *Lowell's Religious Outlook* (1926), pp. 100-113.

PERSONAL. Some of Lowell's simplest and most genuine poetic expression is found in a small group of poems of personal grief. Such are: "The Changeling" (1847) and "The First Snow-Fall" (1849), occasioned by the loss of his first child, his daughter Blanche, and the birth of a second daughter; "Auf Wiedersehen!" (1854), "The Windharp" (1854), and "Ode to Happiness" (*c.* 1854; 1861) reflecting sorrow over the death of his wife in 1853 and marking a turn toward traditionalism; "After the Burial" (1868), lamenting the death of his second daughter Rose; "In the Twilight" (1868), characterized by a strong strain of Celtic mysticism; "Nightwatches" (1877), an exquisite sonnet, recording the bereavement suffered in the death of a woman friend of his declining years. Greatest of all these poems of personal grief was, of course, "Agassiz" (1874), written in Italy upon receipt of the news of his friend's death. Composed swiftly and passionately, it still shows awareness of the conventions of elegiac verse, and finds space for portraits of the Saturday Club as Agassiz knew it.[102]

OCCASIONAL. While Holmes was outstanding as the poet of social gatherings and reunions, Lowell excelled in voicing sentiments of formal public gatherings. "On Board the '76" (1865) was written for Bryant's seventieth birthday, and pays tribute to his services to the cause of freedom. Similar birthday poems were addressed "To Whittier on His Seventy-fifth Birthday" (1882; 1888), and "To Holmes on His Seventy-fifth Birthday" (1884). The poem "To Charles Eliot Norton" (1868) is more informal. Most admired in Lowell's day were the odes: "Ode Recited at the Harvard Commemoration"† (1865), "Ode Read at the One Hundredth Anniversary of the Fight at Concord Bridge" (1875), "Under the Old Elm — Read at Cambridge on the Hundredth Anniversary of Washington's Taking Command of the American Army" (1875), "An Ode for the Fourth of July, 1876" (1876). Of these, the "Commemoration Ode" is most valued, but chiefly because of the Lincoln strophe added afterwards in the *Atlantic* printing for September, 1865. Actually, it was comparatively ineffective as delivered, the real sensation having been the prayer by Phillips Brooks.

MISCELLANEOUS. "The Pioneer" (1847), far from a great poem, may profitably be compared with Whitman's splendid lyric, "Pioneers! O Pioneers!" (1865). "Columbus" (1844; 1848), a much underrated dramatic monologue, is one of but a few poems dealing with the discoverer of America, and contains some imaginative and eloquent lines. "Death of Queen Mercedes" (1878) is an admired sonnet. "Auspex" (1879) is an exquisite bit, notable for effective use of a short line.

---

102 For discussion of circumstances surrounding the writing of the poem, see H. E. Scudder, *James Russell Lowell,* II (1901), p. 176; B. J. Loewenberg, "The Controversy over Evolution in New England, 1859-1873," *NEQ.*, VIII (1935), pp. 232-257.

GENERAL ESTIMATE

AS A POET. *Merits:* (1) wit and humor; (2) technical mastery of (a) ode, (b) sonnet, (c) humorous technical devices such as double rhymes and puns; (3) vigor and earnestness in controversial verse; (4) appreciation of Nature, colored with mystical sensitiveness; (5) mastery of rural dialect; (6) acquaintance with literary tradition; (7) richness of allusion. *Defects:*[103] (1) cheapening through puns, wordplay, etc.; (2) poetry of controversy often mere versified oratory; (3) an excess of didacticism; (4) despite technical facility, a lack of sensuous charm; (5) erudition at best often limiting audience, and frequently bordering on pedantry; (6) nature poetry marked by emotional sensitivity without philosophical or strongly scientific basis; (7) poetry generally imitative.[104]

AS A CRITIC. The tendency among recent critics is to concede to Lowell: (1) historical importance ("the first American with a real historical perspective"), (2) impressive erudition resulting from exceptionally wide reading, (3) sound taste involving threefold evaluation on the basis of historical perspective, organic unity, and elegance of expression together with emphasis upon pleasure to the reader as a proper objective and measure. Charges against him: (1) lack of organization and considered purpose resulting in (a) digressions, (b) substitution of strings of quoted "beauties" for searching analysis; (2) intellectual softness and indolence, making him most at home in the past where reputations are fixed and no difficult decisions are involved; (3) instability as to critical position, illustrated (a) in his attack upon sentimentalism in the "Rousseau" wherein he is really "describing his own symptoms,"[105] (b) in his wavering between the Classic and the Romantic, with a compromise fondness for Dante and Shakespeare; and in his admiration for Dryden and Pope without willingness to accept "decorum" as an ideal; (4) his blunders and unfairness in the judgment of contemporaries, notably Thoreau and Whitman.[106]

---

103 C. H. Grattan, "Lowell," *AM.*, II (1924), pp. 63-69; V. L. Parrington, *Main Currents in American Thought*, II (1927), pp. 63-69; Alfred Kreymborg, *Our Singing Strength* (1929), pp. 116-133; Rica Brenner, *Twelve American Poets before 1900* (1933), pp. 199-228.

104 F. L. Pattee, "A Call for a Literary Historian," in Norman Foerster (editor), *The Reinterpretation of American Literature* (1928), p. 20; Van Wyck Brooks, *The Flowering of New England 1815-1865* (1936), p. 319.

105 Norman Foerster, *American Criticism* (1928), p. 150.

106 Cf. Van Wyck Brooks, *The Flowering of New England 1815-1865* (1936), p. 520. For general comment on Lowell as critic, see Ray Palmer, "James Russell Lowell and Modern Literary Criticism," *IR.*, IV (1877), pp. 264-281; E. S. Parsons, "Lowell's Conception of Poetry," *CCP.*, Language Series II (1908), pp. 67-84; Gustav Pollak, *International Perspective in Criticism* (1914), pp. 58-83; J. J. Reilly, *James Russell Lowell as a Critic* (1915); J. M. Robertson, "Lowell as a Critic," *NAR.*, CCIX (1919), pp. 246-262; H. H. Clark, "Lowell's Criticism of Romantic Literature," *PMLA.*, XLI (1926), pp. 209-228; Norman Foerster, *American Criticism* (1928), pp. 111-156; H. H. Clark, "Lowell — Humanitarian, Nationalist, or Humanist," *SP.*, XXVII (1930), pp. 411-441; Austin Warren, "Lowell on Thoreau," *SP.*, XXVII (1930), pp. 442-461; J. P. Pritchard, "Lowell's Debt to Horace's *Ars Poetica*," *AL.*, III (1931-1932), pp. 259-276; G. E. DeMille, *Literary Criticism in America* (1931), pp. 49-85; J. P. Pritchard, "Aristotle's *Poetics* and Certain American Literary Critics," *C.Weekly*, XXVII (1934), pp. 89-93 (pp. 81-85, 89-93, 97-99); P. H. Boynton, *Literature and American Life* (1936), p. 559.

Chapter VII

WALT WHITMAN: PROPHET OF AMERICAN DEMOCRACY

WALT[ER] WHITMAN, 1819—1892, prose writer, poet.[1] Born in West Hills, Long Island, into humbler Quaker branch of colonial family, moving (1823) to Brooklyn. Began work as office boy and printer's devil (1831). Connected in various editorial capacities with newspapers in and about New York until late '50's, interrupting work at least twice to teach school, and (1848) to go to New Orleans. *Leaves of Grass* (1855), privately printed, with type set by the author. To nurse his brother George, wounded in battle, Walt went (1862) to Virginia and drifted into volunteer service as a nurse in the Washington hospitals. The war over, he obtained (1865) a clerical position first in the Department of the Interior, and, when dismissed on the charge that *Leaves of Grass* was an immoral volume, in the Attorney General's office. There he was employed until stricken by paralysis in 1873, the effect being intensified by the death of his mother. Gradual recovery began with visits (beginning 1876) to Timber Creek, near Camden, New Jersey. Trips to the Rockies (1879), Canada (1880), and Boston (1881) preceded purchase (1884) of property in Camden where he resided until his death.

POETRY AND PROSE BEFORE "LEAVES OF GRASS"

Work before 1855 sporadically fictional,[2] largely journalistic, much of it political in basic interest.[3] Creative writing divided by

---

1 Whitman's separate publications include: *Franklin Evans; or The Inebriate* (1842): *Leaves of Grass*† (1855, 1856, 1860†, 1867†, 1871, 1872, 1881†, 1888, 1891), *Walt Whitman's Drum-Taps* (1865), *Sequel to Drum-Taps* (1865), *Democratic Vistas*† (1871), *Memoranda during the War* (1875), *Two Rivulets, including Democratic Vistas, Centennial Songs, and Passage to India*† (1876), *Specimen Days and Collect*† (1882), *Specimen Days in America* (1887), *November Boughs*† (1888), *Leaves of Grass with Sands at Seventy and A Backward Glance o'er Travel'd Roads* (1889), *Complete Prose Works* (1892), *Autobiographia, or the Story of a Life* (1892), *Calamus: A Series of Letters Written during the Years 1868-1880* (1897), *The Wound Dresser: A Series of Letters Written from the Hospitals in Washington during the War of the Rebellion* (1898), *"Walt Whitman at Home." By Himself* (1898), *Notes and Fragments* (1899), *Walt Whitman's Diary in Canada* (1904), *An American Primer* (1904), *Lafayette in Brooklyn* (1905), *Memories of President Lincoln and Other Lyrics of the War* (1906). For additional writings, see bibliography, pages 305-307.

2 To these years belongs his fictional experiment, *Franklin Evans: or The Inebriate: A Tale of the Times,* published November, 1842, in the *New World.*

3 Floyd Stovall, *Walt Whitman: Representative Selections* (1934), p. xviii *ff.*, analyzes its character; stresses his early adherence to Democracy as represented by Jefferson and Jackson: his coolness to abolitionism balanced by dislike of slavery; simultaneous devotion to States Rights and Union; friendliness to humanitarian reforms. Cf. Cleveland Rodgers and John Black (editors), *The Gathering of the Forces* (1920), reprinting material from the Brooklyn *Daily Eagle* (1846-1847); C. I. Glicksberg, "Walt Whitman the Journalist," *Americana*, XXX (1936), pp. 474-490; Emory Holloway and Ralph Adimari (editors), *"New York Dissected" by Walt Whitman* (1936).

Campbell into two groups:[4] (1) that contributed to newspapers 1838—1844, uniformly imitative and conventional;[5] (2) 1844—1854, showing progress toward *Leaves of Grass,* and in general a transitional stage. Influences responsible for maturing his genius largely conjectural;[6] possibly personal experience; perhaps readings in Greek and Elizebethan classics, in the Bible, Goethe, Rousseau, Coleridge, Carlyle,[7] *Ossian.*[8] Influence of Emerson, acknowledged by Whitman, took also the form of personal encouragement following appearance of First Edition *Leaves of Grass.*[9] Whitman's possible indebtedness to George Sand has been recently urged.[10]

"LEAVES OF GRASS"

Leaves of Grass† (1855). With twelve poems appeared the "Preface," not reprinted with later editions,[11] stressing need of an American literature which (1) is independent, self-sufficient; (2) reflects our national heritage of (a) environment, (b) history, (c) mingled racial elements. Like Carlyle,[12] Whitman makes of his ideal poet a seer, and adds that as the poet of Democracy he must be one of the people, strong physically, representative and typical. Like Wordsworth in the Preface to the *Lyrical Ballads,* he defends the highly individual style in which his imagined poet (strikingly resembling a self-portrait) is to point out the essential and lasting in a world of the trifling and transitory.[13] Actually the

---

4 Killis Campbell, "The Evolution of Whitman as Artist," *AL.*, VI (1934-1935), pp. 254-263.

5 Characterized by Floyd Stovall (*ibid.*, xxi), who would place the dividing line at 1847, as "crudely amateurish, emotionally hollow, and leaden with homiletic pessimism."

6 For compact analysis, see Stovall, *ibid.*, xxii *f.* Of supplementary interest are A. N. Wiley, "Reiterative Devices in *Leaves of Grass,*" *AL.*, I (1929-1930), pp. 161-170; G. W. Allen, "Walt Whitman and Jules Michelet," *EA.*, I (1937), pp. 230-237; S. A. Rhodes, "The Influence of Walt Whitman on André Gide," *R.Rev.*, XXXI (1940), pp. 156-171; F. M. Smith, "Whitman's Debt to Carlyle's *Sartor Resartus,*" *MLQ.*, III (1942), pp. 51-65.

7 Gregory Paine, "The Literary Relations of Whitman and Carlyle with Especial Reference to Their Contrasting Views on Democracy," *SP.*, XXXVI (1939), pp. 550-563; F. M. Smith, "Whitman's Poet-Prophet and Carlyle's Hero," *PMLA.*, LLV (1940), pp. 1146-1164.

8 Cf. F. I. Carpenter, "The Vogue of Ossian in America: A Study in Taste," *AL.*, II (1930-1931), p. 413 (pp. 405-417); Newton Arvin, *Whitman* (1938), p. 182 *f.*

9 Cf. J. B. Moore, "The Master of Whitman," *SP.*, XXIII (1926), pp. 77-89; C. L. F. Gohdes, "Whitman and Emerson," *SR.*, XXXVII (1929), pp. 79-93.

10 Cf. Esther Shephard, *Walt Whitman's Pose* (1938); Newton Arvin, *Whitman* (1938), p. 178 *f.* Whitman had read *Consuelo* and the sequel, *The Countess of Rudolstadt*, repeatedly, the prized feature of *Consuelo* being its emphasis on the moral side of art.

11 The essays prefaced to *As a Strong Bird on Pinions Free* (1872), *Two Rivulets* (1876), and *November Boughs* (1888) also throw light on Whitman's purpose in writing *Leaves of Grass.*

12 Newton Arvin, *Whitman* (1938), p. 182 *f.*, points out the reluctance with which Whitman came later to disagree with Carlyle's view of Democracy.

13 Cf. F. N. Scott, "A Note on Walt Whitman's Prosody," *JEGP.*, VII (1907-1908), pp. 134-153; P. M. Jones, "Influence of Walt Whitman on the Origin of the 'Vers Libre,'" *MLR.*, XI (1916), pp. 186-194; John Erskine, "A Note on Whitman's Prosody," *SP.*, XX (1923), pp. 336-344; Amy Lowell, "Walt Whitman and the New Poetry," *YR.*, XVI (1927), pp. 502-519; Lois Ware, "Poetic Conventions in *Leaves of Grass,*" *SP.*, XXVI (1929), pp. 47-57; A. N. Wiley, "Reiterative Devices in *Leaves of Grass,*" *AL.*, I (1929-1930), pp. 161-170; Leon Howard, "Walt Whitman and the American Language," *AS.*, V (1930), pp. 441-451; G. W. Allen, *American Prosody* (1935), pp. 217-243; M. N. Posey, *Whitman's Debt to the Bible with Special Reference to the Origins of His Rhythms* (Ph.D., Texas, 1938); Sculley Bradley, "The Fundamental Metrical Principle in Whitman's Poetry," *AL.*, X (1938-1939), pp. 437-459.

style of the Preface itself is something between prose and poetry, and in the miscellaneousness of its materials, its disjointed constructions and rhapsodic passages,[14] not greatly differing from some of the poems which follow. Second Edition (1856) enlarged to thirty-two poems by additions, often objectionable. Other important editions: Third, much enlarged (1860); Fourth (1867); and Seventh (1881). The revisions in later editions, much more extensive than generally realized, reduce indelicacy and other violations of taste, break up inordinately long lines, introduce increasingly iambic movement.[15]

WHITMAN'S PURPOSE EXPRESSED IN VERSE

"Song of Myself"† (1855). First, longest, most characteristic, and most important, because in the nature of an announcement of Whitman's program. Chief characteristics: (1) absence of organization; (2) exceptional diversity and vividness of materials made possible by a knowledge of widely-separated regions, and a multitude of occupations; (3) arrangement in characteristic lists with parallel phrasing; (4) liberality in admission of details and phrases generally thought vulgar or indecent; (5) exquisite lyric passages; (6) insistent note of grandiose egoism.[16]

"Song of the Answerer" (1855). Adds to his life purpose as a poet that of bringing about the unification of America.

"Out of the Cradle Endlessly Rocking"† (1859). Probably autobiographical. Exquisitely phrased, delicately and symbolically conceived, represents in the lament of the bird for its dead mate the reward which compensates human love-loss in the creative impulse of the artist.[17]

Among later poems throwing light on his conception of his role as a poet are: "Whoever You Are Holding Me Now in Hand" (1860), in which Whitman sees himself propagating a new religion of love, or comradeship, and supported by admiring followers; "Starting from Paumanok" (1860), emphasizing again the need of comradeship as the binder in the social organism; "Passage to India"† (1868; 1871), which envisages a time when the poet he dreams of shall assemble a new Trinity: God, Nature, and Man; "To Thee Old Cause" (1871), tying his book ("my book and the

14 The Transcendental aspects of Whitman's verse, indicated in part by the admitted impetus from Emerson, have been stressed by various critics. Cf. C[harles] Cestre, "Walt Whitman: Le Mystique, Le Lyrique," *RAA.*, VII (1929-1930), pp. 482-504; Leon Howard, "For a Critique of Whitman's Transcendentalism," *MLN.*, XLVII (1932), pp. 79-85; W. F. Taylor, *A History of American Letters* (1936), p. 227 *ff.*

15 For additional information see Killis Campbell, "The Evolution of Whitman as Artist," *AL.*, VI (1934-1935), pp. 254-263.

16 C. F. Strauch, "The Structure of Walt Whitman's 'Song of Myself,'" *EJCE.*, XXVII (1938), pp. 597-607.

17 For the basis of the poem in a real incident see Emory Holloway, *Whitman: An Interpretation in Narrative* (1926), p. 162.

war are one") to the world-shaking effects of the civil conflict; "The Mystic Trumpeter" (1872) which proclaims the role of his ideal poet as exponent of a new universal freedom.[18]

WHITMAN AND THE WAR

Whitman's attitude in respect to the issues of the war underwent important changes in the years preceding and in the years of the Civil War. From an attitude of toleration of slavery[19] and a lack of respect or liking for Negroes, he advanced (1848) to an advocacy of free soil,[20] and, with passing of the Fugitive Slave Act, to feel rage[21] that Northern white men should be turned into slave-catchers. Entire absence of hatred for the South,[22] dislike of abolitionism and abolitionists, feeling that there were other things — the labor problem for instance — as bad as slavery, and a Quakerish dislike for war[23] kept him out of the war, and his poetry from violent partisanship. Experience as a nurse, however, roused his humane impulses; the personality of Lincoln inspired admiration and affection.

Varying aspects of these complex attitudes are reflected in his poems. "Come Up from the Fields, Father" (1865) is a touching picture of the arrival of bad news such as the poet himself had presumably often dispatched. It is one of the poet's few attempts at character creation and dramatic presentation of a scene. "The Wound-Dresser" (1865) describes realistically his hospital activities. "Over the Carnage Rose Prophetic a Voice" (1860; 1865) stresses the need of Comradeship and reconciliation. So, too, "Turn O Libertad" (1865),[24] "Reconciliation" (1865—1866), "Thick-Sprinkled Bunting" (1865), "Years of the Modern" (1865), and a number of others of the same year. In the South ("To the Leaven'd Soil They Trod," 1865—1866) he hoped to find an audience for his songs. From the past his glance turns forward as in "Thou Mother with Thy Equal Brood" (1872).

Grief over the death of Lincoln is given immortal expression in two great poems. "When Lilacs Last in the Dooryard Bloom'd"† (1865) emphasizes the unity resulting from a common grief. "O Captain! My Captain!"† (1865) has attracted attention aside

---

18 M. W. Guthrie, *Modern Poet-Prophets* (1897), pp. 244-332; F. B. Gummere, *Democracy and Poetry* (1911), pp. 96-148; W. L. Werner, "Whitman's 'The Mystic Trumpeter' as Autobiography," *AL.*, VII (1935-1936), pp. 455-458.

19 Newton Arvin, *Whitman* (1938), p. 24, shows that the poet had given the Mexican War hearty support; that his grandparents (p. 31) owned slaves. Cf. also C. J. Furness, "Walt Whitman's Politics," *AM.*, XVI (1929), pp. 459-466.

20 Newton Arvin, *Whitman* (1938), p. 44.

21 Newton Arvin, *ibid.*, (1938), p. 54.

22 Newton Arvin, *ibid.*, (1938), p. 62.

23 E. L. Masters, *Whitman* (1937), p. 273.

24 T. O. Mabbott, "Walt Whitman's Use of 'Libertad,'" *NQ.*, CLXXIV (1938), p. 367 *f.*

from its intrinsic merits because of its metrical regularity. The poet valued the poem less than did the public.[25]

EXPANDING AMERICA

The optimistic tone of Whitman's war poetry finds support in his grandiose conception of the future of America. The attitude voiced briefly in "Turn O Libertad" and "Thick-Sprinkled Bunting" is given a more memorable and extensive development in "Pioneers! O Pioneers!"† (1865).[26] "Passage to India"† (1868) ties this view to three specific achievements in world unification: completion of the Suez Canal, the Atlantic Cable, and the Union Pacific Railroad. "To a Locomotive in Winter" (1876) shows that, like Thoreau, Whitman found stimulus to his imagination in this mechanical agent of commerce. Important beyond any other single force in insuring this glorious future for America is the concept of comradeship.[27] Because of his emphasis upon Democracy, equalitarianism, and world peace there has been some tendency to regard his thinking as socialistic.[28] He has, however, been credited with first revealing the organic unity of American life,[29] and with incorporating in his writings so much of America that "he is almost a literature."[30] The group of nine poems, "Calamus"† (1860), are so entitled because the plant of this name symbolizes with its close-knit blades the mutual support gained from comradeship.[31]

---

25 E. L. Masters, *Whitman* (1937), p. 129. More than a dozen musical compositions are based on "O Captain! My Captain!" For a bibliography of 183 publications and manuscripts comprising 244 compositions based on his poems, see *Leaves of Music by Walt Whitman* (from the collection of B. C. Landauer; privately printed, 1937). For artistic and educational readings of almost a score of poems from Walt Whitman's *Leaves of Grass*, hear Ralph Bellamy's recordings in Musical Masterpiece Album M-955 (four twelve-inch Victor records, *c.* 1944; $4.50). Ralph Bellamy's dramatic underscoring has been praised by Dorothy Parker, Clifton Fadiman, and William Rose Benét.

26 Cf. Willa Cather's *O Pioneers!* (1913). For discussion of Whitman's relation to the passing of the frontier, see Norman Foerster, "Factors in American Literary History," and J. B. Hubbell, "The Frontier," in Norman Foerster, *The Reinterpretation of American Literature*, pp. 23-38, 39-61; also F. J. Turner, "The Significance of the Frontier in American History" (address before American Historical Association, 1893) in F. J. Turner, *The Frontier in American History* (1920).

27 Cf. H. S. Canby, *Classic Americans* (1932), pp. 313-318, 321-329, 349; H. A. Myers, "Whitman's Conception of the Spiritual Democracy 1855-1856," *AL.*, VI (1934-1935), pp. 239-253; Floyd Stovall, *Walt Whitman* (1934), p. xlvii; H. S. Canby, *Walt Whitman: An American* (1943), p. 65.

28 Cf. V. L. Parrington, *Main Currents in American Thought*, III (1930), pp. 69-86. In a paper, "Vital Contradictions in *Leaves of Grass*," read before the American Literature group of the Modern Language Association on December 29, 1937, Newton Arvin said: "He [Whitman] envisioned, therefore, a classless, unified society of equals and free men, posited on the moral potentialities of human beings. To me it seems disingenuous to deny that this program, if translated into our own generation, is essentially the program of socialism." In discussion following, H. R. Warfel replied that Whitman's insistence upon individualism invalidated such an assertion. Certainly, as Arvin himself points out (*Whitman*, 1938, pp. 241-245), Whitman had no interest in the Fourier movement for co-operation, was never a trades-unionist, and shows no horror over child and sweatshop labor.

29 Van Wyck Brooks, quoted in Norman Foerster, *Toward Standards* (1930), p. 113.

30 "Whitman absorbed so much of the America about him, that he is more than a single writer: he is almost a literature." Lewis Mumford, *The Golden Day* (1926), quoted in Norman Foerster, *Toward Standards*, p. 123.

31 Cf. W. S. Kennedy, *Reminiscences of Walt Whitman* (1896), p. 134. The relation of this manly love to "the passion of Woman-love" which he develops in "Children of Adam" is well stated in Haniel Long, *Walt Whitman and the Springs of Courage* (1938), p. 90.

Outstanding among the "Calamus" group are the following (all written or first published in 1860): "In Paths Untrodden," "Whoever You Are Holding Me Now in Hand," "For You O Democracy," "Recorders Ages Hence," "Behold this Swarthy Face," "I Hear It Was Charged against Me." Outside the "Calamus," however, appears the longer and more complex "Starting from Paumanok" (1860; 1881).

Sensational by reason of their frank treatment of sex were the poems included in "Children of Adam"† (1860, 1867). Intended by Whitman[32] to be "the same to the passion of woman love as the Calamus-Leaves are to adhesiveness, manly love," they exploited physical passion in the face of every civilized taboo and brought a storm of protest. Whitman's wish to banish prudery was honorable; Emerson, Thoreau, and Alcott thought his intention commendable;[33] the language employed, however, made prudery seem a virtue. Lanier, too, who had greeted Whitman's first poetry with enthusiasm, was repelled by these more extreme pieces.[34] Holmes, Whittier, Lowell took an even stronger stand, and the magazines were quite uniformly unfriendly.[35] Outstanding pieces: "I Sing the Body Electric," "Out of the Rolling Ocean the Crowd," "Once I Pass'd through a Populous City,"† "I Heard You Solemn-Sweet Pipes of the Organ." These last poems, tantalizing in their indefiniteness, allude perhaps to real individuals.[36] So, too, "The City Dead-House" (1867) which, despite its grim theme, expresses that absorbing interest in the city's multifarious life which produced "City of Orgies" (1860) where, with a fine egoism, he proclaims himself her laureate: "Mannahatta" ("I was asking . . . ," 1860); and the noble "Crossing Brooklyn Ferry" (1856).

But the country attracted him also. "Song of Myself"† (1855) and "Song of the Broad-Axe"† (1856) amaze one with their

32 See manuscript note, quoted in Haniel Long, *ibid.*, p. 90.

33 On Emerson's reaction see E. L. Masters, *Whitman* (1937), pp. 100, 203. For Thoreau's feeling see V. C. White, "Thoreau's Opinion of Whitman," *NEQ.*, VIII (1935), pp. 262-264, and Walden Edition, II, p. 243; VI, pp. 291, 295 *f.* For an interpretation of Whitman's intention, see Arthur Rickett, *The Vagabond in Literature,* (1906), p. 183 (pp. 169-250).

34 Cf. Haniel Long, *Walt Whitman and the Springs of Courage* (1938), p. 28.

35 Cf. Portia Baker, "Walt Whitman and *The Atlantic Monthly,*" *AL.*, VI (1934-1935), pp. 283-301; also her "Walt Whitman's Relations with Some New York Magazines," *AL.*, VII (1935-1936), pp. 274-301; E. L. Masters, *Whitman* (1937), p. 191 *f.* On Lowell's attitude, see Haniel Long, *ibid.*, p. 30; on Whittier's, see Russell Blankenship, *American Literature* (1931), p. 349. For an interpretation of the general reaction, see V. F. Calverton, *The Liberation of American Literature* (1932), p. 294. On the more favorable English reaction and the reasons therefor, see Emory Holloway, *Whitman: An Interpretation in Narrative* (1926), p. 258; W. S. Monroe, "Swinburne's Recantation of Walt Whitman," *RAA.*, VIII (1930-1931), pp. 347-351; W. B. Cairns, "Swinburne's Opinion of Whitman," *AL.*, III (1931-1932), pp. 125-136; Harold Blodgett, *Walt Whitman in England* (1934); C. L. Gohdes and P. F. Baum, *Letters of William Michael Rossetti concerning Whitman, Blake, and Shelley, to Anne Gilchrist and Her Son* (1934). For an interpretation of Whitman's attitude; see Norman Foerster, *The Reinterpretation of American Literature* (1928), p. 35 *f.*

36 On the rarity of his treatment of individuals, see Bliss Perry, *Walt Whitman* (1906), p. 293; E. L. Masters, *Whitman* (1937), p. 305.

knowledge of occupations and their extraordinary geographical range. Among the multiplicity of elements in "There Was a Child Went Forth" (1855) shown entering into one individual's life, as many are of nature as of man. In "A Song of the Rolling Earth" (1856) the earth becomes a great mother, ministering to her child for whom everything is designed. Part of her ministration is in opportunity for reflection. "On the Beach at Night Alone" (1856) leaves with Whitman the idea of a "vast similitude" which spans the Universe. "On the Beach at Night" (1871) shows him in the heavens something "more immortal even than the stars." "With Husky-Haughty Lips, O Sea!" (1883; 1888—1889) finds the sea itself the comforter. "To Think of Time" (1855) stresses the brevity of the individual life in the endless span of Time. In "A Noiseless Patient Spider" (*c.* 1862, 1868; 1871) he finds a symbol of the place of the soul in the Universe. In "Passage to India" (1871) Whitman approaches more closely than elsewhere to the thought of an encompassing power, while adhering to his favorite concept of the Comrade or Elder Brother.[37] More specifically, in "Chanting the Square Deific" (1865—1866) he names as the four points of the square: (1) Jehovah (Natural Law); Christ (Love); Satan (Free, Individual Will); and Santa Spirita (General Soul).[38]

PROSE WORKS[39]

***Democratic Vistas*†** (1871). Feeling as he did increasingly with advancing years, the urgent problems confronting Democracy, in particular the ignorance, heedlessness, and susceptibility to demagoguery of the masses, the critical danger to Democracy from Poverty, the inadequacy of the parties and politics in general as remedies (necessary though they be), he turned to the possibilities of a great national literature as an educative agency.[40]

***Specimen Days and Collect*†** (1882). A more miscellaneous work, including a considerable body of material, *Memoranda during the War,* which he had published seven years before, and notes which he was accumulating for a poem while convalescing in the charming surroundings at Timber Creek.

---

37 In his earlier poem, "To Him That Was Crucified" (1860), he had spoken of Christ as his co-worker and equal. For comment on his purpose in writing "Passage to India," see his Preface to *Leaves of Grass* and *Two Rivulets* as quoted in Floyd Stovall, *Walt Whitman* (1934), p. 337 *ff.* Cf. also A. H. Strong, *American Poets and Their Theology* (1916), pp. 421-470; E. J. Bailey, *Religious Thought in the Greater American Poets* (1922), pp. 183-228.

38 Cf. Floyd Stovall, *ibid.*, p. 410; also Introduction, pp. xxxvii-xlii. Cf. also Bliss Perry, *Walt Whitman: His Life and Work* (1906), p. 265; E. L. Masters, *Whitman* (1937), p. 266; G. L. Sixbey, "'Chanting The Square Deific'—A Study in Whitman's Religion," *AL.*, IX (1937-1938), pp. 171-195.

39 See Louise Pound, "Introduction" to *Specimen Days, Democratic Vistas, and Other Prose* (1935), especially p. xxix *ff.* (pp. ix-liii); Lionel Trilling, "Sermon on a Text from Whitman," *Nation,* CLV (1945), p. 215 *f.* (pp. 215-216, 218, 220).

40 Emory Holloway, "Whitman as Critic of America," *SP.*, XX (1923), pp. 345-369.

GENERAL ESTIMATE

AS A CRITIC. Long disregarded, Whitman's criticism has of late attracted increasing attention. With little formal education, and unsystematic about his reading, Whitman was nevertheless "better equipped than Poe, probably in quantity, quite certainly in quality." [41] He knew well the Bible and Greek literature, admired Shakespeare,[42] Coleridge, Goethe, Carlyle, Scott, Dickens, and Eliot; cordially disliked Milton, Johnson, Thackeray. His judgments of American contemporaries such as his admiration for Bryant and Emerson are fragmentary and sometimes explainable on personal grounds, yet shrewd and telling.[43] More important are his contributions to critical theory. Though moderated with advancing years, his demand was for a new literature springing from Democracy, for a style growing from within rather than imposed from without. Power he regarded as more important than form. Truly great poetry he believed must spring from a great national spirit. His deep interest in science and his industry in accumulating scientific information parallel his essentially eugenic attitude toward sex. Opposed strongly to certain elements in both Romanticism and Realism, he still had a foot in each camp.[44]

AS A POET. *Merits:* (1) A poetic medium, unique and at times exquisite, founded upon theories sincerely held and courageously maintained in the face of enormous opposition. (2) A lyric gift of the first order, expressing itself upon occasion with poignant tenderness and great verbal felicity. (3) Capacity for employment of conventional verse patterns. (Cf. "Pioneers! O Pioneers!," "O Captain! My Captain!" [1865]). (4) Deep-seated passion for Democracy, social and industrial as well as political. (5) Familiarity with the America of his day unmatched in its geographical, social, and occupational range and in the precision of its detail. (6) Unprecedented interest in urban life and employment of urban themes and details. (7) Knowledge of and sincere affection for rural nature. (8) Bold assertion of the loveliness of the human body, male and female; of the beauty and propriety of all its functions; of the enormous importance of the vital relationships of the sexes; of the need for elimination of all prudery in exchange for

41 Norman Foerster, *American Criticism* (1928), p. 170 (pp. 157-222); M. O. Johnson, "Walt Whitman as a Critic of Literature," *UNSLLC.*, No. 16 (1938), pp. 1-73.

42 Louise Pound, "Walt Whitman and the Classics," *Sw.R.*, X (1925), pp. 75-83; R. C. Harrison, "Walt Whitman and Shakespeare," *PMLA.*, XLIV (1929), pp. 1201-1238; C. J. Furness, "Walt Whitman's Estimate of Shakespeare," *HSNPL.*, XIV (1932), pp. 1-33; H. B. Reed, "The Heraclitan Obsession of Walt Whitman," *Personalist*, XV (1934), pp. 125-138.

43 For quoted comments, see E. L. Masters, *Whitman* (1937), pp. 247-260.

44 For a full discussion, consult Norman Foerster, *American Criticism* (1928), pp. 157-222.

a new complete frankness. *Faults:* (1) Inability to "explore and depict a human soul" (Masters, 305), *i.e.,* to create character. (2) Employment of a style not to be classified as either prose or verse. (3) Monotonous and planless listing of miscellaneous details.[45] (4) A mistaken assumption that banishment of foolish taboos justifies substitution for the higher, more spiritual, and more deeply affectionate sex relationships of an exclusively physical tie.

45 But, it is also claimed, there is an inextricable tie between Whitman's catalogue method and his basic theories and practices: Mattie Swayne, "Whitman's Catalogue Rhetoric," *UTSE* (1941), pp. 162-178; D. W. Schumann, "Enumerative Style and Its Significance in Whitman, Rilke, Werfel," *MLQ.*, III (1942), pp. 171-204.

Chapter VIII

MID-CENTURY MINOR FIGURES: ROMANCERS, ESSAYISTS, POETS

HARRIET [ELIZABETH] BEECHER STOWE, 1811—1896, novelist, humanitarian.[1] One of the nine children of the distinguished Lyman Beecher ("Dr. Cushing" of her last serial, *Poganuc People,* 1878), Mrs. Stowe had six brothers, five of whom became clergymen, and one, Henry Ward, a pulpit orator of fame. Removal of the family in 1832 to Cincinnati, where Lyman Beecher became head of Lane Theological Seminary, brought to Harriet, who had known Negroes only as respected servants in her father's home, her first contacts with slavery. Once at least she visited a plantation where the slaves were happy and the master kind. She saw slaves sold, and her brother had made a river voyage to New Orleans; on the other hand, she was, like her father, a moderate abolitionist, hoping to bring about an improvement in conditions through mutual understanding. Under the stimulating encouragement of Professor Calvin E. Stowe, to whom she was married in 1836, she became increasingly active as a writer. "Immediate Emancipation," a story published in the *New York Evangelist,* January 2, 1845, utilized the idea of being "sold down the river." [2] Removal to Brunswick, Maine (1850), where Professor Stowe had accepted a professorship at Bowdoin College, brought Mrs. Stowe under strong pressure to assist the abolitionist cause with her pen. For a time in the '70's Mrs. Stowe did platform readings from her works. Her residence, for some years at Hartford, Connecticut, was at length removed to Florida, where she died.[3]

Uncle Tom's Cabin; or, Life among the Lowly† (published serially June 5, 1851, to April 1, 1852, in the *National Era,* and in book form, 1852). Sales were enormous; returns substantial (though the dramatic rights and the English sales of one and one-half million copies brought Mrs. Stowe nothing); the resulting fame of the author as great in England as America, and widespread over the Continent.[4]

---

1 For bibliography, see page 307.

2 For sources of other details later incorporated in *Uncle Tom's Cabin* see Catherine Gilbertson, *Harriet Beecher Stowe* (1937), pp. 110 *ff.*

3 High points of her life form the basis of *Harriet,* a play by Florence Ryerson and Colin Clements, produced at the Henry Miller Theater, New York City, March 3, 1943, with Helen Hayes in the title role.

4 Van Wyck Brooks, *The Flowering of New England 1815-1865* (1936), p. 420.

Uncle Tom's Cabin is characterized favorably by: (a) exceptional effectiveness, arising in part from the circumstances of its appearance, and amply demonstrated by its phenomenal sale and translation into thirty-seven languages; partly from the undeniable power of its emotional appeal; (b) sincerity of purpose, as indicated by the intense emotion of the author during its composition, and other recorded biographical evidence; (c) an aim friendly and pacific; conciliatory rather than radical;[5] (d) a reasonably sound basis in personal experience and acquaintance, though of insufficient extent for conclusions so sweeping, or to withstand attacks so searing.[6] On the negative side are to be noted: (a) a strain of sentimentalism deriving from a line of feminine fiction writers on this side of the water and from Dickens' Tiny Tim, Little Nell, and Little Dorrit on the other; (b) the utilization of character types such as the melodrama villain, the sentimental heroine; (c) inaccuracies of detail arising from unfamiliarity with Southern manners; crudities of style arising from haste. As Pattee has shown,[7] the death of Uncle Tom was the first episode written, and, like that of Little Eva, caused its author as much sorrow in the writing as experienced by a multitude of subsequent readers. Of the various dramatic versions which lax laws permitted without advantage to the author, that of George L. Aikin, first seen at Troy, September, 1852, established itself as most successful, and, despite alterations in the handling of the villain, and the introduction of bloodhounds, as perhaps the best.

A Key to Uncle Tom's Cabin (1853). Hostile criticism[8] of *Uncle Tom's Cabin* and denial of the authenticity of sensational incidents contained therein led to Mrs. Stowe's reply in *A Key to Uncle Tom's Cabin,* which defended the characters as not overdrawn, discussed legal aspects of slavery, printed testimony from the lips of former slaves, attacked the clergy for its equivocal attitude.

Dred, A Tale of the Great Dismal Swamp† (1856). Partly as a result of the attacks on *Uncle Tom's Cabin,* had a sounder documentary basis[9] than its predecessor; but, despite a heavy sale on both sides of the Atlantic, never rivalled it in popularity.

The Minister's Wooing† (1859). This romance set in 18th century Puritan New England pleased many, including Lowell, who

5 F. L. Pattee, *The Feminine Fifties* (1940), p. 131, shows that rage against the book was slow in rising in the South, that the first protests came from ardent abolitionists like Garrison, exasperated at its moderation.

6 Cf. Catherine Gilbertson, p. 154; Forrest Wilson, *Crusader in Crinoline* (1941).

7 Cf. F. L. Pattee, *ibid.*, p. 74.

8 Fourteen or more pro-slavery novels appeared immediately in reply. Cf. J. R. Tandy, "Pro-Slavery Propaganda in American Fiction of the Fifties," *SAQ.*, XXI (1922), pp. 41-50, 170-178.

9 J. H. Nelson, "A Note on the Genesis of Mrs. Stowe's *Dred,*" *UKSE.*, VI, No. 4 (1940), pp. 59-64.

had been repelled by the propaganda of her earlier best sellers. Except for a lack of compelling interest, the book is without serious fault.

The Pearl of Orr's Island† (1862). Has salty sea-coast characters and atmosphere, with occasional sentimental scenes to please those readers who had wept over little Eva.

Oldtown Folks† (1869). Deals with the same times as *The Minister's Wooing* and had its setting in Old Natick (South Natick), Massachusetts, where Professor Stowe was born.

JAMES T[HOMAS] FIELDS, 1817—1881, editor, lecturer, minor poet. Partner at twenty-one in the firm known successively as Ticknor, Reed, and Fields; Ticknor and Fields; and Fields, Osgood, and Co., he became in 1861 Lowell's successor as editor of the *Atlantic Monthly,* retiring in 1870.

His poetry, in general undistinguished, was contained in the volumes: *Poems* (1849), *A Few Verses for a Few Friends*† (1858), and *Ballads and Other Verses* (1881), which last contained verses from earlier volumes. Literary taste, coupled with sympathy, integrity, and business acumen, made him a prized intimate of many literary men, and gave value to his volumes: *Yesterdays with Authors*† (1872), *Hawthorne* (1876), *In and Out of Doors with Charles Dickens* (1876), *Underbrush* (1877).

GEORGE WILLIAM CURTIS, 1824—1892, essayist, orator, editor.[10] Born in Rhode Island; a pupil for a time at the Brook Farm school, where he acquired an admiration for Emerson strengthened during later residence at Concord. Foreign travel (1846—1850) provided material for *Nile Notes of a Howadji* (1851), *The Howadji in Syria* (1852), and *Lotus Eating* (1852). *Potiphar Papers*† (1853) which satirized New York social life, is, like *Prue and I*† (1856—1857), imitative of Irving's *Salmagundi* vein. At the same time he exerted a strong influence upon public affairs through such orations as "The Duty of the American Scholar to Politics and the Times" (1856), which pressed home the sin of slavery. Politically independent, he supported Cleveland as a friend of Civil Service reform, against Blaine, whom he regarded as corrupt. He also supported the cause of Woman's Suffrage and urged improved relations between Capital and Labor.[11] Editorship of *Harper's Weekly* (1863—1892), of the department "The Easy Chair" in *Harper's Magazine* and, subsequently, of the magazine itself, gave opportunity for further advancing these ends.

---

10 For bibliography, see page 307.

11 Cf. *Orations and Addresses of George William Curtis,* edited by C. E. Norton (three volumes, 1894).

BAYARD TAYLOR, 1825—1878, lecturer, diplomat, translator, novelist, dramatist, poet, historian.[12] Born in Pennsylvania, of Quaker stock; largely self-educated. His first volume of poems, *Ximena, or the Battle of the Sierra Morena* (1844), was followed by two years' wandering in Europe on which he based *Views A-foot* (1846) which made him known to the public. *Eldorado*† (1850) and *A Book of Romances, Lyrics, and Songs* (1851) record his impressions of California, which he visited during the Gold Rush. Oriental travel (1851—1854), including Admiral Perry's voyage to Japan, bore fruit in *Poems of the Orient* (1854), in which the "Bedouin Song" appeared, and *Poems of Home and Travel* (1855). Helped by N. P. Willis and Horace Greeley to employment in New York, he was for the first years of the Civil War a journalist at Washington; then (1862—1863) secretary to the Legation at St. Petersburg. Short stories contributed to the *Atlantic* in the early '60's, collected in *Tales from Home,* deal effectively with the Quaker surroundings of his boyhood ("Friend Eli's Daughter"), less effectively with spiritualism ("The Confessions of a Medium," "The Haunted Shanty"). Chief novels: *Hannah Thurston* (1863), a regionalistic study of life in Ptolemy, a New York village, in a day when interest in co-operative enterprises was giving way to more urgent issues leading to the Civil War; *John Godfrey's Fortunes* (1864), an autobiographical record of literary experiences in New York City; *The Story of Kennett* (1866), a vividly realistic picture of life in his native town. Once regarded as the most distinguished poet of his generation, and commissioned to write "The National Ode, July 4, 1776," he is remembered today for his "Bedouin Song"† and for his fine translation of *Faust*† (1870—1871) in the original metres; otherwise as an imitator of greater men. His familiarity with the German language led to his appointment (1870) as nonresident professor of German literature at Cornell University, and in 1878 as minister to Germany.

LOUISA MAY ALCOTT, 1832—1888, author of juvenile fiction,[13] and second daughter of Bronson and Abigail (May) Alcott, was born in Germantown, Pennsylvania. Residence in Boston (1834—1840), and at Hosmer Cottage, Concord (1841—1842) was followed by the Fruitlands experiment (1843), in which she was an involuntary, and as she has indicated in "Transcendental Wild Oats,"[14] at times a critical participant. The years (1845—1848) of residence at "Hillside," Concord, to which the family returned after an unhappy interval at Walpole, Massachusetts, provided the setting for much of the narrative of *Little Women*† (1868, 1869). The fever episode, however, and the activities of Mrs.

12 For bibliography, see page 307.

13 For bibliography, see pages 307-308.

14 First printed in the *Independent*, December 8, 1873; reprinted in *Silver Pitchers: and Independence, a Centennial Love Story* (1876).

March (Louisa's mother) as a social worker, belong to a half dozen years when the Alcotts were moving from house to house, and Louisa was for considerable periods alone in Boston. From her middle teens Louisa and her older sister had collaborated on melodramatic tales such as they read in the weekly papers, and on hair-raising dramas which were performed at home by the four sisters.[15] Beginning with the sale (1852) of her first story, Louisa found an increasing public, and in 1860, after the family had re-established a residence at Concord, made her first entrance into the *Atlantic*. *Hospital Sketches* (1863), based upon her experiences at Washington as an untrained army nurse,[16] disclosed powers hitherto unrealized, and won her wide recognition. Five years later, in response to the suggestion of her publisher, who wished a book for girls, she produced *Little Women*. The enormous popularity of the work, a fact of the first importance to Miss Alcott, and a clear indication that she had at last found her right theme and audience, must not lead to the assumption that literature for children was a novelty. Juvenile reading had a long history. Catechisms, religious and secular, gave rise in the dissenting faiths to dialogue story manuals like Defoe's *The Family Instructor* (1715) and *Religious Courtship* (1722), which circulated in enormous numbers.[17] Sugar-coated instruction forms the basis also of the works of Hannah More and of Thomas Day's intolerably priggish and didactic *Sandford and Merton* (1783—1789). From this incubus Miss Alcott largely escaped. Resolutely escewing religious instruction, she kept didacticism at a minimum. Popularity was at the same time stimulated by her general avoidance of any allusion to the political crisis which had so recently divided the country. The fame attained by *Little Women* and its successors is not primarily the result of either structural or stylistic excellence, but of a reality of portraiture seldom matched up to this point in American literature. This is partly true because, as a recent biographer has pointed out,[18] most of the principals are real persons in the family and Concord circle. As she passed, of necessity, in later novels to more imaginative plots, positive identifications become rarer, and there is a more sentimental tone. However, her influence is as much in the direction of realism as romance, and particularly as regards her popularization of genuinely American settings and types.

THOMAS BAILEY ALDRICH, 1836—1907, poet, short-story writer, editor,[19] was New Hampshire born, but broadened in experience, if not in social attitudes, by some years of residence in

15 M. B. Stern, "Louisa Alcott, Trouper," *NEQ.*, XVI (1943), pp. 175-197.
16 M. B. Stern, "Louisa M. Alcott: Civil War Nurse," *Americana*, XXXVII (1943), pp. 296-325.
17 Cf. B. V. Crawford, "Teaching by Dialogue," *PQ.*, III (1924), pp. 23-31.
18 Katherine Anthony, *Louisa May Alcott* (1938), p. 162 *f.*
19 For bibliography, see page 308.

New Orleans. Forced by the death of his father to forego a college education, he came to New York to work as a clerk. His first volume of poems, *The Bells* (1855), came out in his nineteenth year, as luck would have it the same year as *Leaves of Grass*. To any discriminating critic the comparison of the two volumes must have been well calculated to reveal the imitative quality of Aldrich's talent. From occasional contributor to magazines he advanced to assistant editor of the *Home Journal,* then edited by N. P. Willis. In 1865 he moved to Boston where for nine years he edited *Every Saturday* (1866—1874), a Ticknor and Fields publication. It was thus an easy transfer to their *Atlantic Monthly* when, in 1881, Howells resigned the editorship. Under Aldrich's direction (1881—1890) the magazine won foreign praise as "the best edited magazine in the English language."

Without doing anything really well, Aldrich was a respectable craftsman in several fields. As a poet he showed himself a master of form, excelling in slight, delicate verse of the moment.[20] His surprise epistolary novelette, *Marjorie Daw*† (1873), was long reckoned one of the classics of American fiction. *The Stillwater Tragedy* (1880) has its place in the development of the American detective story. Most enduring is, perhaps, *The Story of a Bad Boy*† (1870), an excellent semi-autobiographical narrative. Aldrich was, however, chiefly important by reason of the conservative, genteel quality illustrated in his works and enforced through editorial influence.

ELIZABETH STUART PHELPS [WARD], 1844—1911, writer of popular religious stories.[21] Boston born. Following example of her literary mother, whose given and maiden names she adopted instead of Mary Gray, she began as a writer of tales. Though most were of the "Sunday-school" variety, and exhibit a persistent leaning toward the sentimental and the melodramatic, some like "'Tenty Scran" (*Atlantic,* November, 1860)[22] show remarkable emotional insight for her age, or, like "The Tenth of January" (*Atlantic,* March, 1868) exhibit social consciousness in the then neglected field of industrial life. *The Gates Ajar*† (1868) which, with its sequels *Beyond the Gates* (1883), *The Gates Between* (1887), and *Within the Gates* (1901) had a huge sale on both sides of the Atlantic, seeks to comfort those bereaved in the Civil War by assembling in long pages of conversation those passages from the Bible best calculated to offer assurance of immortality and eventual happiness. Illustrative of her genuine interest in

---

20 E. W. Bowen, "Thomas Bailey Aldrich, a Decade After," *MR.*, LCIX (1917), p. 386 *ff.* (pp. 379-390); Alfred Noyes, *Pageant of Letters* (1940), pp. 246-260.

21 M. A. Bennett, *Elizabeth Stuart Phelps* (1939).

22 A. H. Quinn, *American Fiction* (1936, p. 193), points out that, while "'Tenty Scran" is credited to Mrs. Ward in the *Atlantic Monthly Index*, it is not certainly hers. A passage in *Chapters from a Life* (p. 78) seems to support designation of "What Did She See With?" (*Atlantic*, 1868) as the first piece contributed.

the cause of the working woman, especially those employed in the mills, are her novels, *Hedged In* (1870) and *The Silent Partner* (1871), based on facts derived from government reports. *Doctor Zay* (1882) turns to the professional woman. Of her shorter works the best known is "The Madonna of the Tubs" (1887), though "Jack the Fisherman" (1887) and "A Singular Life" (1895) are both excellent stories. Tributes to her father are contained in *Austin Phelps* (1891) and *Chapters from a Life* (1896).

THE TRIUMPH OF REALISM

(1865-1914)

Chapter IX

THE LOCAL-COLORISTS

HISTORICAL BACKGROUND

General View. (1) Handicapped by postbellum problems and threatened by chaos, the South rebuilt slowly, accelerating its industrial development so that, at the turn of the century, it had become an industrial region. In the North, industrial expansion was rapid. (2) For some forty years after the Civil War, railway construction — aided by local, State, and Federal grants of money, credit, and land — was pushed westward, thereby opening up that region to settlement. Playing a significant role in the development of the West and Northwest were the Baltimore and Ohio Railroad, which had given distinguished service in the Civil War, the Union Pacific, which by connecting with the Central Pacific in 1869 became the first transcontinental railroad, the Northern Pacific, begun in 1870 and completed in 1883, and the Southern Pacific, formed in 1884. (3) Such inventions as the Hoe press and the self-binding reaper, air brakes and Pullman cars, the incandescent light and the motion picture, the typewriter, the telephone, the electric street railways, and the airplane revolutionized transportation and industry. (4) Industrial capital not only increased tremendously in amount and political power, but the national wealth was becoming concentrated in the hands of a few. From 1896 to 1912, "Big Business" attempted to control the government; and by 1910 two hundred of 200,000 non-banking corporations possessed at least forty per cent of all corporate assets. (5) The urban social structure was transformed. From the farm to the city went many people, and became wage earners. This new distribution of the population was further enlarged by millions of immigrants from the United Kingdom, Ireland, and various sections of Europe. The drift of the rural population to the cities, foreign immigration, and the industrial revolution compelled large numbers into a proletariat. (6) By 1870 there were as many as thirty national labor unions. Strikes against employers were often accompanied by violence. Political and social unrest was regimenting society into the opposing classes of labor and capital. (7) There grew up enormous corporations in transportation and industry, and these in turn combined into trusts. Two outstanding monopolists were J. D. Rockefeller and Andrew Carnegie. (8) The new type of public official or statesman no longer was a Henry Clay or a Daniel Webster or a J. C. Calhoun. Men like Roscoe Conkling, A. P. Gorman, M. S. Quay, and J. G. Blaine wished the natural resources of the country transferred to private ownership, believed in providing public aid for private enterprises, but rebelled against any State or Federal interference with such private property. (9) The power of judicial review under the Fourteenth Amendment began to be applied to all State legislation affecting private property, and to social and remedial legislation. (10) Transformed by the Civil War into the majority party, the Republicans, except for four years, stayed in control until 1889. (11) Since the two major parties concerned themselves primarily with the tariff, minor parties took up social and economic problems: among these bodies were the Greenback Party, the People's or Populist Party, the 16-to-1 Silver Men, the Socialist-Labor Party, the Socialist Party. (12) Most important was the Campaign of 1896, the most prominent issue being the gold standard, and the most famous statement of the free silver policy being the "Cross of Gold" speech made by W. J. Bryan. (13) Between 1865 and 1895 new centers of learning appeared, hastening the end of intellectual provincialism: Cornell (1865), Smith (1871), Johns Hopkins (1876), Bryn Mawr (1880), Tuskegee Normal and Industrial Institute (1881), Stanford (1885), University of Chicago (1890). Moreover, under the stimulus of the Morrill Agricultural College Act of 1862, the land-grant colleges and universities grew rapidly; and it has been estimated that among those benefiting from its provisions and those of the second Morrill Act of 1890 are twenty-six state universities and in the South seventeen schools exclusively for Negroes. (14) The Panama Canal was informally opened to commerce in 1914. (15) Triumph of private enterprise. (16) The history of the United States from 1865 to 1914 may be divided into two parts: the period of Reconstruction, and the growth of the United States as a world power: see immediately below.

Reconstruction

Andrew Johnson Administration (1865—1869). *1865:* Thirty-Ninth Congress, refusing to admit the Southern congressmen, appoint a joint committee to consider Reconstruction. Thirteenth Amendment. *1866:* Civil Rights Bill. First permanent transatlantic cable opened. *1867:* Reconstruction Act. Alaska Purchase. National Ku Klux Klan. Granger movement. *1868:* Impeachment and acquittal of President Johnson. Omnibus Act. Fourteenth Amendment.

Ulysses S. Grant Administration (1869—1873; 1873—1877). *1869:* Transcontinental railroad transportation opened. Knights of Labor organized. "Black Friday" scandal. *1870:* Standard Oil

Company chartered. Greenbacks as legal tender declared unconstitutional for debts contracted prior to 1862. Fifteenth Amendment. Enforcement Act. Readmission of Georgia; Reconstruction is completed. *1871:* Tweed Ring in New York City is overthrown. Federal control of federal elections. Indians become national wards. Ku-Klux Act. Legal-tender greenbacks declared unconstitutional. Treaty of Washington signed with Great Britain. Chicago fire. *1872: Crédit Mobilier* scandal. Creation of Yellowstone National Park. General Amnesty Act. Boston fire. *1873:* Coinage Act, later called the "Crime of '73." Slaughterhouse cases. Panic: periodic overexpansion of industrial capitalism produces a series of economic crises (1873—1879; 1893—1897). *1874:* Remington typewriter placed on market. Inflation Bill. Founding of Women's Christian Temperance Union. *1875:* Resumption Act. Peak of Granger movement. Greenback Party organized. Hawaiian Reciprocity Treaty. *1876:* Telephone patented by A. G. Bell. Centennial Exposition. Massacre of Custer's force. Twenty-third Presidential election. *1877:* Invention of the phonograph. Electoral Count Law.

Rutherford B. Hayes Administration (1877—1881). Withdrawal of Federal troops from South Carolina and Louisiana ends the Reconstruction Period and creates the Democratic "Solid South."

Social, Political, and Economic Development: The United States Becomes a World Power

Hayes Administration (continued). *1877:* Railroad and coal strikes throughout East. *1878:* Electric arc light invented. Resumption of specie payment. *1880:* Chinese Exclusion Treaty is signed with China.

James A. Garfield Administration (1881—1881). J. A. Garfield is assassinated four months after he becomes President.

Chester A. Arthur Administration (1881—1885). *1881:* Vice-President C. A. Arthur becomes the twenty-first President. Forming of the Federation of Organized Trades and Labor Unions of the United States and Canada, which in 1886 became the American Federation of Labor. Star-route postal frauds exposed. *1882:* Antipolygamy Act. Chinese Exclusion Act becomes effective. Knights of Columbus. *1883:* Civil Service Reform Act. Tariff and Internal Revenue Act. Beginning of the new steel navy. New York-Brooklyn suspension bridge opened. Letter postage reduced from three cents a half ounce (1851) to two cents a half ounce. *1884:* Federal Bureau of Labor authorized.

Grover Cleveland Administration (1885—1889). *1885:* Letter postage reduced to two cents an ounce. *1886:* Presidential Succession Act. General strike on the Gould railway system promoted by Knights of Labor. Anarchist riot in Haymarket Square, Chicago. First Mergenthaler Linotype used. *1887:* Mexican War Pension Act. Electoral Count Act. Interstate Commerce Act. Indian Allotment Law. *1888:* Second Chinese Exclusion Act. *1889:* Bankruptcy of the French Panama Canal Company. Department of Agriculture becomes an executive department.

Benjamin Harrison Administration (1889—1893). Oklahoma, part of the Indian Territory, opened to settlement. Breaking of the Conemaugh Dam floods Johnstown, Pennsylvania. Pan-American Congress. Australian ballot system adopted in majority of states. *1890:* Sherman Anti-Trust Act. Silver Purchase Act. McKinley Tariff Act. *1891:* International Copyright Law. Forest Reserve Act. Beginning of Populist Party. *1892:* Populist Party is first minor party to cast electoral votes. Many strikes and much violence — in Pennsylvania, Tennessee, Wyoming, and Idaho. Federal troops used to restore order in the West. *1893:* Edison develops the moving-picture apparatus.

Grover Cleveland Administration (Second Term, 1893—1897). World Columbian Exposition. Gold panic. *1894:* "Coxey's Army" demonstrates in Washington. Strike of the American Railway Union: Federal troops employed as protection. Wilson-Gorman Tariff. *1895:* Automobile comes into practical use. Gold reserve is reduced. Bureau of Immigration created. Income tax law declared unconstitutional. Cleveland applies the "Monroe Doctrine" to controversy between Great Britain and Venezuela. *1896:* Rural free delivery begins. President issues proclamation warning Americans not to violate the neutrality laws by aiding the insurrection in Cuba.

William McKinley Administration (1897—1901). *1897:* Dingley Tariff Act. *1898:* Greater New York Charter becomes effective. U.S.S. *Maine* blown up. Spanish-American War. Guam seized. Uniform Bankruptcy Law. Annexation of Hawaii. Treaty of Peace: Spain relinquishes Cuba, cedes Puerto Rico and Guam, and sells the Philippine Islands to United States for $20,000,000. *1899:* Philippine Insurrection. First Hague Conference. Open-Door Policy for China. United States receives Tutuila Island as a naval station. *1900:* Gold Standard Act. Appointment of Philippine Civil Commission. Galveston tornado. Free silver and imperialism are the issues of the twenty-ninth Presidential Election. *1901:* Billion-dollar U. S. Steel Corporation organized. Platt Amendment. Pan-American Exposition. Wall Street Panic. Steel strike of 150,000 workers. First wireless telegram received. President McKinley shot.

Theodore Roosevelt Administration (1901—1905; 1905—1909). Theodore Roosevelt takes oath as the twenty-fifth

President. Hay-Pauncefote Treaty. *1902:* Strike of anthracite coal miners. Newlands Reclamation Act. Isthmian Canal Act. Philippine Government Act. Signing of Reciprocity Act with Canada. *1903:* Expedition Act. Department of Commerce and Labor authorized. Elkins Act. Immigration Act. Treaty with Cuba. Transpacific cable opened between the United States and the Philippines. Recognition of Panama's independence. Panama Canal Treaty. *1904:* Baltimore fire. Louisiana Purchase Exposition. Labor troubles in Colorado, Chicago, and Massachusetts. *1905:* Protocol is signed with Santo Domingo. Lewis and Clark Exposition. Russo-Japanese Treaty of Peace signed at Portsmouth, New Hampshire. Industrial Workers of the World organized. Armstrong Commission investigates life insurance companies. *1906:* San Francisco earthquake and fire. Hepburn Act. Federal Food and Drug Act, and Meat Inspection Act. Third Pan-American Congress. Exclusion of Japanese from San Francisco public schools. R. E. Peary reports that he came within about two hundred miles of the North Pole. Roosevelt is awarded the Nobel Peace Prize. *1907:* J. D. Rockefeller gives $32,000,000 to the General Education Board. Mrs. Russell Sage endows with $10,000,000 the "Sage Foundation." Jamestown Tercentennial Exposition. Second Hague Conference. Stock panic in New York. Around-the-world voyage of the American fleet begins; fleet returns fourteen months later in 1909. *1908:* "Gentlemen's Agreement" with Japan. Wright brothers demonstrate the successful flying machine. Exclusion of Japanese children from San Francisco public schools is rescinded. East River subway tunnel in New York opened. Danbury Hatters' Case. Opening of Hudson Tunnel between Hoboken and New York. Employers' Liability Act. Conference of State Governors at the White House for the conservation of natural resources. Two-cent letter postage with Great Britain goes into effect. China decides to devote the Boxer Fund money to the education of Chinese pupils in the United States. *1909:* North Atlantic Coast Fisheries Treaty. President's salary raised to $75,000 a year.

William H. Taft Administration (1909—1913). Peary reaches the North Pole. Alaska-Yukon-Pacific Exposition. Sixteenth Amendment. Payne-Aldrich Tariff Act. National Conservation Congress meets. Hudson-Fulton Celebration. *1910:* International Waterways Treaty signed with Great Britain. Jury verdict in the Danbury Hatters' Case is against the boycotting union; and the decision is not nullified until the Clayton Act of 1914. Mann-Elkins Act. Postal Savings Bank Act. Theodore Roosevelt outlines the "New Nationalism." Hague Tribunal decision in the North Atlantic Fisheries Arbitration. *1911:* Andrew Carnegie gives $10,-000,000 more to the Carnegie Institute; and ten months later announces a gift of $25,000,000 to establish and maintain the Carnegie Corporation for the Promotion of Education. National Progressive Republican League organized. Supreme Court sustains the decree dissolving the Standard Oil Company of New Jersey and orders the dissolution of the American Tobacco Company. Abrogation of the treaty between Russia and the United States. *1912:* Two-month strike of textile workers at Lawrence, Massachusetts. Mississippi Valley floods. Esch Match Act. Steamship *Titanic* sunk by ice on maiden trip. Formation of Progressive Party under Theodore Roosevelt. Act for operating the Panama Canal. Act authorizing experimental parcel post. Various strikes in co-operation with the Industrial Workers of the World. *1913:* Parcel-post system instituted. Sixteenth Amendment. Webb Liquor Shipment Act.

Woodrow Wilson Administration (1913—1917; 1917—1921). Department of Labor created. Complete wireless message sent from Arlington, Maryland, to Eiffel Tower in Paris, France. W. J. Bryan, Secretary of State, presents a world-peace plan. California anti-alien landownership act. President Wilson publicly denounces lobbying at Washington. Seventeenth Amendment. Woman-suffrage law in Illinois. "Advancement-of-Peace" treaty is signed with San Salvador, the first under Secretary Bryan's plan. World's largest power dam dedicated. President Wilson proclaims strict neutrality as respects Mexican revolution. Serious strike in Colorado mines. Underwood Tariff Act. Owen-Glass Federal Reserve Act. *1914:* Goethals is made Civil Governor of the Canal Zone. Lifting of war-materials embargo from the United States into Mexico. Treaty with Colombia. Federal troops ordered to the Colorado strike district. Cape Cod Canal. President Wilson proclaims a Mother's Day. Outbreak of war in Europe forces stock exchanges to close. Neutrality proclamation. Treaty with Nicaragua. Panama Canal formally opened. Federal Trade Commission Act. Clayton Anti-Trust Act. Panama Canal temporarily closed. Federal Reserve Bank System goes into effect. United States protests British seizures and detention of American cargoes destined to neutral European ports.[1]

GENERAL VIEW OF THE LITERATURE

With the exception of the work of Whitman and Lanier, and of Emily Dickinson, who from about the turn of the century until about 1915 was forgotten, the poetry of the post-Civil War period struck a distinctly minor note. On the other hand, the informal or personal essay continued to be popular — and genteel; a native drama, characterized by a de-emphasis on foreign models and by

1 For a concise outline of historic events after 1914, consult J. A. Krout, *New Outline-History of the United States since 1865* (1949).

a tendency to original themes, emerged in the plays of Bronson Howard, Clyde Fitch, Augustus Thomas, and W. V. Moody; and the American short story, as the result of the efforts of Bret Harte, Brander Matthews, H. C. Bunner, Ambrose Bierce, Stephen Crane, Henry James, Mary E. Wilkins Freeman, Hamlin Garland, and many others, became a distinct literary form. Finally, from the Civil until the World War of 1914, every decade—the gilded '70's, the local-color '80's, the *fin-de-siècle* '90's, and the strenuous 1900's—is reflected in various types of fiction: novels of entertainment, of romance and of history, of realism and social criticism; and in different kinds of nonfiction: nature essays, literary criticism, historical works, political, scientific, religious, and philosophical writings. With the industrialization of the United States came the twilight of romanticism and the dawn of realism; with the triumph of the machine, American literature became for the first time *national* rather than *sectional* in points of view.

Influence of the Frontier. "The Significance of the Frontier in American History" was stated in classic form by F. J. Turner (1861—1932) in a paper so titled when read before the American Historical Association in 1893.[1] His hypothesis, accepted with its implications as being an important part of the whole truth, is that the Frontier has been the one great determinant of American civili-

1 The general Turner philosophy, the chief points of which he had first presented in "The Problems of American History," published in the student periodical, *The Aegis*, November 4, 1892, dominated the writing and interpretation of American History for four decades after its presentation. Previous to his analysis, emphasis had been put upon the germ theory of politics; but Turner, instead of believing that American institutions were only a continuation of European beginnings, emphasized the enforced adaptations of Europeans to their new environment. His is an economic interpretation of history, with heavy underlining of the frontier as the essential formative factor in the development of the American people. While attacks on his theory have been made by J. L. McDougall, G. W. Pierson, B. F. Wright, C. A. Beard, and L. M Hacker, others like D. D. Irvine, M. L. Hansen, J. D. Hicks, D. R. Fox, and F. L. Paxson continue to proclaim the validity of the Turner hypothesis. Probably no one would quarrel with D. R. Fox's statement that F. J. Turner's is "the most famous and influential paper in American historiography," and with Max Farrand's assertion that F. J. Turner "was probably the strongest single influence of his generation upon historical scholarship in America." Consult F. J. Turner, (1) *The Frontier in American History* (collected essays, 1920), (2) *The Significance of Sections in American History* (1932), (3) *The United States: 1830-1850* (posthumously, 1935), (4) *The Earlier Writings of Frederick Jackson Turner*, compiled by E. E. Edwards, with an Introduction by Fulmer Mood (1938); and also Carl Becker in *American Masters of Social Science* edited by H. W. Odum (1927), pp. 271-318; *The Section and Frontier in American History: the Methodological Concepts of Frederick Jackson Turner*, edited by S. A. Rice (1931); Joseph Schafer, "Turner's Frontier Philosophy," *WMH.*, XVI (1932-1933), pp. 451-469; F. L. Paxson, "A Generation of the Frontier Hypothesis: 1893-1932," *Pa.HR.*, II (1933), pp. 34-51; Curtis Nettels, "Frederick Jackson Turner and the New Deal," *WMH.*, XVII (1933-1934), pp. 257-265; E. E. Edwards, *References on the Significance of the Frontier in American History* (U.S. Dept. Agric., Bibliographic Collections, No. 25, 1935; second edition, 1939); Avery Craven, "The 'Turner Theories' and the South," *SHJ.*, V (1939), pp. 291-314; C. A. Beard in *Books That Changed Our Minds*, edited by Malcolm Cowley & Bernard Smith (1939), pp. 59-71; D. D. Irvine, *Beyond Frederick Jackson Turner* (American Military Institute, 1940); G. W. Pierson, "The Frontier and Frontiersmen of Turner's Essays," *PMHB.*, LXIV (1940), pp. 449-478; Murray Kane, "Some Considerations on the Frontier Concept of Frederick Jackson Turner," *MVHR.*, XXVII (1940-1941), pp. 379-400; Avery Craven, "Frederick Jackson Turner, Historian," *WMH.*, XXV (1941-1942), pp. 408-424; G. W. Pierson, "The Frontier and American Institutions: A Criticism of the Turner Theory," *NEQ.*, XV (1942), pp. 224-255; G. W. Pierson, "American Historians and the Frontier Hypothesis in 1941 (I)," *WMH.*, XXVI (1942-1943), pp. 36-60. Read also, page 159, footnote 2.

zation: he declared, in 1893, that the era of expansion had ended and that "the frontier has gone, and with its going has closed the first period of American history."[2] The physical frontier may have had an influence on almost every American author, including not only the local-colorists of the latter part of the nineteenth century, but also previous writers like Crèvecoeur (p. 26), William Byrd (p. 18), Timothy Flint (p. 75), C. S. Kirkland (p. 83), Irving (p. 49), Cooper (p. 65), W. G. Simms (p. 74), A. B. Longstreet (p. 83), and Davy Crockett (p. 83), and later ones like Frank Norris (p. 228), E. W. Howe (p. 206), O. E. Rölvaag (p. 270), Jack London (p. 229), E. L. Masters (p. 274), Sinclair Lewis (p. 271), and Willa Cather (p. 270). The frontier influenced such forms as the ballad and the tall tale (pp. 160-161); it had its own idols at various times, among whom are W. H. Bonny ("Billy the Kid") of New Mexico, J. B. Hickok ("Wild Bill Hickok") of Kansas, Mike Fink of the Ohio and Mississippi Rivers, Paul Bunyan of the Great Lakes region and the Pacific Northwest, Simon Kenton of Kentucky and Ohio, Samuel Houston of Texas, James Bridger of the Great Plains.[3]

Local-Color Movement. Local-color writings are a sifted mixture of romanticism and realism, probably influenced by the works of Washington Irving, by the frontier tradition of tall tales, and by the English and French romantic traditions of Sir Walter Scott, Maria Edgeworth, Bulwer-Lytton, Victor Hugo, Prosper Mérimée, and Bernardin de Saint-Pierre. Local-color fiction is concerned with the commonplace scenes and surface characteristics

2 "Up to our own day American history has been in a large degree the history of the colonization of the Great West. The existence of an area of free land, its continuous recession, and the advance of American settlement westward explain American development. . . . Thus American development has exhibited not merely advance along a single line, but a return to primitive conditions on a continually advancing frontier line . . . . In this advance, the frontier is the outer edge of the wave — the meeting point between savagery and civilization . . . ." As the colonist, "European in dress, industries, tools, modes of travel, and thought," transforms the wilderness, he is in turn mastered by it. "At first, the frontier was the Atlantic coast"; and it was simultaneously the frontier of Europe. "Moving westward, . . . the advance of the frontier has meant steady movement away from the influence of Europe, a steady growth of independence on American lines." The various kinds of frontiers have had several influences on the East and on the Old World: (1) "the frontier promoted the formation of a composite nationality for the American people"; (2) "the advance of the frontier decreased our dependence on England"; (3) it determined the "growth of nationalism and the evolution of American political institutions"; (4) its "nationalizing tendency . . . transformed the democracy of Jefferson into the national republicanism of Monroe and the democracy of Andrew Jackson"; and, most important, (5) it has promoted "democracy here and in Europe."

"From the conditions of frontier life came intellectual traits of profound importance. . . . The result is that to the frontier the American intellect owes its striking characteristics. That coarseness and strength combined with acuteness and acquisitiveness; that practical, inventive turn of mind, quick to find expedients; that masterful grasp of material things, lacking in the artistic but powerful to effect great ends; that restless, nervous energy; that dominant individualism, working for good and for evil, and withal that buoyancy and exuberance which comes with freedom—these are traits of the frontier, or traits called out elsewhere because of the existence of the frontier." All the foregoing quotations are from F. J. Turner's essay, "The Significance of the Frontier."

3 A serviceable bibliography is available in P. H. Boynton, *Literature and American Life* (1936), pp. 660-663.

of a particular locality, and is characterized by accurate use of dialects and speech peculiarities, by careful presentation of character types, of sectional occupations and interests, of codes of conduct. Although such humorists as G. H. Derby ("John Phoenix"), C. H. Smith ("Bill Arp, So Called"), D. R. Locke ("Petroleum V. Nasby"), C. F. Browne ("Artemus Ward"), and H. W. Shaw ("Josh Billings") preceded Bret Harte (p. 161), yet the latter's "Luck of Roaring Camp" may be regarded as the first postbellum local-color story. Such preoccupation with locality was later reborn in a not too dissimilar movement known today as Regionalism.

Ballads and Folk Songs. Of recent years a vast heritage of ballad material has been discovered. Some are remnants of English and Scottish ballads;[4] others are play party singing games, whoppers, Negro hollers and blues, spirituals and work-tunes, chanteys of the sea, songs of the cowboy, the lumberjack, the Indian fighter, the hobo: among railroad workers, "Casey Jones" is a favorite; among Kentucky and Tennessee mountaineers, "The Roving Gambler"; among the Negroes, "John Henry," "The Gospel Train," "The Ram of Darby," "Trouble, Trouble," and "Swing Low, Sweet Chariot"; among hoboes, "Hallelujah, I'm a Bum" and "The Gila Monster Route"; among lumberjacks, "The Jam on Gerry's Rock" and "Louie Sands and Jim McGee"; among the Westerners of the plains, "The Buffalo Skinners"; among the cowboys, "Git Along, Little Dogies," "The Lone Prairie," and "The Old Chisholm Trail"; among chanteymen, "Blow the Man Down" and "A Yankee Ship Came down the River"; and among anthracite miners, "The Avondale Mine Disaster," "The Lick Branch Explosion," and "The Sliding Scale." From such ballads is expected no exquisite choice of words, no perfection of form, no loftiness of theme. But they do reflect the life of isolated communities, and especially that of the everyday American. Moreover, cycles or groups of ballads have grown up around such figures as Jesse James (who is also the hero of some dime novels and numerous folk tales), Frankie and Johnny, John Henry, and Casey Jones.

Other ballads are: "The Jealous Lover of Lone Green Valley," "John Done Saw That Number," "Water-Boy," "A Plantation Serenade," "Satan's a Liah," "All God's Chillun Got Wings," "You Turn for Sugar an' Tea," "De Blues Ain' Nothin'," and "Go Down, Ol' Hannah."

Tall Tales. Narrated with mock solemnity, these frontier anecdotes, so steeped in violent exaggeration or so characterized

4 For a terse summary of the origin, theories of ballad making, definition, classification, characteristics, and metrical form of ballads, see W. B. Otis and M. H. Needleman, *A Survey-History of English Literature* (1938), pp. 100-102. Consult, also, Reed Smith, "The Traditional Ballad in America, 1933," *JAF.*, XLVII (1934), pp. 64-75; and the references given by P. H. Boynton, *Literature and American Life* (1936), pp. 660-663.

by it that they developed into extravaganzas or even folk legends, were told about such characters as Paul Bunyan, Davy Crockett. and Mike Fink.[5] In the writing market there were also literary examples: A. B. Longstreet's *Georgia Scenes* (1835); T. B. Thorpe's *Tom Owen: The Bee-Hunter, The Big Bear of Arkansas* (1841). *Mysteries of the Backwoods* (1846), and *The Hive of "The Bee-Hunter"* (1845); W. T. Thompson's *Major Jones's Courtship* (1843), *Major Jones's Chronicles of Pineville* (1843), and *Major Jones's Sketches of Travel* (1848); A. S. Stephens's *High Life in New York* (1843); the *Odd Leaves of a Louisiana "Swamp Doctor"* (1843) by the pseudonymous "Madison Tensas, M.D."; S. F. Smith's *Sol Smith's Theatrical Apprenticeship* (1845) and *Theatrical Journey-Work* (1854); J. J. Hooper's *Some Adventures of Captain Simon Suggs* (1846) and *The Widow Rugby's Husband* (1851); J. S. Robb's *Streaks of Squatter Life* (1847) and *Far-West Scenes* (1847); J. M. Field's *The Drama in Pokerville* (1847); and C. W. Harris's *Sut Lovingood Yarns* (1867). Finally, the works of Mark Twain abound in such tales.

THE LOCAL-COLORISTS: THE WEST

[FRANCIS] BRETT HARTE, generally known as **BRET HARTE,** 1836—1902, writer of novels, humorous verse. and short stories.[6] Born in Albany, New York, the son of Henry Harte, a teacher of languages, and Elizabeth Ostrander. Lived at Providence, Rhode Island, at Philadelphia, Pennsylvania, at Lowell, Massachusetts, at Brooklyn, New York, and in New York City. Father died (1845). Mother remarried and moved to California, where Bret joined her (1854). Occupied himself variously as druggist's clerk, teacher, and miner. Settled in San Francisco (1860). Married Anna Griswold (1862). Meanwhile, was contributing to the *Golden Era* and the *Northern Californian.* Was made Secretary of the California Mint (1863). Published *The Lost Galleon and Other Tales* (1867), a first collection of poems possessing a measure of originality, humor, and range, as well as occasional bits of local slang. Editor of the newly-begun *Overland Monthly* (1868—1871), in which he published his best short stories subsequently included in *The Luck of Roaring Camp and Other Sketches*, the 1870 volume that brought him, first, fame, and then

---

5 B. A. Botkin, editor, *A Treasury of American Folklore* (1944), with a Foreword by Carl Sandburg.

6 H. W. Boynton, *Bret Harte* (1903); T. E. Pemberton, *The Life of Bret Harte* (1903); H. C. Merwin, *The Life of Bret Harte* (1911); E. W. Bowen, "Francis Bret Harte," *SR.*, XXIV (1916), pp. 287-302; F. L. Pattee, *The Development of the American Short Story* (1923), pp. 220-244; *The Letters of Bret Harte*, edited by G. B. Harte (1926); G. R. Stewart, Jr. "The Bret Harte Legend," *UCC.*, XXX (1928), pp. 338-350; G. R. Stewart, *Bret Harte: Argonaut and Exile* (1931); *Bret Harte*, edited by Joseph Gaer, *California Literary Research Project*, Mimeograph No. 10 (1935); *Calendar of the Francis Bret Harte Letters in the William Andrews Clarke Memorial Library* (Southern California Historical Records Survey Project, 1942); B. A. Booth, "Unpublished Letters of Bret Harte," *AL.*, XVI (1944-1945), pp. 131-142.

a contract from the *Atlantic Monthly* for $10,000 for his year's output. Triumphal trip East (1871); but subsequent work did not fulfill the promise of earlier writings. Declined the post of First Secretary of the American Legation at the Court of Russia. Leaving his family behind, he accepted the U. S. Consulship at Crefeld, Rhenish Prussia (1878). Consul at Glasgow, Scotland (1880—1885). Spent his last years chiefly in London, where he died of cancer of the throat.

POETRY

Representative verse includes "The Mountain Heart's-Ease," "What the Bullet Sang," "The Angelus," "Mrs. Judge Jenkins," "The Society upon the Stanislaus," "Songs without Sense," "The Aged Stranger," and "John Burns at Gettysburg."

"Relieving Guard." Sincere, emotional tribute to the memory of his friend Starr King.

"The Reveille." Not without lyrical feeling.

"Dickens in Camp."† Verses of spirited reverence and impassioned spontaneity, born several hours subsequent to the news reaching San Francisco that Dickens had died.

"Plain Language from Truthful James"† (1870). More familiarly known under the pirated name of "The Heathen Chinee," it is a clever, moralizing, daintily satiric comic ballad of the boomeranging duplicity of Truthful James and Bill Nye in the euchre game with Ah Sin.[7] Expressed in the form of Swinburne's imposing threnody in *Atalanta in Calydon.* Others of his ballads that helped inaugurate local-color in American literature are "Dow's Flat," "Chiquita," "Jim," "In the Tunnel," "Penelope," and "The Stage Driver's Story."

STORIES AND SKETCHES

Condensed Novels and Other Papers (1867). Part I includes stories in excellent imitation of Cooper, Dumas, Bulwer-Lytton, Victor Hugo, Charles Lever, Dickens, and others. Part II is composed of a dozen "Civic Sketches," including the Hawthornean "From a Balcony." Part III, written chiefly after the manner of Washington Irving, has beautiful legends and tales, among which are the "Legend of Monte del Diablo,"† the "Adventure of Padre Vicentio," and, perhaps most significant, "A Night at Wingdam,"† a Dickensian sketch not over-moistened by dripping sentimentality.

The Luck of Roaring Camp and Other Sketches† (1870). Memorable are "Miggles," "Brown of Calaveras," "M'liss," and the three discussed immediately below.

---

7 It is a mistake to believe that Bret Harte had the usual, intolerant California opinion of the Chinese: see, for example, W. P. Fenn, *Ah Sin and His Brethren in American Literature* (1933), pp. 45-71; M. L. Kleim, "The Chinese as Portrayed in the Works of Bret Harte: A Study of Race Relations," *SSR.*, XXV (1940-1941), pp. 441-450.

"The Luck of Roaring Camp."† Somewhat unconventional in language, theme, treatment, and morals,[8] the story was decried by the religious press of California but well received in the East. Compactness of structure; melodramatic denouement. Motif, however, not wholly uncharacteristic of contemporaneous writers.

"The Outcasts of Poker Flat."† Unforgettable characters: the gambler John Oakhurst, the drunken sluice-robber "Uncle Billy," the two prostitutes called "the Duchess" and "Mother Shipton," and the eloping Tom Simson and Piney.

"Tennessee's Partner."† Illustrative of frontier "lynch-law" justice and the bonds of masculine friendship. Scenes have an admirable fidelity. Note use of literary English and camp jargon. Mawkish last paragraph.

Mrs. Skaggs's Husbands and Other Sketches (1873). Includes the popular "The Iliad of Sandy Bar," with its clever, explanatory genesis of the feud between York and Scott and the latter's pathetic-humorous last words.

SUGGESTED MERITS

1. If not the founder of the school of local-color, inclusive of the provincialisms and the dialectal peculiarities, he at least spiced such stories and sketches with dramatic incidents and picturesque scenes, and gave the type wider currency.[10] Writings have a documentary importance; they pioneered in the new manner, they influenced abidingly the development of the short story, they gave a set to the literary treatment of pioneer life in the West. His sheaf of perhaps a half-

SUGGESTED DEFECTS

1. His tales are fabricated out of a few repetitive themes and pat motifs, in part as characteristic of his earlier writings as they seem to be more obviously of his later ones.[9] Depreciated is the indifference to verisimilitude; challenged is the accuracy of his pictures of the miners, and the melodramatic paradoxes of his incongruous situations.[11] Has been charged with the invention of a meretricious dialect and has even been discredited for loosing "a sea of local color."

8 For Harte's own account of the circumstances under which the story was first published, see his "The Rise of the Short Story," *CM.*, LXXX, N.S. VII (1899), pp. 1-8.

9 R. R. Walterhouse has made a comprehensive survey of the stock material in the Western local-color story. Of some eight hundred examples of nineteenth-century Western fiction discussed, about eightscore are by Bret Harte. Consult R. R. Walterhouse, *Bret Harte, Joaquin Miller, and the Western Local Color Story: A Study in the Origins of Popular Fiction* (Ph.D., Chicago, 1939).

10 Granville Hicks is among those who emphasize that, while not possibly the founder of American regionalism, Bret Harte was the first to gain wide popularity following the Civil War. His short stories illuminative of sectional differences gradually were displaced, only to be revived again in such books as Ellen Glasgow's *Barren Ground* (1925), T. S. Stribling's *Teeftallow* (1926), Julia Peterkin's *Scarlet Sister Mary* (1928), G. H. Carroll's *As the Earth Turns* (1933), and Glenway Wescott's *The Apple of the Eye* (1934). See Harry Hartwick, *The Foreground of American Fiction* (1934), p. 146 *f.*; Granville Hicks, *The Great Tradition* (1935), p. 38.

11 "Bret Harte was the most successful purveyor of these meretricious sentimentalities, turning coast pioneers into good copy for distant romantic readers: dealing with mining camps in which no one ever worked; mines that men fought for, found, and gambled with; miners who behaved like opera choruses; women freezing in snowdrifts with never a mention of the cold; Mother Shipton comfortably starving to death in ten days and departing life with an epigram; M'liss, shaggy as a Shetland colt and sleek-souled as Little Eva. Almost all the Western tales, and all of hundreds of others about the West, were built, like sham folklore, from combinations of a few pat themes and motifs that were soon as outworn as the tritest poetic diction. They rang the changes

dozen stories and of about an equal number of poems have a secure place in American literature.	Out of a vast body of writings,[12] no inventive longer plot remains, and too few short pieces.
2. Possesses a sense of moral contrasts. Sincere if unflattering presentation of clerical characters.[13] Repudiates the idea of total depravity, the idea that the minority is of the elect and the majority of the damned. Accepts the thesis that out of evil good may emerge.[14]	2. The West criticized the immoral character of the stories, their vulgarity, obscenity, and tough realism. Others objected to his indictment of Puritanism. One of his artifices, states R. R. Walterhouse, is the "use of a paradoxical moral order"; furthermore, his implicit attitude toward religious institutions is similarly implicit in the works of many other contemporaneous authors.
3. Could apprehend character, drawing individualistic if composite types with a few competent strokes. Rememberable are Oakhurst, M'liss, Jack Hamlin, Yuba Bill, Colonel Starbottle, Tennessee's Partner, Miggles.	3. His perceptive but unanalytical mind could not imagine or create a single enduring character. Eccentricities of figures, theatricality of villains, elemental meretriciousness of heroines. Characterization static despite a succession of opportunistic incidents.
4. Superior in the invention of striking situations and episodes, and in the handling of setting. Had wit, humor of understatement, hard sanity. Grew to distrust saccharinity, and expressed his satire in humorous dialect rhymes and prose parodies.	4. Like his characters, his situations are stock. Cardboard plots dependent upon bizarre details and deficient in the elements of realism and truth to soul. Stagey romanticism and sentimental proclivities.[15]
5. Workmanship and style neater and more skillful than the literary craftsmanship of many of his contemporaries.	5. Diction conventional, sentences show lapses in construction, details are too Dickensian. Stories not only weak but at times incoherent.

---

on the miraculous reforms unconsciously achieved by women and babies, the redeeming grace of loyalty between 'pardners,' the dramatic effect of recognition scenes between long-separated lovers. And they were ridden with type characters: the last man in the deserted camp, the learned recluse, the adopted Indian child or the white child adopted by Indians, the woman disguised as a man, the gallant gambler. Even the Plautine *miles gloriosus*, the cowardly braggart, was translated into the idiom of the mining camp." P. H. Boynton, *Literature and American Life* (1936), p. 648 *f*.

12 Here is a partial list of his publications, the more representative of which are daggered: *Poems* (1871), *East and West Poems* (1871), *M'liss: An Idyl of Red Mountain*† (novelette, 1873), *Two Men of Sandy Bar*† (play, 1876), *Gabriel Conroy*† (novel, 1876), *Thankful Blossom* (1877), *The Story of a Mine* (1878), *Drift from Two Shores* (1878), *The Twins of Table Mountain* (1879), *Jeff Brigg's Love Story*† (novelette, 1880), *Ah Sin*† (play in collaboration with Mark Twain, 1877), *An Heiress of Red Dog*† (1878), *Flip, and Found at Blazing Star* (1882), *On the Frontier* (1884), *Snow-Bound at Eagle's* (1885), *A Phyllis of the Sierras* (1888), *A Waif of the Plains* (1890), *A Sappho of Green Springs*† (1891), *Colonel Starbottle's Client*† (1892), *Barker's Luck* (1896), *Stories in Light and Shadow*† (1898), *Openings in the Old Trail* (1902).

13 In *Tales of the Argonauts* (1875) he presents a gentle picture of Padre Junipero. For the influence upon Harte and his treatment of a vanishing regime of Spanish characters, art, architecture, and miscellanea, consult Carlos Vasquez-Arjona, "Spanish and Spanish-American Influences on Bret Harte," *RH.*, LXXVI (1929), pp. 573-621.

14 L. L. Hazard, "Eden to Eldorado," *UCC.*, XXXV (1933), pp. 107-121.

15 His stock routine includes the same backdrop and the same characters; the purpose is to present mining camp life; the motive is to demonstrate the inherent goodness buried within rough exteriors. One artifice, as R. R. Walterhouse has pointed out, is to pervert the standardized themes and to conclude with an O. Henry ending.

EDWARD EGGLESTON, 1837—1902, short-story writer, historian, novelist. Born in Vevay, Indiana. Strict Methodist upbringing and an education chiefly confined to country elementary schools were later reflected in his writings. At nineteen, upon his return from Minnesota, to which he had gone a year earlier for restoration of health, he became a Methodist circuit rider in Indiana, by which his health was further impaired. For almost a decade he preached in various prairie towns in Minnesota. In 1866, he began editing Sunday-school magazines in Chicago, notably the *Little Corporal,* a paper later incorporated into *St. Nicholas.* Joined the editorial staff of the New York *Independent.* He was founder and for five years pastor in Brooklyn, New York, of a Church of Christian Endeavor (1874—1879), from which he retired to devote himself to writing and historical research.

Relatively unimportant are his short stories, juvenile fiction, and history texts. What are valuable are his candid novelized transcripts of Indiana life that, in the very teeth of melodramatic incidents and unfinished, crude plots, frequently mawkish writing and Sunday-school sentiment, emerge as tales simple in plot and homely of circumstances, with the characterization Dickens-like in clarity and with background, atmosphere, manners, and dialects realized with such fidelity that they document Indiana pioneering as realistically as historical studies in social conditions. His realism is both an outgrowth of his belief that novels are pernicious things which must be purified by or impregnated with ultimate morality and historical materials to which other elements are to be subordinated, and of H. A. Taine's doctrine that stress must be placed upon well-selected facts and environmental influences, that an individual may be explained by the human-culture, outer-environmental formula of race, milieu, and the moment. It has often been observed that his function was historical rather than literary: he added the archetypal figure of the circuit rider, he made prominent the middle border states, he left a folkbook classic of the primitive settlements in the Ohio region.

NOVELS[16]

(1) *The End of the World* (1872). Wooden, stagey Indiana love story concerned with the 1843—1844 delusions of the Millerites or Second Adventists, and more realistic than *The Hoosier Schoolmaster.* (2) *The Mystery of Metropolisville* (1873). As melodramatic a story of a frontier real-estate boom as *The End of the World* is of the Millerites. (3) *The Circuit Rider* (1874). Despite its somewhat raggedy-edged style, is, in its account of Morton Goodwin, a Methodist itinerant preacher in southern Ohio, easily more skillfully constructed and more realistic than the more

16 J. T. Flanagan, "The Novels of Edward Eggleston," *CE.*, V (1944), pp. 250-254.

famous *Schoolmaster.* (4) *The Hoosier Schoolboy* (1883). In part an outgrowth of his earlier *Hoosier Schoolmaster,* indicts rural school conditions. (5) *The Graysons* (1887). Historical tale set in Illinois is perhaps as well-constructed as anything Eggleston wrote, involving Abraham Lincoln's appearance in a trial where he obtains an acquittal (Chapter XXVII) by the device of proving that the chief witness could not have seen the shooting, due to an absence of moonlight. (6) *The Faith Doctor*† (1891). A social satire that is descriptive of the faith-healing beliefs of Christian Scientists. Scenes laid in New York. Smooth style.

The Hoosier Schoolmaster† (1871). Most famous book is a picture of life in backwoods Indiana about 1850, founded upon the experiences of his brother, G. C. Eggleston. Compensating for its Dickensian but over-pious sentimentalism, its impossible villain, its types or caricatures, and its melodramatic climax to a plot that exists primarily for the description of the manners and sentiments of those early days are its realistic depiction of ordinary Hoosiers, its capturing of their plain language, its quite lively, concisely-put substance, and its valuable record of such matters as frontier lawlessness, revival preaching, and back-country conditions.[17]

Roxy† (1878). Interesting realistic Indiana tale of a triangle: despite community conventions, Roxy Adams, a genuine pioneer type, offers to accept the unborn child of her husband Mark Bonamy and Nancy Kirtley, who belongs to the shiftless "poor white" class. Fluent style, analytical characterization.

HISTORIES[17a]

The Beginners of a Nation (1896) and ***The Transit of Civilization*** (1901). Two learned, pleasant volumes in his pioneering cultural history of American life. Account cut short at the year 1700.

JOHN [MILTON] HAY, 1838—1905, author, statesman.[18] Born at Salem, Indiana. Grew up in Pike County, Illinois. Was graduated from Brown University, Rhode Island (1858). Several years later was admitted to the Illinois bar. Assistant private secretary to President Lincoln. For five years after the President's assassination served in the legations at Paris (1865—1867), Vienna (1867—1868), and Madrid (1868—1870). Staff-member of the

17 "Slight as it appears, this story has in it so much of humor as well as of direct observation, that it still persists in print after more than fifty years. . . . He is our pioneer midwest novelist, the first of a long line of writers of western and village life." Hamlin Garland, *The Westward March of American Settlement* (1927), pp. 30, 31.

17a J. A. Rawley, "Edward Eggleston: Historian," *IMH.,* XL (1944), pp. 345-352 (pp. 341-352).

18 J. B. Bishop, *John Hay* (1906); Lorenzo Sears, *John Hay* (1914); *The Life and Letters of John Hay,* edited by W. R. Thayer (two volumes in one, 1929); Tyler Dennett, *John Hay* (1933).

New York *Tribune* (1870—1875). Married Clara Stone, the daughter of the wealthy Cleveland banker Amasa Stone. Assistant Secretary of State (1879—1881) in the administration of President Hayes. United States Ambassador to Great Britain (1897). Secretary of State under McKinley and Theodore Roosevelt (1898—1905).

Miscellaneous writings include *Jim Bludso of the Prairie Bell, and Little Breeches* (1871), *Robert Burns* (1888), *Poems* (1890), *In Praise of Omar* (1898), *Addresses of John Hay* (1906), *Letters from John Hay and Extracts from His Diary*[19] (1908).

POETRY

Verses include "The White Flag" and "A Woman's Love," two love poems; "Liberty," a blank-verse lyric with three quotable lines; "The Stirrup-Cup," simple in its mysticism; "In a Graveyard," "Remorse," and "Through the Long Days," reminiscent of the graveyard tradition in English poetry.

***The Pike County Ballads and Other Pieces*†** (1871). Dialect poems or comic ballads about the Illinois frontier, often described as carrying on the tradition of localism and lingo[20] which had succeeded in Lowell's *Biglow Papers,* was flourishing in the jocular work of Bret Harte, and for a decade or more vastly stimulated popular interest in this type of literature. Most frequently quoted are "Jim Bludso" and "Little Breeches." The other pieces are "Banty Tim," said to be a forerunner of Kipling's "Gunga Din," and "The Mystery of Gilgil," "Golyer," "The Pledge at Spunky Point." Picturesque, crude virility; racy, terse; more genuinely mirroring the feelings of Western life than the ballads of Harte. If not the inaugurator of local-color (Harte is generally recognized as first in the field), Hay is among the early practitioners.

PROSE

Castilian Days (1871). Collection of seventeen sketches on the civilization of Spain — its pastimes, holidays, and customs, its landscape, art, and history, especially its inextricable connection with the Church. Twenty-five years later this travel book of essays

---

19 Hay is an unusually good letter-writer. An excellent introduction to his skill in illuminating the social and political atmosphere of Washington during the Civil War is *Lincoln and the Civil War in the Diaries and Letters of John Hay,* edited by Tyler Dennett (1939).

20 The Pike County folk of his poems were called pristinely vulgar, and as coarse as their language indicated. John Hay himself expressed a wish that the people would forget the half-dozen ballads, even requesting E. C. Stedman not to anthologize "Little Breeches," stating "how odious the very name of that hopeless little fluke is to yours faithfully." On the other hand, A. C. Ward has asserted that nearly "the whole philosophy of Pike County is embraced in the first verses of *Little Breeches*"; moreover, though the *Pike County Ballads* "seem feeble slush to twentieth-century intellectualists, they are nearer to universal experience than bloodless highbrowism is likely to get." In the words of the son, C. H. Hay, "half a century has shown that these rough-hewn models of Western types are destined to outlive all his other poetical efforts."

was still being described as "the bitterest and most infamous attack upon the Catholic Church," and as "obscene."[21] Economy of expression, grace of style, graphic observation.

The Bread-Winners (anonymously, 1883). Early novel of industrial unrest, fomenting the belief that labor unions are led by unconscionable leaders and polemizing in defense of property and vested rights. Plot slight, characters trivial. From its very publication it has been coupled with *Democracy* by Henry Adams (p. 256), generally to the advantage of the latter.[22]

Abraham Lincoln: A History (in collaboration with J. G. Nicolay, ten volumes, 1890). Vivid, monumental, authoritative one-and-a-half-million-word biography of Lincoln, superseded only by Carl Sandburg's six volumes (see p. 275).

[CINCINNATUS HINER (or HEINE)] MILLER, known better as **"JOAQUIN"**[23] **MILLER**, *c.* 1837[24]—1913, gold seeker, lawyer, Indian fighter, judge, newspaper editor, poet, novelist, dramatist.[25] Born in Liberty, Union County, Indiana. Taught to read and write by his father Hulings, a Quaker teacher. Family migrated West (1852), settling on a farm in Oregon (1852—1856). Set out for California and the gold fields (*c.* 1856). While he was living with the Digger Indians (1857), a daughter of his was born to a squaw. For at least three months (1857—1858), attended Columbia College at Eugene, Oregon.[26] Broke jail at Shasta City, to which he had been sentenced for stealing a horse (1859). With Isaac Mossman, established a pony express between Idaho and

---

21 Yet Elihu Root could say of John Hay: "The principles of Christian ethics controlled his judgments and his practice . . . . The scope of his human sympathy was universal. He could write both the Pike County ballads and Castilian Days." *The Dedication of the John Hay Library,* November 10, 1910 (1911), Address by Elihu Root, p. 41 (pp. 39-62).

22 V. L. Parrington, *Main Currents in American Thought,* III (1930), pp. 173-179; Granville Hicks, *The Great Tradition* (1933), pp. 79, 81; Tyler Dennett, *John Hay* (1933), pp. 110-112, 165 *f.*; P. H. Boynton, *Literature and American Life* (1936), pp. 740-742. Easily as significant in the development of proletarian fiction, it may be noted, are "Life in the Iron Mills" (1861) and *John Andross* (1874), both written by Rebecca H. Davis: Parrington, *op. cit.*, p. 60 *f.*; W. F. Taylor, *The Economic Novel in America* (1942), p. 79.

23 The name "Joaquin," which he assumed, came from an article he had published in defense of Joaquin Murietta, a Mexican brigand. See, for example, Hamlin Garland, "The Poet of the Sierras," *Sunset,* XXX (1913), p. 766 *f.* (pp. 765-770).

24 Misstatements in almost every account of Miller's life are in large measure the result of his own commitments. Concerning the date of his birth, for example, Harr Wagner, M. S Peterson, and George Sterling set the year 1841, 1839, and 1835 respectively, but those seem irreconcilable with the date furnished by J. J. Miller, *My Father, C. H. Joaquin Miller, Poet* (1941), p. 8 *f.* Probably closer to 1837 than to 1841 is the date of his birth: consult J. S. Richards, "Joaquin Miller's California Diary," *FM.*, XVI (1935), pp. 35-40; and *California Diary Beginning in 1855 & Ending in 1857,* edited by J. S. Richards (1936).

25 F. L. Pattee, *A History of American Literature since 1870* (1915), pp. 99-115; *The Poetical Works of Joaquin Miller,* edited by S. P. Sherman (1923); George Sterling, "Joaquin Miller," *AM.*, VI (1926), pp. 220-229; Harr Wagner, *Joaquin Miller and His Other Self* (1929); M. S. Peterson, *Joaquin Miller, Literary Frontiersman* (1937); Arlin Turner, "Joaquin Miller in New Orleans," *LHQ.*, XXII (1939), pp. 216-225.

26 Joseph Schafer, "An Historical Survey of Public Education in Eugene, Oregon," *OHSQ.*, II (1901), p. 56 (pp. 55-77); R. A. Gettman, "A Note on Columbia College," *AL.*, III (1931-1932), pp. 480-482.

Oregon (1861). Returned to Eugene (1862). Married Minnie Theresa Dyer ("Minnie Myrtle") in 1862, who bore him three children, left him in 1867, obtained a legal separation in 1869, and died in 1882. Edited the anti-Union *Democratic Register* (1863). For leading a punitive expedition against the Indians, he was rewarded with a judgeship (1866—1869). Published *Specimens* (1868) and *Joaquin et al.* (1869). Drifted to San Francisco (1870), where he joined the California literary society which included Bret Harte, C. W. Stoddard, and Ina Coolbrith. Left for New York. Sailed to England. *Pacific Poems* (1871) and *Songs of the Sierras* (1871). Back to America. From South America he went to England (1872) for a three-year stay, publishing *Life amongst the Modocs* (1873) and *Songs of the Sunlands* (1873). To America (1875). In Italy and on the Continent (1876—1878). *Songs of Italy* (1878). In America (1878—1886). Married Abigail Leland (1883), to whom a daughter was born. *Memorie and Rime* (1884). Purchased a permanent estate, "The Hights," at Oakland, California (1886). *Songs of the Mexican Seas* (1887). *Songs of the Soul* (1896). Represented the Hearst and other newspapers in the Klondike (1897). Probably was present as a newspaper correspondent in Pekin during the Boxer Rebellion (1900). *Chants for the Boer* (1900). *As It Was in the Beginning* (1903). Publication of his complete works (1909—1910). Died at "The Hights" (1913).

EARLY PERIOD

Specimens (1868). Personal, melodramatic, somewhat untamed narrative verse in iambic tetrameter.

***Songs of the Sierras*†** (1871). Byronic accents won him instant acclaim in England. New subject matter and romantic style, yet with some restraint in expression. Compare with its prose counterpart, *Life amongst the Modocs.*

MIDDLE PERIOD

(1) *Songs of the Sunlands* (1873). With its echoes of Swinburne, Mrs. Browning, and the Rossettis, the earliest reflection of his travels contributes little to his permanence as a poet. (2) *Life amongst the Modocs* (1873). Sentimental prose work, pseudo-autobiographical in its core and not too happy in its narrative manipulation. (3) *The One Fair Woman* (1876). Romantic novel. (4) *First Fam'lies of the Sierras* (1875). Prose tale of the Forty-Niners. (5) *The Baroness of New York* (1877). Protracted romantic melody in verse. (6) *Songs of Italy* (1878). Influenced by Browning. (7) *Shadows of Shasta* (1881). Inept prose work, a bit rememberable for its impulsive defense of the Indian. (8) *The Destruction of Gotham* (1886). Novel of class conflict in New York City. (9) *The Danites in the Sierras* (1882). Romantic,

exaggerated, anti-Mormon drama of frontier life. (10) *In Classic Shades* (1890). Less imitative than *Songs of Italy,* are poems on American themes.

FINAL PERIOD

The Building of the City Beautiful (1892). Prose romance ornamented by verses lifted from a contemplated "Life of Christ." Pleads for the Utopian ideal of peace, equality, tolerance, and brotherhood.

***Songs of the Soul*†** (1896). Contains some of his best poems including "The Passing of Tennyson" and "Columbus."

***A Song of Creation*†** (1899). Able stanzas, more than usually poetic in spirit and practical in philosophy. Dramatic nature-portrayals of his journeys from California to Alaska, the Far East, Hawaii, and the return to his native land.

***Overland in a Covered Wagon*†** (1930). Excellent literary story of pioneer life in the Middle West, and the westward exodus to Oregon and California. Is the "introduction" written for the complete edition of his poems.[27]

SUGGESTED MERITS	SUGGESTED DEFECTS
1. Several of his poems possess a swinging, even an impetuous, power, imaginatively sustained in their flights. Master of the iambic tetrameter form.	1. No firm narrative power in poetry. Diction conventional, style journalistic, quality theatrical, bombast tumbling, versification crude. Indebted to European models and forms, especially to those of Byron and Swinburne.
2. As stated by M. S. Peterson, nature for him is essentially drama. A lover of landscape, Miller shows natural scenes in action.[28]	2. A besetting sin is the over-luxuriant descriptive passages. Too often, nature for Joaquin Miller is melodrama.
3. As a romantic troubadour,[29] he sang of primitive strength: his feminine characters are not only Amazonian-maned but also romantically inclined. As a humanitarian, he espoused such oppressed people as the Jews of Palestine, the Mexicans in California, the American Indian, the Southern Confederacy. His myth-making power contributed to the poetic legends and culture of the West.	3. Overindulges in primitivism or the return-to-nature doctrine. His night-pieces or night-settings reveal the sentimental naturalism of a defunct Byronism. Almost all of his work is conventional, bookish, falsely exclamatory, and diluted both in form and concentration. Stigmatized as a poor imitator of the hackneyed Bret-Harte formulas of Far Western fiction.[30] Never thinks out a subject.

27 *Overland in a Covered Wagon,* edited by S. G. Firman (1930).

28 In *Paquita* [*Life amongst the Modocs*], Joaquin Miller depreciates the civilized order and describes an Indian Eden. For his Whitmanesque primitivism, see M. S. Peterson, "Joaquin Miller, an Introductory Sketch," *RAA.*, VIII (1930-1931), pp. 114-121.

29 In thought and phrase Joaquin Miller may have anticipated the poem "Trees" by Joyce Kilmer: B. B. Beebe, "More Letters of Joaquin Miller," *Frontier,* XII (1932), p. 227 *f.* (pp. 223-228).

30 R. R. Walterhouse, *Bret Harte, Joaquin Miller, and the Western Local Color Story: A Study in the Origins of Popular Fiction* (Ph.D., Chicago, 1939), pp. 3, 67.

OTHER LOCAL-COLORISTS: THE WEST

JOSEPH KIRKLAND, 1830—1894, who based his unromantic stories of the Middle West upon his own experiences, as did his mother, Caroline Stansbury Kirkland (p. 83). *Zury, the Meanest Man in Spring County*† (1887) and its sequel *The McVeys* (1888) are a realistic account of Zury (Usury) Prouder, who eventually marries Ann Sparrow McVey, mother of his twins. *The Captain of Company K* (1891), the anonymous prize story of the Detroit *Free Press,* treats the siege of Fort Donelson and the Battle of Shiloh unheroically and spasmodically from the point of view of a soldier. Here, as elsewhere, punning, moralizing, and sentimentality are obvious; but as in the preceding 1887 and 1888 volumes, there is the same fidelity to picturesque idiom and rustic people, the same earthiness of character-depiction.

HELEN [MARIA] HUNT JACKSON, 1831—1885, whom R. W. Emerson (p. 286) thought at least the best woman-poet on the continent, but who today is judged by her novels rather than by her poems. *Mercy Philbrick's Choice* (1876), a novelized study of Emily Dickinson (p. 231), was described by T. W. Higginson (p. 261) as having power, but being "too painful." *Hetty's Strange History* (1877), a story of retribution, is not especially immoral from today's point of view; *A Century of Dishonor*† (1881) is a sound, comprehensive account of the American Indian and governmental mistreatment of him; *Ramona*† (1884) is a romance that indicts the Americans who wipe out Indian villages and seize Spanish and Indian land. Among her poems are "Thought," "Burnt Ships," "Resurgam," and "Gondolieds." She also wrote *Bathmendi: A Persian Tale* (1867), *Verses* (1870), *Saxe Holm's Stories* (Series I, 1874; II, 1878), *Letters from a Cat: Published by Her Mistress* (1879), *The Training of Children* (1882), *Report on the Conditions and Needs of the Mission Indians* (1883), *Sonnets and Lyrics* (1886), *Father Junipero and the Mission Indians* (1902), *Glimpses of California and the Missions* (1902).

[JAMES] MAURICE THOMPSON, 1844—1901, known for his *Hoosier Mosaics*† (1875), a collection of vigorous dialect sketches, and for *Alice of Old Vincennes*† (1900), a best-selling historical romance of the Northwest Territory and George Rogers Clark's 1779 campaign. In addition to nature studies in *By-Ways and Bird Notes* (1885) and *My Winter Garden* (1900), in addition to poetry volumes called *Songs of Fair Weather* (1883) and *Poems* (1892), he wrote such other romantic regional novels as *A Tallahassee Girl* (1881), *His Second Campaign*† (1883), *At Love's Extremes* (1885), *A Banker of Bankersville* (1886), and *The King of Honey Island* (1892).

ALICE FRENCH, 1850—1934, novelist, short-story writer, who, though Massachusetts-born and long resident in Iowa, wrote about the villages of Arkansas under the pseudonym Octave Thanet, showed an interest in such labor problems as co-operatives versus labor unions, and, though a conventional writer, helped found local-color fiction in America. Her short *Stories of a Western Town* (1893), *A Captured Dream and Other Stories* (1897), and *Stories That End Well* (1911) are better known than such novels as *Knitters in the Sun* (1887), *Expiation* (1890), *The Missionary Sheriff* (1897), *The Heart of Toil* (1898), *Man of the Hour* (1905), and *A Step on the Stair* (1913).

E[DGAR] W[ATSON] HOWE, 1853—1937, editor-proprietor whose *The Story of a Country Town* (1883) anticipated *Main Street* by Sinclair Lewis (p. 271) and *Winesburg, Ohio* by Sherwood Anderson (p. 270). Howe's is a powerful, bitter, melodramatic, naturalistic tale of the smugness and cruelty of the Middle Western farm villages of Fairview and Twin-Mounds. Forgotten are *A Moonlight Boy* (1886), *The Confessions of John Whitlock* (1891), and *The Anthology of Another Town* (1920). His autobiography is found in *Plain People* (1929); his aphoristic paragraphing, in *Country Town Sayings* (1911), *The Blessing of Business* (1918), *Ventures in Common Sense* (1919), and *The Indignations of E. W. Howe* (1925).

THE LOCAL-COLORISTS: THE SOUTH

JOEL CHANDLER HARRIS, 1848—1908, essayist, poet, humorist, tale-teller, journalist, creator of "Uncle Remus."[31] Native of Eatonton, in middle Georgia. Married Essie (Esther, Esthel) LaRose (1873), who bore him nine children. Worked on various newspapers, beginning with J. A. Turner's *Countryman* and ending with the Atlanta *Constitution* (1876—1900), where his series of sketches and verses revolving about the antebellum figure of Uncle Remus made him internationally[32] famous: his authentic reproduction of the dialect of a Gullah Afro-American Negro, his humorous, happy, lovable creation of Uncle Remus, his animal stories with plantation life as a background make his papers a unique contribution to Negro folklore.[33] Another phase of his local-color work portrays the Georgia "cracker" or "poor white": *Mingo and Other Sketches in Black and White*† (1884); *Sister Jane: Her Friends and Acquaintances* (1896); *Gabriel Tolliver: A Story of Reconstruction* (1902); *Free Joe and Other Georgian Sketches* (1887); *Tales of the Home Folks in Peace and War* (1898); *The Making of a Statesman and Other Stories* (1902). A frequent statement is that what T. N. Page did for Virginia and G. W. Cable did for Louisiana, J. C. Harris did for Georgia. Part of the nine lines on his tombstone reads: "And while I am trying hard to speak the right word, I seem to hear a voice lifted above the rest, saying: 'You have made some of us happy.' "

UNCLE REMUS SERIES

Uncle Remus: His Songs and Sayings† (1880); *The Tar-Baby and Other Rhymes of Uncle Remus* (1880); *Nights with Uncle Remus*† (1892); *Uncle Remus and His Friends*† (1892); *Told by Uncle Remus* (1905); *Uncle Remus and Brer Rabbit* (1906); *Uncle Remus and the Little Boy* (1910); *Uncle Remus Returns* (1918).

[PATRICIO] LAFCADIO [TESSIMA CARLOS] HEARN, 1850—1904, journalist, translator, essayist, lecturer,

---

31 J. C. Harris, *The Life and Letters of Joel Chandler Harris* (1918) and *Joel Chandler Harris, Editor and Essayist* (1931).

32 The Tar-Baby story, for example, has been translated even into Bengali and African dialects. Consult J. C. Harris's introductions to *Uncle Remus: Songs and Sayings, Nights with Uncle Remus,* and *Uncle Remus and His Friends.*

33 F. M. Warren, "*'Uncle Remus'* and *'The Roman de Renard,'* " *MLN.*, V (1890), pp. 257-270; R. S. Baker, "Joel Chandler Harris," *Outlook*, LXXVIII (1904), pp. 595-603; H. A. Toulmin, Jr., *Social Historians* (1911), pp. 133-164; E. W. Bowen, "Joel Chandler Harris, A Faithful Interpreter of the Negro," *RCR.*, Series 4, XXIII (1919), pp. 357-369; T. E. Ferguson, "Joel Chandler Harris," *TR.*, VI (1920-1921), pp. 214-221; H. W. Mabie, *Commemorative Tributes to Richard Watson Gilder, Joel Chandler Harris, Edward Everett Hale, Carl Schurz, Winslow Homer* (1922), pp. 3-6; C. A. Smith, in *A Short History of American Literature,* edited by W. P. Trent, John Erskine, S. P. Sherman, and Carl Van Doren (1922), pp. 301-310.

folk-lorist, philosopher.[34] Born on the Ionian Island of Santa Maura (Leucadia or Lefcadia). Son of C. B. Hearn, a British surgeon-major, and Rosa Tessima (or Rosa Cerigote) Hearn, a Greek. When his parents separated, Patrick, as he was known to his friends, came under the care of Mrs. Sarah Brenane, a pious Catholic great-aunt. While at St. Cuthbert's College in Yorkshire, as a result of an accident at play, he lost the sight of his left eye, and this caused his right eye to become enlarged. Because the lad voiced pantheistic opinions, he was dismissed. After a two-year stay in a school near Rouen, France, the boy ran off to Paris. Impoverished in London. Finally, emigrated to America (1869). Starved for two years in New York. To Cincinnati, which had been his original destination when sent off to America by Mrs. Brenane. Taught by Harry Watkin[35] how to set type and read proof. His vivid account of the "Tan Yard Case" (1874) made him well-known on the *Enquirer,* for which he worked (1872—1875). Founded the short-lived *Ye Giglampz,* a weekly. Dismissed from the *Enquirer* as a result of his entanglement with Althea Foley, a mulatto woman.[36] Reporter for the *Commercial* (1875—1877), which sent him to New Orleans (1877—1879).[37] Wrote a series of ghostly newspaper sketches, now generally known under the title of "Fantastics." Assistant editor of the *Item* (1878—1881). Within a score of days his five-cent restaurant, "The Hard Times," closed up. On the New Orleans *Times-Democrat* (1881—1887),[38] where his chief work was to make translations from the French and to editorialize on literary topics.[39] Left New Orleans for New York, where he stayed for a time with H. E. Krehbiel, whose wife disliked Hearn's habits. Twice commissioned to Martinique by *Harper's* (1887). Armed with an ambiguous contract and probably influenced by a reading of Percival Lowell's *The Soul of the Far East,* he left New York for Japan (1890).[40] Taught

34 P. E. More, *Shelburne Essays,* Second Series (1905), pp. 46-72; Elizabeth Bisland, *The Life and Letters of Lafcadio Hearn* (two volumes, 1906); E. L. Tinker, *Lafcadio Hearn's American Days* (1924); Oscar Lewis, *Hearn and His Biographers* (1930); Jean Temple, *Blue Ghost* (1931); Kazuo Koizumi, *Father and I* (1935); K. P. Kirkwood, *Unfamiliar Lafcadio Hearn* (1936).

35 *Letters from the Raven,* edited by Milton Bronner (1907), presents Hearn's correspondence with Harry Watkin.

36 *The Japanese Letters of Lafcadio Hearn,* edited by Elizabeth Bisland (1910), pp. vii-ix; Oscar Lewis, *Hearn and His Biographers* (1930), pp. 45-76.

37 Sketches, editorials, and essays that Lafcadio Hearn wrote for the Cincinnati and New Orleans newspapers in his American days are available in several compilations edited separately by C. W. Hutson, Ichiro Nishizaki, and Albert Mordell. Other compilers are Ferris Greenslet, Ryuji Tanabé, Sanki Ichikawa, and Iwao Inagaki.

38 It is said that on orders from Page Baker, editor-in-chief of the *Times-Democrat,* no one was permitted to change even a comma in work submitted by Hearn, who was nicknamed "Old Semicolon" because of his attempts to reform American punctuation.

39 Notorious and severe is Hearn's attack upon Whitman's *Leaves of Grass* on July 30, 1882. In another editorial he described W. D. Howells as "one who carries what he calls 'realism' to the unreal excess of suppressing in his own work all emotion, all enthusiasm, all veritably natural feeling." Writings that are deficient in high color and strong drama did not seem to appeal to Hearn.

40 E. L. Tinker, *Lafcadio Hearn's American Days* (1924), p. 326 *ff.*; Jean Temple, *Blue Ghost* (1931), p. 110 *ff.*

in the middle school of Matsue (1890). Married Setsu Koizumi (1891), a twenty-two-year-old Japanese of a distinguished Samurai family, who bore him three sons and a daughter. Became a Japanese citizen, and assumed the name of Koizumi ("Little Spring") Yakumo. Taught at a government college at Kumamoto. Dismissed (1902) from the faculty of the Imperial University of Tokio, where for almost a decade he had occupied the chair of English literature. Appointed to a Professorship at Waseda University (1904). Died of a heart attack in Tokio (1904). Lectures posthumously published from verbatim trascripts.[41] Posthumously honored by an Imperial Japanese decoration.

Much of his writing is journalistic and facile; yet a sustained feeling for flavored words, a dexterity of style, and an acute observation make him a master of description. Excellently interpretative and stimulating are his lectures on criticism, which illuminate genuine literary experience and put emphasis upon the emotional content of literature.[42]

He is credited with best interpreting the Orient to the Occidental mind; but there remains a controversy regarding the verity of his pictures about Japan. He seems to close his eye to unpleasant realistic facts about that country; and to open it only upon its beauty and poetry, its wisdom and mysticism. Always a romanticist, yet he doubted the Christian creed, and finally embraced the Buddhist faith; always a mystic, yet he depended upon the teachings of Herbert Spencer, even interpreting Japan in that philosopher's terms. However, he may still be recommended as a fairly reliable guide to the better spirit of that country.

AMERICAN WRITINGS

(1) *One of Cleopatra's Nights* (1882), his first book, a volume of stories translated from Gautier; (2) *La Cuisine Creole* (1885), a collection of culinary recipes; (3) *Gombo Zhèbes* (1885), a slight dictionary of Negro-French or Creole proverbs; (4) *Some Chinese Ghosts*† (1887), a group of well-finished Oriental sketches collected from *Harper's;* (5) *Two Years in the French West Indies* (1890), finished sketches resulting from his experiences in Martinique.

Strange Leaves from Strange Literature† (1884). Testifying to his predilection for the exotic, tells of Oriental love and hate, venge-

---

41 A number of students succeeded in taking down not only passages but also complete talks as Lafcadio Hearn lectured to them slowly and simply so that the English could be understood more readily. Such transcriptions have been edited notedly by John Erskine, as well as by such former students of Hearn as Iwao Inagaki (1928) and Shigetsugu Kishi (1941).

42 *Interpretations of Literature* (two volumes, 1915), first selection from Hearn's lectures at the University of Tokio; *Appreciations of Poetry* (1916), second selection; *Life and Literature* (1917) — all three edited by John Erskine. See also *Talks to Writers* (1920), *Books and Habits* (1921), and *Pre-Raphaelite and Other Poets* (1922), likewise edited by John Erskine.

ance and death, in fantastic stories stemming out of such sources as the Anvari-Soheili, the Baitál-Pachísí, the Talmud, and the Kalevala.

Chita: A Memory of Last Island† (1889). Narrative tale, slight in plot but unified by excellent descriptions, was inspired by a tidal wave he saw (1884) while at Grand Isle in the Gulf of the Mississippi.

Youma: The Story of a West-Indian Slave† (1890). Martyr tale of a *da,* the foster-mother and nurse of Mayotte, was founded on fact.

Karma (1890). Thoughtful study of self-revelation. Inferior to *Youma.*

JAPANESE WRITINGS

Included are: *Out of the East* (1895), *Kokoro* (1896), *Gleanings in Buddha-Fields* (1897), *Exotics and Retrospectives* (1898), *In Ghostly Japan* (1899), *Shadowings* (1900), *A Japanese Miscellany* (1901), *Kottō* (1902), *Japan: An Attempt at Interpretation* (1904), *Kwaidan* (1904), *The Romance of the Milky Way* (1905). Best-known is *Glimpses of Unfamiliar Japan*† (two volumes, 1894), a pleasant introduction to its characters and feudal customs; worth the knowing is *Japanese Fairy Tales*†.[43]

GEORGE W[ASHINGTON] CABLE, 1844—1925, depictor of the Creole civilization. Native of New Orleans.[44] Father was a Virginian; mother came of New England ancestry. Enlisted on the Confederate side in the Fourth Mississippi Cavalry (1861—1865). After the war, was successively a surveyor, a contributor for about eighteen months of the column "Drop Shot" in the New Orleans *Daily Picayune,*[45] and a clerk in a cotton agent's office. His attitude on the Negro question proved offensive to his neighbors,[46]

---

43 "That Hearn was such a perfectionist, such a discerning and impassioned collector of these little jewels of folklore, that he lavished such care in comprehending completely the spiritual and historical background from which they sprang, explains why his beautifully misty tales . . . — rhythmically delicate as the web of the golden-spider — are no mere grey translations, but are rather the rainbow reincarnation of the very spirit of those ancient Japanese who first gave substance to the shadow of their ancestral fears by putting into words these spectral myths." E. L. Tinker in his "Prologue" to *Japanese Fairy Tales* (1936), p. 10 (pp. 3-10).

44 E. W. Bowen, "George Washington Cable: An Appreciation," *SAQ.*, XVIII (1919), pp. 145-155; L. L. C. Bikle, *George W. Cable: His Life and Letters* (1928); E. L. Tinker, "A Prologue," in *Old Creole Days* by G. W. Cable, together with *The Scenes of Cable's Romances* by Lafcadio Hearn (The Heritage Press, 1943), pp. vii-xviii.

45 Always a religious man, G. W. Cable showed his Sunday-school bias even in his earliest contributions: E. L. Tinker, "Cable and the Creoles," *AL.*, V (1933-1934), p. 314 *f.* (pp. 313-326); Arlin Turner, "George Washington Cable's Literary Apprenticeship," *LHQ., XXIV* (1941), p. 186 (pp. 168-186).

46 "Cable's inherent variance with the South and her people showed itself throughout his life: First, in his presentation of the Creoles; second, in his attitude towards slavery and the negro question; and, third and fourth, of lesser importance, in his attitude toward the Civil War, and in connection with prison and asylum reform in the South." Margaret Bloom, "George W. Cable," *Bookman,* LXXIII (1931), p. 401 *f.* (pp. 401-403). See also E. L. Tinker, "Cable and the Creoles," *AL.*, V (1933-1934), pp. 313, 318 *f.* (pp. 313-326).

and was a factor in his removing to Northampton, Massachusetts (1884), where he lived until his death.

Representative writings include (1) *The Creoles of Louisiana* (1884), a collection of historical sketches; (2) *The Silent South* (1885), a slight volume that, striving to improve the conditions of the Negro, cast a lance against such evils as the convict-lease system, prisons, and asylums; (3) *John March, Southerner* (1894), problem novel of the Reconstruction anticipating the work of Ellen Glasgow and others; (4) *The Negro Question* (1890), centering about the same problem as his 1885 book; (5) *Strong Hearts* (1899), a collection of stories; and (6) *The Cavalier* (1901), a tale of the Civil War. Other works are *Strange True Stories of Louisiana* (1889), *The Busy Man's Bible* (1891), *Bylow Hill* (1902), *Kincaid's Battery* (1908), *"Posson Jone'" and Père Raphaël* (1909), *The Amateur Garden* (1914), *Gideon's Band* (1914), *The Flower of the Chapdelaines* (1918), and *The Lovers of Louisiana* (1918).[47]

SHORT STORIES

***Old Creole Days*†** (1879). Seven idealized, exotic stories of nineteenth-century New Orleans are adequate representations of quaint Creole life. Its de-emphasis on plot or incident and the accuracy of the reproduced Creole lingo have been challenged; but not the engagingly-etched characters and their deft dialect, the colorful situations and the romantic background of Creole life. In "'Tite Poulette," Cable attacks the tragedies resulting from miscegenation; in "Jean-ah Poquelin," he demonstrates how a community misjudges a former slave-trader; in "Posson Jone'," he portrays, to use his own descriptive words, "an ardent and controlling mutual affection springing into life wholly apart from the passion of sex"; and in "Madame Délicieuse" and "Café des Exilés," he is again vivid and interesting.

***Madame Delphine*†** (1881). Long short story or novelette incorporated into later editions of *Old Creole Days*. Cumulatively overwhelming is the characterization of Madame Delphine. Note the descriptive chapter allotted to each character.

---

47 Ordinary and negligible are most of his romances. Not only did he lack the creative type of mind but his pedagogic excesses slaughtered whatever creative ability he may have possessed. Such is the theory of E. L. Tinker, who nevertheless describes G. W. Cable as "the legitimate father of the literary movement which is producing such splendid fruit in the South today."

To the excessively appreciative R. U. Johnson, Cable "was a man of Puritan instincts who could interpret the Cavalier as no author has done. He portrayed women as understandingly and as sympathetically as Tolstoy. He knew the Creoles by heart, and gives us all the sparkling facets of their attractive character." His style "is composed of many qualities: grace, force, range, suggestiveness, imagination, large and unconventional vocabulary, shimmering humor, easy movement, contrast, tenderness, surprise and dramatic progression to an adequate climax. Thus his style has intense personality." R. U. Johnson believes that, "with the possible exception of Hawthorne and Poe, Cable is the greatest figure in American fiction." R. U. Johnson, "George Washington Cable," *Commemorative Tributes to Cable, Sargent, Pennell* (American Academy of Arts and Letters, 1927), pp. 1-6.

NOVELS

***The Grandissmes: A Story of Creole Life*†** (1880). With the New Orleans of 1803 suffusing its romantic background, this highly picturesque novel appeals by reason of its felicitous plot (out of the fertility of which is born a forest of episodes), sculpturesque character-creations, dramatic happenings, genial humor, and sparkling execution. Its organization could be less diffuse and more proportioned and balanced.

Dr. Sevier (1885). Rambling, shapeless, plotless, moralistic, its saving interest may lie in the characterization of the Doctor and the Richlings. Attacks the corruption of New Orleans.

Bonaventure (1888). Idyl composed of three slight sketches or stories is graced, stylistically, by good descriptions and, narratively, by a lovable Creole among the Acadian descendents on the bayous of Louisiana. Again he is unable to sustain a long plot.

JAMES LANE ALLEN, 1849—1925, short-story writer, novelist.[48] Born in Fayette County, near Lexington, Kentucky. Was graduated from the University of Kentucky, now known as Transylvania College (1872). M.A. (1877). Lack of funds forced him to leave Johns Hopkins University, where he had hoped to study comparative philology. Professor of Latin at Bethany College, West Virginia (1882—1884). To New York (1884), where he settled permanently in 1893. Died in the Roosevelt Hospital.

Characteristic of his writings is an understrain of sadness. His large output reveals an artificial, ornate style, unreal characterization, and deficient plot construction. Publications include (1) *The Blue-Grass Region of Kentucky and Other Kentucky Articles* (1892), a collection contributed to *Harper's* and the *Century;* (2) *The Heroine in Bronze, or a Portrait of a Girl* (1912), a love story of an honorable hero, a book that is for one moment rhetorically graceful and for the next moment dialogistically strained, but consistently shallow; (3) *The Last Christmas Tree: An Idyl of Immortality* (1914), a prose poem printed six years earlier in a magazine; (4) *The Sword of Youth* (1915), a novelette of the Civil War; (5) *A Cathedral Singer* (1916); (6) *The Kentucky Warbler* (1918), inept but noble in purpose; (7) *The Emblems of Fidelity: A Comedy in Letters* (1919), by no means devoid of humor; (8) *The Alabaster Box* (1923), a collection of stories; and (9) *The Landmark* (1925), a posthumous group of short tales.

---

48 L. W. Payne, Jr., "The Stories of James Lane Allen," *SRQ.*, VIII (1900), pp. 45-55; H. A. Toulmin, Jr., *Social Historians* (1911), pp. 101-129; J. W. Townsend, *James Lane Allen* (1928); G. C. Knight, *James Lane Allen and The Genteel Tradition* (1935).

***Flute and Violin and Other Kentucky Tales and Romances*†** (1891). Six carefully-constructed, poetic tales, but coated with a florid style and a priggish point of view. Includes "Flute and Violin," quietly pathetic; "Two Gentlemen of Kentucky"; "King Solomon of Kentucky,"† based upon facts and strong in human interest; and "Posthumous Fame; or a Legend of the Beautiful," which shows the influence of Hawthorne as much as "The White Cowl" and "Sister Dolorosa," two tales criticized by the religious press. For "John Gray," see *The Choir Invisible* (p. 178, below).

***A Kentucky Cardinal: A Story*†** (1894). Entire theme of this pleasant novelette is infused with restrained feeling, sparkling vitality, deep sympathy, and poeticized out-of-door descriptions. With this idyl compare "A Passion in the Desert" by Balzac and *Le Secret du précepteur* by Victor Cherbuliez.

Aftermath (1896). Idyllic sequel to *A Kentucky Cardinal* is inferior in descriptive gems, lightness of jest, and engaging quality.

Summer in Arcady: A Tale of Nature (1896). Original title of *Butterflies: a Tale of Nature* refers to a boy-girl bundling in the lush Kentucky grass. Frank account of seduction and love was protested by critics who avoided considerations of such merits as humorous touches, passionate if verbal strength, and natural, almost vitalized conversation.

***The Choir Invisible*†** (1897). Historical romance, an expanded version of his earlier *John Gray: A Kentucky Tale of the Olden Time* (1893), relates the love of John for the already-married Jessica. Engaging nature-pictures. Slender plot thinned out even further by a tendency to stiffness of dialogue and an excess of sweetness. Title derived from George Eliot's poem beginning "Oh may I join the choir invisible."

***The Reign of Law*†** (1900; English title, *The Increasing Purpose*). Like *Summer in Arcady,* is a graphic love tale of humble farm folk in the Kentucky hemp fields, and like its predecessor aroused a storm of comment.[49] Masculinity of its theme maintained by maturing workmanship, realistic settings, lifelike characters. Partly autobiographical. Includes "The Song of the Hemp," probably his best lyric.

The Mettle of the Pasture (1903). Old-fashionedly puritanical, protractedly dull, reekingly sentimental work dealing with the follies and tragedies of a Southern town's aristocrats.

49 Among his critics was President McGarvey of the College of the Bible in the University of Texas, whose strictures appeared in the Lexington *Leader* on October 8, 1900. That the hero of the story "was made up largely from his own experiences" and that the book's chief purpose "is to degrade Christianity" are among the assertions made. To these J. L. Allen replied. See *Mr. James Lane Allen's Novel, the Reign of Law: A Controversy and Some Opinions concerning It* (New York, 1900).

The Bride of the Mistletoe (1909). First of his planned Christmas trilogy,[50] the queer sketch seems to have phallic worship for its background. Influenced by Maeterlinck.

The Doctor's Christmas Eve (1910). Sequel to *The Bride of the Mistletoe* is more conventional, but as depressing as its 1909 predecessor is weird. Discouraged by the reception of both, Allen suspended the trilogy.

OTHER LOCAL-COLORISTS: THE SOUTH

CONSTANCE FENIMORE WOOLSON, 1840—1894, perhaps our earliest realist, in the modern sense. Wrote *Two Women: 1862* (1877), her only long poem. Two collections of short stories have been commented upon by Henry James (p. 211) for their minuteness of observation and tenderness of feeling: *Castle Nowhere: Lake Country Sketches* (1875), nine stories concerned chiefly with the early French inhabitants near the Great Lakes; and *Rodman the Keeper: Southern Sketches* (1880), ten of the tales having previously been published in outstanding Northern magazines, is appreciative of both Southern and Northern characters: the stories are now exotic and fragrant, now poignant and woeful. Previously she had issued *The Old Stone House* (under pseudonym of Anne March, 1873), a Dickensian novel for children; posthumously, *The Front Yard and Other Italian Stories* (1895) and *Dorothy and Other Italian Stories* (1896), two collections interesting for their character studies of Americans in Italy, where she had lived during her last fifteen years. Excellent tales: "Jeanette," "The Old Agency," "The Lady of Little Fishing," "Solomon," and "Wilhelmina" (in *Castle Nowhere*); "Sister St. Luke," "Felipe," "The South Devil," "Rodman the Keeper," "Old Gardiston," and "In the Cotton Country" (in *Rodman the Keeper*); "The Front Yard" and "The Street of the Hyacinth" (in *The Front Yard*); "Dorothy" and "A Transplanted Boy" (in *Dorothy*).

Although stronger as a writer of short fiction, while in Italy she also wrote five novels first published serially in *Harper's,* in four of which fresh picturings of the South are dominant and in all of which the settings are American. *Anne*† (1882), superior in its early chapters which have the Mackinac region of the Great Lakes as a setting, plotted more complicatedly as the episodic story is moved to an eastern part of the country and the marital difficulties increase. *For the Major*† (1883), a novelette of a wife's self-sacrifice in the small American town of Far Edgerly, is centered on a Black Mountain plantation of the Carolinas. *East Angels*† (1886), slight in plot but a well-written study of a group of characters on a Florida estate near Gracias-a-Dios. In *East Angels* geographic factors have diminished importance, as they have in her next two novels. *Jupiter Lights* (1889), an improbable, slightly morbid study of marital life principally in the South, although both the Lake Superior region and Italy itself also are part of the location. *Horace Chase* (1884), a didactic study with its chief settings in Asheville, North Carolina, and St. Augustine, Florida, yet less melodramatic than *Anne* and *Jupiter Lights* and as well constructed as *East Angels.*

HENRY WOODFIN GRADY, 1850—1889, Georgia journalist who achieved national fame as an orator by "The New South," a speech delivered in New York City at a banquet of the New England Society on December 21, 1886, and who retained his laurels by "The Race Problem in the South," delivered at the annual banquet of the Boston Merchants' Association in December, 1889. Trenchant pen and silver tongue pleaded against tenant farming, advanced forward-looking views on penology, urged fairer treatment of the Negro, recognizing that the South could advance only as the Negro advanced with it. Consult *The New South and Other Addresses* (1904) and *The Complete Orations and Speeches of Henry W. Grady* (1910).

---

50 W. A. Bradley, "James Lane Allen's 'The Doctor's Christmas Eve,'" *Bookman,* XXXII (1910-1911), pp. 640-642; G. C. Knight, "Allen's Christmas Trilogy and Its Meaning," *Bookman,* LXVIII (1928-1929), pp. 411-415.

MARY NOAILLES MURFREE, 1850—1922, whose tales of the Cumberland folk are on the whole real, as are the flashes of humor, eloquent scenes, lifelike Tennesseean mountaineers, and human appeal, and as are the charges that her works are ridden with didactic attitudes, conversational asides, too many descriptions, type characters, sameness of plots, and poorly sustained themes. Under the pen name R. E. Dembry she wrote tenuous society essays; under the pseudonym Charles Egbert Craddock, derived from the name of a minor character in her early incomplete *Allegheny Winds and Waters,* she published her local-color fiction.

Among her juvenile volumes are *Down the Ravine* (1885), an agreeable, moralistic novel, and *The Young Mountaineers* (1897), a collection of wholesome mountain tales. SHORT STORIES: *In the Tennessee Mountains*† (1884), eight local color-stories previously published under her pseudonym C. E. Craddock in the *Atlantic Monthly,* remembered especially for "Drifting Down Lost Creek," "A Playin' of Old Sledge at the Settlemint," and "Electioneerin' on Big Injun Mounting." Its high level of excellence was not reached by any succeeding volume: *The Phantoms of the Foot-Bridge* (1895), *The Young Mountaineers* (1897), *The Bushwhackers* (1899), *The Frontiersmen* (1904), and *The Raid of the Guerrilla* (1912), although "The Mystery of Witch-Face Mountain," leading tale in a collection with that title, is one of her best novelettes even if its ending lacks inevitability. NOVELS: *Where the Battle Was Fought* (1884), a flabbily-plotted novel of Reconstruction in her native Tennessee town of Murfreesboro. *The Prophet of the Great Smoky Mountains*† (1885), a readable, strongly religious novelette, poor in unity but more skilfully organized than her 1884 work. *In the "Stranger People's" Country*† (1891), possibly her most artistic work. *The Story of Old Fort Loudon* (1899), despite a few good episodes and an accurate reproduction of the Fort in the 1760's, is on the whole a poor historical novel. *A Spectre of Power* (1903), another popular documented work with a standardized, competently-done plot. *The Storm Centre* (1905), a Civil War novel, faithful in its setting, false in its sentimentality, with its court-martial description influenced by *Military Law and the Practice of Courts-Martial* (1862). *The Amulet* (1906), where the setting for her final historical novel is Fort Prince George in 1763.

KATE [O'FLAHERTY] CHOPIN, 1851—1904, interpreter of Creole and Cajun life. NOVELS: *At Fault* (1890), tragic domestic drama set in the Cane River region of Louisiana, is a story of character development and disintegration that unfortunately does not fulfill the stylistic and structural promise of the first half. *The Awakening* (1899), wherein the heroine Edna drowns herself, stirred up a tempest of criticism by its morbidity of theme and eroticism of motivation. SHORT-STORY COLLECTIONS: *Bayou Folk* (1894), twenty-three simple, delicate, graceful stories and sketches of the Acadians and Creoles of the Louisiana bayous. Includes "For Marse Chouchoute," a dramatic tale of loyalty and sacrifice; "Désirée's Baby," a great story; and "Ma'am Pélagre," a kind sketch of a woman's character. *A Night in Acadie* (1897), twenty-one tales of the bayou country. Stories again show her deftness with the patois of the people, their feelings and motives. Representative is "Ozème's Holiday," humorous in its pathos. POETRY: Simple, not without merit. "If It Might Be," "I Opened All the Portals Wide," "Love Everlasting," "You and I," "Good Night," "A Fancy," "Life."

IRWIN RUSSELL, 1853—1879, whose dialect verses are among the first to appreciate the Negro character. Both T. N. Page, in his *Befo' de War* (1888), and J. C. Harris, in his introduction to Russell's *Christmas-Night in the Quarters and Other Poems* (1917; an enlarged issue of Russell's *Poems,* published in 1888), have acknowledged their obligations to their predecessor, whose masterpiece is "Christmas-Night in the Quarters," a not too carefully constructed Negro-operetta influenced by Robert Burns, and presenting interesting plantation pictures. When Irwin Russell died, he was only twenty-six years old. (For J. C. Harris and T. N. Page, see pp. 172 and 180.)

THOMAS NELSON PAGE, 1853—1922, distinguished as a leading Southern *genre* writer of regionalism. *Robert E. Lee: The Southerner* (1908) and *Robert*

E. Lee: Man and Soldier (1911) have only a slight academic interest; *Among the Camps* (1891) and *Pastime Stories* (1894) are forgotten juvenile works, and only the autobiographical elements keep *Two Little Confederates* (1888) alive; "Uncle Gabe's White Folks" (1877) is a sympathetic poem in the Negro vernacular, almost the only one remembered from such volumes as *Befo' de War* (in collaboration, 1888) and *The Coast of Bohemia* (1906). *Elsket and Other Stories* (1891), *The Burial of the Guns* (1894), and *Bred in the Bone* (1904) are short-story collections not so well known as *In Ole Virginia* (1887), six local-color stories notable for their inclusion of "Marse Chan," straightforwardly narrating in Negro dialect a Civil War tale inspired by a letter found in the pocket of a dead private. "Polly" (in the same volume) and "Meh Lady" are each a notable story of the reconciliation of prejudices. Among his novels are *On Newfound River* (1891), *Red Rock* (1898), *The Old Gentleman of the Black Stock* (1897), *Gordon Keith* (1903), and *John Marvel, Assistant* (1909); among his nonfiction, *The Old South* (1892), social and historical essays, *Social Life in Old Virginia* (1897), *The Old Dominion* (1908), *Dante and His Influence* (1922), and, notably, *The Negro: The Southerner's Problem* (1904) and *Italy and the World War* (1920), declared by R. U. Johnson to be an astonishing *tour de force* of narrative.

GRACE ELIZABETH KING, 1853—1932. Wrote several historical volumes including: *Jean Baptiste Le Moyne, Sieur de Bienville* (1893), a competent account of the founder of New Orleans. *De Soto and His Men in the Land of Florida* (1898), a tinged tale of the sixteenth-century expedition. *Stories from Louisiana History* (1905), for juveniles. *Mount Vernon on the Potomac* (1929), an account of George Washington's home and grave, and of the patriotic association formed to preserve that landmark. *Memories of a Southern Woman of Letters* (1932), a posthumous sheaf of garrulous, enthusiastic reminiscences.

More important are: *New Orleans: The Place and the People*† (1898), a tender, understanding, colorful, even imaginative chronicle of the foundation and development of the city. *Creole Families of New Orleans* (1921), forty delightful, tactful, and accurate chapters, based on genealogical records, concerned with the oldest families of the city, and the social life and customs of early Louisiana days, particularly in its account of the Pontalba family.

Most important are her short stories and novels, such as: *Monsieur Motte*† (1888) a *New Princeton Review* romance of a family plantation restored to the orphaned Marie Modeste through the efforts of Marcelite, a faithful ex-slave. *Tales of a Time and Place*† (1892), five somewhat impressionistic short stories of New Orleans reprinted from *Harper's,* and *Balcony Stories*† (1893), fourteen tales about the Creole Louisianans reprinted from *Century,* the simplicity, tragedy, and poetry of whose lives are accentuated by quirks of speech, eccentricities of temperament, and quaintness of humor. *The Pleasant Ways of St. Medard*† (1907; 1916), a somewhat discursive but sincere, unvarnished depiction of the struggle of an impoverished New Orleans family for readjustment during post-Civil War days. *La Dame de Ste. Hermine* (1924), a naturally-told historical romance of the settlement of New Orleans by Bienville in the first quarter of the eighteenth century.

JOHN [WILLIAM] FOX, Jr., *c.* 1862—1919, whose novels and novelettes made the mountaineers of the Cumberlands widely known. He never broke away from the romantic formulas of stereotyped heroines and villains, cloying sentimentalism, and somewhat ornate landscape descriptions; yet he wrote easily and pleasantly and accurately of the life and customs of the Kentucky, Tennessee, and West Virginia mountaineers. NOVELS AND NOVELETTES: *A Mountain Europa* (1894), *A Cumberland Vendetta* (1895), *Hell for Sartain* (1897), *The Kentuckians* (1898), *Crittenden* (1900), *The Heart of the Hills* (1913), *Erskine Dale: Pioneer* (1920); but his most popular were *The Little Shepherd of Kingdom Come* (1902) and *The Trail of the Lonesome Pine* (1908).

THE LOCAL-COLORISTS: NEW ENGLAND

SARAH ORNE JEWETT, 1849—1909, creator of "the Sarah Orne Jewett country."[51] Born in South Berwick, Maine. Daughter of Dr. Theodore Jewett, who took her with him on his country calls. Friend of Annie Adams Fields. First woman awarded a Litt.D. by Bowdoin College (1901).

Her publications are *The Story of the Normans* (1877), *Play-Days: A Book of Stories for Children* (1878), *Betty Leicester* (1889), *Betty Leicester's Christmas* (1894), *Letters* (1911), *Verses* (1916), and several volumes of short-stories collected in *Old Friends and New* (1879), *Country By-Ways* (1881), *The Mate of the Daylight and Friends Ashore* (1883), *A White Heron* (1886), *The King of Folly Island, and Other People* (1888), *Strangers and Wayfarers* (1890), *A Native of Winby, and Other Tales*† (1893), *The Life of Nancy* (1895), and *The Queen's Twin, and Other Stories* (1899).

NOVELS

(1) *A Country Doctor* (1884), in which she describes her father's character, reveals her as a short-story writer rather than as a novelist. (2) *A Marsh Island* (1885) relates the love of a wealthy painter Dick Dale and Doris Owen, a New England farmer's daughter. (3) *The Tory Lover* (1901), deviating from her usual forte, is a historical novel dealing with John Paul Jones and the men he recruited from Berwick and concerned with the troubled choice of raising the colors of a new country or of holding aloft those of England.

SHORT-STORY COLLECTIONS

Deephaven† (1877). Bundle of thirteen local-color sketches loosely tied by the colorless device of regarding Deephaven, a Maine seaport town like Berwick, through the eyes of Helen Denis and Kate Lancaster, two summer visitors from Boston. Pervading the accurate, realistic transcriptions of the fading environment she knew so thoroughly is a poetic atmosphere that romanticizes the quiet, everyday incidents and scenes in deteriorating towns or in idyllic villages. Heightening the totality of effect is the utter simplicity and extraordinary fidelity to significant detail.

Tales of New England† (1890). Group of eight stories selected from previous writings includes some of her best: "A Lost Lover," from *Old Friends and New;* "Her Only Son,"† from *The Mate of*

---

51 C. M. Thompson, "The Art of Miss Jewett," *Atl.*, XCIV (1904), pp. 485-497; *Letters of Sarah Orne Jewett*, edited by Annie Fields, (1911); E. M. Chapman, "The New England of Sarah Orne Jewett," *YR.*, III (1913-1914), pp. 157-172; M. H. Shackford, "Sarah Orne Jewett," *SR.*, XXX (1922), pp. 20-26; F. O. Matthiessen, *Sarah Orne Jewett* (1929); Willa Cather, *Not Under Forty* (1936), pp. 76-95.

the Daylight and Friends Ashore; "Miss Tempy's Watchers,"† "Law Lane," and "The Courting of Sister Wisby," all three from *The King of Folly Island, and Other People;* "A White Heron,"† "The Dulham Ladies,"† and "Marsh Rosemary," from *A White Heron.* (Note that two other excellent stories, not included in this collection, might conceivably be incorporated into a selection of her best: "The Flight of Betsy Lane," from *A Native of Winby, and Other Tales* and "The Hiltons' Holiday," from *The Life of Nancy.*)

***The Country of the Pointed Firs*†** (1896). Chapters are rather a series of local-color character sketches very much like those of *Deephaven:* portraits and anecdotes unfolded by a summer visitor to Dunnet, Maine, are all sewn by a thin thread of plot stitched in with a delightful humor, a quiet satire, and a delicate pathos that make this volume and *Deephaven* perhaps her most distinguished work. As in the latter, again portrays a seaport town during the era when New England, drained of its inhabitants who had gone adventuring past the Mississippi, was now made up of deserted farms and dwindling settlements in which only the old people remained.

SUGGESTED MERITS	SUGGESTED DEFECTS
1. A detached spectator, she portrays the social conditions prevalent in the dying Maine settlements. Mature understanding, individual insight, and realism tinctured with a genial optimism characterize her stories. The countryside she created will endure.	1. A romantic, she refused to accept for picturization the headachy, the coarse, and the squalid truths in her New England. Successful with pathetic incidents, she failed when confronted with tragedy. She is never the master of anything beyond a tiny realm. She has left no winged message or lofty vision.
2. Stories dependent on setting and on character molded by environment. Gift of presenting people through mild scenes and simple situations.	2. Absence of plot development. Even her novels are merely a series of sketches threaded thinly by plot. Action desultory, scenes seldom dramatic.
3. Her women, in their struggle to farm the stony New England land and in their determination never to yield to spiritual defeat, represent all Yankees, masculine as well as feminine.	3. Missed the opportunity of a memorable portrayal of Yankee men bustling in the growing Yankee towns. Too fragmentary is her insight into people. Recognize that her vision is confined, that her genius is distinctly feminine.

4. At her best, she writes with effortless simplicity and limpid precision. Her style reminds us of both Hawthorne and the earlier Howells. However, not since Hawthorne, declares Van Wyck Brooks, had anyone "pictured this New England world with such exquisite freshness of feeling."[52]

---

52 Van Wyck Brooks, *New England: Indian Summer, 1865-1915* (1940), p. 353.

MARY E[LEANOR] WILKINS FREEMAN, 1852—1930, playwright, poet, novelist, short-story writer. Lived most of the time in Randolph, Massachusetts, her birthplace. Educated for one year at Mount Holyoke Seminary (1870). Moved to Brattleboro, Vermont (1873). Father died (1883). Upon her marriage to Dr. C. M. Freeman (1902), she moved to Metuchen, New Jersey. Death of husband (1923). Awarded the William Dean Howells medal for fiction (1925). Elected a member of the National Institute of Arts and Letters (1926). Wrote a play, two volumes of verse, a dozen novels, and about 245 short stories.

SHORT-STORY COLLECTIONS

A Humble Romance and Other Stories† (1887). About two dozen grim tales, mirroring New England typical characters and their sodden, joyless consciences. Includes "A Humble Romance," "Old Lady Pingree," "Cinnamon Roses," "An Independent Thinker," "The Bar Light-House," "A Mistaken Charity."

A New England Nun and Other Stories† (1891). Twenty-four gnarly character studies, chiefly about provincial New England women, are representative of Victorian sweetishness and are again influenced by the local-color movement. Louisa Ellis is the "New England Nun"; "Sister Liddy" exists only in the imagination of Polly Moss and in the minds of her fellow paupers. Well-known, too, are "Christmas Jenny" and "Life Everlastin'."

Edgewater People (1918). Collection approximates the high, significant level of her earlier volumes.

The Wind in the Rose Bush (1903). Several convincing ghost-stories, effective in their supernaturalism. Example: "The South-west Chamber."

NOVELS

Pembroke† (1894). Easily breakable into a succession of short stories. Excellent as a study until marred by a happy ending.

The Heart's Highway (1900). Virginia of about 1682 is its historical background. Fails to recapture the swashbuckling romance of the seventeenth century as well as her stark tales do that of rural Yankee life.

The Portion of Labor (1901). Sprawling social work not over-meaningful in its treatment of such industrial problems as wage-cuts and strikes. Protracted, repetitious, platitudinous,[53] yet revelatory of an insight into the character of Robert Lloyd and Ellen Brewster.

---

53 The portion of labor, states the toil-worn Andrew Brewster, is primarily "the growth in character of the laborer."

SUGGESTED MERITS	SUGGESTED DEFECTS
1. Unflinching delineation of the drab-colored, austere Yankee lives of the 1850's, 1860's, and 1870's. Convincing stories of the repressed spinster, the forbearing martyr, the worn-out farmer.	1. Her New England characters are angular and exaggerated. Dickensian caricature. People, as well as events, are seen through feminine eyes. Deficient in her depiction of a developing soul.
2. Uncompromising revelation of the bleak, declining New England regime.	2. Yielded to the temptation of the happy ending.[54] Frequently sentimental.
3. Balzacian realism poignant with a breathless intensity.	3. Morbid objectivity inexorable in its depressing effects. Realism conventional.
4. Master of the short effort dominated by one character.	4. Small power of construction whenever the unit of measure is long.
5. Earlier style appropriately severe and staccato, unbedecked by transitions. Faithful rendition of the Yankee cadences of speech.	5. Style of later period self-conscious and ornamented. Even her earlier stories have a crudeness.

OTHER LOCAL-COLORISTS: NEW ENGLAND

EDWARD EVERETT HALE, 1822—1909, Unitarian clergyman, author of Utopian romances, historical memorials, biographical studies, and an American pioneer in preaching the need of a kind of League of Nations. Most significant literary contributions were the scholarly *France in France* (two volumes, 1887—1888) and the famous tale called "The Man Without a Country" (1863), suggested by a speech made by Vallandigham. Despite the obvious haste of its writing, this story of Philip Nolan has a reality of detail and a power of pathos that make readers forget it was written to influence the election of 1863 and remember only that a man can not set himself apart from the claims of society. "Unless duly authenticated as fiction," says H. W. Mabie, "it will some day be read as history." *Kansas and Nebraska* (1854), an unoriginal but influential record in favor of settling both those states with antislavery people; *If, Yes, and Perhaps* (1868), a collection that includes his best-known tale and, among others, "My Double and How He Undid Me," a wholly fantastic conception written to assert the rights of the individual in a society; *Sybaris and Other Homes* (1869), a Utopian disguise for a tract on social hygiene; *Ten Times One Is Ten* (1871), a novelette which acquired world-wide influence by inspiring "Ten Times One" and "Lend-a-Hand" clubs; *In His Name* (1874), a quasi-historical religious account of Lyons and the twelfth-century Waldenses, a simple, touching, even clever story with a motif as homiletical as the 1871 novelette; *Philip Nolan's Friends* (1877), a romantic story of the real Nolan; *A New England Boyhood* (1893) and *Memories of a Hundred Years* (1902), entertaining autobiographical works, the earlier of which has been designated as "the only noteworthy book about Boston boyhood."

54 "It may be well to add here . . . that the notorious happy ending is bad not because it is happy, but precisely because it is not. A happy ending to a human story profoundly rooted in both character and fate, were it attainable in such a world as the present, would be of an inestimable preciousness. The meretricious happy ending of the conventional short story . . . has no relation to such an one. It is, rather, a feebly propitiatory gesture; an *absit omen;* it is a sop to the slightly neurotic and wholly muddle-headed who ask of art as of life not reality but feigning, not catharsis but conformation in immaturity, not cure but drug." Ludwig Lewisohn, *Expression in America* (1932), p. 286; see, also, p. 291.

MARY [HARTWELL] CATHERWOOD, 1847—1902, whose *The Romance of Dollard* (1888), the first of a series of historical romances concerned with French Canada, the Lakes, and the Mississippi Valley, was declared by Francis Parkman (p. 78) to be a pioneering departure in American fiction. Within six years after "The Hospital Nurse" (1864), her first published story, she became known as a steady contributor to juvenile publications, one of her best books for children being *Heroes of the Middle West: The French* (1898). At various times she lived in different parts of Illinois (Milford, Danville, Fairfield, Chicago), and many of her writings are concerned with that state. Her short stories are excellent examples of local-color fiction; her novels have a place in the history of literary development. Works include *The Story of Tonty* (1890), *The Lady of Fort St. John* (1891), *Old Kaskaskia* (1893), *The White Islander* (1893), *The Spirit of an Illinois Town, and The Little Renault* (1897), *Spanish Peggy; A Story of Young Illinois* (1899), and *Lazarre* (1901), a best seller. *The Chase of Saint-Castin* (1894) is a collection of seven short stories of the French in the New World, six of which had appeared in the *Atlantic Monthly.* Unfinished is the historical novel, *For Tippecanoe* (1902), and still in manuscript is *The Queen Bee,* inspired by the assassination of William McKinley.

CHAPTER X

THE GILDED AGE: CONSERVATISM AND ICONOCLASM

SAMUEL LANGHORNE CLEMENS, known as **MARK TWAIN,** 1835—1910, printer, river pilot, miner, journalist, travel writer, lecturer, publisher, capitalist, novelist, humanitarian.[1] Born in Florida, Missouri, the son of John Marshall Clemens, a Virginian, and Jane Lampton, a Kentucky belle. Settled in Hannibal, Missouri (1839). Death of father (1847). Apprenticed (1848—1853) to his brother Orion, who edited the Missouri *Courier.* Journeyman printer in St. Louis, New York, Philadelphia, and Muscatine (1853—1854). Again worked with his brother Orion, in Keokuk, Iowa (1855). Job printer in Cincinnati (1856—1857). Plan in 1856 to make a quick fortune in South America was aborted by his meeting with Horace Bixby, pilot. Became a pilot's apprentice on the Mississippi, and later a licensed pilot (1857—1861). After a few weeks of officering a not too well organized Confederate militia,[2] he went to Nevada as un-

---

1 W. D. Howells, *My Mark Twain* (1910); A. B. Paine, (1) *Mark Twain: A Biography* (three volumes, 1912); (2) *Mark Twain's Letters* (two volumes, 1917); (3) *Mark Twain's Autobiography* (two volumes, 1924); Van Wyck Brooks, *The Ordeal of Mark* Twain (1920; revised, 1933); Gamaliel Bradford, *American Portraits* (1922), pp. 1-28; A. B. Paine, *Mark Twain's Notebook* (1925); C. H. Grattan, in *American Writers on American Literature,* edited by John Macy (1931), pp. 274-284; Bernard DeVoto, *Mark Twain's America* (1932); M. M. Brashear, *Mark Twain, Son of Missouri* (1934); Edward Wagenknecht, *Mark Twain: The Man and His Work* (1935); Bernard DeVoto, *Mark Twain at Work* (1942); DeLancey Ferguson, *Mark Twain: Man and Legend* (1943), Frank Baldanza, *Mark Twain* (Barnes & Noble, 1961).

MISCELLANEOUS WRITINGS: *Mark Twain's Sketches, New and Old* (1875); *A True Story, and the Recent Carnival of Crime* (1877); *Punch, Brothers, Punch! and Other Sketches* (1878); *Conversation, as It Was by the Social Fireside, in the Time of the Tudors* (1880); *The Stolen White Elephant Etc.* (1882); *Merry Tales* (1892); *The American Claimant* (1892); *The £1,000,000 Bank-Note and Other Stories* (1893); *Pudd'nhead Wilson's Calendar for 1894* (1893); *Tom Sawyer Abroad* (1894); *Those Extraordinary Twins* (1894); *Tom Sawyer, Detective* (1896); *How to Tell a Story and Other Essays* (1897); *English as She Is Taught* (1900); *To the Person Sitting in Darkness* (1901); *Edmund Burke on Croker and Tammany* (1901); *A Double-Barrelled Detective Story* (1902); *My Debut as a Literary Person with Other Essays* (1903); *"A Dog's Tale"* (1903); *Extracts from Adam's Diary* (1904); *King Leopold's Soliloquy* (1905); *Eve's Diary* (1906); *The $30,000 Bequest and Other Stories* (1906); *Christian Science* (1907); *A Horse's Tale* (1907); *Is Shakespeare Dead?* (1909); *Extract from Captain Stormfield's Visit to Heaven* (1909); *Queen Victoria's Jubilee* (1909); *Mark Twain's Letter to the California Pioneers* (1911); *The Curious Republic of Gondour and Other Whimsical Sketches* (1919); *Mark Twain, Able Yachtsman, Interviews Himself on Why Lipton Failed to Lift the Cup* (1920); *The Sandwich Islands* (1920); *Europe and Elsewhere* (1923); *The Quaker City Holy Land Excursion, an Unfinished Play* (1927); *The Adventures of Thomas Jefferson Snodgrass* (1928); *Slovenly Peter* (1935); *Washington in 1868,* a collection of newsletters written in 1868 and edited by Cyril Clemens (1943).

2 F. W. Lorch, "Mark Twain and the Campaign That Failed," *AL.,* XII (1940-1941), pp. 454-470.

remunerated secretary to Orion (1861), secretary to Governor J. W. Nye of Nevada Territory. Unsuccessful as a miner. Reporter on the *Enterprise* in Virginia City, Nevada (1862—1863), where he adopted the pseudonym Mark Twain.[3] Met Artemus Ward. To San Francisco (1864), where he wrote for the *Golden Era,* the *Alta California,* and especially the *Morning Call.* Met Bret Harte. Lectured in San Francisco about the Sandwich Islands (Hawaii), to which he had been sent by the Sacramento *Union* to write travel sketches.[4] Commissioned by that paper to make a world tour, Mark Twain, upon reaching New York by way of the Nicaragua Isthmus, lectured at Cooper Union (1867), and then joined the *Quaker City* steamship excursion to the Mediterranean and Palestine. Returned to America in November of same year. A month or so later, met Olivia Langdon (1867); engaged (1869); married (1870).[5] Became an editor of the Buffalo *Express* (*c.* 1869—1870). Langdon Clemens born (1870); died (1872). Settled in Hartford, Connecticut (*c.* 1871—1891). Olivia Susan Clemens born (1871); died (1896). First journey to England (1872); second (1873—1874). Clara Clemens born (1874). To Bermuda (1877). Two European tours (1878—1879; 1891—1893). Jane Lampton Clemens born (1880); died (1909). Became a partner in the publishing firm of Charles L. Webster Company, which reaped enormous profits from its sales of Grant's *Memoirs* and Mark Twain's own writings, but eventually failed (1893) and left Clemens bankrupt (1894). By the end of January, 1898, he had repaid the enormous debt by means of a world lecture tour (1895, 1896). Returned to America (1900). Litt.D. (Yale, 1901; University of Missouri, 1902; Oxford, 1907). To Europe (1903). Death of Mrs. Clemens (1904). Mark Twain died of angina pectoris at Redding, Connecticut (1910), survived only by his daughter Clara.

---

3 The old river phrase is a Mississippi leadsmen's call signifying two fathoms, or twelve feet. That S. L. Clemens had adopted the pen name before the death of Captain Isaiah Sellers is revealed by the latter's logbook. See G. H. Brownell, "Mark Twainiana," *ABC.,* III (1933), pp. 207-212.

4 For an introduction to Mark Twain's metropolitan journalism from his appearance in San Francisco until his departure in 1866 for New York, see *The Washoe Giant in San Francisco,* edited by Franklin Walker (1938). As for his *Letters from the Sandwich Islands* of 1866, they have been rated by F. L. Pattee as a mishmash of idyllic impressionism and satire, mordant criticism, and laughing-out-loud slapstick.

5 Van Wyck Brooks has built up the psychoanalytical thesis of Mark Twain as a natural artist and rebellious pioneer frustrated by the bourgeois environment in which he found himself, by the puritanical and materialistic respectability represented in his youth by his mother Jane, and in his manhood by his wife Olivia. To Bernard DeVoto, such an interpretation of Mark Twain as the victim of his surroundings is absurd; in his opinion, the potential creativeness of Mark Twain, the early frontier raconteur and untrammeled pioneer, developed naturally and inevitably in his later writings. For a discussion of the two contradictory interpretations, read Van Wyck Brooks, *The Ordeal of Mark Twain* (1920); Bernard DeVoto, *Mark Twain's America* (1932), especially pp. 224-239; Doris and Samuel Webster, "Whitewashing Jane Clemens," *Bookman,* LXI (1925), pp. 531-535; F. L. Pattee, *Mark Twain: Representative Selections* (1935), pp. xxvi-xxx, xxxvi *ff.* (pp. xi-lxiii); DeLancey Ferguson, "The Case for Mark Twain's Wife," *UTQ.,* IX (1939-1940), pp. 9-21. It may be germane, too, to read Sinclair Lewis, "Fools, Liars, and Mr. DeVoto," *SRL.,* XXVII (April 15, 1944), pp. 9-12; and J. D. Adams, "Speaking of Books," *NYTBR.,* April 30, 1944, p. 2, cols. 2-4.

S. L. Clemens has been praised for his simplicity and informality of phrase, bold and incongruous similes, flavored colloquialisms, cadence of speech, and brilliant fragments or episodes, as well as for his cumulative jocosities, irresistible drollery, lifelike delineation of character, convincing narrative, universal appeal,[6] and philosophical insight. Yet he is as often tedious and structureless as not.

Possessing neither a wide background of economic fact and theory nor a comprehensive knowledge of scientific or philosophical methods, he could not voice any profound social criticism; but he had a genuine contempt for all pretense and hypocrisy, and exposed to humorous view the tyrannies of chivalry, of slavery, and of religion.[7] Probably hamstrung in some measure by genteel surroundings and, in later years, by a deterministic pessimism and an inferiority complex,[8] he seems to have succumbed to compromise and appeasement, to have become a member in good standing of the Gilded Age which he himself helped describe. Briefly, he was more of a petit-bourgeois "debunker" than a creator; he is memorable, as Kipling said, "in his indirect influence as a protesting force in an age of iron philistinism." Mark Twain is the greatest American voice of the West of his day.[9]

---

6 Original Mark Twain writings have been located in three dozen different eastern magazines; his works have been translated into a dozen languages: Archibald Henderson, "The International Fame of Mark Twain," *NAR.*, CXCII (1910), pp. 805-815; E. H. Hemminghaus, *Mark Twain in Germany* (1939); F. S. Hellman, *List of Writings by Mark Twain Translated into Certain Foreign Languages* (1939). Moreover, many personages are Mark Twain enthusiasts; the 1939 letterhead of the International Mark Twain Society lists, for example, Benito Mussolini as Honorary President.

7 H. H. Waggoner disagrees with M. M. Brashear's thesis that the distinctive features of Mark Twain's philosophy spring directly from his reading of the literature of the eighteenth century, from the reading of Thomas Paine, and, possibly, Hobbes, Locke, and Hume.

8 In a letter to Mrs. Mary Hallock Foote, Mark Twain confessed: "I'm not the declining sort. I would take charge of the constellations if I were asked to do it. All you need in this life is ignorance and confidence; then success is sure."

9 Despite his inconsistency and desultoriness as a social critic, Mark Twain made an important contribution to the public store of sheer happiness: in the words of F. L. Pattee (*Mark Twain: Representative Selections*, 1935, p. lii [pp. xi-lxiii]), he "made the common people laugh. Who in all the history of literature has done more?"

In *The Economic Novel in America* (1942, p. 146 *f.*) W. F. Taylor puts it vividly: "He expressed them ['the traditions of democracy, in which the interests of the whole citizenry should be preserved'], dramatized them, salted them with his incomparable humor, and helped to store them up in the consciousness of millions of readers. . . . Men read imaginative literature for individual objects, not social; they read for psychological fulfillment, not for the acquiring of ideas about the State or the Machine. They read that they may have life, and have it more abundantly. They read Mark Twain because he offers them, abundantly and intensely, the heightened sense of life they crave. They continue to read him because he offers that heightened sense of life not merely as temporary excitement, but as an enduring nourishment for a thousand deepseated capacities for experience which, amid the monotony of civilized living, too easily go undernourished. By his touch are awakened potentialities stored in men's deepest nerve centers by generation after generation of experience: — the sense of broad incongruity whose voice is bluff laughter; the sensitiveness to superstition that lingers in the subrational part of all our natures; the perennial craving for some picaresque escape from responsibility; the enjoyment of those images of sky and river and wooded shoreline amid which the race has lived for countless generations. The work of Mark Twain is great and permanent work because through it, an universally powerful creative mind ministers to these central and enduring psychological needs of the race. The social criticism of Mark Twain is of enduring significance, not alone because it is in such close accord with our main American tradition, but also because it has been, almost as if by accident, drawn along in the current of an achievement far greater than itself."

TALL TALES

Of the many burlesque and extravagant stories that appear in such volumes as *Innocents Abroad, Roughing It,* and *A Tramp Abroad,* there is probably no single tale as widely known as —

The Celebrated Jumping Frog of Calaveras County (1865). Folk-tale sketch[10] of Jim Smiley and his pet bratachian given wider fame by this more comic version. Printed accidentally, it made Mark Twain nationally famous.

TRAVEL BOOKS[10a]

The Innocents Abroad; or, The New Pilgrims' Progress (1869). Autobiographical account of Mark Twain's steamship tour to Europe and the Holy Land is based on letters sent two years earlier to the San Francisco *Alta California*[11] and the New York *Herald* and *Tribune.* Its pilgrims are real persons; *e.g.,* Dan is Dan Slote, Doctor is Dr. A. R. Jackson, and Charley is Charles A. Langdon, whose sister became Mrs. Clemens. Pokes irreverent fun at Old World sights and peculiarities, shrines and manners; but elegant and reverent at times. Stylistic skill better than in previous writing; good descriptive passages.

Roughing It† (1872). Without so much of the charm of *Innocents Abroad,* but with its characteristic exaggeration, this "record of several years of variegated vagabondizing" is drawn from his journey from St. Louis to Carson City, his adventures in Nevada, and the Sandwich Islands. Episodic presentation glamorizes the Old Far West with all its pioneers and desperadoes and their virility and lustiness.[12]

A Tramp Abroad (1880). Travel narrative of a walking trip (1878) with J. H. Twichell through Germany, Italy, and Switzerland. Very much as they do in *Innocents Abroad,* satire and humor enliven the description of European society, folklore, and history. His undistinguished drawings might well be omitted to make room for more of the serious passages. Uneven, often dull.

---

10 Although unoriginal with Mark Twain, this gambling yarn has been praised by J. R. Lowell as the finest piece of American humor and by W. D. Howells as Mark Twain's most stupendous invention. The Jumping Frog story has been traced to the Sierra mining camps of the early Gold Rush days; two versions preceding that of Mark Twain appeared in the Sonora *Herald* of June 11, 1853, and in the San Andreas *Independent* of December 11, 1858. Consult Oscar Lewis, *The Origin of the Celebrated Jumping Frog of Calaveras County* (1931). As for the possible influence of literary humorists upon Mark Twain, see G. C. Bellamy, "Mark Twain's Indebtedness to John Phoenix," *AL.,* XIII (1941-1942), pp. 29-43.

10a J. D. Adams, "Speaking of Books," *NYTBR.* (June 17, 1945), p. 2; *NYTBR.* (June 24, 1945), p. 2.

11 Between the day he left San Francisco and that on which his excursion steamer sailed from New York, Mark Twain wrote twenty-six weekly letters covering that half-year period; and those missives, which preceded the European letters of 1867, are now available: *Mark Twain's Travels with Mr. Brown,* edited by Franklin Walker and G. E. Dane (1940).

12 It is to be noted that *Roughing It,* as well as some other volumes by Mark Twain, relied measureably upon stock elements in Far Western literature: R. R. Walterhouse, *Bret Harte, Joaquin Miller, and the Western Local Color Story: A Study in the Origins of Popular Fiction* (Ph.D., Chicago, 1939).

Life on the Mississippi† (1883). Autobiographical narrative of Mississippi River life on the steamers plying between St. Louis and New Orleans. First half, transfigured by nostalgic memory and poetic perception, is a series of sketches invested with gusto and continuity; latter part of volume, written about eight years later, while specific, realistic, and not without its graphic passages, and while excelling in anecdotes and reminiscences, lacks the verve and Twainian unity of the earlier chapters.

Following the Equator (1897). Materials, chiefly about Australasia and India, resulted from his world lecture tour. Satirical discussions on imperialistic morality engendered by Cecil Rhodes, the Jameson Raid, and the Boer War. Reveals a forced Mark Twain, and especially anticipates his subsequent pessimistic work.

PERSONALIZED FICTION

The Gilded Age: A Tale of To-day (1873). In collaboration with C. D. Warner, novel satirizes the ruthless individualism and speculative exploitation of public resources during the period of the Reconstruction. As formless a work as the speculative fever and unbridled enterprise of the post-Civil War boom years it describes. Best character: Colonel Beriah Sellers, an American Micawber modelled primarily on Mark Twain's uncle, James Lampton.

The Adventures of Tom Sawyer† (1876). Despite such limitations as incongruous humor, episodic construction, and emotional anachronisms, it is a masterpiece by virtue of permanent commonplaces about nostalgic boyhood experience, by virtue of an assimilative process that makes out of its narrative, unity of tone, realism, and characters a body of engaging mythology, and by virtue of a divergence from the traditional patterns of juvenile fiction.[13] Autobiographical elements; for example, John Briggs became Joe Harper, and Tom Blankenship was the original Huck Finn.[14]

The Adventures of Huckleberry Finn† (1884). Sequel to *Tom Sawyer,* and more profound, is excellent in its character-delineation and nature description, the latter of which acts as a kind of

---

13 Walter Blair, "On the Structure of Tom Sawyer," *MP.*, XXXVII (1940-1941), pp. 75-88.

14 Sequels include not only *Huckleberry Finn* but also *Tom Sawyer Abroad* (1894) and *Tom Sawyer, Detective* (1896). If there are any literary influences upon the writings of Mark Twain, aside from those upon his earlier work, no conclusive evidence has been presented. One distinguished scholar sees in *Tom Sawyer* and *Huckleberry Finn* the influence of Cervantes: O. H. Moore, "Mark Twain and Don Quixote," *PMLA.*, XXXVII (1922), pp. 324-346. Several have observed that the plot of *Tom Sawyer, Detective,* has its source not in a Swedish criminal trial, as Mark Twain stated, but elsewhere: see J. C. Bay, "Tom Sawyer, Detective: The Origin of the Plot," *Essays Offered to Herbert Putnam,* edited by W. W. Bishop and Andrew Keogh (1929), pp. 80-88; A. B. Benson, "Mark Twain's Contacts with Scandinavia," *SSN.*, XIV (1937), pp. 159-167.

soothing interlude to the salty adventures.[15] Stylistic vigor[16] as appropriate as its picaresque structure; as in *Tom Sawyer,* the merits transcend the weaknesses.

***The Tragedy of Pudd'nhead Wilson*†** (1894). David Wilson's "tragic" avocation solves the murder of the Judge. Best pictures are Roxy and her half-breed son Tom. Rich in maxims.

HISTORICAL ROMANCES

The Prince and the Pauper (1882). Carefully constructed historical romance — abundantly veined by humorous situations — cloaks an attack upon the economic and social evils inherent in the English monarchical system during the reign of the boy King, Edward VI.

A Connecticut Yankee in King Arthur's Court (1889). Is an impassioned satire upon the cruelty and oppression, aristocracy and feudalism of Arthurian England. Burlesques the idealistic side of chivalry presented by the *Morte d'Arthur* and the *Idylls of the King.*

***Personal Recollections of Joan of Arc by the Sieur Louis de Conte*†** (1896). Excellent workmanship and delicacy of both feeling and expression heighten the total effect of this romanticized-realistic historical biography.[17] Particularly in his account of her trial and martyrdom does he indict a religious system.

QUESTIONING THEMES

The Man That Corrupted Hadleyburg (1900). Short story of how greed rots away the soul of an entire town. Unsparing analysis of man's frailty under the pressure of money-temptation.

What Is Man? (written, 1893; rewritten, 1898; privately printed, 1906). Platonic dialogue in form but not in philosophical thought

---

15 In the autumn of 1884 an engraving in the volume was so altered that it became improperly suggestive. Later, on the ground that *Huckleberry Finn* would endanger the morals of the young, the Library Committee at Concord, Massachusetts, excluded the book, whereby it became a *cause célèbre.* The latter action was recognized by Mark Twain as "a rattling tip-top puff" which would "sell 25,000 copies for us sure." A. L. Vogelbeck, "The Publication and Reception of *Huckleberry Finn* in America," *AL.,* XI (1939-1940), pp. 260-272; *Adventures of Huckleberry Finn,* edited by Bernard DeVoto (1942), p. liv (pp. ix-lxxvi).

16 He demonstrates, for example, especial competence in representing the nuances of Jim's pronunciation: J. N. Tidwell, "Mark Twain's Representation of Negro Speech," *AS., XVII* (1942), pp. 174-176.

17 When it is recalled that not even in the serious *Joan of Arc* does the discursive and burlesquing spirit entirely desert Mark Twain, then one can expect that kind of tone with more casual themes: for example, in *Slovenly Peter* (*Der Struwwelpeter*) the final lines are:

> "The dog's his heir, and this estate
> That dog inherits, and will ate.*"

"*My child, never use an expression like that. It is utterly unprincipled and outrageous to say ate when you mean eat, and you must never do it except when crowded for a rhyme. As you grow up you will find that poetry is a sandy road to travel, and the only way to pull through at all is to lay your grammar down and take hold with both hands."

between a Young Man and a pessimistic Old Man.[18] Mark Twain's "Dover Beach."

The Mysterious Stranger (1916). Swiftian, allegorical romance interpretable either as a challenge to God's reality or as a presentation of the problem of evil.[19] Influenced by Zolaesque determinism and naturalism. Recalls Voltaire's story of the Hermit in *Zadig*.[20]

WILLIAM DEAN HOWELLS, 1837—1920, poet, dramatist, essayist, critic, editor, novelist.[21] Born in Martin's Ferry, Ohio, the son of William Cooper Howells, printer-journalist and abolitionist. Moved to Hamilton, (1840), to Dayton (1848), to Columbus (1851), to Ashtabula[22] (1852), and to Jefferson, Ohio: had very little formal education. Compositor and reporter for the *Ohio State Journal* (1856—1860), and while in that capacity wrote *The Campaign Life of Abraham Lincoln* (1860), a document which helped elect the Republican candidate and which brought Howells an appointment as United States Consul in Venice (1860—1865). Married Elinor Gertrude Mead (1862), of Brattleboro, Vermont, who bore him one son and two daughters. Returned to America (1865), associating himself for about a year with the New York *Tribune*, the *Times*, and the *Nation* (1865—1866). Assistant editor (1866—1872) and then editor-in-chief (1872—1881) of the *Atlantic Monthly*, from which he resigned. Began serializing his stories in the *Century Magazine*. Settled in New York (1885). A New York traction strike, the Haymarket Riot, and the reading of Tolstoy and Henry George gave body to his socialistic leanings. Conducted the "Editor's Study" in *Harper's Monthly* (1886—1891). Brief editorship of the *Cosmopolitan*. Rebuilt and filled the "Editor's Easy Chair" in *Harper's* (1900—1920). First president of the American Academy of Arts and Letters (1909—1920). For his work in fiction Howells was awarded the gold medal of the National Institute of Arts and Letters (1915). Received honorary degrees from Yale, Columbia, Harvard, Princeton, and Oxford.

PLAYS

His plays vary in merit. They include: "Self-Sacrifice: A Farce-Tragedy" and "The Night before Christmas: A Morality," both of

18 Bernard DeVoto, *Mark Twain at Work* (1942), p. 116 *ff.* (pp. 105-130).

19 G. N. Shuster, "The Tragedy of Mark Twain," *CW.*, CIV (1916-1917), p. 736 (pp. 731-737).

20 F. A. G. Cowper, "The Hermit Story as Used by Voltaire and Mark Twain," *In Honor of the Ninetieth Birthday of Charles Frederick Johnson* (1928), pp. 313-337.

21 Alexander Harvey, *William Dean Howells* (1917); D. G. Cooke, *William Dean Howells* (1922); O. W. Firkins, *William Dean Howells* (1924); Mildred Howells, *The Life and Letters of William Dean Howells* (two volumes, 1928); George Arms and W. M. Gibson, editors, "Five Interviews with William Dean Howells," *Americana*, XXXVII (1943), pp. 257-295.

22 For the influence of the *Ashtabula Sentinel* on young Howells, see E. H. Cady, "William Dean Howells," *OSAHQ.*, LIII (1944), pp. 39-51.

which are between the covers of *The Daughter of the Storage* (1916); at least four comedies, *Out of the Question* (1877), *A Counterfeit Presentment* (1877), *A Previous Engagement* (1897), and *An Indian Giver* (1900); and a score of farces: *The Parlor Car* (1871), *The Sleeping Car* (1883), *The Register* (1884), *The Elevator* (1885), *The Garroters* (1886), *A Sea-Change; or Love's Stowaway: A Lyricated Farce* (1888), *The Mouse-Trap, and Other Farces* (1889), *The Sleeping Car and Other Farces* (1890), *A Letter of Introduction* (1892), *The Unexpected Guests* (1893), *Evening Dress* (1893), *A Likely Story* (1894), *Five O'Clock Tea* (1894), *Room Forty-Five* (1900), *The Smoking Car* (1900), and *Parting Friends* (1911).

POETRY[23]

The Poets and Poetry of the West (1860), which contains a half dozen poems by Howells; *Poems* (1869, 1885, 1901); *Stops of Various Quills* (1895); *The Mother and the Father* (1909); and—

Poems of Two Friends (1860). First book, issued in conjunction with J. J. Piatt (p. 249).

No Love Lost: A Romance of Travel (1869). Hexametric novel or poem savors of Browning in conception and of Longfellow in meter.

BOOKS OF TRAVEL

Three Villages (1884); *Tuscan Cities* (1886); *A Little Swiss Sojourn* (1892); *The Seen and Unseen at Stratford-on-Avon* (1914); *Hither and Thither in Germany* (1920). A revisit to Europe also was recorded in *London Films* (1905), *Certain Delightful English Towns; with Glimpses of the Pleasant Country Between* (1906); *Roman Holidays and Others* (1908); *Seven English Cities* (1909); and *Familiar Spanish Travels* (1913). Perhaps best-known is —

Venetian Life (1866). Collection of a series of letters which had appeared first in the Boston *Advertiser* and which captured the flavor of Italian life, as did *Italian Journeys* (1867), the charmingly written sketches that followed.

SKETCHES AND STORIES

A Day's Pleasure, and Other Sketches (1876); *A Fearful Responsibility, and Other Stories* (three tales, 1881); *Christmas Every Day, and Other Stories Told for Children* (1893); *A Parting and a Meeting* (1896); *Doorstep Acquaintance, and Other Sketches* (1900); *A Pair of Patient Lovers* (five short stories,

---

23 O. W. Firkins, *William Dean Howells* (1924), "Plays and Poems," pp. 234-261.

1901); *The Flight of Pony Baker: A Boy's Town Story* (1902); *Questionable Shapes* (three stories of the occult, 1903) and *Between the Dark and the Daylight; Romances* (1907), both volumes being concerned in general with the supernatural; *The Daughter of the Storage, and Other Things in Prose and Verse* (1916). Of this group, two merit separate attention:

Suburban Sketches (1871). Collection of delightful, realistic miniatures of scenes and characters of Cambridge's horse-car era.

A Fearful Responsibility (1881). Novelette of an American invalid professor in Italy.

LITERARY CRITICISM

Modern Italian Poets (1887); *Literature and Life* (1902); *Imaginary Interviews* (1910); and —

Criticism and Fiction (1891). Best statement of his literary credo, including his antagonism to contemporaneous romantic fiction, and his advocacy of realism, decency, and democracy in American novels.

My Literary Passions (1895). Hodgepodge of interesting comments on many writers, including praise of Tolstoy, is composed of what are platitudes and dogmatisms today, but were realistic correctives in his own period.

Literary Friends and Acquaintances (1900). First-hand recollections about such personalities as Lowell, Longfellow, and Holmes. Many anecdotes.

Heroines of Fiction† (two volumes, 1901). Leading idea that the excellence of a novelist is best indicated by his portrayal of women boomerangs in the general criticism that Howells' own heroines are not too well delineated.

My Mark Twain† (1910). Possibly over-appreciative but of genuine value. Biography declared by Carl Van Doren as "incomparably the finest of all the interpretations of Howells's great friend."

AUTOBIOGRAPHICAL WORKS

Impressions and Experiences (1896), *Years of My Youth* (unfinished, 1916). Consult also *My Literary Passions* (p. 195), *Literary Friends and Acquaintances* (p. 195), *New Leaf Mills* (p. 198), as well as —

A Boy's Town† (1890). Simple, lucid, delightful, penetrating book of memories about Hamilton, Ohio. Written in the third person.

My Year in a Log Cabin (1893). Eagerly reminiscent record of his year on the Little Miami River.

NOVELS DEALING WITH THE MARCHES[24]

Their Wedding Journey (1871). His first novel, this slowly-advancing narrative of the honeymooning Basil and Isabel March to Niagara, the St. Lawrence, Montreal, and Quebec, is more of a travel book or travelogue held together by a slender plot, studied details and manners, delicacy of sentiment, kaleidoscopic description, and the two well-drawn, leading characters.

***A Hazard of New Fortunes*†** (1890). Best work in everyday realism and all but painful idealism. Is a sympathetic approach to the sociological problems of industrial conflict or revolt. Dialectic-speaking Basil denounces economic insecurity. Competent illustration of how competitive capitalism affects the development of different sets of virile characters. Keen observation, mellow wisdom, careful workmanship, excellent analysis of thought and emotion; his most complicated novel, it is also his longest, and its leisurely development of plot becomes somewhat tiring.

An Open-Eyed Conspiracy (1897). Slight novel, with Saratoga as its scene, is somewhat more pleasant because of the conversation of the Marches.

Their Silver Wedding Journey (1899). Longest travel book about Basil and Isabel March, novelized by a coquettish love story, chronicles their sightseeing in Europe, principally Hamburg, Leipzig, Carlsbad, Weimar, and Berlin.

ECONOMIC NOVELS[25]

The Minister's Charge; or, The Apprenticeship of Lemuel Barker (1887). Presents an uninspiring picture of weaklings, of religious conditions, and of the dramatic theme that we are our brothers' keepers. Alive are the comical proletariat figures of Statira Dudley and 'Manda Grier.

---

24 The practice of connecting no fewer than two short stories ("A Circle in the Water" and "A Pair of Patient Lovers") and six novels by the repetition of the characters of Basil and Isabel March leads to the conclusion that in their persons "Howells has incarnated his idea of the normal male and female of our species." The two advance more in years and in vitality with their creator than "in his deepening wisdom," affecting us "variously according to our moods," and representing "pretty faithfully the dull average of humanity. At rare and idealistic moments, . . . we spurn them contemptuously as libels on our kind; and then . . . we welcome them as at least a shade more wise than most. They are in general less constant in their effect, more complete and subtle, than the bookish characters we know, and always a trifle below the level we expect people with their advantages to attain." No one gainsays that, after the manner of both Balzac and Trollope, Howells introduces living personalities again and again; but it is better not to consider him either the Balzac or Trollope of America. See J. F. Muirhead, "W. D. Howells: The American Trollope," *Landmark*, II (1920), pp. 53-56; D. G. Cooke, *William Dean Howells* (1923), p. 156 *ff.*; O. W. Firkins, *William Dean Howells* (1924), p. 74 *f.*

25 W. F. Taylor, "On the Origin of Howells' Interest in Economic Reform," *AL.*, II (1930-1931), pp. 3-14; J. W. Getzels, "William Dean Howells and Socialism," *SS.*, II (1938), pp. 514-517; W. F. Taylor, *The Economic Novel in America* (1942), pp. 214-281; George Arms, "The Literary Background of Howells's Social Criticism," *AL.*, XIV (1942-1943), pp. 260-276.

Annie Kilburne (1888). Laboriously-developed plot unfolds without solving a complex social problem when the thirty-one-year-old Annie returns from Rome and attempts to find her place in a New England town composed of three elements, the older, substantial inhabitants, to which she herself belongs, the "summer people," and the working class. Well-drawn characterization contributes measurably to Howells's indictment of false charity in the economic setup.

A Hazard of New Fortunes.† (See p. 196.)

The Quality of Mercy (1892). Dramatic psychological chronicle wherein not only is the absconding embezzler, Northwick, made responsible for the crime, but also strict social conventions, small-town narrowness — in brief, the social order itself. Loose plot; limited, somber study of moral corruption and crime, both of which are the results of the economic structure.

The World of Chance (1893). Not merely a record of New York literary life, as illustrated by the actions of Shelley Ray, author of *A Modern Romeo;* not merely a love story of Shelley and Peace Denton; but also, via the character of Ansel Denton, a careful consideration of life's insecurity in an industrial world.

A Traveler from Altruria (1894). Utopian romance, which is more delightful than its anemic epistolary sequel, *Through the Eye of the Needle. A Traveler from Altruria,* his most controversial work, is in reality a keen satire of industrial America. Dialogue is brilliant and witty though unexciting; characters are abstractions; potpourri of social and economic ideas eclecticized from several tracts on ideal commonwealths. (Compare with Bellamy's *Looking Backward,* p. 218.)

Through the Eye of the Needle (1907). Sequel to *A Traveler from Altruria,* and inferior to it, describes that idealistic country by means of letters written by Mrs. Homos.

OTHER NOVELS

(1) *Private Theatricals* (*Atlantic,* 1875—1876), or *Mrs. Farrell* (book form, 1921). Rosabel Farrell, an engaging young widow, is one of his most dynamic characters. (2) *Dr. Breen's Practice* (1881). Anti-feminine picture of a woman physician in particular and a satire of the medical profession in general. (3) *A Woman's Reason* (1883).[25a] Sparkling, subtle study, says A. H. Quinn, of feminine nature, of class feeling, and of Bostonian social values. (4) *The Shadow of a Dream* (1890). Novelette of considerable

25a George Arms, "A Novel and Two Letters," *RUL.*, VIII (December, 1944), pp. 9-13.

suspense. (5) *An Imperative Duty* (1893). Weak is the solution to the argumentative statement but tenuous treatment of the problem of miscegenation. (6) *The Coast of Bohemia* (1893). Typical people make this story of a young woman art student at New York a pleasant transcript of manners. (7) *The Day of the Wedding* (1896). Flimsy, formless novelette. (8) *Ragged Lady* (1899). Resumed are the international theme and the love-and-conscience problems. (9) *The Vacation of the Kelwyns* (*c.* 1900; posthumously, 1920). Novel with the scene laid in a New Hampshire community during a summer is meritorious only because of its fair character-delineation. (10) *Letters Home* (1903). Unimportant epistolary narrative. (11) *Miss Bellard's Inspiration* (1905). Slight novelette. (12) *New Leaf Mills* (1913). Semi-autobiographic chronicle of the Ohio Valley mill community of his youth.

A Chance Acquaintance (1873). Tells no exciting love story, yet is a good study of the American *Pride-and-Prejudice* caste spirit. Plot slight, but delicately shaped; dialogue natural; sketches along the St. Lawrence and at Quebec are crisply pleasant. Compare this travelogue with *Their Wedding Journey* (p. 196).

A Foregone Conclusion (1875). Showy, protracted ending can not obscure the integrated descriptive elements, distinct characterization, and artistic plotting. Its personalities have a steadily-growing idyllic kind of reality.

The Lady of the Aroostook (1879). Sparkling romance in a realistic setting of some small town figures among whom is a young New England teacher as the solitary woman passenger on the merchant ship, *Aroostook*. While H. T. Peck exaggerated in calling it the most perfect American story, it is recognizable as a flashing example of Howells' comedy of manners.

The Undiscovered Country (1880). Study in religious sectarianism presents sordid spiritualism and spiritual Shakerism. Affection between Ford and Egeria, daughter of Dr. Boynton, has been called the apotheosis of the Howells love story.

A Modern Instance† (1881). Problem novel dramatizes a story of young love, an unfortunate marriage, growing distrust, a wife's desertion, and eventual divorce. Stern realism, masterly delineation of ordinary people, excellent portrayal of literary and journalistic Boston. Generally regarded as a study in the deterioration of character, while that of *The Rise of Silas Lapham* is one in the development of character; Halleck's anticlimactic discovery lacks inevitability. His most tragic novel, one that, characteristically Howellsian, just misses reaching a decision about fundamental life-and-character realities.

***The Rise of Silas Lapham*†** (1885). Vital characterization of a self-made Vermonter who lost his money but discovered his soul. Cool, felicitous style; excellent construction; human kindliness. So well presented is its theme of moral regeneration that the novel is generally considered his masterpiece.

***Indian Summer*†** (1886). Against a picturesque Florentine setting appear two portraits, one of the loves of a man of forty, the other of the romance of a middle-aged woman. Features the outstanding elements of the love romance, the conscience story, and the international novel. Badinage amusing, repartee brilliant, dialogue masterly, narration gay and stimulating.

April Hopes (1888). Despite the tragic elements of the young love affair between Dan Mavering and Alice Pasner, an almost spiritually-minded heroine, this is a book brightened by sketches of Boston's upper set. Pleasant social satire.

***The Landlord at Lion's Head*†** (1897). Realistic spiritual study of Jeff Durgin makes the work one of his most creative.

***The Kentons*†** (1902). Slight, downy, yet flawless chronicle of an Ohio family who hurry abroad in order to cure their daughter Ellen of a disapproved love affair. Boyne Kenton has been regarded as anticipating a character in Booth Tarkington's *Seventeen* (1916).

The Son of Royal Langbrith (1904). Dramatic statement of a moral problem: Should James Langbrith's tendency to father-worship be destroyed? Dr. Anther's death sets into motion the unfolding to James of Royal Langbrith's true character.

The Leatherwood God (1916). Plot interest centers around a frontier evangelist who is regarded as a god by a small Ohio community of Howells' young manhood. Humor, insight.

SUGGESTED MERITS

1. With Whitman, is probably the most influential writer since the Civil War. From about 1891 to 1915, he dominated the intellectual scene.

As a critic, he encouraged many writers, including Mark Twain (p. 187), Henry James (p. 200), Hamlin Garland (p. 204), Stephen Crane (p. 207), Paul Laurence Dunbar (p. 252), Frank Norris (p. 228), E. D. Howe (p. 206), and Booth

SUGGESTED DEFECTS

1. In no way are his parlor dialogues related to the dramatic one-act play that is independent of mere repartee and treats of deeper emotion.[26]

His literary criticism lacks dispassionate judgment, lacks the truly critical mind. He judges from **a priori** law; he is defeated by ancestral finicality.

Puritan ancestry[27] makes him avoid such depths of human ex-

26 M. J. Moses, *The American Dramatists* (1925), p. 394 *f.*

27 H. G. Belcher, "Howells's Opinions on the Religious Conflicts of His Age as Exhibited in Magazine Articles," *AL.*, XV (1943-1944), pp. 262-278.

Tarkington (p. 269); as a writer of sparkling farce-comedy,[28] he excelled his contemporaries in building up a slight incident and in enlarging surface-character.

His works, spanning two literatures, championed reality[29] in fiction and in many ways mirror in epitome the spiritual and intellectual temper of his era. His very provincialism is what makes him a supreme exponent of the commonplaces of the bourgeois spirit at the close of the nineteenth century.[30]

Truth is his only passion; and his transcripts of American life are strengthened by a selective realism, by a theoretical detachment, and by the crusading understanding that the novel must be an instrument for waging war on the injustices of modern civilization and for socializing the economic structure.

perience as hatred and sexual love. Correct are his portraits of American city and country life, and able are his analyses of native Americans; but, rather than a great interpreter, he is merely an observant reporter. His method is realistic, but the result is sentimental.

Denatured is his realism because it does not dig deep enough; it falls short of reality because he is no protagonist of the very doctrine he preaches.

Tersely, the Howellsian mending-wall attitudes have neighborliness; but they never enter upon adjacent grounds to grapple wholeheartedly with serious problems. In classic fashion, and oft-repeated, O. W. Firkins has phrased this deficiency.[31]

2. He does succeed in telling a reasonably realistic story in a style that has suavity, simple clarity, adroit talk, uniformly excellent dialogue, savory humor, supple grace, felicitous exposition, and solid workmanship. Well-drawn portrayals of the scheming, the tactful, and the witty women.

2. Mattering least is his plot, which often has a Baedeker approach and a somewhat sprawling formlessness. His men lack virility, his women are cute and superficial; his entire approach is passionl ss. The human element is always intruding upon his landscape description. There is an excess of conversation; there are his tendencies to expand trivialities and protract conclusions. Style is that of a painstaking craftsman rather than of a genuine artist.

HENRY JAMES, 1843—1916, critic, novelist.[32] Fortunate in an inheritance of moderate wealth and a home environment of intelligence and intellectual interests; educated by private tutors,

28 A. H. Quinn, *A History of the American Drama from the Civil War to the Present Day* (1937, 1943), pp. 66-81.

29 Present-day critics emphasize that Howells wrote with social conscience and that he saw the possibilities of the American scene. Read G. E. DeMille, "The Infallible Dean," *SR., XXXVI* (1928), pp. 148-156; V. L. Parrington, *Main Currents in American Thought*, III (1930), pp. 241-253; Herbert Edwards, "Howells and the Controversy over Realism in American Literature," *AL.*, III (1931-1932), pp. 239-248; V. F. Calverton, *The Liberation of American Literature* (1932), pp. 375-381; Alfred Kazin, *On Native Grounds* (1942), pp. 3-50.

30 C. H. Grattan, "Howells: Ten Years After," *AM.*, XX (1930), pp. 42-50.

31 In *William Dean Howells* (1924), p. 65, O. W. Firkins states that "adultery is never pictured; seduction never; divorce once and sparingly ('A Modern Instance'); marriage discordant to the point of cleavage, only once and in the same novel with the divorce; crime only once with any fullness ('The Quality of Mercy'); politics never; religion passingly and superficially; science only in crepuscular psychology; mechanics, athletics, bodily exploits or collisions, very rarely."

32 For full bibliography, see pages 308-309.

by study at Harvard, and by foreign travel, James was exception ally well equipped for his career as a professional literary man. Long resident abroad, and deficient in knowledge of any but the Eastern fringe of his native land, James was through his mature years only technically American; and even this distinction disappeared when, just before his death, he became a British citizen. Friendships with E. L. Godkin, C. E. Norton, and W. D. Howells launched him in the middle '60's as a contributor to the New York *Nation,* the *North American Review,* and the *Atlantic,* but his departure shortly afterwards for Europe marked a substantial abandonment of American residence. In France, in the middle '70's, he came to know Flaubert, de Goncourt, Daudet, Maupassant, and Zola; but none influenced him as had his countryman Hawthorne, and as did their predecessor Balzac, and the Russian Turgenev, then resident in Paris. The remainder of his life, except for an occasional visit to America, he spent in Italy and England. The significance of this virtual expatriation in respect to his place in American literature was threefold: it operated to encourage use of European settings, characters, social standards, and points of view strange to Americans; it gave him, understandably, a view of such of his countrymen as appear in his novels through critical Continental eyes; it made him an unpopular personality to American readers, and put him increasingly out of touch with the rising industrialism of America.[33]

33 Writings by Henry James not cited or discussed on pages 200-204 are: NOVELS: *Watch and Ward* (1878); *The Outcry* (1911). NOVELETTES AND SHORT STORIES: *A Passionate Pilgrim and Other Tales* (1875); *The Madonna of the Future and Other Tales* (two volumes, including "Madame de Mauves" and "The Diary of a Man of Fifty," 1879); *An International Episode* (1879); *Four Meetings* (1879); *A Bundle of Letters* (1880); *The Pension Beaurepas* (1881); *The Point of View* (1883); *The Siege of London* (1883); *Tales of Three Cities* (1884); *The Author of Beltraffio* (1885); *Stories Revived* (three volumes, 1885); *A London Life; The Patagonia; The Liar; Mrs. Temperley* (two volumes, 1889); *A Lesson of the Master; The Marriages; The Pupil; Brooksmith; The Solution; Sir Edmund Orme* (1892); *The Real Thing, and Other Tales* (1893); *Picture and Text* (1893); *The Private Life, The Wheel of Time, Lord Beaupre, The Visits, Collaboration, Owen Wingrave* (1893); *Terminations, The Death of the Lion, The Coxon Fund, The Middle Years, The Altar of the Dead* (1895); *Embarrassments* (1896); *In the Cage* (1898); *The Two Magics: The Turn of the Screw, Covering End* (1898); *The Soft Side* (including "The Real Right Thing" and "Miss Gunton of Poughkeepsie," 1900); *The Better Sort* (1903); *Julia Bride* (1909); *The Finer Grain* (1910); *Garbielle de Bergerac* (*Atlantic Monthly,* 1869; book, 1918); *A Landscape Painter* (four stories, 1919); *Travelling Companions* (seven stories, 1919); *Master Eustace* (five stories, 1920). DRAMAS: *Theatricals* ("Tenants" and "Disengaged," 1894); *Theatricals* ("The Album" and "The Reprobate," 1895). ESSAYS AND BIOGRAPHIES: *Transatlantic Sketches* (1875); *French Poets and Novelists* (1878); *Hawthorne* (1879); *Foreign Parts* (1883); *Portraits of Places* (1883); *A Little Tour in France* (1885); *Four Meetings* (1885); *The Art of Fiction* (1885); *Partial Portraits* (1888); *Essays in London and Elsewhere* (1893); *William Wetmore Story and His Friends* (1903); *The Question of Our Speech; The Lesson of Balzac* (two lectures, 1905); *English Hours* (1905); *The American Scene* (1907); *Views and Reviews* (1908); *Italian Hours* (1909); *A Small Boy and Others* (1913); *Notes on Novelists* (1914); *Notes of a Son and Brother* (1914); *England at War: An Essay* (1915); *The Question of the Mind* (1915); *The Middle Years* (1917); *Within the Rim, and Other Essays* (1918). Additional material is available in *Notes and Reviews* (edited by Pierre de Chaignon la Rose, 1921); *Henry James: Letters to A. C. Benson and Auguste Monod* (edited by E. F. Benson, 1930); *Letters of Henry James to Walter Berry* (edited by Mildred Howells, 1928); *The Letters of Henry James*† (edited in two volumes by Percy Lubbock, 1920); *Theatre and Friendship: Some Henry James Letters: With a Commentary* (by Elizabeth Robins, 1932); *Stories of Writers and Artists* (edited with an Essay by F. O. Matthiessen, 1944).

NOVELS

Group I: From RODERICK HUDSON (1875) to THE BOSTONIANS (1886). The essential provincialism of Boston (as James saw it) is presented in *The Europeans* (1878) and *The Bostonians* (1886); of New York, in *Washington Square* (1881). The woman's suffrage movement received none too friendly notice in *The Bostonians* wherein the ardent but fading Olive Chancellor is contrasted with her younger and more attractive disciple, Verena Tarrant.

Other volumes are *The American*† (1877), *Confidence* (novelette, 1880), and —

Roderick Hudson† (1876). Study of an American sculptor in whom opportunities afforded by residence abroad disclosed deficiencies of artistic capacity and personal integrity. Christina Light reappears in *The Princess Casamassima.*

The Portrait of a Lady† (1881). In many ways one of James's noblest works, has as its central figure an American woman, Isabel Archer, well characterized in the title. Resident in Europe and surrounded by an interesting and varied group of characters, she is placed in situations of the most trying sort. Startling and in a way refreshing is the presence of an American newspaper woman, Henrietta Stackpole.

Group II: From THE PRINCESS CASAMASSIMA (1886) to THE SACRED FOUNT (1901). Second group includes *The Reverberator* (novelette, 1888), *The Aspern Papers* (novelette, 1888), *The Other House* (novel, 1896), *The Sacred Fount* (novelette, 1901), and —

The Princess Casamassima (1886). Unusual and, generally speaking, unsuccessful venture into the realm of political and social reform.

The Tragic Muse (1890). Set in England, shows its central character, Nick Dormer, facing a choice between the claims of politics and art, and rejecting the former for the latter.

What Maisie Knew† (1897). In its picture of fast London society through which the innocent and uncomprehending Maisie walks miraculously unscathed, is better than its successor, *The Awkward Age* (1899), but nevertheless one of James's more unpleasant books.

The Spoils of Poynton (printed as ***The Old Thing,*** 1896; present title, 1897). Illustrates the dependent position of woman under English marriage laws.

Group III: THE WINGS OF THE DOVE (1902) and after. *The Ivory Tower* (1917) and *The Sense of the Past* (1917) are incomplete novels, posthumously published. Three masterpieces:

The Wings of the Dove† (1902). Heroine is Milly Theale, avowedly modelled upon his cousin Mary Temple. Poignant appeal of situation.

The Ambassadors† (1903). One of his best constructed novels. Lambert Strether, an American, has the intelligence to discover in Paris what he has missed in America. James has thus at last outlived embarrassment over the folks from home.

The Golden Bowl† (1904). Shows Maggie Verver, an American girl, in the difficult position of discovering that Prince Amerigo, the Italian nobleman she has married, has previously been intimate with Charlotte Stant, the woman who is now Maggie's stepmother. Situation is worked out, of course — as always in James — without recourse to law.

SHORT STORIES

James had both a liking and a genius for the short-story form; but his tendency to elaboration led frequently to an expansion of short-story themes to the dimensions of the novelette. *Daisy Miller*† (1879), which contrasts with devastating effect the manners of what James thought a typical American girl to those of a settled and correct Continental society, had the closest approach to popularity of anything James ever wrote. Outstanding also are: *The Turn of the Screw*† (1898), *A Passionate Pilgrim* (1871), *An International Episode* (1879), *The Liar*† (1889), *The Lesson of the Master*† (1892).

GENERAL ESTIMATE

James's critical essays, while devoted to a variety of topics, include significant statements regarding the art of fiction and the related art of painting with which he was almost equally familiar. His lofty view of the profession of authorship was equalled only by his devotion to its technical aspects. His emphasis upon form was French. He delighted in the well-made novel, adhered closely to a plan, left no loose ends. Interest in the analysis of character, and of that mixture of impulsive response and ratiocination which furnishes the background for conversation, slows up action. Style, too, sometimes dangerously absorbs attention. In his best work he transcends these difficulties.

Other deficiencies are more deeply seated. His orderly, sheltered, celibate, monotonously blameless life had denied him enriching experiences. His almost complete ignorance of business; still worse, his lack of any understanding of the perpetual and ruthless struggle for mere existence which absorbs the attention of a large part of the human race; his chilliness in the treatment of the sex passion; these are qualifications of his claim to supreme rank as a fiction writer. Within his limits he was a noble artist, but his narrow reputation constitutes a fair ultimate judgment of his work.

HAMLIN [HANNIBAL] GARLAND, 1860—1940, short-story writer, novelist, autobiographer, social historian.[34] Born on a farm near West Salem, Wisconsin. Family emigrated to Winneshiek County, Iowa (1869). Entered Cedar Valley Seminary, at Osage, Iowa (1876), from which he was graduated four years later (1881). Tramped through Eastern states. Worked as a carpenter in Illinois and Massachusetts (1882). Staked a claim in McPherson County, North Dakota (1883), sold it (1884), and returned to Boston to qualify himself for teaching. First a pupil, and later (1885) an instructor, in the Boston School of Oratory. Taught and lectured in and about Boston (1885—1889). Visits to Dakota, Iowa, and Wisconsin (1887) provided material for his Mississippi Valley stories. Fourth visit (1889) to his parents at Ordway, Brown County, Dakota Territory, to which they had moved in 1881. Sent on tour by B. O. Flower, socially minded editor of the *Arena,* to investigate labor and farm conditions (1891). Wintered in New York (1892). Settled in Chicago (1893). Purchased house in West Salem, Wisconsin, for his parents (1893). Summered in Colorado, New Mexico, and Arizona (1894, 1895, 1896). Studied the Sioux Indians in North and South Dakota (1897). Wintered in Washington (1897). Six-months' overland trip (1898) into Yukon Valley led to *The Trail of the Gold Seekers* (1899) and *The Long Trail* (1907). Visited England (1899). Married Zulime Taft (1899), who bore him two daughters, Mary Isabel (1904, Wisconsin) and Constance (1907, Chicago). Established family in New York (1915). Elected to the American Academy of Arts and Letters (1918). Won Pulitzer Prize for the best biography of the year with *A Daughter of the Middle Border* (1921). Took family to England (1922). Honorary degree of Litt.D. conferred by the University of Wisconsin (1926). Won the Roosevelt Memorial Association Medal (1931). Moved from New York City to McLaughlin Park, Los Angeles (1932). Honorary degree from Northwestern University (1933). Died of a cerebral hemorrhage.

A strong didactic or propagandistic purpose directs most of his writings. In pursuit of his literary credo of Veritism, he endeavors to be objective in his realism, reproducing colloquial speech faith-

34 E. W. Bowen, "Hamlin Garland, the Middle-West Short-Story Writer," *SRQ.*, XXVII (1919), pp. 411-422; R. R. Raw, "Hamlin Garland, the Romanticist," *SR.*, XXXVI (1928), pp. 202-210; *Hamlin Garland Memorial*, by the Federal Writers' Project of the Works Progress Administration in South Dakota (South Dakota Writers' League, 1939); Claude Simpson, "Hamlin Garland's Decline," *Sw.R.*, XXVI (1940-1941), pp. 223-234.

fully, presenting real-life situations, and possessing genuine depth of feeling; but he is frequently prolix and even tedious, his writings, especially his early work, are crude potboilers, and his social and political attitudes have in them a strong theatrical element. By his very emphasis on only the grinding monotony of Western farm life, his books show a reaction against romanticism and a retention of it. It was he "who became known as the type-symbol of the pioneer in American literature, the dirt farmer who for a time moved westward with his emigrant family but eventually chose to become a back-trailer and created the literary Middle Border."[35]

EARLY PERIOD: REALISM (1887—1894)

Propagandistic are three novels published in 1892: (1) *A Member of the Third House,* concerned with the corrupting legislative influence of the railroads; (2) *A Spoil of Office,* which exposes political rottenness, pictures the growth of the Grange and the Farmer's Alliance, and speaks out in favor of the Populist Party; and (3) *Jason Edwards: An Average Man,* wherein the Single Tax theories of Henry George receive attention. Less ephemeral, too, are (4) *A Little Norsk* (1892), a novelette of a Dakota farm girl whose disheartening marriage individualizes even more sharply the two farmer-characters who years earlier had rescued her; and (5) *Boy Life on the Prairie* (1899), idyllic in its freshness and vigor, much of it included in the later *A Son of the Middle Border.*

Main-Travelled Roads† (1891). Half-dozen Mississippi Valley sketches; five more stories added to later editions. Presentation of farm life in the Middle West cudgels the atrophying influence and the spiritual limitations of rural life. Includes "Under the Lion's Paw,"† through which artistic story of a mortgaged farmer emerges a message openly in favor of land reform; "The Return of the Private,"† keyed against the superficiality of romance by a tale of a fevered soldier who finds at home not a royal welcome but the stern enmeshing dullness of the "daily running fight with nature" and the struggle against the persistent "injustice of his fellow-men"; "Up the Coolly," an allegorical approach to the farmer and the successful citified brother, to the lower and the upper strata of human society; and "A Branch Road," in which a young woman aged prematurely by parents, by a mistreating husband, and by a narrow farm life, is forced to overlook conventional morality.

Crumbling Idols (1894). Little book of essays pleads a bit vaporously for "veritism," or an honest realism founded on ob-

---

35 J. T. Flanagan, "Hamlin Garland, Occasional Minnesotan," *M.Hist.,* XXII (1941), p. 157 (pp. 157-168); W. F. Taylor, *The Economic Novel in America* (1942), pp. 148-183.

servation; but the veritist or realist must also be an idealist, writing of what is and suggesting what is to be: by picturing the ugliness and warfare, he conjures up the converse picture of beauty and peace. Theory derived in part from Eugene Veron's *Esthetics* and Max Nordau's *Conventional Lies;* also, from Eggleston's *Hoosier Schoolmaster,* Ed Howe's *Story of a Country Town,* and Joseph Kirkland's *Zury.*

MIDDLE PERIOD: ROMANCE (1895—1916)

(1) *The Captain of the Gray-Horse Troop* (1902) champions the Sioux Indians who are being exploited by white settlers; (2) *Hesper* (1903), far from strong in its realistic dealings with the labor war among the independent miner, the union miner, and the capitalistic operator in the Cripple Creek gold mines; (3) *Cavanagh, Forest Ranger* (1910), weak novel gaining its value from the delineation of that phase of our national life where a Federal conservation program meets the resistance of cattle barons; (4) *Other Main-Travelled Roads* (1910), short stories selected from two earlier books, (5) *Prairie Folks* (1893) and (6) *Wayside Courtships* (1897); and —

Rose of Dutcher's Coolly (1895). Transitional novel, strong in its realities, romantic in its conclusion. Later chapters belie the promise of the earlier ones. Part-reflection of his Chicago experiences; charming descriptive bits.

FINAL PERIOD: AUTOBIOGRAPHY (1917-1940)

A Son of the Middle Border† (serialized, 1914; book, 1917). Bittersweet autobiographical narrative documents not only his struggle and growth and success until 1893 but also the history of pioneer days on the Western frontier.[36] Stylistic infelicities. Self-written account complemented by *A Daughter of the Middle Border* (1921), concerned with his later years, especially his marriage; *Trail-Makers of the Middle Border* (1926);[37] and *Back-Trailers from the Middle Border* (1928), as semifictional as the preceding two.

Roadside Meetings (1930). Account of his literary friendships, followed by the longish, garrulous, and more or less inconsequen-

---

36 "Our material pioneering is done," opines Hamlin Garland as he re-sketches "the thrust of the pioneer and the steady expansion of the nation's plowed lands." He is glad that he "was born early enough to catch the dying echoes of their songs, to bask in the failing light of their fires." Hamlin Garland, "The Westward March of Settlement," *FT.*, XII (1934-1935), pp. 499-505, a reprint of pp. 11-27 and p. 34 of the 1927 *Reading with a Purpose* pamphlet given in footnote 37.

37 In his own words, *A Son of the Middle Border* and its introductory volume, *Trail-Makers of the Middle Border,* taken together, "present the homely everyday history of a group of migrating families from 1840 to 1895, a most momentous half century of western social development. They are as true to the home-life of the prairie and the plains as my memory will permit." Hamlin Garland, *The Westward March of American Settlement* (*Reading with a Purpose* series, 1927), p. 33.

tial recollections in *Companions on the Trail* (1931), *My Friendly Contemporaries* (1932), and *Afternoon Neighbors* (1934).

STEPHEN CRANE, 1871—1900, journalist, short-story writer, novelist.[38] Born in Newark, New Jersey. Attended Claverack College, a military academy three miles east of Hudson, New York (*c.* 1887—1890). Entered Lafayette College (1890—1891). Transferred to Syracuse University (1891), where he spent less time in the classroom than on the baseball field.[39] Reporter for the *Herald* and the *Tribune*. To Cuba (1896), where his more than two-day struggle subsequent to the sinking of the steamer *Commodore* inspired "The Open Boat." Experiences as correspondent during the Greco-Turkish War resulted in *Active Service* (1899), a loose, wooden-charactered, journalistic novel.[40] Much better reporting in *Wounds in the Rain* (1900), an outgrowth of his Spanish-American activities in Cuba: includes two fine civil war stories, "The Price of the Harness" and "An Episode of War." From England[41] he went to Germany, where at Badenweiler he died from tuberculosis.[42] Buried at Elizabeth, New Jersey.

Volumes include *Whilomville Stories* (1900), excellent in its discernment of child psychology, from playfulness to brutality (representative are "Lynx-Hunting," "Shame," and "The Carriage-Lamps"); *Great Battles of the World* (1901), an indifferent historical study; *Last Words* (1902), a compilation of early stories and sketches; *The O'Ruddy* (1903), an experimental satiric romance completed by Robert Barr.

NOVELETTE AND NOVEL

Maggie: A Girl of the Streets (1893). Naturalistic, impression-

---

38 Thomas Beer, *Stephen Crane*, with an introduction by Joseph Conrad (1923); *The Work of Stephen Crane*, edited by Wilson Follett, (1925): Volume II, Introduction by R. H. Davis, pp. ix-xx; D. H. Dickason, "Stephen Crane and the *Philistine*," *AL.*, XV (1943-1944), pp. 279-287, *Letters*, ed. R. W. Stallman and L. Gilkes (1960).

39 Fresh material dealing with Crane's preparatory school and college attendance, covering the years 1888 to 1892, is presented by L. U. Pratt, "The Formal Education of Stephen Crane," *AL.*, X (1938-1939), pp. 460-471, in an endeavor to modify certain accepted views of Crane; *e.g.*, that he could not himself dri'l well at the military school. Supplement material with Harvey Wickham, "Stephen Crane at College," *AM.*, VII (1926), pp. 291-297; M. J. French, "Stephen Crane, Ball Player," *SUAN.*, XV (January, 1934), p. 3*f.*; Claude Jones, "Stephen Crane at Syracuse," *AL.*, VII (1935-1936), pp. 82-84.

40 Intended as potboilers were such books as *Active Service* and *The O'Ruddy*. "Suppose," supposes Sherwood Anderson correctly, "he did put a pretty little patent-leather finish on some of his later tales. Take him for what he was—his importance."

41 "There was no tumult in the high world of letters English because Stephen Crane had rented a villa named Ravensbrook at Oxted in Surrey and proposed to make a stay. He was even snubbed with a vengeance." The foregoing statement by Thomas Beer in *Stephen Crane* (1923), p. 161 *ff.*, is refuted by F. M. Ford, *Mightier than the Sword* (1938), p. 46 *ff.* (pp. 38-58).

42 Many legends about Stephen Crane made the rounds, ranging from the allegation that he was the natural son of Grover Cleveland to that which had him murdered by an actress in Chicago. Of more significance in his life was the part played by his wife, Cora Howorth Stewart Taylor, who also suffered the abuse heaped upon him. Thomas Beer, *Stephen Crane* (1923), "Appendix," p. 243 *ff.* (pp. 243-248); Mrs. Joseph Conrad, "Recollections of Stephen Crane," *Bookman*, LXIII (1926), pp. 134-137; Carl Bohnenberger and N. M. Hill (editors), "The Letters of Joseph Conrad to Stephen and Cora Crane," *Bookman*, LXIX (1929), pp. 225-235, 367-374.

istic novelette printed at author's expense under the pseudonym "Johnston Smith" has been placed by Wilson Follett as "a cornerstone of American fictional history." Reportorial, episodic analysis of environmental victimization; influenced by Zola's *L'Assommoir.* Note that characters are types, and that the conversation strives for realism by its grim, repetitive vacuity. Should be compared with Crane's *George's Mother* (1896).

***The Red Badge of Courage*†** (1895). Novel of the Civil War, lyrical and intense in its objective, developmental dissection of a raw recruit's soul[43] under gunfire. Vivid, direct, impersonal; bristles with a particularized idiom, burning perception, poetic prose-images. Indebted to talks with General J. B. Van Petten of Claverack College and other veterans,[44] to the *Century's* "Battles and Leaders of the Civil War," and to W. F. Hinman's *Corporal Si Klegg and His "Pard"* (1887).[45] Uncertain is the indebtedness to Zola's *La Débâcle* and to Tolstoy's *War and Peace* and *Sevastopol.*

SHORT-STORY COLLECTIONS

The Little Regiment, and Other Episodes of the American Civil War (1887; issued in England as *Pictures of the War,* 1916). Half-dozen short-stories including "A Mystery of Heroism," described by Carl Van Doren as "pure, concentrated Crane"; "Three Miraculous Soldiers," easily of tantamount rank with the perhaps better-known "A Grey Sleeve"; and "The Little Regiment,"† perfect in a surface contempt that conceals the inarticulate love of two brothers even at the very moment when each is voicing what is not meant.

The Open Boat and Other Tales of Adventure (1898). Among the eight stories are "An Illusion in Red and White," as ironically grim as "The Monster"; "The Bride Comes to Yellow Sky," a lifelike, risible tale admired by Willa Cather; "Horses — One Dash," of autobiographical value as are "The Third Violet" and "The Open Boat"[46]; and the title-story,† its frequently-praised first

43 Critical opinion comments frequently that Henry Fleming becomes almost an abstraction. That is similarly an operative factor in *Maggie* of which the first version calls the characters simply "the girl," "the girl's mother," and "the girl's brother." In *The Red Badge of Courage* Henry so loses all identity that Joseph Conrad once misstated that the hero is not given a personal name. Wilson Follett, "The Second Twenty-Eight Years," *Bookman,* LXVIII (1928-1929), pp. 532-537.
For another and possibly a better account of a recruit's sensations in battle, read J. W. DeForrest, "The First Time under Fire," *Harper's,* XXIX (1864), pp. 475-482.

44 L. U. Pratt, "A Possible Source of *The Red Badge of Courage,*" *AL.,* XI (1939-1940), pp. 1-10.

45 H. T. Webster, "William F. Hinman's *Corporal Si Klegg* and Stephen Crane's *The Red Badge of Courage,*" *AL.,* XI (1939-1940), pp. 285-293.

46 Crane loved horses and the sea. "And his passage on this earth was like that of a horseman riding swiftly in the dawn of a day fated to be short and without sunshine." Joseph Conrad, "Stephen Crane," *Bookman,* L (1919-1920), p. 531 (pp. 529-531). Elsewhere, Harvey Wickham cautions that Crane was not the pliable, soft fellow "created by the sentimentalizing imagination of Conrad's declining years." See also Amy Lowell's opinion, page 209, footnote 48.

sentence[47] opening up a circumstantial, objective, tense narrative of an open boat manned by three shipwrecked men and Crane: the cadences of his prose rise and fall with the waves of grim humor and graphic details.

The Monster and Other Stories (1899). At least three of its seven tales are meritorious: "The Monster,"† where a Negro, while rescuing a boy, suffers facial disfigurement: a horror tale focused within the capricious lens of a cruel, intolerant community, and snapped with painful realism and trenchant sympathy; "The Blue Hotel,"† a superlative story, praised by H. L. Mencken for its austere economy, brilliant dramatic effect, Conradian dignity, and epic sweep, and possibly Crane's only story which deliberately moralizes; and "The Third Violet," chiefly valuable, according to Wilson Follett, as an autobiographical transcript concerned with a hopeless love affair of 1891 and a short period in 1893: but it is more than that — as in "The Little Regiment," inscrutable motives compel lies to issue out of each character in this romantic novelette of a young artist.

POETRY COLLECTIONS[48]

The Black Riders and Other Lines (1895). Volume of staccato, unrimed poems merciless in their epigrammatized piercing beneath smug surfaces into the futile angularity of our hearts and souls; *e.g.,* attacks religion. Its so-called free-verse form possibly influenced by the Bible and by Emily Dickinson; anticipatory of the Imagists. Representative: "God fashioned the ship of the world carefully"; "Should the wide world roll away"; "A man went before a strange God."

War Is Kind and Other Lines (1899). Title poem, as well as several others, is as good as anything he ever wrote; on the whole, however, collection is not an improvement upon *The Black Rider* volume. Representative: "A newspaper is a collection of half-injustices"; "Wayfarer"; "A man said to the universe."

REFORMERS, HISTORIANS, AND PHILOSOPHERS

HENRY GEORGE, 1839—1897, pioneer in American political economy; ranked by John Dewey as America's greatest social philosopher. Henry George's system of economics (he himself disliked the phrase "Single Tax," and used it perhaps only once in *Progress and Poverty*) has been attacked as fallacious and his doctrines as untenable (Arthur Crump, 1884; E. H. Johnson, 1910 — see also below): his is "one of the most extreme doctrines of Communism," stated the Duke of Argyll

47 "None of them knew the colour of the sky" is as famous as "The red sun was pasted in the sky like a wafer," the latter of which appears in *The Red Badge of Courage.*

48 Despite her declarations that his poetry is static and even more adolescent than his prose, Amy Lowell concludes: "He died too soon. . . . He ranks in America somewhat as Chatterton ranks in England. A boy, spiritually killed by neglect. A marvellous boy, potentially a genius, historically an important link in the chain of American poetry." *The Work of Stephen Crane,* edited by Wilson Follett (1925): Volume VI, Introduction by Amy Lowell, p. xxix (pp. ix-xxix).

in 1884 (although Karl Marx regarded *Progress and Poverty* as "simply an attempt to rescue the rule of capitalism — in fact, to rear it anew upon a firmer basis than its present one. This cloven hoof, together with the donkey's ears, peeps unmistakably out of the declamation by Henry George"). J. F. Muirhead concludes that the practical statesman will not confiscate private property on land, but will simply confiscate rent or appropriate rent by taxation, and abolish all taxation except that on land values; John Dewey, in a radio address (193-?), stated: "I do not claim that George's remedy is a panacea that will cure by itself all our ailments. *But I do claim that we cannot get rid of our basic troubles without it.*" Despite the infusion of error which his theory may contain, he will undoubtedly be remembered, as Arthur Birnie said, for his belief in social justice, his fidelity to a social ideal. More than six million copies of his books in English alone have been circulated, as well as translations in many languages.

For more information, consult D. C. Pedder, *Henry George and His Gospel* (1908), A. N. Nichols, *The Single Tax Movement in the United States* (1916), C. B. Fillebrown, *Henry George and the Economists* (1916), R. A. Sawyer, *Henry George and the Single Tax* (a Catalogue of the Collection in the New York Public Library, 1926), Henry George, Jr., *The Life of Henry George* (1930), L. F. Post, *The Prophet of San Francisco* (1930), G. R. Geiger, *The Philosophy of Henry George* (1933), J. F. Muirhead, *Land and Unemployment* (1935; introduction by Garnet Smith), Ernest Teilhac, *Pioneers of American Thought in the Nineteenth Century* (translated by E. A. J. Johnson, 1936), A. J. Nock, *Henry George* (1939), Arthur Birnie, *Single-Tax George* (1939), and [L. F. Post], "The Single Tax," in *The Encyclopedia Americana,* XXV (1941), pp. 34-39.

THREE IMPORTANT VOLUMES

Our Land and Land Policy, National and State (1871). Only forty-eight pages, yet his first thorough attempt to set forth a solution to the problem of "advancing poverty with advancing wealth." Advocated the abolition of land monopoly by transferring all taxes from labor and its products into one tax on the value of land, thereby solving the problem of absorbing the "unearned increment." Proposal, made in the fifth section of pamphlet, later became known as the single tax theory, more fully developed in

Progress and Poverty — An Inquiry into the Cause of Industrial Depressions and of Increase of Want with Increase of Wealth† (1878). Logical, comprehensive, scientific inquiry into the fundamental cause of industrial upsets and involuntary poverty explains why tycoons and paupers multiply together, and wherein lies the remedy to that man-made condition. Attacks the doctrine of Malthus, and the "wages-fund" theory; advances the "unearned increment" theory, that the land value of every community is enough to pay all its necessary public expenses. Was attacked and condemned by Thomas Huxley, Goldwin Smith, Leo XIII, Frederic Harrison, John Bright, and Joseph Chamberlain. Examples of the Single Tax principles in application are found in such places as Canada, Brazil, Argentine, South Africa, Australia, New Zealand, and the United States. Order of 200,000-word exposition could be improved; much of its matter irrelevant. On the whole, exposition clear, message attractive, thinking original and compelling, sincerity fervent. This volume is the political bible of thousands.

Protection or Free Trade (1885). An examination of the tariff question as it affects the interests of labor; also, a persuasive attack upon free-trade fallacies. As stated by D. C. Pedder, the ultimate " 'robber' " of the working man's earnings is Private Property in Land," and, as emphasized by G. R. Geiger, unrestricted *laissez-faire* meant the abolition not only of tariffs but of all taxes, and demanded, in the words of Henry George, "the treatment of the land as the common property in usufruct of the whole people."

JOHN FISKE, 1842—1901, musician, Harvard lecturer, American history professor at Washington University in St. Louis, letter-writer, popularizer of American history, philosopher. Value lies not in originality as an investigator, thinker, or scholar, but in interpretation of the work of others; in facts well presented, style lucidly attractive and almost magnetic, in characterization and in history dramatically and philosophically presented. PHILOSOPHY: *Outlines of Cosmic Philosophy* (1874), declared even twenty-five years later to be the best single interpretation of Herbert Spencer, clearing away that thinker's alleged confusions and adding propositions, including Fiske's important contribution to the theory of evolution — that regarding the prolonged period of human infancy when compared with the shorter infancy of the lower animals. *The Destiny of Man* (1884), first and best of a series, is an unfolding of " 'the growing predominance of the psychical life,' " (thereby encouraging a belief in Immortality), and is usually coupled with *The Idea of God* (1885), which stressed the historic differences between the old and the new Theism: both works, according to Fiske, contain the outline of a theory of religion to be elaborated upon later. *Through Nature to God* (1899), a plea for the junction of scientific and of religious thought, with an emphasis on the universal roots of love and selfishness. *Life Everlasting* (1901), a small posthumous book. HISTORY: *The Critical Period of American History, 1783-1789* (1888), his best interpretative work, and *The Beginnings of New England* (1889), which, like the 1888 volume, employs the Comtean ideas of sociological evolution as applied to American history. His best scholarly contribution is *The Discovery of America* (1892). Outdated is *Civil Government in the United States* (1890); of value as a military history is *The American Revolution* (1891), much better organized than *New France and New England* (posthumously, 1902). Fiske wrote more than a dozen other works, including *Essays: Historical and Literary* (two posthumous volumes, 1902), estimates of such lives as Thomas Hutchinson, Alexander Hamilton, Thomas Jefferson, and Daniel Webster.

WILLIAM JAMES, 1842—1910, psychologist, philosopher. Early philosophical thinking fought against Hegelianism and attempted to reconcile the British empirical tradition, to which he adhered, with religion; middle period evaluated moral, social, and religious questions; final period, his most productive, attempting the achievement of a systematic philosophy, denied the existence of consciousness and thereby began such movements as neo-realism and behaviorism. Irwin Edman and H. W. Schneider declare as Kantian the background of his philosophy; R. B. Perry believes that in its most general aspect the philosophy of William James is dedicated to the doctrine of empiricism. As John Dewey puts it, William James's power of literary expression has enriched philosophic literature. Just if commonplace is the saying that of the pair of extraordinary brothers, the novelist Henry James (p. 200) wrote like a psychologist, while the psychologist William wrote like a novelist. Many of the latter's most popular books originally appeared as lectures before semi-popular audiences.

VOLUMES

***The Principles of Psychology*†** (two volumes, 1890). Preface defines his "positivistic" method. Endeavors throughout work to prove that conscious experience is connected from the start, and sets the foundations of his theory of experience. Stream-of-thought conception does for consciousness what his empiricism strives to do for the field of experience. Sources include the works of Wundt, Helmholtz, Fechner, James Ward, and Carl Stumpf. Deft in factual observation and psychological introspection; successful convergence of empiricistic and idealistic elements. Curiously, by virtue of citations from other psychologists, this is practically his only work that is technical in style.

Psychology: Briefer Course (1892). Preface of this abridgment of his two-volumed *Principles* avows that approximately two-fifths is either new or re-done, while the rest is " 'scissors and paste.' "

The Will to Believe, and Other Essays in Popular Philosophy (1897). Doctrines influenced by Renouvier. Lead-article states thesis: "Our passional nature not only lawfully may, but must, decide an option between propositions, whenever it is a genuine option that cannot by its nature be decided on intellectual grounds."

Human Immortality: Two Supposed Objections to the Doctrine (1898). Harvard University Ingersoll Lecture of 1897 examines the objection that thought is a brain function, and defends the possibility of immortality.

Talks to Teachers on Psychology: and to Students on Some of Life's Ideals (1899). Popular volume consists partly of addresses before women's colleges and in the main of public lectures to teachers.

The Varieties of Religious Experience: A Study in Human Nature† (1902). Consolidates his spiritual resources, favors an empirical approach to religion. Signalized, declares John Dewey, "the function of his psychological method in a definite philosophic attitude"; challenges, says J. M. Moore, the entire European and "Platonic" tradition; is, declare Irwin Edman and H. W. Schneider, "one of the most significant applications of his psychology of belief." Keen introspection, felicitous style.

Pragmatism: A New Way for Some Old Ways of Thinking† (1907). Lowell Institute and Columbia University lectures, the preface to which differentiates between "pragmatism" and "radical empiricism." Note that the conception of pragmatism as a method may have begun with William James about two decades earlier rather than with the publication of *Psychology* in 1890, as is generally believed.

A Pluralistic Universe (1909). Lectures given at Manchester College, Oxford.

The Meaning of Truth: A Sequel to "Pragmatism" (1909). Significant for a preface that defines "radical empiricism," explains James's relation to Schiller and Dewey, and summarizes the subject of pragmatism.

On Some of Life's Ideals (1912). "On a certain Blindness in Human Beings" and "What Makes Life Significant?" are two essays among others in this popular volume collected from previous works.

ESSAYS

Letter on the Philippine Tangle (1899). Anti-imperialistic statement.

"Address on Philippine Question" (1903). Calls upon American liberals to stand firm as the party of conscience against imperialism.

"The Ph.D. Octopus" (1903). Laments the emphasis on the doctor's degree as developmental of artificial standards.

"The Energies of Men" (1907). Deals, says Perry, "with the human reserves brought into play in emergencies."

"The Moral Equivalent of War" (1910). Favors conscription of youth for manual work as a substitute for war in order to develop discipline and other martial virtues.

EDITED VOLUMES

Some Problems of Philosophy (edited by H. M. Kallen, 1911). Introductory textbook in philosophy prepared by the editor from an unfinished manuscript.

Essays in Radical Empiricism (edited by R. B. Perry, 1912). Systematic endeavor to set forth the doctrine of radical empiricism, a term that may perhaps symbolize the real message of James. Theme is often that of modified dualism. Eighth essay, written in French, is a summary of James's attitude toward the epistemological problem.

Collected Essays and Reviews (edited by R. B. Perry, 1920). Includes: "The Psychological Theory of Extension" (1889), a compact reply to G. C. Robertson concerning James's position as regards space perception. "Plea for Psychology as a Natural Science" (1892) urges the explanation of "mental states" in terms of physical, organic, and physiological conditions. "The Physical Basis of Emotion" (1894), a reassertion of the James-Lange theory of emotions and a reply to criticisms by such men as Wundt and Lehmann.

The Letters of William James (edited by Henry James, two volumes, 1920). Vivid, lucid, racy; wealth of illustration, variety of interest.

JACOB AUGUST RIIS, 1849—1914, Danish-born "police reporter, reformer, useful citizen"; "knight in the slums." Used flashlight and camera, lantern slides and newspaper columns and reports to committees to attack Mulberry Bend tenement conditions, excoriate social malpractice, expose municipal corruption, and work for constructive reform. Most popular are *How the Other Half Lives* (1890), self-explained by its title, and *The Making of an American* (1901), an appealing autobiography. Other books: *The Children of the Poor* (1892); *Out of Mulberry Street* (1898); *A Ten Years' War* (1900); *The Battle with the Slum* (1902); *Children of the Tenements* (1903); *Is there a Santa Claus?* (1904). Also wrote *Theodore Roosevelt: The Citizen* (1904): it was T. R. who for years had assisted Jacob Riis.

WILLIAM JENNINGS BRYAN, 1860—1925, orator, advocate of free silver, thrice an unsuccessful candidate for the Presidency, Secretary of State during Wilson's administration, militant defender of Fundamentalism: regarded by one group as "an opportunist Galahad" (C. W. Thompson's characterization) and by another as the "Great Commoner" (it was Bryan who founded *The Commoner,* a newspaper, at Lincoln, Nebraska, in 1901). President F. D. Roosevelt has quoted Bryan's statement: "I respect the aristocracy of learning. I deplore the plutocracy of wealth but I thank God for the democracy of the heart"; and the President has added that it was sincerity "which served him [Bryan] so well in his lifelong fight against sham and privilege and wrong." Concerning Bryan's attitude about the hypothesis of evolution, H. E. Fosdick has labeled it "sincere but appalling obscurantism."

Fame came with Bryan's "Cross of Gold" speech at the 1896 Democratic national convention at Chicago; his oration was fired by lucidity of language and contagion of faith. A thick volume but thin production reporting his travels and speeches during his campaign is *The First Battle* (1896); disfigured, according to E. L. Masters, by a biographical sketch by Mrs. Bryan, whose writing lacks quality and taste. Bryan's James Sprunt Lectures were published in *In His Image* (1922), where the bases for arguments, as outlined by T. V. Smith, are three large assumptions: "(1) a distrust of human nature *überhaupt,* (2) an undisguised emphasis upon human feelings as over against reflection, and (3) an extravagant optimism based upon factors confessedly outside of human control." Other publications: *Under Other Flags* (1904), *A Tale of Two Conventions* (1912), *Famous Figures of the Old Testament* (1923), *Christ and His Companions of the New Testament* (1925). In 1925 appeared *The Memoirs of William Jennings Bryan,* "By Himself and His Wife, Mary Baird Bryan."

JANE ADDAMS, 1865—1935, reformer, humanistic liberal, sociologist. Founder in Chicago of Hull House (1889), the first social settlement of America; provider of the first public playground in Chicago (1894). Branded a Pacifist in 1917; given the Nobel Peace Prize in 1931. "If the under dog was always right," Floyd Dell quotes Miss Addams as saying, "one might quite easily try to defend him. The trouble is that very often he is but obscurely right, sometimes only partially right, and often quite wrong, but perhaps he is never so altogether wrong and pig-headed and utterly reprehensible as he is represented by those who add the possession of prejudice to the other almost insuperable difficulties in understanding him."

Among her works: *Democracy and Social Ethics*† (1902) is in fundamental agreement with Tolstoy's point that the brotherhood of man must depart from mere lip talk and arrive at the very heart of facts. *The Spirit of Youth and the City Streets*† (1909) reflects her sympathy with childhood. *Twenty Years at Hull House*† (1910) was followed two decades later by *The Second Twenty Years at Hull House*† (1930), which is an epitome of her generous, heroic work directed toward "a complete mobilization of the human spirit." *The Long Road of Woman's Memory* (1916) is a gem republished in *The Excellent Becomes the Permanent*† (1932), memorial addresses. She also wrote *Newer Ideals of Peace* (1907), *A New Conscience and an Ancient Evil* (1912), and *Peace and Bread in Time of War* (1922; reprinted 1945).

Chapter XI

DEMOCRACY AND THE COMMON MAN: NOVELISTS AND SHORT-STORY WRITERS

AMBROSE [GWINETT] BIERCE, 1842—*c.* 1914, journalist, critic, poet, short-story writer;[1] once overrated as "the one commanding figure in America in our time."[2] Born in Horse Cave, Meigs County, Ohio. Attended the Kentucky Military Institute. Enlisted (1861) in Company C of the Ninth Indiana Volunteers and served throughout the Civil War.[3] Brevetted Major for distinguished service. To San Francisco, where he contributed to the *Argonaut* and edited the *News-Letter.* Married Mary Ellen Day (1871), who bore him two boys (Day, 1872; Leigh, 1874) and one daughter (Helen, 1876): the older son was murdered as a result of a love affair, the younger died of pneumonia. In England (1872—1876), where he was a staff-member of *Fun,* where he contributed to *Hood's Comic Almanac,* and where he published under the pseudonym Dod Grile three compilations of biting, sardonic sketches in *The Fiend's Delight* (1872), *Nuggets and Dust Panned Out in California* (1872), and *Cobwebs from an Empty Skull* (1874) — titles indicative of his taste for the macabre. Returned to San Francisco (1876), where his column "Prattle,"[4] which had originated as "The Town Crier" in the *News-Letter* (1869), was continued in the *Argonaut* (1877—1879) and in the *Wasp*[5] (1881—1886), and finally found its way into Hearst's *Examiner* (1887—1899), established him as literary dictator of

1 *The Letters of Ambrose Bierce,* edited by B. C. Pope, with a memoir by George Sterling (1922); *Twenty-One Letters of Ambrose Bierce,* edited by Samuel Loveman (1922); Carey McWilliams, *Ambrose Bierce* (1929); Walter Neale, *Life of Ambrose Bierce* (1929); Vincent Starrett, *Ambrose Bierce* (1929); J. S.. Goldstein, "Edwin Markham, Ambrose Bierce, and *The Man With a Hoe,*" *MLN.,* LVIII (1943), pp. 165-175.

2 Percival Pollard, *Their Day in Court* (1909), p. 238: revelatory of contemporaneous opinion.

3 Several of his war stories have been traced to actual occurrences. Chief source about Bierce himself is the Rolls of his regiment: Napier Wilt, "Ambrose Bierce and the Civil War," *AL.,* I (1929-1930), pp. 260-285.

4 *Selections from Prattle,* with a foreword by J. H. Jackson, and compiled by C. D. Hall (The California Literary Pamphlets: Number Three, 1936).

5 Franklin Walker, *The Wickedest Man in San Francisco* (1941).

the Pacific coast.[6] To Washington as Hearst correspondent[7] for the New York *American* (1897). Contributed to Hearst's *Cosmopolitan* (1905—1909). Disappeared into Mexico (1913), where probably a year later he died.[8]

SHORT-STORY VOLUMES

***Tales of Soldiers and Civilians*†** (1891); retitled ***In the Midst of Life*†**[9] (1892). Twenty-six grim horror tales. Examples: (1) "A Horseman in the Sky," a vignette admirably constructed; as brilliant as "A Son of the Gods," but attaining its conclusion by the trick of somewhat remote coincidence. (2) "An Occurrence at Owl Creek Bridge," a psychological *tour de force* ingeniously detailing the spectacular introspective escape of a Confederate spy in the illusory interval between the adjusting of the noose and the fall to the end of the rope. (3) "Chickamauga," stark in its realism, of a deaf-mute child almost gamboling through a shell-torn battlefield loaded with decaying bodies until the youngster comes upon his burned-down house and his mother's bullet-stricken body. (4) "A Son of the Gods," in which, sans conversation and sans characterization, human emotions propel men to die the very death the reconnoitering rider sacrifices himself to save them from: as magnetic a study as "A Horseman in the Sky," and even surpassing the latter in artistry. (5) "One of the Missing," where the menacing stare of an empty gun barrel which kills Jerome Searing presents an opportunity to demonstrate such Biercean characteristics as the evocation of stark horror, a bizarre plot told with simple clarity, veridical description, devastating emotional tension, austere verbal leashing, and accurate psychology. Should be compared with the apotheosis of military fortitude as represented in "A Son of the Gods." In a way, the story and its atavistic terror are remin-

---

6 On page 6 of his introduction to George Sterling's *The Testimony of the Suns* (1927), Oscar Lewis has described Bierce as "our Rhadamanthus of letters, from whose decision there was no appeal. With a scratch of his pen he made or broke reputations, literary or otherwise."

7 The New York *Journal*, on February 4, 1901, printed four lines by Bierce:

"The bullet that pierced Goebel's breast
Cannot be found in all the West;
Good reason; it is speeding here
To stretch McKinley on his bier,"

which, it is said, may have inspired the assassination of McKinley.

8 The disappearance of "Bitter Bierce" renewed the stories about his name, including those of marital incompatibility and the deaths of his two sons, and the legends that he indulged in dismantling holy crosses and exhuming corpses. Of his actions or fate after his departure to Mexico, no authentic trace is available. For an account of the various stories about his dramatic disappearance, see Carey McWilliams, "The Mystery of Ambrose Bierce," *AM.*, XXII (1931), pp. 330-337.

9 Each of the ten stories about soldiers in the first edition ends with the death of "the young, the beautiful, and the brave." *In the Midst of Life* added some stories and omitted others.

iscent of "The Man and the Snake." Possibly influenced by Poe.[10] (6) "The Eyes of the Panther," an excellent terror tale of an animal's influence on a girl's life.

Can Such Things Be?† (1893). Twenty-four stories, one of the most notable being "The Death of Halpern Frayser," in which the morbidity of the poem beginning "Enthralled by some mysterious spell, I stood" contributes to the verisimilitude and unalloyed atmosphere of an intricately-developed tale.

POETRY COLLECTIONS[11]

Black Beetles in Amber (1892) and ***Shapes of Clay*** (1903). The first is a volume of epigrams in verse, bitter in strength, obviously influenced by Horace, Juvenal, Dryden, Pope, and other satirists; the second is another collection of satirical verse launched at individuals. On the whole, his poetry is trivial and conventional.

Representative Poems: "An Invocation,"[12] anticipatory here and there of Kipling's "Recessional"; "Another Way," "Reminded," "Geotheos," "The Passing Show," "Presentment," "A Word to the Wise," "Death of Grant."

OTHER WORKS

The Monk and the Hangman's Daughter (1892). Unusual psychological document of sustained horror skillfully adapted from a German medieval romance. Simple, direct, almost flawless style. Final version[13] differs in two or three ways from *Der Mönck von Berchtesgaden* of Richard Voss, but is on the whole a literal or a closely-paraphrased translation.

---

10 That Bierce was familiar with Poe is evident, for example, from the chess-player in "Moxon's Master," a dramatic, even powerful, story; but the two should not receive the same classification. Where Poe's supernaturalism is unlicensed and a *tour de force,* Bierce's is restrained, and resembles more the manner of Fitz-James O'Brien (p. 224) than that of Poe: compare, as a case in point, "The Damned Thing" with O'Brien's "What Was It?" Bierce's horror tales are in the Gothic tradition, with tonal echoes of "Monk" Lewis and Mary Shelley, of Maturin, Ingemann, and Hoffman.

No further proof is needed of Bierce's knowledge of Poe, but it is well to recall the Poe Hoax of 1899, when with Herman Scheffauer and Carroll Carrington, Bierce conceived the plan of printing Scheffauer's "The Sea of Serenity" in the *Examiner* as a poem by Edgar Allan Poe.

11 Antagonism to emotional utterance and impatience with sentimental reform account, it is said, for Bierce's failure as a poet. "I think it quite likely that his hatred of romantic and sentimental poets may be traced to the revulsion which he must have experienced in later years toward this idyllic love affair [with his first love, Fatima Wright] and the poems and letters in which it was commemorated," is the theory of Carey McWilliams, "Ambrose Bierce and His First Love," *Bookman,* LXXV (1932), p. 259 (pp. 254-259).

12 A judicious editorial evaluating the poem appeared in the San Francisco *Examiner* of July 5, 1888; and is reprinted in full in *An Invocation,* with a critical introduction by George Sterling, and an explanation by Oscar Lewis (1928), pp. 9-13.

13 Vincent Starrett declares the novelette to be the joint production of Bierce and G. Adolphe Danziger. Bierce attributes the first English version to Adolph DeCastro, and therein lies a tale. For the nature and extent of the collaboration, read Adolph DeCastro, "Ambrose Bierce as He Really Was," *AP.,* XIV (October, 1926), p. 38 *ff.* (pp. 28-44); Adolph DeCastro, *Portrait of Ambrose Bierce* (1929), pp. 275-279, pp. 310-317; Carey McWilliams, *Ambrose Bierce* (1929), pp. 215-218; Frank Monaghan, "Ambrose Bierce and the Authorship of *The Monk and the Hangman's Daughter,* *AL.,* II (1930-1931), pp. 337-349.

Fantastic Fables (1899). Aesopian collection applied to contemporaneous economics and politics. Occasionally humorous, most frequently cynical.

The Cynic's Word Book (1906); retitled ***The Devil's Dictionary*** (1911). Collection of definitions, incisively astute, caustically skeptical, and blisteringly ironic, addressed to those "who prefer dry wines to sweet, sense to sentiment, wit to humor, and clean English to slang," reflecting Bierce's nineteenth-century aversions to labor unions, democracy, and socialism.[14]

Antepenultimata (1909). Essays critical of our civilization. Volume includes *Ashes of the Beacon* and *The Shadow on the Dial* (1909).

SUGGESTED MERITS	SUGGESTED DEFECTS
1. Permanence rests on fewer than a dozen stories; best are founded on Civil War experiences. Veridical approach and circumstantial details create an atmosphere of all-enveloping malignity and a philosophy of ironic despair. Life-like sketches.	1. Limitation of theme and mood. Of more than threescore short stories, only two or three deal with a subject other than death. Implausible, abnormal situations. Pathological types rather than emergent characters. Gothicism.
2. Concerned less with terror than with a mocking revelation of human weakness, ironic fright, and a divination of atavistic, cosmic fear. Master of the macabre tale.	2. Ghoulish horror heaped upon horror produces a revulsion of feeling. Too many melodramatic elements. Over-used exclamation-mark attitude.
3. Surprise endings justifiable in some stories.	3. Trick plots, snap denouements.
4. Intellectualized humor, comprised of extreme overstatement and extreme understatement, furnishes emotional relief.	4. Facetiously, laboriously humorous. Unbecoming jocularity; e.g., in "The Damned Thing" and in "A Watcher by the Dead."
5. At his best, acridity of phrase, delicate sense of the shades of meaning, verbal vigor and restraint, a chiselled chastity and economy of style.[15] Huge bulk of satirical writing, often provocative.	5. Ninety-five per cent of all his writings is journalistic, of which the larger bulk is polemical in nature—and trite. Fluency overflows into claptrap work. Neither original nor profound. No sustained effort in the field of satire.

14 Bierce displayed an eruptive contempt for the masses: he ridiculed the trial-by-jury system, attacked labor methods and unionization, and rejected Utopias and communism.

15 No prodigality of adjectives and adverbs bloats his sentences; no wayward saffron imagery bedizens his verse. In his *Write It Right* (1909), Bierce gives a blacklist of literary faults or *Don'ts* for writers; but even a Prescriptive Grammarian nods. When George Sterling queries whether or not the word "throbs" used only four stanzas earlier should be retained, Bierce answers: "Yes, sure." See eighth stanza on page 3 of the "Facsimile of the Original Manuscript" in George Sterling's *The Testimony of the Suns*, introduction by Oscar Lewis, with a memoir of Ambrose Bierce by A. M. Bender (1927). The "Facsimile" has notes by George Sterling in black ink and comments by Ambrose Bierce in red.

EDWARD BELLAMY, 1850—1898, short-story writer, novelist.[16] Native of Chicopee Falls, Massachusetts. One year at Union College. To Europe (1868). Admitted to the bar in Hampden County, Massachusetts. Staff-member of the New York *Evening Post* (1871). Editorial writer and book reviewer for the Springfield *Union* (1872—1876). Connected with the Berkshire *Courier*. Married Emma Sanderson. Birth of Paul (1884); of Marion (1886).[17] Founded the Springfield *Daily News* (1880); and the *New Nation* (1891). Lecturing, traveling, and writing on behalf of Nationalism[18] contributed to the development of tuberculosis. After returning from Colorado, to which he had gone for relief, he died at Chicopee Falls.

Writings include *Six to One: A Nantucket Idyl* (1878), a novel resulting from a voyage to Hawaii; *Miss Ludington's Sister* (1884), a romance as psychic as *Dr. Heidenhoff's Process; The Blindman's World and Other Stories* (1898);[19] and—

The Duke of Stockbridge (serialized, 1879; book form, 1900). Proletarian-historical novel describes with accuracy the struggle between debtor-farmers and their creditors, the background being the Shays's Rebellion (1786—1787).[20]

Dr. Heidenhoff's Process (1880). Psychological account praised by W. D. Howells as "one of the finest feats in the region of romance which I had known."[21]

Looking Backward, or 2000—1887† (1888). Utopian romance is the *vade mecum* of Nationalism. Originally, planned as "a mere literary fantasy, a fairy tale of social felicity"; ultimately, "became

16 A. E. Morgan, *Edward Bellamy* (1944).

17 Bellamy confesses that he kept postponing the examination of society's economic problem until the birth of his children "gave the problem of life a new and more solemn meaning." Thus, "it was in the fall or winter of 1886 that I sat down to my desk with the definite purpose of trying to reason out a method of economic organization by which the republic might guarantee the livelihood and material welfare of its citizens on a basis of equality correspondng to and supplementing their political equality. There was no doubt in my mind that the proposed study should be in the form of a story." [The story became *Looking Backward.*] Edward Bellamy, "How I Wrote 'Looking Backward,'" *LHJ.*, II (April, 1894), p. 2. It has been noted that *Symzonia*, probably by J. C. Symmes, anticipated "such instrumental utopias of the late nineteenth century as Bellamy's *Looking Backward*": J. O. Bailey, "An Early American Utopian Fiction," *AL.*, XIV (1942-1943), p. 293 (pp. 285-293).

18 The first of the four characteristics of the Nationalist spirit and of the men and women engaged in it is unselfishness. The second "is a tolerant and charitable attitude toward the critical and the indifferent — toward our opponents." Patriotism is third. Finally, the Nationalist movement "must contain as a condition of success . . . its present spirit of conservatism as to methods, combined with uncompromising fidelity to ends." Edward Bellamy, "Looking Forward," *Nationalist*, II (1889), pp. 1-4.

19 Van Wyck Brooks, *New England: Indian Summer, 1865-1915* (1940), pp. 384-388.

20 Occurring during the final quarter of the nineteenth century was an awakening interest in social reform: in England, among others, were William Morris and Arnold Toynbee; in Russia, Leon Tolstoy and Peter Kropotkin; in Germany, Karl Marx and Friedrich Engels; and, in America, Jane Addams.

21 In the prefatory sketch to *The Blindman's World and Other Stories* (1898), p. v (pp. v-xiii). Therein, too, Howells declares that only by Hawthorne is Bellamy's romantic imagination surpassed (p. xiii).

the vehicle of a definite scheme of industrial reorganization."[22] Provocative in its efforts to outline an American form of socialism achieved by gradual and orderly democratic steps.[23] Influenced the economic novels of W. D. Howells.[24]

Equality (1897). Sequel to *Looking Backward* is a kind of economic treatise with a filamentous plot.[25]

FRANCIS MARION CRAWFORD, 1854—1909, short-story writer, playwright, literary critic, cosmopolitan novelist.[26] Born at Bagni di Lucca in northern Italy, the son of Thomas Crawford, an eminent sculptor. Educated at St. Paul's School, Concord, New Hampshire (1866—1869); at Cambridge, England (1870—1871); at Karlsruhe and at Heidelberg, Germany (1871—1873); and at Rome. His study of Sanskrit in India, where he was converted to Catholicism and where for almost two years he was editor of the *Indian Herald* at Allahabad, was only one indication of his bent for language-mastery, for he ultimately knew fifteen or more tongues, including French, German, Italian, Spanish, Swedish, Bohemian, Turkish, Russian, as well as Latin and Greek. To America (1881), where he entered Harvard University, con-

22 Edward Bellamy, "How I Came to Write 'Looking Backward,'" *Nationalist,* I (1899), pp. 1-4. See also, page 218, footnote 17.

23 The system advocated in *Looking Backward* is a modified form of socialism, to which Bellamy gave the name Nationalism in order to avoid any potential tie-up to Marxism. Fundamental principles of the plan of action included the nationalization of industries, the attainment of both economic and political equality, the gradual acquisition by peaceful methods of the means of production and distribution, and the appeal to every class of society. Economic modifications are predicated upon education and understanding. Consult W. F. Phillips, "Edward Bellamy — Prophet of Nationalism," *WR.,* CL (1898). pp. 498-504; A. B. Forbes, "The Literary Quest for Utopia, 1880-1900," *SF.,* VI (1927-1928), pp. 182-184 (pp. 179-189); J. H. Franklin, "Edward Bellamy and the Nationalist Movement," *NEQ.,* XI, (1938), pp. 747-751 (pp. 739-772); R. L. Shurter, "The Writing of *Looking Backward,*" *SAQ.,* XXXVIII (1939), pp. 255-261. In this connection, see also Edward Bellamy, "'Looking Backward' Again," *NAR.,* CL (1890) pp. 351-363, an answer to the criticisms made by General F. A. Walker in the February *Atlantic;* Mrs. J. B. Shipley, *The True Author of Looking Backward* (1890), a pamphlet demonstrating the resemblance of Edward Bellamy's ideas to those of August Bebel; and G. A. Sanders, *Reality: Or Law and Order vs. Anarchy and Socialism* (1898), a reply to *Looking Backward* and *Equality;* W. F. Taylor, *The Economic Novel in America* (1942), pp. 184-213; C. A. Madison, "Edward Bellamy, Social Dreamer," *NEQ.,* XV (1942), pp. 444-466; Elizabeth Sadler, "One Book's Influence: Edward Bellamy's 'Looking Backward,'" *NEQ.,* XVII (1944), pp. 530-555.

24 W. F. Taylor, "On the Origin of Howells' Interest in Economic Reform," *AL.,* II (1930-1931), pp. 3-14.

25 *Equality,* says J. H. Franklin, "was an effort to develop many of the ideas suggested in *Looking Backward* and to answer questions that had been raised since 1888"; unlike *Looking Backward,* which "had enough plot to carry the reader rather pleasantly through the intricate economics of the future," states R. L. Shurter, "*Equality* is . . . devoted to filling in the gaps in the social structure described in *Looking Backward.*" W. D. Howells rated *Equality* as Bellamy's most inartistic work, concluding: "I felt that it was not enough to clothe the dry bones of its sociology with paper garments out of 'Looking Backward.'" *Loc. cit.* Franklin, p. 771; Shurter, p. 261; Howells, p. xi.

26 F. T. Cooper, *Some American Story Tellers* (1911), pp. 1-26; Hugh Walpole, "The Stories of Francis Marion Crawford," *YR.,* XII (1923), pp. 674-691; M. H. Elliott, *My Cousin F. Marion Crawford* (1934); Grace Chapman, "Francis Marion Crawford," *LM.,* XXX (1934), pp. 244-253; A. H. Quinn, *American Fiction* (1936), pp. 385-403.

tributed to the *Critic* and the *New York World,* and finally, at the suggestion of his uncle, Samuel Ward, wrote the fame-bringing *Mr. Isaacs* (1882). Went abroad, wintered at Constantinople, where he was soon married, and at last settled permanently (*c.* 1884) at Sorrento, on the Bay of Naples, where, except for occasional visits to America, he spent the rest of his life largely in a villa overlooking the Isles of the Sirens.

Of his more than twoscore novels the best are customarily said to be his fifteen studies of Italian life, especially the *Saracinesca* cycle about one Roman family out of which emerge real portraits of such men as Saracinesca, Sant' Ilario, Giacinto, Spicca, and Orsino.

STORIES OF CONTEMPORARY LIFE

(1) *An American Politician* (1884), superficial political novel. (2) *The Three Fates* (1892), faultily-constructed, repetitive, cynical, partly-autobiographical tale. (3) *Katherine Lauderdale* (1894), as protracted as its sequel, *The Ralstons* (1895), but less melodramatic.

Mr. Isaacs† (1882). Story of British India, informed with the exotic quality of an imagination as mystical as its atmosphere, moves forward in a steady current of dramatic narration unimpeded by lengthened conversations and philosophic discussions. Style could be more even, construction could be less crude; but these possible imperfections are buried beneath an Oriental coloring that appealed to readers in a decade that was responding to local-color fiction, beneath a new, strange environment that anticipated by several years the bold work of Kipling, and beneath a fertile yarn told with sentiment and surging narrative flow.

GERMAN NOVELS

(1) *Dr. Claudius*† (1883), interesting plot, good dialogue, clearly-drawn characters, fair construction, and well-bred tone; also autobiographical.[27] (2) *Greifenstein* (1889), sentimental romance. (3) *A Cigarette-Maker's Romance*† (1890), displays excellent sense of good melodrama, faithful tone, and perfect form.[28]

HISTORICAL ROMANCES

(1) *Zoroaster* (1885), tragic tale; deft depiction of Jewish and Persian characters. (2) *Khaled* (1891), effective supernaturalism,

---

27 A. B. Benson, "Marion Crawford's *Dr. Claudius,*" *SSN.*, XII (1932-1933), pp. 77-85.

28 [Anonymous], "The Novels of Mr. Marion Crawford," *ER.*, CCIV (1906), pp. 63-72 (pp. 61-80).

especially dramatic in its concluding part. (3) *Via Crucis*† (1898), realistic portrait-paintings of historical characters; story rapid in movement but rather conventional; background artificial. (4) *In the Palace of the King*† (1900), adroitly-managed romance; while swifter of movement than *Via Crucis* and more unified in spite of complicated plot, is below the latter's level. (5) *Marietta*† (1901), competent in its characterization of Zorzi. (6) *Arethusa* (1907), gracious love story. (7) *Stradella* (1909), improbable tale.

ITALIAN NOVELS

(1) *A Roman Singer* (1884), pleasant story, simple in style and thin in plot, partly biographized by Crawford's own strivings at opera singing. (2) *To Leeward* (1884), melodramatic tale. (3) *Marzio's Crucifix*† (1887), primarily a unified character study; not completely free from melodrama and sentimentality. (4) *Saracinesca*† (1887), a love story set among high Italian society of 1865. Is the first of a series of novels treating of several generations of a patrician Italian family. (5) *Sant' Ilario*† (1889), second member of trilogy is more involved in plot than *Saracinesca*. (6) *Don Orsino*† (1892), third book in the *Saracinesca* series is an interesting story of a genuine sacrifice. (7) *Children of the King* (1892), village tragedy, with such adequately-realized persons as Sebastino and Ruggiero. (8) *Pietro Ghisleri* (1893), elaborate, involved, yet persuasive plot. (9) *Casa Braccio* (1895), realistic and emotional in earlier part, and memorably commonplace in second part. (10) *Taquisara* (1896), a story of attempted defraudation. (11) *The Heart of Rome* (1903), competently realistic characterizations of Sabina Conti. (9) *Corleone* (1896), an inferior sequel in the *Saracinesca* series. (10) *The White Sister* (1909), an appealing story.

OTHER WRITINGS

The Novel: What It Is† (1893). Monograph is a genuine contribution to the literature of criticism. Evaluates the novel as "a marketable commodity," the first object of which "is to amuse and interest the reader." States that in "art of all kinds the moral lesson is a mistake"; regards the purpose-novel as "a violation of the social contract." The novel should deal largely with love. "What am I, a novel-writer, trying to do? I am trying to make little pocket-theatres out of words."[29] His own works exemplify these theories.

Wandering Ghosts (1911). Collection of seven ocean ghost-tales, the creepiest of which is "The Upper Berth."†

---

29 F. M. Crawford, *The Novel: What It Is* (1893), pp. 8, 11, 18, 19, 57.

SUGGESTED MERITS	SUGGESTED DEFECTS
1. His forty-five novels testify to a sane cosmopolitan knowledge of history, architecture, politics, and life. He is a conservative historian of a glamorous past set in backgrounds selected from the world over and, in many cases, variegated by personal observation. F. M. Crawford is "the historian of a dead past."	1. Neither an original nor even an interesting philosophy of life is present in his intellectually-novelized world. Never are his ideas or conclusions brilliant, daring, or unusual; always they are deficient in any kind of social message. As Chapman says, he "has become the historian of a dead past."
2. In moving actions lies his forte, to which are coupled a deft and an astonishing narrative power and unremitting zest.	2. All the devices of melodrama are utilized by his plots, which on occasion are slight in development. His novels are merely journalizations.
3. Excellent characterization of honest gentlemen and idealistic women. Like his settings, his characters are frequently outgrowths of personal knowledge.	3. Crawford's heroes are a bit too noble and his women too wooden. Lacking concreteness, his characterizations are somewhat general and indistinct.
4. Style is easy and flowing, lucid and bright, spiced by energy and gusto. Convincing dialogue.	4. Style is shallow and without distinction. Specifically in the historical novels is his dialogue dull.

H[ENRY] C[UYLER] BUNNER, 1855—1896, novelist, short-story writer, master of *vers de société*.[30] Born at Oswego, New York. Editor of (1878—1896) and chief contributor to *Puck*. Died at Nutley, New Jersey.

As a novelist, he will not be remembered; as a short-story writer, he pioneered with sketches of New York life, foreshadowing the work of O. Henry (p. 268) and contributing much towards the perfection of short-story mechanics; as a poet, he is painstaking and charming, spontaneous and hearty, and adept and fecund in difficult French verse forms.

NOVELS

(1) *A Woman of Honor* (1883). Immature work founded on his unacted drama *Faith,* regarded by the author himself as artificial or even theatrical. (2) *The Midge* (1886). Admirably individualized are the New York bachelor-doctor and his orphan waif in this charming novelettish story, the locale of which is the French quarter of the City. (3) *The Story of a New York House* (1887). From their mansion in Greenwich Village to impoverished extinction go three generations of the Dolphs. Structurally inferior to

30 B. W. Wells, "Henry Cuyler Bunner," *SR.*, V (1897), pp. 17-32; Brander Matthews, *The Historical Novel and Other Essays* (1901), pp. 165-189; Brander Matthews, *Recreations of an Anthologist* (1904), pp. 186-208; G. E. Jensen, *The Life and Letters of Henry Cuyler Bunner* (1939).

The Midge, but stylistically superior. (4) *The Runaway Browns* (1892). Anemic and characterless, but fairly clever and not unpleasant tale of the adventures of Paul and Adele, a young puppet-like couple who ultimately discover the bluebird of happiness at their own drab hearth.

SHORT STORIES

"A Letter and a Paragraph," a vigorous and pathetic tale that appeared in *In Partnership* (1884), written in collaboration with Brander Matthews; "Zadoc Pine," the lead-tale in *Zadoc Pine and Other Stories* (1891), described by B. W. Wells as "full of the healthiest naturalistic inspiration and the most proudly confident Americanism"; "Square-Five Fathom," which deserves wider recognition; "Natural Selection: A Romance of Chelsea Village and East Hampton Town," anathema to those who believe in a classless society. The volume *More "Short Sixes"* (1894) was a carefully finished group of stories that succeeded the more vitalized —

"Short Sixes" (1891). Tales totaling a baker's dozen have been admired for their deft cleverness and piquant individuality, their effective character sketches and telling situations, their native fertility and interpretative artistry. Avowedly influenced by the *contes* of Maupassant. Best-known are "Colonel Brereton's Aunty," "The Two Churches of 'Quawket," "Zenobia's Infidelity," "The Tenor," which is ankle-deep in tragedy rather than in broad fun, and "The Love-Letters of Smith," basically no more funny than "A Letter and a Paragraph," even though the undiscerning may laugh at the "shattering of an ideal" in the latter, and at the epistolary wooing of the "little seamstress" in the former.

"Made in France": French Tales Told with a United States Twist (1893). Collection of ten of Maupassant's stories[31] that captures the spirit and the form of the French originals without being a literal translation; if the stories fail, it is not attributable to any deficiency in construction or competent compactness or humorous touch, but in ephemerality. Yet this volume and *Love in Old Cloathes and Other Stories* (1896), which contains seven stories, in some ways represent his best work as a prose artist.

Jersey Street and Jersey Lane (1896). Tales and essays possess a strength ripened by a mellow maturity of perception and delicacy.

---

31 His debt to Guy de Maupassant is clear, yet Bunner's stories are usually so Americanized that they are more like his than those of the Frenchman. Compare, for example, the treatment of "Father Dominick's Convert" with its French counterpart, the "Confession de Théodule Sabot."

Furthermore, giving play to "a spirit of tricksy humor that Maupassant would have appreciated, the most French of all these ten tales 'with a United States twist' is not derived from the French but is Bunner's own invention — a fact no reviewer of the volume ever knew enough to find out." Brander Matthews, *The Historical Novel and Other Essays* (1901), p. 179 (pp. 165-189).

POETRY

Airs from Arcady and Elsewhere (1884) is composed of about fifty graceful, unenergized poems; *Rowen: "Second-Crop" Songs* (1892), another volume of verses, is stylistically somewhat firmer of touch; *The Poems of H. C. Bunner* (1896) is his final collection. His flowing style is clever and polished; his verses are wholesome in their humor and kindly in their satire.

REPRESENTATIVE POEMS

"Behold the Deeds" (1878), a chant-royal voiced by Adolphe Culpepper Ferguson, whose landlady's simple expedient keeps him within his room on Saturday nights; "Atlantic City," an agreeable explanation of his displeasure with that city; "Holiday Home" and "Robin's Song," two lilting lyrics; "The Appeal to Harold," the vigor and the originality of which have been commented upon; "Yes" and "Candor," a couple of humorous love poems; "To Her," a happy lyric; "Da Capo," revelatory of the irony of love as "Strong as Death" is of love and death; "A Pitcher of Mignonette," a triolet; "The Chaperon" and "She Was a Beauty," two of his better-known kindly, familiar poems; and "Shake, Mulleary and Go-ethe," approved by Alfred Kreymborg.

OTHER NOVELISTS AND SHORT-STORY WRITERS

JOHN WILLIAM DE FOREST, 1826—1906, realistic writer. Best fictional work, *Miss Ravenel's Conversion from Secession to Loyalty*† (1865; 1867), a study of the Civil War, excellent in its characterization of Mrs. Larue, Lieutenant-Colonel John Carter, and Lillie Ravenel, surely among the earliest realistic heroines in American fiction. Excellent non-fictional book, *History of the Indians of Connecticut* (1851), not yet superseded as a source for information about that state's tribes. Other novels: *Witching Times* (1857), *Seacliff* (1859), *Overland* (1871), *Kate Beaumont* (1872), *Irene the Missionary* (1879), the locale of each being respectively Massachusetts, Connecticut, New Mexico and California, South Carolina, and Syria. *The Wetherel Affair* (1873), a mystery novel; *Honest John Vane* (1875) and *Playing the Mischief* (1875), political stories; *The Bloody Chasm* (1881) and *A Lover's Revolt* (1898), the former a Civil War romance, the latter a Revolutionary War novel; *Oriental Acquaintance* (1856) and *European Acquaintance* (1858), accounts of his years abroad in England, Germany, Italy, and the Near East (1846—1848, 1850—1855).

FITZ-JAMES O'BRIEN, *c.* 1828—1862, Irish-born journalist, poet, playwright, and story writer. Arrived in New York in 1852. *A Gentleman from Ireland* (1854) kept the stage for forty years. *Ballads of Ireland* (1856) and *The Poems and Stories of Fitz-James O'Brien* (edited by William Winter, 1881) make available verses, for the most part jingling and commonplace, and short stories, at their best crisply written and rococo, yet also stiltedly conversational and fatuously sentimental. Obligations to Hoffman are evident in "The Wondersmith,"† in which Herr Hippe is burned to death because wooden puppets become inhabited by souls escaping when the stopper has accidentally fallen out of the imprisoning bottle; his debt to Poe is apparent in "The Lost Room," ghostly with its visitants, gloomy in its setting, weird in its music. Other stories of the uncanny are "Mother of Pearl," where a hashish-eating woman murders her child and tries to knife her sleeping spouse; "The Bohemian," with mesmerism as its subject; "A Terrible Night," where a dreamer swings an axe on his best friend; "What Was It?,"† the story of a dangerous, invisible presence; and "The Diamond Lens,"† where the inventor goes mad after his atomic, sylph-like inamorata dies soon after the evaporation of the water-drop in which she is enclosed.

LEW[IS] WALLACE, 1827—1905, soldier, lawyer, diplomat, painter, poet, novelist; described by A. J. Beveridge as "dreamer of beautiful dreams for better things for his fellow-men; and wielder of a sword and pen which helped those dreams come true." NOVELS: *The Fair God* (1873), a historical work that brought recognition; *Ben Hur: A Tale of the Christ*† (1880; dramatized 1899), a romantic best seller that has been translated into European and Oriental languages, and transcribed in braille; *The Prince of India* (1893), founded on the story of the Wandering Jew. *Commodus* (1877), a play, later became part of *The Wooing of Malkatoon* (1898), a protracted poem. Last page of his two-volume *Lew Wallace: An Autobiography* (1906) is signed S. E. W.; the work in some measure is probably that of his wife, Susan Elston Wallace.

S[ILAS] WEIR MITCHELL, 1829—1914, nerve specialist, medical writer, poet, novelist. Psychological analysis plays an important role in such novels as *In War Time* (1885), *Roland Blake* (1886), *Characteristics* (1892), *Dr. North and His Friends* (1900), *Circumstance* (1901), *Constance Trescot* (1905), *John Sherwood: Iron Master* (1911), and *Westways* (1913). The French Revolution is the background of picaresque *The Adventures of Francois* (1898); post-Revolutionary Philadelphia, of *The Red City* (1907); colonial Philadelphia, of his greatest historical novel, *Hugh Wynne: Free Quaker*† (1897). Other volumes: *The Hill of Stories and Other Poems* (1883), *Cup of Youth and Other Poems* (1889), and *Philip Vernon: A Tale in Prose and Verse* (1895). Most rewarding poems are "Lines to Deserted Study" (1856) and "Ode on a Lycian Tomb" (1899).

FRANK R. [or **FRANCIS RICHARD**] **STOCKTON,** 1834—1902, novelist, short story writer. CHIEF BOOKS: *Rudder Grange* (1879), humorous novel followed by such sequels as *The Rudder Grangers Abroad* (1891), *Pomona's Travels* (1894), and *John Gayther's Garden* (1902), contains an entertaining portrayal of a phase of American life, written in a droll vein. *The Lady or the Tiger and Other Stories* (1884), its title piece becoming sensationally popular; its continuation, "The Discourager of Hesitancy," is less well known. *The Casting Away of Mrs. Lecks and Mrs. Aleshine* (1886), an almost thrilling fantasy or novelette, simple in plot; its sequel is *The Dusantes* (1888). Other writings are: *The Late Mrs. Null* (1886), an ingeniously-plotted, amusing novel; *The Great War Syndicate* (1889), an excellent tale; *Ardis Claverden* (1890), a pretentious work; *The Adventures of Captain Horn* (1895), where two rememberable characters are Mrs. Horn and Mrs. Cliff; *Mrs. Cliff's Yacht* (1896), which is soon hot upon the trailless sea in pursuit of pirates; *The Great Stone of Sardis* (1898), a droll novelette of the dominating Mrs. Black; *Personally Conducted* (1889), a formal travel book; *Kate Bonnet* (1902), a strongly-told, satirical romance of a pirate's daughter, now related in a restrained, now in a swashbuckling manner. CHILDREN'S BOOKS: *Ting-a-ling* (1870), *Roundabout Rambles in Lands of Fact and Fancy* (1872), *Tales Out of School* (1875), *A Jolly Fellowship* (1880), *The Story of Viteau* (1884). SHORT-STORY COLLECTIONS: *The Floating Prince and Other Tales* (1881), *A Christmas Wreck* (1886), *The Bee-Man of Orn and Other Fanciful Tales* (1887), *The Queen's Museum* (1887), *Amos Killbright: His Adscititious Experiences, with Other Stories* (1888), *The Clocks of Rondaine* (1892), *The Watchmaker's Wife* (1893), *Fanciful Tales* (1894), *A Chosen Few* (1895), *A Story-Teller's Pack* (1897), *Afield and Afloat* (1900), *The Magic Egg* (1907). INDIVIDUAL SHORT STORIES: "Our Story," "The Queen's Museum," "The Griffin and the Minor Canon," "The Transferred Ghost," "The Philopena," "Amos Killbright," "Lost Dryad," "The Spectral Mortgage," "The Remarkable Wreck of the Thomas Hyke."

ALBION WINEGAR TOURGÉE, 1838—1905, Ohio-born writer, utilized his experiences as a Union officer, carpetbagger, editor, jurist, and diplomat to attack race prejudice, champion Negro rights, and propagandize political beliefs about post-war Reconstruction through realistically-depicted if tractlike novels; and was variously followed in treatment of the era by C. F. Woolson (p. 179), T. N. Page (180), G. W. Cable (p. 175), J. C. Harris (p. 172), G. E. King (p. 181), and Ellen Glasgow (p. 270). *'Toinette* (1874), republished as *A Royal Gentleman* (1881), a study of the love of a Southern attorney for his octoroon slave; covers the period 1858—1867; makes the point that the Southerner regards 'Toinette as chattel. *Figs and Thistles* (1879), semi-autobiographical, and possibly a disguised account of J. A. Garfield. *A Fool's Errand*† (1879), semi-autobiographic novel recording his doctrinal beliefs about the post-war South and his growing disillusionment with the methods of Reconstruction. *Bricks without Straw* (1880), another story of reconstruction: marriage to Mollie Ainslie, a New England schoolteacher, converts Hesden Le Mayne, a Southerner, to a Yankee point of view about social and economic betterment of Negroes. *John Eax and Mamelon* (1882), local-color novelettes of the reconstruction era in the South. *Pactolus Prime* (1890), less persuasive than *'Toinette* as a study of the relationship between the Negro and the White. *An Appeal to Caesar* (1884), a political tract written to influence Republican policies as respects an educational system in the South. *The Continent* (1882—1884), a weekly literary magazine which showed his dislike of the Ku Klux Klan, as did his *Eighty-nine* (1888), "a prognostication of the year to come."

EDWARD NOYES WESTCOTT, 1846—1898, successful Syracuse banker. *David Harum, A Story of American Life* (1898), a posthumously published novel described by blurbs of the day as having a slight but clearly defined plot, as being a gold mine of pregnant philosophy, as presenting a character realistically wrought out, and as winning affection by its humanity. *The Teller* (1901) includes a short story, his letters, and an account of his life.

RICHARD HARDING DAVIS, 1864—1916, journalist, playwright, romancer. Most famous are *Gallegher and Other Stories* (1891), *Van Bibber and Others* (1892), and *Ranson's Folly* (1902). Among his two dozen plays are *The Orator of Zephata City* (1899), *The Dictator* (1904; 1906), *"Miss Civilization"* (1905; 1906), *The Galloper* (1909), and *The Zone Police* (1914). Books of travel and correspondence include *The West from a Car-Window* (1892), *About Paris* (1895), *Three Gringos in Venezuela and Central America* (1896), *Cuba in War Time* (1897), *With Both Armies in South Africa* (1900), *With the French in France and Salonika* (1916). *Soldiers of Fortune* (1897) and *The Bar Sinister* (1903) are representative novels.

FRANCES [ELIZA] HODGSON BURNETT, 1849—1924, Anglo-American novelist. *That Lass o' Lowrie's*† (1877), a novel of the coal mines in the "Pit" district of Yorkshire, and *Little Lord Fauntleroy* (1886), popular among children, are her most famous. *Esmeralda* (1881), a novel dramatized by William Gillette; *Sara Crewe, or What Happened at Miss Minchin's* (1888), a dramatization of an early book; *Editha's Burglar* (1888), Augustus Thomas' dramatization of her story; *A Lady of Quality* (1896), later dramatized; *The Making of a Marchioness* (1901), a small book; *The Shuttle* (1907), the basis of which is an international marriage, was finished after much difficulty; *A Fair Barbarian* (1881), which puts a Western girl into an English town; *The Secret Garden* (1911), often regarded as a Christian Science book as is *The Dawn of a To-morrow; White People* (1917), which she herself described as "a strange story perhaps, but it says things which will perhaps make love seem near, even when, to mortal sense, it is far away."

HAROLD FREDERIC, 1856—1898, whose general theme and general group of characters are repeated in every novel except such romantic works about English life as *March Hares* (1896), *Gloria Mundi* (1898), *The Market Place* (1898), and, primarily, *The Damnation of Theron Ware*† (1896), an unevenly-written novel understanding in its delineation of an unsophisticated Methodist preacher and critical of an Evangelical sect. Semi-autobiographical is the superficially realistic *Seth's Brother's Wife* (1887); anticipatory of *The Damnation of Theron Ware* is *The Lawton Girl* (1887); sympathetic with Abolitionism is *The Copperhead* (1894); historical are *In the Valley* (1890), which is concerned with the Revolutionary War, and *Marsena and Other Stories of the Wartime* (1895), concerned with the Civil

War. Among his outdated writings are *The Young Emperor: William II of Germany* (1891), *The New Exodus* (1892), *Mrs. Grundy* (1896), and *The Return of the O'Mahoney* (1898).

HENRY BLAKE FULLER, 1857—1929, who with mild irony and gentle humor wrote novels of Italy and of his native Chicago. POETRY: *The New Flag* (1899), vulgar diatribes against such public figures as McKinley, Theodore Roosevelt, and Lodge; *Lines Long and Short* (1917), brief biographies in free verse. DRAMA: *The Puppet-Booth* (1896), a series of short, deft, aphoristic, pictorial, symbolic, and dramatic sketches, is a return to his earlier romantic mood of 1891 and 1892; *The Fan* (1925) and *The Coffee House* (1925), both translated from Goldoni. SHORT STORIES: *From the Other Side* (1898), four tales with a transatlantic setting; *The Last Refuge* (1900), a whimsical fable of the City of Happiness, is a return to his idealistic manner; *Under the Skylights* (1901), three satires upon the cultural pretensions of his native city, including in "The Downfall of Abner Joyce" a picture of Hamlin Garland; *Waldo Trench and Others* (1908), like the 1898 volume, concerned with Europeans and Americans travelling abroad, chiefly in Italy. NOVELS: *The Chevalier of Pensieri-Vani* (1890), a masterpiece of episodes quaint of incident, delicate of structure, and high in irony, was followed by *The Châtelaine of La Trinité* (1892), akin in form and structure, similarly flavored by a romantic mood and an ageless satire: both, it is said, influenced Thornton Wilder's *The Cabala* (1926). *The Cliff-Dwellers* (1893), a realistic novel of bourgeois strivings and high society. *With the Procession* (1895), another indictment of social and economic Chicago life. *On the Stairs* (1918), a sardonic picture of a self-made American drawn to exemplify Fuller's made-to-order theory of novel-compounding. *Bertram Cope's Year* (1919), a delicate and an unprogressive handling of a perilous theme, a one-year association of a University of Chicago instructor and a hermaphroditic young man. *Gardens of This World* (1929), a poised, romantic continuation of his earlier novels. *Not on the Screen* (1930), an acid satire of the self-made Embert Howell and of the hackneyed formulas of motion pictures.

CHARLES MONROE SHELDON, 1857—1946, pastor, editor, novelist. Of his three-dozen books, it is *In His Steps* (serial, 1896—1897; book form, 1897), which has been published in a score of languages and which sold over twenty-two million copies (many of these are said to have been distributed free by religious organizations). It is the story of a modern minister who acts out the thesis, "What Would Jesus Do?" Only the Bible and Shakespeare have had a wider distribution.

PAUL LEICESTER FORD, 1865—1902, novelist, historian, bibliographer. HISTORY: *The Writings of Thomas Jefferson* (ten volumes, 1892—1894); *The True George Washington* (1896). BIBLIOGRAPHY: *Websteriana* (1882); *Some Materials for a Bibliography of the Official Publications of the Continental Congress* (1888). NOVELS: *The Honorable Peter Stirling* (1894), generally recognized as a portrait of Grover Cleveland; *The Story of an Untold Love* (1897), unsatisfactory in its characterization of women; *Janice Meredith* (1899), a novel of New Jersey life that reaches into Revolutionary Philadelphia as well as into Virginia and New York, and authentic in its colonial atmosphere, but also sentimental.

DAVID GRAHAM PHILLIPS, 1867—1911, playwright, essayist, reformer, journalist. His twenty-three novels, frequently motivated by sex elements in order to enhance reader-interest, are documentations of the commercial, political, and social relations at the turn of the century, their purposes being an exposure of evils and the indoctrination of "an ideology compounded of democracy, nationalism, and socialism" (J. C. McCloskey).

The Great God Success (1901), which modified Joseph Pulitzer's liking for Phillips, is a bold presentation of the man-woman relationship and of the business frauds of modern Croesuses. *The Golden Fleece* (1903), through its theme of a fortune-hunting earl lashed out at European democracy. *The Master-Rogue* (1903), the autobiography of a great financier. *The Cost* (1904), nucleated by the effect of a secret marriage, deals a bit melodramatically with business chicanery and political intrigue. *The Plum Tree*† (1905), a well-sustained study of a political boss, *The Social Secretary* (1905), deals with romance and snobbery in Washington, just as *The Deluge* (1905) does with those same elements and also with Wall Street manipulation in New York. *Light-Fingered Gentry*† (1907), about insurance scandals. *The Second Generation*† (1907), about the successful Hiram Ranger, whose story focuses the conflict between the evils of wealth and the virtues of toil. *The Fashionable Adventures of Joshua Craig* (1909), whose portrait of Margaret Severance helped cause the murder of Phillips, blends a bit of national corruption with a larger portion of love. *Old Wives for New* (1908), meritorious in its description, characterization, and perhaps in its theme that the loss of a husband's love coincides with the loss of a woman's beauty. *The Hungry Heart*† (1909), a convincingly- and dramatically-told romance, much better done than *White Magic* (1910). *The Husband's Story* (1910), about feminine social ambitions as related by Godfrey Loring. *The Price She Paid* (1912), resembling *Susan Lenox* in its tale of a woman's struggle for independence. *Susan Lenox: Her Fall and Rise*† (1908; 1917), his greatest novel, an epic of slum life, political corruption, and a courtesan's struggle for independence.

Also published: *The Reign of Guilt* (1905), muckraking articles; *The Worth of a Woman* (1908), one-act play about a woman who will not use her pregnancy to force a man into marriage.

[BENJAMIN] FRANK[LIN] NORRIS, 1870—1902, born in Chicago, settled in San Francisco (1884), studied art in London and Paris (1887—1889), attended the University of California (1890—1894), where his writings were regarded as lacking "syntactical perfection," went to Harvard (1894—1895), acted as a reporter in South Africa (1895—1896), remained for two years a staff member of the *Wave*, a genuine force in San Francisco journalism, was a correspondent during the Spanish-American War, and became connected with Doubleday, Page, and Company, which he persuaded to publish Dreiser's *Sister Carrie* (p. 269). His many limitations as a technical novelist and as a social philosopher unable to conceal his merits: he is sincere, vigorous, daring; he is a hater of special privilege; tersely, beneath his self-conscious, credible, novelistic world of realism is a heart of romanticism. NOVELS: *Moran of the Lady Letty* (1898), a Stevensonian-Kiplingesque sea romance of adventure off the coast of California, its splashiness of writing and recklessness of plausibility amply redeemed by a stress on detail and a moderate power of movement illustrative of the Norris to come. *McTeague*† (1899), the first publication of which was criticized for the accident that happens to Owgooste, an event deleted from subsequent editions, is astonishingly authentic in its study of an animalistic San Francisco dentist, of human greed and environmental sordidness, although C. H. Grattan rates its ending as incongruous and melodramtic. *Blix* (1900), a partly autobiographic story of his wooing of Jeannette Black, whom he married, pictures clearly and buoyantly the San Francisco of the late nineties as well as his own experiences. *A Man's Woman* (1900), popular, highly-keyed novel of Arctic exploration obviously influenced by Zola: often quoted is the author's own description of it as "a kind of theatrical sort with a lot of niggling analysis to try to justify the violent action of the first few chapters." *The Octopus*† (1901), the first of his "Epic of the Wheat" trilogy (followed by *The Pit,* where the product was marketed, and *The Wolf,* where the wheat was eaten — the latter of which was never written), is, despite some disjointedness and a melodramatic anticlimax, a well-organized, multiple drama, the principal action being the struggle between the wheat growers and the Southern Pacific Railroad for the fertile San Joaquin Valley: frank in its sexual imagery, its massive allegory is concerned with the economic forces operative in a segment of American life. *The Pit* (1903), decidedly thinner in its theme and even in its realism than *The Octopus,* is a romance of the business struggle in the Chicago grain market. *The Wolf,* left unwritten, was to present a European famine relieved by the importation and consumption of American wheat: the preceding two volumes had dealt respectively with the production and the distribution. *Vandover and the Brute*† (1894—1895; posthumously, 1914), novel with a San Francisco background, noted by P. H. Bixler as possessing a starkly realistic yet essentially juvenile theme, is a Zolaistic portrayal of degeneration, even if not too progressively motivated: the dominant theme, states W. F. Taylor, is "the outbreak of destructive passion even within the pale of civilized society" (*cf.* with Norris' *Lauth,* a two-part tale of the brute instinct to kill that bursts out of the supposedly civilized student Lauth).

MISCELLANEOUS: *Yvernelle* (1891), a jingling narrative poem in three cantos, written while at the University of California, as were such other adventures in verse as "Brunhilde" (1890) and "Crepusculum" (1892); *A Deal in Wheat, and Other Stories of the New and Old World* (1903), collected from *Everybody's, Century, Collier's Weekly,* New York *Herald,* and elsewhere; *The Responsibilities of the Novelist* (1903), a statement of his artistic credo, and other literary essays: *e.g.*, "The Novel with a 'Purpose' " discusses methods and principles he followed in writing *The Octopus:* to Norris, the noblest form of the novel is the sociological type; *The Joyous Miracle* (1906), a novelette; *The Third Circle* (1909), stories collected from the *Wave, Argonaut, Smart Set,* and other publications; *Frank Norris of The Wave* (1931), short fiction.

JACK [or **JOHN GRIFFITH**] **LONDON,** 1876—1916, sociological essayist, short-story writer, novelist.

From 1900 on Jack London wrote three plays, entitled *Scorn of Woman* (1906), *Theft* (1910), and *The Acorn Planter* (1916); several general books, such as *Revolution* (1910), a baker's dozen of sociological and other essays, and *The Cruise of the Snark,* sixteen articles on the South Sea; and about forty novels and short-story collections. Often lacking are evenness and quality of writing; usually his novels are a string of short stories that tie up a single tale.

NOVELS: *A Daughter of the Snows* (1902), an episodic novel revealing his inability to picture "any woman above the working class" and "his conception of the supremacy of the Anglo-Saxon race." *The Call of the Wild*† (1903), capital episodic tale of the dog Buck affirms London's belief in adaptation as the only means of survival and his emphasis on atavism. This novel, influenced by E. R. Young's *My Dogs in the Northland,* has freshness of romance and realism of atmosphere. *The Sea-Wolf* (1904), successful in its opening chapters but weak toward the end of the book, perhaps even marred by the introduction of Maude Brewster, this novel makes an attack on the Nietzschean superman idea by telling of the literary-minded Humphrey Van Weyden who falls into the power of a sea-captain, Wolf Larsen, the incarnation of Nietzsche's primitive, ruthless blond beast. *The Game* (1905), a well-conceived, tragically-ending picture of the trade of prizefighting, influenced Gene Tunney temporarily to abandon his career. Compare *The Game* with *The Abysmal Brute* (1913), another brief prize-fight novel. *Before Adam* (1906), influenced considerably by Stanley Waterloo's *The Story of Ab,* is a dramatization of evolution and the life of prehistoric people. *White Fang* (1906), a dog-book tract that may belong with the "nature-faking" against which Theodore Roosevelt campaigned. *The Iron Heel*† (1908), the only American book listed by Bukharin in his full bibliography on communism, is a remarkable prophecy of a fascist revolution in 1932 and reaffirms his faith in an ultimate equalitarian golden age. *Martin Eden*† (1909), semi-autobiographical novel popularly, perhaps mistakenly, regarded as an indictment of individualism, of the Nietzschean superman idea. *Burning Daylight* (1910), an idealistic success story episodically brilliant; socialistic ideas in the latter half of book are propaganda, but made an integral part of the novel. *Smoke Bellew* (1912), Christopher Bellew's adventures in the Klondike. *John Barleycorn*† (1913), simple, moving autobiographical novel is a tract against alcoholic drink. *The Valley of the Moon*† (1913), a propagandizing novel, parts of which are excellent; it contains, in the opinion of Irving Stone, the greatest thinking and writing of Jack London. *The Star Rover*† (1915), an underrated novel. *Jerry of the Islands* (posthumous, 1917), a pleasant story of an Irish setter pup's adventures in the New Hebrides.

SHORT-STORY COLLECTIONS: *The Son of the Wolf*† (1900), eight of its nine stories having appeared in the *Overland Monthly; The God of His Fathers*† (1901), eleven Klondike stories, better than the earlier volume; *Children of the Forest*† (1902), a series of ten Alaskan-Indian tales; *Tales of the Fish Patrol* (1905), adventure stories abundant in action and incident; *Love of Life and Other Stories* (1907), among which are some of his best Alaskan tales; *The Strength of the Strong* (1914), which includes "South of the Slot," a convincing proletarian story which had appeared five years earlier in the *Saturday Evening Post;* and *On the Makaloa Mat* (posthumous, 1919), seven tales.

OTHER WORKS: *The Kempton-Wace Letters* (1903), a series of philosophical letters on love from Herbert Wace (Jack London) to Dane Kempton (Anna Strunsky, a seventeen-year-old Russian Jewess). She is the proponent of the romantic, and he of the realistic, love attitudes. *The War of the Classes* (1905), a collection of socialistic essays influenced, as in *People of the Abyss,* by his experiences as a vagabond. *The Road* (1907), a narrative of his hobo experiences, usable as a source book on tramp life. *The People of the Abyss* (1913), Jack London's own favorite, is a fresh, vigorous, and sincere work about the underprivileged East-enders of London.

Chapter XII

CONVENTION AND REVOLT IN POETRY

EMILY [ELIZABETH] DICKINSON, 1830—1886, poet.[1] Daughter of Edward Dickinson, a prominent lawyer of Amherst, Massachusetts, and for twoscore years treasurer of Amherst College. Educated at Amherst Academy. Beginning of friendship with Susan Gilbert (1846), the "Sister Sue" who in 1856 married her brother Austin and to whom went much of her poetry and prose. Went to South Hadley Female Seminary, now Mount Holyoke College (1847—1848), where she rebelled against the observance of Christmas as a fast day.[2] While at Washington, D. C., with her father, who had become a member of Congress, she is said to have experienced a brief and shadowy love affair with a married Philadelphian minister (1854).[3] Her circle of friends included B. F. Newton, a law student in her father's office; the Reverend Charles Wadsworth of Philadelphia, whom she met in 1854; Thomas Wentworth Higginson, who visited her at Amherst in 1870 after exchanges of letters covering eight years; Dr. J. G. Holland, at that time one of the most successful men of letters in the United States; and Helen Hunt Jackson, who is said to have modeled the heroine of *Mercy Philbrick's Choice* (1876) upon the character of Emily, as did Susan Glaspell in her 1931 Pulitzer Prize play, *Alison's House* (p. 279). Emily seldom left her home after she was twenty-six years old, and, following her father's death (1874), became the town's recluse.[4] Died of

---

1 T. W. Higginson, "Emily Dickinson's Letters," *Atl.*, LXVIII (1891), pp. 444-456; *Letters of Emily Dickinson*, edited by M. L. Todd (two volumes, 1894; new and enlarged one-volume edition, 1931); *The Life and Letters of Emily Dickinson*, edited by M. D. Bianchi (1924). Mrs. Bianchi does not acknowledge that the source for her text is Mrs. Todd's 1894 edition: see M. U. Schappes, "Errors in Mrs. Bianchi's Edition of Emily Dickinson's Letters," *AL.*, IV (1932-1933), pp. 369-384.
Genevieve Taggard, *The Life and Mind of Emily Dickinson* (1930); M. D. Bianchi, *Emily Dickinson Face to Face* (1932); G. F. Whicher, *This Was a Poet* (1938); M. T. Bingham, *Ancestors' Brocades* (1945).

2 S. R. McLean, "Emily Dickinson at Mount Holyoke," *NEQ.*, VII (1934), pp. 25-42.

3 Many have endeavored to pry under this experience in the hope of a clue to Emily's renunciation of "the world, the flesh, and publication"; but perhaps no investigator has succeeded in identifying the man who may have inspired her love poems, who may have played a decisive part in shaping her life after she was twenty-four years old. Among those suggested as her lover are George Gould, Charles Wadsworth, B. F. Newton, and E. B. Hunt. Perhaps identification is impossible because there was none. F. J. Pohl, "The Emily Dickinson Controversy," *SR.*, XLI (1933), pp. 467-482; G. F. Whicher, *This Was a Poet* (1938), p. viii, p. 320.

4 Emily may not have been the recluse pictured by most critics; for years she was "in surprisingly close relation with the plain people of her time," and she may have "had her feet more firmly set in bourgeois soil than we have lately been led to believe." Consult MacGregor Jenkins, *Emily Dickinson, Friend and Neighbor* (1930); Margaret Bloom, "Emily Dickinson and Dr. Holland," *UCC.*, XXXV (1932-1933), pp. 96-103; Van Wyck Brooks, *New England: Indian Summer, 1865-1915* (1940), pp. 316-329.

Bright's disease.

Except for an early verse valentine, only two of her poems, neither of which was offered by her for publication, were printed during her lifetime.[5] Her request that all her manuscripts and correspondence be destroyed was not followed. Some posthumous volumes including about 925 poems are: *Poems*† (1890), *Poems: Second Series*† (1891), *Poems: Third Series*† (1896),[6] *The Single Hound* (1914), *Further Poems* (1929), *Poems: Centenary Edition* (1930), *Unpublished Poems* (1936) and *Bolts of Melody*† (1945).

Her editors usually classify her poems under the headings "Life," "Nature," "Love," "Time and Eternity," "The Single Hound," and "Further Poems."[7]

LETTERS

While, on the whole, her poems are more revealing than her letters, yet the latter possess a significant complementing intimacy: the poems reveal her mind and soul, whereas the letters record her external life, including her capacity for friendship. Infrequent reference to natural loveliness. Compacted idiom sometimes obscure; sense of humor keen. Mystic in faith, yet skeptical of religious formulas.[8]

INDIVIDUAL POEMS

"A bird came down the walk"; "After great pain a formal feeling"; "Because I could not stop for death"; "Elysium is as far as to"; "The heart asks pleasure first"; "I died for beauty, but was scarce"; "I heard a fly buzz when I died"; "I never saw a moor"; "I like to see it lap the miles"; "I had no time to hate"; "I dreaded that first robin so"; "I'll tell you how the sun rose"; "I taste a liquor never brewed"; "If you were coming in the fall"; "My life closed twice before its close"; "The soul selects her own society"; "This quiet Dust was Gentlemen and Ladies"; "Alter? When the hills do"; "Bring me the sunset in a cup"; "Hope is a subtle glutton"; "Much madness is divinest sense"; "I started early, took my dog"; "There is no frigate like a book."

---

5 The "Valentine Extravaganza" was printed in the *Springfield Republican* of February 26, 1852, as was "A narrow fellow in the grass," entitled "The Snake," on February 14, 1866. "Success," the third poem, was published by Helen Hunt Jackson in *A Masque of Poets* (1878).

6 Contrary to the popular impression, her poems were the subject of discussion when published; not until 1900 and for the following fifteen years did she fall into obscurity. See A. M. Wells, "Early Criticism of Emily Dickinson," *AL.*, I (1929-1930), pp. 243-259; A. L. Hampson, "Foreword" in M. D. Bianchi's *Emily Dickinson Face to Face* (1932), pp. ix-xx.

7 This arrangement by the editors of her poems has little if any significance in relation to Emily's mind. Not only were many of the titles supplied by the editors, but, for example, M. L. Todd also had to choose from a list of alternative words which Emily often left with her manuscript. There have been demands for better editing; and there has been a need for determining the sequence of her poems, for that would illuminate our knowledge of Emily's growth as a poet. For a listing of about one-fifth of the poems that have been printed, with their possible chronological date, see G. F. Whicher, "A Chronological Grouping of Some of Emily Dickinson's Poems," *Colophon,* Part Sixteen, No. 2 (1934), ninth and following pages (unnumbered).

8 Paul Kurth, "Emily Dickinson in Her Letters," *Thought,* IV (1929), pp. 430-439.

SUGGESTED MERITS	SUGGESTED DEFECTS
1. Eccentric vision enriched by a variety of imagery and an exotic quality of imagination.[9]	1. Lack of a consistent alertness to science and humanitarianism, to worldly struggles and social quests.[10]
2. Gnomic compactness of expression compels mental vigilance, while spontaneity of words animates connotative meanings. Concerned more with thought and mood than with technique.[11]	2. Excessive concision results in cryptic, symbolic epigrammatism, puzzling by its incoherent versicles, baffling in its verbal and metaphysical obscurantism, and lacking in both finished expression and subtlety.
3. Faithful, introspective intimacy with her mental experiences is illuminated by flashes of, so to speak, dissimilar resemblances and unexpected conclusions. Studied carelessness and deceptive monotony unfold an originality of insight and a subtlety of mood. Prodigal of the metaphor, her characteristic figure.	3. Although some nature poems are of deft delicacy and distinctive insight, most are superficial, and limited to the nature of a New England garden. As Yvor Winters phrases it, beautiful lines and passages are wasted in the desert of crudities. Her music is staccato and singsong;[12] her conceits are exaggerated.
4. Hopeless rhymes, slipshod lapses, anacoluthic meters, and abandonment even of assonance[13]	4. Truncated lines, sterile rhymes, and dislocated syntax are not to be accounted for as the deliberately

9 Conrad Aiken has declared her poetry "perhaps the finest by a woman in the English language," and Martin Armstrong has quarreled only with the "perhaps"; Ludwig Lewisohn has rated her among the few great woman poets of all literature. She has been labeled "a New England Nun," "a modern Sappho," and "the flower of American Transcendentalism." To Harry Hansen, Emily is the greatest woman poet of America; and to Yvor Winters she may be "one of the greatest lyric poets of all time."

In 1915 F. L. Pattee said of Emily: "Her poems are disappointing. Critics have echoed Higginson, until Emily Dickinson has figured, often at length, in all the later histories and anthologies, but it is becoming clear that she was overrated. To compare her eccentric fragments with Blake's elfin wildness is ridiculous. They are mere conceits, vague jottings of a brooding mind; they are crudely wrought, and, like their author's letters, which were given to the public later, they are colorless and for the most part lifeless. They reveal little either of Emily Dickinson or of human life generally. They should have been allowed to perish as their author intended."

Yet a few years later F. L. Pattee revised his opinion: Emily's poems, he stated, "are startlingly, even crudely, original. . . . Some of them remind one of the work of Blake. They are the record of the inner life of an abnormally sensitive soul, — fragments, lyrical ejaculations, childish conceits, little orphic sayings often illogical and meaningless, lines and couplets at times that are like glimpses of another world, spasmodic cries, always brief, always bearing upon the deepest things that life knows, — love, death, nature, time, eternity."

The prevailing criticism seems weighted in the direction of A. L. Hampson's appraisal: "The translation of quite ordinary everyday experiences into moments of startling beauty, the lightning and humorous acceptance of everything from bees and birds, and flowers, to death, to loneliness and to light, all streaming through her mind into the scheme of the world, give one a fresh sense of life. The unerring aim of her words pins her quick understanding quivering to the page. Her words and concerns may range from a Whim, capitalized, to a profound realization of the meaning and effect of experience common to us all."

The foregoing statements are quoted from F. L. Pattee, *A History of American Literature since 1870* (1915), p. 340 *f.*, F. L. Pattee, *Century Readings for a Course in American Literature* (1926), p. 700; A. L. Hampson, *Emily Dickinson: A Bibliography* (1930), p. 6. See also D. G. Van Der Vat, "Emily Dickinson (1830-1886)," *ES.*, XXI (1939), pp. 241-260.

10 Edward Sapir, "Emily Dickinson, a Primitive," *Poetry*, XXVI (1925) pp. 97-105.

11 G. W. Allen, *American Prosody* (1935), pp. 307-320.

12 A number of her poems have been set to music.

13 Taking issue with M. D. Bianchi's declaration that Emily, when she chose, abandoned "even assonance, writing in metre alone, like a Greek," R. P. Blackmur avers that it is better to say that Emily wrote like an Italian "with recurring pairs of stressed syllables."

are deliberate, have a definite charm, and possess beauties within the comprehension of the poetic soul.[14] Only about one in twelve poems is written in irregular meter. Excellent utilization of the subjunctive mood.[15]

5. Notable are the Emersonian concept of compensation,[17] the Puritan asceticism, and the Puritan theme of renunciation. Her poetry is predominantly mystical and psychological, rather than irreligious. Humanitarianism subordinated to individual responsibility, physical love to divine.[18]

6. Sense of action obtained by activized verbs and masculinized phrases, yet without detriment to the delicate grace and womanliness of her mind and nature.[19] A precursor of the Imagist school.[20]

chosen devices of a master craftsman.[16] Narrow range apparent in her preferred employment of octosyllabic quatrains or couplets, of the iambic or trochaic meter, of the four-stress line. Overuses the subjunctive mood.

5. Religious emancipation and spiritual freedom have a place; but one bred in the Calvinist tradition can not condone the irreverence manifested by her questionings of the theological traditions of Puritanism.

6. If meriting praise for exactitude of observation, quickness of intellect, and slyness of humor, then also requiring depreciation for clumsiness of style, poverty of language, and slipshodness of technique. Not consciously a progenitor of free verse.

SIDNEY LANIER, 1842—1881, musician, critic, poet.[21] Born in Macon, Georgia. Entered Oglethorpe College (1856) at Midway, Georgia, the college now located near Atlanta. After graduation (1860), was appointed a tutor (1860—1861). Enlisted in the Confederate Army with the Macon Volunteers (1861). Was captured while signal officer on the blockade-runner *Annie,*

---

14 Her utterances, declares T. W. Higginson, have "an uneven vigor sometimes exasperating, seemingly wayward, but really unsought and inevitable." At her perversities and lapses and tyrannies Conrad Aiken first sighs — and then realizes their positive charm. Somehow, say critics, such irregularities as the carelessness of meter and anacoluthon are too excellent to be ascribed to spontaneous self-expression. Most explicit is the claim that, with the exception of the nonsense verse written for her brother's children, all instances of irregular rhymes have artistic significance: Susan Miles, "The Irregularities of Emily Dickinson," *LM.*, XIII (1925-1926), pp. 145-158.

15 G. B. Sherrer, "A Study of Unusual Verb Constructions in the Poems of Emily Dickinson," *AL.*, VII (1935-1936), pp. 37-46.

16 Yvor Winters, *Maule's Curse* (1938), pp. 149-165.

17 F. O. Matthies[s]en, " 'Midsummer in the Mind,' " *SRL.*, XIII, No. 12 (January 18, 1936), p. 12.

18 *The Life and Letters of Emily Dickinson*, edited by M. D. Bianchi (1924), pp. 88-105; Katherine Brégy, "Emily Dickinson: A New England Anchoress," *CW.*, CXX (1924-1925), pp. 344-354; C. K. Trueblood, "Emily Dickinson," *Dial*, LXXX (1926), pp. 301-311. R. W. Brown, *Lonely Americans* (1929), pp. 235-257; Desmond Powell, "Emily Dickinson," *CCP.*, General Series No. 200, Study Series No. 19 (1934), pp. 1-12; D. G. Van Der Vat, "Emily Dickinson, (1830-1886)," *ES.*, XXI (1939), pp. 241-260; R. P. Blackmur, *The Expense of Greatness* (1940), 106-138.

19 W. H. Finch, "The Poetry of Emily Dickinson," *RL.*, II (1933), p. 199 (pp. 194-202).

20 Amy Lowell, *Poetry and Poets* (1930), pp. 88-108.

21 H. M. Jones in *American Poetry*, edited by P. H. Boynton (1918), pp. 670-675; Gamaliel Bradford, *American Portraits* (1922), pp. 58-83; S. T. Williams in *American Writers on American Literature*, edited by John Macy (1931), pp. 327-341; A. H. Starke, *Sidney Lanier* (1933); Lincoln Lorenz, *The Life of Sidney Lanier* (1935); Richard Webb and E. R. Coulston, *Sidney Lanier* (1941).

and was incarcerated at the Federal prison at Point Lookout, Maryland (1864), from which he was released after four months (1865). Conditions in the Union prison had developed a latent tuberculosis,[22] against which he struggled the rest of his brief life shackled by poverty and discouragement; most of his life he described as having been "merely not dying." Married Mary Day, of Macon (1867), to whom were born four sons: Charles Day, 1865; Sidney, 1870; Henry Wysham, 1874; and Robert, 1880. Taught in a country academy at Prattville, Alabama (1867—1868). Severe hemorrhage (1868) forced his return to Macon, where he practised law in his father's office (1869—1872). Another breakdown sent him off to recuperate at Austin, Texas (1872),[23] at which town he was recognized as an artistic flutist. Returned to Macon (1873). Flutist in Peabody Symphony Orchestra at Baltimore (1873). Played at New York for Dr. Leopold Damrosch (1874). Wrote the words for a cantata to be sung at the Centennial Exhibition (1876). Published *Sketches of India* (1876), *Florida* (1876), and, most important, *Poems* (1877). Lectured at Peabody Institute (1878). Published *The Boy's Froissart* (1878). Appointed by President Gilman as Lecturer in English at the Johns Hopkins University (1879).[24] Published *The Boy's King Arthur* (1881), *The Boy's Mabinogion* (1881), and *The Boy's Percy* (1882). Died of consumption at Lynn, North Carolina. Buried in Greenmount Cemetery, Baltimore, Maryland. Over his grave is a Georgian boulder upon which is a bronze tablet bearing a line-inscription from "Sunrise":

I-AM-LIT-BY-THE-SUN

POETRY

(1) "Nirvana" (1868; 1868), an early poem epithalamic in intent and personal in its approach toward sectional and national problems. (2) "Acknowledgment" (1874—1875; 1876), four Shakespearean sonnets, of which the best is III: "If I do ask, How God can dumbness keep." (3) "The Mocking Bird," a sonnet on the mystery in the workings of nature: one of several poems declared by H. A. Beers to be "the most characteristically Southern poetry . . . written in America."[25] (4) "Song of the Chattahoochee" (*c.* 1877; 1883), popular work, quiet in simplicity, competent in rhythmic schemes, mainly in iambics, and Tennysonian in music and color: often criticized are the unpoetic lines (ll. 44 *ff.*) linking Duty with forces of gravity. (5) "Night and Day" (1866; 1884),

22 To the question, "Where would you like to live?" Lanier answered: "Somewhere where lungs are not necessary to Life." J. S. Short, "Sidney Lanier, 'Familiar Citizen of the Town,'" *MHM.*, XXXV (1940), p. 135, Question 23 (pp. 121-146).

23 J. S. Mayfield, *Sidney Lanier in Texas* (1932).

24 J. S. Short, "Sidney Lanier at Johns Hopkins," *JHAM.*, V (1916-1917), pp. 7-24.

25 H. A. Beers, *A Short History of American Literature* (1906), p. 212.

an early jingling poem inspired by Shakespeare and as favorably reminiscent of him as is "The Marsh-Song — At Sunset."

A second group may be made of his religious promptings: (1) "How Love Looked for Hell," a pre-Raphaelite poem wherein Love, guided by Mind and Sense, who have "become psychological knights rather than mere abstractions,"[26] fails in its quest for Hell, for wherever Love went Hell could not be. (2) "The Stirrup-Cup" (1877; 1877), based on Highlander custom, Elizabethan and flawless in its courageous challenge. (3) "The Crystal" (1880; 1880), somewhat tainted by elaborate images and poetical devices, but withal a beautiful, confessional tribute to "Jesus, good Paragon";[27] (4) "A Ballad of Trees and the Master" (1880; 1880), concerned with the hour that Jesus spent in the garden on the Mount of Olives just before his crucifixion: instinct with the simplicity of medieval worship and demonstrating that Lanier can, as in "The Revenge of Hamish," be simple and easy and terse, even if the thought could be clearer.[28] (5) "Remonstrance" (1878—1879; 1883), a denouncement of conventional religious creeds and Church intolerance.

Among his poems that illustrate Lanier's concern with the economic plight of people are: (1) "The Jacquerie" (1868), an unfinished, long work, chiefly in blank verse, not wholly lacking in dignity despite a joyous note by which it is dominated: superb are the lyric, "May the maiden," as beautiful in its way as Lanier's "Evening Song" (1876; 1877), and the song, "The hound was cuffed, the hound was kicked." (2) "The Raven Days" (1868; 1868). a gloomy, fairly graphic picture of the "dark Raven days" of Reconstruction. (3) "Thar's More in the Man Than Thar Is in the Land" (1869-1871), a realistic dialect poem likewise concerned with the plight of the South after the Civil War, but minimizing environmental influences upon success or failure and exaggerating the lift-oneself-by-the-bootstrap view.

"Corn"† (1874; 1875). Long, uneven poem, composed chiefly of pentameter lines, original in conception and execution and American in theme. Latter half (ll. 111-200) is an agrarian attack[29] on the cotton-trade, "on games of Buy-and-Sell," with the farmer waking too late after being victimized by "squandering scamps and quacks."

---

26 Philip Graham, "Lanier and Science," *AL.*, IV (1932-1933), p. 290 (pp. 288-292).

27 "The Crystal" is the greatest Lanier poem because "it combines the most of critical judgment with the clearest confession of his faith in Christ": A. H. Strong, *American Poets and Their Theology* (1916), p. 407 (pp. 371-418).

28 Its triple rhyme precludes a somewhat general conclusion that such rhyme is unsuitable in serious verse: G. R. Stewart, Jr., *The Technique of English Verse* (1930), p. 170.

29 R. P. Warren, "The Blind Poet: Sidney Lanier," *AR.*, II (1933-1934), pp. 27-45; Aubrey Starke, "The Agrarians Deny a Leader," *ibid.*, II (1933-1934), pp. 534-553; J. C. Ransom, "Hearts and Heads," *ibid.*, II (1933-1934), pp. 554-571; J. A. Shackford, "Sidney Lanier as Southerner," *SR.*, XLVIII (1940), pp. 153-173, 348-355, 480-493.

"The Symphony"† (1875; 1875). Arraignment, in complex versification and varied cadences, of Trade and its evils is important as a revelation of his philosophy.[30] Each instrument — violins, flute, clarinet, horn, hautboy — is personified; each participates in the allegory of life, discussing industrialistic claws and the social questions of the day. Oft-quoted is the last line: "Music is Love in search of a word," which may be the symbolic key to the poem's message.

"Psalm of the West"† (1876; 1876). Of a united nation this Centennial Ode sings: it could be less vague, less prolix, and less forced — and more clearly expressed. Both the opening and the prettified parable of the tournament between the heart and the head have been praised; but if any part redeems the whole, it is the series of eight Miltonic sonnets on Columbus. Note its dozen-and-a-half metrical forms.

"The Revenge of Hamish"† (1878; 1878). Objectivity, terseness, and the absence of conceits all heighten this heroic border tale or ballad, successful both in its narrative and its experiment with the lagaoedic dactylic meter. Plot possibly derived from an episode in William Black's novel, *Macleod of Dare* (Chapter III) and Charles Mackaye's *Maclaine's Child.*

"Hymns of the Marshes."† Only four of six projected hymns were completed: "Sunrise" (1880; 1882), "Individuality" (1878—1879; 1882), "Marsh-Song — At Sunset" (1878—1880; 1882), and "The Marshes of Glynn" (1878; 1879). Some long, sweeping, suspended, noble movements vitiated by melodic conceits, an occasionally obtrusive background, and "the *reductio ad absurdum*" of the tendency to "nympholeptic longing."[31] However, the full day's record of a moving spiritual experience, simple and mature and profound, of a vision of the greatness of God, is socialized by an opulent rhythmic background and by sensitized religious sympathies, by a tandem of moods symphonizing with the rising and setting sun flooding the marshes and inextricably connected to the everyday struggles. As analyzed by G. W. Allen, "The Marshes of Glynn" is in anapestic measure, employing initial truncation and the shifting both of accents and of the number of syllables in the line from one to seventeen.

PROSE WORKS

In addition to the popular editions of such old favorites as Froissart, King Arthur, Percy, and the Mabinogion (see preceding material), Lanier also published *Tiger-Lilies, a Novel* (1867), an

30 G. B. Oxnam, "Sidney Lanier: A Prophet of the Social Awakening," *MR.*, XCIX (1917), pp. 86-90.

31 Norman Foerster, *Nature in American Literature* (1923), p. 232 (pp. 221-273).

immature, somewhat luxuriant work about his experiences in the Civil War; *Music and Poetry* (1898); and *Retrospects and Prospects: Descriptive and Historical Essays* (1899).

***The Science of English Verse*†** (1880). Basic conception is that poetry is essentially a form of music, is essentially the rhythm of language: music and verse, theorizes Lanier, are obedient to and governed by identical laws of composition, in rhyme, rhythm, vowel assonance, alliterations, and phrasings. At odds with the fundamental system which bases English verse upon accent or stress-measurement, he conceives of melody as dependent upon time-measurement, conceives of melody as the product of rhythm, tone, and color. His assertion is that syllables of spoken words have definite time-relations grouped by the habituated speaking voice; it is possible to vary meter, to stress alliteration, and to develop onomatopoeia until the poetic mold becomes a synthesis of the forms of poetry interpreted in terms of music.[32]

The English Novel and the Principle of Its Development (1883). Like his posthumous *Shakspere and His Forerunners* (two volumes, 1902), this volume is less an original discussion than an elaboration of recognized facts and older critical opinions. Both volumes "show the same fresh interest in old problems, the same atmosphere of discovery in well-mapped fields."[33]

32 What of the professional reception of Lanier's prosodic theories? J. P. Dabney, *The Musical Basis of Verse* (1901), p. viii, declares Lanier's "the first deliberate attempt to analyse verse upon its true lines; viz., by musical notation." While a bit too difficult for the general reader, and not completely logical within itself, yet "Lanier's supreme glory is that he was a pioneer." According to A. H. Tolman, *The Views about Hamlet and Other Essays* (1904), p. 109 *f.* (pp. 107-113), Lanier is absolutely right in his broad position on the subject of verse-rhythm; and according to T. S. Omond, *English Metrists in the Eighteenth and Nineteenth Centuries* (1907), p. 185 (pp. 177-186), *The Science of English Verse* is valuable for principles rather than conclusions — but George Saintsbury, *A History of English Prosody,* III (1910), p. 493 *f.*, refuses to accept Lanier on any terms, for which he is in turn cudgeled by Harriet Monroe, *Poets & Their Art* (1926), p. 268 *f.* (pp. 268-284), for not taking sides "in 'the battle of Accent versus Quantity.' " Since Lanier's work, she declares, "there is no longer any excuse for persistence in the old error" that English verse is "accentual" while the rhythm of classic verse is "quantitative": "English verse is as quantitative as Greek verse." On the other hand, Henry Lanz, *The Physical Basis of Rime* (1931), p. 178 *f.*, while believing erroneous Lanier's conviction "that English verse has for its basis not accent but strict musical quantity," acknowledges that in *Music and Poetry* (1898) Lanier "was on the right track with regard to the nature of the relation between musical sounds and human words." In like vein, J. C. Andersen, *The Laws of Verse* (1928), p. 179 *f.*, regards as untenable Lanier's prosodic theory, and also as dangerous the insistence on the musical regularity of poetry, the representation of "the rhythm of poetry by musical notation, or indeed by any system of symbols." More recently W. L. Schramm, "Approaches to a Science of English Verse," *UIS.*, No. 46 (1935), p. 5, avers that his monograph points "the way toward the science of verse Lanier could have written if he had lived in a day when the forces of sound had been harnessed and measured." It is important to remember that Lanier neither started any school of poetry nor has had many avowed imitators.

Consult also Edwin Mims, *Sidney Lanier* (1905), pp. 352-359; Bliss Perry, *A Study of Poetry* (1920), p. 171 *f.*; H. C. Thorpe, "Sidney Lanier: A Poet for Musicians," *MuQ.*, XI (1925), pp. 373-382; A. H. Starke, *Sidney Lanier* (1933), p. 333 *ff.*; Aubrey Starke, "Lanier's Appreciation of Whitman," *A.Schol.*, II (1933), p. 406 *f.* (pp. 398-408). For additional references, see footnote 13.

33 F. W. Cady laments that "a thesis so obvious has usurped the attention of a writer upon the novel," for it "does not appear to need the patient elaboration which it receives." What a pity, concurs Gamaliel Bradford, "to see such a splendid intelligence wearing itself out for futile results." F. W. Cady, "Sidney Lanier," *SAQ.*, XIII (1914), p. 158 (pp. 156-173); Gamaliel Bradford, *American Portraits* (1922), p. 70 (pp. 61-83).

SUGGESTED MERITS	SUGGESTED DEFECTS
1. Gift of melody, of rhythms that march and flow and of cadences that linger. Versatility in conventional meters.[35]	1. Both his bookishness[34] and mechanical theory of verse thin out spontaneity of utterance. Because of exquisite music, the message suffers dilution.
2. Voicing the suffering that arises out of the conflict between the old and the new economic-social structures, he indicts the malign inhumanities of modern commercialism.[36]	2. Seeping into the poems are a consumptive sentimentality and a hectic moral goodness that artificializes his diction and feminizes his imagery.
3. Deep, religious nature unobtrusively permeates his writings. High ethics of conception, provocativeness of thought, nobility of spirit.[37]	3. Workmanship does not always conceal his moralizing tendencies.[38] Deficient in originality of thought.
4. Excellent work is rooted in the Georgia soil, and flowers into Southern themes; yet he is distinctly American in subject. Spontaneous evocations of beauty. Between the Civil War and the turn of the century, no Southern poet is more outstanding.	4. Not completely free from the faults of his day, even his best poetry is crippled by hounded conceits, by strained metaphors, by opulent diffuseness, by gaudy preciosity, and by manneristic gestures.

EDWARD ROWLAND SILL, 1841—1887, educator, essayist, poet.[39] Born in Windsor, Connecticut. Orphaned when about twelve years old, yet he was educated at Phillips Exeter Academy and at the Western Reserve College preparatory school. Was graduated from Yale (1861), where he was an editor of the *Yale Literary Magazine*. Spent five years in California, which he had reached by way of Cape Horn, and where he held odd jobs in a post office, on a ranch, and in a bank, and where he read law and studied medicine. Returning East (1866), he soon quit study-

---

34 Philip Graham, "Lanier's Reading," *UTSE.*, No. 11 (University of Texas Bulletin, No. 3133: September 1, 1931).

35 G. W. Allen, *American Prosody* (1935), pp. 277-301 (pp. 277-306).

36 N. B. Fagin, "Sidney Lanier: Poet of the South," *JHAM.*, XX (1931-1932), pp. 231-241; Philip Graham, "Lanier and Science," *AL.*, IV (1932-1933), pp. 288-292.

37 M. S. Kaufman, "Sidney Lanier, Poet Laureate of the South," *MR.*, LXXXII (1900), pp. 94-107; H. N. Snyder, *Sidney Lanier* (1906); E. B. Pollard, "The Spiritual Message of Sidney Lanier," *HR.*, LXXIV (1917), pp. 91-95; T. A. Doyle [Sister], "The Indomitable Courage of Sidney Lanier," *CW.*, CLVI (1942-1943), pp. 293-301.

38 His devotion to the Ruskin theory that morality is the criterion of artistic worth led him to attack writings wholly lacking or deficient in moral purity. To Lanier the ideal is George Eliot, while Richardson and Zola are diseased; yet meriting recall is Lanier's opinion that Whitman's *Leaves of Grass* was worth a million of *Atalanta in Calydon.* (However, Lanier was offended by the subsequent editions.)

39 W. B. Parker, *Edward Rowland Sill* (1915); E. L. Baker, "Edward Rowland Sill," *OM.*, LXXXIII (1925), pp. 154-155, 175-176, Alfred Kreymborg, *Our Singing Strength* (1929), pp. 183-192 (pp. 172-192); Newton Arvin, "The Failure of E. R. Sill," *Bookman, LXXII* (1930-1931), pp. 581-589; *Around the Horn,* by E. R. Sill, edited with an Introduction by S. T. Williams and B. D. Simison (1944). In preparation by S. T. Williams is a collection of E. R. Sill's correspondence: *SRL.*, XXVII (January 8, 1944), p. 13.

ing at the Harvard Divinity School, taking a teaching position in Brooklyn and working as literary critic on the New York *Evening Mail.* Married Elizabeth Newberry Sill, a first cousin. After being principal of the high school and superintendent of the elementary grades at Cuyahoga Falls, Ohio (1868—1871), and after teaching high school English at Oakland, California (1871—1874), he accepted the chair of English literature at the University of California (1874—1883). Resigned on account of ill health (1883). Spent his last years at Cuyahoga Falls, contributing either anonymously to the *Atlantic* and other publications, or under the pseudonym Andrew Hedbrooke. Died unexpectedly after a minor operation in a Cleveland hospital.

Both in scope and style E. R. Sill was a minor poet, yet none of his contemporaries wrote so many beautifully-sustained lyrics. His two most widely quoted are "Opportunity" and "The Fool's Prayer," but these may not be his best. Recurring are the moods of optimism and despair, especially of negation; even his trifling essays on literary and educational topics, though charmingly treated, manifest a congenital discontent. Deficient in power or depth his poetry is, as in creative imagination or passion, but it is musical and impregnated by simplicity and spontaneity, playful humor and Yankee understatement, frank didacticism, classic delicacy, and a questioning skepticism.

WORKS

The Hermitage and Other Poems† (1868), *The Venus of Milo and Other Poems*† (1883), *Poems*† (1887), *Hermione and Other Poems* (1899), *The Prose of Edward Rowland Sill* (1900), *The Poems of Edward Rowland Sill* (1902).

INDIVIDUAL POEMS

"A Memory," "Opportunity," "Roland," "Five Lives," "The Fool's Prayer," "Christmas in California," "Momentous Words," "The Departure of the Pilot," "A Prayer for Peace," "The Agile Sonneteer," "Tranquillity," "Life," "Morning," "A Tropical Morning at Sea," "Tempted," "On Second Thought."

JOHN B[ANNISTER] TABB, 1845—1909, poet-priest.[40] Born in Amelia County, Virginia. A weak optic nerve interfered with a normal childhood, disqualified him for service with the Con-

---

40 M. S. Pine [pseudonym of Sister Mary Pauline Finn], *John Bannister Tabb* (1915); J. B. Jacobi, "The Large Philosophy in the Little Poems of Father Tabb," *ACQ.*, XL (1915), pp. 33-47; J. B. Kelly, "The Poetry of a Priest," *CW.*, CIII (1916), pp. 228-233; Katherine Brégny, "Of Father Tabb," *CW.*, CXIV (1921-1922), pp. 308-318; J. M. Tabb, *Father Tabb* (1921); F. A. Litz, *Father Tabb* (Ph.D., Johns Hopkins, 1924); G. N. Shuster, "Father Tabb and the Romantic Tradition," *Month*, CXLIV (1924), pp. 516-525; *The Poetry of Father Tabb*, edited by F. A. Litz (1928); Aubrey Starke, "Father John Tabb: A Checklist," *ABC.*, VI (1935), pp. 101-104; Gordon Blair, *Father Tabb* (1940).

federate army, and a year before his death caused total blindness. While returning from Bermuda as a Confederate blockade-runner on the *Siren,* he was captured by the Federal ship *Keystone State* and imprisoned for seven months at Point Lookout, Maryland, where he formed a firm friendship with a fellow-prisoner, Sidney Lanier (p. 234),[41] who probably was an influence upon his style and whom he later celebrated in several poems. Went to Baltimore to study music, a lifetime passion. Was received into the Catholic Church (1872). Was graduated from St. Charles' College, Ellicot City, Maryland (1875), which he had entered three years previously in order to study for the priesthood. Taught at the St. Peter's Boys' School, Richmond (1875—1877). Ordained priest in the Baltimore cathedral (1884). Taught Latin, Greek, and English grammar in St. Charles' College (1878—1909). Buried in Hollywood cemetery, Richmond.

Father Tabb is said to be the best American representative echoing the seventeenth-century English metaphysical poets and is recognized as a forerunner of the imagistic school: he is as religious a poet as Richard Crashaw and as sanely devotional as George Herbert, yet also as lucid and varied in theme as Robert Herrick and as vigorously pictorial as Emily Dickinson. Among his negative characteristics are an unbridled tendency to punning, a wilfulness if elfishness of phrasing, and an intricacy of conceits; among his most positive virtues are a delicate, compressed utterance, a superb cameo-chiseling, and a mystical reflectiveness. Apparent spontaneity and metrical skill are the result of careful workmanship. His poetry is primarily religious in feeling; his sympathy is as intuitive as his insight is metaphysical; yet his symbols are often of the simplest and most natural. In the works of Nature, which is most consistently the background of his brief musical lyrics and quatrains, Father Tabb sees the reflection of the Omnipotent Being. He is a minor poet, but a true one.

WORKS

Poems (1882), *An Octavo to Mary* (1893), *Poems* (1894), *Bone Rules; or Skeleton of English Grammar* (1897),[42] *Lyrics* (1897), *Child Verse: Poems Grave and Gay* (1899), *Two Lyrics* (1902), *Later Lyrics* (1902), *The Rosary in Rhyme* (1904), *Later Poems* (1910).

---

41 For a number of mutual letters from J. B. Tabb and Sidney Lanier, see Gordon Blair, *Father Tabb* (1940), pp. 40-54, 55-65.

42 *Bone Rules,* his most important prose work, inaugurated, says Katherine Brégny, a new fashion in textbooks. Among sentences to be corrected were:

"Lay still," his mother often said,
When Washington had went to bed.
But little Georgie would reply:
"I set up, but I can not lie."

Compare with page 192, footnote 17.

REPRESENTATIVE POEMS

(1) RELIGIOUS: "The Recompense" (1891), "Communion" (1892), "Son of Mary" (1892), "Blossom" (1892), "Father Damien" (1892), "Evolution" (1894), "The Incarnation" (1894), "Resurrection" (1894), "A Lenten Thought" (1894), "Out of Bounds" (1894), "Magdalen" (1894), "Faith" (1895), "Inspiration" (1895), "Fiut Lux" (1910). (2) ABOUT HIS BLINDNESS: "A Sunset Song" (1908), "Going Blind" (1908), "Loss" (1909), "The Image-Maker" (1909), "Waves" (1909), "Blind," beginning "Again as in the desert way" (1909). (3) ABOUT LANIER: "Love's Hybla" (1892), "At Lanier's Grave" (1892), "Cloistered" (1893), "To Sidney Lanier" (1894), "My Star" (1894), "In Touch" (1909), "On the Forthcoming Volume of Lanier's Poems." (4) MISCELLANEOUS POEMS: "Killdee" (1886), "Transition" (1887), "To the Wood-Robin" (1889), "The Sunbeam" (1892), "Fern Song" (1894), "Golden-Rod" (1894), "At the Year's End" (1897), "An April Bloom" (1897), "The Rain-Pool" (1902).

[WILLIAM] BLISS CARMAN, 1861—1929, so-called Poet-Laureate of Canada who lived the greater part of his life in the United States.[43] Born in Fredericton, New Brunswick, Canada. Educated at Collegiate Institute, Fredericton (1872—1878), at the University of New Brunswick (1879—1881; A.B., 1884), at Edinburgh (1882—1883), and at Harvard (1886—1888). To New York (*c.* 1889), where he became an office-editor of the *Independent* (1890—1893). Edited the *Chap Book*. Received the Lorne Pierce Medal from the Royal Society of Canada (1929). Summered in the Catskills with the M. L. King family. Died of cerebral hemorrhage at the home of Dr. Thomas Tunney, New Canaan, Connecticut, at whose home he had lived for several years. Buried in Forest Hill Cemetery in his native province of New Brunswick.

CHIEF VOLUMES OF POETRY

(1) *Low Tide on Grand Pré*† (1893), an intensely unified work. (2) *Songs of Vagabondia* (1894), *More Songs from Vagabondia* (1896), and *Last Songs from Vagabondia* (1901), three collections, written jointly with Richard Hovey (see page 244). Reminiscent of Stevenson in their joy and somewhat factitious in their Bohemianism, include joyous love lyrics, jolly verses, irresponsible tavern-songs, and some more serious endeavors, but none of them anemic. (3) *Behind the Arras: A Book of the Unseen* (1895), strong in unity, deep in mysticism: most notable are

---

43 *Later Poems,* with an Appreciation by R. H. Hathaway, (1922), pp. vii-xxii; Odell Shepard, *Bliss Carman* (1923); R. H. Hathaway, "The Poetry of Bliss Carman," *SR.,* XXXIII (1925), pp. 469-483; James Cappon, *Bliss Carman* (1930), Part I, pp. 1-253; C. G. D. Roberts, "Bliss Carman," *DR.,* IX (1929-1930), pp. 409-417; X (1930), pp. 1-9; W. I. Morse, *Bliss Carman* (1941).

"Behind the Gamut," described by James Cappon as "a metaphysic in verse," and "Behind the Arras," especially successful in the earlier part. (4) *From the Green Book of the Bards* (*Pipes of Pan,* No. II, 1903), wherein his personality is as manifest as in *Low Tide on Grand Pré.* (5) *Songs of the Sea-Children* (*Pipes of Pan,* No. III, 1904), a beautiful, impressive book filled with love poems, and with verses as physical and masculine in their abandon as those in *Ballads of Lost Haven* (1897). (6) *From the Book of Valentines* (*Pipes of Pan,* No. V, 1905), includes the excellent piece called "The Great Release." (7) *Sappho: One Hundred Lyrics* (1911) is on the whole a continuation of *Songs of the Sea-Children.* (8) *Daughters of Dawn* (1913) and (9) *Earth Deities* (1914), written in conjunction with Mary Perry King, are effective poem-dances. (10) *Far Horizons* (1925) differs from *April Airs* (1916) and *Wild Garden* (1929) in that its subject is the Canadian West.

MISCELLANEOUS VOLUMES OF POETRY AND PROSE

Among his other works are *St. Kavin* (1894), *A Seamark* (1895), *At Michaelmas* (1895), *The Girl in the Poster* (1897), *By Aurelian War* (1898), *The Vengeance of Noel Brassard* (1899), *Winter Holiday* (1899), *Christmas Eve at St. Kavin's* (1901), *From the Book of Myths* (*Pipes of Pan,* No. I, 1902), *Ode for the Coronation* (1902), *Songs from a Northern Garden* (*Pipes of Pan,* No. IV, 1904), *The Rough Rider and Other Poems* (1909), *The Gate of Peace* (1909), and *Echoes from Vagabondia* (1912).

A certain simplicity and elegance mark the several volumes of essays on the conduct and vision of life. While his prose has a measure of thought-value, "often illuminated with a naive clear-sightedness,"[44] yet it never announces any surprising departures from modern thought. His essays are available in *The Kinship of Nature* (1904), *The Friendship of Art* (1904), *The Poetry of Life* (1905), and *The Making of Personality* (1907).

REPRESENTATIVE POEMS

"A Vagabond Song," "A Captain of the Press Gang," "The Gravedigger," "Hem and Haw," "Daisies," "The Sailing of the Fleets," "A Rover's Song," "A Spring Feeling," "An Autumn Garden," "The Joys of the Road," "A Sea Child," "The Deserted Pasture," "Hack and Hew," "'Lord of My Heart's Elation,'" "Marian Drury," "Song, 'Love, by that loosened hair.'"

---

44 Julian Hawthorne, *Bliss Carman: 1861-1929* (1929), reprinted from *The San Francisco Chronicle* of June 16, 1929.

SUGGESTED MERITS	SUGGESTED DEFECTS
1. Strong intellectual tendencies, the quality of which is in sympathy with American thought and democracy.	1. Neither the accents of originality nor of depth appear in the great mass of his work, which is distinctly inferior.
2. His philosophy is veined by transcendental reverie and ample humanity.	2. Unconcerned with the pressing social problems of the day. Not only mystical but sometimes esoteric.
3. He is a lyricist of nature, characteristically Canadian.	3. Wanderlustful philosophy is but "hobohemianism" and self-conscious boisterousness.
4. Piquant turns of fancy, genial carelessness of style, artistic mastery of verse technique, its flowing rhythms and classic forms.	4. Lapses into flabby didacticism, wearisome repetition, poetic commonplace, hair-trigger versifying. Later music is facile — but thin and diluted.

RICHARD HOVEY, 1864—1900, art student, student at the General Theological Seminary in New York, actor, journalist, lecturer in Alcott's Concord school of philosophy, Professor of English at Barnard College, poet, and dramatist. Born in Normal, Illinois, the son of the President of State Normal University, formerly a major-general in the United States Army. Spent his boyhood in Washington, D. C. Editor of the *Dartmouth* and the *Aegis* at Dartmouth, from which he was graduated in 1885. In Europe, he came to know Maurice Maeterlinck, whose *Pelléas and Mélisande* and seven other plays he translated. Married Mrs. Henrietta Russell (1893). Died suddenly in New York. Of him critics generally say that his too-early death cut short years of experimentation which gave promise of a poetic career of high distinction.[45]

The Laurel: An Ode (1889). Title-poem is addressed to Mary Day Lanier, and reveals an indebtedness to the musical influence of Sidney Lanier. Although the flavor of Whitman and of other poets is in this collection, Louis Untermeyer states that the book "gave promise of that extraordinary facility which often brought Hovey perilously close to mere technique."

Songs from Vagabondia (1894), ***More Songs from Vagabondia*** (1896), and ***Last Songs from Vagabondia*** (1901). All three volumes were written in partnership with the Canadian-born poet Bliss Carman (see page 242), and in revolt against the tradition of complacency and inanity of the period, and its bankruptcy of out-of-door ideas. For five years the people responded to their vagabond call for freedom from the artificial life, captivated by their compelling exuberance and continuous abandon, their happy-go-

45 Henry Leffert, *Richard Hovey* (M.A., New York University, 1927).

lucky, impetuous stanzas, their lyric singing of gipsy-like comradeship and masculine joy, their persistent optimism and complete wholesomeness.

Along the Trail (1898). Incorporates the early verses of the volumes that had appeared in 1880, 1889, 1891, and 1893.

To the End of the Trail (1908). Representative collection of his later and maturer lyrics edited by Mrs. Hovey.

REPRESENTATIVE POEMS

"At the Crossroads," prevailingly anapestic and illustrative of his poetry of good fellowship; "Spring: An Ode," a rapturous cry with its interludial "Stein Song" sung in numerous colleges; "Seaward," a worthy elegy on the death of T. W. Parsons; "Three of a Kind," telling of the joys on a hike during autumnal days; "Unmanifest Destiny," his most famous lyric, the patriotism or chauvinism of which should be compared with that of "The Battle of the Kegs" by Francis Hopkinson (page 31), "The Battle-Field" by W. C. Bryant (page 57), and "Laus Deo!" by J. G. Whittier (page 115). Additional poems are "After Business Hours," "The Sea Gypsy," "Love in the Winds," "Comrades," "Men of Dartmouth," "A Dream of Sappho," "Contemporaries," "To Rudyard Kipling," "Among the Hills," "The Wander-Lovers," "Barney McGee," "The Word of the Lord from Havana," and "Accident in Art."

Launcelot and Guenevere: A Poem in Five Dramas (five volumes, 1907). General title of a comprehensive, uncompleted cycle of three poetic trilogies, each to be composed of a masque and two dramas. Taking the old Malory story, Hovey removes the Tennysonian sentimentality, minimizes the glamorous trappings of a bygone age and its comedy of manners, poeticizes and sometimes theatricalizes the incidents, substitutes the noble, tragic love of Launcelot and Guenevere for the ideal purity of King Arthur, and plannedly weights the tale with its inward significance and the psychological problems born out of it and involved in "a harmonody of ethics."

Of this ambitious cycle of poetic masques and dramas based on the *Morte d'Arthur,* only five were published: (1) *The Quest of Merlin* (1891), a lyrical masque, noble in conception, but somewhat immature in execution and lacking in human interest. (2) *The Marriage of Guenevere* (1891—1895; 1895), a tragedy excellent in its characterization of Guenevere[46] and showing a gain over *The Quest of Merlin* in marked beauty and power. (3) *The Birth of Galahad* (1898), a romantic drama, which measurably sustains

46 The Guenevere of Tennyson sins and comes to repentance and remorse; the Guenevere of Morris appeals to our tender heart and asks human sympathy; and the Guenevere of Hovey loves, never sins, never repents: *The Holy Graal and Other Fragments,* edited by Mrs. Richard Hovey (1907), p. 14 (pp. 11-20).

the atmosphere created and puts blood into the anemic knights. (4) *Taliesin: A Masque*† (1900), masterly in the utilization of at least thirty meters, best in workmanship, in restrained and intensive power, and in spiritual mood. (5) *The Holy Graal and Other Fragments* (1907), parts of the unfinished dramas which indicate the scope and purport of the projected cycle, and, in Bliss Carman's words, "its essential profundity, seriousness, and wisdom."

WILLIAM VAUGHN MOODY, 1869—1910, poet, dramatist.[47] Born in Spencer, Indiana. Sixth child of Francis B. Moody and Henrietta E. Story. Attended the Pritchett Institute of Design at Louisville, Kentucky. Taught at a district school near New Albany, Indiana, to which his family had moved in 1870. Prepared for two years at Riverview Academy, a military school at Poughkeepsie, New York. Worked his way through Harvard (1889—1893). Travelled abroad, tutoring a wealthy pupil (1892—1893). A.B., Harvard (1893). Harvard Graduate School (1893—1895). Went abroad (1894). Instructor of English at the University of Chicago (1895), becoming an assistant professor by the time he left (1901). *Poems* (1901). Nominally connected with the college until 1907. In collaboration with R. M. Lovett, published the successful *A History of English Literature* (1902). Made four trips into the Far West (1901, 1904, 1906, 1909) and three more to England and Europe (1902, 1907, 1909). Litt.D., Yale University (1908). Harriet Converse Brainerd,[48] whom he had met in 1905, obtained a divorce in order to marry Moody (1909). Died (1910).

DRAMATIC TRILOGY IN VERSE

The Fire Bringer (1904). Theme, conjecturally influenced by Leopardi's *History of the Human Race,* utilizes the old Greek myth of Prometheus to explain the supremacy of good over evil, and the essential unity of God and the world.[49] General stiffness and heaviness of expression masked by picturesque diction and poetic image of as high an order as its blank verse. Dominant figure is Prometheus. Best-known lyrics: "Of wounds and sore defeat," and "I stood within the heart of God."

---

47 *The Poems and Plays of William Vaughn Moody* (two volumes, 1912), with an "Introduction" by J. M. Manly, pp. vii-xlvi; W. M. Payne, "William Vaughn Moody," [a book review] *Dial,* LIII (1912), pp. 484-486; C. M. Lewis, "William Vaughn Moody," *YR.,* N. S. II (1912-1913), pp. 688-703; Paul Shorey, "The Poetry of William Vaughn Moody," *UR.,* N. S. XIII (1927), pp. 172-200; N. F. Adkins, "The Poetic Philosophy of William Vaughn Moody," *TR.,* IX (1924), pp. 97-112; *Selected Poems of William Vaughn Moody,* edited by R. M. Lovett (1931), pp. ix-xcii.

48 *Letters to Harriet,* edited by Percy MacKaye, (1935), "II. Harriet Converse Tilden (Moody)," pp. 435-438; also, "Introduction," pp. 5-13 (pp. 3-71).

49 M. H. Shackford, "Moody's *The Fire Bringer* for To-Day," SRQ., XXVI (1918), pp. 407-416.

The Masque of Judgment (1900). Most complicated of his three closet dramas advancing the general theme of the inseparableness of God and man. Most important figure is Raphael. Psychologic power.

The Death of Eve (1912). Purpose was to detail how mankind searches for reconciliation with God. Only the first act is complete, yet this dynamic blank-verse fragment is a key to the meaning of the trilogy. More plainly-styled and orderly than its preceding members; psychological characterization, excellent dramaturgy. Perhaps familiar with *La Vision d'Eve* of Léon Dierx.[50]

PROSE PLAYS

The Great Divide (1909); originally called *A Sabine Woman* (1906). Amateurish work, brocaded with theatricalism, is concerned with the conflict between the cultures of the East and West. Blank verse with occasional lyrics. Spectacular success on Broadway.

The Faith Healer (1909). Potboiler of a revivalist who self-questions the clash between the material and the spiritual.

POETRY COLLECTIONS AND LETTERS

Gloucester Moors and Other Poems (1901). Includes: (1) "Gloucester Moors," which gives beautiful, humanitarian utterance to a preoccupation with the problem of the economic underdog; (2) "Good Friday Night," a simple, well-imaged, finished narrative poem based upon an Eastertide procession at Sorrento, Italy; it is as arresting and profound as "Second Coming" (1905), an emotional, partly-narrative poem which also grew out of a personal experience;[51] (3) "Road-Hymn for the Start," possibly only a surface-covered poem of vagabondage; (4) "An Ode in Time of Hesitation,"[52] as eloquent in form as in thought: an intelligent patriotism that does not subscribe to the Stephen Decatur toast of "my country, right or wrong"; (5) "The Quarry," suggested by the partition of China, is an appeal in behalf of helpless nations; (6) "On a Soldier Fallen in the Philippines," another penetrating thrust against imperialistic aims; (7) "Until the Troubling of the

50 C. M. Lewis, "William Vaughn Moody," *YR.*, N. S. II (1912-1913), p. 695 *ff.* (pp. 688-703).

51 Moody's "study of life of Jesus in the New Testament was one that absorbed him constantly, and he has left a record of this absorption in two poems — Good Friday Night and Second Coming." Harriet C. Moody in a letter to Mrs. G. N. Veeder in 1921: G. N. Veeder, *Concerning William Vaughn Moody* (1941), p. 9.

52 F. J. and Adaline Glasheen, "Moody's 'An Ode in Time of Hesitation,'" *CE.*, V (1943-1944), pp. 121-129.

Waters," a spiritual study; (8) "Jetsam," in blank verse; (9) "The Brute," whose personification as machinery conjures up a prophetic vision of economic relief and social changes, is Whitmanesque in its strength, Ruskinian in its approach to the machine's destructiveness of beauty, and happy-ended in its conclusion that the lost beauty will be restored and good will emerge; (10) "The Menagerie," reminiscent in manner of older poets, over-familiar in style, ironic in humor, and grotesque in realism, is concerned with the theory of evolution and its implications; (11) "The Golden Journey," original and thrilling; (12) "Heart's Wild-Flower," a lyric of exquisite phrasing and melody; (13) "On the River," another good piece; (14) "Song-Flower and Poppy," a two-part poem that attempts a synthesis of things religious and things worldly; (15) "The Daguerreotype," a thoughtful tribute to his mother, masculine in its directness, poignant in utterance and clairvoyant despite some strange strayings of fancy and vision.

Second Coming, and Later Poems (1912).[53] Among the better poems are: (1) "Old Pourquoi" (1904), with its strain of sheer grotesquery and imaginative strength; (2) "I Am the Woman," a melodic outburst veined with compacted imagery; (3) "The Moon-Moth," whose totality of meaning may be debatable but not its highly sensuous lyricism and daring imagery; (4) "The Fountain," another application, according to N. F. Adkins, of his thesis of body-and-spirit unity. For "Second Coming," see "Good Friday Night," p. 247.

LETTERS[54]

Revelatory of his poetic mind — meticulous phrasing, sensitive image-making faculty, mischievous touches of humor, spiritual passion. Florid. His *Letters to Harriet* (1901—1909) sketch the Broadway of his time.

SUGGESTED MERITS	SUGGESTED DEFECTS
1. Modern spirit who confronted expedient actions and questioned the eternal in America's soul. Revered and championed womanhood.	1. Substance, ideas, and feelings entangled by ornate threads of reflection and over-luxuriance of emotion. Obscurity; vague idealism.
2. More a poet than a philosopher. Adequacy of expression, concreteness of image, eloquence of verse. Favorite forms are the drama and the ode; yet his genius is primarily lyrical.	2. Turgidity and opulence of work, especially true of early verse. A transitional figure: his phraseology and style are academic and forced, echoing or akin to the older English poets.

53 See *The Poems and Plays of William Vaughn Moody*, edited by J. M. Manly (two volumes, 1912).

54 *Some Letters of William Vaughn Moody*, edited by G. D. Mason (1912); *Letters to Harriet*, edited by Percy MacKaye (1935), pp. 3-71, pp. 381-411.

OTHER LYRISTS

RICHARD HENRY STODDARD, 1825—1903, poet, critic, editor. AUTOBIOGRAPHY: *Recollections Personal and Literary* (1903). POETRY: *Songs of Summer* (1857), *The King's Bell* (1863), *Abraham Lincoln: An Horatian Ode* (1865), *Poems* (1851, 1880), *The Lion's Cub* (1890). In a letter dated March 7, 1897, William Sharp called Stoddard "the foremost living lyric poet of America"; but if Stoddard is remembered it is not as a writer of original verse: although his work has melody, imagery, even charm, it is predominantly artificial, imitative, and sentimental. His score of Oriental poems, three-fourths of which appear in *The Book of the East* (1871), has gained recognition as the first considerable collection of adaptations of Chinese poetry in our literature: the translations were an excellent source of the Chinese part of Longfellow's *Poems of Place* (p. 249).

JOHN JAMES PIATT, 1835—1917, journalist, poet; recently called (by Clare Dowler, 1936) a "representative figure of a momentous period." Verses are neither memorable nor profound; subject matter not unoriginal — but the verses do express the spirit of the frontier. VOLUMES: *Poems of Two Friends* (with W. D. Howells, 1860); *Poems in Sunshine and Firelight* (1866); *Western Windows and Other Poems* (1868, 1872, 1877); *The Pioneer's Chimney and Other Poems* (1871); *Landmarks and Other Poems* (1872); *Poems of House and Home* (1878); *The Union of American Poetry and Art* (anthology, 1879—1880); *Odes in Ohio and Other Poems* (1897); and *Pencilled Fly-Leaves: A Book of Essays in Town and Country* (1880). REPRESENTATIVE POEMS: "The Western Pioneer," "Taking the Night Train," "Passengers," "Walking to the Station," "Snow Falling," "Sonnet — In 1862," "Torch-Light in Fall-Time," "The Morning Street," and "At Kilcolman Castle."

WILL CARLETON, 1845—1912, short-story writer, scenario-writer, versisifier, lecturer. Of his twelve collections of poetry, including *City Ballads* (1885), *City Legends* (1889), and *City Festivals* (1892), his best is *Farm Ballads*† (1873). Range as limited as his imagination, but his genuine sentiment and quaint humor popularized country domestic life. "Betsy and I Are Out" is a homely ballad so successful that it encouraged the penning of "Out of the Old House Nancy," "Over the Hill to the Poor House," "Gone With a Handsomer Man," and "Over the Hill from the Poor House." Other verses are "Cover Them Over," a dirge in memory of Civil War heroes; "The New Church Organ," a humorous ballad; and that famous brace, "Betsy and I Are Out" and "How Betsy and I Made Up."

EMMA LAZARUS, 1849—1887, New York poet whose sonnet beginning "Give me your tired, your poor" is carved on the pedestal of the Statue of Liberty, and who has been labeled (by Philip Cowen, 1929) as "the one poet of first rank American Jewry has yet produced." *Poems and Translations* (1867), a serious, even melancholy, volume. *Admetus and Other Poems* (1871), dedicated to Emerson, is concerned primarily with classic themes. *Alide* (1874), an historical prose romance based on an episode between Goethe and Frederika Brion. *The Spagnoletto* (1876), a colorful tragedy in verse dealing with Italian life of the seventeenth century. *Poems and Ballads of Heine* (1881), an excellent translation. *Songs of a Semite*† (1882), made known best by "The Dance to Death," a moving poetic drama partly based upon factual scenes of Jewish life in Germany during the Middle Ages. *By the Waters of Babylon* (1887), a prose poem presenting pictures of Jews throughout the centuries. "Russian Christianity vs. American Judaism" (1882), a reply to an attack upon the Jews made by Madame Ragozin; "An Epistle from Joshua Ibn Vives," a poem founded on an incident of Spanish-Jewish life in the fifteenth century; "An Epistle to the Jews," a series of stimulating essays that resulted eventually in the founding of the Hebrew Technical Institute; "The Banner of the Jew," "The New Ezekiel," and "The Crowing of the Red Cock," three representative poems available in *The Poems of Emma Lazarus* (two volumes, 1889). See, also, *Emma Lazarus: Selections from Her Poetry and Prose,* edited, with an Introduction, by M. V. Schappes (1944), pp. 7-20, 103-105.

JAMES WHITCOMB RILEY, 1849—1916, homespun rhymer, the "Hoosier Poet" to whose memory a hospital was erected by popular subscription at a cost exceeding two million dollars. Verse-contributions to the Indianapolis *Journal* contain much of the substance of his poetry. Pen names included "The Bad Haroun," "Old E. Z. Mark," "Doc Marigold," and especially "Benj. F. Johnson," under which *nom de plume* Riley once interviewed himself. *The Lockerbie Book* (edited by H. H. Howland, 1911) is a 611-page memorial to the fact that Riley also wrote non-dialect verse, one touched with his characteristic quaint quality; but his genius was for the homely Hoosier vernacular. REPRESENTATIVE NON-DIALECT POEMS: "Bereaved," "The Poet of the Future," "The Name of Old Glory," "The Boy Patriot," "The Soldier," "The Brook-Song," "The Circus-Day Parade," "The Man in the Moon," "A Life-Lesson." REPRESENTATIVE DIALECT POEMS: "That-Air Young-Un," "The Old Swimmin'-Hole," "Nothin' to Say," "Kingry's Mill," "Griggsby's Station," "Down Around the River," "The Old Man and Jim," "Knee-Deep in June," "Little Orphant Annie," "The Raggedy Man," "Granny," "When the Frost is on the Punkin." REPRESENTATIVE READINGS: "The Old Soldier's Story," "The Peanut Story" or "Object Lesson." REPRESENTATIVE VOLUMES (often of mingled verse and prose): *The Old Swimmin'-Hole and 'Leven More Poems* (1883), *Afterwhiles* (1887), *Pipes o'Pan at Zekesbury* (1888), *Rhymes of Childhood* (1890), *Green Fields and Running Brooks* (1892), *Poems Here at Home* (1893), *Book of Joyous Children* (1902).

EUGENE FIELD, 1850—1895, columnist, journalist, humorist, poet. Best remembered for his "Sharps and Flats" department in the Chicago *Daily News,* for his bold renderings of Horace (Field called his house "Sabine Farm"), and for two sentimental poems, "Dutch Lullaby" (better known as "Wynken, Blynken, and Nod") and "Little Boy Blue," the latter said by C. H. Dennis to have its germ in "Christmas Treasures." Of his compact volume, *Culture's Garland* (1887), Field said: "I am not ashamed of this little book, but like the boy with the measles, I am sorry for it in spots." Verse collections include *A Little Book of Western Verse*† (1889), *Echoes from a Sabine Farm* (in collaboration, 1891), *Second Book of Verse* (1892), *Love Songs of Childhood* (1894). PROSE VOLUMES: *A Little Book of Profitable Tales*† (1893), *The Holy-Cross and Other Tales* (1893), *The Love Affairs of a Bibliomaniac* (1896).

EDWIN [CHARLES] MARKHAM, 1852—1940, who achieved national popularity when his "The Man with the Hoe" appeared in the San Francisco *Examiner* of December 20, 1899. That poem, inspired by Millet's painting, has been described by Mark Sullivan as the "most extraordinary phenomenon of the 'Mauve Decade,'" and elsewhere as "the battle cry of the next thousand years"; but the poem is more a rhetorical protest than a true picture. In addition to *The Man with the Hoe and Other Poems* (1899), he published a number of other volumes, including *Lincoln and Other Poems* (1901), the title-poem of which is a great utterance; and *Children in Bondage* (in collaboration 1914), which attempts "A Complete and Careful Presentation of the Anxious Problem of Child Labor — its Causes, its Crimes, and its Cure" (Chapters II—XI and XIV being Markham's). He has recorded many of his poems on phonograph records.

Edwin Markham, states William Rose Benét, "has always been a dogmatic poet, but with a great liberality of spirit and an accomplished knowledge of versification. . . . His lyrics, sonnets, and epigrams are interesting though many of them slide off the mind. . . . Elsewhere I must admit that, while I admire the energy of this poet and his idealism, I find much that dates considerably in language and manner of expression. The craftsmanship is not adept enough, the moral too obvious."

FRANK DEMPSTER SHERMAN, 1860—1916, mathematician, Columbia professor of architecture and graphics, genealogist, versifier. Facile poems are compact, inevitable, even exquisite; subjects of his *vers de société* are often archaic. His light verses for children were frequently signed "Felix Carmen." *Madrigals and Catches* (1887), a debonair first book; *New Waggings of Old Tales* by Two Wags (the other being J. K. Bangs; 1888); *Lyrics for a Lute* (1890); *Little-Folk Lyrics* (1892); *Lyrics of Joy* (1904); *A Southern Flight* (with Clinton Scollard, 1905).

INDIVIDUAL POEMS: "Moonrise," "An Avowal," "Behind Her Fan," "At Midnight," "The Rose's Cup," "A Greeting for Spring," "Confession," "Engaged," "Her Guitar," "Her China Cup," "Breath of Song," "A Tear Bottle," "Life," "Awake, Awake," "Dies Ultima."

CLINTON SCOLLARD, 1860—1932, university professor, historical novelist, poet who used French verse-forms, imitated Bliss Carman and Richard Hovey's songs of the open road (p. 242), and almost invariably wrote derivatively. Published or edited at least threescore books, including *Pictures in Song* (1884), *Giovio and Giulia* (metrical romance, 1892), *Lawton* (ode, 1900), *Count Falcon of the Eyrie* (novel, 1903), *Songs of a Syrian Lover* (1912), *The Singing Heart* (lyrics and other poems, selected by his wife, Jessie B. Rittenhouse, 1934).

LOUISE IMOGEN GUINEY, 1861—1920, essayist, poet. By her own admission her prose was disciplined by such writers as Sir Thomas Browne, Jeremy Taylor, Edmund Burke, Lamb, Hazlitt, Newman, and Stevenson; her poetry, by Sidney, Spenser, the Caroline lyricists, Shelley, Wordsworth, and Matthew Arnold. Sometimes abstruse is her humor, often scholarly are her writings. In her work, states J. B. Rittenhouse, three notes predominate — the valorous, the Celtic, and the mystical.

Blessed Edmund Campion (1908), a monograph on the heroic Jesuit, resulted from her deep Catholic sympathies; but she never completed an anthology of Recusant Poets from the time of Surrey to that of Pope. In addition to her published piece of hagiography she issued volumes of essays: *Goose Quill Papers* (1885), noted for deliberate archaism, quaint pictures, delicate but scholarly humor. *'Monsieur Henri'* (1892), deft sketch of the Vendean war and of its hero, Henri de la Rochejaquelin. *A Little English Gallery* (1894), portraits of Farquhar, Vaughan, Lady Danvers, and others. *Patrins* (1897), a delectable series of fancies. POETRY: *Songs at the Start* (1884), her earliest book; *The White Saul and Other Poems* (1887); *A Roadside Harp* (1893); *The Martyr's Idyl and Shorter Poems* (1900); and *Happy Ending* (1909; revised 1927), her own collection, as she said, of "the less faulty half" of all her published poetry. POEMS: "Tarpeia," "On Some Old Music," "Last Faun," "The White Sail," "The Knight Errant," "Vigil-at-Arms," "To a Dog's Memory," "The Yew Tree," "Athassel Abbey," "Song of the Lilac," "Tryste Noël," "A Friend's Song for Simoisius," "Borderlands," "The Squall," "Deo Optimo Maximo," "The Outdoor Litany," "By the Trundle Bed," "Nocturne," "Beati Mortui," "The Inner Fate," "St. Francis Endeth His Sermon," "The Wild Ride," "Astraea," "Winter Boughs," "Summum Bonum," "The Colour-Bearer."

JOHN KENDRICK BANGS, 1862—1922, humorist. Wrote at least sixty books, including such volumes of verse as *Cobwebs from a Library Corner* (1899), *Songs of Cheer* (1910), *Echoes of Cheer* (1912), and *The Foothills of Parnassus* (1914); such juvenile writings as *Tiddledywink Tales* (1891) followed successively by *The Tiddledywink's Poetry Book* (1892), *In Camp with a Tin Soldier* (1892), *Half-Hours with Jimmieboy* (1893), and *The Mantel-Piece Minstrels* (1896); and such miscellany as *The Idiot* (1895), a series of papers, *Mr. Bonaparte of Corsica* (1895), a burlesque biography made funnier by the H. W. McVickar illustrations, *A Rebellious Heroine* (1896), a well-done satirical novelette of deterministic writers, *The Bicyclers* (1896), a collection of four related farces satirizing contemporaneous fads, *Paste Jewels* (1897), seven episodic tales of a married couple's servant problem, and *Ghosts I Have Met and Some Others* (1898). Best-known is *A House-Boat on the Styx*† (1896), Hadean in its humor, genial in its presentation of diverse personages and their Associated Shades, lucky in its illustrations by Peter Newell. The endeavors of the Associated Shades under the leadership of Sherlock Holmes to retake their club house is told in the sequel, *The Pursuit of the House-Boat*† (1897), a best seller, better than its predecessor yet less popular. Another Styxian chronicle is *The Enchanted Typewriter* (1899).

MADISON [JULIUS] CAWEIN, 1865—1914, who, between the publication of *Blooms of the Berry* (1887) and *The Cup of Comus* (1915), issued at least thirty-four books, including the five-volume compilation of *Poems* (1907).

Over-facile and prolific pen makes Nature its theme; limns rural scenes consummately. Representative among his fifteen hundred or more poems: "The Twilight Moth," "A Flower of the Field," "Prayer for Old Age," "The Rain-Crow," "Evening on the Farm," "Dirge: What Shall Her Silence Keep?," "At the End of the Road," "To a Wind-Flower," "Wood-Words," "Under Arcturus," "Ghosts," "The Feud," "A Threnody," "Proem" to *Myth and Romance,* "Requescat," "The Man Hunt," "The Wind in the Pines," "A Voice in the Wind," "Here Is the Place Where Loveliness Keeps House," "Unrequited," "Deserted," "In the Shadow of the Beeches."

GEORGE STERLING, 1869—1926, playwright, poet. Verse forms traditional, allusions classical, romanticism exotic: alienated the radical thinker; imagery either lush or condensed, philosophic creed depressing and fatalistic: alienated the ordinary reader. Yet wrote good sonnets and simple lyrics. *The Testimony of the Suns* (1903), his first excellent long work; *A Wine of Wizardry* (1907), sheer in imagery, and extravagantly praised by Ambrose Bierce (p. 214) as one of the greatest American poems; *Lilith* (1919), symbolic drama of the poetic soul in its search for beauty; *Robinson Jeffers: The Man and the Artist* (1926), a prose appreciation; and *Sonnets to Craig* (1928), of which few of the approximately one hundred are memorable. INDIVIDUAL POEMS: "Autumn in Carmel," "Illusion," "The Day," "To a Girl Dancing," "Three Sonnets by the Night Sea," "Man," "At the Grave of Serra," "Three Sonnets on Oblivion," "The Black Vulture," "Beyond the Breakers," "Omnia Exeunt in Mysterium," "The Voice of the Dove," "Willy Pitcher," "Ode on the Centenary of the Birth of Robert Browning," "Night in Heaven."

THOMAS AUGUSTINE DALY, 1871—1948, journalist, poet. Best known for his dialect verse, available in *Canzoni* (1906), which ran to about fifty thousand copies, *Carmina* (1909), *Madrigali* (1912), *McAroni Ballads* (1919), *McAroni Medleys* (1931). PROSE: *Herself and the Household* (1924), *The House of Dooner* (with Christopher Morley, 1928). REPRESENTATIVE POEMS: "To a Thrush," "The Living-Room," "The Blossomy Barrow," "Ballade of Summer's Passing," "To a Tenant," "Song for April," "Waiting for the Train," "What the Flag Sings," "A Song for September."

PAUL LAURENCE DUNBAR, 1872—1906, novelist, short-story writer, poet. Pathos and unforced humor characterize his short stories, but, unlike his novels, his short stories perhaps distort social history; and those two qualities are endearing in his poetry, too. His earlier verses express the aspirations and the folk temperament of the Negro worker, while his later ones, often written in literary English, reflect, as in his novels, a growing attachment to his befriending white acquaintances. Perhaps therein is a clue to his failure to mirror a race soul while blending successfully the emotional whimsies, sentiments, and forces anchored within his people.

NOVELS: *The Uncalled* (1898), in which Dunbar and his wife are hero and heroine, is nevertheless concerned more with white than with Negro characters. Despite some excellent passages and fair plotting, it adds nothing to his reputation. It was dramatized for the radio by Meredith Page and broadcast in 1937. *The Love of Landry* (1900), a mid-Victorian romance with Colorado as its setting. Its characters are not closely associated with Negro life. *The Fanatics* (1901), an artificial novel of a social-political problem generated by the Civil War in a little Ohio town. *The Sport of the Gods*† (1902), where the main participants are Negroes. *The Uncalled* and *The Love of Landry* are both amateurish; but in the former, Dunbar denounced the hypocrisy of orthodox religion. In *The Fanatics* and in *The Sport of the Gods,* he demonstrates a sympathy; but in the latter he debunks southern gentility. At no time, however, do his novels, chiefly in the "plantation tradition," show more than promise.

STORIES AND SKETCHES: Of his six-dozen generally mediocre stories published in four separate volumes, some memorable ones are: "Anner 'Lizer's Stumblin' Block," "A Family Feud," and "The Trial Sermons on Bull-Skin" (all three from *Folks from Dixie,*† 1898, twelve stories), "The Last Fiddling of Mordaunt's Jim" (from *In Old Plantation Days,* 1903, twenty-five stories), and "The Lynching of

Jube Benson" (from *The Heart of Happy Hollow,* 1904, sixteen stories). Twenty short stories also appeared in *The Strength of Gideon* (1900).

POETRY: (1) *Oaks and Ivy* (1893), influenced by Irwin Russell and J. W. Riley. Romantic echoes appear in later volumes as well. (2) *Majors and Minors* (1895), not so good as his first volume, yet called by Benjamin Brawley "the most notable collection of poems ever issued by a Negro in the United States." (3) *Lyrics of Lowly Life*† (1896), chiefly a selection of the better poems in the two preceding collections. Other volumes: *Lyrics of Hearthside*† (1899), *Poems of Cabin and Field* (1899), *Candle-Lightin' Time* (1901), *Lyrics of Love and Laughter*† (1903), *Li'l' Gal* (1904), *Lyrics of Sunshine and Shadow*† (1905), *Howdy Honey Howdy* (1905), *Joggin' Erlong* (1906), *Chrismus Is A Comin'* (1907), *Lyrics of Lowly Life* (1908), *Speakin' o' Christmas* (1914), *The Complete Poems of Paul Laurence Dunbar* (1913, 1938).

INDIVIDUAL POEMS: "The Poet and His Song," "Ere Sleep Comes Down to Soothe the Weary Eyes," "Fulfilment," "We Wear the Mask," "When Malindy Sings," "Life," "The Corn-Stalk Fiddle," "The Spellin'-Bee," "When de Co'n Pone's Hot," "On the Sea Wall," "Love's Apotheosis," "Love," "At Candle-Lightin' Time," "Whistling Sam," "Encouragement," "When Dey 'Listed Colored Soldiers," "Ode to Ethiopia," "The Haunted Oak."

Chapter XIII

NATIONALISM AND COSMOPOLITANISM: ESSAYISTS, CRITICS, AND PLAYWRIGHTS

JOHN BURROUGHS, 1837—1921, teacher, poet, literary critic, essayist, naturalist.[1] Born on a farm just north of Roxbury, New York. Intermittent formal schooling included about a term each at Ashland Collegiate Institute and Cooperstown Seminary. Teacher in Illinois. Married Ursula North (1857). Taught at East Orange, New Jersey (1859). Contributed to the *Atlantic Monthly* (1860) and to the New York *Leader* (1861). Clerk in the Treasury Department at Washington (1864—1873), where he met Whitman.[2] U. S. Bank Examiner (1873—1884). Settled down (1884) on a farm at West Park on the Hudson, where nature lovers pilgrimaged to his cabin "Slabsides" and his house "Riverby." Honorary degrees from Colgate, Yale, and the University of Georgia. Recipient of the gold medal of the Academy of Arts and Letters (1916). Died in Ohio (1921), on his way home from a short visit to southern California, where a chest abscess had developed and had been operated upon unsuccessfully. Laid to rest on his boyhood farm. Unveiled exactly a year later (1922) on the Boyhood Rock near Woodchuck Lodge at Roxbury-in-the-Catskills was a bronze tablet, its two-line epigraph being a quotation from his most famous poem, "Waiting":

I STAND AMID THE ETERNAL WAYS
AND WHAT IS MINE SHALL KNOW MY FACE

Whether consciously or not, the early effusions of John Burroughs were characterized by the defects of the Johnsonian style; later, the unsigned essay "Expression" which appeared in the *Atlantic* (1860) was so dressed up with a few surface Emersonian mannerisms that it was mistaken for the idiom of that American

1 Clara Barrus, *John Burroughs, Boy and Man* (1920); John Burroughs, *My Boyhood, With a Conclusion by His Son Julian Burroughs* (1922); Clifton Johnson, *John Burroughs Talks* (1922); Norman Foerster, *Nature in American Literature* (1923), pp. 264-305; W. S. Kennedy, *The Real John Burroughs* (1924); Clara Barrus, *The Life and Letters of John Burroughs* (two volumes, 1925); Clara Barrus, *The Heart of Burroughs' Journals* (1928); C. H. Osborne, *The Religion of John Burroughs* (1930).

2 Clara Barrus, "Whitman and Burroughs as Comrades," *YR.*, XV (1925-1926), pp. 59-81.

philosopher.[3] John Burroughs first began to find himself in "From the Back Country," a series of unfinished but fresh articles in the New York *Leader* (1861); and, twenty years later, in *Pepacton* (1881), finally mastered the craft of nature writing.

The charm of Uncle John of Woodchuck is a personal emanation felt only in a leisurely reading of his nature essays, which are an excellent medium for his chatty and mellow style, delightful humor, familiar dignity, and simple architecture. It is in his objective materials that he succeeds best, in his concern with the outward life of nature — primarily because of his power of sympathetic rather than original observation. His few books on literary criticism merit a bit more attention; his later volumes on human topics, contemporary science, and philosophical problems make no profound contribution except as they reveal a belief in evolution, a reverent if creedless faith, and a Bergsonian mysticism. The Sage of Slabsides is basically a see-er and not a seer;[4] with John Muir, he developed in America a literary *genre,* the nature essay. Only Emerson and Thoreau are better.[5]

WORKS

Notes on Walt Whitman as Poet and Person (1867), the first biographical-critical study of the Good Gray Poet, later expanded into *Walt Whitman: A Study* (1896);[6] *Wake-Robin* (1871), *Winter Sunshine* (1875), *Birds and Poets* (1877), *Locusts and Wild Honey* (1879), *Pepacton* (1881), *Fresh Fields* (1884), *Signs and Seasons* (1886), *Indoor Studies* (1889), *Riverby* (1894), *The Light of Day* (1900), *Literary Values* (1902), *The Life of Audubon* (1902), *Far and Near* (1904), *Ways of Nature* (1905), *Bird and Bough* (poems, 1906), *Camping and Tramping with Roosevelt* (1907), *Leaf and Tendril* (1908), *Time and Change* (1912), *The Summit of the Years* (1913), *The Breath of Life* (1915), *Under the Apple Trees* (1916), *Field and Study* (1919), *Accepting the Universe* (1920), *Under the Maples* (1921), *The Last Harvest* (1922).

HENRY [BROOKS] ADAMS, 1838—1918, historian, a pioneer of the seminar method of study; called, overratedly, "the

---

3 Frequently John Burroughs declared that Emerson was his spiritual father; for example: "In taking this line from Emerson for the title of an essay on Henri Bergson, I would indicate at once the aspect of his philosophy that most appeals to me." John Burroughs, "A Prophet of the Soul," *Atl.,* CXIII (1914), p. 120 (pp. 120-132).

4 D. L. Sharp, *The Seer of Slabsides* (1921), p. 3.

5 J. H. DeLoach, *Rambles with John Burroughs* (1912), pp. 93-107; Bliss Perry, "John Burroughs as a Man of Letters," *HGM.,* XXX (1921-1922), pp. 328-333.

6 It is generally recognized that a large part of *Notes on Walt Whitman as Poet and Person* was written by Walt Whitman himself: consult F. P. Hier, Jr., "The End of a Literary Mystery," *AM.,* I (1924), pp. 471-478.

Aristotle of America."[7] Instead of studying Civil Law at Berlin (1858), spent most of his time upon trips, once as far down as Italy. Returned to the United States (1860). Secretary to his father, Charles Francis Adams, at the American Embassy in London (1861—1868). Back to Washington, D. C. (1868). Through the influence of his father, became a teacher of medieval history at Harvard (1870—1877), and edited *The North American Review*. Married Marian Hooper, of Boston and Beverly Farms, Massachusetts (1872). To Europe (1872—1873). By taking cyanide of potassium, Marian committed suicide (1885).[8] Visited South Seas (1890) and Normandy (1895). Visit to Paris Exposition (1900), where the huge dynamo affected his speculative mind.

Democracy — An American Novel (anonymously, 1880). Rather incompetent novelizing, but significant for its understanding if satirical documentation of social and political Washington, corrupted by irresponsible ambition. Its major political theme is treated more fully in *The Education of Henry Adams*.[9] Originals of the main characters include Rutherford B. Hayes, nineteenth President of the United States ("Old Granite"), James G. Blaine (Senator Silas P. Ratcliffe), Mrs. Bigelow Lawrence, Miss Fanny Chapman, James Lowndes, and Emily Beale. (See, also, Hay's *Bread-Winners*, p. 168; Mark Twain's *The Gilded Age*, p. 191.)

John Randolph (1882). Historical work. Light touch and interpretative spirit possibly outbalanced by inexpert judgment.[10] Inferior to his *The Life of Albert Gallatin* (1879) and *The Writings of Albert Gallatin* (1879).

Esther — A Novel (pseudonymously, 1884). By "Frances Snow Compton." Measures a woman's mental recognition of religious faith against a spiritual conflict. As in *Democracy*, concerned with political faith, so in *Esther*, concerned with religious faith, the chief character is a feminine soul in search of truth — anticipatory of the symbolism of the Virgin of Chartres; yet the central conflict of both trivial novels is alike. By modelling Esther Dudley

---

7 Henry Adams, *The Degradation of the Democratic Dogma*, with an "Introductory Note" by Brooks Adams (1919), pp. v-xiii; *A Cycle of Adams Letters 1861-1865*, edited by W. C. Ford, (two volumes, 1920). J. T. Adams, *Henry Adams* (1933); R. V. Shumate, "The Political Philosophy of Henry Adams," *APSR.*, XXVIII (1934), pp. 599-610; Edgar Johnson, "Henry Adams: The Last Liberal," *SS.*, I (1936-1937), pp. 362-377; M. I. Baym, "William James and Henry Adams," *NEQ.*, X (1937), pp. 717-742; R. P. Blackmur "Henry Adams: Three Late Moments," *KR.*, II (1940), pp. 7-29; Oscar Cargill, "The Mediaevalism of Henry Adams," in *Essays and Studies in Honor of Carleton Brown* (1940), pp. 296-329.

8 Katharine Simonds, "The Tragedy of Mrs. Henry Adams," *NEQ.*, IX (1936), pp. 564-582.

9 Although he had liberal opinions, Henry Adams probably thought none too highly of *hoi polloi*. While Walt Whitman regarded society as evolutive of a genuine democracy, Henry Adams arrived at a "mystical pantheism with the love of the Virgin as force, and Chartres Cathedral as society," W. H. Jordy, "Henry Adams and Walt Whitman," *SAQ.*, L (1941), pp. 132-145.

10 For a criticism of Adams's treatment of John Randolph, consult the twoscore references in W. C. Bruce, *John Randolph of Roanoke* (two volumes, 1922). And for critical studies of *Randolph* and Adams' other works see George Hochfield, *Henry Adams* (Barnes & Noble, 1962).

partly[11] upon the character of Marian Adams, the author gives an insight into his own spiritual biography. Stephen Hazard is in some ways Henry Adams. Fair realism, persuasive talk, considerate irony, intellectualized action, excellent understanding of feminine emotions.[12]

History of the United States during the Administrations of Jefferson and Madison (1885—1891).[13] Political and diplomatic history large in bulk, and generally praised for its charming style, gift of narration and characterization, masterly research, philosophical reflection.[14] Except for the early chapters, perhaps not fully appreciative of basic economic and social phenomena.

***Mont-Saint-Michel and Chartres*†** (privately printed, 1904; published 1913). Critical work subtitled "A Study of Thirteenth-Century Unity" fuses medieval theology, philosophy, and mysticism, medieval sociology and economics, medieval art, romance, and literature into a dynamic worship of a world distant from the chaos of his own times and presided over by the Virgin Mother of Jesus.[15] In this contrasting study of the architectural structures raised in the martial eleventh and halcyon thirteenth centuries, where the religious theme of *Esther* receives profounder expression, the mellow humor and intricate learning, the unique insight and escapist promptings build up a prose-poem tribute to the Virgin, apotheosis of womankind.

A Letter to American Teachers of History (1910). By adopting Lord Kelvin's second law of thermodynamics[16] (the law of the dissipation of energy), Adams tilts a lance against evolution as a doctrine of ultimate perfectibility. Dynamic theory urges recognition

---

11 By no means completely, for his marriage to the charming Marian was happy: Katharine Simonds, "The Tragedy of Mrs. Henry Adams," *NEQ.*, IX (1936), pp. 564-582.

12 Marian Adams, who lost her father several months after *Esther* appeared, may have obtained from it a suicide hint: the heroine, after losing her invalid father, feels impelled "to get out of life itself rather than suffer such . . . misery of helplessness." Also playing its tragic part was, possibly, twelve years of childlessness.

13 Published as follows: *History of the United States of America during the Second Administration of Thomas Jefferson* (1885), *History of the United States of America during the First Administration of James Madison 1809-1813* (1888), *History of the United States of America during the First Administration of Thomas Jefferson* (two volumes, 1889), *History of the United States of America during the Second Administration of Thomas Jefferson* (two volumes, 1890), *History of the United States of America during the First Administration of James Madison* (two volumes, 1890), *History of the United States of America during the Second Administration of James Madison* (three volumes, 1891).

14 "Written strictly in accord with scientific principles, the nine-volume work still stands as one of the outstanding achievements of American historiography and a monument to the scientific theory of history." James Stone, "Henry Adams's Philosophy of History," *NEQ.*, XIV (1914), p. 540 (pp. 538-548). See also W. C. Ford, "Henry Adams, Historian," *Nation*, CVI (1918), p. 674 *f*; Yvor Winters, *The Anatomy of Nonsense* (1943), pp. 69-87 (pp. 23-87).

15 P[hyllis] Blanchard, "The Education of Henry Adams," *MH.*, IV (1920), pp. 232-242; H. L. Creek, "The Mediaevalism of Henry Adams," *SAQ.*, XXIV (1925), pp. 86-97; James Brodrick, "The Quest of Henry Adams," *Month*, CLXX (1937), pp. 301-309, 397-406.

16 It is becoming apparent that it was Brooks Adams who helped make a philosopher out of Henry. Previously it had been generally believed that Henry influenced the thought in *The Law of Civilization and Decay* (1895), written by his brother Brooks. See C. A. Beard's introduction to *The Law of Civilization and Decay* (1943), pp. 3-53; and also H. E. Barnes, "Brooks Adams on World Utopia," *CuH.*, VI (1944), pp. 1-6.

of the principle that, instead of evolving toward a state of perfection, human thought or society is a substance or an organism subject to the law of degradation, and hence destined for senescence and decay. Doctrine, applied to history, is generally characterized as futilitarian.

The Education of Henry Adams† (privately printed, 1907; posthumously, 1918). Pioneering attempt to effect a continuity between European medievalism and American modernism, and to achieve a synthesis of all human knowledge. Subtitled "A Study of Twentieth-Century Multiplicity," this partial, but nevertheless, intellectual autobiography[17] chronicles the evolution — or devolution — from unity in the adoration of Our Lady of Chartres to chaos or "multiplicity," valiantly groping to expound the dualism by utilizing philosophy, physics, and mathematics, by resorting to such theories as the law of phase and the second law of thermodynamics, and by endeavoring to achieve an historical reconciliation between the Virgin of the thirteenth century and the Dynamo of the twentieth.[18] Odyssey of introspective maladjustment despite consistent efforts to comprehend the world about him. Later chapters (especially xxv, xxxiii, xxxiv) are an exercised discussion of his dynamic theory of history[19] (see *A Letter to American Teachers of History*): his ultimate conclusion is that Chaos is the law of nature, while Order is the dream of man.[20] Arterializing its vigorous scepticism and alert humor, its absorptive knowledge, rich expressiveness, and extraordinary substance are veins of desperate pessimism, of disintegrative pathos, and of philosophic anarchism.[21]

---

17 Noted for its frank admissions, yet his reportorial autobiography has its reticences; excluded are, for example, twenty years of his life, including the years of his marriage. To the Freudian the absence of the sexual theory as an explanation of life may be one reason for his will to power.

18 Eugene O'Neill's melodramatic *Dynamo* (1929), wherein it becomes a divine symbol, is perhaps a travesty or satire of the mind of Henry Adams.

19 To Adams's theory many serious demurrers have been raised. Meriting study is the doctrine that laws governing the material world may influence the destiny of man. Consult G. H. Sabine, "Henry Adams and the Writing of History," *UCC.*, XXVI (1924), pp. 31-46; R. A. Hume, "Henry Adams's Quest for Certainty," in *Stanford Studies in Language and Literature,* edited by Hardin Craig (1941), pp. 361-373.

20 "According to his theory of history, . . . the teacher was at best helpless, and, in the immediate future, silence next to good-temper was the mark of sense. After midsummer, 1914, the rule was made absolute."

The foregoing quotation from the "Editor's Preface" signed by Henry Cabot Lodge in *The Education of Henry Adams* (1918) has special significance if it was written, as J. T. Adams states, by Henry Adams.

21 Henry's apologia for being a failure is a deceptive pose, cautions Brooks Adams as he reminds us that, by ordinary standards, his brother Henry succeeded as a writer, a teacher, and an historian. Granted that Henry's life is not wholly the American tragedy he desires us to believe, yet his restless journeyings do point up for him the meaninglessness and futility of life. A more appropriate name for *The Education of Henry Adams* might be "Why Education Failed to Educate Henry Adams," an aptly-titled article by W. D. Sheldon, *SR.*, XXVIII (1920), pp. 54-65; while H. S. Canby, *The Education of Henry Adams* (1942), p. xii (pp. ix-xiii), states that the "full title of his book . . . might run something like this: — 'How I Educated Myself in the Nature of the Nineteenth Century; and Learning what it was Like in Reference to Me, went on and tried to Discover where it was Going; Made some brilliant Guesses, but could see no Final Solution hopeful for Man; and so Resolved that my use of Education had led only to a Demonstration of the Extent of Human Ignorance.' " See also Carl Becker, "The Education of Henry Adams," *AHR.*, XXIV (1918-1919), pp. 422-434.

The Prayer to the Virgin of Chartres (*c.* 1904; published 1920). Poem important chiefly for the light it throws upon his spiritual history.[22] Meditate, for example, upon "Ourselves we worship and we have no Son."

Letters. Reveal him once again the master of that ironic note and detached intellectuality prominent in *The Education of Henry Adams.*

GAMALIEL BRADFORD, 1863—1932, called by John Macy "the supreme," but not necessarily the best biographer of our time. Born in Boston at Bowdoin and Allston Streets. Of direct descent in the eighth generation from Governor William Bradford of Plymouth Colony (see p. 4). To Europe for a year (1878). Forced by ill health to withdraw from Harvard, which he had entered in 1882. Married Helen Hubbard Ford (1886). Summered in continental Europe (1887). All his life he suffered seriously from illness, almost always working at a typewriter rigged up ingeniously near his bed, where he did most of his secretaryless writing. A financial competence inherited from his mother freed him from financial worry. Died at his home in Wellesley Hills, Massachusetts, from an inherited disease.[23]

Gamaliel Bradford developed in his own way a method[24] of writing brief "portraits" or "psychographs"[25] of historical figures of

22 Mabel LaFarge, "Henry Adams: A Niece's Memoirs," *YR.*, IX (1920), p. 284 *f.* (pp. 271-285); Ferner Nuhn, "Henry Adams and the Hand of the Fathers," *A.Pr.*, V (1940), pp. 51-56.

23 His mother, Clara Crowninshield Kinsman Bradford, died from consumption at the age of twenty-nine, only five years after her marriage, attaining even then a greater age than any others in the large family of which she was a member. Consult C. K. Bolton, "Gamaliel Bradford: A Memoir," *MHS.*, LXV (1933), pp. 81-91.

24 "Arrived today at the first reading of Paine's *Works,* and instantly perceive what I had not quite fathomed before, the secret of his greatness, such as he is. The man is a writer. I should say that this is apt to be my method of getting at a subject. I take first the outside sources, the secondary matter, the hearsay and gossip of those less likely to know, and then get to the heart, the essential biographies, and the man's own words. Perhaps this is a mistake. I may get prejudices from the unreliable sources that I do not afterwards eradicate. But I somehow feel as if this were the more natural form of approach, what one would adopt in real life, and so far it seems to work reasonably well, besides that in some cases my method is quite different." *The Journal of Gamaliel Bradford, 1883-1932,* edited by Van Wyck Brooks (1933); dated June 11, 1922, p. 306.

25 To Bradford the word "portrait" is unsatisfactory, for a painter "takes a man only at one special moment of his life and [the portrait] may therefore be quite untrue to the larger lives of his character," whereas a psychographer "endeavors to grasp as many particular moments as he can and to give his reader not one but the enduring sum total" of the "vast complex of influences that have gone to building up that face and figure." Psychography is not bound to "the chronological pattern of narrative biography" (John Macy) that is an integral part of portrait-writing; nor is psychography "bound to present an elaborate sequence of dates, events, and circumstances, of which some are vital to the analysis of the individual subject, but many are merely required to make the narrative complete" (Gamaliel Bradford).

What, positively, is this new style of biography? "Out of the perpetual flow of actions and circumstances that constitutes a man's whole life," psychography "seeks to extract what is essential, what is permanent and so vitally characteristic" — it "is the condensed, essential, artistic presentation of character," which is quite distinct from individuality, and "is the sum of qualities or of generalized habits of action." A psychograph "seeks to extricate from the fleeting, shifting, many-colored tissues of a man's long life, those habits of action, usually known as qualities of character," which are the slow, almost unalterable product of inheritance and training. Its art is "to disentangle these habits from the immaterial, inessential matter of biography, to illustrate them by touches of speech and action that are significant, and by those

varied eras and countries, and produced no fewer than one hundred fourteen such character studies of men and women,[26] of whom at least half are American. Neither inventing nor standing alone in this kind of fluid, creative biography, yet his personal application of "soul-writing" made him prominent. Paired off with his breadth of sympathy[27] and scholarly detachment are adequate craftsmanship and a historian's zeal, all best sustained in his miniatures rather than in such life-size, full-length psychographs as those devoted to Pepys, Darwin, Moody, and even Lee.

His indefatigable activity as a writer produced two thousand poems, eight novels, of which only three were published, fifteen plays, of which only one was printed but not a single one produced, and numerous other works.[28]

AMERICAN CHARACTER STUDIES

(1) *Types of American Characters* (1895), concerned with the pessimist, the idealist, the epicurean, the philanthropist, the man of letters, the American out-of-doors, and the scholar, this series of essays is a pale and abstract foreshadow of his later psychographic portraits. (2) *Lee the American*† (1912), generally applauded as the work whereby he comes into his own as psychographer.[29] (3) *Damaged Souls*† (1923), easily his best-known

only. . . ." Consult Edward Wagenknecht, "Gamaliel Bradford," *BLM.*, II, No. 4 (1922), pp. 177-184; Gamaliel Bradford, *A Naturalist of Souls* (1926), p. 5 *f.*; M. D. Woodruff, "Gamaliel Bradford: A Searcher of Souls," *SAQ.*, XXVIII (1929), pp. 419-428; John Macy, "Gamaliel Bradford: Portrayer of Souls," *Bookman*, LXXV (1932), pp. 144-146; Dale Warren, "Gamaliel Bradford: A Personal Sketch," *SAQ.*, XXXIII (1933), p. 14 *f.* (pp. 9-18).

26 A complete alphabetical list of all appears in Dale Warren, "Gamaliel Bradford: A Personal Sketch," *SAQ.*, XXXIII (1933), pp. 15-18 (pp. 9-18). Consult also L. H. Hough, "A Magnificent and Meticulous Dilettante," *RL.*, II (1933), pp. 271-284.

27 His deep interest in other people's lives made it possible for him to enter sympathetically into the lives of Darwin, a gentleman scholar; of Lee, a gentleman warrior; of Pepys, a likeable rogue; and of Moody, a robust gospeler.

28 Published volumes of poetry are *A Pageant of Life* (1904), early poems; *A Prophet of Joy* (1920), a long narrative poem; and *Shadow Verses* (1920), a group of poems. *Unmade in Heaven* (1917), in four acts, is his only printed play. The novels are *The Private Tutor* (1904), *Between Two Masters* (1906), and *Matthew Porter* (1908). In addition to *Lee the American* (1912), the Civil War also provided material for *Confederate Portraits* (1914), *A Portrait of General George Gordon Meade* (1915), *Union Portraits* (1916). Further studies of Americans appear in *Types of American Characters* (1895), *American Portraits, 1875-1900* (1922), *Damaged Souls* (1923), *D. L. Moody: A Worker in Souls* (1927), *As God Made Them* (1929). Other works include *The Soul of Samuel Pepys* (1924), *The Haunted Biographer* (1927), *Early Days in Wellesley* (1929), *Daughters of Eve* (1930), *The Quick and the Dead* (1931), *Biography and the Human Heart* (1932), *Saints and Sinners* (1932), and *Portraits and Personalities*, edited by M. A. Bessey (1933).

29 But it was not until H. L. Mencken's appreciative review of *American Portraits* appeared in the New York Evening Post *Literary Review* of April 8, 1922, that Bradford's popularity began. However, it is not amiss to question in a measure H. L. Mencken's statement that "This Bradford is the man who invented the formula of Lytton Strachey's 'Queen Victoria,'" for Bradford himself admitted that even the word "psychograph" is not his own invention: see "Appendix" to *Lee the American* (1912), pp. 269-283, and "Psychography" in *A Naturalist of Souls* (1917), pp. 3-25. Dated April 11, 1922, Bradford's letter of gratefulness to H. L. Mencken is available in *The Letters of Gamaliel Bradford, 1918-1931*, edited by Van Wyck Brooks (1934), p. 105 *f.*

book.[30] (4) *D. L. Moody: A Worker in Souls* (1927), a fairly satisfactory discussion of the average evangelistic attitudes toward religion.

TRANSATLANTIC CHARACTER STUDIES

(1) *A Naturalist of Souls* (1917) deals wholly with people across the Atlantic; (2) *Bare Souls* (1924), concerned in part with transatlantic figures; (3) *Darwin* (1926), a sympathetic portrayal of the negative-nihilistic approach to religion.

WOMEN CHARACTER STUDIES

(1) Devoted to Europeans, chiefly French and of the eighteenth century, is *Portraits of Women* (1916); (2) to wives, reformers, and educators, *Portraits of American Women* (1916); (3) to those whose husbands are eminent, *Wives* (1925); (4) to the daily life of Elizabethan women and the women of Elizabethan literature, the posthumous *Elizabethan Women* (1936).

AUTOBIOGRAPHY

(1) *The Journal of Gamaliel Bradford, 1883-1932* (1933),[31] a description of his inner life, of his resolute fifty-year battle against sickness and infirmity; (2) *The Letters of Gamaliel Bradford, 1918-1931* (1934), a description of his social life; and —

***Life and I*†** (1928). Beautiful spiritual autobiography, reverent but frank in its discussion of the problems of religion. Originally planned as *Christ and I* (out of eight chapters the last four are: "Christ and I," "Christ and Not-I," "Christ and More than I," "Christ and I and God"), it is memorable for a penetrating consideration of Jesus and the New Testament.

OTHER ESSAYISTS AND CRITICS

THOMAS WENTWORTH HIGGINSON, 1823—1911, clergyman, novelist, historian, essayist, biographer. AUTOBIOGRAPHY: (1) *Army Life in a Black Regiment* (1870), describes his war experiences, including his adventures as colonel of the first Negro regiment of freed slaves. (2) *Cheerful Yesterdays* (1898), about his contemporaries, written indoors during a two-year illness. (3) *Malbone* (1869), his only romance, in which his wife is the novel's Aunt Jane. MISCELLANEOUS: *Oldport Days* (1873), essays descriptive of the Newport of his day; *History of the United States for Young People* (1874), well done; *The Monarch of Dreams* (1886),

30 As Van Wyck Brooks has noted, Bradford had an all-American mind, one identical with that of Amy Lowell and Robert Frost, of John Dewey and S. E. Morison, and one that made instinctive efforts to attach itself "whole-heartedly to the life of the country, . . . to nationalize itself" at a critical moment in our history. Bradford's study of Robert E. Lee is an instance of this; but less frequently noted is his *Damaged Souls*, where a prominent aim is to reveal the human and more attractive elements in such characters as Benedict Arnold, Aaron Burr, and John Brown. Abused and damaged their souls may be, but not damned.

31 *The Journal*, edited by Van Wyck Brooks, represents only about one-seventh of the length of the manuscript, which totals 1,400,000 words.

imaginative tale; *An Afternoon Landscape* (1888), first volume of verse; *Henry Wadsworth Longfellow* (1902) and *John Greenleaf Whittier* (1902), both in the *American Men of Letters Series.*

CHARLES DUDLEY WARNER, 1829—1900, surveyor, lawyer, essayist, novelist, editor of the *American Men of Letters Series.* ESSAYS: *My Summer in a Garden* (1870; title-page dated 1871), a series of humorous, mellow nature-essays. *Backlog Studies* (1873), graceful social and literary discussions. *As We Were Saying* (1891) and *As We Go* (1893), two little books possessing his characteristically urbane wit, mellow grace, and, perhaps, basic shallowness. *The Relation of Literature to Life*† (1896), contains "his deepest and most earnest convictions." TRAVEL SKETCHES: *My Winter on the Nile* (1876) and *In the Levant* (1877), a graphic record of a visit to the Orient during 1875 and 1876; *Our Italy* (1891), an account of Southern California. TRILOGY OF NOVELS: *A Little Journey in the World* (1889), how Rodney Henderson accumulates a great fortune in the stock market; *The Golden House* (1894), how the great fortune is fraudulently misused; and *That Fortune* (1899), how Rodney's money, accumulated by ruthless methods, is lost. For *The Gilded Age,* written in collaboration with Mark Twain, see page 191. BIOGRAPHIES: *Captain John Smith* (1881); *Washington Irving* (1881).

JOHN MUIR, 1838—1914, Scottish-American explorer, naturalist, teacher. Nature-philosophy is theistic, yet he is an evolutionist. Unaffected, descriptive style is exemplified in his *Letters to a Friend* (1915) as well as in his other writings. *The Story of My Boyhood and Youth* (1913) is exactly that, telling of Scotland, America, and the University of Wisconsin. In *Our National Parks*† (1901) appears some of his best work. His and his gallant dog's narrow escape during a glacier storm is recounted in *Stickeen* (1909). Also wrote *My First Summer in the Sierra* (1911), *The Yosemite*† (1912), *Travels in Alaska* (a series of explorations made during the summers of 1879, 1880, 1881; published 1915), *Steep Trails* (1918), and *The Mountains of California*† (1894), especially noteworthy, illustrated by Muir himself, and famous for its discussions of "The Water-Ouzel," "A Wind-Storm in the Forests," "The River Floods," and "The Douglas Squirrel."

RICHARD WATSON GILDER, 1844—1909, editor, poet, man-of-affairs. To Brander Matthews, his essays are tender, mellow, and flavored; to Ferris Greenslet, his letters have vivacity, sincerity, and abiding charm; to H. W. Mabie, his poetry possesses vitality and charm, reveals a delicate touch invigorated by sensitive imagination, conviction, and thought — but on the whole his productions are not especially memorable. Of his nine principal volumes of poetry the best is his first, *The New Day* (1875), a cycle of love sonnets. Prose includes *Lincoln the Leader; and Lincoln's Genius for Expression* (1909) and *Grover Cleveland: A Record of Friendship* (1910).

W[ILLIAM] C[RARY] BROWNELL, 1851—1928, perhaps the most discerning literary critic of his day. *French Traits: An Essay in Comparative Criticism* (1889), a straight-thinking, sympathetic, penetrating study of American as well as French life. *French Art* (1892), charming expository criticism. *Victorian Prose Masters* (1901), dispassionate, occasionally recondite, but never less than admirable in its judgments, apparently influenced by Matthew Arnold. *American Prose Masters*† (1909), more spontaneous and original than the 1901 volume: perhaps this 1909 collection of critical estimates identifies him with the New Humanists. *Criticism* (1914), a little volume, as stimulating in its rhythm and restraint as all his works. *Standards* (1917), seven well-written short papers, broad of perception and austere of taste. *The Genius of Style* (1924), which favors discipline and centrality of taste as against impulse and sentimentality. Other volumes are: *Democratic Distinction in America* (1927); *The Spirit of Society* (1927); *William Crary Brownell* (an Anthology of His Writings together with Biographical Notes and Impressions of the Later Years, by Gertrude Hall Brownell, 1933).

HENRY VAN DYKE, 1852—1933, minister, professor of English at Princeton, ambassador, poet, critic, short-story writer, essayist. *The Reality of Religion* (1884) was the first of a series of theological books, followed by *The Story of the*

Psalms (1887), *Sermons to Young Men* (1893), *The Christ Child in Art* (1894), and *The Poetry of the Psalms* (1900). Originally preached as a Christmas sermon, *The Story of the Other Wise Man*† (1896) was subsequently published in short-story form, as was his *The First Christmas Tree* (1897); both have been translated into several Oriental and numerous European languages. *Essays in Application* (1905) is a volume of literary criticism not so well known as *The Poetry of Tennyson* (1889), a sympathetic study. Popular were the essays in such collections as *Little Rivers*† (1895) and *Fisherman's Luck* (1899), and his short fiction in *The Ruling Passion*† (1901), his first book of stories, *The Blue Flower* (1902), a translation from the German of Novalis, and *The Unknown Quantity* (1912), inspired by the death of a favorite daughter. Published also were *The Builders, and Other Poems* (1897), *The Toiling of Felix, and Other Poems* (1900), *Music and Other Poems* (1904), *The Spirit of America* (a translation of his Sorbonne lecture, 1908—1909; 1910), *The Grand Canyon and Other Poems* (1914), *Companionable Books* (1923), and *Chosen Poems* (1933). REPRESENTATIVE POEMS: "The Arrow," "Four Things," "America for Me," "Love and Light," "Joy and Duty," "Work," "Might and Right."

GEORGE EDWARD WOODBERRY, 1855—1930, professor, poet, biographer, critic, editor. His interpretations of Poe, Shelley, Milton, and Hawthorne have understanding and urbanity, if not too much color and warmth. Popular are "The Secret" and "O, Inexpressible as Sweet," two lyrics; "At Gibraltar," two sonnets; and "The North Shore Watch," a beautiful threnody. Volumes include: *A History of Wood-Engraving* (1883), *Edgar Allan Poe* (1885; enlarged 1909), *The North Watch Shore and Other Poems* (1890), *Studies in Letters and Life* (1890), *The Complete Poetical Works of Percy Bysshe Shelley*† (1892), *Heart of Man* (1899), *Makers of Literature* (1900), *Nathaniel Hawthorne*† (1902), *America in Literature* (1903), *The Torch* (1905), *Swinburne* (1905), *The Appreciation of Literature* (1907), *Ralph Waldo Emerson* (1907), *The Inspiration of Poetry* (1910), *The Flight and Other Poems* (1914), *North Africa and the Desert* (1917), *Ideal Passion: Sonnets* (1917), *The Roamer* (1920), *Selected Letters* (with an introduction by Walter De La Mare, 1933), *Selected Poems* (1933).

ELBERT HUBBARD, 1856—1915, "go-getting" essayist; "Ad Man Superbus, Salesman Maximus" (to quote Burton Bigelow, 1931). Edited the *Philistine* 1895—1915) and the *Fra* (1908—1917), magazines. Best known is "A Message to Garcia," a "small homily" that has reached a sale of forty million copies. Perhaps his masterpiece is *Little Journeys,* a series of one hundred and seventy essays about his little pilgrimages to the homes of great men; begun in 1894, these little journeys continued for fourteen years.

SAMUEL McCHORD CROTHERS, 1857—1927, minister, essayist. *The Gentle Reader* (1903) introduced him widely to the American public; and his familiar, mellow essays, often synonymous with sermons, have flashes of spiritual insight: his writings, Bliss Perry once described, "mount to Paradise by the stairway of surprise," while his *Ralph Waldo Emerson: How to Know Him* (1921), J. F. Newton states, is "the best book ever written in interpretation" of the American philosopher. Volumes include: *Members of One Body* (1894), *The Pardoner's Wallet* (1905), *The Endless Life* (1905), *By the Christmas Fire* (1908), *Among Friends* (1910), *Humanly Speaking* (1912), *The Pleasures of an Absentee Landlord* (1916), *The Dame School of Experience* (1919), and *The Cheerful Giver* (1923).

ERNEST [or EVAN] THOMPSON SETON or ERNEST SETON THOMPSON, 1860—1946, English-born artist, naturalist, author. Illustrates his own books. *Wild Animals I Have Known* (1898), his most famous, has had a great influence in stirring up an interest in nature. *Lives of Game Animals* (four volumes, 1925—1928), said to be perhaps the best work in its field, won the Daniel Giraud Elliott medal. D. C. Peattie, however, has described Seton's *Great Historic Animals* (1937) as mawkish in style and lacking in sincerity; Seton, says the critic, is nature-faking. His *Lives of Game Animals,* a preliminary of which appeared in 1909 as *Life Histories of Northern Animals,* is excellent, concedes D. C. Peattie; but even in that book, generally said to be a foremost work on American mammals, Seton shows a tendency "toward a false humanizing of animals." In addition to *Trail of an Artist-Naturalist* (1940), an autobiography, Seton has published *A List of the Mammals of Manitoba* (1886), *Biography of a Grizzly* (1900), *Lives of the Hunted* (1901), *Woodcraft and Indian Lore* (1912), *Biography of an Arctic Fox* (1937), and *Buffalo Wind* (1938).

FINLEY PETER DUNNE, 1867—1936, journalist, editor, satirist-creator of "Mr. Dooley," an Irish saloonkeeper who in penetrating brogue voiced opinions of events and leaders, of selfishness and injustice. "Anger, and a warm sympathy for the underprivileged," says Franklin P. Adams, "underlay almost all the 'Dooley' sketches . . . . Most of them, on the surface, are dated; . . . ." *Mr. Dooley in Peace and War* (1898), instantly-successful essays clipped from the *Evening Journal* and the *Post*. *Mr. Dooley in the Hearts of His Countrymen* (1898), the dedication to which was called "in questionable taste" by the *Dial*. *Mr. Dooley's Philosophy* (1900), which opened with a review of Roosevelt's *Rough Riders*. *Observations of Mr. Dooley* (1906), praised by W. P. Trent, W. D. Howells, and H. W. Boynton. *Mr. Dooley Says* (1910), which contains the famous political satire on the Payne-Aldrich tariff. For Mr. Dooley at his best, see *Mr. Dooley at His Best* (edited by Elmer Ellis, 1938).

PLAYWRIGHTS

AUGUSTUS THOMAS, 1857—1934, who wrote at least threescore popular plays, including a series of earthy comedies. Adapted F. H. Burnett's *Editha's Burglar* (one-act play, 1883), later expanded into *The Burglar* (four-act play, 1889); wrote *Mrs. Leffingwell's Boots* (1905), a farce. *Alabama* (1891), *In Mizzoura* (1893), *Arizona*† (1899), *Colorado* (1902), and *Rio Grande* (1916) are "state" comedies, their background thoroughly American; *The Witching Hour* (1907), *The Harvest Moon* (1909), and *As A Man Thinks* (1911) are psychopathic studies. Perhaps his best known is *The Copperhead* (1918), a Civil War play.

DAVID BELASCO, 1859—1931, actor, producer of more than three hundred plays, realistic playwright. When twelve years old, wrote a play, *Jim Black; or, the Regulator's Revenge*. In collaboration with J. A. Herne, wrote *Hearts of Oak* (1879), a realistic adaptation of an English melodrama, *The Mariner's Compass*, by H. J. Leslie; with Henry C. De Mille, *John Delmer's Daughters; or, Duty* (1883), an unsuccessful domestic comedy; *The Wife* (1887), with a better stage history; *Lord Chumley* (1888), a domestic drama; and also *The Charity Ball* (1889) and *Men and Women* (1890). *La Belle Russe* (1881), frank in its exposition of feminine wickedness and excellent in craftsmanship; *The Stranglers of Paris* (1881), a "shocker" founded on Adolphe Belot's French novel, *Les Etrangleurs de Paris; The Girl I Left Behind Me* (with Franklin Fyles, 1893), a melodrama of suspense. *The Heart of Maryland*† (1895), a Civil War drama inspired by the poem, "Curfew Shall Not Ring To-night!" and famous for its bell-clapper scene; *Naughty Anthony* (1899), a farce; *Madame Butterfly*† (1900), a delicate, poignant, one-act dramatization of a story by J. L. Long, and made into an opera by Puccini (1906); *The Darling of the Gods* (with J. L. Long, 1902), romantic tragedy; *The Girl of the Golden West* (1905), which became the libretto of an Italian opera by Puccini (1910); *The Return of Peter Grimm* (1911; 1920), where the spiritual interest is plausible and charming; and *Van Der Decken* (1915), the theme of which is "The Flying Dutchman."

CLYDE [WILLIAM] FITCH, 1865—1909, at least thirty of whose sixty farces, society dramas, historical plays, and problem plays were original, dealt with American subjects, and reflected American social life, while the others were adaptations or dramatizations of other pieces. *Beau Brummel*† (1890), written for Richard Mansfield, was his first triumph; *The Moth and the Flame* (1898) showed the French influence in theatrical effect; *The Stubbornness of Geraldine* (1902) was successful partly because of its unusual pitching-steamer stage-set; *Captain Jinks of the Horse Marines* (1901), a pleasing farce; *The Climbers*† (1901), while its comedy is deficient in creative power, is a faithful representation of contemporaneous manners; *The Girl with the Green Eyes*† (1902), a serious study of the pathologically jealous Jinny

Tillman; *Her Own Way* (1903) and *Her Great Match* (1905), constructed expressly for Maxine Elliott, as the earlier simply-plotted, theatrically-effective *Barbara Frietchie* (1899) was for Julia Marlowe, and *Nathan Hale* (1899) was for Nat Goodwin; *The Truth*† (1906), its every character distinct, and containing, in the opinion of W. L. Phelps, incomparably the best last act Fitch ever wrote; and *The City*† (1909), among his most virile studies. One of the daring plays of its time is *Sappho* (1900), a dramatization of Alphonse Daudet's romance: William Winter anathematized it as "dark, dull and stupid," dirty in character and pernicious in quality, a "reeking compost of filth and folly that the crude and frivolous Clyde Fitch has dug out of it [the novel] with which to mire the stage."

JOSEPHINE PRESTON PEABODY, 1874—1922, poet, dramatist. POETRY VOLUMES: *The Wayfarers*† (1898), her first book of light lyric verse; *The Singing Leaves* (1903); *The Book of the Little Past*† (1908); *The Singing Man*† (1911); *Collected Poems* (1927). PLAYS: *Fortune and Men's Eyes* (1900), a one-act drama about Shakespeare and founded on that poet's sonnets; *Marlowe* (1901), five-act poetic drama; *The Wings* (1905), one-act play introducing Cerdic and King Aelfric of seventh-century Northumbria; *The Piper* (1909; 1910), four-act drama whose charm veneered some structural defects: this depiction of the struggle between Christianity and the power of the Devil was awarded the first prize in the Stratford-on-Avon competition, and was produced in America as well as in England; *The Wolf of Gubbio* (1913), a three-act drama about St. Francis of Assisi, Brother Leo, and Brother Juniper, depicting the conflict between love and greed as effectively as *The Piper* does between Christianity and the Devil; *The Portrait of Mrs. W.* (1922), biographical prose play about Mary Wollstonecraft and William Godwin, with such other figures as Southey, Mrs. Siddons, young Shelley, and Mrs. Symes. INDIVIDUAL POEMS: "The Source," "I Shall Arise," "Stay at Home," "The House of the Road," "Alms," "Alison's Mother to the Brook," "Woman-Vigil," "Cradle Song," "To a Dog."

YESTERDAY AND TODAY

CHAPTER XIV

REPRESENTATIVE AUTHORS

HISTORICAL BACKGROUND

1914: Beginning of First World War. *1917:* Entrance of United States in First World War. *1918:* The Armistice. *1919:* The Treaty of Versailles. *1919:* Ratification of Prohibition Amendment. *1920:* Formation of League of Nations. *1920:* Woman Suffrage Amendment. *1921:* Restriction of Immigration. *1927:* Lindbergh's Non-Stop Flight to Paris. *1929:* Depression and Panic. *1930:* Hawley-Smoot Tariff. *1933:* Creation of AAA and NRA. *1935:* Social Security Act. *1935:* National Labor Relations Act. *1938:* Wages and Hours Act. *1940:* National Conscription Act. *1941:* Lend-Lease Bill. *1941:* Pearl Harbor. *1945:* Release of Atomic Energy. *1945:* Surrender of Germany and Japan. *1945:* San Francisco Conference. *1945:* First Truman Administration. *1947:* Truman Doctrine. *1949:* North Atlantic Pact. *1949:* Second Truman Administration. *1953—:* Eisenhower Administration.

GENERAL VIEW OF THE LITERATURE[1]

After the First World War, American literature reflected the swiftly changing economic, cultural, and social conditions. An era of prosperity followed a brief period of postwar disillusionment. Then came nationalistic isolationism, social conservatism, and popular interest in anything big, exciting, spectacular, from crime waves to violent industrial strikes. This relatively prosperous era of superficial values, however, saw the development of the largest number of gifted writers in any decade of the twentieth century: for example, Sinclair Lewis, whose realistic novels of social analysis satirized American life; Willa Cather, with her conservative, sincere, dignified portraiture of individual American characters; F. Scott Fitzgerald, who drew sharp pictures of rebellious, maladjusted personalities; William Faulkner, dissector of the psychological peculiarities and disintegrating characters of individuals and families; Thornton Wilder, clarifier of modern mores by reference to the past; Ernest Hemingway, realistic, skeptical, objective, deliberately tough in attitude; John Dos Passos, staccato critic of the capitalistic way of life; and many others.

---

1 For the most comprehensive and reliable survey and bio-bibliography of today's writers, consult F. B. Millett, *Contemporary American Authors* (1940). Useful is S. J. Kunitz and Howard Haycraft, *Twentieth Century Authors* (1942).

The decade 1930 to 1939 witnessed a complete reversal in the social climate and creative scene: deep economic depression, rapid social reform, disillusion, pessimism. Proletarian literature rose and then declined. American authors sought deeper, serious, lasting values. Eloquent works of protest were created by Sinclair Lewis, John Steinbeck, Dos Passos, James T. Farrell, Waldo Frank, Erskine Caldwell, Maxwell Anderson, Elmer Rice, Clifford Odets, and Sidney Kingsley.

Looking backward over the first half of this century one sees that American literature acquired distinctive character in several directions: (a) in romantic works about social realities, such as big business, racketeering and crime, and culture on a mass scale; (b) in realistic, technically skillful portrayals of individuals and groups; (c) in experimental works stressing frank vignettes about the American scene, without much attention to form. The two world wars brought into sharpest relief the widespread tension arising from a mixture of optimism and fear, loneliness and "one-worldness"; the writers seemed to be searching for something more fundamental than scientific or material progress and its concomitant commercialization of culture. During the Second World War, Hemingway, Steinbeck, and journalists such as John Hersey and Ernie Pyle contributed excellent graphic reporting on the feelings and experiences of the common soldier at the front. The postwar years have seen the continuance of uncertainty and tension, at home and abroad, stimulating an intensified search for deeper values and basic ideals for the guidance of American life.

SHORT-STORY WRITERS AND NOVELISTS

Gertrude [Franklin Horn] Atherton, 1857—1948, short-story writer, novelist. NOVELS[2]: *The Doomswoman* (1892), *The Californians* (1898), *The Conqueror*† (1902), *Rezánov* (1906), *Julia France and Her Times* (1912), *The Sisters-in-Law* (1921), *Black Oxen*† (1923), *The Immortal Marriage* (1927), *The Sophisticates*

---

2 To conserve space, the classifications of authors have been made as flexible as they are broad. Often, severer grouping is possible, and, for certain purposes, may be desirable. For example, the writings of Stewart Edward White can be separated as follows: FICTION OF THE FAR WEST: *The Claim Jumpers* (1901), *The Westerners* (1901), *Blazed Trail Stories* (1904), *Arizona Nights* (1907), *The Killers* (1920), *The Long Rifle* (1932). FICTION OF THE FAR NORTH: *Conjuror's House* (1903), *The Silent Places* (1904), *Skookum Chuck* (1925), *Secret Harbour* (1926), *Pole Star* (in collaboration, 1935), *Wild Geese Calling* (1940). FICTION OF THE LUMBER-WOODS: *The Blazed Trail* (1902), *The Riverman* (1908), *The Rules of the Game* (1913) — and, again, *Blazed Trail Stories* (1904). FICTION OF CALIFORNIA: *Gold* (1913), *The Gray Dawn* (1915), *The Rose Dawn* (1920), *On Tiptoe* (1922), *Ranchero* (1933), *Folded Hills* (1934). FICTION OF AFRICA: *The Leopard Woman* (1916), *Simba* (1918), *Back of Beyond* (1927). FICTION OF MYSTERY: *The Mystery* (in collaboration, 1907), *The Sign at Six* (1912). THE OUT-OF-DOORS AND ADVENTURE: *The Mountains* (1904), *The Pass* (1906), *Camp and Trail* (1907), *The Cabin* (1911), *The Land of Footprints* (1912), *African Campfires* (1913), *The Rediscovered Country* (1915), *Lions in the Path* (1926). JUVENILE: *The Magic Forest* (1903), *The Adventures of Bobby Orde* (1911). HISTORICAL AND PHILOSOPHICAL WORKS: *The Forty-Niners* (1918), *Daniel Boone: Wilderness Scout* (1922), *Credo* (1925), *Why Be a Mud Turtle* (1928), *Dog Days* (1930), *Old California: In Picture and Story* (1937), *Betty Book* (1937), *Across the Unknown* (in collaboration, 1939), *The Unobstructed Universe* (1940), *The Road I Know* (1942), *The Stars Are Still There* (1946), *Job of Living* (1948).

(1931), *The House of Lee* (1940), *Horn of Life* (1942). AUTOBIOGRAPHY: *Adventures of a Novelist* (1932). HISTORY: *Golden Gate Country*† (1945). BIOGRAPHY: *My San Francisco: A Wayward Biography*† (1946).

Owen Wister, 1860—1938, humorist, poet, biographer, short-story writer, novelist. BIOGRAPHY: *Ulysses S. Grant* (1900), *The Seven Ages of Washington* (1907), *Roosevelt*† (1930). SHORT STORIES: *Lin McLean* (1897), *The Jimmyjohn Boss* (1900), *Philosophy 4*† (1903), *When West Was West* (1928). NOVELS: *The Virginian*† (1902), *Lady Baltimore* (1906).

Edith [Newbold Jones] Wharton, 1862—1937, short-story writer, novelist. POEMS: *Artemis to Actaeon* (1909), *Twelve Poems* (1926). AUTOBIOGRAPHY: *A Backward Glance* (1934). LITERARY CRITICISM: *The Writing of Fiction* (1925). TRAVEL: *Italian Backgrounds* (1905), *A Motor-Flight through France* (1908), *In Morocco* (1920). SHORT STORIES: *The Greater Inclination* (1899), *Crucial Instances* (1901), *The Descent of Man* (1904), *The Hermit and the Wild Woman* (1908), *Tales of Men and Ghosts* (1910), *Xingu*† (1916), *Here and Beyond* (1926), *Certain People* (1930), *Human Nature* (1933), *The World Over* (1936), *Ghosts* (1937). NOVELS: *The Touchstone* (1900), *The Valley of Decision* (two volumes, 1902), *Sanctuary* (1903), *The House of Mirth*† (1905), *The Fruit of the Tree* (1907), *Madame de Treymes* (1907), *Ethan Frome*† (1911), *The Reef* (1912), *The Custom of the Country* (1913), *Summer* (1917), *The Marne* (1918), *The Age of Innocence*† (1920), *The Glimpses of the Moon* (1922), *A Son at the Front* (1923), *False Dawn* (1924), *New Year's Day* (1924), *The Old Maid* (1924), *The Spark* (1924), *The Mother's Recompense* (1925), *Twilight Sleep* (1927), *The Children* (1928), *Hudson River Bracketed* (1929), *The Gods Arrive* (1932), *The Buccaneers* (unfinished, 1938). MISCELLANEOUS: *The Decoration of Houses* (in collaboration, 1904), *Fighting France, from Dunkerque to Belfort* (1915), *Best Short Stories* (1958).

William Sydney Porter, better known by his pseudonym **O. Henry,** 1867—1910, short-story writer. SHORT STORIES: *Cabbages and Kings* (1904), *The Four Million*† (1906), *The Trimmed Lamp* (1907), *Heart of the West* (1907), *The Voice of the City*† (1908), *The Gentle Grafter* (1908), *Roads of Destiny* (1909), *Options*† (1909), *Strictly Business* (1910), *Whirligigs* (1910). POSTHUMOUSLY PUBLISHED: *Sixes and Sevens* (1911), *The Gift of the Wise Men* (1911), *Rolling Stones* (1912), *Waifs and Strays* (1917), *O. Henryana* (poetry and short stories, 1920), *Letters to Lithopolis from O. Henry to Mabel Wagnalls* (1922), *Postscripts* (1923), *O. Henry Encore* (1939). DRAMATIZATIONS: *Lo* (with F. P. Adams, 1909), *The World and the Door* (*c.* 1909), *Alias Jimmy Valentine* (dramatization of "A Retrieved Reformation" by Paul Armstrong, 1910), *The Third Ingredient* (by Catherine Robertson, 1912), *The Double-Dyed Deceiver* (1913), *Roads of Destiny* (1918), *The Memento* (photoplay, 1920), *Cabbages and Kings* (photoplay, 1922), *A Caballero's Way* (photoplay, 1929). INDIVIDUAL STORIES: "A Municipal Report," "The Church with an Overshot Wheel," "The Memento," "The Gift of the Magi," "The Last Leaf," "The Furnished Room," "The Guardian of the Accolade," "Thimble, Thimble," "A Retrieved Reformation," "An Unfinished Story," "The Skylight Room," "A Lickpenny Lover," "The Double-Dyed Deceiver," "A Service of Love," "Mammon and the Archer," "The Pendulum," "The Enchanted Kiss," "The Third Ingredient," "The Ransom of Red Chief," "The Shamrock and the Palm," "Let Me Feel Your Pulse," "Two Renegades." COMPLETE WORKS (1953).

Robert Herrick, 1868—1938, editor, novelist, educator. SHORT STORIES: *Literary Love-Letters* (1896), *The Master of the Inn*† (1908). NOVELS: *The Man Who Wins* (1897), *The Gospel of Freedom* (1898), *The Web of Life* (1900), *The Real World* (1901), *The Common Lot* (1904), *The Memoirs of an American Citizen*† (1905), *Together* (1908), *A Life for a Life* (1910), *The Healer* (1911), *His Great Adventure* (1913), *One Woman's Life* (1913), *Clark's Field*† (1914), *Homely Lilla* (1923), *Waste* (1924), *Chimes* (1926), *The End of Desire* (1932), *Sometime* (1933).

[Newton] Booth Tarkington, 1869—1946, illustrator, humorist, literary critic, essayist, playwright, short-story writer, novelist. REMINISCENCES: *The World Does Move* (1928). LETTERS: *Your Amiable Uncle: Letters to His Nephews* (1949).

PLAYS: *Monsieur Beaucaire* (in collaboration with E. G. Sutherland, 1901), "Cameo Kirby" (*c.* 1907), *The Man from Home*† (in collaboration with H. L. Wilson, 1908), *The Gibson Upright* (in collaboration, 1919), *Clarence* (1921), *Mister Antonio* (1935). NOVELS: *The Gentlemen from Indiana*† (1899), *Monsieur Beaucaire*† (1900), *The Conquest of Canaan* (1905), *Penrod*† (1914), *Penrod and Sam* (1916), *Seventeen* (1916), *Alice Adams*† (1921), *Gentle Julia* (1922), *Women* (1925), *Growth* (a trilogy, 1927: *The Magnificent Ambersons,* 1918; *The Turmoil,* 1915; *National Avenue* [*The Midlander,* 1923]), *The Plutocrat* (1927), *Penrod Jashber* (1929), *Presenting Lily Mars* (1933), *Little Orvie* (1934), *Kate Fennigate* (1943), *Image of Josephine* (1945), *Show Piece* (unfinished, 1947). OTHER: *On Plays, Playwrights and Playgoers* (1959).

Winston Churchill, 1871—1947, short-story writer, playwright, novelist. PLAY: *Dr. Jonathan* (1919). RELIGION: *The Unchartered Way* (1940). NOVELS: *The Celebrity* (1898), *Richard Carvel*† (1899), *The Crisis*† (1901), *The Crossing*† (1904), *Coniston* (1906), *Mr. Crewe's Career* (1908), *A Modern Chronicle* (1910), *The Inside of the Cup*† (1913), *A Far Country* (1915), *The Dwelling-Place of Light* (1917).

Theodore [Herman Albert] Dreiser, 1871—1945, poet, playwright, essayist, novelist. POETRY: *Moods, Cadenced and Declaimed* (1926). PLAYS: *Plays of the Natural and the Supernatural* (1916), *The Hand of the Potter* (1918). DESCRIPTION AND TRAVEL: *The Color of a Great City* (1923), *My City* (1929). POLITICAL AND SOCIAL PHILOSOPHY: *Hey Rub-a-Dub* (1920), *Dreiser Looks at Russia* (1928), *Tragic America* (*c.* 1931), *The Living Thoughts of Thoreau* (edited, 1939), *Concerning Dives and Lazarus* (1940), *America Is Worth Saving* (1941). AUTOBIOGRAPHY: *A Traveler at Forty* (1913), *A Hoosier Holiday* (1916), *A Book about Myself* (1922), *Dawn* (1931). SHORT STORIES: *Free* (1918), *Twelve Men* (1919), *Chains* (1927), *A Gallery of Women* (two volumes, 1929). NOVELS: *Sister Carrie* (1900), *Jennie Gerhardt*† (1911), *The Financier* (1912), *The Titan* (1914), *The "Genius"*† (1915), *An American Tragedy*† (two volumes, 1925), *The Bulwark* (1946), *The Stoic* (1947). LETTERS (1959).

Stewart Edward White, 1873—1946, psychical researcher, writer of juvenile works, historian, journalizer of dog stories, short-story writer, novelist. NOVELS: *The Claim Jumpers* (1901), *The Westerners* (1901), *The Blazed Trail*† (1902), *The Rules of the Game* (1910), *The Story of California* (trilogy, 1927: *Gold,* 1913; *The Gray Dawn,* 1915; *The Rose Dawn,* 1920), *The Long Rifle* (1932), *Ranchero* (1933), *Wild Geese Calling* (1940). TRAVEL: *The Pass* (1906), *The Land of Footprints* (1912), *African Camp Fires* (1913), *Lions in the Path* (1926). SPIRITUALISM: *The Unobstructed Universe* (1940), *The Road I Know* (1942), *The Stars Are Still There*† (1946), *Job of Living*† (1948). MISCELLANEOUS: *The Cabin* (the strenuous life, 1911), *The Forty-Niners* (history, 1918), *Daniel Boone* (biography, 1922). (See also page 269, footnote 2.)

Zona Gale, 1874—1938, poet, short-story writer, novelist. PLAYS: *Miss Lulu Bett*† (1921), *Mister Pitt* (1924; 1925). POEMS: *The Secret Way* (1921). REMINISCENCES: *When I Was a Little Girl* (1913), *Portage, Wisconsin, and Other Essays* (1928). SHORT STORIES: *Friendship Village* (1908), *Neighborhood Stories* (1908), *Peace in Friendship Village* (1919), *Yellow Gentians and Blue* (1927), *Bridal Pond* (1930), *Old-Fashioned Tales* (1933). NOVELS: *Romance Island* (1906), *Birth* (1918), *Miss Lulu Bett*† (1920), *Faint Perfume* (1923), *Preface to a Life* (1926), *Borgia* (1929), *Papa La Fleur* (1933).

Ellen [Anderson Gholson] Glasgow, 1874—1945, novelist. ESSAYS: *A Certain Measure*† (1943). POETRY: *The Freeman and Other Poems* (1902). SHORT STORIES: *The Shadowy Third* (1923). NOVELS: *The Descendant* (1897), *The Voice of the People* (1900), *The Battle-Ground* (1902), *The Deliverance* (1904), *The Wheel of Life* (1906), *The Ancient Law* (1908), *The Romance of a Plain Man* (1909), *The Miller of Old Church* (1911), *Virginia* (1913), *Life and Gabriella* (1916), *The Builders* (1919), *One Man in His Time* (1922), *Barren Ground*† (1925), *The Romantic Comedians*† (1926), *They Stooped to Folly* (1929), *The Sheltered Life* (1932), *Vein of Iron* (1935), *In This Our Life*† (1941). AUTOBIOGRAPHY: *The Woman Within* (1954).

Gertrude Stein, 1874—1946, experimentalist, short-story writer. AUTOBIOGRAPHY: *The Autobiography of Alice B. Toklas*† (1933). SHORT STORIES: *Three Lives: Stories of the Good Anna, Melanctha, and the Gentle Lena*† (1909). OTHER WRITINGS: *Four Saints in Three Acts*† (opera, 1934), *The World . . . Is Round* (children's book, 1939), *Paris France* (impressions, 1940), *What Are Masterpieces* (lectures, 1940), *Ida* (novel, 1941), *Wars I Have Seen*† (1945), *Brewsie and Willie*† (1946), *Four in America* (essays, 1947), *First Reader and Three Plays*† (1948), *Last Operas and Plays* (edited by Carl Van Vetchen, 1949).

O[le] E[dvart] Rölvaag, 1876—1931, Norwegian-American novelist. TRANSLATED FROM THE NORWEGIAN: *Giants in the Earth*† (1927), *Peder Victorious*† (1929), *Pure Gold* (1930), *Their Fathers' God*† (1931), *The Boat of Longing* (1933).

Sherwood Anderson, 1876—1941, essayist, playwright, short-story writer, novelist. SHORT-STORY COLLECTIONS: *Winesburg, Ohio*† (1919), *The Triumph of the Egg* (1921), *Horses and Men* (1923), *Death in the Woods* (1933). NOVELS: *Windy McPherson's Son* (1916), *Marching Men* (1917), *Poor White*† (1920), *Many Marriages* (1923), *Dark Laughter*† (1925), *Beyond Desire* (1932), *Kit Brandon* (1936). ESSAYS AND STUDIES: *The Modern Writer* (1925), *Sherwood Anderson's Notebook* (1926), *Hello Towns!* (1928), *Nearer the Grass Roots* (1929), *Perhaps Women* (1931), *Puzzled America* (1935), *A Writer's Conception of Realism* (1939), *Home Town* (1940). POETRY: *Mid-American Chants* (1918), *A New Testament* (1927). PLAYS: *Winesburg and Others* (1937), *Above Suspicion* (1941). AUTOBIOGRAPHY: *A Story-Teller's Story*† (1924), *Tar: A Midwest Childhood* (1926), *Sherwood Anderson's Memoirs*† (1942). INDIVIDUAL POEMS: "Evening Song," "Chicago," "The Lame One," "American Spring Song," "Song of Industrial America." MISCELLANY: *Sherwood Anderson Reader* (1947), *Letters* (1953).

Willa [Sibert] Cather, 1874?—1947, poet, short-story writer, essayist. POETRY: *April Twilights* (1903). ESSAYS: *Not under Forty* (1936), *On Writing: Critical Studies on Writing as an Art*† (essays and letters, with a foreword by Stephen Tennant, 1949). SHORT STORIES: *The Troll Garden* (1905), *Youth and the Bright Medusa* (1920), *Obscure Destinies* (1932), *The Old Beauty and Others* (1948). NOVELS: *Alexander's Bridge* (1912), *O Pioneers!*† (1913), *The Song of the Lark* (1915), *My Antonia*† (1918), *One of Ours* (1922), *A Lost Lady*† (1923), *The Professor's House* (1925), *My Mortal Enemy* (1926), *Death Comes for the Archbishop*† (1927), *Shadows on the Rock* (1931), *Lucy Gayheart* (1935), *Sapphira and The Slave Girl* (1940). INDIVIDUAL POEMS: "The Palatine," "In Media Vita," "Spanish Johnny," "In Rose Time," "Poppies in Ludlow Castle." OTHER: *Writings From* (her) *Campus Years* (1950).

Upton [Beall] Sinclair, 1878— , writer of children's books, of studies in health, in telepathy, in religion, of plays and short stories, of political and social studies, of novels. AUTOBIOGRAPHY: *American Outpost* (1932). STUDIES: *The Profits of Religion* (1918), *The Brass Check*† (1919), *The Goose-Step: A Study of American Education* (1923), *The Goslings* (1924), *Mammonart*† (1925), *I, Governor of California, and How I Ended Poverty: A True Story of the Future* (1933), *Upton Sinclair Presents William Fox* (1933), *Personal Jesus; Portrait and Interpretation* (1952). NOVELS: *King Midas* (1901), *The Journal of Arthur Stirling* (1903), *Manassas* (1904), *The Jungle*† (1906), *The Metropolis* (1908), *King Coal* (1917), *Jimmie Higgins* (1919), *100%, the Story of a Patriot* (1920), *Oil!* (1927), *Boston*† (two volumes, 1928), *Mountain City* (1930), *Roman Holiday* (1931), *The Flivver King* (1937), *World's End* (1940), *Between Two Worlds* (1941), *Dragon's Teeth*† (1942), *Dragon Harvest* (1945), *World to Win* (1946), *Presidential Mission* (1947), *One Clear Call* (1948), *O Shepherd, Speak!* (1949), *Another Pamela* (1950), *The Enemy Had It Too* (1950), *The Return of Lanny Budd* (1953).

[James] Branch Cabell, 1879–1958, poet, short-story writer, critic, essayist, novelist. HISTORY: *The St. Johns*† (in collaboration, 1943). POETRY: *From the Hidden Way* (1916), *Sonnets from Antan* (1929). SHORT STORIES: *The Line of Love* (1905), *Gallantry* (1907), *Chivalry* (1909), *The Certain Hour* (1916), *The Music from Behind the Moon* (1926), *The White Robe* (1928). LITERARY CRITICISM: *Joseph Hergesheimer* (1921), *The Lineage of Lichfield* (1922), *Some of Us*

(1930), *Preface to the Past* (1936). ESSAYS: *Beyond Life* (1919), *Straws and Prayer-Books* (1924), *Special Delivery* (1933), *Ladies and Gentlemen* (1934), *Let Me Lie* (1947). AUTOBIOGRAPHY: *These Restless Heads* (1932). NOVELS: *The Eagle's Shadow* (1904), *The Cords of Vanity* (1909), *The Soul of Melicent* (1913: its later edition is called *Domnei*, 1920), *The Rivet in Grandfather's Neck* (1915), *The Cream of the Jest* (1917), *Jurgen*† (1919), *Figures of Earth*† (1921), *The High Place* (1923), *The Silver Stallion* (1926), *Something about Eve* (1927), *The Way of Ecben* (1929), *Smirt* (1934), *Smith* (1935), *Smire* (1937), *The King Was in His Counting-House* (1938), *Hamlet Had an Uncle* (1940), *The First Gentleman of America* (1942), *There Were Two Pirates*† (1946), *Devil's Own Dear Son* (1949). OTHER AUTOBIOGRAPHY: *Quiet, Please* (1952), *As I Remember It* (1955).

Ernest Poole, 1880—1950, novelist. SHORT STORIES: *The Little Dark Man* (1925). STUDIES: *"The Dark People"* (1918), *The Village* (1918), *Nurses on Horseback* (1932), *Great White Hills of New Hampshire*† (1946). AUTOBIOGRAPHY: *The Bridge* (1940). BIOGRAPHY: *Giants Gone* (1943). NOVELS: *The Voice of the Street* (1906), *The Harbor*† (1915), *His Family* (1917), *His Second Wife* (1918), *Blind* (1920), *Beggars' Gold* (1921), *Millions* (1922), *Danger* (1923), *The Avalanche* (1924), *The Hunter's Moon* (1925), *With Eastern Eyes* (1926), *Silent Storms* (1927), *The Car of Croesus* (1930), *The Destroyer* (1931), *Great Winds* (1933), *One of Us* (1934), *Nancy Flyer: A Stagecoach Epic*† (1949).

Joseph Hergesheimer, 1880—1954, novelist. AUTOBIOGRAPHICAL: *The Presbyterian Child* (1923), *From an Old House* (1925). SHORT STORIES: *The Happy End* (1919), *Quiet Cities* (1928). NOVELS: *The Lay Anthony* (1914), *Mountain Blood* (1915), *The Three Black Pennys*† (1917), *Gold and Iron* (three novelettes, 1918), *Java Head*† (1919), *Linda Condon* (1919), *The Bright Shawl* (1922), *Cytherea* (1922), *Balisand* (1924), *Tampico* (1926), *Swords and Roses* (1929), *The Party Dress* (1930), *The Limestone Tree* (1931), *The Foolscap Rose* (1934). MISCELLANEOUS: *San Cristóbal de la Habana* (sketches, 1920), *Sheridan* (biography, 1931).

Julia [Mood] Peterkin, 1880—1961, novelist. NOVELS: *Black April* (1927), *Scarlet Sister Mary*† (1928), *Bright Skin* (1932). SHORT STORIES: *Green Thursday* (1924). NEGRO STUDY: *Roll, Jordan, Roll* (in collaboration with Doris Ulmann, 1933).

Carl Van Vechten, 1880— , music critic, novelist. NOVELS: *Peter Whiffle*† (1922), *The Blind Bow-Boy* (1923), *The Tattooed Countess* (1924), *Nigger Heaven* (1926), *Spider Boy* (1928), *Parties* (1930). MISCELLANEOUS: *The Tiger in the House* (on cats, 1920), *Excavations* (on music, 1926), *Sacred and Profane Memories* (autobiographical essays, 1932).

[Harry] Sinclair Lewis, 1885—1951, critic, playwright, novelist. SHORT STORIES: *Selected Short Stories* (1935). PLAYS: *Dodsworth* (dramatized by Sidney Howard, 1934), *Jayhawker* (in collaboration with Lloyd Lewis, 1935), *It Can't Happen Here* (in collaboration with J. C. Moffit, 1936), *Arrowsmith* (dramatized by Orson Welles, 1939). NOVELS: *Our Mr. Wren* (1914), *The Trail of the Hawk* (1915), *The Innocents* (1917), *The Job* (1917), *Main Street*† (1920), *Babbitt*† (1922), *Arrowsmith*† (1925), *Elmer Gantry* (1927), *The Man Who Knew Coolidge* (1928), *Dodsworth*† (1929), *Ann Vickers* (1933), *Work of Art* (1934), *It Can't Happen Here* (1935), *The Prodigal Parents* (1938), *Bethel Merriday* (1940), *Gideon Planish*† (1943), *Cass Timberlane* (1945), *Kingsblood Royal*† (1947), *God-Seeker* (1949), *Our Mr. Wrenn* (1951), *World So Wide* (1951). LETTERS (1952).

Elizabeth Madox Roberts, 1886—1941, short-story writer, poet, novelist. SHORT STORIES: *The Haunted Mirror* (1932) *Not by Strange Gods* (1941). POEMS: *In the Great Steep's Garden* (1915), *Under the Tree* (1922), *Song in the Meadow* (1940). NOVELS: *The Time of Man*† (1926), *My Heart and My Flesh*†

(1927), *Jingling in the Wind* (1928), *The Great Meadow* (1930), *A Buried Treasure* (1931), *He Sent Forth a Raven* (1935), *Black Is My Truelove's Hair* (1938). INDIVIDUAL POEMS: "A Ballet Song of Mary," "Child Asleep," "Water Noises," "The Sky," "The Pilaster," "Woodcock of the Ivory Beak," "Shells in Rocks."

Wilbur Daniel Steele, 1886— , short-story writer, novelist. PLAYS: *The Terrible Woman* (1925), *Post Road* (in collaboration, 1935), *How Beautiful with Shoes* (in collaboration, 1935). NOVELS: *Storm* (1914), *Isles of the Blest* (1924), *Taboo* (1925), *Meat* (1928), *Sound of Rowlocks* (1938), *That Girl from Memphis*† (1945). SHORT STORIES: *Land's End* (1918), *The Shame Dance* (1923), *Urkey Island*† (1926), *The Man Who Saw through Heaven* (1927), *Tower of Sand* (1929), *Best Stories* (collection, 1946), *Full Cargo* (short stories, 1951).

Mary Ellen Chase, 1887— , textbook writer, essayist, novelist. NOVELS: *Uplands* (1927), *Mary Peters*† (1934), *Silas Crockett*† (1935), *Dawn in Lyonesse* (1938), *Windswept*† (1941). MISCELLANEOUS: *The Girl from the Big Horn Country* (juvenile literature, 1916), *The Golden Asse and Other Essays* (1929), *Constructive Theme Writing for College Freshmen* (1929), *A Goodly Heritage* (autobiography, 1932), *The Bible and the Common Reader*† (1944), *Jonathan Fisher*† (a biography, 1948), *Plum Tree*† (tale, 1949), *Recipe for a Magic Childhood* (1951), *Readings From the Bible* (1952), *The White Gate* (1954), *Sailing The Seven Seas* (1958).

Floyd Dell, 1887— , dramatist, essayist, novelist. BIOGRAPHY: *Upton Sinclair* (1927). AUTOBIOGRAPHY: *Homecoming* (1933). PLAYS: *The Angel Intrudes* (1918), *Little Accident* (1928). STUDIES: *Were You Ever a Child?* (1919), *Intellectual Vagabondage* (1926), *The Outline of Marriage* (1926-1927), *Love in the Machine Age* (1930). NOVELS: *Moon-Calf*† (1920), *The Briary-Bush* (1921), *Janet March* (1923), *Runaway* (1923), *An Old Man's Folly* (1926), *An Unmarried Father* (1927), *Love without Money* (1931), *Diana Stair* (1932).

Edna Ferber, 1887— , short-story writer, playwright, novelist. SHORT STORIES: *Buttered Side Down* (1912), *They Brought Their Women* (1933), *One Basket*† (1947). PLAYS: *$1200 a Year* (with Newman Levy, 1920), *The Eldest* (1925). See also George S. Kaufman, page 284. NOVELS: *Dawn O'Hara, the Girl Who Laughed* (1911), *So Big*† (1924), *Show Boat*† (1926), *Cimarron* (1930), *Saratoga Trunk*† (1941), *Great Son* (1945), *Giant*† (1952), *Ice Palace* (1958).

James Boyd, 1888—1944, novelist. PLAY: *One More Free Man* (1941). NOVELS: *Drums*† (1925), *Marching On* (1927), *Long Hunt* (1930), *Roll River* (1935), *Bitter Creek* (1939). POETRY: *Eighteen Poems* (1944).

Christopher [Darlington] Morley, 1890—1957, columnist, humorist, essayist, poet, novelist. ESSAYS: *Shandygaff* (1918), *History of an Autumn* (1938). POETRY: *The Rocking Horse* (1919), *Chimneysmoke* (1921), *Parson's Pleasure* (1923), *Mandarin in Manhattan* (1933), *Middle Kingdom: Poems, 1929-1944*† (1944), *Spirit Level and Other Poems* (1946), *Old Mandarin*† (1947). NOVELS: *Parnassus on Wheels* (1917), *The Haunted Bookshop* (1919), *Where the Blue Begins* (1922), *Thunder on the Left* (1925), *Human Being* (1932), *Swiss Family Manhattan* (1932), *The Trojan Horse* (1937), *Kitty Foyle* (1939), *Murder with a Difference*† (three crime novels, 1946), *Man Who Made Friends with Himself*† (1949). REMINISCENCES: *John Mistletoe* (1931), *Thorofare* (1942). SHORT STORIES: *Tales from a Rolltop Desk* (1921). TRAVEL: *Hasta la Vista* (1935). OMNIBUS VOLUME: *Morley's Variety* (1944). INDIVIDUAL POEMS: "In an Auction Room," "Parsons' Pleasure," "Of a Child That Had Fever," "The Dogwood Tree," "At a Window Sill," "Two Sonnets to Themselves."

Conrad Richter, 1890— , novelist. NOVELS: *The Sea of Grass* (1937), Trilogy: *The Trees* (1940), *The Fields* (1946), *The Town* (1950, Pulitzer Prize).

Pearl S[ydenstricker] Buck, 1892— , translator, pamphleteer, biographer, short-story writer, novelist, winner of Nobel Prize for Literature for 1938. NOVELS: *The Good Earth*† (1931), *Sons* (1932), *A House Divided* (1935), *Dragon Seed*† (1942), *The Promise*† (sequel, 1943), *Pavilion of Women* (1946), *Peony* (1948), *Kinfolk*† (1949), *God's Men* (1951), *Hidden Flower* (1952), *Come, My Beloved* (1953), *Letter From Peking* (1957). OTHER: *Of Men and Women*† (social conditions, 1941), *Today and Forever* (stories of China, 1941), *American Unity and Asia*† (1942), *Chinese Children Next Door*† (for children, 1942), *Water-Buffalo Children*† (stories of her childhood, 1943), *What America Means to Me*† (1943), *China in Black and White*† (woodcuts, 1945), *Yu Lan, Flying Boy of China*† (1945), *Talk about Russia*† (1945), *Tell the People: Talks about the Mass Education Movement* (1945), *How It Happens: Talk about the German People*, 1914-1933 (1947), *The Big Wave*† (for children, 1948), *American Argument*† (1949), *My Several Worlds* (1954).

Ruth Suckow, 1892— , short-story writer, novelist. SHORT STORIES: *Iowa Interiors*† (1926), *Children and Older People* (1931), *Some Others and Myself* (1952). NOVELS: *Country People* (1924), *The Odyssey of a Nice Girl* (1925), *The Bonney Family* (1928), *Cora* (1929), *The Kramer Girls* (1930), *The Folks*† (1934). OMNIBUS VOLUMES: *Carry-Over* (1936), *New Hope* (1941).

John Phillips Marquand, 1893—1960, novelist. NOVELS: *The Late George Apley*† (1937, Pulitzer Prize), *Wickford Point* (1939), *H. M. Pulham Esquire*† (1941), *So Little Time* (1943), *Point of No Return* (1949), *Melville Goodwin, U.S.A.* (1951), *Sincerely, Willis Wayde* (1955), *Women and Thomas Harrow* (1958).

Evelyn [D.] Scott, 1893— , poet, novelist. PLAY: *Love* (1920). SHORT STORIES: *Ideals* (1927). POEMS: *Precipitations* (1920), *The Winter Alone* (1930). AUTOBIOGRAPHY: *Escapade* (1923), *Background in Tennessee* (1937). NOVELS: *The Narrow House* (1921), *Narcissus* (1922), *The Golden Door* (1925), *Migrations* (1927), *The Wave*† (1929), *Blue Rum* (pseudonymously, 1930), *A Calendar of Sin* (two volumes, 1931), *Eva Gay* (1933), *Breathe upon These Slain* (1934), *Bread and a Sword* (1937), *Shadow of the Hawk* (1941).

Rachel [Lyman] Field, 1894—1942, illustrator, adapter, biographer, poet, writer of children's books and verses, novelist. ADAPTATIONS AND ARRANGEMENTS: *The White Cat and Other Old French Fairy Tales by Mme. La Comtesse D'Auloy* (1928), *People from Dickens* (1935). BIOGRAPHY: *God's Pocket* (1934). CHILDREN'S VERSES: *The Pointed People* (1924), *Christmas Time*† (1941). PLAY: *Rise Up, Jennie Smith*† (1918). STORY OF CHRISTMAS EVE: *All Through the Night*† (1940). NOVELS: *Time Out of Mind* (1935), *All This, and Heaven Too*† (1938), *And Now Tomorrow*† (1942).

Robert [Gruntal] Nathan, 1894— , poet, novelist. POETRY: *Youth Grows Old* (1922), *A Cedar Box* (1929), *A Winter Tide* (1940), *Dunkirk: A Ballad* (1942), *Morning in Iowa*† (1944), *Darkening Meadows* (1945), *Green Leaf* (1950), *The Married Man* (1962). NOVELS: *Peter Kindred* (1919), *Autumn* (1921), *The Puppet Master* (1923), *Jonah* (1925), *One More Spring*† (1933), *Road of Ages*† (1935), *The Barley Fields*† (1938: *The Fiddler in Barley*, 1926; *The Woodcutter's House*, 1927; *The Bishop's Wife*, 1928; *There Is Another Heaven*, 1929; *The Orchid*, 1931), *Journey of Tapiola* (1938), *Winter in April* (1938), *Portrait of Jennie* (1940), *They Went On Together*† (1941), *Journal for Josephine*† (1943), *But Gently Day* (1943), *Mr. Whittle and the Morning Star*† (1947), *Long After Summer*† (1948), *River Journey* (1949), *Adventures of Tapiola* (1950), *Married Look* (1950), *Innocent Eve* (1951), *Train in the Meadow* (1953), *Sir Henry* (1955), *So Love Returns* (1958), *Star in the Wind* (1962).

Katherine Anne Porter, 1894— , short-story writer, novelist, critic. NOVELS: *Pale Horse, Pale Rider* (three short novels: *Old Mortality*, *Noon Wine*, and title story, 1939), *Ship of Fools* (1962). STORIES: *Hacienda* (1934), *Flowering Judas and Other Stories* (1935), *The Leaning Tower and Other Stories* (1957).

F[rancis] Scott [Key] Fitzgerald, 1896—1940, short-story writer, novelist, PLAY: *The Vegetable; or, From President to Postman* (1923). SHORT STORIES: *Flappers and Philosophers* (1920), *Tales of the Jazz Age* (1922), *All the Sad Young Men* (1926), *Taps at Reveille* (1935), *Pat Hobby Stories* (1962). NOVELS: *This Side of Paradise*† (1920), *The Beautiful and Damned* (1922), *The Great Gatsby*† (1925), *Tender Is the Night* (1934), *The Last Tycoon* (1941). OTHER: *The Crack-Up* (1945).

Louis Bromfield, 1896—1956, playwright, novelist. ECONOMIC POLICY: *A Few Brass Tacks* (1946). FARM LIFE: *Pleasant Valley*† (1945), *Malabar Farm*† (1948). PLAYS: *The House of Women* (1927). *Times Have Changed* (1935), *De Luxe* (1935). SHORT STORIES: *Awake and Rehearse* (1929), *It Takes All Kinds* (1939), *Kenny* (1947). NOVELS: *The Green Bay Tree*† (1924), *Possession* (1925), *Early Autumn*† (1926), *A Good Woman* (1927), *The Strange Case of Miss Annie Spragg* (1928), *Twenty-Four Hours* (1930), *The Farm*† (1933), *The Rains Came* (1937), *Night in Bombay* (1940), *Until the Day Break* (1942), *Mrs. Parkington*† (1943), *What Became of Anna Bolton?* (1944), *Colorado* (1947), *Malabar Farm* (1948), *Out of the Earth* (1950), *Mr. Smith* (1951).

John [Roderigo] Dos Passos, 1896— , poet, playwright, novelist. POETRY: *A Pushcart at the Curb* (1922). TRAVEL BOOKS: *Rosinante to the Road Again* (1922), *Orient Express* (1927), *In All Countries* (1934), *Journeys between Wars* (1938), *State of the Nation* (1944). PERSONAL NARRATIVE: *Tour of Duty* (1946). PLAYS: *The Garbage Man* ("The Moon is a Gong," 1926), *Airways, Inc.* (1928), *Fortune Heights* (1933). SOCIAL THEORY: *The Ground We Stand On*† (1941). NOVELS: *One Man's Initiation — 1917* (1920), *Three Soldiers*† (1921), *Streets of Night* (1923), *Manhattan Transfer*† (1925), *The 42nd Parallel* (1930), *1919* (1932), *The Big Money* (1936), (*U.S.A.*† trilogy, 1937), *Adventures of a Young Man* (1939), *Number One* (1943), *First Encounter* (1945), *Grand Design* (1949), *Prospect Before Us* (1950), *Chosen Country* (1951), *Midcentury* (1961).

Thornton [Niven] Wilder, 1897— , playwright, novelist. PLAYS: *The Angel That Troubled the Waters* (1928), *The Long Christmas Dinner* (1931), *Our Town*† (1938), *The Skin of Our Teeth* (1942), *The Matchmaker* (1954). NOVELS: *The Cabala* (1926), *The Bridge of San Luis Rey*† (1927), *The Woman of Andros* (1930), *Heaven's My Destination* (1935), *Ides of March*† (1948).

William [Harrison] Faulkner (or Falkner) 1897—1962, poet, novelist, winner of Nobel Prize for Literature for 1949. SHORT STORIES: *These 13* (1931), *Miss Zilphia Gant* (1932), *Doctor Martino* (1934), *Go Down, Moses* (1942). POEMS: *The Marble Faun* (1924), *Salmagundi* (essays and poems, 1932), *A Green Bough* (1933). NOVELS: *Soldiers' Pay* (1926), *Mosquitoes* (1927), *Sartoris* (1929), *The Sound and the Fury*† (1929), *As I Lay Dying*† (1930), *Sanctuary* (1931), *Light in August* (1932), *Pylon* (1935), *Absalom, Absalom!* (1936), *The Unvanquished* (1938), *The Wild Palms* (1939), *The Hamlet* (1940), *Intruder in the Dust*† (1948), *Requiem for a Nun* (1951), *A Fable* (1954), *The Town* (1957), *The Mansion* (1959), *The Reivers* (1962).

Ernest [Miller] Hemingway, 1899—1961, short-story writer, novelist. SHORT STORIES: *Men without Women*† (1927), *Winner Take Nothing* (1933). NOVELS: *The Sun Also Rises* (1926), *The Torrents of Spring* (1926), *A Farewell to Arms*† (1929), *To Have and Have Not* (1937), *For Whom the Bell Tolls*† (1940), *Across the River and into the Trees* (1950), *The Old Man and the Sea*† (1952). Nobel Prize 1954. OTHER: *Three Stories and Ten Poems* (1923), *In Our Time* (1924), *Death in the Afternoon* (about bullfighting, 1932), *Green Hills of Africa* (about big-game hunting and other matters, 1935), *The Fifth Column and the First Forty-Nine Stories* ("The Fifth Column" is a play; 1938), *Men at War* (a short-story collection edited by Hemingway, 1942). OMNIBUS VOLUME: *The Viking Portable*

Library: Hemingway (1944), *Collected Stories* (1950).

Vincent Sheean, 1899— , political writer, novelist, biographer. POLITICAL STUDIES: *An American among the Riffi* (1926), *The New Persia* (1927), *Personal History*† (1935), *Not Peace But a Sword*† (1939), *This House Against This House* (1946). NOVELS: *God and Magog* (1929), *Sanfelice* (1936), *A Certain Rich Man* (1947), *Rage of Soul* (1952), *Lilly* (1954). BIOGRAPHY: *Lead, Kindly Light* (Gandhi, 1949), *Indigo Bunting* (Edna St. Vincent Millay, 1951), *Mahatma Gandhi* (1955).

Glenway Wescott, 1901— , short-story writer, novelist. POEMS: *The Bitterns* (1920), *Natives of Rock* (1925). ESSAYS: *Fear and Trembling* (1932). BELLES-LETTRES: *A Calendar of Saints for Unbelievers* (in collaboration, 1932). LIBRETTO: *The Dream of Audubon* (1940). SHORT STORIES: *Like a Lover* (1926), *Good-Bye, Wisconsin* (1928), *The Babe's Bed* (1930). NOVELS: *The Apple of the Eye* (1924), *The Grandmothers*† (1927), *Apartment in Athens*† (1945).

Thomas [Clayton] Wolfe, 1900—1938, short-story writer, novelist.[3] AUTOBIOGRAPHICAL SKETCH: *The Story of a Novel* (1936). NOVELS: *Look Homeward, Angel*† (1929), *Of Time and the River* (1935), *The Web and the Rock* (1939), *You Can't Go Home Again* (1940). OTHER: *The Hills Beyond* (shorter works, 1941), *Letters to His Mother* (1943), *Portable Thomas Wolfe* (1946), *Mannerhouse* (play written *c.* 1926; published 1946), *From Death to Morning* (stories 1935), *A Stone, A Leaf, A Door* (poems, 1945).

Oliver [Hazard Perry] LaFarge, 1901—1963, editor, short-story writer, novelist, ethnologist. NOVELS: *Laughing Boy*† (1929), *The Enemy Gods* (1937), *Copper Pot*† (1942). STUDIES: *Tribes and Temples* (in collaboration, two volumes, 1926-1927), *The Year Bearer's People* (in collaboration, 1931), *The Changing Indian*† (essays, edited, 1942), *Santa Eulalia: The Religion of a Cuchumátan Indian Town*† (1947). MISCELLANY: *All the Young Men* (stories, 1935), *As Long as the Grass Shall Grow* (1940), *Raw Material*† (autobiography, 1945), *Eagle in the Egg* (on air transportation, 1949), *The American Indian* (1960).

John [Ernst] Steinbeck, 1902— , short-story writer, novelist. SHORT STORIES: *Nothing So Monstrous* (1936), *The Long Valley* (1938). NOVELS: *Tortilla Flat*† (1935), *Of Mice and Men*† (1937), *The Grapes of Wrath* (1939), *Cannery Row*† (1945), *Wayward Bus* (1947), *The Pearl* (1947), *East of Eden*† (1952), *Sweet Thursday* (1954), *The Short Reign of Pippin IV* (1957), *The Red Pony* (1959), *The Winter of our Discontent* (1961). OTHER: *The Forgotten Village*† (1941), *Sea of Cortez*† (in collaboration, 1941), *Bombs Away* (1942), *Portable Steinbeck* (1943), *Russian Journal* (1948), *Burning Bright* (play, 1950), *Travels With Charley* (1962).

Philip Wylie, 1902— , journalist, editor, novelist. NOVELS: *Heavy Laden* (1928), *Night Unto Night* (1944), *Opus 21*† (1949), *The Disappearance*† (1951). OTHER: *Generation of Vipers* (1942), *An Essay on Morals* (1947).

Erskine [Preston] Caldwell, 1903— , critic, short-story writer, novelist, SHORT STORIES: *Kneel to the Rising Sun and Other Stories*† (1935), *Georgia Boy*† (1943), *Stories* (1944), *American Earth,* (collection, 1950), *Episodes in Palmetto* (1950), *The Courting of Susie Brown* (1952), *Complete Stories* (1953), *Gulf Coast Stories* (1956). NOVELS: *Tobacco Road*† (1932), *God's Little Acre* (1933), *Trouble in July* (1940), *All Night Long* (1942), *Tragic Ground* (1944), *House in the Uplands* (1946), *Sure Hand of God* (1947), *This Very Earth* (1948), *Place Called Estherville* (1949), *Claudelle Inglish* (1959), *Jenny By Nature* (1961), *Close to Home* (1962). OTHER: *Say Is This the U.S.A.* (in collaboration, 1941), *Call It Experience* (1951).

3 For biog., criticism, and bibliog. see Richard Walser, *Thomas Wolfe* (Barnes & Noble, 1961).

James Gould Cozzens, 1903— , novelist. NOVELS: *Confusion* (1924), *Michael Scarlett* (1925), *Cock Pit* (1928), *The Son of Perdition* (1929), *S.S. San Pedro*† (1931), *The Last Adam* (1933), *Castaway* (1934), *Men and Brethren* (1936), *Ask Me Tomorrow* (1940), *The Just and the Unjust*† (1942), *Guard of Honor* (1948), *By Love Possessed* (1957).

James T[homas] Farrell, 1904— , critic, short-story writer, novelist. SHORT STORIES: *The Short Stories of James T. Farrell, with an Introduction by Robert M. Lovett* (1937), includes three previous volumes: *Calico Shoes* (1934), *Guillotine Party* (1935), *Can All This Grandeur Perish?* (1937); *$1,000 a Week* (1942), *To Whom It May Concern* (1944). NOVELS: *Studs Lonigan*† (1935); a trilogy: *Young Lonigan* (1932), *The Young Manhood of Studs Lonigan* (1934), *Judgment Day* (1935); *Tommy Gallagher's Crusade* (1939), *Ellen Rogers* (1941), *My Days of Anger* (1943), the fourth book in the saga of *Danny O'Neill*, the previous ones being *A World I Never Made* (1936), *No Star Is Lost* (1938), and *Father and Son* (1940), *The Road Between* (1949), *This Man and This Woman* (1951), *Yet Other Waters* (1952). OTHER WRITINGS: *A Note on Literary Criticism* (1936), *The League of Frightened Philistines* (1946), *The Fate of Writing in America* (1946), *When Boyhood Dreams Come True* (stories, sketches, essays, and a play, 1946), *Literature and Morality* (essays, 1947), *Truth and Myth about America* (1949), *Frontier and James Whitcomb Riley* (1951), *Reflections at Fifty* (1954), *My Baseball Diary* (1957).

Christopher Isherwood, 1904— , short-story writer, novelist, translator, playwright. PLAYS: (in collaboration with W. H. Auden) *The Dog Beneath the Skin* (1935), *The Ascent of F. 6.* (1936), *On the Frontier* (1938). SHORT STORIES: *The Berlin Stories*† (1946). NOVELS: *The Memorial* (1932), *Lions and Shadows* (1938), *Prater Violet*† (1945), *The World in the Evening* (1952).

John [Henry] O'Hara, 1905— , short-story writer, novelist. SHORT STORIES: *The Doctor's Son and Other Stories* (1935), *Files on Parade* (1939), *Pipe Night*† (1945), *Hellbox* (1947), *Sermons and Soda Water* (1961). NOVELS: *Appointment in Samarra* (1934), *Butterfield 8* (1935), *Hope of Heaven* (1938), *Pal Joey* (1940), *Rage to Live* (1949), *Farmers Hotel* (1951), *From the Terrace* (1958), *Ten North Frederick* (1955). OTHER: *Sweet and Sour* (1954).

Robert Penn Warren, 1905— , editor, biographer, poet, short-story writer, novelist. POEMS: *Thirty-Six Poems* (1935), *Eleven Poems on the Same Theme*† (1942), *Seected Poems*† (1944), *You Emperors . . .* (1960). SHORT STORIES: *Circus in the Attick* (1948). NOVELS: *Night Rider* (1939), *At Heaven's Gate* (1943), *All the King's Men*† (1946), *World Enough and Time* (1950), *Band of Angels* (1955), *The Cave* (1959), *Wilderness* (1961). OTHER: *Selected Essays* (1958).

William Saroyan, 1908— , novelist, playwright, short-story writer. NOVELS: *Human Comedy* (1943), *Adventures of Wesley Jackson* (1946), *Papa, You're Crazy* (1957). PLAYS: *Three Plays* (1940), includes *My Heart's in the Highlands* (1939), *The Time of Your Life* (1939), and *Love's Old Sweet Song* (1941), *Three Plays* (1941), *Razzle Dazzle* (1942), *Get Away, Old Man* (1944), *Jim Dandy*† (1947), *Three Plays* (1949), *Hello Out There* (1949). SHORT STORIES: *The Daring Young Man on the Flying Trapeze and Other Stories*† (1934), *My Name is Aram* (1940), *Dear Baby*† (1944), *Saroyan Special*† (1949), *The Assyrian and Other Stories* (1950), *Tracy's Tiger* (1951), *Rock Wagram* (1951). OTHER WRITINGS: *Fables* (1942), *Bicycle Rider in Beverly Hills* (autobiography, 1952), *Twin Adventures . . .* (1950), *The Cave Dwellers* (play, reviews, essays, 1958).

Walter van Tilburg Clark, 1909— , teacher, novelist. NOVELS: *The Ox-Bow Incident*† (1940), *The City of Trembling Leaves* (1945), *The Track of the Cat*† (1949), *The Watchful Gods* (1950), *Tim Hazard* (1951).

Frederic Prokosch, 1908— , poet, novelist. POEMS: *The Assassins* (1936), *The Carnival* (1938), *Death at Sea*† (1941), *Chosen Poems*† (1947). NOVELS: *The Asiatics*† (1935), *The Seven Who Fled*† (1937), *Night of the Poor* (1939), *The Skies of Europe* (1941), *Conspirators* (1943), *Age of Thunder* (1945), *Idols of the Cave* (1946), *Storm and Echo* (1948), *Nine Days to Mukalla* (1953), *A Tale for Midnight* (1955).

Howard Fast, 1914— , war correspondent, short-story writer, novelist. NOVELS: *Two Valleys* (1932), *Citizen Tom Paine*† (1943), *Freedom Road*† (1944), *The American* (biography of John Peter Altgeld, 1946), *Spartacus* (1952).

John Hersey, 1914— , novelist. NOVELS: *A Bell for Adano*† (1944, Pulitzer Prize winner), *Hiroshima*† (1946), *The Wall*† (1950), *A Single Pebble* (1956), *The Child Buyer* (1960).

Carson McCullers, 1917— , novelist, short-story writer. NOVELS: *The Heart Is a Lonely Hunter*† (1940), *Reflections in a Golden Eye* (1941), *The Member of the Wedding*† (1946), *Clock Without Hands* (1961). PLAY: *Square Root of Wonderful* (1958). COLLECTION: *The Ballad of the Sad Café* (novels and stories to 1951).

Truman Capote, 1924— , novelist and short-story writer. SHORT STORIES: *A Tree of Night* (1950). NOVELS: *Other Voices, Other Rooms*† (1948), *The Grass Harp* (1951), *Breakfast at Tiffany's* (1958). ESSAYS: *Local Color* (1950).

POETS

Lizette Woodworth Reese, 1856—1935, poet. FICTIONAL FRAGMENT: *Worleys* (1936). REMINISCENCES: *A Victorian Village* (1929), *The York Road* (1931). POETRY: *A Branch of May* (1887), *A Handful of Lavender* (1891), *A Quiet Road* (1896), *A Wayside Lute* (1909), *Spicewood* (1920), *Wild Cherry* (1923), *Selected Poems*† (1926), *Little Henrietta* (1927), *White April* (1930), *Pastures* (1933), *The Old House in the Country* (1936).

Edwin Arlington Robinson, 1869—1935, poet. BIOGRAPHICAL: *Selected Letters* (1940), *Untriangulated Stars: Letters to Harry de Forest Smith, 1890-1905* (1947). PLAYS: *Van Zorn* (1914), *The Porcupine* (1915). POETRY: *The Torrent and The Night Before*† (1896), *The Children of the Night* (1897), *Captain Craig* (1902), *The Town down the River* (1910), *The Man against the Sky* (1916), *Merlin* (1917), *Lancelot* (1920), *The Three Taverns* (1920), *Avon's Harvest* (1921), *Roman Bartholow* (1923), *The Man Who Died Twice*† (1924), *Dionysus in Doubt* (1925), *Tristram*† (1927), *Sonnets, 1889-1927* (1928), *Cavender's House* (1929), *The Glory of the Nightingales* (1930), *Matthias at the Door* (1931), *Nicodemus* (1932), *Talifer* (1933), *Amaranth* (1934), *King Jasper* (1935), *Collected Poems*† (1937). INDIVIDUAL POEMS: "Mr. Flood's Party," "Miniver Cheevy," "Flammonde," "For a Dead Lady," "The Sheaves," "Eros Turannos," "Richard Cory," "The Master," "Luke Havergal," "The House on the Hill," "The Gift of God," "The Man against the Sky," "Ben Jonson Entertains a Man from Stratford," "Veteran Sirens," "The Poor Relation," "Firelight," "The Field of Glory," "Calverly," "John Evereldown," "The Mill," "George Crabbe," "Bewick Finzer," "The Dark Hills."

Edgar Lee Masters, 1869–1950, novelist, poet. BIOGRAPHY: *Vachel Lindsay*† (1935), *Whitman* (1937), *Mark Twain* (1938). AUTOBIOGRAPHY: *Across Spoon River* (1936). VERSE PLAYS: *Maximilian* (1902), *Lee* (1926), *Jack Kelso* (1928), *Godbey* (1931). NOVELS: *Mitch Miller* (1920), *Children of the Market Place* (1922), *Skeeters Kirby* (1923), *Mirage* (1924), *The Tide of Time* (1937). POETRY: *A Book of Verses* (1898), *Spoon River Anthology*† (1915), *The Great Valley* (1916), *Songs and Satires* (1916), *Toward the Gulf* (1918), *Starved Rock* (1919), *Domesday*

Book (1920), *The Open Sea* (1921), *The New Spoon River* (1924), *The Fate of the July* (1929), *Lichee Nuts* (1930), *The Serpent in the Wilderness* (1933), *Invisible Landscapes* (1935), *Poems of People* (1936), *The New World* (1937), *Illinois Poems* (1941), *Along the Illinois* (1942). MISCELLANEOUS: *The Tale of Chicago* (history, 1933), *The Living Thoughts of Emerson* (edited, 1940), *The Sangamon* (river-history, 1942). INDIVIDUAL POEMS: "My Light with Yours," "Ann Rutledge," "Lucinda Matlock," "Petit, the Poet," "Editor Whedon," "Morgan Oakley," "By the Waters of Babylon," "Ship-Shoe Lovey," "Hare Drummer," "Howard Lamson," "The Loom," "A Curious Boy," "The Seven Cities of America," "Widows," "Week-End by the Sea."

Amy [Lawrence] Lowell, 1874—1925, critic, poet. BIOGRAPHY: *John Keats*† (two volumes, 1925). LITERARY CRITICISM: *Six French Poets* (1915), *Tendencies in Modern American Poetry*† (1917). POEMS: *A Dome of Many-Colored Glass* (1912), *Sword Blades and Poppy Seed*† (1914), *Men, Women, and Ghosts* (1916), *Can Grande's Castle* (1918), *Pictures of the Floating World* (1919), *Fir-Flower Tablets* (in collaboration with Florence Ayscough, 1921), *Legends* (1921), *A Critical Fable* (1922), *What's o'Clock* (1925), *East Wind* (1926), *Ballads for Sale* (1927). INDIVIDUAL POEMS: "Patterns," "Lilacs," "Apology," "Madonna of the Evening Flowers," "Solitaire," "Meeting-House Hill," "A Gift," "A Decade," "The City of Falling Leaves," "Four Sides to a House," "The Dinner Party," "Little Ivory Fingers Pulled with String," "Venus Transiens," "A Rhyme out of Motley." CORRESPONDENCE (with F. Ayscough) 1946. COMPLETE POETICAL WORKS (1955).

Robert [Lee] Frost, 1874—1963, poet. PLAYS: *A Way Out* (1929), *Snow* (1941). POETRY: *A Boy's Will* (1913), *North of Boston*† (1914), *Mountain Interval*† (1916), *New Hampshire*† (1923), *Selected Poems* (1923), *West-Running Brook* (1928), *Collected Poems* (1930), *A Further Range*† (1936), *Collected Poems*† (1939), *A Witness Tree*† (1942), *Come In* (selected by Louis Untermeyer, 1943), *Masque of Reason*† (1945), *Masque of Mercy*† (1947), *Steeple Bush*† (1947), *Complete Poems*† (1949). INDIVIDUAL POEMS: "Stopping by Woods on a Snowy Evening," "An Old Man's Winter Night," "Birches," "Mending Wall," "The Road Not Taken," "The Death of the Hired Man," "After Apple-Picking," "Home Burial," "Fire and Ice," "The Sound of the Trees," "The Runaway," "My November Guest," "The Fear," "To Earthward," "Spring Pools," "The Aim Was Song," "Two Tramps in Mud Time," "Our Singing Strength," "For Once, Then Something," "Acquainted with the Night," "To Edward Thomas," "Not to Keep," "The Hill Wife," "Good-Bye and Keep Cold," "The Onset," "The Oven Bird," "Come In," "Departmental," "Happiness Makes Up in Height," "Revelation," "The Wood-Pile," "Mowing," "Reluctance," "The Code," "A Servant to Servants," "Putting in the Seed," "A Time to Talk," "The Cow in Apple Time," "Brown's Descent," "Hard Not to Be King." OTHER: *A Talk for Students* (1956), *Aforesaid* (1954), *In The Clearing* (poems, 1962).

William Ellery [Channing] Leonard, 1876—1945, playwright, translator, essayist, poet. TRANSLATIONS: *The Fragments of Empedocles* (1908), *T. Lucretius Carus. Of the Nature of Things* (1916). STUDIES: *The Poet of Galilee* (1909). AUTOBIOGRAPHY: *The Locomotive-God*† (1927). POEMS: *Sonnets and Poems* (1906), *The Vaunt of Man* (1912), *The Lynching Bee* (1920), *Two Lives*† (1922), *Tutankhamen and After* (1924), *This Midland City* (1930), *Man against Time: An Heroic Drama*† (1945). INDIVIDUAL POEMS: "Indian Summer," "The Image of Delight," "To the Victor," "The Pied Piper," "Tom Mooney," and sonnets from *Two Lives:* "O how came I that loved stars, moon, and flame," "This afternoon on Willow-Walk alone," "Thrice summer and autumn passed into the west," "We act in crises not as one who dons," "The Cosmic Rhythms have old right of way."

Carl [August] Sandburg, 1878— , poet. CHILDREN'S BOOKS: *Rootabaga Stories* (1922), *Rootabaga Pigeons* (1923), *Abe Lincoln Grows Up* (1928), *Early Moon* (poems, 1930), *Potato Face* (1930). BIOGRAPHY: *Abraham Lincoln: The Prairie Years*† (two volumes, 1926), *Steichen, the Photographer* (1929), *Mary Lincoln, Wife and Widow* (in collaboration with P. M. Angle, 1932), *Abraham*

Lincoln: The War Years† (four volumes, 1939), *Lincoln Collector* (Oliver Barrett, 1950). HISTORY: *Storm over the Land* (1942). POETRY: *Chicago Poems* (1916), *Cornhuskers* (1918), *Smoke and Steel* (1920), *Slabs of the Sunburnt West* (1922), *Selected Poems*† (1928), *Good Morning, America* (1928), *The People, Yes*† (1936), *Complete Poems*† (1950, Pulitzer Prize). HISTORICAL NOVEL: *Remembrance Rock*† (1948). MISCELLANEOUS: *The Chicago Race Riots* (social study, 1919), *The American Songbag* (editor, 1927), *Home Front Memo* (miscellany, 1943). AUTOBIOGRAPHY: *Always the Young Strangers*† (1952). INDIVIDUAL POEMS: "Chicago," "Grass," "Four Preludes on Playthings of the Winds," "Prayers of Steel," "Nocturne in a Deserted Brickyard," "Cool Tombs," "Psalm of Those Who Go Forth before Daylight," "Losers," "Old Timers," "Under the Harvest Moon," "Caboose Thoughts," "The Man with the Broken Fingers," "The People Will Live On," (from *The People, Yes*), "Prairie," "Broken-Face Gargoyles," "At a Window," "Joy," "Three Spring Notations on Bipeds," "Buttons," "Plunger," "Wilderness," "To a Contemporary Bunk-Shooter," "Take a Letter to Dmitri Shostakovich," "The Fireborn Are at Home in Fire." OTHER: *Harvest Poems 1910-1960* (1960).

[Nicholas] Vachel Lindsay, 1879—1931, poet. AUTOBIOGRAPHY: *Adventures while Preaching the Gospel of Beauty* (1914), *A Handy Guide for Beggars* (1916). POETRY: *The Tree of Laughing Bells* (1905), *Rhymes to Be Traded for Bread* (1912), *General William Booth Enters into Heaven*† (1913), *The Congo*† (1914), *The Chinese Nightingale*† (1917), *The Daniel Jazz* (1920), *The Golden Whales of California* (1920), *Collected Poems* (1923), *Going-to-the-Sun* (1923), *The Candle in the Cabin* (1926), *Going-to-the-Stars* (1926), *Johnny Appleseed* (1928), *Every Soul Is a Circus* (1929). MISCELLANEOUS: *The Golden Book of Springfield* (1920), *The Litany of Washington Street* (1929), *Letters of Nicholas Vachel Lindsay to A. Joseph Armstrong* (edited by A. J. Armstrong, 1940). INDIVIDUAL POEMS: "General William Booth Enters into Heaven," "The Eagle That Is Forgotten," "Abraham Lincoln Walks at Midnight," "The Leaden-Eyed," "The Chinese Nightingale," "The Congo," "A Negro Sermon: Simon Legree," "Aladdin and the Jinn," "A Net to Snare the Moonlight," "The Ghosts of the Buffaloes," "John Brown," "The Daniel Jazz," "Nancy Hanks, Mother of Abraham Lincoln," "On the Building of Springfield," "Prologue to 'Rhymes to Be Traded for Bread,' " "In Praise of Johnny Appleseed," "The Flower of Mending," "Where Is the Real Non-Resistant?"

Wallace Stevens, 1879—1955, poet. POETRY: *Harmonium* (1923), *Ideas of Order* (1935), *Owl's Clover* (1936), *The Man with the Blue Guitar* (1937), *Parts of a World*† (1942), *Notes toward a Supreme Fiction*† (1943), *Transport to Summer* (1947), *Collected Poems* (1957), INDIVIDUAL POEMS: "Peter Quince at the Clavier," "The Worms at Heaven's Gate," "The Emperor of Ice-Cream," "Le Monocle de Mon Oncle," "Sea Surface Full of Clouds," "Domination of Black," "Anecdote of the Jar," "The Paltry Nude Starts on a Spring Voyage," "Tattoo," "The Snow Man," "To the One of Fictive Music," "Cortège for Rosenbloom," "Homunculus et la Belle Etoile," "Tea at the Palaz of Hoon," "Bouquet of Belle Scavoir," "Asides on the Oboe," "The Pleasures of Merely Circulating," "Six Discordant Songs." MISCELLANY: *Necessary Angel: Essays in Reality and the Imagination* (1951).

William Carlos Williams, 1883—1963, physician, poet, translator. POETRY: *Collected Poems* (1951). AUTOBIOGRAPHY (1951). SHORT STORIES: *Make Light of It* (collected stories, 1950), *The Farmers' Daughters* (1961).

Sara Teasdale, 1884—1933, poet. POETRY: *Sonnets to Duse* (1907), *Helen of Troy* (1911), *Rivers to the Sea* (1915), *Love Songs* (1917), *Flame and Shadow* (1920), *Dark of the Moon* (1926), *Stars To-Night* (1930), *Strange Victory* (1933), *Collected Poems*† (1937). INDIVIDUAL POEMS: "I Shall Not Care," "Arcturus," "Let It Be Forgotten," "Spring Night," "The Answer," "The Long Hill," "Debt," "Over the Hill," "Barter," "Winter Night Song," "There Will Come Soft Rains," "Blue Squalls," "Come," "Song for Colin," "Night Song at Amalfi," "The Look," "Spring in War Time," "Effigy of a Nun," "The Flight," "On the Sussex Downs."

Elinor [Hoyt] Wylie, 1885—1928, poet, novelist. NOVELS: *Jennifer Lorn* (1923), *The Venetian Glass Nephew* (1925), *The Orphan Angel* (1926), *Mr. Hodge & Mr. Hazard* (1928). POETRY: *Incidental Numbers* (1912), *Nets to Catch the Wind* (1921), *Black Armour* (1923), *Angels and Earthly Creatures*† (1928), *Trivial Breath* (1928), *Last Poems* (1943). INDIVIDUAL POEMS: "The Eagle and the Mole," "Let No Charitable Hope," "Hymn to Earth," "Velvet Shoes," "Escape," "Castilian," "O Virtuous Light," "Birthday Sonnet," "Prophecy," "Atavism," "Peregrine," and sonnets from *One Person:* "The Little Beauty That I Was Allowed—," "I Hereby Swear That to Uphold Your House," "Before I Die, Let Me Be Happy Here," "Upon Your Heart, Which Is the Heart of All."

Ezra [Loomis] Pound, 1885— , translator, editor, essayist, poet, Nazi propagandist. ESSAYS, STUDIES, AND LITERARY CRITICISM: *The Spirit of Romance* (1910), *Pavannes and Divisions* (1918), *Instigations* (1920), *Indiscretions* (1923), *Antheil and the Treatise on Harmony* (1924), *ABC of Reading* (1934), *Make It New* (1934), *Polite Essays* (1937), *Culture* (1938). POETRY: *A Lume Spento* (1908), *Exultations*† (1909), *Personae*† (1909), *Provença* (1910), *Canzoni* (1911), *Ripostes* (1912), *Lustra* (1916), *Quia Pauper Amavi* (1919), *Umbra* (1920), *A Draft of XVI Cantos* (1925), *Selected Poems* (1928), *A Draft of XXX Cantos*† (1930), *Eleven New Cantos, XXXI-XLI* (1934), *Cantos*† (1948), *Pisan Cantos*† (1948), *Collected Poems* (1950). MISCELLANEOUS: *Sonnets and Ballads of Guido Cavalcanti* (translation, 1912), *Gaudier-Brzeska* (biography, 1916), *Certain Noble Plays of Japan* (edited, 1916), *'Noh,' or Accomplishment* (in collaboration with Ernest Fenollosa, 1916). INDIVIDUAL POEMS: "Ballad of the Goodly Fere," "The River-Merchant's Wife: A Letter," "Dance Figure," "A Virginal," "The Return," "Envoi (1919)," "Further Instructions," "Exile's Letter," "The Garden," "Canto XIII: 'Kung Walked,' " "Francesca," "Immortality," "The Tree," "The Spring," "Ortus," "The Study in Aesthetics." LETTERS: 1907-1941 (1950). TRANSLATIONS (1953).

John Hall Wheelock, 1886— , poet. POETRY: *Verses by Two Undergraduates* (in collaboration with Van Wyck Brooks, 1905 — see p. 289), *The Human Fantasy* (1911), *The Belovéd Adventure* (1912), *Love and Liberation* (1913), *Dust and Light* (1919), *The Black Panther* (1922), *The Bright Doom* (1927), *Poems, 1911-1936*† (1936). INDIVIDUAL POEMS: "The Fish-Hawk," "Sunday Evening in the Common," "Nirvana," "This Quiet Dust," "All My Love for My Sweet," "The Thunder-Shower," "Pitiless Beauty," "Prayer to the Sun," "The Dear Mystery," "The Black Panther," "Autumn," "Along the Beaches," "Love and Liberation," "The Undiscovered Country." *Poems Old and New* (1956), *The Gardener . . .* (1961).

John Gould Fletcher, 1886—1950, translator, essayist, poet. HISTORY: *Arkansas*† (1947). TRANSLATIONS: Elie Faure's *The Dance over Fire and Water* (1926), J. J. Rousseau's *The Reveries of a Solitary* (1927). BIOGRAPHY: *Paul Gauguin: His Life and Heart* (1921), *John Smith—Also Pocahontas* (1928). AUTOBIOGRAPHY: *Life Is My Song* (1937). STUDIES: *The Crisis of the Film* (1929), *The Two Frontiers* (1930). POETRY: *Irradiations* (1915), *Goblins and Pagodas* (1916), *Japanese Prints* (1918), *Breakers and Granite* (1921), *Parables* (1925), *Branches of Adam* (1926), *The Black Rock* (1928), *XXIV Elegies* (1935), *The Epic of Arkansas* (1936), *Selected Poems*† (1938), *South Star* (1941), *Burning Mountain*† (1946). INDIVIDUAL POEMS: "Blue Symphony," "Mexican Quarter," "The Stevedores," "Vision," "Lincoln," "Heat," "White Symphony," "Down the Mississippi," "Embarkation," "The Swan," "The Groundswell."

[John] Robinson Jeffers, 1887—1962, poet. POETRY: *Flagons and Apples* (1912), *Californians* (1916), *Tamar* (1924), *Roan Stallion, Tamar, and Other Poems*† (1925), *The Women at Point Sur* (1927), *Cawdor* (1928), *Dear Judas* (1929), *Descent to the Dead* (1931), *Thurso's Landing* (1932), *Give Your Heart to the Hawks* (1933), *Solstice* (1935), *Such Counsels You Gave to Me* (1937), *The Selected Poetry of Robinson Jeffers*† (1938), *Be Angry at the Sun* (1941), *The Double Axe and Other Poems* (1948). INDIVIDUAL POEMS: "Shine, Perishing Republic," "To the Stone-Cutters," "Night," "Hurt Hawks," "Age in Prospect," "Promise of Peace," "Meditation on Saviors," "Fog," "The Door," "Fire on the Hills,"

"I Shall Laugh Purely," "Post Mortem," "The Tower beyond Tragedy," "Salmon-Fishing," "Prescription of Painful Ends," "The Tree Toad," "Pelicans," "Tor House," "May — June, *1940*." OTHER: *Medea* (1946), *Hungerfield* (1954).

John Crowe Ransom, 1888— , editor, critic, poet. LITERARY CRITICISM: *The World's Body* (1938), *The New Criticism* (1941). POETRY: *Poems about God* (1919), *Chills and Fever*† (1924), *Grace after Meat* (1924), *Two Gentlemen in Bonds* (1927), *Selected Poems*† (1945). MISCELLANEOUS: *God without Thunder* (a defense of orthodoxy, 1930), *I'll Take My Stand* (an agrarian anthology, 1930), *Topics for Freshman Writing* (1935), *A College Primer of Writing* (1943). INDIVIDUAL POEMS: "Here Lies a Lady," "Piazza Piece," "Captain Carpenter," "Two in August," "Antique Harvesters," "Janet Walking," "Blue Girls," "Amphibious Crocodile," "Number Five," "In Process of a Noble Alliance," "April Treason."

T[homas] S[tearns] Eliot, 1888— , American-born poet who became a British subject in 1927; winner of the Nobel Prize for Literature in 1948. CRITICISM: *Ezra Pound: His Metric and Poetry* (1917), *The Sacred Wood*† (1920), *Homage to John Dryden* (1924), *Shakespeare and the Stoicism of Seneca* (1927), *For Lancelot Andrews*† (1928), *Tradition and Experiment in Present-Day Literature* (1929), *Selected Essays, 1917-1932*† (1932), *John Dryden: The Poet, the Dramatist, the Critic* (1932), *The Use of Poetry and the Use of Criticism* (1933), *After Strange Gods*† (1934), *Elizabethan Essays* (1934), *The Idea of a Christian Society* (1940), *Music of Poetry* (1942), *A Choice of Kipling's Verse* (editor, 1943), *Notes Toward the Definition of Culture*† (1949). PAGEANT: *The Rock* (1934). PLAYS: *Murder in the Cathedral* (1935), *The Family Reunion* (1939), *The Cocktail Party* (1950). POETRY: *Prufrock and Other Observations* (1917), *Poems*† (1919), *The Waste Land*† (1922), *Ash-Wednesday*† (1930), *Collected Poems, 1900-1935*† (1936), *East Coker* (1940), *Burnt Norton* (1941), *The Dry Salvages* (1941), *Little Gidding* (1942), *Four Quartets*† (1943). INDIVIDUAL POEMS: "Sweeny Among the Nightingales," "Portrait of a Lady," "Love Song of J. Alfred Prufrock," "Gerontion," "La Figlia che Piange," "Whispers of Immortality," "A Song for Simeon," "The Hippopotamus," "Morning at the Window," "Ash-Wednesday: I, II," "The Hollow Men," "Marina," "Journey of the Magi," "Rhapsody on a Windy Night." OTHER: *Complete Poems and Plays* (1952), *The Confidential Clerk* (play, 1954).

Conrad [Potter] Aiken, 1889— , editor, critic, poet, novelist, short-story writer. SHORT-STORY COLLECTIONS: *Bring! Bring!* (1925), *Costumes by Eros!* (1928), *Collected Short Stories* (1960). NOVELS: *Blue Voyage* (1927), *Great Circle* (1933), *King Coffin* (1935); *Conversation* (1939). EDITOR: *Selected Poems of Emily Dickinson* (1924), *American Poetry, 1671-1928* (1929). LITERARY CRITICISM: *Scepticisms*† (1919). POETRY: *Earth Triumphant* (1914), *The Jig of Forslin* (1916), *Turns and Movies* (1916), *Nocturne of Remembered Spring* (1917), *The Charnel Rose* (1918), *The House of Dust* (1920), *Punch: The Immortal Liar* (1921), *Priapus and the Pool* (1922), *The Pilgrimage of Festus* (1923), *Selected Poems*† (1929), *John Deth* (1930), *Preludes for Memnon* (1931), *Landscape West of Eden* (1934), *Time in the Rock* (1936), *And in the Human Heart* (1940), *Brownstone Eclogues* (1942), *The Soldier* (1944), *The Kid* (1947), *Divine Pilgrim* (1949), *Skylight One*† (1949). INDIVIDUAL POEMS: "This Is the Shape of the Leaf," "And in the Hanging Gardens," "When Trout Swim down Great Ormond Street," "Morning Song of Senlin," "Music I Heard with You," "Prelude VI: 'Rimbaud and Verlaine,'" "Portrait of One Dead," "The Wedding," "Sound of Breaking," "The Room," "Tetélestai," "There Is Nothing Moving Here." AUTOBIOGRAPHY: *Ushant* (1952). OTHER: *Collected Poems* (1953), *Reviewer's ABC* (criticism to 1958).

Edna St. Vincent Millay, 1892—1950, poet. HUMOR: *Distressing Dialogues* (pseudonymously, 1924). PLAYS: *Aria da Capo* (1920), *The Lamp and the Bell* (1921), *Two Slatterns and a King* (1921), *The King's Henchman*† (in collaboration with Deems Taylor, 1926-1927), *The Princess Marries the Page* (1932). POEMS: *Renascence* (1917), *A Few Figs from Thistles* (1920), *Second April* (1921), *The Ballad of the Harp-Weaver* (1922), *The Harp-Weaver and Other Poems*† (1923),

The Buck in the Snow (1928), *Fatal Interview*† (1931), *Wine from These Grapes* (1934), *Huntsman, What Quarry?* (1939), *Make Bright the Arrow* (1940), *Collected Sonnets* (1941), *Murder of Lidice* (1942), *Collected Lyrics* (1943). INDIVIDUAL POEMS: "Euclid Alone Has Looked on Beauty Bare," "Dirge Without Music," "Renascence," "God's World," "The Poet and His Book," "Moriturus," "Oh, Sleep Forever in the Latmian Cave," "Thou Art Not Lovelier than Lilacs," "Afternoon on a Hill," "I Shall Go Back," "Elaine," "Elegy before Death," "Passer Mortuis," "Afternoon on a Hill," "What Lips My Lips Have Kissed," "Recuerdo," "Say What You Will," "Autumn Chant," "What's This of Death." OTHER: *Letters* (ed. A. R. MacDougall, 1952), *Mine the Harvest* (last poems, 1954), *Collected Poems* (1956).

Archibald MacLeish, 1892— , social writer, poet. PLAY: *Destroyers*† (1942). SATIRE: *Infernal Machine*† (with Robert de San Marzano, 1947). STUDIES: *The Irresponsibles* (1940), *The American Cause* (1941), *A Time to Speak* (prose collection, 1941), *American Opinion and the War* (1942), *A Time to Act*† (selected addresses, 1943). PLAYS: *Nobodaddy* (1926), *Panic* (1935), *The Destroyers* (1942), *The Fall of the City* (1937), *Air Raid* (1938), *J.B.* (1958). POETRY: *The Happy Marriage* (1924), *The Pot of Earth* (1925), *Streets in the Moon* (1926), *The Hamlet of A. MacLeish* (1928), *New Found Land* (1930), *Conquistador*† (1932), *Frescoes for Mr. Rockefeller's City* (1933), *Public Speech* (1936), *Land of the Free* (1938), *America Was Promises* (1939), *Actfive, and Other Poems*† (1948), *Poems, 1917-1952* (1952). INDIVIDUAL POEMS: "You, Andrew Marvel," "The End of the World," "Ars Poetica," "The Too-Late Born," "Immortal Autumn," "Bernál Díaz' Preface to His Book," "Burying Ground by the Ties," "L'an Trentiesme de Mon Eage," "Memorial Rain," "Land of the Free," "Speech to Those Who Say Comrade," "The Western Sky," "Speech to a Crowd," "Epistle to Be Left in the Earth," "The Fall of the City," "The Spanish Dead," "The Reconciliation."

Dorothy [Rothschild] Parker, 1893— , short-story writer, poet. SHORT STORIES: *Laments for the Living* (1930), *After Such Pleasures* (1933), *Here Lies* (collected stories, 1939). POETRY: *Enough Rope* (1926), *Sunset Gun* (1928), *Death and Taxes* (1931). COLLECTED POEMS: *Not So Deep as a Well* (1936). OMNIBUS VOLUME: *The Viking Portable Library: Dorothy Parker* (stories and poems, 1944). INDIVIDUAL POEMS: "Somebody's Song," "Inventory," "Bohemia," "Fighting Words," "Résumé," "Biographies."

E[dward] E[stlin] Cummings, 1894—1962, poet, essayist. POETRY: *Tulips and Chimneys* (volume of poems, 1922), *Collected Poems* (1938). ESSAYS AND JOURNALS: *The Enormous Room* (Life and Letters Series, 1930), *Anthropos—The Future of Art* (1945), *Santa Claus: A Morality* (1946), *EIMI* (journal of a trip to Russia, 1948). OTHER: *i: six nonlectures* (1953), *Poems, 1923-1954* (1954), *95 Poems* (1958).

Stephen Vincent Benét, 1898—1943, translator, editor, playwright, novelist, poet. HISTORY: *America*† (1945). RADIO SCRIPTS: *We Stand United*† (1945). SHORT STORIES: *Tales before Midnight* (1939). PLAYS: *The Headless Horseman* (1937), *The Devil and Daniel Webster* (1939), *Freedom's a Hard-Bought Thing* (*c.* 1941). NOVELS: *The Beginning of Wisdom* (1921), *Young People's Pride* (1922), *Jean Huguenot* (1923), *Spanish Bayonet* (1926). POETRY: *Five Men and Pompey* (1915), *Young Adventure* (1918) *Heavens and Earth* (1920), *The Ballad of William Sycamore, 1790-1880* (1923), *King David* (1923), *Tiger Joy* (1925), *John Brown's Body*† (1928), *Ballads and Poems, 1915-1930* (1931), *Nightmare at Noon* (1940), *They Burned the Books* (1942), *Western Star* (unfinished, 1943). COLLECTIONS: *Selected Works*† (two volumes, 1942), *The Last Circle*† (1946). INDIVIDUAL POEMS: "The Ballad of William Sycamore," "The Mountain Whippoorwill," "The Hider's Song," "The Guns," "Litany for Dictatorships," "Rain after a Vaudeville Show," "Listen to the People" (dramatic radio-script poem), "Song about Children." SELECTED LETTERS (1960).

Malcolm Cowley, 1898— , translator, editor, poet, critic. POETRY: *Blue Juniata* (1929), *Dry Season* (1941). REMINISCENCES: *Exile's Return*† (1934).

EDITOR: *After the Genteel Tradition: American Writers since 1910* (1937), *Books That Changed Our Minds* (in collaboration with Bernard Smith, 1939). INDIVIDUAL POEMS: "The Urn," "The Hill above the Mine," "Blue Juniata," "For St. Bartholomew's Eve," "The Farm Died," "William Wilson," "Towers of Song," "Winter: Two Sonnets." CRITICISM: *The Literary Situation* (1954).

[Harold] Hart Crane, 1899—1932, poet. POETRY: *White Buildings* (1926). *The Bridge* (1930), *Collected Poems*† (1933). INDIVIDUAL POEMS: "To Brooklyn Bridge," "Praise for an Urn," "For the Marriage of Faustus and Helen," "The River" (from *The Bridge*), "Royal Palm," "Repose of Rivers," "Voyages: II," "Cutty Sark," "The Hurricane," "Lachrymae Christae." LETTERS (1952).

Léonie [Fuller] Adams, 1899 , translator, poet. POETRY: *Those Not Elect* (1925), *High Falcon* (1929), *This Measure* (1933), *Poems: A Selection* (1954). INDIVIDUAL POEMS: "Country Summer," "The Mount," "The River in the Meadows," "April Mortality," "Never Enough of Living," "Bell Tower."

[James] Langston Hughes, 1902— , short-story writer, novelist, poet. CHILDREN'S BOOK: *Popo and Fifina: Children of Haiti* (in collaboration with Arna Bontemps, 1932). SHORT STORIES: *The Ways of White Folks* (1934), *Laughing to Keep from Crying* (1952). NOVEL: *Not without Laughter* (1930). POEMS: *The Weary Blues*† (1926), *Fine Clothes to the Jew* (1927), *The Big Sea*† (1940), *Shakespeare in Harlem*† (1942), *Fields of Wonder* (1947), *One-Way Ticket* (1949), *Montage of a Dream Deferred* (1951). OTHER: *Poetry of the Negro, 1746-1949* (anthology, with Arna Wendell, 1949), *The First Book of Negroes* (1952), *Famous American Negroes* (1954), *Simple Speaks His Mind* (1950), *Simple Takes a Wife* (1953), *Best of Simple* (1961).

George Dillon, 1906— , translator, poet. POETRY: *Boy in the Wind* (1927), *The Flowering Stone*† (1931). INDIVIDUAL POEMS: "Boy in the Wind," "Memory of Lake Superior," "The Noise of Leaves," "April's Amazing Meaning," "Compliment to Mariners," "The Hours of the Day," "Women without Fear," "The Hard Lovers," "The Dead Elm on the Hilltop."

W[ystan] H[ugh] Auden, 1907 , poet, essayist, playwright. POEMS: *The Age of Anxiety* (collection, Pulitzer Prize, 1947), *Collected Poetry* (1945), *Collected Shorter Poems, 1930-1944* (1950), *Nones* (1951), *The Shield of Achilles* (1955). OTHER: *Journey to a War* (with Christopher Isherwood, 1939), *The Enchafèd Flood* (1950), *Some Notes on Grimm and Anderson* (1952). PLAYS: (See section on Christopher Isherwood.)

Peter Viereck, 1916— , poet. POETRY: *Terror and Decorum* (collection, Pulitzer Prize, 1948), *Strike Through the Mask* (1950), *The Unadjusted Man* (1956).

IMPORTANT PLAYWRIGHTS

Percy [Wallace] MacKaye, 1875—1956, translator, essayist, poet, playwright. BIOGRAPHY: *Epoch* (two volumes, 1927). FOLK TALES: *Tall Tales of the Kentucky Mountains* (1926). OPERA: *Rip Van Winkle* (in collaboration, 1919). MASQUES: *Sanctuary: A Bird Masque* (1914), *Caliban by the Yellow Sands* (1916), *The Evergreen Tree* (1917). PLAYS: *The Canterbury Pilgrims* (1903), *Jeanne d'Arc* (1906), *Sappho and Phaon* (1907), *Mater* (1908), *The Scarecrow*† (1908), *Anti-Matrimony* (1910), *To-Morrow* (1912), *Yankee Fantasies* (1912), *Washington: The Man Who Made Us* (1920), *This Fine-Pretty World* (1924), *Kentucky Mountain Fantasies* (1928). POETRY: *Discoveries and Inventions; Victories of the American Spirit* (1950), *My Lady Dear, Arise* (songs and sonnets, 1951). OTHER: *The Mystery of Hamlet* (four verse plays, 1950), *Poog's Pasture* (autobiography, 1951), *Poog and the Caboose Man* (1952).

Rachel Crothers, 1878—1958, director, playwright. PLAYS: *The Three of Us*†

(1906; 1916), *A Man's World*† (1909; 1915), *He and She* (1911), *Ourselves* (1912; 1913), *Young Wisdom* (1913; 1914), *Old Lady 31*† (1916; *c.* 1923), *Nice People*† (1920), "Everyday" (1921), *Mother Carey's Chickens*† (in collaboration with K. D. Wiggin, 1917; 1925), *Mary the Third* (1923), *Expressing Willie*† (1924), *A Lady's Virtue* (1925), *Let Us Be Gay* (1929), "As Husbands Go"† (1931), *When Ladies Meet*† (1932), *Susan and God*† (1938).

Susan Glaspell, 1882—1948, novelist, playwright. SHORT STORIES: *Lifted Masks* (1912). BIOGRAPHY: *The Road to the Temple*† (1926). NOVELS: *The Glory of the Conquered* (1909), *The Visioning* (1911), *Fidelity* (1915), *Brook Evans* (1928), *Fugitive's Return* (1929), *Ambrose Holt and Family* (1931), *The Morning Is Near Us* (1940), *Norma Ashe* (1942), *Judd Rankin's Daughter*† (1945). INDIVIDUAL PLAYS AND PERFORMANCE YEAR: *Suppressed Desires* (1914), *Trifles*† (1916), *Close the Book* (1917), *Woman's Honor* (1918), *Tickless Time* (1918), *Bernice* (1919), *Inheritors* (1921), *The Verge* (1921), *Allison's House*† (1930).

Maxwell Anderson, 1888—1959, editor, essayist, poet, playwright. POEMS: *You Who Have Dreams* (1925). ESSAYS: *The Essence of Tragedy and Other Footnotes and Papers* (1939), *Off Broadway*† (1947). PLAYS: *Sea Wife* (mimeographed, 1926), *Both Your Houses* (1933), *Candle in the Wind* (1941), *Journey to Jerusalem* (1941), *Eve of St. Mark* (1942), *Joan of Lorraine*† (1947), *Anne of the Thousand Days*† (1948). COLLECTIONS: *Three American Plays* (in collaboration with Lawrence Stallings, 1926), includes *What Price Glory*† (1924); *Eleven Verse Plays* (1940), includes *Elizabeth the Queen*† (1930), *Night Over Taos* (1932), *Mary of Scotland* (1933), *Valley Forge* (1934), *Winterset*† (1935), *The Wingless Victory* (1936), *High Tor*† (1937), *The Masque of Kings* (1936), *The Feast of Ortolans* (1938), *Second Overture* (1938), *Key Largo* (1939), *Lost in the Stars* (dramatization of Alan Paton's novel, *Cry, the Beloved Country,* 1950), *Barefoot in Athens* (1951), *The Bad Seed* (adaptation, 1955). VERSES FOR MUSIC (with Kurt Weill): "It Never Was Anywhere You" (1938), "September Song" (1938).

Eugene [Gladstone] O'Neill, 1888—1953, dramatist. PLAYS: *Beyond the Horizon*† (1920), *Chris Christopherson* (1920: subsequently rewritten as *Anna Christie*), *The Straw* (1921), *Gold* (1921: originally the one-act play, *Where the Cross Is Made,* 1918), *The Emperor Jones*† (1920; 1921), *Anna Christie*† (1921), *The First Man* (1922), *The Hairy Ape* (1922), *All God's Chillun Got Wings* (1924), *Welded* (1924), *Desire under the Elms*† (1924; 1925), *The Fountain* (1925; 1926), *The Great God Brown* (1926), *Marco Millions* (1927), *Lazarus Laughed* (1927), *Strange Interlude*† (1928), *Dynamo* (1929), *Mourning Becomes Electra*† (trilogy, 1931), *Ah Wilderness*† (1933), *Days without End* (1934), *Iceman Cometh*† (1946). ONE-ACT PLAYS: *Recklessness* (1914), *The Web* (1914), *Warnings* (1914), *Thirst* (1914), *Fog* (1914), *Before Breakfast* (1916), *Bound East for Cardiff* (1916), *In the Zone* (1917; 1919), *The Long Voyage Home* (1917), *The Sniper* (1917), *The Moon of the Caribbees* (1918; 1919), *The Rope* (1918; 1919), *The Dreamy Kid* (1919; 1920), *Exorcism* (1920). OTHER: *Lost Plays* (1950), *A Moon for the Misbegotten* (1952), *Long Day's Journey Into Night* (1956), *A Touch of the Poet* (1957).

George S. Kaufman, 1889—1961, journalist, director, playwright. PLAYS: All in collaboration: *Dulcy*† (1921), *To the Ladies* (1923), *Beggar on Horseback* (1924), *Merton of the Movies* (1925). *Once in a Lifetime* (1930), *Merrily We Roll Along* (1934), *You Can't Take It with You*† (1936), *I'd Rather Be Right* (1937), *The American Way* (1939), *The Man Who Came to Dinner* (1939), *George Washington Slept Here* (1940). *Minick* (1924), *The Royal Family*† (1928), *Dinner at Eight* (1932), *Stage Door*† (1936), *The Land Is Bright* (1941). *Of Thee I Sing*† (1932), *Let 'Em Eat Cake* (1933). *June Moon* (1930). *The Dark Tower* (1934). *First Lady* (1935). *Small Hours* (1951), *The Solid Gold Cadillac* (1954).

Sidney [Coe] Howard, 1891—1939, versatile writer. PLAYS: *They Knew What They Wanted*† (1925), *Silver Cord*† (1927), *Ghost of Yankee Doodle* (1938).

Elmer [L.] Rice, 1892— , novelist, playwright. NOVELS: *A Voyage to Purilia* (1930), *Imperial City* (1937), *The Show Must Go On* (1949). PLAYS: *The Adding Machine*† (1923), *Street Scene*† (1929), *Counsellor-at-Law* (1931), *Two on an Island*† (1940), *Flight to the West* (1941), *A New Life*† (1944), *Dream Girl* (1946), *Grand Tour* (1952), *The Winner* (1954).

S[amuel] N[athaniel] Behrman, 1893— , adapter, playwright. PLAYS: *Bedside Manners* (1924), *The Second Man*† (1927), *Brief Moment* (1934), *Biography*† (1933), *Rain from Heaven*† (1934), *End of Summer* (1936), *No Time for Comedy* (1939), *The Talley Man* (1941), *The Pirate*† (1943), *Dunnigan's Daughter*† (1946). OTHER WRITINGS: *Amphitryon 38* (by Jean Giraudoux, from the French, 1938), *Jacobowsky and the Colonel* (original play by Franz V. Werfel, 1944); *Josef Duveen* (a biography, 1949); *Jane* (a play based on a story by W. Somerset Maugham, 1952), *Portrait of Max* (1960).

Ben Hecht, *c.* 1893—1964, essayist, short-story writer, novelist, playwright. SHORT STORIES AND SKETCHES: *A Thousand and One Afternoons in Chicago* (1922), *Tales of Chicago Streets* (1924), *Broken Necks* (1926), *The Champion from Far Away* (1931), *A Book of Miracles* (1939), *Collected Stories* (1945), *The Cat That Jumped out of the Story* (1947). NOVELS: *Erik Dorn*† (1921), *Fantazius Mallare* (1922), *Gargoyles* (1922), *The Florentine Dagger* (1923), *Humpty Dumpty* (1924), *The Kingdom of Evil* (1924), *Count Bruga* (1926), *A Jew in Love* (1931), *I Hate Actors!* (1944). PLAYS: *The Master Poisoner* (with Maxwell Bodenheim, 1918), *The Front Page*† (with Charles MacArthur, 1928), *The Wonder Hat* (with Kenneth Goodman, 1933), *Twentieth Century* (with Charles MacArthur, 1933), *The Great Magoo* (with Gene Fowler, 1933), *To Quito and Back* (1937), *Ladies and Gentlemen* (with Charles MacArthur, 1941), *Fun to be Free* (1941). OTHER: *A Guide for the Bedevilled*† (on Anti-Semitism, 1944), *A Child of the Century* (autobiog., 1954).

Paul [Eliot] Green, 1894— , compiler, critic, playwright. NOVEL: *The Laughing Pioneer* (1932). SHORT STORIES: *Wide Fields* (1928), *Salvation on a String*† (1946), *Dog on the Sun* (1949). ESSAYS: *Hawthorn Tree* (1944). INDIVIDUAL PLAYS: *Your Fiery Furnace* (1923), *The Lord's Will* (1925), *In Abraham's Bosom*† (1926), *The Field God* (1927), *In the Valley* (1928), *The House of Connelly*† (1931), *Tread the Green Grass* (1931), *Roll Sweet Chariot* (1935), *Hymn to the Rising Sun*† (1936), *Johnny Johnson* (in collaboration, 1937), *The Lost Colony* (1937), *The Critical Year* (1939), *Franklin and the King* (1939), *The Highland Call* (1941), *Common Glory*† (1948), *Faith of our Fathers* (1950).

Philip Barry, 1896—1949, dramatist. PLAYS: *You and I*† (1923; 1925), *In a Garden* (1925; 1926), *White Wings* (1926; 1927), *Cock Robin* (in collaboration, 1928; 1929), *Holiday*† (1928; 1929), *Hotel Universe*† (1930), *Tomorrow and Tomorrow* (1931), *The Animal Kingdom* (1932), *The Joyous Season* (1934), *Bright Star* (1935), *Here Come the Clowns* (1938: novelized the same year into *War in Heaven*), *The Philadelphia Story* (1939), *Liberty Jones* (1941), *Without Love* (1943), *Second Threshold* (1951).

Robert [Emmett] Sherwood. 1896—1955, editor, essayist, novelist, playwright. PLAYS: *The Road to Rome* (1927), *Reunion in Vienna*† (1932), *Idiot's Delight*† (1936), *Abe Lincoln in Illinois* (1939), *There Shall Be No Night*† (1940). HISTORY: *Roosevelt and Hopkins: An Intimate History*† (1948).

Lillian Hellman, 1905— , playwright. PLAYS: *The Children's Hour*† (1934), *Days to Come* (1936), *The Little Foxes*† (1939), *Watch on the Rhine*† (1941), *The Searching Wind*† (1944), *Another Part of the Forest* (1946), *Montserrat* (1949), *The Autumn Garden* (1951), *Toys in the Attic* (1960).

Sidney Kingsley, 1906— , playwright. *Men in White* (1933), *Dead End*† (1936), *Patriots*† (1943), *Detective Story*† (1949), *Darkness at Noon*† (1951).

Clifford Odets, 1906— , playwright. PLAYS: *Awake and Sing*† (1935), *Waiting for Lefty*† (1935), *Till the Day I Die*† (1935), *Golden Boy*† (1937), *Night Music* (1940), *Clash by Night* (1942), *Country Girl* (1951).

Mary Coyle Chase, 1907— , playwright. PLAYS: *Now You've Done It* (1937), *Too Much Business* (1938), *Harvey*† (1944, Pulitzer Prize winner), *Bernardine* (1952), *Mrs. McThing*† (1952).

Tennessee Williams [Thomas Lanier] 1914— , playwright, novelist. PLAYS: *Battle of Angels* (1940), *The Glass Menagerie*† (1944), *You Touched Me* (1946), *A Streetcar Named Desire*† (1947, Pulitzer Prize winner), *Summer and Smoke* (1948), *The Rose Tattoo* (1950), *I Rise in Flames, Cried the Phoenix* (1951), *Cat on a Hot Tin Roof* (1955), *Orpheus Descending* (1957), *Suddenly Last Summer* (1958), *Sweet Bird of Youth* (1959), *Period of Adjustment* (1961), *The Night of the Iguana* (1961). OTHER: *The Roman Spring of Mrs. Stone* (novel, 1950), *One Arm and Other Stories* (1954).

Arthur Miller, 1915— , playwright, novelist. PLAYS: *The Man Who Had All the Luck* (1944), *Situation Normal* (1944), *All My Sons*† (1947), *Death of a Salesman*† (1949), *An Enemy of the People* (adaptation of Ibsen's play, 1951), *The Crucible* (1953), *A Memory of Two Mondays* (1957), *A View from the Bridge* (1957), *The Misfits* (1961). NOVEL: *Focus* (1945).

ESSAYISTS, CRITICS, EDUCATORS, PHILOSOPHERS

Agnes Repplier, 1858—1950, editor, critic, essayist. ESSAYS: *Books and Men* (1888), *Point of View* (1891), *Essays in Miniature* (1892), *Essays in Idleness* (1893), *In the Dozy Hours* (1894), *Compromises* (1904), *Americans and Others* (1912), *Counter-Currents* (1916), *Under Dispute* (1924), *To Think of Tea!* (1932), *In Pursuit of Laughter* (1936), *Eight Decades*† (1937). AUTOBIOGRAPHY: *In Our Convent Days* (1905), "A Happy Half-Century" in *A Happy Half-Century and Other Essays* (1908). MISCELLANEOUS: *Philadelphia: The Place and the People* (history, 1898), *The Fireside Sphinx* (about cats, 1912), *Père Marquette, Priest, Pioneer, and Adventurer* (biography, 1929), *Mère Marie of the Ursulines* (biography, 1931), *Junípero Serra* (biography, 1933).

John Dewey, 1859—1952, educator, philosopher. PSYCHOLOGY: *Psychology*† (1887), *How We Think* (1909), *Human Nature and Conduct*† (1922). LOGIC: *Studies in Logical Theory* (1903), *Essay in Experimental Logic* (1916), *Logic: The Theory of Inquiry* (1938). ETHICS: *Outlines of a Critical Theory of Ethics* (1891), *Ethics* (in collaboration with J. H. Tufts, 1908). POLITICAL AND SOCIAL PHILOSOPHY: *The Influence of Darwin in Philosophy and Other Essays* (1910), *Reconstruction in Philosophy* (1920), *Experience and Nature*† (1925), *The Quest for Certainty* (1929), *Impressions of Soviet Russia and the Revolutionary World, Mexico — China — Turkey* (1929), *Individualism: Old and New* (1930), *Philosophy and Civilization* (1931), *Art as Experience*† (1934), *Liberalism and Social Action* (1935), *Intelligence in the Modern World: John Dewey's Philosophy* (edited by Joseph Ratner, 1939), *Freedom and Culture* (1939), *Problems of Men*† (1946). EDUCATION: *The School and Society*† (1899), *The Child and the Curriculum*† (1902), *Moral Principles in Education*† (1909), *Interest and Effort in Education*† (1913), *Democracy and Education* (1916), *Experience and Education*† (1938), *The Bertrand Russell Case* (with H. M. Kallen, 1942), *Essays for Conference* (1950). BIOGRAPHY: *David Dubinsky; a Pictorial Biography* (1952).

George Santayana, 1863—1952, poet, educator, philosophical writer. VERSE PLAY: *Lucifer; a Theological Tragedy* (1899). NOVEL: *The Last Puritan*† (1935). MEMOIRS: *Persons and Places*† (1944), *Middle Span*† (1945), *My Host the World* (1953). POETRY: *Sonnets . . .* (1894), *A Hermit of Carmel* (1901), *Poems* (1922). STUDIES: *The Sense of Beauty* (1896), *Interpretations of Poetry and Religion* (1900), *The Life of Reason; or The Phases of Human Progress*† (five volumes: I —

Introduction and Reason in Common Sense, 1905; II — *Reason in Society,* 1905; III — *Reason in Religion,* 1905; IV — *Reason in Art,* 1905; V — *Reason in Science,* 1906), *Three Philosophical Poets: Lucretius, Dante, and Goethe* (1910), *Winds of Doctrine* (1913), *Egotism in German Philosophy* (1916; the 1940 edition adds a New Preface, and a postscript: "The Nature of Egotism and the Moral Conflicts That Disturb the World"), *Philosophical Opinion in America* (1918), *Character & Opinion in the United States* (1920), *Soliloquies in England and Later Soliloquies* (1922), *Scepticism and Animal Faith*† (1923), *Dialogues in Limbo* (1925), *Platonism and the Spiritual Life*† (1927), *The Genteel Tradition at Bay* (1931), *Some Turns of Thought in Modern Philosophy* (1933), *Obiter Scripta* (edited by Justus Buchler and Benjamin Schwartz, 1936), *The Philosophy of Santayana*† (edited by Irwin Edman, 1936), *The Philosophy of George Santayana*† (edited by P. A. Schlipp, 1940), *The Realms of Being*† (four volumes: I — *The Realm of Essence,* 1927; II — *The Realm of Matter,* 1930; III — *The Realm of Truth,* 1938; IV — *The Realm of Spirit,* 1940), *Realms of Being* (one-volume edition, 1942), *Idea of Christ in the Gospels, or, God in Man*† (1946), *Knowing and the Known* (in collaboration with A. F. Bentley, (1949), *Dominations and Powers: Reflections on Liberty, Society, and Government* (1951). INDIVIDUAL POEMS: ODES: "My Heart Rebels against My Generation," "Gathering the Echoes of Forgotten Wisdom," "Of Thee the Northman by His Bleachéd Wisdom." SONNETS: "O World, Thou Choosest Not the Part," "Slow and Reluctant Was the Long Descent," "I Would I Might Forget that I Am," "Have Patience: It Is Fit that in This Wise," "Sweet Are the Days when We Wander with No Hope," "'Tis Love That Moveth the Celestial Spheres," "As in the Midst of Battle There Is Room," "As When the Sceptre Dangles from the Hand," "After Grey Vigils, Sunshine in the Heart," "O World, Thou Choosest Not the Better Part"; and such pieces as "Gabriel," "Easter Hymn," "Good Friday Hymn," "On the Death of a Metaphysician," "The Rustic at the Play," "On a Piece of Tapestry."

Paul Elmer More, 1864—1937, translator, editor, essayist, critic, scholar. BIOGRAPHY: *Benjamin Franklin* (1900). AUTOBIOGRAPHY: *Pages from an Oxford Diary* (1937). PHILOSOPHICAL STUDIES: *Platonism* (1917), *The Religion of Plato* (1921), *Hellenistic Philosophies* (1923), *The Christ of the New Testament* (1924), *The Catholic Faith* (1931). CRITICAL ESSAYS: *Shelburne Essays* (eleven volumes: First Series, 1904; Second, 1905; Third, 1905; Fourth, 1906; Fifth, 1908; Sixth, 1909; Seventh, 1910; Eighth,† 1913; Ninth, 1915; Tenth, 1919; Eleventh, 1921), *The Demon of the Absolute*† (1928), *Selected Shelburne Essays*† (1935).

Irving Babbitt, 1865—1933, editor, translator, critic, scholar. ESSAYS AND STUDIES: *Literature and the American College* (1908), *The New Laokoön*† (1910), *The Masters of Modern French Criticism* (1912), *Rousseau and Romanticism*† (1919), *Democracy and Leadership* (1924), *On Being Creative* (1932), *Spanish Character* (1940).

George Ade, 1866—1944, columnist, syndicate-writer, novelist, playwright, fabulist. FABLES: *Fables in Slang*† (1899), *More Fables*† (1900), *Forty Modern Fables*† (1901), *The Girl Proposition* (1902), *People You Knew*† (1903), *Breaking into Society* (1904), *True Bills* (1904), *I Knew Him When —* (1910), *Knocking the Neighbors* (1912), *Ade's Fables* (1914), *Hand-Made Fables*† (1920), *Thirty Fables in Slang* (1933). SHORT STORIES AND NOVELS: *Artie* (1896), *Pink Marsh* (1897), *Doc' Horne* (1899), *Circus Days* (1903), *In Babel* (1903), *The Slim Princess* (1907), *Bang! Bang!* (1928), *Stories of the Streets and the Towns* (1941). PLAYS AND PRODUCTION YEAR: *Ki-Ram or The Sultan of Sulu* (1902), *Peggy from Paris* (1903), *The Napoleon* (1903) *The County Chairman*† (1903), *The College Widow*† (1904), *Our New Minister* (1904), *The Shogun* (1904), *The Bad Samaritan* (1905), *Just out of College* (1905), *Marse Covington* (1906), *Artie* (1907), *Father and the Boys* (1907), *The Fair Co-Ed* (1908), *The Old Town* (1909), *Nettie* (1914), *The Mayor and the Manicure* (printed, 1923). MISCELLANEOUS: *In Pastures New* (humorous travel sketches, 1906), *Verses and Jingles* (1911), *Single Blessedness and Other Observations* (essays, 1922), *The Old-Time Saloon* (essays, 1931), *One Afternoon with Mark Twain* (1939), *The Permanent Ade: [The] Living Writings of George Ade*† (edited by Fred C. Kelly, 1947).

Charles A[ustin] Beard, 1874—1948, editor, historian, political science, educator. POLITICAL AND HISTORICAL STUDIES: *An Introduction to the English Historians* (1906), *The Development of Modern Europe* (in collaboration with J. H. Robinson, two volumes, 1907-1908), *American Government and Politics* (1910), *American City Government* (1912), *The Supreme Court and the Constitution* (1912), *An Economic Interpretation of the Constitution*† (1913), *Economic Origins of Jeffersonian Democracy*† (1915), *The Economic Basis of Politics* (1922), *The Rise of American Civilization*† (in collaboration with Mary R. Beard, two volumes, 1927), *The American Leviathan* (in collaboration with William Beard, 1930), *A Charter for the Social Sciences* (1932), *The Idea of National Interest* (in colaboration with G. H. E. Smith, 1934), *The Open Door at Home* (in collaboration with G. H. E. Smith, 1934), *America in Midpassage* (in collaboration with Mary R. Beard: volume III of *The Rise of American Civilization,* 1930), *A Balance Sheet of American History* (1940), *The Old Deal and the New Deal* (1940), *A Foreign Policy for America* (1940), *American Spirit* (in collaboration with M. R. Beard, 1942), *The Republic* (1943), *A Basic History of the United States* (with M. R. Beard, 1944), *The Economic Basis of Politics* (1945), *American Foreign Policy in the Making: 1932-1940*† (1946), *President Roosevelt and the Coming of the War 1941*† (1948).

[Charles] William Beebe, 1877—1962, scientist, explorer. STUDIES: *Two-Bird Lovers in Mexico* (1905), *The Log of the Sun* (1906), *Our Search of a Wilderness* (1910), *Tropical Wild Life in British Guiana* (1917), *Jungle Peace*† (1918), *Pheasants: Their Lives and Homes* (1926), *Galapagos: World's End* (1924), *Jungle Days* (1925), *The Arcturus Adventure* (1926), *Pheasant Jungles* (1927), *Beneath Tropic Seas* (1928), *Nonsuch: Land of Water* (1932), *Half Mile Down.* (1934). *Book of Bays* (1942), *High Jungle*† (1949). EDITOR: *The Book of Naturalists* (1944).

James Truslow Adams, 1878—1949, pamphleteer, editor, biographer, historian. HISTORICAL AND BIOGRAPHICAL STUDIES: *Notes on the Families of Truslow, Horler, and Horley from English Records* (1920), *The Founding of New England* (1921), *The Epic of America*† (1931), *History of the United States* (five volumes, 1933—1937), *The Living Jefferson* (1936), *Empire on the Seven Seas: The British Empire* (1940), *The American: The Making of a New Man* (1943), *Frontiers of American Culture*† (1944), *Big Business in a Democracy* (1945). EDITED AND COMPILED WORKS: *Hamiltonian Principles: Extracts from the Writings of Alexander Hamilton* (1928), *Jeffersonian Principles: Extracts from the Writings of Thomas Jefferson* (1928), *Atlas of American History*† (1943), *Album of American History* (four volumes, 1944-1948).

Henry Seidel Canby, 1878—1961, textbook writer, editor, critic. TEXTBOOK: *Handbook of English Usage* (in collaboration with J. B. Opdycke, 1942), *Book of the Short Story*† (revised edition, in collaboration with Robeson Bailey, 1948). BIOGRAPHY: *Thoreau*† (1939), *Walt Whitman* (1943). INFORMAL RIVER-HISTORY: *The Brandywine* (1941). REMINISCENCES: *The Age of Confidence*† (1934), *Alma Mater: The Gothic Age of the American College* (1936), *Family History*† (1945), *American Memoir*† (1947). STUDIES: *The Short Story* (1902), *The Short Story in English* (1909), *A Study of the Short Story* (1913), *Everyday Americans* (1920), *Definitions* (First Series, 1922; Second, 1924), *American Estimates* (1929), *Classic Americans*† (1931), *Turn West, Turn East; Mark Twain and Henry James* (1951).

Dorothy Canfield [Dorothea Frances Canfield Fisher], 1879—1958, editor, translator, playwright, short-story writer, novelist, educator. TRANSLATION: *Life of Christ by Giovanni Papini* (1923). CHILDREN'S BOOK: *Made-to-Order Stories* (1925). SHORT STORIES: *The Real Motive* (1916), *Fables for Parents* (1937), *Tell Me a Story* (collection, 1950). NOVELS: *The Squirrel-Cage* (1912), *The Bent Twig*† (1915), *The Brimming Cup*† (1921), *Seasoned Timber* (1939), ESSAYS AND STUDIES IN LITERATURE AND IN EDUCATION: *Corneille and Racine in England* (1904), *A Montessori Mother* (1912), *The French School at Middlebury* (c. 1923), *Our Young Folks*† (1943). TALES FOR CHARACTER

EDUCATION: *Nothing Ever Happens, and How It Does*† (with Sarah N. Cleghorn, 1940), *American Portraits*† (drawings and biographical sketches, 1947). MISCELLANY: *Fair World for All; the Meaning of the Declaration of Human Rights* (1952).

H[enry] L[ouis] Mencken, 1880—1956, journalist, editor, essayist, critic. AUTOBIOGRAPHY: *Days of H. L. Mencken* (1947), omnibus volume including *Happy Days* (1940), *Newspaper Days* (1941), and *Heathen Days* (1943). AMERICAN USAGE AND VOCABULARY: *The American Language*† (1919; supplements, 1945, 1948). STUDIES: *George Bernard Shaw* (1905), *The Philosophy of Friedrich Nietzsche* (1908), *A Book of Prefaces*† (1917), *In Defense of Women* (1918), *Prejudices*† (Six Series: 1919, 1920, 1922, 1924, 1926, 1927), *The American Credo* (in collaboration with G. J. Nathan, 1920), *Notes on Democracy* (1926), *James Branch Cabell*† (1927), *Selected Prejudices*† (1927), *Treatise on the Gods* (1930), *Treatise on Right and Wrong* (1934). MISCELLANEOUS: *Ventures into Verse* (1903), *A Book of Burlesques* (1916), *Europe after 8:15* (in collaboration, 1914), *Making a President* (1932), and, in collaboration with G. J. Nathan, the two plays, *The Artist* (1912), and *Heliogabalus* (1920), *Christmas Story*† (1946), *Chrestomathy*† (1949). OTHER: *New Dictionary of Quotations . . .* (1942), *Letters* (1961).

Stuart P[ratt] Sherman, 1881—1926, editor, critic, educator. CRITICISM: *On Contemporary Literature*† (1917), *Matthew Arnold: How to Know Him*† (1917), *Americans* (1922), *The Genius of America* (1923), *My Dear Cornelia* (1924), *Points of View*† (1924), *Critical Woodcuts* (1926), *The Main Stream* (1927), *The Emotional Discovery of America and Other Essays* (1932). BIOGRAPHICAL: *Life and Letters of Stuart P. Sherman* (two volumes, 1929). EDITOR: *The Cambridge History of American Literature* (in collaboration, four volumes, 1917-1921).

Ludwig Lewisohn, 1883—1955, short-story writer, playwright, novelist, editor, translator, critic. AUTOBIOGRAPHY: *Up Stream: An American Chronicle*† (1922), *Mid-Channel: An American Chronicle* (1929). NOVELS: *The Broken Snare* (1908), *For Ever Wilt Thou Love* (1939), *Renegade*† (1942), *Breathe Upon These* (1944), *Case of Mr. Crump* (1947, but originally published in Paris in 1926), *Anniversary*† (1947), *In a Summer Season* (1955). CRITICISM: *Expression in America* (1937; published also in 1937 under the title *The Story of American Literature*). EDITOR: *Among the Nations: Three Tales and a Play about Jews* (1948), *Goethe: The Story of a Man* (two volumes, 1949), *Unambo* (translation of the novel of war in Israel, 1952). OTHER: *The American Jew* (1950), *The Magic Word* (1950).

Max [Forrester] Eastman, 1883— , poet, translator, political writer, critic. POETRY: *Lot's Wife* (1942). TRANSLATOR: *The History of the Russian Revolution* (translated from the Russian of Leon Trotsky, three volumes, 1932-1933). POLITICAL STUDIES: *Marx, Lenin and The Science of Revolution* (1926), *Marxism: Is It Science?* (1940), *Stalin's Russia and the Crisis in Socialism* (1940). AUTOBIOGRAPHY: *Enjoyment of Living*† (1948). STUDIES: *Enjoyment of Poetry*† (1913), *The Literary Mind: Its Place in an Age of Science* (1931), *Art and the Life of Action* (1934), *Artists in Uniform*† (1934), *Enjoyment of Laughter*† (1936), *Heroes I Have Known* (1942), *Enjoyment of Poetry* (1951), *Great Companions* (1959). WORKS: *Poems of Five Decades* (1954).

Ring[gold] W[ilmer] Lardner, 1885—1933, columnist, sports writer, humorist, short-story writer. HUMOR: *Treat 'Em Rough* (1918), *What of It?* (1925), *The Story of a Wonder Man* (1937), *First and Last* (1934). SHORT STORIES: *Gullible's Travels* (1917), *How to Write Short Stories*† (1924), *The Love Nest*† (1926), *Round Up* (1929). NOVELS: *You Know Me Al* (1916), *The Big Town* (1921). MISCELLANEOUS: *Bib Ballads* (rhymes, 1915), *June Moon* (play in collaboration with G. S. Kaufman, 1930), *Portable Ring Lardner*† (1946).

Louis Untermeyer, 1885— , novelist, parodist, biographer, translator, poet, critic, editor. BIOGRAPHY: *Heinrich Heine: Paradox and Poet*† (1937). SELECTED WORK: *Selected Poems and Parodies of Louis Untermeyer* (1935). EDITOR: *Modern American Poetry* (1919), *Modern British Poetry* (1920), *Modern American and British Poetry* (1922), *American Poetry from the Beginning to Whitman*† (1931),

The Book of Living Verse: English and American Poetry from the Thirteenth Century to the Present Day (1932), *The Albatross Book of Modern Living Verse: English and American Poetry of the Later Nineteenth and of the Twentieth Centuries* (1933), *The New Modern American & British Poetry* (1939), *Stars to Steer By*† (1941), *Treasury of Great Poems* (1942), *Treasury of Laughter*† (1946), *An Anthology of the New England Poets from Colonial Times to the Present Day*† (1948), *Best Humor Annual* (in collaboration with R. E. Shiken, 1951, 1952), *Early American Poets* (1952), *Magic Circle; Stories and People in Poetry* (1952).

Carl [Clinton] Van Doren, 1885–1950, novelist, short-story writer, biographer, historian, critic, editor. AUTOBIOGRAPHY: *Three Worlds*† (1936). BIOGRAPHY: *Benjamin Franklin*† (three volumes, 1938). LITERARY CRITICISM: *Contemporary American Novelists, 1900-1920* (1922). EDITOR: *Tales by Washington Irving* (1918). *The Borzoi Reader* (1936), *The American Novel, 1789-1939* (1940), *Letters and Papers of Benjamin Franklin and Richard Jackson, 1753-1785*† (1947). HISTORY: *Secret History of the American Revolution* (1941), *Meeting in January: The Story of a Crisis Now for the First Time Fully Told . . .*† (1943), *Great Rehearsal: The Story of the Making and Ratifying of the Constitution*† (1948).

Van Wyck Brooks, 1886—1963, poet, translator, essayist, critic. BIOGRAPHY: *The Ordeal of Mark Twain*† (1920), *The Pilgrimage of Henry James*† (1925), *The Life of Emerson* (1932). STUDIES: *The Wine of the Puritans* (1908), *America's Coming-of-Age*† (1915), *Letters and Leadership* (1918), *Emerson and Others* (1927), *Sketches in Criticism* (1932), *The Flowering of New England, 1815-1865*† (1936), *New England: Indian Summer*† (1940), *On Literature Today*† (1941), *Opinions of Oliver Allston* (1941), *The World of Washington Irving* (1944), *The Times of Melville and Whitman* (1947), *A Chilmark Miscellany*† (1948), *The Confident Years* (1952), *Days of the Phoenix* (1957), *Dream of Arcadia* (1958), *Howells* (1959), *From the Shadow of the Mountain* (1961), *Fenellosa and His Circle* (1962).

Norman Foerster, 1887— , editor, compiler, textbook writer, critic. TEXTBOOKS: *Sentences and Thinking* (in collaboration, 1919), *Writing and Thinking* (in collaboration, 1931). EDITOR: *American Poetry and Prose: A Book of Readings, 1607-1916* (1925), *The Reinterpretation of American Literature* (1928), *Humanities after the War*† (1944). CRITICISM: *Nature in American Literature: Studies in the Modern View of Nature* (1923), *Toward Standards: A Study of the Present Critical Movement in American Letters*† (1930), *The Future of the Liberal College* (1938), *Humanities and the Common Man: The Democratic Role of the State Universities* (1946).

Robert [Charles] Benchley, 1889—1945, dramatic critic, humorist. HUMOROUS ESSAYS: *Of All Things*† (1921), *The Early Worm* (1927), *20,000 Leagues under the Sea; or, David Copperfield* (1928), *The Treasurer's Report*† (1930), *No Poems; or, Around the World Backwards and Sideways* (1932), *My Ten Years in a Quandary, and How They Grew* (1936), *After 1903 — What?* (1938), *Inside Benchley* (1942), *Benchley Beside Himself*† (1943), *Benchley —— or else!*† (1947), *Chips Off the Old Benchley* (1949), *The Benchley Roundup* (1954).

Waldo [David] Frank, 1889— , editor, translator, biographer, novelist, lecturer. ESSAYS AND STUDIES: *The Art of the Vieux Colombier* (1918), *The Re-Discovery of America: An Introduction to a Philosophy of American Life*† (1929), *Chart for Rough Water: Our Role in a New World*† (1940). HISTORY AND TRAVEL: *Virgin Spain* (1926; revision, 1942), *South American Journey*† (1943). NOVELS: *City Block*† (1922), *Chalk Face* (1924), *Summer Never Ends* (1941), *Island in the Atlantic*† (1946), *Invaders* (1948), *Not Heaven* (1953). BIOGRAPHY: *Birth of a World* (Bolivar, 1951). OTHER: *The Jew In Our Day* (1944).

Walter Lippmann, 1889— , columnist, editor, political writer. ETHICS: *A Preface to Morals*† (1929). POLITICAL AND SOCIAL STUDIES: *A Preface to Politics*† (1913), *Drift and Mastery* (1914), *The Stakes of Diplomacy* (1915), *The Political Scene* (1919), *Liberty and the News* (1920), *Public Opinion* (1922), *The*

Phantom Public (1925), *The Method of Freedom* (1934), *An Inquiry into the Principles of the Good Society* (1937), *Some Notes on War and Peace* (1940), *U. S. Foreign Policy: Shield of the Republic* (1943), *U. S. War Aims* (1944), *Inquiry into the Principles of the Good Society* (1944), *Cold War: A Study in U. S. Foreign Policy* (1947), *Essays in the Public Philosophy* (1955), *The Communist World and Ours* (1959).

Lewis Mumford, 1895— , editor, critic. EDITOR: *The American Caravan* (1927). BIOGRAPHY: *Herman Melville* (1929). STUDIES: *The Story of Utopias* (1922), *Sticks and Stones* (1924), *The Golden Day*† (1926), *The Brown Decades* (1931), *Technics and Civilization*† (1934), *The Culture of Cities* (1938), *Faith for Living* (1940), *The South in Architecture*† (1941), *Social Foundations of Post-War Building* (1943), *New World Theme* (in collaboration, 1943), *The Condition of Man*† (1944), *City Development: Studies in Disintegration and Renewal*† (1945), *Values for Survival* (1946), *Green Memories: The Story of Geddes Mumford*† (1947), *Conduct of Life* (1951), *Art and Technics* (1952), *The City in History* (1961).

Edmund Wilson, 1895— , poet, novelist, editor, essayist, critic. MUSICAL COMEDY: *The Evil Eye* (book by Edmund Wilson, Jr., 1915-1916). POEMS: *Poets, Farewell!* (1929). NOVEL: *I Thought of Daisy* (1929). PLAYS AND DIALOGUES: *Discordant Encounters* (1926), *This Room and This Gin and These Sandwiches* (1937), *Little Blue Light* (1950). EDITOR: *Shock of Recognition* (collection of American writings, 1943). SKETCHES AND TRAVELS: *Travels in Two Democracies* (1936), *Europe without Baedeker* (1947). CRITICISM: *Axel's Castle* (on the literature of 1870-1930, 1931), *The Triple Thinker: Ten Essays* (1938), *The Wound and the Bow* (1941), *The Boys in the Back Room: Notes on California Novelists* (1941), *Triple Thinkers: Twelve Essays* (1949), *Classics and Commercials* (1950), *Shores of Light* (1952). OTHER: *The American Jitters* (1932), *A Study in the Writing and Acting of History* (1940), *Note-Books of Night* (1942), *Memoirs of Hecate County*† (1946), *A Piece of My Mind* (1956), *Apologies to the Iroquois* (1959).

Bernard [Augustine] DeVoto, 1897—1955, editor, textbook writer, novelist, essayist, historian. TEXTBOOK: *The Writers' Handbook* (in collaboration, 1927). NOVELS: *The Crooked Mile* (1924), *The Chariot of Fire* (1926), *The House of Sun-Goes-Down* (1928), *We Accept with Pleasure* (1934), *Advance Agent*† (1942), *Woman in the Picture* (1944), *Mountain Time*† (1947). ESSAYS AND STUDIES: *Mark Twain's America*† (1932), *Minority Report* (1940), *Mark Twain at Work*† (1942), *Year of Decision, 1846*† (1943), *Literary Fallacy* (1944), *Across the Wide Missouri*† (1947), *The World of Fiction* (1950), *The Hour* (1951), *The Course of Empire* (1952).

John Gunther, 1901— , journalist, author, political writer. STUDIES: *Inside Europe* (1936), *Inside Asia* (1939), *Inside Latin America* (1941), *Inside the U.S.A.* (1947), *Roosevelt in Retrospect* (1950), *The Riddle of MacArthur* (1951), *Caesar of the Pacific* (1951), *Inside Russia Today* (1958), *Meet the Congo* (1959), *Inside Europe Today* (1961). NOVEL: *The Troubled Midnight* (1962).

Granville Hicks, 1901— , editor, poet, biographer, novelist, critic. SOCIAL STUDIES: *John Reed: The Making of a Revolutionary* (with John Stuart, 1936), *I Like America . . .* (1938), *Small Town* (1946). NOVELS: *Only One Storm*† (1942), *Behold Trouble* (1944), *There Was a Man in Our Town* (1952), *Where We Came Out* (1954). CRITICISM: *The Great Tradition* (American Literature since the Civil War, 1933).

Jacques Barzun, 1907— , educator, writer. STUDIES: *The French Race: Theories of Its Origin* (1932), *Race: A Study in Modern Superstition* (1937), *Of Human Freedom* (1939), *Darwin, Marx, Wagner* (1941), *Romanticism and the Modern Ego* (1943), *Teacher in America* (1945), *Berlioz and the Romantic Century* (1950), *God's Country and Mine* (1954), *House of Intellect* (1959), *Classic, Romantic and Modern* (1961).

Thomas Merton, 1915— , philosopher, poet, biographer. AUTOBIOGRAPHY: *The Seven Storey Mountain* (1948). PHILOSOPHICAL AND RELIGIOUS STUDIES: *The Waters of Siloe* (1949), *Seeds of Contemplation* (1949), *Ascent to Truth* (1951), *The Sign of Jonas* (1953). BIOGRAPHY: *Exile Ends in Glory—The Life of a Trappistine, Mother M. Berchmans* (1948). POETRY: *The Tears of the Blind* (collection, 1949), *Figures for an Apocalypse* (1947).

APPENDIX

SUPPLEMENTARY BIBLIOGRAPHIES

WILLIAM ELLERY CHANNING, 1780—1842 (pp. 87-88)

WORKS: *The Works of William E. Channing* (six volumes, 1841-1843).

BIOGRAPHY AND CRITICISM: Chadwick, J. W., *William Ellery Channing, Minister of Religion* (1903); Channing, W. H., *Memoir of William Ellery Channing* (three volumes, 1848); Eliot, C. W., *Four American Leaders* (1906); Ladu, A. I., "Channing and Transcendentalism," *AL.*, XI (1939-1940), pp. 129-137; Spiller, R. E., "A Case for Channing," *NEQ.*, III (1930), pp. 55-81.

RALPH WALDO EMERSON (pp. 88-98)

WORKS: *The Complete Works of Ralph Waldo Emerson*, Centenary Edition, edited by E. W. Emerson (twelve volumes, 1903-1932); *The Journals of Ralph Waldo Emerson*, edited by E. W. Emerson and W. E. Forbes (ten volumes, 1909-1914); *The Letters of Ralph Waldo Emerson*, edited by R. L. Rusk (six volumes, 1939); *The Correspondence of Thomas Carlyle and Ralph Waldo Emerson, 1834-1872*, edited by C. E. Norton (two volumes, revised ed., 1888); "The Emerson-Thoreau Correspondence," edited by F. B. Sanborn, *Atl.*, LXIX (1892), pp. 577-596, 736-753; *Emerson-Clough Letters*, edited by H. F. Lowry and R. L. Rusk (1934); *Uncollected Lectures by Ralph Waldo Emerson: Reports of Lectures on American Life and Natural Religion*, reprinted from the *Commonwealth*, edited by Clarence Gohdes (1932); *The Uncollected Writings, Essays, Addresses, Poems, Reviews and Letters by Ralph Waldo Emerson*, edited by C. C. Bigelow (1912); *Young Emerson Speaks: Unpublished Discourses on Many Subjects* by Ralph Waldo Emerson, edited by A. C. McGiffert, Jr. (1938); *Ralph Waldo Emerson: Representative Selections*, with Introduction, Bibliography, and Notes, edited by F. I. Carpenter (1934); *The Heart of Emerson's Journals*, edited by Bliss Perry (1926); *Ralph Waldo Emerson's Reading . . . Together with Some Unpublished Letters*, by K. W. Cameron (1941); G. S. Hubbell, *A Concordance to the Poems of Ralph Waldo Emerson* (1932); H. A. Pochmann, "The Emerson Canon," *UTQ.*, XII (1943), pp. 476-484.

BIBLIOGRAPHY: Carpenter, F. I. (ed.), *Ralph Waldo Emerson, Representative Selections*, with Introduction, Bibliography, and Notes (1934); Cooke, G. W., *Bibliography of Ralph Waldo Emerson* (1908).

BIOGRAPHY: Brooks, Van Wyck, *The Life of Emerson* (1932); *The Flowering of New England 1815-1865* (1936), consult Index, p. 542; Cabot, J. E., *A Memoir of Ralph Waldo Emerson* (two volumes, 1887); Emerson, E. W., *Emerson in Concord* (1889); Firkins, O. W., *Ralph Waldo Emerson* (1915); Garnett, Richard, *Life of Ralph Waldo Emerson* (1888); Gay, R. M., *Emerson: A Study of the Poet as Seer* (1928); Hastings, Louise, "Emerson in Cincinnati," *NEQ.*, XI (1938), pp. 443-469; Hoeltje, H. H., "Ralph Waldo Emerson in Iowa," *IJHP.*, XXV (1927), pp. 236-276; "Emerson's Venture in Western Land," *AL.*, II (1930-1931), pp. 438-440; "Ralph Waldo Emerson in Minnesota," *M.Hist.*, XI (1930), pp. 145-159; "Emerson in Virginia," *NEQ.*, V, (1932), pp. 753-768; "Emerson, Citizen of Concord," *AL.*, XI (1939-1940), pp. 367-378; *The Sheltering Tree: A Story of the Friendship of Ralph Waldo Emerson and Amos Bronson Alcott* (1943); Holmes, O. W., *Ralph Waldo Emerson* (1885); Meeks, L. H., "The Lyceum in the Early West," *IMH.*, XXIX (1933), pp. 87-95; Michaud, Régis, *Emerson: The Enraptured Yankee* (1930); Nye, R. B., "Emerson in Michigan and the Northwest," *Mi.HM.*, XXVI (1942), pp. 159-172; Russell, Phillips, *Emerson: The Wisest American* (1929); Sanborn, F. B., *The Personality of Emerson* (1903); Scudder, Townsend, *The Lonely Wayfaring Man* (1936); Townsend Scudder, III, "Emerson's British Lecture Tour, 1847-1848," *AL.*, VII (1935-1936), pp. 15-36, 166-180; Stewart, Randall, "The Concord Group," *SR.*, XLIV (1936), pp. 434-446; Thompson, F. T., "Emerson and Carlyle," *SP.*, XXIV (1927), pp. 438-453; Warfel, H. R., "Margaret Fuller and Ralph Waldo Emerson," *PMLA.*, L (1935), pp. 576-595; Woodberry, G. E., *Ralph Waldo Emerson* (1907); Woodbury, C. J., *Talks with Ralph Waldo Emerson* (1890); Wright, L. M., "Culture through Lectures," *IJHP.*, XXXVIII (1940), pp. 115-162.

Pochmann, H. A., "Emerson and the St. Louis Hegelians," *AGR.*, X (1944), pp. 14-17.

CRITICISM: Abbott, J. P., *Emerson and The Conduct of Life* (Ph.D., Iowa, 1939); Adams, J. T., "Emerson Re-read," *Atl.*, CXLVI (1930), pp. 484-492; Allen, G. W., *American Prosody* (1935), pp. 91-126; Arnold, Matthew, *Discourses in America* (1885), pp. 138-207; Beach, J. W., "Emerson and Evolution," *UTQ.*, III (1933-1934), pp. 474-497; Benton, Joel, *Emerson as a Poet* (1883); Brittin, N. A., "Emerson and the Metaphysical Poets," *AL.*, VIII (1936-1937), pp. 1-21; Brooks, Van Wyck, *America's Coming-of-Age* (1915), pp. 70-85; *Emerson and Others* (1927), pp. 3-105; Brownell, W. C.,

American Prose Masters (1909), pp. 131-204; Burke, Kenneth, "Acceptance and Rejection," *So.R., II* (1936-1937), pp. 600-632; Calverton, V. F., *The Liberation of American Literature* (1932), p. 248; Canby, H. S., *Classic Americans* (1931), pp. 143-183; Cannon, C. W., *The Influences Determining Emerson's Conception of Jesus* (Ph.D., Iowa, 1936-1937); Carpenter, F. I., "Immortality from India," *AL.*, I (1929-1930), pp. 233-242; "William James and Emerson," *AL.*, XI (1939-1940), pp. 39-57; *Emerson and Asia* (1930); "Points of Comparison Between Emerson and William James," *NEQ.*, II (1929), pp. 458-474; Cestre, Charles, "Emerson Poete," *EA.*, IV (1940), pp. 1-14; "La Pedagogie d'Emerson," *AUP.*, IV (1929), pp. 302-318; "Le Romantisme d'Emerson," *RAA.*, VII (1929), pp. 1-18; "Thoreau et Emerson," *ibid.*, VII (1929), pp. 213-230; Charvat, William, *Emerson and Catholicism* (Ph.D., Iowa, 1940); "American Romanticism and the Depression of 1837," *SS.*, II (1937-1938), p. 80 (pp. 67-82); Christy, Arthur, *The Orient in American Transcendentalism* (1932), pp. 61-185; Clark, H. H., "Emerson and Science," *PQ.*, X (1931), pp. 225-260; Commager, H. S., "Tempest in a Boston Tea Cup," *NEQ.*, VI (1933), pp. 651-675; Crothers, S. M., *Ralph Waldo Emerson: How to Know Him* (1921); Dillaway, Newton, *Prophet of America: Emerson and the Problems of To-day* (1936); Downs, L. H., *Emerson and Dr. Channing* (Ph.D., Iowa, 1940); Elliott, G. R., "On Emerson's 'Grace' and 'Self-Reliance,'" *NEQ.*, II (1929), pp. 93-104; Foerster, Norman, *Nature in American Literature* (1923), pp. 37-68; *American Criticism* (1928), pp. 52-111; Flanagan, J. T., *Emerson and the State* (Ph.D., Minnesota, 1934); "Emerson and Communism," *NEQ.*, X (1937), pp. 243-261; "Emerson as a Critic of Fiction," *PQ.*, XV (1936), pp. 30-45; [Flewelling, R. T.], "Emerson and the Middle Border," *Personalist*, XVI (1935), pp. 295-309; "Emerson and Adolescent America," *ibid.*, XX (1939), pp. 343-352; Foster, C. H., *Emerson's Theory of Poetry* (1939); Gilman, Margaret, "Baudelaire and Emerson," *R.Rev.*, XXIV (1943), pp. 211-222; Glicksberg, C. I., "Bryant on Emerson the Lecturer," *NEQ.*, XII (1939), pp. 530-534; Gohdes, Clarence, "Some Remarks on Emerson's *Divinity School Address*," *AL.*, I (1929-1930), pp. 27-31; Gray, H. D., *Emerson: a Statement of New England Transcendentalism as Expressed in the Philosophy of Its Chief Exponent*, Stanford Publications, University Series, No. 29 (1917); Harrison, J. S., *The Teachers of Emerson* (1910); Hartwig, G. H., "Emerson on Historical Christianity, *HJ.*, XXXVII (1938-1939), pp. 405-412; Hazard, Lucy, *The Frontier in American Literature* (1927), p. 150 *ff.*; Hazlitt, Henry, "Emerson" in Macy, John (ed.), *American Writers on American Literature* (1931), pp. 81-96; Hotson, Clarence, "The Christian Critics and Mr. Emerson," *NEQ.*, XI (1938), pp. 29-47; Huggard, W. A., "Emerson and the Problem of War and Peace," *UIS.*, V (No. 5, 1938); James, Henry, *Partial Portraits* (1888), pp. 1-33; Jorgenson, C. E., "Emerson's Paradise under the Shadow of Swords," *PQ.*, XI (1932), pp. 274-292; Kern, A. C., "Emerson and Economics," *NEQ.*, XIII (1940), pp. 678-696; Kreymborg, Alfred, *Our Singing Strength* (1929), pp. 67-83; Ladu, A. I., "Emerson: Whig or Democrat," *NEQ.*, XIII (1940), pp. 434-437 (pp. 419-441); Lowell, J. R., *My Study Windows* (1871), pp. 375-384; MacMechan, Archibald (ed.), *Carlyle on Heroes and Hero-Worship, and the Heroic in History* (1901), p. 344; McQuiston, Raymer, "The Relation of Ralph Waldo Emerson to Public Affairs," *UKHS.*, III, No. 1 (1923); Macy, John, *The Spirit of American Literature* (1913), pp. 45-76; Marchand, Ernest, "Emerson and the Frontier," *AL.*, III (1931-1932), pp. 149-174; Matthiessen, F. O., *American Renaissance* (1941), pp. 3-75; Michaud, Régis, *Autour d'Emerson* (1924); *L'Esthétique d'Emerson* (1927); Miller, Perry, "Jonathan Edwards to Emerson," *NEQ.*, XIII (1940), p. 589 *ff.*; Moore, J. B., "Emerson on Wordsworth," *PMLA.*, *XLI*, N.S. XXXIV (1926), pp. 179-192; "Thoreau Rejects Emerson" *AL.*, IV (1932-1933), pp. 241-256; More, P. E., *Shelburne Essays*, First Series (1904), pp. 71-84; *ibid.*, Eleventh Series (1921), pp. 69-94; "Emerson," *CHAL.*, I (1917), pp. 349-362; Parrington, V. L., *Main Currents in American Thought*, II (1927), pp. 386-399; Perry, Bliss, *Emerson Today* (1931); Pritchard, J. P., *Return to the Fountains: Some Classical Sources of American Criticism* (1942), pp. 44-60; Sandeen, E. E., *Emerson as an American* (Ph.D., Iowa, 1940); Santayana, G. E., in *Interpretations of Poetry and Religion* (1900), pp. 217-233; Silver, Mildred, "Emerson and the Idea of Progress," *AL.*, XII (1940-1941), p. 7 *ff.* (pp. 1-19); Silver, R. G., "Ellery Channing's Collaboration with Emerson," *AL.*, VII (1935-1936), pp. 84-86; Smith, Bernard, *Forces in American Criticism* (1939), p. 91 *ff.*, (pp. 66-133); Spencer, B. T., "A National Literature, 1837-1855," *AL.*, VIII (1936-1937), pp. 125-159; Strauch, C. F., "The Background for Emerson's 'Boston Hymn,'" *AL.*, XIV (1942-1943), pp. 36-47; Thompson, F. T., "Emerson's Indebtedness to Coleridge," *SP.*, XXIII (1926), pp. 55-76; "Emerson and Carlyle," *ibid.*, XXIV (1927), pp. 438-453; "Emerson's Theory and Practice of Poetry," *PMLA.*, XLIII (1928), pp. 1170-1184; Thwing, C. F., "The American Scholar: Emerson's Phi Beta Kappa Address (1837)," *HJ.*, XXXVI (1937-1938), pp. 119-131; Tolles, F. B., "Emerson and Quakerism," *AL.*, X (1938-1939), pp. 142-165; Ustick, W. L., "Emerson's Debt to Montaigne," *WUV.*, IX, Fourth Series, No. 2 (1922), pp. 245-262; Vance, W. S., "Carlyle in America before *Sartor Resartus*," *AL.*, VII (1935-1936), pp. 363-375; Wahr, F. W., *Emerson and Goethe* (Ph.D., Michigan, 1915); Williamson, George, "Emerson the Oriental," *UCC.*, XXX (1928), pp. 271-288; Winters, Yvor, *Maule's Curse* (1938), pp. 125-146; Young, C. L., *Emerson's Montaigne* (1941).

Davis, M. R., "Emerson's 'Reason' and the Scottish Philosophers," *NEQ.*, XVII (1944), pp. 209-228; Huggard, W. A., "Emerson's Philosophy of War and Peace," *PQ.*, XII (1943), pp. 370-375; Turpie, M. C., "A Quaker Source for Emerson's Sermon on the Lord's Supper," *NEQ.*, XVII (1944), pp. 95-101.

HENRY DAVID THOREAU (pp. 98-101)

WORKS: *Collected Works*, Manuscript and Walden Editions; alike except for manuscript insertions (twenty volumes, 1906). To this have been added: "The Service," edited by F. B. Sanborn (1902); "Sir Walter Raleigh," edited by Henry A. Metcalf (1905); some journal material bearing on the Minnesota and Staten Island trips, edited by F. B. Sanborn (1905); "Godfrey of Boulogne" in *Unpublished Poems by Bryant and Thoreau* (1907); "The Moon" (1927); "Life" (1930); and "The Transmigration of the Seven Brahmans," a translation from the *Harivansa* of Langlois, edited by Arthur Christy (1932); *Collected Poems*, edited by Carl Bode (1943).

BIBLIOGRAPHY: Allen, F. H., *Bibliography of Henry David Thoreau* (1908); Crawford, B. V., *Henry David Thoreau: Representative Selections* (1934); pp. lix-lxix; Harding, Walter, "A Bibliography of Thoreau in Poetry, Fiction, and Drama," *BBDI.*, XVIII (May-August, 1943), pp. 15-18; Taylor, W. F., *History of American Letters* (1936), pp. 159-167; Wade, J. S., "A Contribution to a Bibliography from 1909 to 1936 of Henry David Thoreau," *Journal of the New York Entomological Society*, XLVIII (1939), pp. 163-203; White, W., *A Henry David Thoreau Bibliography, 1908-1937;* (printed in the *Bulletin of Bibliography*, XVI, [1938], pp. 90-92, 111-113, 131-132; XVI [1939], pp. 163, 181-182, 199-202); published separately (1939). For detailed current bibliography, refer to the Thoreau Society Bulletin, Box 762, Chapel Hill, N. C. (Raymond Adams).

BIOGRAPHY: Adams, Raymond, "Thoreau at Harvard," *NEQ.*, XIII (1940), pp. 24-33; Atkinson, J. B., *Henry Thoreau, the Cosmic Yankee* (1927); Bazalgette, Léon, *Henry Thoreau, Bachelor of Nature*, translated by Van Wyck Brooks (1924); Berry, E. G., "Thoreau in Canada," *DR.*, XXIII (1943), pp. 68-74; Boyd, David, "The Rebel Idealist," *Americana*, XXX (1936), pp. 89-118, 286-323; Canby, H. S., *Thoreau* (1939); Channing, W. E., *Thoreau: The Poet-Naturalist* (1873): revised and enlarged by F. B. Sanborn (1902); Christy, Arthur, "A Thoreau Fact-Book," *Colophon*, Part 16, No. 9 (1934); Emerson, E. W., *Henry Thoreau as Remembered by a Young Friend* (1917); Flanagan, T. T., "Thoreau in Minnesota," *M.Hist.*, XVI (1935), pp. 35-46; Hatch, B. L., in *Papers in Honor of Andrew Keogh* (1938), pp. 317-324; Hoeltje, H. H., "Thoreau in Concord Church and Town Records," *NEQ.*, XII (1939), pp. 349-359; McGill, F. T., "Thoreau and College Discipline," *NEQ.*, XV (1942), pp. 349-353; Sanborn, F. B., *The Life of Henry David Thoreau* (1917); Straker, R. L., "Thoreau's Journey to Minnesota," *NEQ.*, XIV (1941), pp. 549-555; Van Doren, Mark, *Henry David Thoreau: A Critical Study* (1916).

CRITICISM: Adams, Raymond, "Thoreau's Literary Apprenticeship," *SP.*, XXIX (1932), pp. 617-629; Benson, A. B., "Scandinavian Influences in the Writings of Thoreau," *SSN.*, XVI (1941), pp. 201-211, 241-256; Brooks, Van Wyck, *The Flowering of New England 1815-1865* (1936), pp. 286-302, 359-373, 422-442; Burroughs, John, *Indoor Studies* (1889), pp. 1-42; *Literary Values* (1902), pp. 217-223; "A Critical Glance into Thoreau," *Atl.*, CXXIII (1919), pp. 777-786; *The Last Harvest* (1922), pp. 103-171; Canby, H. S., "Henry David Thoreau," in *Classic Americans* (1931); Introduction, *Henry David Thoreau. Works* (1937); "Two Women," *NAR.*, CCXLVIII (1939-1940), pp. 18-32; "Thoreau in Search of a Public," *A.Schol.*, VIII (1939), pp. 431-444; Carpenter, F. I., *Emerson and Asia* (1930); Christy, Arthur, *The Orient in American Transcendentalism* (1932); Cook, R. L., *The Concord Saunterer* (1940), including a discussion of "The Nature Mysticism of Thoreau" and "Original Letters by Thoreau"; Crawford, B. V., Introduction, Bibliography, and Notes to *Henry David Thoreau: Representative Selections* (1934); Deevy, E. S., Jr., "A Re-examination of Thoreau's 'Walden,'" *QRB.*, XVII (1942), pp. 1-11; Dreiser, Theodore, *The Living Thoughts of Thoreau* (1939); Emerson, R. W., "Thoreau," *Atl.*, X (1862), pp. 239-249; Walden Edition, *Thoreau*, Vol. I; Foerster, Norman, "The Intellectual Heritage of Thoreau," *TR.*, II (1917), pp. 192-212; "Thoreau as Artist," *SR.*, XXIX (1921), pp. 2-13; *Nature in American Literature* (1923), pp. 69-142; Gohdes, Clarence, "Henry Thoreau, Bachelor of Arts," *CJ.*, XIII (1928), pp. 323-336; Johnston, Edgar, *A Treasury of Biography* (1941), p. 274 *f.*; Keiser, Albert, *The Indian in American Literature* (1933), pp. 209-232; Lee, Harry, *More Day to Dawn* (1941); Lorch, F. W., "Thoreau and the Organic Principle in Poetry," *PMLA.*, LIII (1938), pp. 286-302; Lowell J. R., *A Fable for Critics* (1848); *My Study Windows* (1871), pp. 193-209; Mackaye, James, *Thoreau, Philosopher of Freedom* (1930), pp. vii-xvi; MacMechan, Archibald, *CHAL.*, II (1927), pp. 1-15; Madison, C. A., "Henry David Thoreau: Transcendental Individualist," *Ethics*, LIV (1944), pp. 110-123; Manning, C. A., "Thoreau and Tolstoy," *NEQ.*, XVI (1943), pp. 234-243; Matthiessen, F. O., *American Renaissance* (1941), pp. 76-119, 153-157, 162-175; Moore, J. B., "Thoreau Rejects Emerson," *AL.*, IV (1932-1933), pp. 241-256; More, P. E., "A Hermit's Notes on Thoreau," *Shelburne Essays*, First Series (1904), pp. 1-21; "Thoreau and German Romanticism," *ibid.*, Fifth Series (1908), pp. 106-131; Mumford, Lewis, *The Golden Day: A Study in American Literature and Culture* (1934), pp. 108-120; Parrington, V. L., *Main Currents in American Thought* II (1927), pp. 400-413; Pritchard, J. M., *Return to the Fountains: Some Classical Sources of American Criticism* (1942), pp. 61-77; Raysor, T. M., "The Love Story of Thoreau," *SP.*, XXIII (1926), pp. 457-463; Seldes, Gilbert, "Thoreau" in Macy, John (ed.), *American Writers on American Literature* (1936), pp. 164-176; Shepard, Odell, Preface to *The Heart of Thoreau's Journals* (1927); Introduction to *Henry David Thoreau: A Week on the Concord and Merrimack Rivers* (1921); Sherman, S. P., *Main Stream* (1926), pp. 37-47; Stevenson, R. L., *Familiar Studies of Men and Books* (1892), pp. 129-171; Stewart, Randall, "The Concord Group," *SR.*, XLIV (1936), pp. 434-446; Taylor, W. F., *A History of American Letters* (1936), pp. 158-167; Templeman, W. D., "Thoreau, Moralist of the Picturesque," *PMLA.*, XLVII (1932), pp. 864-889; Walcutt, C. C., "Thoreau in the Twentieth Century," *SAQ.*, XXXIX (1940), pp. 168-184; Warren, Austin, "Lowell on Thoreau," *SP.*, XXVII (1930), pp. 442-461; White, Viola C., *The Concord Saunterer: Including a Discussion of the Nature Mysticism of Thoreau and a Check List of Thoreau Items in the Abernethy Library of Middlebury College* (1940); Wood, J. P., "English and American Criticism of Thoreau," *NEQ.*, VI (1933), pp. 733-746.

Hinkley, E. B., "Thoreau and Beston, two observers of Cape Cod," *NEQ.*, IV (1931). pp. 216-229; Peattie, D. C., "Is Thoreau a Modern?" *NAR.*, CCXLV (1938), pp. 159-169; Wells, H. W., "An Evaluation of Thoreau's Poetry," *AL.*, XVI (1944-1945), pp. 99-109.

[AMOS] BRONSON ALCOTT (pp. 101-102)

WORKS: *Observations on the Principles and Methods of Infant Instruction* (1830); *Conversations on the Gospels Held in Mr. Alcott's School Unfolding the Doctrine and Discipline of Human Culture* (1836, 1837); *Tablets* (1868); *Concord Days* (1872); *Table Talk* (1877); *New Connecticut* (1881); *Sonnets and Canzonets* (1882); *Ralph Waldo Emerson: an Estimate of his Character and Genius: in Prose and Verse* (1865, 1882); *Journals,* selected and edited by Odell Shepard (1938).

BIOGRAPHY: B[ates], E. S., "Alcott, Amos Bronson," *DAB.*, I (1928), pp. 139-141; Hoeltje, H. H., *The Sheltering Tree* (1943); Morrow, H. W., *The Father of Little Women* (1927); Sanborn, F. B., and Harris, W. T., *A. Bronson Alcott, His Life and Philosophy* (1893); Shepard, Odell, *Pedlar's Progress* (1937).

CRITICISM: Blankenship, Russell, *American Literature* (1931), pp. 312-315; Carpenter, F. I., "Bronson Alcott: Genteel Transcendentalist," *NEQ.*, XIII (1940), pp. 34-48; Christy, Arthur, *The Orient in American Transcendentalism* (1932); Edgell, D. P., "Bronson Alcott's 'Gentility,'" *NEQ.*, XIII (1940), pp. 699-705; "Bronson Alcott's 'Autobiographical Index,'" *NEQ.*, XIV (1941), pp. 704-715; Gohdes, Clarence, "Alcott's 'Conversation' on the Transcendental Club and *The Dial*," *AL.*, III (1931-1932), pp. 14-27; Gross, H. B., Jr., "Notes on *Pedlar's Progress*," *AL.*. X (1938-1939), pp. 216-222; Haefner, G. E., *A Critical Estimate of the Educational Theories and Practices of Amos Bronson Alcott* (Ph.D., Columbia, 1937); Higginson, T. W., *Carlyle's Laugh and Other Surprises* (1909), pp. 75-91; *Contemporaries* (1899), pp. 22-33; Hoeltje, H. H., "Some Iowa Lectures and Conversations of Amos Bronson Alcott," *IJHP.*, XXIX (1931), pp. 375-401; McCuskey, Dorothy, *Bronson Alcott, Teacher* (1940); Sears, C. E., *Bronson Alcott's Fruitlands* (1915); Shepard, Odell, "Sunken Treasure," *SRL.*, XVI (Mar. 27, 1937), p. 15 *f.*; Stewart, Randall, "The Concord Group," *SR.*. XLIV (1936), pp. 434-446; Warren, Austin, "The Orphic Sage: Bronson Alcott," *AL.*, III (1931-1932), pp. 3-13; "The Concord School of Philosophy," *NEQ.*, II (1929), pp. 199-233; Wellek, René, "The Minor Transcendentalists and German Philosophy," *NEQ.*, XV (1942), pp. 656-666; Willis, F. L. H., *Alcott Memoirs* (1915).

SARAH MARGARET FULLER (pp. 102-103)

WORKS: *Eckermann's Conversations with Goethe*—a translation from the German of Eckermann (1839); *Correspondence of Fraülein Günderode and Bettina von Arnim,* translated in collaboration with Minna Wesselhoeft (1842); *Summer on the Lakes, in 1843* (1844); *Woman in the Nineteenth Century* (1844); *Papers on Literature and Art* (1846); *At Home and Abroad, or, Things and Thoughts in America and Europe,* edited by her brother (1856); *Life Without, and Life Within; or Reviews, Narratives, Essays and Poems,* edited by A. B. Fuller (1859); *Love-Letters of Margaret Fuller 1845-1846,* with an introduction by Julia Ward Howe (1903); *The Writings of Margaret Fuller,* selected and edited by Mason Wade (1941). In addition to *Summer on the Lakes* and *Woman in the Nineteenth Century,* includes thirteen of her Critical Essays, her letters relative to the Roman Revolution, twenty-five new letters, and selected passages from the Memoirs.

BIOGRAPHY AND CRITICISM: Anthony, Katharine, *Margaret Fuller* (1920); A[nthony], K[atherine], "Fuller, Sarah Margaret," *DAB.*, VII (1931), pp. 63-66; Barbour, F. M., "Margaret Fuller and the British Reviewers," *NEQ.*, IX (1936), pp. 618-625; Bell, Margaret, *Margaret Fuller* (1930); Black, Ladbroke, *Some Queer People* (1931), pp. 55-74; Blankenship, Russell, *American Literature* (1931), pp. 319-322; Bradford, Gamaliel, *Portraits of American Women* (1919), pp. 131-163; Braun, F. A., *Margaret Fuller and Goethe* (1910); Burton, Roland, *Margaret Fuller as Literary Critic* (Ph.D., Iowa, 1941); Carpenter, R. V., "Margaret Fuller in Northern Illinois," *JISHS.*, II (1910), pp. 7-27; Derby, J. B., *Margaret Fuller: A Biographical Study* (Ph.D., Yale, 1932); Emerson, R. W., Channing, W. H., and Clarke, J. F. (eds.), *Memoirs of Margaret Fuller Ossoli* (two volumes,, 1852); Fuller, F. T., "Hawthorne and Margaret Fuller Ossoli," *LW.*. XVI (1885), pp. 11-15; Hess, M. W., "Conversations in Boston, 1839," *CW.*. CXLIX (1939), pp. 309-317; Higginson, T. W., *Margaret Fuller Ossoli* (1884); McMaster, H. N., "Margaret Fuller as a Literary Critic," *UBS.*, VII (1928); Madison, C. M., "Margaret Fuller: Transcendental Rebel," *An.R.*, II (1942), pp. 422-438; Parrington, V. L., *Main Currents in American Thought,* II (1927), pp. 426-434; Rostenberg, Leona, "Margaret Fuller's Roman Diary," *JMH.*, XII (1940), pp. 209-220; Stern, M. B., "Margaret Fuller's Schooldays in Cambridge," *NEQ.*, XIII (1940), pp. 207-222; "Margaret Fuller's Stay in Providence 1837-1838," *Americana,* XXXIV (1940), pp. 353-369; "Margaret Fuller and *The Dial*," *SAQ.*, XL (1941), pp. 11-21; "Margaret Fuller's Summer in the West (1843)," *Mi.HM.*, XXV (1941), pp. 300-330; *The Life of Margaret Fuller* (1942); Stewart, Randall, "The Concord Group," *SR.*, XLIV (1936), pp. 434-446; Wade, Mason, *Margaret Fuller* (1940), which contains good bibliography; Warfel, H. R., "Margaret Fuller and Ralph Waldo Emerson," *PMLA.*, L (1935), pp. 576-594; Wellek, René, "The Minor Transcendentalists and German Philosophy," *NEQ.*, XV (1942), pp. 677-679 (pp. 652-680).

THEODORE PARKER (p. 104)

WORKS: *Works,* edited by F. C. Cobbe (fourteen volumes, 1863-1870); Centenary Edition (fifteen volumes, 1907-1911). Chief individual works: *A Discourse of Matters Pertaining to Religion* (1842); *A Letter to the People of the United States Touching the Matter of Slavery* (1848); *Transcendentalism: A Lecture* (1876).

BIOGRAPHY AND CRITICISM: Blankenship, Russell, *American Literature* (1931), pp. 315-319; Chadwick, J. W., *Theodore Parker, Preacher and Reformer* (1900); C[hristie], F. A., "Parker, Theodore," *DAB.*, XIV (1934), pp. 238-241; Commager, H. S., "The Dilemma of Theodore Parker," *NEQ.*, VI (1933), pp. 257-277; "Tempest in a Boston Tea Cup," *ibid.* (1933), pp. 651-675; "Theodore Parker, Intellectual Gourmand," *A.Schol.*, III (1934), pp. 257-265; *Theodore Parker* (1936); Frothingham, O. B., *Theodore Parker* (1874); Higginson, T. W., *Contemporaries* (1899), pp. 34-59; Ladu, A. I., "The Political Ideas of Theodore Parker," *SP.*, XXXVIII (1941), pp. 106-123; Mead, E. D., *Emerson and Theodore Parker* (1910); Parrington, V. L., *Main Currents in American Thought,* II (1927), pp. 414-425; Weiss, John, *Life and Correspondence of Theodore Parker* (two volumes, 1864); Wellek, René, "The Minor Transcendentalists and German Philosophy," *NEQ.*, XV (1942), pp. 669-679 (pp. 652-680).

JONES VERY (p. 104)

Twenty-seven of Very's sonnets were printed by James Freeman Clarke in the *Western Messenger,* March, April, 1839. *Essays and Poems* (1839), edited by Emerson, contained three essays, nine lyrics, and fifty-six sonnets.

WORKS: *Poems and Essays,* with a sketch by J. F. Clarke, and preface by C. A. Bartol (1886).

BIOGRAPHY AND CRITICISM: Baker, Carlos, "Emerson and Jones Very," *NEQ.*, VII (1934), pp. 90-99; Bartlett, W. I., "Early Years of Jones Very — Emerson's 'Brave Saint.'" *EIHS.*, LXXIII (1937), pp. 1-23; "Jones Very — The Harvard Years," *ibid.*, LXXIV (1938), pp. 213-238; *Jones Very: Emerson's "Brave Saint"* (1942); Bradford, Gamaliel, *Biography and the Human Heart* (1932), pp. 185-212; Proudfoot, B. W., *Jones Very: A Bibliographical Study* (Ph.D., Chicago, 1918); Winters, Yvor, *Maule's Curse* (1938), pp. 125-146; 219-232.

WILLIAM ELLERY CHANNING, 1818—1901 (p. 105)

WORKS: *Poems of Sixty-Five Years by Ellery Channing,* edited by F. B. Sanborn (1902); "A Concord Note-Book," *Critic,* XLVII, (1905), pp. 76-81, 121-128, 267-272; *Thoreau, the Poet-Naturalist* (1873, 1902).

BIOGRAPHY AND CRITICISM: Emerson, R. W., "Walks with Ellery Channing," *Atl.*, XC (1902), pp. 27-34; Sanborn, F. B., "The Maintenance of a Poet," *Atl.*, LXXXVI (1900), pp. 819-825; Silver, R. G., "Ellery Channing's Collaboration with Emerson," *AL.*, VII (1935-1936), pp. 84-86.

ORESTES AUGUSTUS BROWNSON (pp. 105-106)

WORKS: *Complete Works,* edited by H. F. Brownson (1882-1887).

BIOGRAPHY AND CRITICISM: Brownson, H. F., *Orestes A. Brownson's Early Life, Middle Life, Latter Life* (three volumes, 1898-1900); Conroy, P. B., "The Role of the American Constitution in the Political Philosophy of Orestes A. Brownson," *Cath.HR.*, XXV (1939), pp. 271-286; Cook, T. I., and Leavelle, A. B., "Orestes A. Brownson's *The American Republic,*" *RP.*, IV (1942), pp. 77-90, 173-193; Corrigan, Sister M. F., *Some Social Principles of Orestes A. Brownson* (1939); Frese, J. R., S.J., "Brownson on Know Nothingism," *USCHRS.*, XXVII (1937), pp. 52-73; Maynard, Theodore, *Orestes Brownson* (1943); Michel, V. G., *The Critical Principles of Orestes A. Brownson* (Dissertation, Catholic University, Washington, D.C., 1918); Mims, H. S., "Early American Democratic Theory and Orestes Brownson," *SS.*, III (1939), pp. 166-188; Parsons, Wilfred, S.J., "Brownson, Hecker and Hewit," *CW.*, CLIII (1941), pp. 396-408; Rowland, J. P., "Brownson and the American Republic Today," *CW.*, CLII (1940-1941), pp. 537-541; Ryan, Thomas, "Brownson Speaks of England," *ibid.*, pp. 426-429; Schlesinger, A. M., Jr., "Orestes Brownson: An American Marxist before Marx," *SR.*, XLVII (1939), pp. 317-323; *Orestes A. Brownson* (1939); Wellek, René, "The Minor Transcendentalists and German Philosophy," *NEQ.*, XV (1942), pp. 669-679; Whalen, Doran, *Granite for God's House: The Life of Orestes Brownson* (1914).

LeBreton, D. R., "Orestes Brownson's Visit to New Orleans in 1855," *AL.*, XVI (1944-1945), pp. 110-114.

HENRY WADSWORTH LONGFELLOW (pp. 107-113)

WORKS: *Complete Works,* Riverside Edition (eleven volumes, 1886). To this the Standard Library Edition of 1891 adds the three-volume *Life* by Samuel Longfellow; Flanders, B. H., "An Uncollected Longfellow Translation," *AL.*, VII (1935-1936), pp. 205-207; Hatfield, J. T., "An Unknown Prose Tale by Longfellow," *AL.*, III (1931-

1932), pp. 136-148; "The Longfellow — Freiligrath Correspondence," *PMLA.*, XLVIII (1933), pp. 1223-1293; Richards, I. T., "Longfellow in England: Unpublished Extracts from His Journal," *PMLA.*, LI (1936), pp. 1123-1140; Thompson, Ralph, "Additions to Longfellow Bibliography including a New Prose Tale," *AL.*, III (1931-1932), pp. 303-308.

BIOGRAPHY: B[ronson], W. C., "Longfellow, Henry Wadsworth," *DAB.*, XI (1933), pp. 382-387; Carpenter, G. R., *Henry Wadsworth Longfellow* (1901); Dana, H. W. L., "Chronicles of the Craigie House: The Coming of Longfellow," *CHSA.*, XXV (1939), pp. 19-60; Gorman, H. S., *A Victorian American, Henry Wadsworth Longfellow* (1926); Higginson, T. W., *Henry Wadsworth Longfellow* (1902); *Old Cambridge* (1899), pp. 111-144; Kennedy, W. S., *Henry W. Longfellow* (1882); Longfellow, Samuel, *Life of Henry Wadsworth Longfellow* (three volumes, 1891); Norton, C. E., *Henry Wadsworth Longfellow: A Sketch of His Life* (1907); Robertson, E. S., *Life of Henry Wadsworth Longfellow* (1887); Rossetti, W. M., *Lives of Famous Poets* (1878), pp. 338-391; Thompson, Lawrance, *Young Longfellow* (1938); Underwood, F. H., *Henry Wadsworth Longfellow* (1882).

Gohdes, Clarence, *American Literature in Nineteenth-Century England* (1944), pp. 99-126.

CRITICISM: Allen, G. W., *American Prosody* (1935), pp. 154-192; Bailey, E. J., *Religious Thought in the Greater American Poets* (1922), pp. 108-136; Boynton, P. H., *Literature and American Life* (1936); Bradford, Gamaliel, *Biography and the Human Heart* (1932), pp. 37-62; Brooks, Van Wyck, *The Flowering of New England, 1815-1865* (1936), pp. 147-171, 303-308, 443-450, 508-512, *passim.* Also, *New England: Indian Summer* (1940), pp. 25-27; Chamberlin, W. A., "Longellow's Attitude toward Goethe," *MP.*, XVI (1918), pp. 57-76; Clausen, Julius, "Longfellow and Scandinavia," *ASR.*, XVI (1928), pp. 732-740; Elliott, G. R., *The Cycle of Modern Poetry* (1929), pp. 64-82; Gavigan, W. V., "Longfellow and Catholicism," *CW.*, CXXXVIII (1933), pp. 42-50; Goggio, Emilio, "Italian Influences on Longfellow's Works," *R.Rev.*, XVI (1925), pp. 208-222; Gohdes, Clarence, "Longfellow and His Authorized British Publishers," *PMLA.*, LV (1940), pp. 1165-1179; Hatfield, J. T., *New Light on Longfellow with Special Reference to His Relations to Germany* (1933); Howells, W. D., *Literary Friends and Acquaintances* (1900), pp. 71, 178-211; "The Art of Longfellow," *NAR.*, CLXXXIV (1907), pp. 472-485; Jones, H. M., "The Longfellow Nobody Knows," *Outlook*, CXLIX (1928), pp. 577-579, 586; "Longfellow" in Macy, John (ed.), *American Writers on American Literature* (1931), pp. 105-124; Kaufman, Paul, in Foerster, Norman, *Reinterpretation of American Literature* (1928), pp. 114-138; Keiser, Albert, *The Indian in American Literature* (1933), pp. 189-208; Kreymborg, Alfred, *Our Singing Strength* (1929), pp. 97-115; Long, W. O., *Literary Pioneers: Early American Explorers of European Culture* (1935), pp. 159-198; More, P. E., *Shelburne Essays*, Fifth Series (1908), pp. 132-157; Osborne, C. S. and Osborne, Stellanova, *Schoolcraft — Longfellow — Hiawatha* (1942); Parrington, V. L., *Main Currents of American Thought*, II (1927), pp 439-441; Pattee, F. L., *The First Century of American Literature, 1770-1870* (1935), pp. 515-536; *The Feminine Fifties* (1940), pp. 167-176; *Side-Lights on American Literature* (1922), pp. 210-249; Perry, Bliss, *Park-Street Papers* (1908), pp. 107-140; Poe, E. A., *The Literati: Some Honest Opinions . . .* (1850), pp. 292-334, 334-362, 363-374; Thompson, L. R., "Longfellow's Original Sin of Imitation," **Colophon, N.S. I** (1935), pp. 97-106; Trent, W. P., *Longfellow and Other Essays* (1910), pp. 3-35; "Longfellow," *CHAL.*, II (1927), pp. 32-41; Whitman, I. L., *Longfellow and Spain* (1927).

JOHN GREENLEAF WHITTIER (pp. 113-117)

WORKS: *The Writings of John Greenleaf Whittier* (seven volumes, 1888-1889); Scudder, H. E. (ed.), *The Complete Poetical Works of John Greenleaf Whittier* (1894).

BIBLIOGRAPHY: **Currier, T. F., *A Bibliography of John Greenleaf Whittier* (1937).**

BIOGRAPHY: Bennett, Whitman, *Whittier, Bard of Freedom* (1941); Carpenter, G. R., *John Greenleaf Whittier* (1903); Currier, T. F., *Elizabeth Lloyd and the Whittiers* (1939); Higginson, T. W., *John Greenleaf Whittier* (1902); Kennedy, W. S., *John Greenleaf Whittier: His Life, Genius, and Writings* (1882, 1895); Lewis, G. K., *John Greenleaf Whittier; His Life and Work* (1913); Linton, W. J., *Life of John Greenleaf Whittier* (1893); Mordell, Albert, *Quaker Militant: John Greenleaf Whittier* (1933); Perry, Bliss, *John Greenleaf Whittier: A Sketch of His Life, with Selected Poems* (1907); Pickard, S. T., *Life and Letters of John Greenleaf Whittier* (two volumes, 1894); *Whittier as a Politician* (1900); *Whittier-Land* (1904); Pollard, J. A., "Whittier's Early Years 1807-1836," (Ph.D., Yale, 1937); Shackford, M. H., "Whittier and Some Cousins," *NEQ.*, XV (1942), pp. 467-496; Snyder, E. D., "Whittier's Letters to Ann Elizabeth Wendell," *BFHA.*, XXIX (1940), pp. 69-92; Stearns, Bertha-Monica, "John Greenleaf Whittier, Editor," *NEQ.*, XIII (1940), pp. 280-304; Underwood, F. H., *John Greenleaf Whittier: A Biography* (1884); Woodberry, G. E., *Makers of Literature* (1900), pp. 302-323.

CRITICISM: Allen, G. W., *American Prosody* (1935), pp. 127-153; Bailey, E. J., *Religious Thought in the Greater American Poets* (1922), pp. 70-107; Christy, Arthur, "Orientalism in New England: Whittier," *AL.*, I (1929-1930), pp. 372-392; "The Orientalism of Whittier," *ibid.*, V (1933-1934), pp. 247-257; Eastburn, I. K., *Whittier's Relation to German Life and Thought* (1915); Foerster, Norman, *Nature in American Literature* (1923), pp. 20-36; Gosse, Edmund, *Portraits and Sketches* (1912), pp. 137-147; Griswold, M. J., "American Quaker History in the Works of Whittier, Hawthorne, and Longfellow," *Americana*, XXXIV (1940), pp. 220-263; Howe, W. D., "Whittier" in

Macy, John (ed.), *American Writers on American Literature* (1931), pp. 125-134; Kreymborg, Alfred, *Our Singing Strength* (1929), pp. 84-96; Lowell, J. R., *The Function of the Poet and Other Essays* (1920), pp. 127-140; More, P. E., *Shelburne Essays*, Third Series (1907), pp. 28-53; Parrington, V. L., *Main Currents in American Thought*, II (1927), pp. 361-370; Perry, Bliss, *Park-Street Papers* (1908), pp. 173-201; Pray, F. M., *A Study of Whittier's Apprenticeship as a Poet* (Ph.D., Pennsylvania State College, 1930); Strong, A. H., *American Poets and Their Theology* (1916), pp. 107-158; Taylor, E. E., *John Greenleaf Whittier: Poet, Reformer, Mystic* (1913); Woodberry, G. E., *Makers of Literature* (1900), pp. 302-323.

Adkins, N. F., "Two Uncollected Prose Sketches of Whittier," *NEQ.*, VI (1933), pp. 364-371; Currier, T. F., "Whittier and the *New England Weekly Review*," *NEQ.*, VI (1933), pp. 589-597, Pickard, John B., *John Greenleaf Whittier* (Barnes & Noble, 1961).

NATHANIEL HAWTHORNE (pp. 117-121)

WORKS (collected and edited): Lathrop, G. P., (ed.), *The Complete Works of Nathaniel Hawthorne* (twelve volumes, 1883); *The Writings of Nathaniel Hawthorne* (twenty-two volumes, 1900); *Passages from the American Notebooks* (1868); *Passages from the English Notebooks* (1870); *Passages from the French and Italian Notebooks* (1871); *The American Notebooks by Nathaniel Hawthorne*, edited by Randall Stewart (1932); *The English Notebooks by Nathaniel Hawthorne*, edited by Randall Stewart (1941); Pickard, S. T. (ed.), *Hawthorne's First Diary* (1897); *Love Letters of Nathaniel Hawthorne 1839-41 and 1841-63* (two volumes, 1907); Arvin, Newton (ed.), *The Heart of Hawthorne's Journals* (1929); or *Letters of Hawthorne to William D. Ticknor, 1851-1864* (two volumes, 1910); Stewart, Randall (ed.), "Hawthorne and Politics: Unpublished Letters to William B. Pike," *NEQ.*, V (1932), pp. 237-263; "Hawthorne's Contributions to *The Salem Advertiser*," *AL.*, V (1933-1934), pp. 327-341; "Two Uncollected Reviews by Hawthorne," *NEQ.*, IX (1936), pp. 504-509; Blodgett, Harold, "Hawthorne as Poetry Critic: Six Unpublished Letters to Lewis Mansfield," *AL.*, XII (1940-1941), pp. 173-184; Turner, Arlin, *Hawthorne as Editor: Selections from His Writings in the American Magazine of Useful and Entertaining Knowledge* (1941).

WORKS (individual): *Fanshawe* (1828); *Twice-Told Tales* (1837, 1842); *Grandfather's Chair* (1841); *Famous Old People* (1841); *Liberty Tree* (1841); *Biographical Stories for Children* (1842); *The Celestial Railroad* (1843); *Mosses from an Old Manse* (1846); *The Scarlet Letter* (1850); *The House of the Seven Gables* (1851); *A Wonder-Book for Girls and Boys* (1851); *The Snow Image, and Other Twice-Told Tales* (1852); *The Blithedale Romance* (1852); *The Life of Franklin Pierce* (1852); *Tanglewood Tales* (1853); *A Rill from the Town Pump* (1857); *The Marble Faun* (1860); *Our Old Home* (1863); *Septimius Felton* (1872); *The Dolliver Romance* (1876); *Dr. Grimshawe's Secret* (1883); *Sketches and Studies* (1883).

BIOGRAPHY: Arvin, Newton, *Hawthorne* (1929); Bridge, Horatio, *Personal Recollections of Nathaniel Hawthorne* (1893); Brownell, W. C., *American Prose Masters* (1909), pp. 63-130; Conway, M. D., *Life of Nathaniel Hawthorne* (1890); Gates, L. E., *Studies and Appreciations* (1900), pp. 92-109; Gorman, H. S., *Hawthorne: A Study in Solitude* (1927); Hawthorne, Julian, *Nathaniel Hawthorne and His Wife* (two volumes, 1884); Hawthorne, Manning, "Hawthorne and 'The Man of God,'" *Colophon*, N.S. II (1937), pp. 262-282; "Hawthorne's Early Years," *EIHC.*, LXXIV (1938), pp. 1-21; "Nathaniel Hawthorne Prepares for College," *NEQ.*, XI (1938), pp. 66-88; "Parental and Family Influences on Hawthorne," *EIHC.*, LXXVI (1940), pp. 1-13; "Nathaniel Hawthorne at Bowdoin," *NEQ.*, XIII (1940), pp. 246-279; "The Friendship between Hawthorne and Longfellow," *EL.*, XXXIX (1940), pp. 25-30; James, Henry, *Hawthorne* (1879); Lathrop, G. P., *A Study of Hawthorne* (1876); Mather Jackson, E. A., *Nathaniel Hawthorne: A Modest Man* (1940); Metzdorf, R. F., "Hawthorne's Suit against Ripley and Dana," *AL.*, XII (1940-1941), pp. 235-241; Miller, H. P., "Hawthorne Surveys His Contemporaries," *AL.*, XII (1940-1941), pp. 228-235; Morris, Lloyd, *The Rebellious Puritan: Portrait of Mr. Hawthorne* (1927); Parrington, V. L., *Main Currents in American Thought*, II (1927), pp. 442-450; Stewart, Randall, *The American Notebooks by Nathaniel Hawthorne* (1932); "Hawthorne's Speeches at Civic Banquets," *AL.*, VII (1935-1936), pp. 415-423; "The Concord Group," *SR.*, XLIV (1936), pp. 434-446; Warren, Austin, *Hawthorne* (1934); Woodberry, G. E., *Nathaniel Hawthorne* (1902). Hall, L. S., *Hawthorne: Critic of Society* (1944).

CRITICISM: Astrov, Vladimir, "Hawthorne and Dostoevski as Explorers of the Human Conscience," *NEQ.*, XV (1942), pp. 296-319; Blair, Walter, "Color, Light, and Shadow in Hawthorne's Fiction," *NEQ.*, XV (1942), pp. 74-94; Bromfield, Louis, "Hawthorne" in Macy, John (ed.), *American Writers on American Literature* (1931), pp. 97-104; Brooks, Van Wyck, *America's Coming-of-Age* (1915), pp. 64-70; "Retreat from Utopia," *SRL.*, XIII (Feb. 22, 1936), pp. 3-4, 14, 16, 18; Brown, E. K., "Hawthorne, Melville, and 'Ethan Brand,'" *AL.*, III (1931-1932), pp. 72-75; Canby, H. S., *Classic Americans* (1931), pp. 226-262; Carpenter, F. I., "Puritans Preferred Blondes: The Heroines of Melville and Hawthorne," *NEQ.*, IX (1936), pp. 253-272; "Scarlet A Minus," *CE.*, V (1944), pp. 173-180; Chandler, E. L., *A Study of the Sources of the Tales and Romances Written by Nathaniel Hawthorne before 1853*, Smith College Studies in Modern Languages, VII, No. 4 (1926); Dony, Francoise, "Romantisme et Puritanisme chez Hawthorne, á propos de la 'Lettre Pourpre,'" *EA.*, IV (1940), pp. 15-30; Doubleday, N. F., "Hawthorne and Literary Nationalism," *AL.*, XII (1940-1941), pp. 447-453; "Hawthorne's Criticism of New England Life," *CE.*, II (1941), pp. 639-653; "Hawthorne's Satirical Allegory," *CE.*, III (1942), pp. 325-337; Erskine, John, *Leading*

American Novelists (1910), pp. 179-273; Faust, Bertha, *Hawthorne's Contemporaneous Reputation* (1939); Foster, C. H., "Hawthorne's Literary Theory," *PMLA.*, LVII (1942), pp. 241-254; Griswold, M. J., "American Quaker History in the Works of Whittier, Hawthorne and Longfellow," *Americana*, XXXIV (1940), pp. 220-263; Hawthorne, Julian, "The Salem of Hawthorne," *Century*, XXVIII, N.S. VI (1884), pp. 3-17; [Howells, W. D.], "Nathaniel Hawthorne," *Atl.*, V (1860), pp. 614-622; Lawrence, D. H., "Studies in Classical American Literature," *Eng.R.*, XXVIII (1919), pp. 404-417; Matthiessen, F. O., *American Renaissance* (1941), pp. 179-368; Michaud, Régis, *The American Novel To-day* (1928), pp. 25-46; Miller, H. P., "Hawthorne Surveys His Contemporaries," *AL.*, XII (1940-1941), pp. 228-235; More, P. E., *Shelburne Essays*, First Series (1904), pp. 22-70; *ibid.*, Second Series (1905), pp. 173-187; Orians, G. H., "New England Witchcraft in Fiction," *AL.*, II (1930-1931), pp. 54-71; "Scott and Hawthorne's *Fanshawe*," *NEQ.*, XI (1938), pp. 388-394; "The Sources and Themes of Hawthorne's 'The Gentle Boy,'" *ibid.*, XIV (1941), pp. 664-678; Perry, Bliss, *The Amateur Spirit* (1904), pp. 119-139; Poe, E. A., "*Twice Told Tales* reviewed," *Graham's*, XX (1842), pp. 254, 298-300; "Tale-Writing: Nathaniel Hawthorne," *Godey's Lady's Book*, XXXV (1847), pp. 252-256 (the foregoing reviews will be found quoted in whole or in part in various anthologies); Rahv, Philip, "The Dark Lady of Salem," *PR.*, VIII (1941), pp. 362-381; Reed, A. L., "Self-Portraiture in the Work of Nathaniel Hawthorne," *SP.*, XXIII (1926), pp. 40-54; Schneider, H. W., *The Puritan Mind* (1930), pp. 256-264; Stephen, Leslie, *Hours in a Library*, I (1875), pp. 204-237; Stewart, Randall, "Hawthorne in England: The Patriotic Motive in the Note-Books," *NEQ.*, VIII (1935), pp. 3-13; "Hawthorne's Contributions to *The Salem Advertiser*," *AL.*, V (1933-1934), pp. 327-341; "Hawthorne and the Civil War," *SP.*, XXXIV (1937), pp. 91-106; Streeter, R. E., "Hawthorne's Misfit Politician and Edward Everett," *AL.*, XVI (1944-1945), pp. 26-28; Thorp, Willard, "Did Melville Review *The Scarlet Letter*," *AL.*, XIV (1942-1943), pp. 302-305; Trollope, Anthony, "The Genius of Nathaniel Hawthorne," *NAR.*, CXXIX (1879), pp. 203-222; Turner, Arlin, "Autobiographical Elements in Hawthorne's *The Blithedale Romance*," *UTSE.*, XV (1935), pp. 39-63; "A Note on Hawthorne's Revisions," *MLN.*, LI (1936), pp. 426-429; "Hawthorne's Methods of Using His Source Materials," *Studies for William A. Read* (1940), pp. 301-312; "Hawthorne's Literary Borrowings," *PMLA.*, LI (1936), pp. 543-562; "Hawthorne and Reform," *NEQ.*, XV (1942), pp. 700-714; Van Doren, Carl, *The American Novel* (1939), pp. 58-83; Waples, Dorothy, "Suggestions for Interpreting *The Marble Faun*," *AL.*, XIII (1941-1942), pp. 224-239; Warren, Austin, "Hawthorne's Reading," *NEQ.*, VIII (1935), pp. 480-497; Winters, Yvor, *Maule's Curse* (1938), pp. 3-22; Wright, Nathalia, "Hawthorne and the Praslin Murder," *NEQ.*, XVI (1942), pp. 5-14.

Burnham, P. E., "Hawthorne's *Fanshawe* and Bowdoin College," *EIHC.*, LXXX (1944), pp. 131-138; Chandler, E. L., "Hawthorne's *Spectator*," *NEQ.*, IV (1931), pp. 289-330; Gallup, D. C., "On Hawthorne's Authorship of 'The Battle-Omen,'" *NEQ.*, IX (1936), pp. 690-699; Gerber, J. C., "Form and Content in *The Scarlet Letter*," *NEQ.*, XVII (1944-1945), pp. 25-55; Hungerford, E. B., "Hawthorne Gossips about Salem," *NEQ.*, VI (1933), pp. 445-469; Pearson, N. H., "A Sketch by Hawthorne," *NEQ.*, VI (1933), pp. 136-144, Arlin Turner, *Nathaniel Hawthorne* (Barnes & Noble, 1961).

OLIVER WENDELL HOLMES (pp. 121-126)

WORKS: *Works*, Riverside Edition (thirteen volumes, 1891); *The Writings of Oliver Wendell Holmes*, Standard Library Edition (thirteen volumes, 1892), virtually identical save for the inclusion of the Morse *Life and Letters;* Scudder, H. E., *The Complete Poetical Works of Oliver Wendell Holmes*, Cambridge Edition (1895); Turner, E. S., "The 'Autocrat's' Theology: Unpublished Letters of Oliver Wendell Holmes," *Putnam's*, VI (1909), pp. 662-667; Clark, H. H., *Major American Poets* (1936), bibliography, pp. 882-886; Hayakawa, S. I., and Jones, H. M., *Oliver Wendell Holmes: Representative Selections*, with Introduction, Bibliography, and Notes (1939); Ives, G. B., *A Bibliography of Oliver Wendell Holmes*, (1907).

BIOGRAPHY: Eliot, C. W., "Oliver Wendell Holmes," *HGM.*, XXXI (1923), pp. 457-465; Emerson, E. W., *The Early Years of the Saturday Club, 1855-1870* (1918), Fields, Annie, *Authors and Friends* (1898), pp. 107-157; Higginson, T. W., *Cheerful Yesterdays* (1901): consult Index, p. 370; *Contemporaries* (1899), pp. 168-191; *Old Cambridge* (1900), pp. 75-108; Howe, M. A. DeW., *Holmes of the Breakfast-Table* (1939); Howells, W. D., *Literary Friends and Acquaintance* (1900), pp. 146-177, originally in *Harper's*, December, 1896; Jerrold, Walter, *Oliver Wendell Holmes* (1893); Morse, J. T., *Life and Letters of Oliver Wendell Holmes* (two volumes, 1896); Ticknor, Caroline (ed.), *Dr. Holmes's Boston* (1915); Trowbridge, J. T., "Recollections of Oliver Wendell Holmes," *Atl.*, XCI (1903), pp. 600-605; Underwood, F. H., "Oliver Wendell Holmes," *Scribner's*, XVIII (1879), pp. 117-127; Winter, William, *Old Friends* (1909), pp. 107-131.

CRITICISM: Allen, G. W., *American Prosody* (1935), pp. 193-212; Bailey, E. J., *Religious Thought in the Greater American Poets* (1922), pp. 137-157; Brooks, Van Wyck, *The Flowering of New England, 1815-1865* (1936), pp. 343-358; Burroughs, John, *Literary Values and Other Papers* (1904): see Index, p. 261; Chesterton, G. K., Introduction to *The Autocrat of the Breakfast-Table* (1904); Clark, H. H., *Major American Poets* (1936), pp. 886-892; "Oliver Wendell Holmes, a Reinterpretation," *NEQ.*, XII (1939), pp. 19-34; Curtis, G. W., *Literary and Social Essays* (1895), pp. 205-236; Fuller, H. DeW., "Holmes" in Macy, John (ed.), *American Writers on American Literature* (1931), pp. 153-163; Grattan, C. H., "Oliver Wendell Holmes," *AM.*, IV (1925), pp. 37-41; Hayakawa, S. I., "Holmes's Lowell Institute Lectures," *AL.*, VIII (1936-1937), pp. 281-290; Howe, M. A. DeW., *American Bookmen* (1902), pp. 265-286;

Knickerbocker, W. S., "His Own Boswell: A Note on the Poetry of Oliver Wendell Holmes," *SR.*, XLI (1933), pp. 454-456; Kreymborg, Alfred, *Our Singing Strength* (1929), pp. 134-150; Lang, Andrew, *Adventures Among Books* (1905), pp. 81-96; Lerner, Max, *The Mind and Faith of Justice Holmes* (1943); Macy, John, *The Spirit of American Literature* (1913), pp. 155-171; Matthews, Brander, *CHAL.*, II (1918), pp. 224-240; Obendorf, C. P., *The Psychiatric Novels of Oliver Wendell Holmes* (1943); Parrington, V. L., *Main Currents in American Thought*, II (1927), pp. 451-459; Pritchard, J. P., *Return to the Fountains: Some Classical Sources of American Criticism* (1942), pp. 90-98; Savage, M. J., "The Religion of Holmes's Poems," *Arena*, XI (1894), pp. 41-54; Strong, A. H., *American Poets and Their Theology* (1916), pp. 319-367; Taylor, W. F., *A History of American Letters* (1936); Trent, W. P., and Erskine, John, *Great American Writers* (1912), pp. 149-158; Wendell, Barrett, *A Literary History of America* (1911), pp. 407-425: Werner, D. L., *The Idea of Union in American Verse 1776-1876* (1932): Williams, M. L., *The Impact of Science upon Religion in the "Authentic Brahmin"* (Ph.D., Michigan, 1938); Withington, Robert, "The Patriotism of the Autocrat," *HGM.*, XXXVI (1927-1928), pp. 523-532.

JAMES RUSSELL LOWELL (pp. 126-133)

WORKS: *The Complete Writings of James Russell Lowell* (sixteen volumes, 1904), includes Norton, C. E. (ed.), *Letters of James Russell Lowell* (two volumes, 1894; enlarged 1904) and Scudder, H. E., *James Russell Lowell* (two volumes, 1901); Scudder, H. E. (ed.), *The Complete Poetical Works of James Russell Lowell* (1897); Howe, M. A. DeW., *New Letters of James Russell Lowell* (1932); Gilder, J. B. (ed.), *Impressions of Spain* (1899).

BIOGRAPHY: Brown, E. E., *Life of James Russell Lowell* (1877); Dole, N. H., biographical sketch in *The Early Poems of James Russell Lowell* (1892); Eliot, C. W., "James Russell Lowell as a Professor," *HGM.*, XXVII (1918-1919), pp. 482-491; Golann, Ethel, "A Lowell Autobiography," *NEQ.*, VII (1934), pp. 356-364; Greenslet, Ferris, *James Russell Lowell* (1905); Hale, E. E., *James Russell Lowell and His Friends* (1899); Hale, E. E., Jr., *James Russell Lowell* (1899); Higginson, T. W., *Book and Heart* (1897), pp. 47-54; *Old Cambridge* (1899), pp. 147-196; Howells, W. D., *Literary Friends and Acquaintance* (1900), pp. 212-250; Lowell, A. L., *Memoir of James Russell Lowell* (1896); Sanborn, F. B., "The Home and Haunts of Lowell," *NEM.*, N.S. V (1891), pp. 275-302; Smalley, G. W., "Mr. Lowell in England," *Harper's*, XCII (1895-1896), pp. 788-801; Stead, W. T., *Character Sketches* (1891); Stearns, F. P., *Cambridge Sketches* (1905), pp. 83-112; Thayer, W. R., *Letters of John Holmes to James Russell Lowell and Others* (1917); "James Russell Lowell as a Teacher," *Scribner's*, LXVIII (1920), pp. 473-480; Underwood, F. H., *James Russell Lowell: A Biographical Sketch* (1882); *The Poet and the Man. Recollections and Appreciations of James Russell Lowell* (1893); Wendell, Barrett, *Stelligeri and Other Essays* (1893), pp. 205-217.

CRITICISM: Allen, G. W., *American Prosody* (1935), pp. 244-276; Altick, R. D., "Was Lowell an Historical Critic?," *AL.*, XIV (1942-1943), pp. 250-259; Bailey, E. J., *Religious Thought in the Greater American Poets* (1922), pp. 158-182; Bail, H. V., "James Russell Lowell's Ode Recited at the Commemoration of the Living and Dead Soldiers of Harvard University, July 21, 1865," *PBSA.*, XXXVII (1943), pp. 169-202; Beatty, R. C., *James Russell Lowell* (1942); Boynton, P. H., *Literature and American Life* (1936): consult Index, p. 914; Brooks, Van Wyck, *America's Coming-of-Age* (1915), pp. 92-105; *The Flowering of New England 1815-1865* (1936), pp. 311-322, 515-525; Brownell, W. C., *American Prose Masters* (1909), pp. 271-335; Chadwick, J. W., "James Russell Lowell," *Uni.R.*, XXXVI (1891), pp. 436-455; Clark, H. H., "Lowell's Criticism of Romantic Literature," *PMLA.*, XLI, N.S. XXXIV (1926), pp. 209-228; "Lowell—Humanitarian, Nationalist, or Humanist?," *SP.*, XXVII (1930), pp.411-441; Curtis, G. W., *James Russell Lowell: An Address* (1892); DeMille, G. E., *Literary Criticism in America* (1931), pp. 49-85; Duncan, E. H., "Lowell's 'Battle of the Kettle and Pot,'" *AL.*, XV (1943-1944), pp. 127-138; Foerster, Norman, *American Criticism* (1928), pp. 111-156; *Nature in American Literature* (1923), pp. 143-175; Hudson, W. H., *Lowell and His Poetry* (1914); James, Henry, *Essays in London and Elsewhere* (1893), pp. 44-80; Jenkins, W. G., "Lowell's Criteria of Political Values," *NEQ.*, VII (1934), pp. 115-141; Kreymborg, Alfred, *Our Singing Strength* (1929), pp. 116-133; Lovett, R. M., "Lowell" in Macy, John (ed.), *American Writers on American Literature* (1931), pp. 177-189; Macy, John, *The Spirit of American Literature* (1913), pp. 189-209; Mims, Edwin, "Lowell as a Citizen," *SAQ.*, I (1902), pp.27-40; Palmer, Ray, "James Russell Lowell and Modern Literary Criticism," *IR.*, IV (1877), pp. 264-281; Parrington, V. L., *Main Currents in American Thought*, II (1927), pp. 460-472; Parsons, E. S., "Lowell's Conception of Poetry," *CCP.*, Language Series II, No. 20 (1908), pp. 67-84; Pattee, F. L., "A Call for a Literary Historian," in Foerster, Norman, *The Reinterpretation of American Literature* (1928), p. 20; Perry, Bliss, "James Russell Lowell," *HGM.*, XXVII (1918-1919), pp. 482-491; Pollak, Gustav, *International Perspective in Criticism* (1914), pp. 58-83; Pritchard, J. P., *Return to the Fountains: Some Classical Sources of American Criticism* (1942), pp. 99-118; Reilly, J. J., *James Russell Lowell as a Critic* (1915); Robertson, J. M., "Lowell as Critic," *NAR.*, CCIX (1919), pp. 246-262; Savage, M. J., "The Religion of Lowell's Poems," *Arena*, IX (1893-1894), pp. 705-722; Shea, L. M., *Lowell's Religious Outlook* (1926); Strong, A. H., *American Poets and Their Theology* (1916), pp. 267-317; Thorndike, A. H., *CHAL.*, II (1927), pp. 245-257; Woodberry, G. E., *Makers of Literature* (1900), pp. 324-349.

WALT WHITMAN (pp. 134-142)

WORKS: *The Complete Writings of Walt Whitman,* edited by R. M. Bucke, T. B. Harned, and H. L. Traubel, with bibliographical and critical contributions by O. L. Triggs (ten volumes, 1902); *Letters Written by Walt Whitman to His Mother,* edited by T. B. Harned (1902); *Walt Whitman's Diary in Canada,* edited by W. S. Kennedy (1904); *The Letters of Anne Gilchrist and Walt Whitman,* edited with an introduction by T. B. Harned (1918); *The Gathering of the Forces,* edited by Cleveland Rodgers and John Black (two volumes, 1920); *The Uncollected Poetry and Prose of Walt Whitman,* edited with an introduction by Emory Holloway (two volumes, 1921); *The Half-Breed and Other Stories by Walt Whitman,* edited by T. O. Mabbott (1927); *Walt Whitman's Workshop,* edited with an introduction by C. J. Furness (1928); *I Sit and Look Out,* edited by Emory Holloway and Vernolian Schwartz (1932); *Walt Whitman and the Civil War: A Collection of Original Articles and Manuscripts,* edited by C. I. Glicksberg (1933); *New York Dissected,* by Walt Whitman, edited with an introduction by Emory Holloway and Ralph Adimari (1936); R. M. Bucke (ed.), *Calamus* (Letters of Walt Whitman to Peter Doyle, 1897); Emory Holloway, "Some New Whitman Letters," *AM.,* XVI (1929), pp. 183-188; R. G. Silver, "Seven Letters of Walt Whitman," *AL.,* VII (1935-1936), pp. 76-81; "Thirty-One Letters of Walt Whitman," *ibid.,* VIII (1936-1937), pp. 417-438; "Whitman's Earliest Signed Prose: A Correction," *AL.,* IX (1937-1938), p. 458; S. T. Williams, "The Adrian Van Linderen Collection of Walt Whitman," *YULG.,* XV (1941), pp. 49-53.

BIBLIOGRAPHY: Allen, G. W., "Walt Whitman Bibliography 1918-1934," *BBDI.,* XV (1934), pp. 84-88, 106-109; "Walt Whitman Bibliography 1935-1942," *BBDI.,* XVII (1943), p. 209 *f.*; American Art Association, *Catalogue of Manuscripts, Autograph Letters, etc., of Walt Whitman* (1936); Holloway, Emory, *CHAL.,* II (1927), pp. 551-581; *Index to Early American Periodical Literature, 1728-1870, No. 3 Walt Whitman* (1941); McCain, Rea (comp.), "Walt Whitman in Italy: A Bibliography," *BBDI.,* XVII (1941), pp. 66-67, 92-93; Monroe, W. S., "Recent Walt Whitman Literature in America," *RAA.,* VIII (1930-1931), pp. 138-141; Shay, Frank, *The Bibliography of Walt Whitman* (1920); Stovall, Floyd, *Walt Whitman: Representative Selections,* with Introduction, Bibliography, and Notes (1934), pp. liii-lx; Triggs, O. L., in *The Complete Writings of Walt Whitman,* X (1902), pp. 139-233; Wells, Carolyn, and Goldsmith, A. F., *A Concise Bibliography of the Works of Walt Whitman* (1922).

BIOGRAPHY: Arvin, Newton, *Whitman* (1938); Bailey, John, *Walt Whitman* (1926); Barrus, Clara, *Whitman and Burroughs, Comrades* (1931); Barton, W. E., *Abraham Lincoln and Walt Whitman* (1928); Baxter, Sylvester, "Walt Whitman in Boston," *NEM.,* N.S. VI (1892), pp. 714-721; Bazalgette, Léon, *Walt Whitman: The Man and His Work* (1920); Bradley, Sculley, "Walt Whitman on Timber Creek," *AL.,* V (1933-1934), pp. 235-246; Brinton, D. G.: Traubel, H. L., "A Visit to West Hills," in *Walt Whitman Fellowship Papers, 1894-1899;* No. 10, December, 1894; Bucke, R. M., *Walt Whitman* (1883); "Memories of Walt Whitman," *Whitman Fellowship Papers* (1894); Canby, H. S., *Walt Whitman* (1943); Carpenter, G. R., *Walt Whitman* (1909); Catel, Jean, *Walt Whitman: La Naissance du Poète* (1929); Chapman, J. J., *Emerson and Other Essays* (1898), pp. 111-128; Conway, M. D., *Autobiography, Memories and Experiences* (two volumes, 1904); Deutsch, Babette, *Walt Whitman: Builder for America* (1942); Eliot, C. N. (ed.), *Walt Whitman as Man, Poet and Friend* (1915); Fausset, Hugh L'Anson, *Walt Whitman: Poet of Democracy* (1942); Glicksberg, C. I., "Walt Whitman in 1862," *AL.,* VI (1934-1935), pp. 264-282; *Walt Whitman and the Civil War* (1933); "Walt Whitman, the Journalist," *Americana,* XXX (1936), pp. 474-490; Gould, E. P., *Anne Gilchrist and Walt Whitman* (1900); Holloway, Emory, *Whitman: An Interpretation in Narrative* (1926); "Whitman on the War's Finale," *Colophon,* I (1930); "Whitman as His Own Press-Agent," *AM.,* XVIII (1929), pp. 482-488; "Whitman as Journalist," *SRL.,* VIII (1932), pp. 677, 679-680; "Walt Whitman's Visit to the Shakers," *Colophon,* XIII (1930); Josephson, Matthew, *Portrait of the Artist as an American* (1930), pp. 139-198; Keller, E. L., *Walt Whitman in Mickle Street* (1921); Kennedy, W. S., *The Fight of a Book for the World* (1926); *Reminiscences of Walt Whitman* (1896); Masters, E. L., *Whitman* (1937); Molinoff, Katherine, *Some Notes on Whitman's Family* (1941); Morris, H. S., *Walt Whitman: A Brief Biography with Reminiscences* (1929); O'Connor, W. D., *The Good Gray Poet* (1866); Perry, Bliss, *Walt Whitman: His Life and Work* (1906); Rogers, Cameron, *The Magnificent Idler* (1926); Sixbey, G. L., "Whitman's War Years" (Ph.D., Yale, 1941); Traubel, Horace, *With Walt Whitman in Camden* (three volumes, 1906-1914); Trowbridge, J. T., "Reminiscences of Walt Whitman," *Atl.,* LXXXIX (1902), pp. 163-175; Wecter, Dixon, "Walt Whitman as Civil Servant," *PMLA.,* LVIII (1943), pp. 1094-1109; Winwar, Frances, *American Giant: Walt Whitman and His Times* (1941).

CRITICISM: Allen, G. W., *American Prosody* (1935), pp. 217-243; "Walt Whitman's 'Long Journey' Motif," *JEGP.,* XXXVIII (1939), pp. 76-95; Bailey, E. J., *Religious Thought in the Greater American Poets* (1922), pp. 183-228; Baker, Portia, "Walt Whitman's Relations with Some New York Magazines," *AL.,* VII (1935-1936), pp. 274-301; "Walt Whitman and *The Atlantic Monthly,*" *ibid.,* VI (1934-1935), pp. 283-301; Baldensperger, Fernand, "Walt Whitman and France," *CUQ.,* XXI (1919), pp. 298-309; Blankenship, Russell, *American Literature* (1931), pp. 348-367; Blodgett, Harold, *Walt Whitman in England* (1934); Born, Helena, *Whitman's Ideal Democracy* (1902); Boyd, Ernest, *Literary Blasphemies* (1927), pp. 186-212; Bradford, Gamaliel, *Biography and the Human Heart* (1932), pp. 65-93; Bradley, Sculley, "The Fundamental Metrical Principle in Whitman's Poetry," *AL.,* X (1938-1939), pp. 437-459; "Walt Whitman and the Postwar World," *SAQ.,* XLII (1943); pp. 220-224; Brenner, Rica, *Twelve American Poets before 1900* (1933), pp. 229-266; Brooks, Van Wyck, *America's Coming-of-Age*

(1915), pp. 109-129; *Sketches in Criticism* (1932), pp. 178-189; Burke, Kenneth, "Acceptance and Rejection," *So.R.*, II (1936-1937), pp. 600-632; Burroughs, John, *Whitman, A Study* (1896); Cairns, W. B., "Walt Whitman," *YR.*, N.S. VIII (1939), pp. 737-754; "Swinburne's Opinion of Whitman," *AL.*, III (1931-1932), pp. 125-135; Calverton, V. F., *The Liberation of American Literature* (1932): consult Index entries, p. 499; Campbell, Killis, "The Evolution of Whitman as Artist," *AL.*, VI (1934-1935), pp. 254-263; Canby, H. S., *Classic Americans* (1932), pp. 308-351; Carpenter, F. I., "Immortality from India," *AL.*, I (1929-1930), p. 240 *f.*, (pp. 233-242); "The Vogue of Ossian in America," *ibid.*, II (1930-1931), pp. 413-417 (pp. 405-417); Cestre, C[harles], "Walt Whitman, L'Inadapté," *RAA.*, VII (1929-1930), pp. 385-408; "Walt Whitman: Le Mystique, Le Lyrique," VII (1929-1930), pp. 482-504; "Walt Whitman, Le Poète," *RAA.*, VIII (1930-1931), pp. 19-41; Chapman, J. J., *Emerson and Other Essays* (1898), pp. 111-128; Cooke, A. L., "Whitman's Indebtedness to the Scientific Thought of His Day," *UTSE.*, No. 14 (1934), pp. 89-115; "Whitman's Background in the Industrial Movements of His Time," *ibid.*, No. 15 (1935), pp. 76-91; Daggett, G. H., *Whitman's Poetic Theory* (Ph.D., North Carolina, 1941); DeSelincourt, Basil, *Walt Whitman: A Critical Study* (1914); Dowden, Ernest, *Studies in Literature 1789-1877* (1892), pp. 468-523; Ellis, Havelock, *The New Spirit* (1892), pp. 89-132; Erskine, John, "A Note on Whitman's Prosody," *SP.*, XX (1923), pp. 336-344; Falk, R. P., "Walt Whitman and German Thought," *JEGP.*, XL (1941), pp. 315-330; Foerster, Norman, *American Criticism* (1928), pp. 157-222; *Nature in American Literature* (1923), pp. 176-220; *The Reinterpretation of American Literature* (1928), pp. 23-28; Frank, Waldo, *The New America* (1922), pp. 220-240; Furness, C. J., "Walt Whitman's Politics," *AM.*, XVI (1929), pp. 459-466; "Walt Whitman's Estimate of Shakespeare," *HSNPL.*, XIV (1932), pp. 1-33; Gohdes, Clarence, and Baum, P. F., *Letters of W. M. Rossetti concerning Whitman, Blake, and Shelley* (1934); Gohdes, C. L. F., "A Note on Whitman's Use of the Bible as a Model," *MLQ.*, II (1941), pp. 105-108; "Whitman and Emerson," *SR.*, XXXVIII (1929), pp. 79-93; Goodale, David, "Some of Walt Whitman's Borrowings," *AL.*, X (1938-1939), pp. 202-213; Gosse, Edmund, *Leaves and Fruit* (1927), pp. 205-211; Gummere, F. B., *Democracy and Poetry* (1911), pp. 96-148; Harrison, R. C., "Walt Whitman and Shakespeare," *PMLA.*, XLIV (1929), pp. 1201-1238; Hayes, Will, *Walt Whitman, the Prophet of the New Era* (1921); Hintz, H. W., *The Quaker Influence in American Literature* (1940), pp. 59-65, 66-75; Holloway, Emory, "Whitman as Critic of America," *SP.*, XX (1923), pp. 345-369; "Notes from a Whitman Student's Scrapbook," *A.Schol.*, II (1933), pp. 269-278; "Whitman's Embryonic Verse," *Sw.R.*, X (1925), pp. 28-40; Howard, Leon, "Walt Whitman and the American Language," *AS.*, V (1930), pp. 441-451; "For a Critique of Whitman's Transcendentalism," *MLN.*, XLVII (1932), pp. 79-85; Howe, M. A. DeW., *American Bookmen* (1902), pp. 222-241; Huneker, James, *Ivory Apes and Peacocks* (1915), pp. 22-31; Hungerford, Edward, "Walt Whitman and His Chart of Bumps," *AL.*, II (1930-1931), pp. 350-384; James, Henry, *Views and Reviews* (1908), pp. 101-110; Johnson, M. O., "Walt Whitman as a Critic of Literature," *UNSLLC.*, No. 16 (1938), pp. 1-73; Jones, P. M., "Influence of Walt Whitman on the Origin of the 'Vers Libre,'" *MLR.*, XI (1916), pp. 186-194; Jordy, W. H., "Henry Adams and Walt Whitman," *SAQ.*, XL (1941), pp. 132-145; Kreymborg, Alfred, *Our Singing Strength* (1929), pp. 206-230; Lafourcade, Georges, "Swinburne and Walt Whitman," *MLR.*, XXII (1927), pp. 84-86; Law-Robertson, Harry, "Walt Whitman in Deutschland," *GBDP.*, XLII (1935); Long, Haniel, *Walt Whitman and the Springs of Courage* (1938); Lowell, Amy, "Walt Whitman and the New Poetry," *YR.*, XVI (1926-1927), pp. 502-519; *Poetry and Poets* (1930); Lucas, F. L., *Authors Dead and Living* (1926); Macphail, Andrew, *Essays in Puritanism* (1905), pp. 223-273; Macy, John, *The Spirit of American Literature* (1913), pp. 210-247; *The Critical Game* (1922), pp. 203-211; Mathews, J. C., "Walt Whitman's Reading of Dante," *UTSE.*, No. 3926 (1939), pp. 177-179; Matthiessen, F. O., *American Renaissance: Art and Expression in the Age of Emerson and Whitman* (1941), pp. 517-625; Mercer, D. F., *Leaves of Grass and the Bhagavad Gita* (Ph.D., California, 1933); Monroe, Harriet, *Poets & Their Art* (1926), pp. 179-184; Monroe, W. S., "Swinburne's Recantation of Walt Whitman," *RAA.*, VIII (1930-1931), pp. 347-351; Moore, J. B., "The Master of Whitman," *SP.*, XXIII (1926), pp. 77-89; More, P. E., *Shelburne Essays*. Fourth Series (1907), pp. 180-211; Mumford, Lewis, *The Golden Day* (1926), pp. 121-138; Myers, H. A., "Whitman's Consistency," *AL.*, VIII (1936-1937), pp. 243-257; "Whitman's Conception of the Spiritual Democracy, 1855-1856," *AL.*, VI (1934-1935), pp. 237-253; Oppenheim, James, "Walt Whitman" in Macy, John (ed.), *American Writers on American Literature* (1936), pp. 258-273; Paine, Gregory, "The Literary Relations of Whitman and Carlyle with Especial Reference to their Contrasting Views on Democracy," *SP.*, XXXVI (1939), pp. 550-563; Parrington, V. L., *Main Currents in American Thought*, III (1930), pp. 69-86; Parsons, O. W., "Whitman the Non-Hegelian," *PMLA.*, LVIII (1943), pp. 1073-1093; Pattee, F. L., *A History of American Literature since 1870* (1915), pp. 163-185; *The Feminine Fifties* (1940), pp. 37-49; Pound, Louise, "Walt Whitman and the Classics," *Sw.R.*, X (1925), pp. 75-83; "Walt Whitman and Italian Music," *AM.*, VI (1925), pp. 58-63; "Walt Whitman and the French Language," *AS.*, I (1926), pp. 421-430; "Walt Whitman's Neologisms," *AM.*, IV (1925), pp. 199-201; Pucciani, O. F., *The Literary Reputation of Walt Whitman in France* (Dissertation, Harvard, 1943); Rascoe, Burton, *Titans of Literature* (1932), pp. 391-394; Reed, H. B., "The Heraclitan Obsession of Walt Whitman," *Personalist*, XV (1934), pp. 125-138; Rickett, Arthur, *The Vagabond in Literature* (1906), pp. 169-205; Riethmueller, R. H., *Walt Whitman and the Germans* (1906); Santayana, George, *Interpretations of Poetry and Religion* (1900), pp. 166-216; Scott, F. N., "A Note on Walt Whitman's Prosody," *JEGP.*, *VII* (1907-1908), pp. 134-153; Shephard, Esther, *Walt Whitman's Pose* (1938); Sherman, S. P., *Americans* (1922), pp. 153-185; Sixbey, G. L., "'Chanting The Square Deific'—A Study in Whitman's Religion," *AL.*, IX (1937-1938), pp. 171-195; Smith, F. M., "Whitman's Poet-Prophet and Carlyle's Hero," *PMLA.*, LV (1940), pp. 1146-1164; "Whitman's Debt to Carlyle's *Sartor Resartus*,"

MLQ., III (1942), pp. 51-65, Stedman, E. C., *Poets of America* (1885), pp. 349-395; Stevenson, R. L., *Familiar Studies of Men and Books* (seventh edition, 1892), pp. 91-127; Stovall, Floyd, *Walt Whitman: Representative Selections* (1934); Strachey, J. St. L., *American Soundings* (1926), pp. 233-245; Strong, A. H., *American Poets and Their Theology* (1916), pp. 421-470; Swinburne, A. C., *Complete Works*, edited by Gosse, Edmund, and Wise, T. J., XVI (1926), pp. 377-444; Symonds, J. A., *Walt Whitman: A Study* (1893); Taylor, W. F., *A History of American Letters* (1936), pp. 225-238; Traubel, H. L., Bucke, R. M., and Harned, T. B. (eds.), *In Re Walt Whitman* (1893); Triggs, O. L., "Walt Whitman," *Poet Lore*, V (1893), pp. 289-305; Ware, Lois, "Poetic Conventions in *Leaves of Grass*," *SP.*, XXVI (1929), pp. 47-57; Wiley, A. N., "Reiterative Devices in *Leaves of Grass*," *AL.*, I (1929-1930), pp. 161-170; White, V. C., "Thoreau's Opinion of Whitman," *NEQ.*, VIII (1935), pp. 262-264.

HARRIET [ELIZABETH] BEECHER STOWE (pp. 143-145)

WORKS: *Uncle Tom's Cabin* (1852); *A Key to Uncle Tom's Cabin* (1853); *Dred: A Tale of the Great Dismal Swamp* (1856); *The Minister's Wooing* (1859); *The Pearl of Orr's Island* (1862); *Oldtown Folks* (1869); *Poganuc People* (1878).

BIOGRAPHY: Beecher, C. (ed.), *Autobiography, Correspondence, Etc., of Lyman Beecher* (two volumes, 1864-1865); Crow, M. F., *Harriet Beecher Stowe* (1913); Fields, Annie (ed.), *Life and Letters of Harriet Beecher Stowe* (1897); Gilbertson, Catherine, *Harriet Beecher Stowe* (1937); MacArthur, R. A., *The Story of Harriet Beecher Stowe* (1922); Rourke, C. M., *Trumpets of Jubilee* (1927), pp. 89-148; Stowe, C. E., *Life of Harriet Beecher Stowe* (1889); Stowe, C. E., and L. B., *Harriet Beecher Stowe* (1911); Stowe, H. B., *Sunny Memories of Foreign Lands* (1854); Stowe, L. B., *Saints, Sinners, and Beechers* (1934), pp. 154-235; Twitchell, J. H., "Harriet Beecher Stowe" in Gilder, J. L., and J. B. (eds.), *Authors at Home* (1889), pp. 315-322; Ward, E. S. P., *Chapters from a Life* (1896), pp. 131-140; Wilson, Forrest, *Crusader in Crinoline* (1941).

CRITICISM: Adams, J. R., *A Critical Study of the Works of Harriet B. Stowe* (Ph.D., So. California, 1940); Bradford, Gamaliel, *Portraits of American Women* (1919), pp. 101-130; Brown, H. R., *The Sentimental Novel in America, 1789-1860* (1940), pp. 241-280; Erskine, John, *Leading American Novelists* (1910), pp. 275-323; Guerry, W. A., "Harriet Beecher Stowe," *SR.*, VI (1898), pp. 335-344; Klingberg, F. J., "Harriet Beecher Stowe and Social Reform in England," *AHR.*, XLIII (1938), pp. 542-552; McDowell, Tremaine, "The Use of Negro Dialect by Harriet Beecher Stowe," *AS.*, VI (1930-1931), pp. 322-326; Maclean, G. E., *"Uncle Tom's Cabin" in Germany* (1910); Maxfield, E. K., " 'Goody Goody' Literature and Mrs. Stowe," *AS.*, IV (1928-1929), pp. 189-202; Parrington, V. L., *Main Currents in American Thought*, II (1927), pp. 371-378; Pattee, F. L., *The Feminine Fifties* (1940), pp. 130-145; Phelps, W. L., *Howells, James, Bryant, and Other Essays* (1924), pp. 181-206; Purcell, J. M., "Mrs. Stowe's Vocabulary," *AS.*, XIII (1938), p. 230 *f.*, Sanborn, F. B., "Mrs. Stowe and Her Uncle Tom," *BS.*, LXVIII (1907), pp. 674-683; Shoup, F. A., "Uncle Tom's Cabin Forty Years After," *SR.*, II (1893-1894), pp. 88-104; Tandy, J. R., "Pro-Slavery Propaganda in American Fiction of the Fifties," *SAQ.*, XXI (1922), pp. 41-50, 170-178.

GEORGE WILLIAM CURTIS (p. 145)

Adams, E. L., "George W. Curtis and his Friends," *MB.*, XIV (1939), pp. 291-303, 353-366; Cary, Edward, *George William Curtis* (1894); Chadwick, J. W., "Recollections of George William Curtis," *Harper's*, LXXXVI (1892-1893), pp. 469-476; *George William Curtis* (1893); Chamberlain, H. H., *George William Curtis and His Antecedents* (1893); Godwin, Parke, *George William Curtis, A Commemorative Address . . .* (1893); Hale, E. E., "Curtis, Whittier, and Longfellow" in *Five Prophets of Today* (1892).

BAYARD TAYLOR (p. 146)

BIOGRAPHY AND CRITICISM: Beatty, R. C., "A Mind Divided," *AR.*, III (1934), pp. 77-95; *Bayard Taylor: Laureate of the Gilded Age* (1936) — reviewed by Sculley Bradley, *AL.*, VIII (1936-1937), pp. 474-477; Flanagan, J. T., "Bayard Taylor's Minnesota Visits," *M.Hist.*, XIX (1938), pp. 399-418; Hansen-Taylor, Marie, and Scudder, H. E., *Life and Letters of Bayard Taylor* (two volumes, 1884); Hellman, G. S., "Three Unpublished Letters of Bayard Taylor," *SRL.*, XXIV, No. 22 (1941), pp. 12-15; Schultz, J. R. (ed.), *The Unpublished Letters of Bayard Taylor* (1937); Smyth, A. H., *Bayard Taylor* (1896); Warnock, Robert, "Unpublished Lectures of Bayard Taylor," *AL.*, V (1933), pp. 123-132; "Bayard Taylor's Unpublished Letters to His Sister Annie," *AL.*, VII (1935-1936), pp. 47-55.

LOUISA M. ALCOTT (pp. 146-147)

WORKS: *Flower Fables, or Fairy Tales* (1855); *Hospital Sketches* (1863); *Moods* (1865; rewritten 1882); *Little Women* (1868, 1869); *Camp and Fireside Stories* (1869); *An Old-Fashioned Girl* (1870); *Little Men* (1871); *Aunt Jo's Scrap Bag* (1872-1882); *Work, A Story of Experience* (1873); *Eight Cousins* (1875); *Rose in Bloom* (1876); *Silver Pitchers* (1876); *A Modern Mephistopheles* (1877); *Under the Lilacs* (1878); *Jack and Jill* (1880); *Proverb Stories* (1882); *Spinning-Wheel Stories* (1884); *Lulu's*

Library (1886-1889); *Jo's Boys, and How They Turned Out* (1886); *A Garland for Girls* (1888); *Comic Tragedies Written by "Jo" and "Meg" and Acted by the "Little Women"* (1893).

BIBLIOGRAPHY: Gulliver, Lucile, *Louisa May Alcott: A Bibliography*, with Appreciation by Cornelia Meigs (1932); Stern, M. B., "Louisa May Alcott's Contributions to Periodicals, 1868-1888," *MB.* (1943), pp. 411-420.

BIOGRAPHY AND CRITICISM: Alcott, J. S. P., "The 'Little Women' of Long Ago," *GH.*, LVI (1913), pp. 182-189; Anthony, Katharine, *Louisa May Alcott* (1938); Bradford, Gamaliel, *Portraits of American Women* (1919), pp. 165-194; Brown, M. H., *Memories of Concord* (1926); Cheney, E. D. (ed.), *Louisa May Alcott. Her Life, Letters, and Journal* (1889, 1928); *Reminiscences* (1902); Clark, A. M. L., *The Alcotts in Harvard* (1902); Crawford, B. V., "Teaching by Dialogue," *PQ.*, III (1924), pp. 23-31; Gerould, K. F., "Miss Alcott's New England," *Atl.*, CVIII (1911), pp. 180-186; Gowing, Clara, *The Alcotts as I Knew Them* (1909); Higginson, T. W., *Short Studies of American Authors* (1906), pp. 61-67; James, Henry, *Notes and Reviews* (1921), pp. 49-58; Meigs, Cornelia, *Invincible Louisa* (1933); Morrow, H. W., *Father of Little Women* (1927); Moses, Belle, *Louisa May Alcott: Dreamer and Worker* (1909); Porter, M. S., *Recollections of Louisa May Alcott* (1893); Roller, Bert, "When Jo Died," *SR.*, XXXVI (1928), pp. 164-170; Sanborn, F. B., *Recollections of Seventy Years* (1909); "Reminiscences of Louisa M. Alcott," *Ind.*, LXXII (1912), pp. 469-502; Sears, C. E., *Bronson Alcott's Fruitlands* (1915); Shepard, Odell, *Pedlar's Progress* (1937); Spofford, H. P., "Louisa May Alcott," *Chaut.*, IX (1888-1889), pp. 160-162; Stearns, F. P., *Sketches from Concord and Appledore* (1895), pp. 69-88; Talbot, Marion, "Glimpses of the Real Louisa May Alcott," *NEQ.*, XI (1938), pp. 731-738; Ticknor, Caroline, *May Alcott: A Memoir* (1929); Whitman, Alfred, "Miss Alcott's Letters to Her 'Laurie,'" *LHJ.*, XVIII (1901), No. 11, p. 4; Willis, F. L. H., *Alcott Memoirs* (1915); Winterich, J. T., "Romantic Stories of Books: *Little Women*," *PW.*, CXX (1931), pp. 607-611.

Stern, M. B., "Louisa M. Alcott: Civil War Nurse," *Americana*, XXXVII (1943), pp. 296-325; "Louisa Alcott, Trouper," *NEQ.*, XVI (1943), pp. 175-197; [Strunsky, Simeon], "Topics of the Times," *NYT.*, December 14, 1944.

THOMAS BAILEY ALDRICH (pp. 147-148)

CHIEF WORKS: *The Story of a Bad Boy* (1870); *Marjorie Daw, and Other People* (1873); *The Stillwater Tragedy* (1880); *From Ponkapog to Pesth* (1883); *Two Bites at a Cherry, with Other Tales* (1894); *Ponkapog Papers* (1903); *Works of Thomas Bailey Aldrich* (eight volumes, 1896); *The Poems of Thomas Bailey Aldrich* (1897).

BIOGRAPHY AND CRITICISM: Aldrich, Mrs. T. B., *Crowding Memories* (1920); Cowie, Alexander, "Indian Summer Novelist," *NEQ.*, XV (1942), pp. 608-621; Greenslet, Ferris, *The Life of Thomas Bailey Aldrich* (1908); Grattan, C. H., "Thomas Bailey Aldrich," *AM.*, V (1925), pp. 41-45; More, P. E., *Shelburne Essays*, Seventh Series (1910), pp. 138-152; Perry, Bliss, *Park-Street Papers* (1908), pp. 143-170; Vedder, H. C., *American Writers of Today* (1894), pp. 104-123.

HENRY JAMES (pp. 200-204)

BIBLIOGRAPHY: Phillips, Le Roy, *A Bibliography of Henry James* (1930); Richardson, L. N. (ed.), *Henry James: Representative Selections*, with Introduction, Bibliography, and Notes (1941); Taylor, W. F., *A History of American Letters* (1936), pp. 556-559.

BIOGRAPHY: Benson, A. C., *Memories and Friends* (1924), pp. 214-228; Bosanquet, Theodora, *Henry James at Work* (1924); Brooks, Van Wyck, *The Pilgrimage of Henry James* (1925); "Henry James of Boston," *SRL.*, XXII (July 15, 1940), pp. 3-4, 16-17; Burr, A. R., (ed.), *Alice James: Her Brothers* (1934); Colvin, Sidney, *Memories and Notes of Persons and Places* (1921); Gosse, Edmund, *Aspects and Impressions* (1922), pp. 17-53; Grattan, C. H., *The Three Jameses* (1932); James, Henry, Jr. (ed.), *Letters of William James* (1920); *Letters of Charles Eliot Norton* (1913); *Letters of Robert Louis Stevenson* (1899); MacKenzie, Compton, "Henry James," *LLT.*, XXXIX (1943), pp. 147-155; Warren, Austin, *The Elder Henry James* (1934).

CRITICISM: Arvin, Newton, "Henry James and the Almighty Dollar," *HH.*, VII (1934), pp. 434-443; Barzun, Jacques, "James the Melodramatist," *KR.*, V (1943), pp. 508-521; Beach, J. W., *The Method of Henry James* (1918); *The Twentieth-Century Novel* (1932), pp. 177-228; Blackmur, R. P., *Art of the Novel: Critical Prefaces, by Henry James* (1934), pp. vii-xxxix; "In the Country of the Blue," *KR.*, V (1943), pp. 595-617; Boyd, Ernest, *Literary Blasphemies* (1927), pp. 213-226; Bradford, Gamaliel, *American Portraits* (1922), pp. 171-196; Brewster, Dorothy, and Burrell, Angus, *Dead Reckonings in Fiction* (1924), pp. 19-41; Brooks, Van Wyck, *The Pilgrimage of Henry James* (1925); "Henry James of Boston," *SRL.*, XXII (July 15, 1940), pp. 3-4, 16-17; Brownell, W. C., *American Prose Masters* (1909), pp. 339-400; Canby, H. S., *Definitions: Essays in Contemporary Criticism*, First Series (1922), pp. 278-281; Cantwell, Robert, "A Little Reality," *HH.*, VII (1934), pp. 494-505; Cary, E. L., *The Novels of Henry James* (1905); Cestre, Charles, "La France dans l'Oeuvre de Henry James," *RAA.*, X (1932), pp. 1-13, 112-122; Conrad, Joseph, "Henry James: An Appreciation," *NAR.*, CLXXX (1905), pp. 102-108; CCIII (1916), pp. 585-591; DeMille, G. E., *Literary Criticism in America* (1931), pp. 158-181; Edel, Leon, "The Exile of Henry James,"

UTQ., II (1932), pp. 520-532; "Henry James: The War Chapter," *UTQ.*, X (1940-1941), pp. 125-138; "Henry James and the Poets," *Poetry*, LXII (1943), pp. 328-334; *Henry James: Les Annees Dramatiques* (1931); *The Prefaces of Henry James* (1931); Edgar, Pelham, *Henry James, Man and Author* (1927); Elton, Oliver, *Modern Studies* (1907), pp. 245-284; Ferguson, Frances, "James's Idea of Dramatic Form," *KR.*, V (1943), pp. 495-507; Follett, H. T. and Wilson, *Some Modern Novelists* (1918), pp. 75-98; Follett, Wilson, "The Simplicity of Henry James," *AR.*, I (1923), pp. 315-325; Forbes, E. L., "Dramatic Lustrum: A Study of the Effect of Henry James's Theatrical Experience on His Later Novels," *NEQ.*, XI (1938), pp. 108-120; Ford (Hueffer), Ford, Madox, *Henry James: A Critical Study* (1913); *Portraits from Life* (1937), pp. 1-20; "Techniques," *So.R.*, I (1935-1936), pp. 20-35; Garland, Hamlin, *Roadside Meetings* (1930), pp. 454-465; Gosse, Edmund, "Henry James," *LM.*, I (1920), pp. 673-684; II (1920), pp. 29-41; Hackett, Francis, *Horizons: A Book of Criticism* (1918), pp. 74-82, 268-273; Hale, E. E., "The Impressionism of Henry James," *UCFP.*, II (1931), pp. 3-17; Hartwick, Harry, *The Foreground of American Fiction* (1934), pp. 341-368; Herrick, Robert, "A Visit to Henry James" in *The Manly Anniversary Studies in Language and Literature* (1923), pp. 229-242; "Henry James" in Macy, John (ed.), *American Writers on American Fiction* (1931), pp. 298-316; Hicks, Granville, *The Great Tradition* (1933), pp. 100, 105-124; Howells, W. D., "Mr. Henry James's Later Work," *NAR.*, CLXXVI (1903), pp. 125-137; *ibid.*, CCIII (1916), pp. 572-584; Hughes, H. L., *Theory and Practice in Henry James* (1926); Josephson, Matthew, *Portrait of the Artist as American* (1930), pp. 70-138, 268-288; Kelley, C. P., "The Early Development of Henry James," *UISLL.*, XV, Nos. 1-2 (1930); Lowell, J. R., *The Function of the Poet and Other Essays* (1920), pp. 105-114; Lubbock, Percy, "Henry James," *QR.*, CCXXVI (1916), pp. 60-74; *The Craft of Fiction* (1921), pp. 145 *ff.*, 156 *ff.*, 172 *ff.*, 189 *ff.*; MacKenzie, Compton, "Henry James," *LLT.*, XXXIX (1943), pp. 147-155; Macy, John, *The Spirit of American Literature* (1913), pp. 324-339; Matthews, Brander, "Henry James and the Theater," *Bookman*, LI (1920), pp. 389-395; Matthiessen, F. O., *American Renaissance* (1941), pp. 292-305, 351-368; "James and the Plastic Arts," *KR.*, V (1943), pp. 533-550; "Henry James's Portrait of the Artist," *PR.*, XI (Winter, 1944), pp. 71-87; Phelps, W. L., *The Advance of the English Novel* (1916), pp. 302-330; *Howells, James, Bryant, and Other Essays* (1924), pp. 123-155; Porter, K. A., "The Days Before," *KR.*, V (1943), pp. 481-494; Pound, Ezra, *Instigations* (1920), pp. 106-167; Rahv, Philip, "The Heiress of All the Ages," *PR.*, X (1943), pp. 227-247; Randell, W. R., "The Art of Mr. Henry James," *FR.*, CV, N.S. XCIX (1916), pp. 620-632; "Henry James as Humanist," *ibid.*, CXVI, N.S. CX (1921), pp. 458-469; Read, Herbert, *The Sense of Glory* (1929), pp. 205-228; Roberts, Morley, *Henry James's Criticism* (1929); Russell, John, "Henry James and the Leaning Tower," *NSN.*, N.S. XXV (1943), p. 254 *f.*; Scott, Dixon, *Men of Letters* (1923), pp. 78-110; Seldes, G. V., "Henry James: An Appreciation," *HM.*, LIII (1911), pp. 92-100; Sherman, Stuart, *On Contemporary Literature* (1917), pp. 226-255; *The Emotional Discovery of America* (1932), pp. 35-47; Spender, Stephen, "The School of Experience in the Early Novels," *HH.*, VII (1934), pp. 417-433; "A Modern Writer in Search of a Moral Subject," *LM.*, XXXI (1934), pp. 128-133; *The Destruction Element: A Study of Modern Writers and Beliefs* (1935), pp. 11-110; Swinnerton, Frank, *The Georgian Scene* (1934), pp. 19-39; Underwood, J. C., *Literature and Insurgency* (1914), pp. 41-86; Van Doren, Carl, *The American Novel* (1940), pp. 163-189; Vivas, Eliseo, "Henry and William James: Two Notes," *KR.*, V (1943), pp. 580-594; Warren, Austin, "Myth and Dialectic in the Later Novels," *ibid.*, pp. 551-568; West, Rebecca, *Henry James* (1916); Wharton, Edith, "Henry James in His Letters," *QR.*, CCXXXIV (1920), pp. 188-202; *A Backward Glance* (1934), pp. 169-196; Wilson, Edmund, *The Triple Thinkers: Ten Essays on Literature* (1938), pp. 122-164; Winters, Yvor, "Henry James and the Relation of Morals to Manners," *AR.*, IX (1937), pp. 482-503; *Maule's Curse* (1938), pp. 169-216.

Matthiessen, F. O., *Henry James: The Major Phase* (1944); "The Painter's Sponge and Varnish Bottle: Henry James's Revision of *The Portrait of a Lady*," *AB.*, I (1944), pp. 49-68; George Stevens, "The Return of Henry James," *SRL.*, XXVIII (March 3, 1945), pp. 7-8, 30, 32-33.

INDEX

The aim of this *Index* is to cover all substantial references to authors, titles, and the like. No attempt is made to direct the reader to every subject or to every proper name mentioned in the handbook. Note, especially, the omission in this *Index* of the hundreds of titles in the final chapter (pages 268-294).

Abbot, Jacob, 82
Abolitionist, The, 88
"Abraham Davenport," 116
Abraham Lincoln: A History, 168
Abraham Lincoln: An Horatian Ode, 59
Account of the History, Manners, and Customs of the Indian Nations . . ., 112
"Acknowledgment," 235
Acorn Planter, The, 229
Active Service, 207
Adams, Henry [Brooks], 255-259
Adams, James Truslow, 290
Adams, John (c. 1705-1740), 20
Adams, John (1735-1826), 36
Adams, Léonie Fuller, 285
Adams, Samuel, 31
Addams, Jane, 213
"Address on Philippine Question," 212
Ade, George, 289
Admetus and Other Poems, 249
"Adventure of Padre Vicentio," 162
"Adventure of the German Student," 51
"Adventures in a Perambulator," 113
Adventures of Captain Bonneville, 52
Adventures of Captain Horn, The, 225
Adventures of Francois, The, 225
Adventures of Huckleberry Finn, The, 191
Adventures of Tom Sawyer, The, 191
Advertisements for the . . . Planters of New-England, or Anywhere, 2
"Advice to Authors," 39
Advice to the Privileged Orders, 41
Aeneid, 105
Afloat and Ashore, 67
"After a Lecture on Shelley," 125
"After a Lecture on Wordsworth," 125
"After the Burial" 132
"After the Curfew," 125
Aftermath (J. L. Allen), 178
Aftermath (H. W. Longfellow), 112
Afternoon Landscape, An, 262
Afternoon Neighbors, 207
"Agassiz," 132
Age of Reason, The, 32, 33
Ah Sin, 162
Ah Sin (drama), 164 *footnote*
Aiken, Conrad [Potter], 233 footnote, 283
Airs from Arcady and Elsewhere, 224
Airs of Palestine, 58
"Al Aaraaf," 61
Alabama, 264
Alabaster Box, The, 177
Alcott, [Amos] Bronson, 95, 101, 102, 299
Alcott, Louisa May, 146-147, 307-308
Alcuin, 42
Aldrich, Thomas Bailey, 113, 147-148, 308
Algerine Captive, The, 41
Alhambra, The, 51
Alice of Old Vincennes, 171
Alide, 249
Alison's House, 231
"All Here," 125
"Allegash and East Branch, The," 99
Allegheny Winds and Waters, 180
Allen, Ethan, 45
Allen, James Lane, 177-179
Allen, Paul, 46
Allston, Washington, 80
Alnwick Castle, with Other Poems, 53
Along the Trail, 245
Alsop, George, 13
Alsop, Richard, 45
Ambassadors, The, 203
"Ambitious Guest, The," 119
"America," 65
"America Independent," 38
American, The, 202
American Democrat, The, 67
American Dictionary of the English Language, An, 44
American Humor (Early Sentiment and Romance, 1810-1865), 76-78
"American Liberty," 38
American Magazine, 19
American Ornithology, 25
American Politician, An, 220
American Primer, An, 134 *footnote*
American Prose Masters, 262
American Revolution, The, 211
American Scholar, The, 89, 91, 92, 97
"American Writers," 79
Ames, Fisher, 45
Ames, Nathaniel, 20
Among My Books, 127, 130
Among the Camps, 181
"Among the Hills," 116
Amulet, The, 180
"Amy Wentworth," 116
Anderson, Maxwell, 286
Anderson, Sherwood, 171, 272
"Angels of Buena Vista, The," 117
"Annabel Lee," 62
Anne, 179
"Anner 'Lizer's Stumblin' Block," 252
Annie Kilburne, 197
Antepenultimata, 217
Anthology of Another Town, The, 171
Anti-Slavery Papers of James Russell Lowell, The, 127 *footnote*
Anti-Slavery Poems, 58
Appeal to Caesar, An, 226
"Appeal to Harold, The," 224
Appreciations of Poetry, 174 *footnote*
April Airs, 243
April Hopes, 199
Ardis Claverden, 225

Arethusa, 221
Arizona, 264
Army Life in a Black Regiment, 261
Arp, Bill (pseud.), 83, 160
"Art" (Emerson's *Essays*), 93
"Art" (Emerson's *Society and Solitude*), 97
Artemus Ward (pseud.), 76-77, 160
Artemus Ward, His Works Complete, 77
Arthur, Chester A., 154
Arthur Mervyn, 42
As a Man Thinks, 264
As a Strong Bird on Pinions Free, 135 footnote
As It Was in the Beginning, 169
As We Go, 262
As We Were Saying, 262
Ashes of the Beacon, 217
Aspern Papers, The, 210
Astoria, 51
Asylum; or, Alonzo and Melissa, The, 46
"At Dartmouth," 126
At Fault, 180
"At Gibraltar," 263
At Love's Extremes, 171
"At the Burns Centennial," 131
"At the Crossroads," 245
"At the Saturday Club," 125
Atherton, Gertrude [Franklin Horn], 269-270
"Atlantic City," 224
"Atlantides, The," 101
"Attack, The," 58
Auden W[ystan] H[ugh], 285
Audubon, John James, 84
"Auf Wiedersehen!," 132
"Auspex," 132
Austin, William, 82
Austin Phelps, 149
Autobiography (Peter Cartwright), 75
Autobiography (Benjamin Franklin), 27, 28, 29
Autobiography, or the Story of a Life, 134
Autobiography of Benjamin Franklin, The, 27, 28, 29
Autocrat of the Breakfast-Table, The, 122, 123
"Avondale Mine Disaster, The," 160
Awakening, The, 180
"Away Down South," 64
Awkward Age, The, 201

Babbitt, Irving, 289
"Bacchus," 98
Back-Trailers from the Middle Border, 206
Backwoodsman, The, 54
Bacon, Delia S., 84
"Bacon's Epitaph, Made by His Man," 2
Balcony Stories, 181
Baldwin, Joseph Glover, 83
Ballad, 159, 160
"Ballad of the Boston Tea-Party, A," 124
"Ballad of the Oysterman, The," 124
"Ballad of Trees and the Master, A," 236
Ballads, 159, 160
Ballads and Other Poems, 107
Ballads and Other Verses, 145
Ballads of Ireland, 224
Ballads of Lost Haven, 243
Bangs, John Kendrick, 250, 251
Banker of Bankersville, A, 171
Bankrupt, The, 75
"Banner of the Jew, The," 249
"Banty Tim," 167
"Bar Light-House, The," 184
Bar Sinister, The, 226
"Barbara Frietchie," 115, 265
Bare Souls, 261
"Barefoot Boy, The," 116
Barker, James Nelson, 46
Barlow, Joel, 40-41
Barnard, John, 20
Baroness of New York, The, 169
Barry, Philip, 287
Bartleby, the Scrivener, 72
Bartram, John, 45
Bartram, William, 25
Barzun, Jacques, 293
Bateman, Mrs. Sidney Frances, 83
"Battle-Field, The," 57, 245
Battle of Bunkers Hill, The, 43
"Battle of Lake Erie, The," 39
"Battle of Niagara," 79
"Battle of the Kegs, The," 31, 245
Battle-Pieces and Aspects of the War, 73
Bay Psalm Book, The, 7, 10
Bayou Folk, 180
Beard, Charles A[ustin], 290
Beau Brummel, 264
Beauchampe, 74
"Beauties of Santa Cruz, The," 37, 39
"Beautiful Dreamer," 64
"Beauty," 97
"Bedouin Song," 146
Beebe, [Charles] Williams, 290
Beers, Ethel Lynn, 81
Befo' de War, 180, 181
Before Adam, 229
Before the Curfew and Other Poems, 122
Beginners of a Nation, The, 166
Beginnings of New England, The, 211
"Behavior," 97
Behind the Arras: A Book of the Unseen,
Behind the Gamut, 243
"Behold the Deeds," 224
"Behold this Swarthy Face," 139
Behrman, S[amuel] N[athaniel], 287
Belasco, David, 264
Belfry of Bruges and Other Poems, 107
Bellamy, Edward, 218-219
Bells, The (T. B. Aldrich), 148
"Bells, The" (E. A. Poe), 62
"Beloved, in the noisy city here," 130
Ben Hur: A Tale of the Christ, 225
Benchley, Robert [Charles], 292
"Benedicite," 116
Benét, Stephen Vincent, 284
Benezet, Anthony, 45
"Benito Cereno," 72
Benj. F. Johnson (pseud.), 250
"Berenice," 63
Bertram Cope's Year, 227
Betrothal, The, 74
"Betsy and I Are Out," 249
Between the Dark and the Daylight, 195
Beverley, Robert, 20
Beyond the Gates, 148
Bianca Visconti, 53
"Bibliolatres," 131
Bicyclers, The, 251
Bierce, Ambrose [Gwinett], 214-217, 252; merits and defects, 217; other works, 216-217; poetry collections, 216; short-story volumes, 215-216
"Big Bear of Arkansas, The," 83
Biglow Papers, The, 127, 128, 131
"Bill and Joe," 125
Bill Arp So Called (pseud.), 83, 160
Bill Arp, So Called, A Side Show of the Southern Side of the War, 83
Billings, Josh (pseud.), 76, 160
Billy Budd, 73
"Billy the Kid," 159
Biographical and Critical Miscellanies, 77
Bird, Robert Montgomery, 82
"Birds of Killingworth, The," 112
Birth of Galahad, The, 245
"Birthday of Daniel Webster," 124
"Birthmark, The," 119
Black Beetles in Amber, 216
"Black Cat, The," 63

"Black Fox of Salmon River," 58
Black Riders and Other Lines, The, 209
Blair, James, 20
Bland, Richard, 45
Bleeker, Ann Eliza, 45
Blessed Edmund Campion, 251
Blessing of Business, The, 171
Blindman's World and Other Stories, The, 218
Blithedale Romance, The, 103, 118, 120, 121
Blix, 228
Bloody Chasm, The, 224
Bloody Tenent of Persecution for Cause of Conscience, The, 6
Bloody Tenent Yet More Bloody . . ., The, 6
"Blow the Man Down," 160
Blue Flower, The, 263
"Blue Hotel, The," 209
Blue-Grass Region of Kentucky and Other Kentucky Articles, The, 177
Body of Liberties, The, 9
"Bohemian, The," 224
Bolts of Melody, 232
Boker, George Henry, 74-75
Bonaventure, 177
Bone Rules, 241
Bonifacius, 8
Bonny, W. H., 159
Book of Romances, Lyrics, and Songs, 146
Book of the East, The, 249
"Books," 97
Border Beagles, 74
Boston Gazette, 19
"Boston Hymn," 98
Boston News-Letter, 19
Boston Quarterly Review, 105
Bostonians, The, 201
Boucher, Jonathan, 45
Boy Life on the Prairie, 205
Boyd, James, 274
Boyleston, Zabdiel, 20
Boylston Prize Dissertations, 122
Boynton, P. H., 164 *footnote*
"Boys, The," 125
Boy's Froissart, The, 235
Boy's King Arthur, The, 235
Boy's Mabinogion, The, 235
Boy's Percy, The, 235
Boy's Town, A, 195
Bracebridge Hall, 51
Brackenridge, Hugh Henry, 24, 43-44
Bradford, Andrew, 19
Bradford, Ebenezer, 46
Bradford, Gamaliel, 259-261; American character studies, 260-261; autobiography, 261; "psychographs," 259-260; trans-Atlantic character studies, 261; women character studies, 261
Bradford, William, 4
Bradstreet, Ann, 10-11
"Brahma," 97
Brainard, John Gardiner Calkins, 58
"Branch Road, A," 205
Brattle, Thomas, 9
Bravo, The, 67
Bread-Winners, The, 168
Bred in the Bone, 181
"Breeze's Invitation, The," 101
Briar Cliff, 54
Bricks without Straw, 226
"Bride Comes to Yellow Sky, The," 208
Bride of the Mistletoe, The, 179
Bridger, James, 159
Briggs, Charles F., 82
"British Prison Ship, The," 37, 38
Broken Battalions, The, 65
Bromfield, Louis, 276
Brook Farm, 87, 105
Brooks, Charles Timothy, 81
Brooks, Maria Gowen, 80
Brooks, Van Wyck, 292
"Brother Jonathan's Lament for Sister Caroline," 124
"Brother where dost thou dwell," 101
Brown, Charles Brockden, 24, 42-43
Brown, David Paul, 82
Brown, William Hill, 41
"Brown of Ossawatomie," 115
Browne, Charles Farrar, 76-77, 160
Brownell, Henry Howard, 81
Brownell, W[illiam] C[rary], 262
Brownson, Orestes Augustus, 105-106, 300
"Brunhilde," 229
"Brute, The," 248
Bryan, William Jennings, 213
Bryant, William Cullen, 54-57
"Bryant's Seventieth Birthday," 125
Buccaneer and Other Poems, The, 58
Buck, Pearl S[ydenstricker], 274-275
Bucktails, The, 54
"Buffalo Skinners, The," 160
Building of the City Beautiful, The, 170
Building of the Ship, The, 111
Bulkley, John, 20
Bunce, Oliver Bell, 84
Bunker Hill, 46
Bunner, H[enry] C[uyler], 222-224; novels, 222-223; representative poems, 234; short stories, 223-224
Bunyan, Paul, 159
Burglar, The, 264
Burial of the Guns, The, 181
Burk, John D., 46
Burnett, Frances [Eliza] Hodgson, 226, 264
Burning Daylight, 229
"Burns," 117
"Burnt Ships," 171
Burritt, Elihu, 79
Burroughs, John, 254-255
Burwell Papers, 2
Bushwhackers, The, 180
Busy-Body papers, 27, 29
Butler, James, 46
Butler, William Allen, 81
Butterflies: a Tale of Nature, 178
By the Waters of Babylon, 249
Byles, Mather, 20
Byrd, William, of Westover, 18
By-Ways and Bird Notes, 171
Cabell, [James] Branch, 272-273
Cable, George Washington, 175-177; novels, 177; short stories, 176
"Café des Exilés," 176
Calamus: A Series of Letters . . ., 134 *footnote,* 138
Calaynos, 74
Caldwell, Erskine [Preston], 277
Calef, Robert, 9
"Calef in Boston," 115
Calhoun, John C., 79
Call of the Wild, The, 229
Calvinism, 2-3
"Cambridge Thirty Years Ago," 129
Campaign Life of Abraham Lincoln, The, 193
Can Such Things Be?, 216
Canby, Henry Seidel, 290
"Candor," 224
Canfield, Dorothy, 290-291
Canzoni, 252
Capote, Truman, 279
"Captain Barney's Victory," 39
Captain Jinks of the Horse Marines, 264
Captain of Company K, The, 171
Captain of the Gray-Horse Troop, The, 206
Captured Dream and Other Stories, The, 171
Careful and Strict Enquiry into the Modern Prevailing Notions of . . . Freedom of Will . . ., A, 17

Carey, Henry Charles, 80
Carey, Mathew, 83
Carleton, Will, 249
"Carlyle," 130
Carman, [William] Bliss, 242-244; chief volumes of poetry, 242-243; merits and defects, 244; miscellaneous volumes of poetry and prose, 243
"Carolina," 64
Carpenter, John Alden, 113
"Carriage-Lamps, The," 207
Carruthers, William Alexander, 82
Cartwright, Peter, 75
Carver, Jonathan, 45
Cary, Alice, 81
Cary, Phoebe, 81
Casa Braccio, 221
Cases of Conscience concerning Evil Spirits, 7
"Casey Jones," 160
"Cask of Amontillado, The," 63
"Cassandra Southwick," 115
Castilian Days, 167
Casting Away of Mrs. Lecks and Mrs. Aleshine, The, 225
Castle Nowhere: Lake Country Sketches, 179
"Cathedral, The" (J. R. Lowell), 131
Cathedral, The (J. R. Lowell), 127
Cathedral Singer, A, 177
Cather, Willa [Sibert], 138 *footnote*, 272
Catherwood, Mary [Hartwell], 186
Cavalier, The, 176
Cavanagh, Forest Ranger, 206
Cawein, Madison [Julius], 251-252
Celebrated Jumping Frog of Calaveras County, The, 190
"Celestial Railroad, The," 119
Century of Dishonor, A, 171
Chainbearer, The, 67
"Chambered Nautilus, The," 125
Chance Acquaintance, A, 198
"Changeling, The," 132
Channing, William Ellery (1780-1842), 87-88, 129, 296
Channing, William Ellery (1818-1901), 105, 300
"Chanting the Square Deific," 140
Chant for the Boer, 169
"Chaperon, The," 224
Chapters from a Life, 148 *footnote*, 149
"Character," 96
Characteristics, 225
Charity Ball, The, 264
Charlemont, 74
Charles Egbert Craddock (pseud.), 180
Chase, Mary Coyle, 288
Chase, Mary Ellen, 274
Chase of Saint-Castin, The, 186
Châtelaine of La Trinité, The, 227
"Chaucer," 130
Chauncey, Charles (1592-1672), 13
Chauncey, Charles (1705-1787), 17
Cheerful Yesterdays, 261
Chesebrough, Caroline, 82
Chestnut Tree, The, 41
"Chesuncook," 99
Chevalier of Pensieri-Vani, The, 227
"Chicamauga," 215
Child, Lydia Maria, 82
Children in Bondage, 250
"Children of Adam," 138 *footnote*, 139
Children of the Forest, 229
Children of the King, 221
"Chiquita," 162
Chita: A Memory of Last Island, 175
Chivers, Thomas Holley, 81
Choir Invisible, The, 178
Chopin, Kate [O'Flaherty], 180
Christ and I, 261
Christian Citizen, 79
Christian Philosopher . . . , The, 8
Christmas Every Day, and Other Stories Told for Children, 194
"Christmas Jenny," 184
"Christmas-Night in the Quarters," 180
Christmas-Night in the Quarters and Other Poems, 180
"Christmas Treasures," 250
Christus: A Mystery, 113
Chronicle of the Conquest of Granada, A, 51
Church, (Colonel) Benjamin, 13
Church-Government and Church-Covenant Discussed, 7
Churches Quarrel Espoused, The, 15
Churchill, Winston, 271
Cigarette-Maker's Romance, A, 220
"Cinnamon Roses," 184
"Circle in the Water, A," 196 *footnote*
"Circles," 93
Circuit Rider, The, 165
Circumstance, 225
City, The, 265
"City Dead-House, The," 139
"City in the Sea, The," 62
"City of Orgies," 139
"Civic Sketches," 162
"Civil Disobedience," 99
Civil Government in the United States, 211
"Civilization," 97
Clara Howard, 43
Clarel, 73
Clark, Lewis Gaylord, 81
Clark, Walter van Tilburg, 278
Clark, Willis Gaylord, 81
Clarke, James Freeman, 106
Clay, Henry, 79
Clemens, Samuel Langhorne, 76, 187-193; merits and defects, 189; personalized fiction, 191-192; questioning themes, 192-193; tall tales, 190; travel books, 190-191
Clements, Colin, 143 *footnote*
Cleveland, Grover, 154-155
Clever Stories of Many Nations, 80
Cliff-Dwellers, The, 227
Cliffton, William, 46
Climbers, The, 264
Clio I and II, 58
Clio III, 58
Coast of Bohemia, The, 181, 198
Cobwebs from an Empty Skull, 214
Cockings, George, 45
Coffee House, The, 227
Coleridge-Taylor, Samuel, 112
Collected Essays and Reviews, 212
Collection of Essays and Fugitiv Writings, A, 44
Colman, Benjamin, 20
Colon (pseud.), 41, 44
"Colon and Spondee" papers, 41, 44
"Colonel Brereton's Aunty," 223
Colonel Starbottle's Client, 164 *footnote*
Colonial Period, The (1607-1763), 1-20; Renaissance and Puritan Influences, 1-13; Rise of Rationalism and Democracy, 14-20
Colorado, 264
Columbiad, The, 40
"Columbus" (J. R. Lowell), 32
"Columbus" ("Joaquin" Miller), 170
"Come Up from the Fields, Father," 137
"Come Where My Love Lies Dreaming," 64
Commentaries on American Law, 80
Commodus, 225
Common Sense, 32, 33
Companions on the Trail, 207
Compendious Dictionary, 44
"Compensation," 94
Condensed Novels and Other Papers, 162
Conduct of Life, The, 90, 96

"Confessions of a Medium, The," 146
Confessions of John Whitlock, The, 171
Confidence, 201
Confidence-Man: His Masquerade, The, 73
Connecticut Wits, The, 39-41
Connecticut Yankee in King Arthur's Court, A, 192
Conquest of Canaan, The, 40
Conrad, Robert Taylor, 83
"Conscience is instinct bred in the house," 101
"Considerations by the Way," 97
Conspiracy of Pontiac, The, 78
Constance Trescott, 225
"Contagiousness of Puerperal Fever, The," 122
"Contemplations," 11
"Contentment," 124
Continent, The, 226
Contrast, The, 41
"Conversations," 101, 103
Conversations on Some of the Old Poets, 126
Conversations on the Gospels Held in Mr. Alcott's School . . . , 101
Convert: or Leaves from My Experience, The, 106
Cook, Ebenezer, 13
Cooke, Ebenezer, 13
Cooke, John Esten, 82
Cooke, Philip Pendleton, 81
Coombe, Thomas, 45
Cooper, James Fenimore, 65-69, 74, 129; historical novels, 69; Leather-Stocking Tales, 67-68; merits and defects, 66, 69; sea stories, 68-69; social criticism, 67
Coplas de Manrique, 110
Copperhead, The, 226, 264
Coquette, The, 46
Corleone, 221
"Corn," 236
Cost, The, 227
Cotton, Ann, 2
Cotton, John (1584-1652), 13
Cotton, John, of Queen's Creek, 2
"Cotton Boll, The," 64
Count Falcon of the Eyrie, 251
Counterfeit Presentment, A, 194
Country Doctor, A, 182
Country of the Pointed Firs, The, 183
Country Town Sayings, 171
"Courage," 97
"Courting of Sister Wisby, The," 183
Courtship of Miles Standish, The, 108, 110, 112
Courtship of Miles Standish and Other Poems, The, 107
"Cover Them Over," 249
Cowley, Malcolm, 284-285
Cox, William, 84
Coxe, Daniel, 20
Cozzens, Frederick S., 83
Cozzens, James Gould, 278
Craddock, Charles Egbert (pseud.), 180
Cranch, Christopher Pearse, 104-105
Crane, [Harold] Hart, 285
Crane, Stephen, 207-209; novelette and novel, 207-208; poetry collections, 209; short-story collections, 208-209
Crater, The, 67
Crawford, Francis Marion, 219-222; German novels, 220; historical romances, 220-221; Italian novels, 221; merits and defects, 222; other writings, 221-222; stories of contemporary life, 220
Crayon Miscellany, The, 51
Creole Families of New Orleans, 181
Creoles of Louisiana, The, 176
"Crepusculum," 229
Crèvecoeur, Hector St. John de (pseud.), 26
Crèvecoeur, Michel-Guillaume Jean de, 26
Crisis, The, 32
Critical Fable, A, 128
Critical Period of American History, The, 211
Criticism and Fiction, 195
Critique of Pure Reason, 85
"Croaker Papers," 53
Crockett, Davy [David], 76 *footnote,* 83
"Cross of Gold" Speech, 213
"Crossing Brooklyn Ferry," 139
Crothers, Rachel, 285-286
Crothers, Samuel McChord, 263
"Crowing of the Red Cock, The," 249
Cruise of the Snark, The, 229
Crumbling Idols, 205
"Cry to Arms, A," 64
"Crystal, The," 236
Culprit Fay, and Other Poems, The, 53
"Culture," 97
Culture's Garland, 250
Cummings, E[dward] E[stlin], 284
Cummins, Maria S., 82
"Curfew Shall Not Ring To-night," 264
Curtis, George William, 129, 145, 307
Custis, George Washington Parke, 82
Cynic's Word Book, The, 217

"Da Capo," 224
"Daguerreotype, The," 248
Daisy Miller, 198, 203
Daly, Thomas Augustine, 252
Damaged Souls, 260, 261
Damnation of Theron Ware, The, 266
"Damned Thing, The," 216, 217
Dana, Richard Henry, Jr., 73
Dana, Richard Henry, Sr., 58
"Dance to Death, The," 249
Danckaerts, Jasper, 13
Dane, Clemence, 116
Danforth, Samuel, 13
Danites in the Sierras, The, 169
Darling of the Gods, The, 264
Darwin, 261
Daughter of the Middle Border, A, 204, 206
Daughter of the Snows, A, 229
Daughter of the Storage, The, 194
Daughter of the Storage, and Other Things in Prose and Verse, The, 195
Daughters of Dawn, 243
Davenport, John, 6
David Harum, A Story of American Life, 226
Davies, Samuel, 20
Davis, Rebecca H., 168 *footnote*
Davis, Richard Harding, 226
Dawes, Rufus, 81
Dawn of a To-morrow, The, 226
Dawson, William, 20
Day, Thomas, 147
Day of Doom, The, 11
Day of the Wedding, The, 198
"Days," 97
Day's Pleasure, and Other Sketches, A, 194
"Deacon's Masterpiece, The," 124
"Dead Master, The," 59
Deal in Wheat, and Other Stories of the New and Old World, A, 229
Death of Eve, The, 247
Death of General Montgomery, The, 43
"Death of Halpern Frayser, The," 216
"Death of Lincoln," 57
"Death of Minnehaha, The," 112
"Death of Queen Mercedes," 132
Declaration of Independence, 27, 30, 31, 33, 34
Decline and Fall of the English System of Finance, 32-33
Deephaven, 182, 183
Deerslayer, The, 68
Defence of the Constitution of the United States of America, 36
Defoe, Daniel, 147

De Forest, John William, 224
Deism, 24, 34, 38
Dell, Floyd, 274
Deluge, The, 228
Dembry, R. C. (pseud.), 180
Democracy (J. R. Lowell), 129
Democracy — An American Novel, 256
Democracy and Other Addresses, 127
Democracy and Social Ethics, 213
Democratic Vistas, 134 *footnote*, 140
Dennie, Joseph, 44-45
Denton, Daniel, 20
Der Struwwelpeter, 192 *footnote*
Derby, George Horatio, 83, 160
Description of New England, A, 2
"Désirée's Baby," 180
De Soto and His Men in the Land of Florida, 181
Destiny of Man, The, 211
Destruction of Gotham, The, 169
"Devil and Tom Walker, The," 51
Devil's Dictionary, The, 217
De Voto, Bernard [Augustine], 293
Dewey, John, 209, 210, 288
Dial, The, 87, 89, 94, 102, 103, 105
Dialogue between Franklin and the Gout, 27
"Diamond Lens, The," 225
Diary (Increase Mather), 7
Diary of Cotton Mather, 9
Diary of Samuel Sewell, 1674-1729, 10
"Dickens in Camp," 162
Dickinson, Emily [Elizabeth], 171, 231-233; individual poems, 232; letters, 232; merits and defects, 233
Dickinson, John, 30-31
Dickinson, Jonathan, 20
Dillon, George, 285
"Discourager of Hesitancy, The," 225
Discourses on Davila, 36
Discovery of America, The, 211
Discovery of the Great West, The, 78
Dissertation on Liberty and Necessity, . . . , A, 27
Dissertations on the English Language, 44
Divers Opinions of Yours Trooly, Petroleum V. Nasby, 76
Diverting History of John Bull and Brother Jonathan, The, 54
Divina Commedia, 107 *footnote*, 110
Divine Comedy, The, 59, 112, 113
"Divine Tragedy, The," 113
Divinity School Address, 89, 91
Dix, Dorothea [Lynde], 79
D. L. Moody: A Worker in Souls, 261
Dr. Breen's Practice, 197
Dr. Claudius, 220
"Dr. Heidegger's Experiment," 119
Dr. Heidenhoff's Process, 218
Dr. North and His Friends, 225
Dr. Sevier, 177
Doctor Zay, 149
Doctor's Christmas Eve, The, 179
Dod Grile (pseud.), 214
Dogood papers, 27, 29
"Domain of Arnheim, The," 63
"Domestic Life," 97
Don Orsino, 221
Doorstep Acquaintance, and Other Sketches, 194
"Dorothy," 179
Dorothy and Other Italian Stories, 179
"Dorothy Q.," 124
Dos Passos, John [Roderigo], 276
"Douglas Squirrel, The," 262
Douglass, William, 20
Down the Ravine, 180
Down-Easters, The, 79
"Downfall of Abner Joyce, The," 227
"Dow's Flat," 162
Drake, Joseph Rodman, 53
Drama, 23, 41, 74, 82-83, 264-265
Drama in Pokerville, The, 161
Dramatists (Early Sentiment and Romance), 82-83
Dramatists (Romantic Period, 1810-1865), 74-75
Dramatists (1865-1914), 264-265
Dramatists (since 1914), 283-285
Dreams of a Day, and Other Poems, The, 58
Dred, A Tale of the Great Dismal Swamp, 144
Dreiser, Theodore [Herman Albert], 228, 271
"Drifting," 58
"Drifting down Lost Creek," 180
"Drop Shot," 175
"Drowne's Wooden Image," 119
"Dryden," 130
Dudley, Paul, 20
Duke of Stockbridge, The, 218
Dulany, Daniel, 45
"Dulham Ladies, The," 183
Du Maurier, Daphne, 116
Dunbar, Paul Laurence, 252-253; novels, 252; poetry, 253; stories and sketches, 252-253
Dunlap, William, 46
Dunne, Finley Peter, 264
Dunton, John, 20
Dusantes, The, 225
"Dutch Lullaby," 250
Duty of the American Scholar to Politics and the Times, The, 145
Dwight, Theodore, 45
Dwight, Timothy, 40
"Each and All," 97
Eagle, The, 44
Early Prose Writings, 127
Earth Deities, 243
East Angels, 179
Eastman, Max [Forrester], 291
"Easy Chair, The," 145
"Ebb and Flow, The," 12
Echo, The (Richard Alsop and Theodore Dwight), 45
Echo, The (C. F. Hoffman), 80
Edgar Huntly; or Memoirs of a Sleep-Walker, 43
Edgewater People, 184
Edict of the King of Prussia, An, 29
Editha's Burglar, 226, 264
"Editor's Easy Chair," 193
"Editor's Study," 193
Education of Henry Adams, The, 258, 259
Edwards, Jonathan, 15-17
Eggleston, Edward, 165-166, 206
Eighty-nine, 226
"Eldorado" (E. A. Poe), 62
Eldorado (Bayard Taylor), 146
"Eleanora," 63
"Electioneerin' on Big Injun Mounting," 122
Elegy on the Times, An, 40
Elevator, The, 194
Eliot, John, 10
Eliot, T[homas] S[tearns], 283
Elizabethan Women, 261
"Eloquence," 97
Elsie Venner, 122, 123
Elsket and Other Stories, 181
Embargo; or, Sketches of the Times, The, 54
Emblems of Fidelity: A Comedy in Letters, The, 177
Embury, Emma Catherine Manley, 81
Emerson, Ralph Waldo, 85, 85-98, 129, 171, 296-297; essays and addresses, 90-97; merits and defects, 92, 98; poetry, 97-98; supplementary bibliography, 296-297
"Emerson the Lecturer," 130
"Encantadas, or Enchanted Isles, The," 72
Enchanted Typewriter, The, 251
End of the World, The, 165

"Endicott and the Red Cross," 120
"Energies of Men, The," 212
English, Thomas Dunn, 81
English Novel and the Principle of Its Development, The, 238
English Poets of the Nineteenth Century, The, 122
Enlightenment, Prose of the, 24-25
"Enthralled by some mysterious spell I stood," 216
Enthusiasm Described and Caution'd Against, 17
Ephemera, The, 27
"Epic of the Wheat" trilogy, 228
"Episode of War, An," 207
"Epistle from Joshua Ibn Vives, An," 249
"Epistle to the Jews, An," 249
Equality, 219
Esmeralda, 226
Essay for the Recording of Illustrious Providences, An, 7
Essays (R. W. Emerson), 89, 92, 95
Essays: Historical and Literary, 211
Essays in Application, 263
Essays in Radical Empiricism, 212
"Essays of Robert Slender, The," 38
Essays to Do Good, 8
Esther — A Novel, 256
"Eternal Goodness, The," 117
"Ethnogenesis," 64
"Eureka," 61
European Acquaintance, 224
Europeans, The, 201, 224
Eutaw, 74
"Eutaw Springs," 39
Evangeline, 107, 108, 110, 111
Evans, Nathaniel, 37
Evening Dress, 194
"Evening Song," 236
Examination into the Leading Principles of the Federal Constitution, An, 44
Excellent Becomes the Permanent, The, 213
"Excursion to Canada," 99
"Experience," 95, 97
Expiation, 171
"Expression," 254
"Eyes of the Panther, The," 216
"Fable," 97
Fable for Critics, A, 127, 128
"Facts and Traditions respecting . . . Intermittent Fever in New England," 122 footnote
Fair Barbarian, A, 226
Fair God, The, 225
Faith Doctor, The, 166
Faith Healer, The, 247
Falkner, William [Harrison], 276
"Fall of the House of Usher, The," 62, 63
"Family Feud, A," 252
Family Instructor, The, 147
Fan, The, 227
Fanatics, The, 252
Fancy's Show Box, 120
"Fanny," 53
Fanny Forester (pseud.), 84
Fanshawe, 117
Fantastic Fables, 217
"Fantastics," 173
Far Horizons, 243
Far-West Scenes, 161
Farewell Address, 36
"Farewell of a Virginia Slave Mother, The," 115
Farewell Sermon, 17
Farm Ballads, 249
Farmer Refuted, A, 35
"Farming," 97
Farrago, 44
Farrell, James T[homas], 278
Fashionable Adventures of Joshua Craig, The, 228
Fast, Howard, 279
"Fate," 96
Father Bombo's Pilgrimage, 37
"Father Dominick's Convert," 223 *footnote*
"Father of American poetry," 138
"Father of American prose," 38
Faulkner, William [Harrison], 276
Faust ([F.] Henry Hedge), 104
Faust (Bayard Taylor), 146
Fay, Theodore Sedgwick, 82
Fearful Responsibility, A, 195
Fearful Responsibility and Other Stories, A, 194
Federalist, The, 35, 36
"Felipe," 179
Felix Carmen (pseud.), 250
Female Poets of America, The, 58
Ferber, Edna, 274
Fessenden, Thomas Green, 46
Few Verses for a Few Friends, A, 145
Field, Eugene, 250
Field, Rachel, 275
Fields, James T[homas], 145, 161
Fiend's Delight, The, 214
Figs and Thistles, 226
Finch, Francis Miles, 81
Fink, Mike, 159
Fire Bringer, The, 246
Fireside Travels, 127
Firkins, O. W., 200 *footnote*
First Battle, The, 213
First Christmas Tree, The, 263
"First-Day Thoughts," 117
First Fam'lies of the Sierras, 169
"First Snow-Fall, The," 131, 132
Fisherman's Luck, 263
Fiske, John, 210-211
Fitch, Clyde [William], 264-265
Fitzgerald, F[rancis] Scott [Key], 276
Five O'Clock Tea, 194
"Flesh and the Spirit, The," 11
Fletcher, John Gould, 282
"Flight of Betsy Lane, The," 183
Flight of Pony Baker: A Boy's Town Story, The, 195
Flint, Timothy, 75
"Flood of Years, The," 57
Florida, 235
"Flute and Violin," 178
Flute and Violin and Other Kentucky Tales and Romances, 178
Fly-ing Dutchman, The, 80
Foerster, Norman, 292
Folger, Peter, 13
Folk Songs, 160
Folks from Dixie, 252
Following the Equator, 191
Fool's Errand, A, 226
"Fool's Prayer, The," 240
"For Marse Chouchoute," 180
"For the Burns Centennial Celebration," 125
For the Major, 179
For Tippecanoe, 186
"For Whittier's Seventieth Birthday," 125
"For You O Democracy," 139
Forayers, The, 74
Ford, Paul Leicester, 227
Foregone Conclusion, A, 198
"Forerunners," 97
"Forest Hymn, A," 55, 57
"Foresters, The," 25
Forrest, (Colonel) Thomas, 46
Fortune and Men's Eyes, 265
Foster, Hannah W., 46
Foster, Stephen Collins, 64
"Fountain, The" (W. C. Bryant), 57
"Fountain, The" (W. V. Moody), 248
Fountain and Other Poems, The (W. C. Bryant), 55
"Four Constitutions, The," 11
"Four Elements, The," 11
"Four Monarchies, The," 11
Four Poems, 127
"Four Seasons, The," 11
Fourierism, 103
Fox, [William] John, Jr., 181

France in France, 185
Frances Snow Compton (pseud.), 256
Francesca da Rimini, 75
Francis Berrian, or the Mexican Patriot, 75
Frank, Waldo [David], 292
Frankie and Johnny, 160
Franklin, Benjamin, 19, 26-29
Franklin Evans; or The Inebriate, 134 footnote
Frank Norris of the Wave, 229
Frederic, Harold, 226-227
Free Joe and Other Georgian Sketches, 172
Freeman, Mary E[leanor] Wilkins, 184-185; merits and defects, 185; novels, 184-185; short-story collections, 184
French, Alice, 171
French Art, 262
French Traits: An Essay in Comparative Criticism, 262
Freneau, Philip, 23, 37-39, 124
"Friend Eli's Daughter," 146
"Friendship," 93
Friendship of Art, The, 243
"From a Balcony," 162
From the Book of Valentines, 243
From the Green Book of the Bards, 243
From the Other Side, 227
"Front Yard, The," 179
Front Yard and Other Italian Stories, The, 179
Frontier, influence of the, 158
Frontiersmen, The, 180
Frost, Robert [Lee], 280
Fruitlands, 102, 146
Full and Candid Account of the Delusion Called Witchcraft, A, 9
Full Vindication, A, 35
Fuller, Henry Blake, 227
Fuller, [Sarah] Margaret, 102-103, 105, 129, 299
Function of the Poet and Other Essays, The, 127
Fur Hunters of the Far West, 75
Further Poems, 232

Gabriel Conroy, 164 footnote
Gabriel Tolliver: Story of Reconstruction, 172
Gale, Zona, 271
Gallegher and Other Stories, 226
Galloway, Joseph, 45
Game, The, 229
Game with the Abysmal Brute, The, 229
Garden, Alexander, 20
Gardens of This World, 227
Garfield, James A., 154
Garland, Hamlin [Hannibal], 204-207; early period: realism, 205-206; final period: autobiography, 206-207; general estimate, 204-205; middle period: romance, 206
Garrison, William Lloyd, 84, 114
"Garrison of Cape Ann, The," 115
Garroters, The, 194
Gates Ajar, The, 148
Gates Between, The, 148
General History of Virginia, the Summer Isles, and New England, The, 2
General Magazine and Historical Chronicle, 19, 27
General View of American Literature: Early Sentiment and Romance, 49, 65; Renaissance and Puritan Influences, 1-2, 10; Rise of Rationalism and Democracy, 14-20; Romantic Period, 74; Struggle for Independence, 23-25; Transcendentalism, 85-87; Triumph of Realism, 157-161
Genius of Style, The, 262
Gentleman from Ireland, A, 224
George, Henry, 209-210
George Fox Digg'd out of His Burrows, 6
"George the Third's Soliloquy," 38
George's Mother, 208
Georgia Scenes, 76 *footnote*, 83, 161
German Influence on Transcendentalism, 85
Gettysburg Address, 79, 104
"Gifts," 96
"Gila Monster Route, The," 160
Gilded Age, The: Conservatism and Iconoclasm (Chap. X), 187-213
Gilded Age: A Tale of To-Day, The, 191, 262
Gilder, Richard Watson, 262
"Giles Corey of the Salem Farms," 113
Giovio and Giulia, 251
"Girdle of Friendship, The," 126
Girl I Left Behind Me, The, 264
Girl of the Golden West, The, 264
Girl with the Green Eyes, The, 264
"Git Along, Little Dogies," 160
"Give All to Love," 93 *footnote*, 97
"Give me your tired, your poor," 249
"Glance behind the Curtain, A," 131
Glasgow, Ellen [Anderson Gholson], 271
Glaspell, Susan, 231, 286
Glaucus, 75
Gleanings in Europe: England, 67
Gleanings in Europe: France, 67
Gleanings in Europe: Italy, 67
Glimpses of Unfamiliar Japan, 175
Gloria Mundi, 226
"Glory of, and the Grace in the Church Set Out, The," 12
"Gloucester Moors," 247
Gloucester Moors and Other Poems, 247
Godey's Lady's Book, 83
Godfrey, Thomas, 19
God of His Fathers, The, 229
"God Save the Rights of Man," 38
God's Controversy with New-England, 12
Godwin, Parker, 129
"Gold Bug, The," 63
Golden Bowl, The, 203
Golden Fleece, The, 227
Golden House, The, 262
"Golden Journey, The," 248
"Golden Legend, The," 113
"Golyer," 167
Gombo Zhèbes, 174
"Gondolieds," 171
"Good Friday Night," 247
"Good Night," 180
"Good Word for Winter, A," 130
Goodrich, Samuel Griswold, 83
Gookin, Daniel, 13
Goose Quill Papers, 251
"Gospel Train, The," 160
Grady, Henry Woodfin, 179
Grammatical Institute of the English Language, The, 44
Grandfather's Chair, 117-118
Grandissimes: A Story of Creole Life, The, 177
"Grandmother's Story of Bunker-Hill Battle," 124
Granite, 116
Grant, Anne McVickar, 46
Grant, Ulysses S., 153-154, 188
Graves, John, 13
"Gray," 130
"Gray Champion, The," 117, 119
Grayson, William John, 81
Graysons, The, 166
Great Battles of the World, 207
Great Christian Doctrine of Original Sin Defended, The, 17
Great Divide, The, 247
"Great God, I ask thee for no meaner pelf," 101
Great God Success, The, 227
Great Historic Animals, 263
Great Release, The, 243
"Great Stone Face, The," 119
Great Stone of Sardis, The, 225

"Great truths are portions of the soul of man," 131
Great War Syndicate, The, 225
Greeley, Horace, 84
Green, Joseph, 20
Green, Paul [Eliot], 287
"Green River," 57
Greene, Albert Gorton, 81
Greene, Asa, 83
Greenfield Hill, 40
Greifenstein, 220
"Grey Sleeve, A," 208
Greyslaer: A Romance of the Mohawk, 80
Griswold, Rufus Sargent, 84
Guardian Angel, The, 122, 123
Guiney, Louise Imogen, 251
Gunther, John, 293
"Gwine to Run All Night; or, De Camptown Races," 64
Hale, Edward Everett, 185
Half-Way Covenant, The, 7
Haliburton, Thomas Chandler, 83
Hall, James, 83
Hall, Sarah Josepha B., 83
Halleck, Fitz-Greene, 53
"Hallelujah, I'm a Bum," 160
Halpine, Charles Graham, 81
"Hamatreya," 97
Hamilton, Alexander, 35
Hammond, John, 13
"Hampton Beach," 116
Hanging of the Crane, The, 108, 113
Hannah Thurston, 146
Happy Ending, 251
"Hard Times, The," 173
Harmony of Interests, Agricultural, Manufacturing, and Commercial, 80
Harriet, 143 *footnote*
Harris, C. W., 161
Harris, Joel Chandler, 172, 180
Harrison, Benjamin, 155
Hart, Joseph C., 82
Harte, Bret, 161-164; see **Harte, [Francis] Brett**
Harte, [Francis] Brett, 161-164, 167; merits and defects, 163-164; poetry, 162; stories and sketches, 162-163
Harvest Moon, The, 264
Hasty Pudding, The, 40
"Hatteras," 39
"Haunted Palace, The," 62
"Haunted Shanty, The," 146
Hawthorne, Nathaniel, 103, 105, 117-121, 145, 302-303; merits and defects, 118; romantic novels, 120-121; short stories, 119-120.
"Hawthorne and the Story-Teller's Art," 60
Hay, John [Milton], 166-168; poetry, 167; prose, 166-168
Hayes, Rutherford B., 154
Hayne, Paul Hamilton, 64-65
Hazard of New Fortunes, A, 196, 197
Headsman, The, 67
Hearn, [Patricia] Lafcadio [Tessima Carlos], 172-175; American writings, 174-175; Japanese writings, 175; merits and defects, 174
Heart of Happy Hollow, The, 253
Heart of Maryland, The, 264
Heart of Rome, The, 221
Heart of Toil, The, 171
Heart's Highway, The, 184
Hearts of Oak, 264
"Heart's Wild-Flower," 248
Heartsease and Rue, 127
"Heathen Chinee, The," 162
Hecht, Ben, 287
Heckewelder, J. G. E., 112
Hedge, [Frederic] Henry, 87, 104
Hedged In, 149
Hedge's Club, 87, 104
Heidenmauer, The, 67
"Height of the Ridiculous," 124
Hellman, Lillian, 287
Hemingway, Ernest [Miller], 276-277
Henry, Patrick, 30
Henry Wadsworth Longfellow, 262
Hentz, Caroline Lee Whiting, 82
Hentz, Nicholas Marcellus, 82
Her Great Match, 265
"Her Only Son," 182
Her Own Way, 265
Hergesheimer, Joseph, 273
Heroes of the Middle West: The French, 186
Heroine in Bronze, or a Portrait of a Girl, The 177
Heroines of Fiction, 195
"Heroism," 93
Herrick, Robert, 270
Hersey, John, 279
Hesper, 206
Hetty's Strange History, 171
Hiawatha, 108, 110, 111-112
"Hiawatha's Wedding Feast," 112
Hickok, J. B., 159
Hicks, Granville, 293
Higginson, Thomas Wentworth, 171, 261-262
High Life in New York, 161
"Highland Light, The," 99
Hill, George, 80
"Hilton's Holiday, The," 183
His Second Campaign, 171
Historians, 77, 209-213
Historical Background: Colonial Period (1607-1763), 1, 14; Revolutionary Period (1763-1810), 22-23, 29-30; Romantic Period (1810-1865), 48; Triumph of Realism (1865-1914), 152-157
"History," 93
History and Annals in New England (Rationalism and Democracy), 17-18
History of English Literature, A, 246
History of Massachusetts, 119
History of New York . . . by Diedrich Knickerbocker, A, 51, 52
History of the Dividing Line Run in the Year 1728, 18
History of the Expedition . . . of Captain Lewis and Clark, 26
History of the Indians of Connecticut, 224
History of the Indian Tribes of the United States, 112
History of the Life and Voyages of Christopher Columbus, A, 51
History of the Navy, 66
History of the Plymouth Plantation, 4
History of the Reign of Ferdinand and Isabella, the Catholic, 77
History of the United Netherlands, 77
History of the United States during the Administrations of Jefferson and Madison, 257
History of the United States for Young People, 261
Hitchcock, Enos, 46
Hive of "The Bee-Hunter," The, 161
Hoffman, Charles Fenno, 80
"Holiday Home," 224
Holmes, Oliver Wendell, 78, 121-126, 303-304; essays and novels, 123; general estimate as a poet, 126; poetry, 123-126
Holy Graal and the Other Fragments, 246
Home as Found, 67
Homeopathy and Its Kindred Delusions, 122
Homeward Bound, 67
Honest John Vane, 224
Honorable Peter Stirling, The, 227
Hooker, Thomas, 13
Hooper, Johnson Jones, 83, 161
Hoosier Mosaics, 171
"Hoosier Poet," 250

Hoosier Schoolboy, The, 166
Hoosier Schoolmaster, The, 165, 166, 206
Hope, James Barron, 81
Hopkins, Lemuel, 45
Hopkins, Stephen, 45
Hopkinson, Farncis, 31
Horace Chase, 179
"Horseman in the Sky, A," 215
"Horses — One Dash," 208
Horse-Shoe Robinson, 73
Horseshoe Robinson (drama), 83
"Hospital Nurse, The," 186
Hospital Sketches, 147
"Hound was cuffed, the hound was kicked, The," 236
"House of Night, The," 37-39
House of the Seven Gables, The, 117, 118, 120
House-Boat on the Styx, 251
Houston, Samuel, 159
Hovey, Richard, 242, 244-246
"How Betsy and I Made Up," 249
"How Love Looked for Hell," 236
"How the Old Horse Won the Bet," 124
How the Other Half Lives, 213
Howadji in Syria, The, 145
Howard, Sidney [Coe], 286
Howe, E[dgar] W[atson], 171, 206
Howe, Julia Ward, 81
Howells, William Dean, 68, 193-200; autobiographical works, 195; books of travel, 194; economic novels, 196-197; literary criticism, 195; merits and defects, 199-200; novels dealing with the Marches, 196; other novels, 197-199; plays, 193-194; poetry, 194; sketches and stories, 194-195
Howe's Masquerade, 120
Hubbard, Elbert, 263
Hubbard, William, 13
Huckleberry Finn, Adventures of, 191
Hugh Wynne: Free Quaker, 225
Hughes [James] Langston, 285
Hulton, Ann, 45
Human Immortality: Two Supposed Objections to the Doctrine, 212
"Humble Romance, A," 184
Humble Romance and Other Stories, A, 184
Humorous Poems, 122
Humphreys, David, 45
Hungry Heart, The, 228
"Hurricane, The," 39
Husband's Story, The, 228
"Huskers, The," 116
"Huswifery," 12
Hutchinson, Thomas, 119
Hutton, Joseph, 46
"Hymn," 97
"Hymn of Trust, A," 125
Hymns, 55
"Hymns of the Marshes," 237
Hyperion, 107, 108

"I am the Woman," 248
"I Cannot Forget with What Fervid Devotion," 56
"I Hear It Was Charged against Me," 139
"I Heard You Solemn Sweet Pipes of the Organ," 139
"I Opened All the Portals Wide," 180
"I Sing the Body Electric," 139
"Ichabod," 115, 124
Idea of God, The, 211
Idiot, The, 251
"If It Might Be," 180
If, Yes, and Perhaps, 185
Iliad of Homer, The, 55
Iliad of Sandy Bar, The, 163
"Illusion in Red and White, An," 208
"Illusions," 97
"I'm guided in the darkest night," 101
Imaginary Interviews, 195
Imperative Duty, An, 197
Impressions and Experiences, 195
"In a Graveyard," 167
In and Out of Doors with Charles Dickens, 145
In Classic Shades, 170
In His Image, 213
In His Name, 185
In His Steps, 227
"In Honor of . . . Queen Elizabeth," 11
In Mizzoura, 264
In Old Plantation Days, 252
In Ole Virginia, 181
In Partnership, 223
"In Paths Untrodden," 139
"In School-Days," 116
"In the Cotton Country," 179
In the Levant, 262
In the Midst of Life, 215
In the Palace of the King, 221
In the "Strange People's" Country, 180
In the Tennessee Mountains, 180
"In the Tunnel," 162
"In the Twilight," 132
In the Valley, 226
In War Time, 225
"Incident in a Railroad Car, An," 131
Increasing Purpose, The, 178
"Independent Thinker, An," 184
"Indian Burying Ground, The," 39
Indian Giver, An, 194
Indian Summer, 199
"Indian-Summer Reverie," 131
Indian Tribes of the United States, 83
Indignations of E. W. Howe, 171
"Individuality," 237
"Inferno," (H. W. Longfellow), 113
"Inferno," (T. W. Parsons), 59
Innocents Abroad; or The New Pilgrim's Progress, The, 190
"Inscription for the Entrance to a Wood," 56
"Inspiration," 101
"Intellect," 93
International Episode, An, 203
Interpretations of Literature, 174 footnote
Irene the Missionary, 224
"Iron Gate, The," 125
Iron Gate, and Other Poems, The, 122
Iron Heel, The, 229
Irving, Washington, 49-52, 145
Isherwood, Christopher, 278
Israel Potter: His Fifty Years of Exile, 72
"Israfel," 62
Italian Journey, 194
Italy and the World War, 181
Ivory Tower, The, 203

"Jack the Fisherman," 149
Jackson, Helen [Maria] Hunt, 171, 231
"Jacquerie, The," 236
"Jam on Gerry's Rocks, The," 160
"Jamaica Funeral, The," 37
Jamaica Inn, 116
James, Henry, 198, 200-204, 308-309; general estimate, 203-204; novels, 202-203; short stories, 203; supplementary bibliography, 308-309
James, Jesse, 160
James, William, 211-213; edited volumes, 212-213; essays, 212; volumes, 211-212
Jane Talbot, 43
Janice Meredith, 227
Jason Edwards: An Average Man, 205
Jean Baptiste Le Moyne, Sieur de Bienville, 181
"Jeanette," 179
"Jeanie with the Light Brown Hair," 64
Jeff Brigg's Love Story, 164 footnote
Jeffers, [John] Robinson, 282-283
Jefferson, Thomas, 33-35
Jerry of the Islands, 229
Jersey Street and Jersey Lane, 223
Jesse James, 160

"Jetsam," 248
Jewett, Sarah Orne, 182-183; merits and defects, 183; novels, 182; short-story collections, 182-183
"Jim," 162
Jim Black; or, the Regulator's Revenge, 264
"Jim Bludso," 167
Joaquin et al., 169
John Andross, 168 *footnote*
John Barleycorn, 229
John Delmer's Daughters; or, Duty, 264
John Eax and Mamelon, 226
"John Endicott," 113
John Gayther's Garden, 225
John Godfrey's Fortunes, 146
"John Gray," 178
John Gray: A Kentucky Tale of the Olden Time, 178
John Greenleaf Whittier, 262
"John Henry," 160
John Lothrop Motley: A Memoir, 122
John March, Southerner, 176
John Marr and Other Sailors, 73
John Phoenix (pseud.), 160
John Randolph, 256
John Sherwood: Iron Master, 225
Johnson, Edward, 13
Johnson, R. U., 176 *footnote*
Johnson, Samuel, 45
Johnston Smith (pseud.), 208
Jones, Hugh, 20
Jones, Joseph Stevens, 83
Joseph and His Brethren, 41
Josh Billings (pseud.), 76, 160
Josh Billings, Farmers Allminax, 76
Josh Billings, His Sayings, 76
Josselyn, John, 13
Journal (S. K. Knight), 18
Journal (John Winthrop), 5
Journal (John Woolman), 25
Journal of Gamaliel Bradford, The, 259 *footnote*, 261
Journalism, 19, 79-80, 83-84
Journals (R. W. Emerson), 93 *footnote*
Journey to the Land of Eden in the Year 1733, A, 18
Joyous Miracle, The, 229
Judd, Sylvester, 82
Judgement of Solomon, The, 41
Judson, Edward Z. C., 84
Judson, Emily C., 84
Jupiter Lights, 179
Juvenile Poems . . . with The Prince of Parthia. a Tragedy, 19

Kansas and Nebraska, 185
Kant, Immanuel, 85
Karma, 175
Kate Beaumont, 224
Kate Bonnet, 225
Katherine Lauderdale, 220
Kaufman, George S., 286
"Keats," 129
Kempton-Wace Letters, The, 230
Kennedy, John Pendleton, 73-74
Kent, James, 80
Kenton, Simon, 159
Kentons, The, 199
Kentucky Cardinal: A Story, A, 178
Kentucky Warbler, The, 177
Key, Francis Scott, 65
Key into the Language of America, A, 6
Key to Uncle Tom's Cabin, A, 144
Khaled, 220
"Khan's Devil, The," 117
King, Grace Elizabeth, 181
King of Folly Island, and Other People, The, 183
King of Honey Island, The, 171
"King Robert of Sicily," 112
"King Solomon of Kentucky," 178
Kingsley, Sidney, 287
Kinship of Nature, The, 243
Kirkland, Caroline Matilda Stansbury, 83
Kirkland, Joseph, 171, 206
Kittredge, Walter, 81
Knickerbocker School, The, 49-54
Knight, Sarah Kemble, 17-18
Knitters in the Sun, 171
Kobboltozo, 105
"Kossuth," 117
"Ktaadn and the Maine Woods," 99

La Belle Russe, 264
La Cuisine Creole, 174
La Dame de Ste. Hermine, 181
La Farge, Oliver [Hazard] Perry, 277
"La Grisette," 124
La Maison d'Or, 126
Ladd, Joseph Brown, 45
"Lady Eleanore's Mantle," 119
Lady Jane and Other Poems, The, 53
"Lady of Little Fishing, The," 179
Lady of Quality, A, 226
Lady of the Aroostook, The, 198
Lady or the Tiger and Other Stories, The, 225
Lafayette in Brooklyn, 134 *footnote*
Lamar, Mirabeau Buonaparte, 81
Landlord at Lion's Head, The, 199
Landmark, The, 177
Lanier, Sidney, 234-239, 242; merits and defects, 239; poetry, 235-237; prose works, 237-238
Lardner, Ring[gold] W[ilmer], 291
La Salle and the Discovery of the Great West, 78
Last Christmas Tree: An Idyl of Immortality, The, 177
"Last Fiddling of Mordaunt's Jim," 252
"Last Leaf, The," 125
Last of the Huggermuggers, The, 105
Last of the Mohicans, The, 68
Last Poems (J. R. Lowell), 127
Last Refuge, The, 227
Last Songs from Vagabondia, 242, 244
"Last Walk in Autumn, The," 116
Last Words, 207
Late Mrs. Null, The, 225
Late Regulations respecting the British Colonies . . . Considered, 30-31
"Latest Form of Infidelity, The," 92
Latest Literary Essays and Addresses (J. R. Lowell), 127
"Latter-Day Warnings," 124
Launcelot and Guenevere: A Poem in Five Dramas, 245
Laurel: An Ode, The, 244
"Laus Deo!," 115, 245
Lauth, 229
"Law Lane," 183
Lawson, James, 82
Lawson, John, 20
Lawton, 251
Lawton Girl, The, 226
Lay of the Scottish Fiddle, The, 54
"Lay Preacher," 44
Lazarre, 186
Lazarus, Emma, 249
Leacock, John, 46
Leatherwood God, The, 199
Leaves from Margaret Smith's Journal, 114
Leaves of Grass, 134, 134 *footnote*, 135, 148, 173 *footnote*
Leaves of Grass with Sands at Seventy and A Backward Glance o'er Travel'd Roads, 134 *footnote*
Lectures on Art, and Poems, 80
Lee, Samuel, 13
Lee the American, 260, 261
Leeds, Daniel, 20
Legaré, Hugh S., 83
Legaré, James Matthews, 81

"Legend of Brittany, A," 131
"Legend of Monte del Diablo," 160
"Legend of Rabbi Ben Levi, The," 112
"Legend of Sleepy Hollow, The," 51
"Legend of the Arabian Astrologer," 51
"Legend of Two Discrete Statues," 51
Leggett, William, 84
Leland, Charles Godfrey, 83
Leonard, Daniel, 45
Leonard, William Ellery Channing, 280
Leonor de Guzman, 74
Leslie, Charles Robert, 84
Leslie, Eliza, 84
Lesson of the Master, The, 203
Letchford, Thomas, 13
"Letter and a Paragraph, A," 223
"Letter from a Gentleman in Boston, to Mr. George Wishart, A," 17
Letter of Introduction, A, 194
Letter . . . on the Character of the English Nation, 31
Letter on the Philippine Tangle, 212
Letter to American Teachers of History, A, 257, 258
Letter to His Countrymen, A, 67
Letters (Henry Adams), 259
Letters (Emily Dickinson), 232
Letters (J. R. Lowell), 129
Letters (John Winthrop), 5
Letters from a Farmer in Pennsylvania, 31
Letters from an American Farmer, 26
Letters from Under a Bridge, 53
Letters Home, 198
Letters of a British Spy, The, 80
Letters of Cato, The, 33
Letters of Fabius, 31
Letters of Gamaliel Bradford, 1918-1931, The, 260 *footnote,* 261
Letters of Jonathan Oldstyle, 50
Letters of William James, The, 213
Letters to a Friend, 262
Letters to Harriet, 248
Lew Wallace: An Autobiography, 225
Lewis, Meriwether, 26
Lewis, Sinclair, 171, 273
Lewisohn, Ludwig, 185 footnote, 291
"Lexington," 124
Liar, The, 203
"Liberty," 167
"Liberty Song," 31
"Lick Branch Explosion, The," 160
"Life," 180
Life amongst the Modocs, 169, 170 *footnote*
Life and Adventures of Dr. Dodimus Duckworth, The, 83
Life and Death of John of Barneveld, The, 77
Life and I, 261
Life and Sayings of Mrs. Partington, 83
Life and Writings of Major Jack Downing, 76
"Life Everlastin'," (M. E. W. Freeman), 184
Life Everlasting (John Fiske), 211
Life Histories of Northern Animals, 263
"Life in the Iron Mills," 168 *footnote*
Life of Albert Gallatin, The, 256
"Life of Charles Brockden Brown," 77
"Life of Christ," 170
Life of George Washington, The, 37
Life of Nancy, The, 183
Life of Oliver Goldsmith, The, 52
Life of Washington, 52
Life on the Mississippi, 191
"Lifetime, A," 57
Light-Fingered Gentry, 228
"Light-winged Smoke, Icarian bird," 101
"Lightning-Rod Man, The," 72
Likely Story, A, 194
Lilith, 252
Lincoln, Abraham, 79
Lincoln and Other Poems, 250
Lindsay, [Nicholas] Vachel, 281
Lines Long and Short, 227
Lionel Lincoln, 69
Lippmann, Walter, 292-293
Literary Friends and Acquaintances, 195
Literary Remains, 58
"Literati, The," 60
Literature and Life, 195
"Little Boy Blue," 250
"Little Breeches," 167
Little English Gallery, A, 251
Little Journey in the World, A, 262
Little Journeys, 263
Little Lord Fauntleroy, 226
Little Norsk, A, 205
"Little Regiment, The," 209
Little Regiment and Other Episodes of the American Civil War, The, 208
Little Rivers, 263
Little Shepherd of Kingdom Come, The, 181
Little Swiss Sojourn, A, 194
Little Women, 146, 147
"Littlepage Manuscripts," 67
Lives of Game Animals, 263
"Living Temple, The," 125
Livingston, William, 20
Local-Color Movement, 159
Local-Colorists, The (Chapter IX), 152-186; New England, 182-186; The South, 172-181; The West, 161-171
Locke, David Ross, 76, 160
Lockerbie Book, The, 250
Lockwood, Ralph Ingersoll, 82
Logan, 79
Loiterings of Travel, 53
London, Jack [or **John Griffith],** 229-230; novels, 229; other works, 230; short-story collections, 229-230
"Lone Prairie, The," 160
Long Road of Woman's Memory, The, 213
Longfellow, Henry Wadsworth, 107-113, 249, 300-301; merits and defects, 108-110; sonnets, 113; supplementary bibliography, 300-301
"Longing for Heaven," 11
Longstreet, Augustus B., 76 *footnote,* 83, 161
Looking Backward, or 2000-1887, 218, 219
Lord, William Wilberforce, 81
Lord Chumley, 264
Lost Galleon and Other Tales, The, 161
"Lost Lover, A," 182
"Lost Occasion, The," 115
Lost Room, The, 224
Lotus Eating, 145
"Louie Sands and Jim McGee," 160
"Love," 93
"Love Everlasting," 180
Love in Old Cloathes and Other Stories, 223
"Love-Letters of Smith, The," 223
Love of Landry, The, 252
Love of Life and Other Stories, 230
Lover's Revolt, A, 224
Love's Calendar, Lays of the Hudson, and Other Poems, 80
Low, Samuel, 46
"Low in the eastern sky," 101
Low Tide on Grand Pré, 242, 243
Lowell, Amy [Lawrence], 128, 280
Lowell, James Russell, 76, 91 *footnote,* 126-133, 304; general estimate as a poet and as a critic, 133; major works, 128-129; other prose, 129-130; other verse, 130-131
Lowell, Maria White, 81

Lowell, Percival, 173
Lowell, Robert Traill Spence, 82
"Luck of Roaring Camp, The," 160, 163
Luck of Roaring Camp and Other Sketches, The, 161, 162
"Lynching of Jube Benson, The," 252-253
"Lynx-Hunting," 207
Lyrics of Lowly Life, 253

"Ma'am Pelágre," 180
"Mabel Martin," 115
M'Fingal, 40
McCullers, Carson, 279
McHenry, James, 80
MacKaye, Percy [Wallace], 285
McKinley, William, 155, 215 footnote
MacLeish, Archibald, 284
McTeague, 228
McVeys, The, 171
Madame Butterfly, 264
"Madame Délicieuse," 176
Madame Delphine, 176
"Made in France": French Tales Told with a United States Twist, 223
Madison, James, 36
Madison Tensas, M.D. (pseud.), 161
"Madonna of the Tubs, The," 149
Madrigals and Catches, 250
Maggie: A Girl of the Streets, 207
Magnalia Christi Americana; or The Ecclesiastical History of New-England, 8,115
Magnolia Cemetery "Ode," 64
Mahomet and His Successors, 52
Maid Who Binds Her Warrior's Sash, The, 58
Main Street, 171, 272
Main-Travelled Roads, 205
Maine Woods, The, 99
Major Jones's Chronicles of Pineville, 161
Major Jones's Courtship, 83, 161
Major Jones's Sketches of Travel, 161
Majors and Minors, 253
Making of a Marchioness, The, 226
Making of an American, The, 213
Making of a Statesman and Other Stories, The, 172
Making of Personality, The, 243
Malbone, 261
"Man and the Snake, The," 215
Man of the Hour, 171
Man That Corrupted Hadleyburg, The, 192
"Man with the Hoe, The," 250
Man with the Hoe and Other Poems, The, 250
"Man without a Country, The," 185
Mann, Horace, 84
"Mannahatta" ("I was asking . . ."), 139
"Manners," 96
Man's Woman, A, 228
Manuductio ad Ministerium, 8-9
Map of Virginia, A, 2
Marble Faun, The, 118, 121
March, Anne (pseud.), 179
March Hares, 226
Marchioness Ossoli: see Fuller, [Sarah] Margaret, 102-103
"Marco Bozzaris," 53
Mardi: And a Voyage Thither, 71
Marietta, 221
Mariner's Compass, The, 264
Marjorie Daw, 148
Market Place, The, 226
Markham, Edwin [Charles], 250
Markoe, Peter, 46
Mark Twain (pseud.), 187-193: see **Clemens, S. L.**
Marlowe, 265
Marquand, J[ohn] P[hilip], 275
Marriage of Guenevere, The, 245
"Marse Chan," 181
Marsena and Other Stories of the Wartime, 226
Marsh Island, A, 182
"Marsh Rosemary," 183
"Marsh-Song — At Sunset," 236, 237
Marshall, John, 36-37
"Marshes of Glynn, The," 237
Martin Eden, 229
Marx, Karl, 210
Mary Gray (pseud.), 148
Marzio's Crucifix, 221
Mason, (Captain) John, 13
Masque of Judgment, The, 247
"Masque of the Red Death, The," 63
"Massaccio," 131
"Massachusetts to Virginia," 115
Master-Rogue, The, 227
Masters, Edgar Lee, 279-280
Mate of the Daylight and Friends Ashore, The, 182-183
Mather, Cotton, 7-9, 115, 119
Mather, Increase, 7
Mather, Richard, 7, 10
Mather Dynasty, The, 7-9
Mathews, Cornelius, 84
"Maud Muller," 117
"May the Maiden," 236
"May-Day," 97
May-Day and Other Pieces, 90
Mayhew, Jonathan, 20
Maylem, John, 20
Mayo, William Starbuck, 82
"Maypole of Merry-Mount, The," 4, 119
Meaning of Truth: A Sequel to "Pragmatism," The, 212
Meat out of the Eater, 12
Mechanism in Thought and Morals, 123
Medical Essays 1842-1882, 122
"Meditation Eight," 12
"Meditation Three," 12
Meek, Alexander Beaufort, 81
"Meeting, The," 117
"Meh Lady," 181
Melanie and Other Poems, 53
Mellen, Grenville, 81
Mellichampe, 74
Melville, Herman, 70-73; poetry, 73; prose, 70-73
Member of the Third House, A, 205
Memoirs, 188
Memoirs of William Jennings Bryan, The, 213
"Memorable Victory of Paul Jones, The," 39
Memoranda during the War, 134 footnote, 140
Memorial to the Legislature of Massachusetts, 79
Memorie and Rime, 169
"Memories," 116
Memories of a Hundred Years, 185
Memories of a Southern Woman of Letters, 181
Memories of President Lincoln, and Other Lyrics of the War, 134 footnote
Men and Women, 264
"Menagerie, The," 248
Mencken, H[enry] L[ouis], 291
Mercy Philbrick's Choice, 171, 231
"Merrimack, The," 116
Merry-Mount, 77
Merton, Thomas, 294
"Message to Garcia, A," 263
Mettle of the Pasture, The, 178
"Mezzo Cammin," 113
Michael Angelo: A Fragment, 113
Michel-Guillaume Jean De Crèvecoeur, 26
Midge, The, 222-223
"Midnight Consultation, A," 38
Miles, Nathan, 45
Miles Standish, Courtship of, 108
Miles Wallingford, 67
Millay, Edna St. Vincent, 283-284
Miller, Arthur, 288

Miller, Cincinnatus Hiner [or Heine], 168-170: see **Miller, "Joaquin"**
Miller, "Joaquin," 168-170; early period, 169; final period, 170; merits and defects, 170; middle period, 169-170
"Milton," 130
Mingo and Other Sketches in Black and White, 172
Minister's Charge; or, The Apprenticeship of Lemuel Barker, The, 196
Minister's Wooing, The, 144, 145
"Miriam," 116
Miss Bellard's Inspiration, 198
Miss Ludington's Sister, 218
Miss Ravenel's Conversation from Secession to Loyalty, 224
"Miss Tempy's Watchers," 183
Missionary Sheriff, The, 171
"Mistaken Charity, A," 184
Mr. Bonaparte of Corsica, 251
"Mr. Dooley," 264
Mr. Dooley at His Best, 264
Mr. Dooley in Peace and War, 264
Mr. Dooley in the Hearts of His Countrymen, 264
Mr. Dooley Says, 264
Mr. Dooley's Philosophy, 264
Mr. Isaacs, 220
Mrs. Cliff's Yacht, 225
Mrs. Farrell, 197
Mrs. Leffingwell's Boots, 264
Mrs. Skaggs's Husbands and Other Sketches, 163
Mitchell, Isaac, 46
Mitchell, Jonathan, 13
Mitchell S[ilas] Weir, 225
M'liss: An Idyl of Red Mountain, 164 *footnote*
Moby-Dick; or, The Whale, 71
"Mocking Bird, The," 235
Modern Chivalry, 43
Modern Instance, A, 198
Modern Italian Poets, 195
"Moll Pitcher," 115
Monaldi, 80
Monarch of Dreams, The, 261
Monikins, The, 67
Monk and the Hangman's Daughter, The, 216
'Monsieur Henri,' 251
Monsieur Motte, 181
"Monster, The," 208, 209
Monster and Other Stories, The, 209
Mont-Saint-Michel and Chartres, 257
"Monument Mountain," 57
Moody, William Vaughn, 246-248; dramatic trilogy in verse, 246-247; letters, 248; merits and defects, 248; poetry collections and letters, 247-248; prose plays, 247
"Moon-Moth, The," 248
Moonlight Boy, A, 171
Moore, Clement Clarke, 81
Moosehead Journal, A, 129
"Moral Equivalent of War, The," 212
Morals of Chess, 27
Moran of the Lady Letty, 228
More, Hannah, 147
More, Paul Elmer, 289
More "Short Sixes," 223
More Songs from Vagabondia, 242, 244
More Wonders of the Invisible World, 9
"Morituri Salutamus," 113
Morley, Christopher [Darlington], 274
Morrell, William, 13
Morris, George Pope, 53-54
Mortal Antipathy, A, 122, 123
Morton, Sarah Wentworth, 45
Morton, Thomas, 4
Morton's Hope, 77
Mosses from an Old Manse, 117
Moth and the Flame, The, 264
Mother and the Father, The, 194
"Mother of Pearl," 224
Motley, John Lathrop, 77-78
"Mount Vernon on the Potomac," 181
Mountains of California, The, 262
Mouse-Trap, and Other Farces, The, 194
Mowatt [Ritchie], Anna Cora, 83
"Moxon's Master," 216
"MS. Found in a Bottle," 60, 63
Muir, John, 262
Mumford, Lewis, 293
"Murders in the Rue Morgue, The," 63
Murfree, Mary Noailles, 180
Murray, Judith Sargent, 46
Murray, Lindley, 46
"Musketaquid," 97
"My Aunt," 124
"My Double and How He Undid Me," 185
My Friendly Contemporaries, 207
My Literary Passions, 195
"My Lost Youth," 112
"My Love, I have no fear that thou shouldst die," 130
My Mark Twain, 195
"My Old Kentucky Home, Good Night," 64
"My Playmate," 116
"My Psalm," 117
My Study Windows, 127, 130
My Summer in a Garden, 262
My Winter Garden, 171
My Winter on the Nile, 262
My Year in a Log Cabin, 195
Myers, Peter Hamilton, 82
Mysteries of the Backwoods, 161
Mysterious Stranger, The, 193
"Mystery of Gilgil, The," 167
"Mystery of Heroism, A," 208
"Mystery of Marie Roget, The," 63
Mystery of Metropolisville, The, 165
Mystery of Witch-Face Mountain, The, 180
Mystic Trumpeter, The, 137

Narrative of Surprising Conversions, 16
"Narrow fellow in the grass, A," 232 *footnote*
Nasby, Petroleum V. (pseud.), 76, 160
Nasby Papers, The, 76
Nathan, Robert Gruntal, 275
Nathan Hale, 265
"National Ode, July 4, 1776, The," 146
Native of Wimby, and Other Tales, A, 183
"Nativity, The," 113
"Natural Selection: A Romance of Chelsea Village . . .," 223
Naturalist of Souls, A, 261
Nature (R. W. Emerson), 85, 89, 90
"Nature" (R. W. Emerson), 95
"Nature" (H. W. Longfellow), 113
"Nature and Treatment of Neuralgia, The," 122 *footnote*
Nature of True Virtue, The, 17
Naughty Anthony, 264
Neal, John, 79
"Near the Lake," 54
"Nearing the Snow-Line," 126
Negro Question, The, 176
Negro: The Southerner's Problem, The, 181
"Nellie Bly," 64
"Nellie Was a Lady," 64
"New Church Organ, The," 249
New Day, The, 262
New England Boyhood, A, 185
New England Courant, 19
"New England Nun, A," 184
New England Nun and Other Stories, A, 184
"New England Reformers," 95

"New England Tragedies, The," 113
New English Canaan, 4
"New Ezekiel, The," 249
New Flag, The, 227
New France and New England, 211
New Leaf Mills, 195, 198
New Orleans: The Place and the People, 181
New Roof, The, 31
"New South, The," 179
New South and Other Addresses, 179
New Views of Christianity, Society, and the Church, 105
New Voyage to Carolina, A, 20
New Waggings of Old Tales, 250
Newell, Robert Henry, 83
Newtonian rationalism, 24
Nicolay, J. G., 168
"Night and Day," 235
"Night at Wingdam, The," 162
"Night before Christmas: A Morality, The," 193
Night in Acadie, A, 180
Nights with Uncle Remus, 172
"Nightwatches," 132
Nile Notes of a Howadji, 145
"Nirvana," 235
No Love Lost: A Romance of Travel, 194
Noah, Mordecai Manuel, 82
"Noiseless Patient Spider, A," 140
"Nominalist and Realist," 96
Norris, [Benjamin] Frank[lin], 228-229
"North Shore Watch, The," 263
Northern Colonies (Rationalism and Democracy), 19-20
Northern Novelists (Early Sentiment and Romance), 82
Northern Poets (Early Sentiment and Romance), 54-59, 80-81
Norton Andrews, 92
Norton, John, 13
Norwood, (Colonel) Henry, 13
Not on the Screen, 227
Notes and Fragments, 134 *footnote*
Notes on the Mind, 16
Notes on . . . Virginia, 34
Notes on Walt Whitman as Poet and Person, 255
Notions of the Americans, 67
Nott, Henry Junius, 82
Novel, The (Revolutionary Period), 24, 41-44
Novel: What It Is, The, 221
"Novel with a 'Purpose', The," 229
Novelists (1865-1914), 214-230
November Boughs, 134 *footnote*, 135 *footnote*
Nuggets and Dust Panned Out in California, 214
Nydia: A Tragic Play, 75

"O Captain! My Captain!," 137, 141
O. Henry (pseud.), 270
"O, Inexpressible as Sweet," 263
Oak Openings, The, 67
Oakes, Urian, 13
Oaks and Ivy, 253
O'Brien, Fitz-James, 216 *footnote*, 224-225
Observations of Mr. Dooley, 264
"Occurrence at Owl Creek Bridge, An," 215
Octopus, The, 228, 229
Odd Leaves of a Louisiana "Swamp Doctor," The, 161
"Ode for the Fourth of. July, 1876, An," 132
"Ode Inscribed to W. H. Channing," 98
"Ode in Time of Hesitation, An," 247
"Ode Read at the One Hundredth Anniversary of the Flight at Concord Bridge,"132
Ode Recited at the Commemoration of the Living and Dead Soldiers . . ., 127
"Ode Recited at the Harvard Commemoration," 132
"Ode to Happiness," 132
Odell, Jonathan, 45
Odets, Clifford, 288
Odyssey of Homer, The, 55
Of Being, 16
Of Insects, 16
Oglethorpe, James E., 20
"Oh Fairest of the Rural Maids," 57
O'Hara, John [Henry], 278
O'Hara, Theodore, 81
"Old Age," 97
"Old Agency, The," 179
Old Bachelor, The, 80
"Old Black Joe," 64
"Old Chisholm Trail, The," 160
Old Continental, The, 54
Old Creole Days, 176
"Old Folks at Home," 64
Old Friends and New, 182
"Old Gardiston," 179
Old House at Sudbury, The, 59
Old Ironsides, 122
"Old Ironsides," 123
"Old Lady Pingree," 184
"Old Pourquoi," 248
Old South, The, 181
Old Stone House, The, 179
Old Thing, The, 201
"Old Uncle Ned," 64
Old Wives for New, 228
Oldport Days, 261
Oldtown Folks, 145
Oliver Oldschool, Esq. (pseud.), 44
Omoo: A Narrative of Adventures in the South Seas, 71
"On a Certain Blindness in Human Beings," 212
"On a Certain Condescension in Foreigners," 130
"On a Soldier Fallen in the Philippines," 247
"On Board the '76," 132
On Some of Life's Ideals, 212
"On the Anniversary of the Storming of the Bastile," 38
"On the Beach at Night," 140
"On the Beach at Night Alone," 140
"On the Capture of Certain Fugitive Slaves near Washington," 131
On the Causes and Cure of Smoky Chimneys, 27
"On the Connecticut River," 58
"On the Death of a Friend's Child," 131
"On the Death of Joseph Rodman Drake," 53
On the Makaloa Mat, 230
"On the River," 248
On the Stairs, 227
"On the Uses of Great Men," 96
"Once I Pass'd through a Populous City," 139
One Fair Woman, The, 169
"One-Hoss Shay," 124
One of Cleopatra's Nights, 174
"One of the Missing," 215
O'Neill, Eugene [Gladstone], 286
"Open Boat, The," 207, 208
Open Boat and Other Tales of Adventure, The, 208
Open-Eyed Conspiracy, 196
"Opportunity," 240
Oregon Trail, The, 78
Oriental Acquaintance, 224
Oriental Contribution to Transcendentalism, 86
"Oriental Maxims," 116
"Origin of Didactic Poetry, The," 128-129
Origin of the Feast of Purim, The, 41

Ormond, 42
Orpheus C. Kerr Papers, The, 83
"Orphic Sayings," 102
"Orphics," 101
O'Ruddy, The, 207
Ossoli, Margaret: see Fuller [Sarah] Margaret, 102-103
Other House, The, 201
Other Main-Travelled Roads, 206
Otis, James, 30
"Our Autocrat," 117
"Our Country's Call," 57
Our Hundred Days in Europe, 122
Our Italy, 262
Our Land and Land Policy, National and State, 210
"Our love is not a fading earthly flower," 130
"Our Master," 117
Our National Parks, 262
Our Old Home, 117, 118
"Our River," 116
"Outcasts of Poker Flat, The," 163
Outlines of Cosmic Philosophy, 211
"Out of the Cradle Endlessly Rocking," 136
Out of the Question, 194
"Out of the Rolling Ocean the Crowd," 139
Outre-Mer, 107
"Over-Heart, The," 116
"Over-Soul, The," 86, 92, 94, 116
"Over the Carnage Rose Prophetic a Voice," 137
Over the Teacups, 122, 123
Overland, 224
Overland in a Covered Wagon, 170
"Ozème's Holiday," 180

Pacific Poems, 169
Pactolus Prime, 226
Page, Thomas Nelson, 180-181
Pageant of Life, A, 260 *footnote*
Pages from an Old Volume of Life, 122
Paine, Robert Treat, 46
Paine, Thomas, 32-33
"Pair of Patient Lovers, A," 194, 196 *footnote*
Pair of Patient Lovers, A, 194
"Palatine, The," 115
Papers on Literature and Art, 129
Paquita, 170 *footnote*
"Paradiso," 113
Parker, Dorothy [Rothschild], 284
Parker, Theodore, 104, 300
Parkman, Francis, 78
Parlor Car, The, 194
Parsons, Thomas William, 59
Parting and a Meeting, A, 194
Parting Friends, 194
"Parting Hymn," 125
Partisan, The, 74
"Passage to India," 136, 138, 140
"Passing of Tennyson, The," 170
Passionate Pilgrim, A, 203
Paste Jewels, 251
Pastime Stories, 181
Pathfinder, The, 68
Patrins, 251
Paul Fane, 53
Paul Redding: A Tale of the Brandywine, 58
"Paul Revere's Ride," 112
Paulding, James Kirke, 54
Peabody, Elizabeth, 101, 103
Peabody, Josephine Preston, 265
Pearl, The, 79
Pearl of Orr's Island, The, 145
Pelléas and Mélisande, 244
Pembroke, 184
Pencilings by the Way, 53
"Penelope," 162
Penhollow, Samuel, 19
"Penman of the Revolution, The," 30
Pennsylvania Magazine; or American Monthly Museum, 32
People of the Abyss, The, 230
Percival, James Gates, 58
Percy, George, 13
Personal Narrative, 17
Personal Recollections of Joan of Arc by the Sieur Louis de Conte, 192
Personally Conducted, 225
Peterkin, Julia [Mood], 273
Petroleum V. Nasby (pseud.), 76, 160
Phantoms of the Foot-bridge, The, 180
"Ph.D. Octopus, The," 212
Phelps, Elizabeth Stuart, 148-149
Philip Nolan's Friends, 185
Phillips, David Graham, 227-228
Philosophers (The Gilded Age), 209-213
"Philosophy of Composition, The," 62
Phoenixiana, 83
"Physical Basis of Emotion, The," 212
Piatt, John James, 194, 249
Piazza Tales, The, 72
"Pictures from Appledore," 131
Pictures of the War, 208
Pierpont, John, 58
Pierre; or, The Ambiguities, 72
Pietro Ghisleri, 221
Pike County Ballads and Other Pieces, The, 167
Pilot, The, 68
Pinckney, Edward Coote, 81
Pioneer, 126
"Pioneer, The," 132
Pioneers, The, 68
"Pioneers! O Pioneers!," 138, 138 *footnote*, 141
Piper, The, 265
"Pipes at Lucknow, The," 117
Pit, The, 228
"Pitcher of Mignonette, A," 224
"Plain Language from Truthful James," 162
Plain People, 171
Plain Truth, 33
Platform of Church Discipline, A, 7
"Playin' of Old Sledge at the Settlemint, A," 180
Playing the Mischief, 224
Plays and Poems (G. H. Boker), 75
"Plea for Captain John Brown, A," 99
"Plea for Psychology as a Natural Science," 212
Pleasant Ways of St. Medard, The, 181
"Pledge at Spunky Point, The," 167
Plum Tree, The, 227
Pluralistic Universe, A, 212
Poe, Edgar Allan, 59-63, 129, 216 *footnote*; criticism, 61; merits and defects, 60-61, 63; poetry, 61-62; short stories, 62-63
Poe Hoax, 216
Poems (J. G. C. Brainard), 58
Poems (M. [J.] Cawein), 251
Poems (W. E. Channing), 105
Poems (R. W. Emerson), 90
Poems (J. T. Fields), 145
Poems (Emily Dickinson), 232
Poems (O. W. Holmes), 122
Poems (W. D. Howells), 194
Poems (Sidney Lanier), 235
Poems (H. W. Longfellow), 107
Poems (J. R. Lowell), 126
Poems (W. V. Moody), 246
Poems (J. G. Percival), 58
Poems (Irwin Russell), 180
Poems ([J.] M. Thompson), 171
Poems and Ballads of Heine, 249

Poems and Stories of Fitz-James O'Brien, The, 224
Poems and Translations, 249
Poems: Centenary Edition, 232
Poems; Chiefly in the Scottish Dialect, 25
Poems of H. C. Bunner, The, 224
Poems of Henry Timrod, 64
Poems of Home and Travel, 146
Poems of Paul Hamilton Hayne, 64-65
Poems of Place, 249
Poems of the Orient, 146
Poems of the War, 75
Poems of Two Friends, 194
Poems on Several Occasions, 37
Poems on Slavery, 109
Poems, Sacred, Passionate, and Humorous, The, 53
Poems: Second Series (Emily Dickinson), 232
Poems: Second Series (J. R. Lowell), 127
Poems: Third Series (Emily Dickinson), 232
"Poet, The," (R. W. Emerson), 95
Poet at the Breakfast-Table, 122, 123
Poetical Works of Fitz-Greene Halleck, The, 53
"Poetry: A Metrical Essay," 125
Poetry of Life, The, 243
Poetry of Tennyson, The, 263
Poets and Poetry of the West, The, 194
Poganuc People, 143
Political Essays, 127
"Political Litany, A," 38
Political Prose (Revolutionary Period), 29-37
"Politics," 96
"Polly," 181
Pomona's Travels, 225
Poole, Ernest, 273
Poor Richard's Almanac, 27
"Pope," 130
Porter, Katherine Anne, 275
Porter, William Sydney, 270
Portion of Labor, The, 184
Portrait, The, 58
Portrait of a Lady, The, 201
Portrait of American Women, 261
Portrait of Mrs. W., The, 265
Portraits of Women, 261
"Posson Jone'," 176
"Posthumous Fame; or a Legend of the Beautiful," 178
Potiphar Papers, 145
Pound, Ezra [Loomis], 282
"Power," 96
"Power of Fancy, The," 39
Power of Sympathy, The, 41
Pragmatism: A New Way for Some Old Ways of Thinking, 212
Prairie, The, 68
Prairie Folks, 206
"Prattle," 214
Prayer to the Virgin of Chartres, The, 259
"Preacher, The," 117
Prentice, George Dennison, 81
Prescott, William Hickling, 77
"Present Crisis, The," 131
Present State of Virginia, The (James Blair), 20
Present State of Virginia, The (Hugh Jones), 20
Preston, Margaret J., 81
Pretty Story, A, 31
Previous Engagement, A, 194
"Price of the Harness, The," 207
Price She Paid, The, 228
Pride of the Village, The, 52
Primitivism, 24
Prince, Thomas, 20
Prince and the Pauper, The, 192
Prince of India, The, 225
Prince of Parthia, The, 19
Princess Casamassima, The, 201
Principles of Psychology, The, 211
Private Theatricals, 197
"Problem, The," 97
"Problems of American History, The," 158
"Proem," 116
Professor at the Breakfast Table, The, 122, 123
Progress and Poverty, 209, 210
Progress: A Satirical Poem, 80
Progress of Dulness, The, 39
Progress to the Mines, in the Year 1732, A, 18
Prokosch, Frederic, 279
Prologue to "Songs in Many Keys," 124
Prometheus (J. R. Lowell), 131
"Prometheus" (J. G. Percival), 58
Prometheus Part II with Other Poems, 58
Prompter, The, 44
"Prophecy of Samuel Sewall, The," 115
Prophet of Joy, A, 260 *footnote*
Prophet of the Great Smoky Mountains, The, 180
Prose Writers of Germany, 104
Protection or Free Trade, 210
"Prudence," 93
Prue and I, 145
"Psalm of Life, A," 110
"Psalm of the West," 237
Psychographs, 259
"Psychological Theory of Extension, The," 212
Psychology: Briefer Course, 211, 212
Publick Occurrences, 19
Puppet-Booth, The, 227
"Purgatorio" (H. W. Longfellow), 113
Purgatorio (T. W. Parsons), 59
Puritan Poetry (Renaissance and Puritan Influences), 10-12
Puritan theology, 2-3
Puritans, The (Renaissance and Puritan Influences), 2-4
"Purloined Letter, The," 63
Pursuit of the House-Boat, The, 251

Quakerism, principles of, 18
Quality of Mercy, The, 197
"Quarry, The," 247
Queen Bee, The, 186
Queries of Highest Consideration, 6
Quest of Merlin, The, 245
Questionable Shapes, 195

"Rabbi Ishmael," 117
"Race Problem in the South, The," 179
Ragged Lady, 198
Raid of the Guerrilla, The, 180
Rainbow, The, 80
Ralph Waldo Emerson (O. W. Holmes), 122
Ralph Waldo Emerson (G. E. Woodbury), 263
Ralstons, The, 220
"Ram of Darby, The," 160
Ramona, 17, 171
Randall, James Ryder, 81
"Randolph of Roanoke," 115
Ransom, John Crowe, 283
Ranson's Folly, 226
"Rappaccini's Daughter," 119
Rationalism, development of, 24
"Raven, The," 62
Raven and Other Poems, The, 60
"Raven Days, The," 236
Read, Thomas Buchanan, 58
Reality of Religion, The, 262
Rebellious Heroine, A, 251
Recollection of the Last Ten Years, 75
"Reconciliation," 137
Reconstruction Period, 153-154
Record of a School, The, 101
"Recorders Ages Hence," 139
Red Badge of Courage, The, 208

Red City, The, 225
Red Rover, 68
Redburn: His First Voyage, 70, 71
Redskins, The, 67
Reese, Lizette Woodworth, 279
Reformers, (The Gilded Age), 209-213
Register, The, 194
Reign of Guilt, The, 228
Reign of Law, The, 178
Relation of Literature to Life, The, 262
"Relieving Guard," 162
Religious Courtship, 147
Religious Writing in New England (Rise of Rationalism and Democracy), 14-17
"Remarkable Providences," 7
Remarks on American Literature, 88, 91 *footnote*
"Remonstrance," 236
"Remorse," 167
Renaissance and Puritan Influences, 1-13
Report on a National Bank, 35
Report on Manufactures, 35
Report on Public Credit, 35
Repplier, Agnes, 288
Representative Men, 90, 96
"Republican Genius of Europe, The," 38
"Requital," 117
Resolutions, 16
"Response," 116
Responsibilities of the Novelist, The, 229
"Resurgam," 171
Return of Peter Grimm, The, 264
"Return of the Private, The," 205
"Reveille, The," 162
"Revenge of Hamish, The," 236, 237
Reverberator, The, 201
Revolution, 229
Revolution, The (1763-1783), 22
Revolutionary Period, The (1763-1810), 21-46
"Rhodora, The," 97
"Rhoecus," 131
Rice, Elmer [L.], 287
Rich, Richard, 13
Richter, Conrad, 274
Richard Hurdis, 74
Right of the British Colonists Asserted and Proved, 30
Rights of Man, The, 32, 33
Riis, Jacob August, 213
Riley, James Whitcomb, 250
Rio Grande, 264
"Rip Van Winkle," 51, 52
Ripley, George, 87
Rise of Silas Lapham, The, 198, 199
Rise of the Dutch Republic, The, 77
"Rise of the Short Story, The," 163 *footnote*
"Rising Glory of America, The," 37
[Ritchie], Anna Cora Mowatt, 83
River Floods, The, 262
"River swelleth more and more, The," 100-101
Road, The, 230
"Road-Hymn for the Start," 247
Roadside Meetings, 206
Robb, J. S., 161
Robert E. Lee: Man and Soldier, 180-181
Robert E. Lee: The Southerner, 180
Roberts, Elizabeth Madox, 273-274
"Robin's Song," 224
Robinson, Edwin Arlington, 279
Robinson Jeffers: The Man and the Artist, 252
Rocky Mountains: or, Scenes, Incidents, and Adventures . . . of Captain B. L. E. Bonneville, The, 52 *footnote*
Roderick Hudson, 201
"Rodman the Keeper," 179
Rodman the Keeper: Southern Sketches, 179
Roger Malvin's Burial, 120
Rogers, John, 13
Rogers, (Major) Robert, 46
Roland Blake, 225
Rölvaag, O[le] E[dvart], 272
Roman Singer, A, 221
Romantic Period, The (1810-1865), 47-149
Room Forty-Five, 194
Roosevelt, Theodore, 155-156
Root, George Frederick, 81
Rose of Dutcher's Coolly, 206
"Rose of the Alhambra, The," 51
Ross, Alexander, 75
Roughing It, 190
Round Table, The, 127
"Rousseau," 133
"Rousseau and the Sentimentalists," 130
"Roving Gambler, The," 160
Rowen: "Second-Crop" Songs, 224
Rowlandson, Mary, 5
Rowson, Susanna H., 46
Roxy, 166
Royal Gentleman, A, 226
Rudder Grange, 225
Rudder Grangers Abroad, The, 225
Rules by Which a Great Empire May Be Reduced to a Small One, 27
Ruling Passion, The, 263
Runaway Browns, The, 223
Rush, Benjamin, 45
Rush, Rebecca, 82
Russell, Irwin, 180
"Russian Christianity vs. American Judaism," 249
Ryan, Abram Joseph, 81
Ryerson, Florence, 143 *footnote*

"Sabbath Scene, A," 115
Sacred Fount, The, 201
"Saga of King Olaf, The," 112
Salmagundi: or The Whim-Whams . . ., 50, 52
Sandburg, Carl [August], 168, 280-281
Sandford and Merton, 147
Sands, Robert Charles, 83
Sandys, George, 12
Sant' Ilario, 221
Santayana, George, 288-289
Sappho (Clyde Fitch), 265
Sappho of Green Springs, A, 164 *footnote*
Sappho: One Hundred Lyrics (Bliss Carman), 243
Sara Crewe, or What Happened at Miss Minchin's, 226
Saracinesca, 221
Sargent, Epes, 84
Saroyan, William, 278
Satanstoe, 66, 67
Saxe, John Godfrey, 80
Scarlet Letter, The, 117, 118, 120, 121
Schoolcraft, Henry R., 83, 112
Science of English Verse, The, 238
Scollard, Clinton, 251
Scorn of Woman, 229
Scott, Evelyn [D.], 275
Scout, The, 74
Sea-Change: or Love's Stowaway . ., A, 194
Sea Lions, The, 67
"Sea-Shore," 97
Sea-Wolf, The, 229
Seabury, Samuel, 35, 45
Seacliff, 224
Seaside and the Fireside, The, 107
Seasonable Thoughts on . . . Religion in New-England, 17
"Seaward," 245
Seccomb, John, 20
"Second Coming," 247, 248
Second Generation, The, 228
Second Twenty Years at Hull House, The, 213
"Secret, The," 263
Secret Garden, The, 226

Sedgwick, Catharine Maria, 82
Sedgwick, Susan Ridley, 82
Seen and Unseen at Stratford-on-Avon, The, 194
Selected Poems (R. W. Emerson), 90
"Self-Reliance," 92, 93, 94
"Self-Sacrifice: A Farce-Tragedy," 193
Sense of the Past, The, 203
Sentiments on Small Pox Inoculation, 8
Sequel to Drum-Taps, 134 *footnote*
*Sermon Preach'd at the Election..1669,A.*6]
Sermons (Samuel Davis), 20
Seton, Ernest [or **Evan**] **Thompson,** 263-264
Seven Songs, 31
Seven Tales of My Native Land, 117
Seventy Six, 79
Several Poems . . . By a Gentlewoman in New-England, 11
Several Reasons Proving that Inoculating Is a Lawful Practice, 7
Sewall, Samuel, 9-10
"Shadow," 63
Shadow of a Dream, The, 197
Shadow on the Dial, The, 217
Shadows of Shasta, 169
Shadow Verses, 260 *footnote*
"Shake, Mulleary and Go-ethe," 224
"Shakespeare Once More," 130
"Shame," 207
Shapes of Clay, 216
"Sharps and Flats," 250
Shaw, Henry Wheeler, 76, 160
Shaw, John, 46
Sheean, Vincent, 277
Sheldon, Charles Monroe, 227
"Shepherd of King Admetus, The," 131
Shepard, Thomas, 5
"Sheridan's Ride," 58
Sherman, Frank Dempster, 250-251
Sherman, Stuart P[ratt], 291
Sherwood, Robert [Emmett], 287
"She Was a Beauty," 224
Shillaber, Benjamin P., 83
"Shoemakers, The," 116
"Short Sixes," 223
Short Story, 50, 61, 158
Short-Story Writers (1865-1914), 214-230
Shuttle, The, 226
"Significance of the Frontier in American History, The," 158, 159
Sigourney, Lydia Huntley, 80
Silent Partner, The, 149
Silent South, The, 176
Sill, Edward Rowland, 239-240
Silver Pitchers: and Independence, a Centennial Love Story, 146 *footnote*
Simms, William Gilmore, 74
Simple Cobbler of Aggawam . . ., The, 9
Sincere Convert, The, 5
Sinclair, Upton [Beall], 272
Singing Heart, The, 251
Single Hound, The, 232
"Singular Life, A," 149
Sinners in the Hands of an Angry God, 17
Sister Carrie, 228
"Sister Dolorosa," 178
Sister Jane: Her Friends and Acquaintances, 172
"Sister Liddy," 184
"Sister St. Luke," 179
Sisters, The, 116
Six to One: A Nantucket Idyl, 218
"Skeleton in Armor, The," 110
Sketch Book of Geoffrey Crayon, Gent., 51
Sketches of American Policy, 44
Sketches of Eighteenth Century America, 26
Sketches of India, 235
Sketches of Switzerland, 67
Sketches of the Life and Character of Patrick Henry, 80
"Skipper Ireson's Ride," 116
Slavery, 88
"Slavery in Massachusetts," 99
Sleeping Car and Other Farces, The, 194
"Sliding Scale, The," 160
Slovenly Peter, 192 *footnote*
"Sluggish smoke curls up from some deep dell, The," 101
Smith, Charles Henry, 83, 160
Smith, (Captain) John, 2
Smith, Samuel Francis, 65
Smith, Seba, 76
Smith, Sol[omon Franklin], 161
Smith, William (1727-1803), 19, 33
Smith, William (1728-1793), 20
Smoke Bellew, 229
Smoking Car, The, 194
"Snake, The," 232 *footnote*
Snelling, William Joseph, 83
Snow-Bound, 110, 114
"Snow-Storm, The," 97
Social Secretary, The, 227
"Society and Solitude," 97
Society and Solitude, 90, 97
Sol Smith's Theatrical Apprenticeship, 161
Soldiers of Fortune, 226
Some Adventures of Captain Simon Suggs, 83, 161
Some Chinese Ghosts, 174
Some Considerations on the Keeping of Negroes, 25
Some Problems of Philosophy, 212
Son of Royal Langbrith, The, 199
"Son of the Gods, A," 215
Son of the Middle Border, A, 205, 206, 206 *footnote*
Son of the Wolf, The, 229
"Song-Flower and Poppy," 248
"Song for American Freedom, A," 31
Song of Creation, A, 170
Song of Hiawatha, The, 107, 111
"Song of Marion's Men," 57
"Song of Myself," 136, 139
"Song of the Answerer," 136
"Song of the Broad-Axe," 139
"Song of the Chattahoochee," 235
"Song of the Hemp, The," 178
"Song of the Rolling Earth, A," 140
Songs at the Start, 251
Songs from Vagabondia, 244
Songs in Many Keys, 122
Songs of a Semite, 249
Songs of Fair Weather, 171
Songs of Italy, 169, 170
Songs of Many Seasons, 122
Songs of the Mexican Seas, 169
Songs of the Sea-Children, 243
Songs of the Sierras, 169
Songs of the Soul, 169, 170
Songs of the Sunlands, 169
Songs of Vagabondia, 242
Sonnets (H. W. Longfellow), 113
Sonnets: A Sequence on Profane Love, 75
Sonnets to Craig, 252
Soul of the Far East, The, 173
Soundings from the Atlantic, 122
"South Devil, The," 179
"South of the Slot," 230
Southern Colonies, The (Rationalism and Democracy), 18, 20
Southern Novelists (Early Sentiment and Romance), 82
Southern Poets (Early Sentiment and Romance), 59-65, 81-82
Southern Writers (Colonial Period), 2
"Southwest Chamber, The," 184
Southworth, Emma D. E. N., 82
Sovereignty & Goodness of God Together, The, 5
Spagnoletto, The, 249
Spanish Student, The, 107, 111

Sparks, Jared, 52
Sparrowgrass Papers, The, 83
Specimen Days and Collect, 134 *footnote,* 140
Specimen Days in America, 134 *footnote*
Specimens, 169
"Spectre Bridegroom, The," 51
Spectre of Power, A, 180
Speech against Writs of Assistance, 30
Spelling Book, 44
"Sphinx, The," 97
Spirit of America, The, 263
Spirit of Youth and the City Streets, The, 213
Spirit-Rapper: An Autobiography, The, 106
"Spiritual Laws," 94
Spoil of Office, A, 205
Spoils of Poynton, The, 201
Sport of the Gods, The, 252
Spotswood, Alexander, 18
"Spring: An Ode," 245
Spy, The, 54, 66, 69
"Square-Five Fathom," 223
Squibob Papers, The, 83
"Stage Driver's Story, The," 162
Standards, 262
Stansbury, Joseph, 45
"Stanzas on Freedom," 131
Star Rover, The, 229
"Star-Spangled Banner, The," 65
"Starting from Paumanok," 136, 139
Statesmen of Literary Note, 79
"Statesman's Secret, The," 124, 126
Steele, Wilbur Daniel, 274
Steere, Richard, 19
Stein, Gertrude, 272
"Stein Song," 245
Steinbeck, John [Ernst], 277
Step on the Stair, A, 171
Stephens, A. S., 161
Sterling, George, 217 *footnote,* 252
"Stethoscope Song, The," 124
Stevens, Wallace, 281
Stickeen, 262
Stillwater Tragedy, The, 148
"Stirrup-Cup, The" (John Hay), 167
"Stirrup-Cup, The" (Sidney Lanier), 236
Stith, William, 20
Stockton, Frank R. [or Francis Richard], 225
Stoddard, Richard Henry, 58-59, 249
Stoddard, Solomon, 20
Stops of Various Quills, 194
Stories from Louisiana History, 181
Stories in Light and Shadow, 164 *footnote*
Stories of a Western Town, 171
Stories That End Well, 171
Storm Centre, The, 180
Story, William Wetmore, 81
Story of a Bad Boy, The, 148
Story of a Country Town, The, 171, 206
"Story of a New York House, The," 222
Story of an Untold Love, The, 227
Story of Kennett, The, 146
Story of My Boyhood and Youth, The, 262
Story of Old Fort Loudon, The, 180
Story of the Other Wise Man, The, 263
"Stout Gentleman, The," 51
Stowe, Harriet [Elizabeth] Beecher, 143-145, 307
Strachey, William, 13
Stradella, 221
Strange Leaves from Strange Literature, 174
Stranglers of Paris, The, 264
"Stratford on Avon," 51
Streaks of Squatter Life, 161
"Street of the Hyacinth, The," 179
Strength of Gideon, The, 253
Strength of the Strong, The, 230
"Strong as Death," 224
Strong Hearts, 176
Stubbornness of Geraldine, The, 264
"Study of Thirteenth-Century Unity, A," 257
Suburban Sketches, 195
"Success" (Emily Dickinson), 232 *footnote*
"Success" (R. W. Emerson), 97
Suckow, Ruth, 275
Summary View of the Rights of British America, A, 34
"Summer by the Lakeside," 116
Summer in Arcady: A Tale of Nature, 178
Summer on the Lakes, 103
"Sun-Day Hymn, A," 125
"Sunrise," 237
"Sunset on the Bearcamp," 116
Susan Lenox: Her Fall and Rise, 228
"Susanna," 64
Sut Lovingood Yarns, 161
Swallow Barn, 73
"Swing Low, Sweet Chariot," 160
Sword of Youth, The, 177
Sybaris and Other Homes, 185
Sylphs of the Seasons, with Other Poems, 80
"Sympathy," 101
"Symphony, The," 237
"Symposium, The," 87

Tabb, John B[annister], 240-242
Tablet, The, 44
Taft, William H., 156-157
Tailfer, Patrick, 20
Taine, H. A., 165
Tales from Home, 146
Tales of a Time and Place, 181
Tales of a Traveller, 51
Tales of a Wayside Inn, 59, 112
Tales of New England, 182
Tales of Soldiers and Civilians, 215
Tales of the Fish Patrol, 229
Tales of the Grotesque and Arabesque, 60
Tales of the Home Folks in Peace and War, 172
Tales of the Times, A, 134 *footnote*
Taliesin: A Masque, 246
Talks to Teachers on Psychology: and to Students on Some of Life's Ideals, 212
Tall Tales, 159, 160-161
Tallahassee Girl, A, 171
Tamerlane and Other Poems, 59
"Tan Yard Case," 173
Taquisara, 221
Tar-Baby and Other Rhymes of Uncle Remus, The, 172
Tarkington, [Newton] Booth, 270-271
Tayleure, Clifton W., 83
Taylor, Bayard, 146, 307
Taylor, Edward. 12
Taylor, W. F., 189, footnote
Teasdale, Sara, 281
"Tell-Tale Heart, The," 63
Teller, The, 226
"Telling the Bees," 116
Ten Great Religions, 106
Ten Times One Is Ten, 185
"Tennessee's Partner," 163
Tenney, Tabitha, 46
"Tenor, The," 223
Tenth Muse Lately Sprung Up in America, The, 11
"Tenth of January, The," 148
"'Tenty Scran," 148
"Terminus," 97
Terrible Night, A, 224
Testimony of the Suns, The, 217 *footnote,* 252
"Thanatopsis," 54, 55, 56
"Thar's More in the Man than Thar Is in the Land," 236
That Fortune, 262
That Lass o' Lowrie's, 226
Theatrical Journey-Work, 161
Theft, 229

Their Silver Wedding Journey, 196
Their Wedding Journey, 196, 198
Theodore de la Guard (pseud.), 9
Theodore Roosevelt: The Citizen, 213
Theology Explained and Defended, 40
"There Was a Child Went Forth," 140
"Thick-Sprinkled Bunting," 137, 138
"Thine Eyes Still Shined," 93 *footnote*, 97
Third Circle, The, 229
"Third Violet, The," 208, 209
Thirty Poems, 55
Thomas, Augustus, 264
Thomas, Fredrick William, 82
Thompson, Daniel Pierce, 82
Thompson, Ernest Seton, 263-264
Thompson, [James] Maurice, 171
Thompson, William Tappan, 83, 161
Thomson, Mortimer Neal, 83
Thoreau, Henry David, 94, 95, 98-101, 129, 133, 297-299; prose, 99-100; poetry, 100-101; supplementary bibliography, 297-299
"Thoreau" (J. R. Lowell), 130
Thoreau: The Poet-Naturalist, 105
Thorpe, Thomas Bangs, 83, 161
"Thou Mother with Thy Equal Brood," 137
"Thought," 171
Three Fates, The, 220
"Three Friends of Mine," 113
Three Memorial Poems, 127
"Three Miraculous Soldiers," 208
"Three of a Kind," 245
"Threnody," 97
Through Nature to God, 211
Through the Eye of the Needle, 197
"Through the Long Days," 167
Ticknor, Francis Orray, 81
Ticknor, George, 84
Timoleon, etc., 73
Timrod, Henry, 64
Tinker, E. L., 175 *footnote*
"'Tite Poulette," 176
"Titmouse, The," 97
"To a Caty-Did," 124
"To a Locomotive in Winter," 138
"To a Waterfowl," 57
"To a Wild Honeysuckle," 39
"To an Author," 39
"To an Insect," 124, 126
"To Charles Eliot Norton," 132
"To Ellen at the South," 93 *footnote*, 97
"To Helen," 61
"To Her," 224
"To Him That Was Crucified," 140 *footnote*
"To Holmes on His Seventy-Fifth Birthday," 132
To Leeward, 221
"To My Dear and Loving Husband," 11
"To My Readers," 126
"To Sylvius," 39
"To the Dandelion," 131
"To the Fringed Gentian," 57
"To the Humble-Bee," 97
"To the Leaven'd Soil They Trod," 137
"To the Memory of the Brave Americans," 39
"To Thee Old Cause," 136
"To Think of Time," 140
"To Whittier on His Seventy-fifth Birthday," 132
"To W. L. Garrison," 131
'Toinette, 226
Told by Uncle Remus, 172
Tom Owen: The Bee-Hunter . . ., 161
Tom Sawyer, Adventures of, 191
Tom Sawyer Abroad, 191 *footnote*
Tom Sawyer, Detective, 191 *footnote*
"Tomo Cheeki, the Creek Indian in Philadelphia," 39
Tompson, Benjamin, 13
"Too Young for Love," 126
Tortesa the Usurer, 53
Tory Lover, The, 182
Tour on the Prairies, A, 51
Tourgée, Albion Winegar, 225, 226
"Town Crier, The," 214
Tragedy of Pudd'nhead Wilson, The, 192
Tragic Muse, The, 201
Trail-Makers of the Middle Border, 206, 206 *footnote*
Trail of an Artist-Naturalist, 264
Trail of the Lonesome Pine, The, 181
Tramp Abroad, A, 190
Transcendental Club, 86, 89, 104
"Transcendental Wild Oats," 146
Transcendentalism: Brook Farm, 87; group activities, 86-87; major and minor figures, 85-106; origin of concept, 85, 86; *The Dial*, 87
Transformation, 121
Transit of Civilization, The, 166
"Transplanted Boy, A," 179
Traveler from Altruria, A, 197
Travels in Alaska, 262
Travels in New-England and New-York, 40
Travels through North and South Carolina, Georgia, East and West Florida, 25
Treatise concerning Religious Affections, A, 16
"Trial Sermons on Bull-Skin, The," 252
"Trouble, Trouble," 160
True Relation of Such Occurences and Accidents of Note as Have Happened in Virginia . . . , A, 2
Trumbull, John, 39-40
Truth, The, 265
Tucker, George, 82
Tucker, Nathaniel Beverley, 82
Tuckerman, Henry Theodore, 84
Turrell, Ebenezer, 20
Turrell, Jane, 20
"Turn O Libertad," 137, 138
Turn of the Screw, The, 203
Turner, Frederick J., 158-159
Twain, Mark (pseud.), 187-193: see **Clemens, S. L.**
Twenty Years at Hull House, 213
Twice-Told Tales, 117, 118
Two Admirals, The, 68
"Two Churches of 'Quawket, The," 223
"Two Gentlemen of Kentucky," 178
Two Little Confederates, 181
Two Men of Sandy Bar, 164 *footnote*
"Two Rabbi[n]s, The," 117
Two Rivulets including Democratic Vistas, Centennial Songs, and Passage to India, 134 *footnote*, 135 *footnote*
Two Women: 1862, 179
Two Years Before the Mast, 73
Two Years in the French West Indies, 174
Tyler, Royall, 24, 41
Typee: A Peep at Polynesian Life, 70
Types of American Characters, 260

"Ulalume," 62
Uncalled, The, 252
"Uncle Gabe's White Folks," 181
"Uncle Ned," 64
"Uncle Remus," 172
Uncle Remus and Brer Rabbit, 172
Uncle Remus and His Friends, 172
Uncle Remus and the Little Boy, 172
Uncle Remus: His Songs and Sayings, 172
Uncle Remus Returns, 172
Uncle Remus Series, 172
Uncle Tom's Cabin; or, Life among the Lowly, 143-144
"Under the Lion's Paw," 205
"Under the Old Elm," 132
Under the Skylights, 227

"Under the Violets," 125
"Under the Willows," 131
Under the Willows and Other Poems, 127
Underbrush, 145
Underhill, (Captain) John, 13
Undiscovered Country, The, 198
Unexpected Guests, The, 194
"Union and Liberty," 124
"Unitarian Christianity Most Favorable to Piety," 88
United States Democratic Review, 105
Unknown Quantity, The, 263
Unmade in Heaven, 260 *footnote*
"Unmanifest Destiny," 245
Unpublished Poems, 232
Untermeyer, Louis, 291-292
"Until the Troubling of the Waters," 247-248
"Up the Coolly," 205
"Upon the Burning of Our House," 11
"Upon the Death of G. B. [General Bacon]," 2
Upside Down, or Philosophy in Petticoats, 66
Urania: A Rhymed Lesson, 122
"Uriel," 97
"Utility and Importance of Direct Exploration in Medical Practice, The," 122 *footnote*

Vacation of the Kelwyns, The, 198
"Valentine Extravaganza," 232 *footnote*
Valley of the Moon, The, 229
Van Bibber and Others, 226
Van Der Decken, 264
Van Doren, Carl [Clinton], 292
Vandover and the Brute, 228
Van Vechten, Carl, 273
Varieties of Religious Experience: A Study in Human Nature, The, 212
Vassell Morton, 78 *footnote*
Venetian Life, 194
Ventures in Common Sense, 171
Very, Jones, 104, 300
Via Crucis, 221
Victorian Prose Masters, 262
Viereck, Peter, 285
Views A-foot, 146
Views and Reviews, 73
Vigil of Faith and Other Poems, 80
Vindication of the Government of New England Churches, A, 15
Vision of Columbus, The, 40
"Vision of Sir Launfal, The," 131
Vision of Sir Launfal, The, 127, 129, 131
"Voiceless, The," 125
Voices of the Night, 107
"Voluntaries," 98
"Voyage of the Good Ship Union," 124

"Waiting," 254
"Waiting, The," 116
Wakefield, 119
Walden; or, Life in the Woods, 99
Waldo Trench and Others, 227
Wallace, Lew[is], 225
Walt Whitman: A Study, 255
"Walt Whitman at Home." By Himself, 134 *footnote*
Walt Whitman: Prophet of American Democracy (Chapter VII), 134-142
Walt Whitman's Diary in Canada, 134 *footnote*
Walt Whitman's Drum-Taps, 134 *footnote*
Wandering Ghosts, 221
War Is Kind and Other Lines, 209
War of the Classes, The, 230
Ward, Artemus (pseud.), 76-77, 160
Ward, Elizabeth Stuart Phelps, 148-149
Ward, Nathaniel, 9
Ware, William, 82
Warner, Charles Dudley, 262
Warner, Susan Bogert, 82
Warren, Caroline Matilda, 46
Warren, Mercy Otis, 46
Warren, Robert Penn, 278
"Warren's Address to the American Soldiers," 58
"Washers of the Shroud, The," 131
Washington, George, 36
Washington Square, 201
Watcher by the Dead, A, 217
"Water-Ouzel, The," 262
Water Witch, The, 68
Way to Wealth, The, 27, 28
Wayfarers, The, 265
Ways of the Spirit and Other Essays, 104
Wayside Courtship, 206
"Wealth," 97
Webber, Charles Wilkins, 82
Webster, Daniel, 79
Webster, Noah, 44
Week on the Concord and Merrimack Rivers, A, 99, 100
Weems, Mason Locke, 83
"Weird Gathering, The," 115
Welby, Amelia Ball Coppuck, 81
Weld, Thomas, 10
"Wellfleet Oysterman, The," 99
"Wendell Phillips," 131
Wept of Wish-ton-Wish, The, 69
Wescott, Glenway, 277
West, The (Early Sentiment and Romance), 75
Westcott, Edward Noyes, 226
Western Writers (Early Sentiment and Romance), 83
"Westminster Abbey," 51
Westward Ho!, 54
Westward March of American Settlement, The, 206 *footnote*
Westways, 225
Wetherel Affair, The, 224
Wharton, Edith [Newbold Jones], 270
"What Did She See With?," 148
What Is Man?, 192
What Maisie Knew, 201
"What Makes Life Significant?," 212
"What Was It?," 216 *footnote*, 224
"Whate'er we leave to God, God does," 101
Wheatley, Phillis, 45
Wheeler, Thomas, 13
Wheelock, John Hall, 282
"When Lilacs Last in the Dooryard Bloom'd," 137
"When Winter fringes every bough," 101
Where the Battle Was Fought, 180
Whicher, Mrs. Frances, 83
Whilomville Stories, 207
Whistle, The, 27
Whitaker, Alexander, 13
White, (Father) Andrew, 12
White, Stewart Edward, 269 *footnote*, 271
"White Cowl, The," 178
White Fang, 229
"White Flag, The," 167
White-Footed Deer and Other Poems, The, 55
"White Heron, A," 183
White Heron, A, 183
White-Jacket; or, The World in a Man-of-War, 70, 71
White Magic, 228
White People, 226
White Sister, The, 221
Whitefield, George, 117
Whitman, Walt[er], 132, 133, 134-142, 173 *footnote*, 256, 305-307; expanding America, 138-140; general estimate as a critic and as a poet, 141-142; *Leaves of Grass,* 134, 135-136; poetry and prose before *Leaves of Grass,* 134-135; prose works, 140; supplementary bibliography, 305-307; Whitman and the War, 137-138; Whitman's purpose expressed in verse, 136

Whittier, John Greenleaf, 113-117, 124, 301-302; important poem, 114-115; important prose piece, 114; shorter poems, 115-117
"Whoever You Are Holding Me Now in Hand," 136, 139
Whole Book of Psalms Faithfully Translated into English Metre, The, 7, 10
Widow Rugby's Husband, The, 161
Widow's Marriage, The, 74
Wieland, 42
Wife, The, 264
Wigglesworth, Michael, 11-12
Wilcox, Carlos, 80
Wild Animals I Have Known, 263
Wild Bill Hickok, 159
Wild Garden, 243
Wilde, Richard Henry, 81
Wilder, Thornton [Niven], 276
"Wilhelmina," 179
Willard, Emma Hart, 80
Willard, Samuel, 20
William Crary Brownell, 262
Williams, John (1664-1729), 20
Williams, John (1761-1818), 45
Williams, Roger, 5-6
Williams, Tennessee [Lanier, Thomas], 288
Williams, William Carlos, 281
Willis, Nathaniel Parker, 53
Wilson, Alexander, 25
Wilson, Edmund, 293
Wilson, James, 45
Wilson, John, 13
Wilson, William, 81
Wilson, Woodrow, 157
Will to Believe and Other Essays in Popular Philosophy, The, 211
Wind in the Rose Bush, The, 184
"Wind Storm in the Forests, A," 262
"Windharp, The," 132
Wine of Wizardry, A, 252
Winesburg, Ohio, 171
Wing-and-Wing, 68
Wings, The, 265
Wings of the Dove, The, 203
Winslow, Edward, 13
"Winter Piece, A," 57
Winthrop, John (1588-1649), 4-5
Winthrop, John (1714-1779), 20
Winthrop, Theodore, 82
Wirt, William, 80
Wise, Henry Augustus, 82
Wise, John, 14-15
Wister, Owen, 270
Witch of Wenham, The, 115
"Witchcraft," 130
Witching Hour, The, 264
Witching Times, 224
"With Husky-Haughty Lips, O Sea!," 140
With the Procession, 227
Witherspoon, John, 45
"Within the circuit of this plodding life," 100
Within the Gates, 148
Wives, 261
Wolcott, Roger, 20
Wolf, The, 228
Wolf of Gubbio, The, 265
Wolfe, Thomas [Clayton], 277
Wolfert's Roost, 52
Woman in the Nineteenth Century, 103
Woman of Honor, A, 222
"Woman's Love, A," 167
Woman's Reason, A, 197
Wonders of the Invisible World, 119
"Wondersmith, The," 224
Wood, Sarah Sayward Barrell Keating, 46
Woodberry, George Edward, 263
Woodcraft, 74
"Woodman, Spare that Tree," 54
"Woodnotes I," 97
"Woodnotes II," 97
Woodworth, Samuel, 82
"Woof of the sun, ethereal gauze," 101
Wooing of Malkatoon, The, 225
Woolman, John, 25
Woolson, Constance Fenimore, 179
Word of Remembrance and Caution to the Rich, A, 25
"Wordsworth," 130
Work, Henry Clay, 81
"Works and Days," 97
World a Mask, The, 75
World of Chance, The, 197
"Worship," 97
"Worth of a Woman, The," 228
"Wound-Dresser, The," 137
Wounds in the Rain, 207
"Wreck of Rivermouth, The," 115
"Wreck of the Hesperus, The," 110
Write It Right, 217 footnote
Writings of Albert Gallatin, The, 256
Writings of Roger Williams, The, 6
Writings of Samuel Adams, The, 31
Writings of Washington, The, 52
Wyandotté, 69
Wylie, Elinor [Hoyt], 282
Wylie, Philip, 277
"Wynken, Blynken, and Nod," 250

Ximena, or the Battle of the Sierra Morena, 146

Ye Giglampz, 173
Yankee in Canada, with Anti-Slavery and Reform Papers, A, 99
"Yankee Ship Came down the River, A," 160
Year's Life, A, 126
Years of My Youth, 195
"Years of the Modern," 137
"Yellow Violet, The," 56
Yemassee, The, 74
"Yes," 224
Yesterdays with Authors, 145
"You and I," 180
Youma: The Story of a West-Indian Slave, 175
"Young Goodman Brown," 119
Young Mountaineers, The, 180
Yvernelle, 229

"Zadoc Pine," 223
Zadoc Pine and Other Stories, 223
"Zenobia's Infidelity," 223
Zoroaster, 220
Zury, the Meanest Man in Spring County, 171, 206